Talking American History

An Informal Narrative History of the United States

TALKING AMERICAN HISTORY

An Informal Narrative History of the United States

Ron Briley

SUNSTONE
PRESS

SANTA FE

Sunstone books may be purchased for educational, business, or sales promotional use.
For information please write: Special Markets Department, Sunstone Press,
P.O. Box 2321, Santa Fe, New Mexico 87504-2321.

Book and cover design › R. Ahl
Printed on acid-free paper
∞

Library of Congress Cataloging-in-Publication Data

Names: Briley, Ron, 1949- author.
Title: Talking American history : an informal narrative history of the
    United States / by Ron Briley.
Description: Santa Fe, New Mexico : Sunstone Press, [2019] | Includes
    bibliographical references. | Summary: "An informal narrative political
    history of the United States told from a progressive perspective"--
    Provided by publisher.
Identifiers: LCCN 2019041728 | ISBN 9781632932884 (paperback) | ISBN
    9781611395839 (epub)
Subjects: LCSH: United States--Politics and government. | United
    States--History. | Liberalism.
Classification: LCC JK275 .B75 2019 | DDC 973--dc23
LC record available at https://lccn.loc.gov/2019041728

WWW.SUNSTONEPRESS.COM

SUNSTONE PRESS / POST OFFICE BOX 2321 / SANTA FE, NM 87504-2321 /USA
(505) 988-4418 / ORDERS ONLY (800) 243-5644 / FAX (505) 988-1025

For my mentors Pete Petersen and Dick Heath
and
The students of Sandia Preparatory School
Who taught me so much.

Contents

Introduction

Industrialist Henry Ford is touted to have dismissed the study of history by describing the discipline as one damned thing after another. Unfortunately, generations of history students in both the schools and universities might agree with Ford after suffering through endless formal lectures and massive textbooks filled with facts to be memorized. And the knowledge explosion of the internet has not necessarily made matters any better as our understanding of history is weighed down by even more "facts," although this information is now available with one click on our computers. Buried under the avalanche of historical detail, students feel overwhelmed, and they understandably turn toward the more pragmatic STEM education with possible careers in science and engineering. Yet, these upcoming scientists are desperately in need of comprehending the historical and cultural context in which their research and discoveries will be implemented. In addition, academic specialization makes it difficult to make historical generalizations as scholars observe that there are significant exceptions to any historical argument. Thus, professional historians tend to qualify their conclusions with such phrases as "research appears to suggest" or "based on this case study one might argue." As the disruptive political campaign of 2016, with its considerable confusion over the roles of immigration, religious liberty, race, civil rights for all Americans, foreign policy, gun violence, terrorism, and foreign policy, demonstrated, all inhabitants of the United States need a better understanding of their national history, within an international context, that will provide a foundation for debate and civil discourse.

Talking American History is an attempt to address the crisis in American history by providing an informal narrative history of the United States from the Colonial period to the present day addressed to the intelligent general reader rather than the professional historian. History, while requiring the application of analytical tools, is fundamentally a story with many strands that interconnect over the course of time. This organizational structure of *Talking American History* is, therefore, rather traditional, employing a chronological approach centered around a rather old-fashioned political framework. However, the contributions of contemporary historians regarding the roles of race, gender, and class will be incorporated into the narrative. In the interest of full disclosure, it is reasonable to expect some information regarding the background and historical orientation of the storyteller.

I was raised in a poor white family with little in the way of education. My father dropped out of elementary school during the Great Depression. He was the hardest working person I have ever known, but his labors led him to an early grave rather than the elusive American dream. My mother was a high school graduate who raised two sons and entered the workforce as a bookkeeper. To earn additional money for essentials, the entire family worked, often alongside my grandparents, in the cotton fields of the Texas Panhandle. Chopping cotton, hoeing the weeds around the cotton plants, and picking cotton during the late summer and early fall were back-breaking labor that I have never forgotten. There were few books in the home, but for some reason I loved reading. Despite my enthusiasm for books, my grades were average at the best, and there was no consideration of college.

That assumption changed when I learned that student deferments were available as the draft allotments for the Vietnam War increased. Although my high school grades were rather shaky, I was accepted at the regional college, West Texas State University. My academic deficiencies were monitored by a young professor from Iowa, Dr. Peter Petersen, and I fell in love with a world of books and scholarship that I had never before experienced. The undergraduate years were difficult as, in addition to compensating for the gaps in my academic background, I had to support a young family on part time jobs and student loans. While Canyon, Texas was somewhat of a political backwater and hardly a bastion of leftist politics, I, nevertheless, identified with the protest movements opposing the Vietnam War, racial segregation, and economic inequality. I gravitated toward the small number of dissidents in the campus chapter of Students for a Democratic Society and identified with the counterculture, although my work and family responsibilities left little time for recreational drugs. Approaching the study of American history within this historical and cultural framework, I believed that I had discovered the reasons for my family's poverty in the exploitive nature of American capitalism and politics under the sway of large corporations. While today I perceive such political and economic questions as more complex, I still find considerable truth within these youthful assumptions.

After earning undergraduate and master's degrees in history from West Texas State University, I applied to a number of PhD programs—most of which were located in the Midwest. Although I was accepted to several doctoral programs, and came close to attending the University of Iowa, I selected the University of New Mexico in Albuquerque because it was number one in my pocketbook, offering me a tuition waiver and graduate assistantship in my first year of study. Perceiving $3,600 annually as a large salary, I enthusiastically embraced my studies under the guidance of Professor Gerald Nash, with whom I got along personally but disagreed regarding politics and interpretations of American history. For my dissertation subject I decided to focus upon four Midwestern progressive members of the Senate Farm Bloc during the 1920s, a topic which resonated with my own political orientation.

After completing my written and oral comprehensive examinations for the doctorate, along with preliminary research in the National Archives and Library of Congress, I found myself in somewhat of an economic crisis when my graduate assistantship expired. Accordingly, I decided to teach in the schools while writing my dissertation—an extremely difficult task with the expenditure of time required by teaching, researching, and writing. After two years at a Catholic junior high school with some classes approaching fifty students, in 1978 I accepted a position with an Albuquerque prep school, Sandia Preparatory School. With my educational background, I had no understanding of what an independent preparatory school entailed. Sandia Prep, however, was a small struggling institution and displayed none of the pretentious class consciousness of the stereotypical prep school. The school proved to be an excellent match for me, and I threw myself into the job which became more a way of life than an occupation as the school grew. In addition to teaching both middle and high school history classes, I served as a class sponsor, academic adviser, chaperoned dances and school trips, coached softball, established a Model United Nations program, and eventually ended up serving twenty-six years as the assistant head of school. Beyond these many duties at Sandia Prep, I taught history for twenty years at the University of New Mexico, Valencia campus.

These obligations, however, rendered it virtually impossible to complete my dissertation. After a number of busy years, I, nevertheless, again felt the urge to pursue historical scholarship, but I had lost interest in the Senate Farm Bloc. It finally occurred to me that engaging in historical writing and research from my primary location in the schools could be a liberating experience. I did not have to worry about attaining tenure and decided to pursue topics that would be of greater personal interest—although others would hopefully be motivated to read my work. Accordingly, I have completed seven books, along with numerous scholarly articles and encyclopedia pieces, on the popular culture topics of film, music, and sport—especially baseball—within historical and political context. The growth of Sandia Preparatory School also offered me an opportunity to develop and teach courses on American History Through Film and World Cinema. The school was also able to help with some travel funding that allowed me to share my research with colleagues at academic conferences. It occurred to me that perhaps it was possible to pursue a traditional academic career from a high school base. Although my teaching duties always came first, I was able to assume an active role within historical organizations such as the American Historical Association (AHA), Society for History Education (SHE), and Organization of American Historians (OAH), and I was fortunate to receive summer Fulbright study opportunities in the Netherlands, Japan, and Yugoslavia. During my forty-year teaching career, I was honored with teaching awards from the AHA, OAH, SHE, National Council for History Education, and the New Mexico Golden Apple. But the most important legacy of my teaching career is the continuing friendship of many former colleagues and students.

This rather lengthy background of my teaching and academic career does not mean that *Talking American History* is intended to be some type of teaching memoir or methods textbook. That is the topic for another book. Rather, *Talking American History* is an interpretative history, and it is only fair that the reader have some grasp of the author's prejudices. Of course, readers should take some inventory of their own assumptions and preconceptions. Thus, it makes considerable difference from whose perspective the story is told. History is not unlike the same accident which eyewitnesses describe so differently. It matters from whose perspective events are viewed. For example, the topic of Western expansion is considerably skewed when perceived from the angle of Anglo pioneers as opposed to the Sioux warrior or Mexican farmer whose land and way of life are being lost. The American Revolution is subject to varying interpretations depending upon whether one is a Patriot, Loyalist, landed gentry, yeoman farmer, merchant, sailor, pioneer, Native American, enslaved black, or a woman.

Challenging the myth of objectivity does not mean all opinions are meaningful and relevant, but rather that there is room for multiple readings of the past based upon the analysis of historical evidence such as primary documents. Thus, history might be considered as a civil and intelligent conversation one has at a cocktail party where varying perspectives are introduced, argued, and respected. Nevertheless, in book form this conversation does tend to be a bit one-sided, but the narrator, who certainly does have a point of view, does not claim omnipotence due to some graduate school classes. Instead, it is the hope of the author that *Talking American History* will stimulate a dialogue in which readers in disagreement with the arguments presented will pursue historical inquiry to refute the author. In many ways history is an argument in which the participants are similar to lawyers presenting their cases in briefs with some decorum for respecting multiple historical interpretations and approaches. Yet, why is it necessary to relegate such disagreements to a more formal court of law? It is the aim of *Talking American History* to present civil historical debate as essential to a functioning democracy as we sample the dip and engage in some historical conversation at our stimulating cocktail party in which discourse expands beyond the more mundane considerations of celebrity gossip.

Of course, the audience for *Talking American History* should not necessarily be confined to the cocktail circuit, as students not of drinking age might find this more informal approach to the study of history a little more interesting than that of a traditional textbook preparing students for an Advanced Placement examination in American history. Thus, *Talking American History* is a story or narrative without the vast array of charts, graphs, maps, photographs, and political cartoons which illustrate and sometimes clog textbooks with so much detail that is nearly impossible to decipher any narrative thread or argument, furthering Ford's contention that history is nothing more than one damned thing after another. To maintain its focus upon telling a story, *Talking American History* will not include endnotes or long passages from primary documents; although a brief bibliography of leading scholarship will be included for each chapter. While internet sources will be de-emphasized for the sake of narrative, the arguments put forth in *Talking American History* should send students back to their computers with a greater appreciation for the subtle role of interpretation and nuance in the discipline of history. In the final analysis, the narrative traditional approach of *Talking American History* is now nontraditional and might serve as welcome relief or a supplement to the orthodoxy of the Advanced Placement test.

Whether the reader is a student or a history buff—somewhat of a strange term as it is difficult to conceive of a serious science or mathematics scholar referring to themselves as an amateur enthusiast—*Talking American History* also seeks to introduce some sense of levity to the study of history. Perhaps history is too important to be left to the professional historians. The study of the past can often be rather depressing as we investigate topics such as war, genocide, disease, poverty, racism, gender discrimination, colonialism, and torture which all too often document a lack of respect for our common humanity. If we do not sometimes smile at the human condition, we may be constantly reduced to tears. Accordingly, *Talking American History* proposes to include some sense of humor in our conversation.

As is suggested above, *Talking American History* reflects the background of its author, and before we begin our journey through American history, it is only fair to explicitly rather than implicitly share my perspective. While there are many exceptional stories and individuals within the American experience, *Talking American History* will not subscribe to the idea of American exceptionalism. The notion that the Founding Fathers, many of whom were slave owners, were guided by God to establish the Constitution and American form of government that would serve as a beacon of liberty and spread its divine mission of freedom to the world is rather simplistic and assumes a degree of superiority that does not quite fit with the more conflicted history of the United States. An intolerant tradition is evident in the Puritan witchcraft trials, genocidal treatment of Native Americans, racial slavery, exploitation of workers and immigrants, sexism, homophobia, territorial expansion, and imperialism. Thus, Americans are not always innocent as proponents of American exceptionalism would have us believe. On the other hand, it is equally simplistic to perceive America as the Great Satan whose only mission is greed and the exploitation of global resources.

Therefore, *Talking American History* subscribes to what one might term the progressive interpretation of American history. Rather than simply embracing American nationalism and assuming that the nation's leaders and flag must be followed, another view of patriotism, as articulated by Frances Wright in 1823 during what may have been the first Fourth of July oration delivered by a woman, argues that rather than blind obedience, the true test of patriotism is whether the nation is living up to its founding principles. In the case of the United States, this would mean adhering to the principles enunciated in the Declaration of Independence that all men are created equal with certain inalienable rights. From this progressive perspective, the story of America is the struggle to extend this principle to all citizens which is embodied in the abolition of slavery, women's suffrage, union movement, immigration reform, Civil Rights Movement, and efforts to obtain equality for members of the LGBTQ community. This sense of progress in bringing equality of opportunity to all citizens, however, has not been without opposition and periods of regression and retreat in regard to basic human rights. And the contemporary political scene indicates considerable flux in regard to the expansion of these individual rights. While the Supreme Court has recognized same sex marriage, many states have pushed back with religious liberty laws allowing discrimination against the LGBTQ community. In addition, demagogic politicians denouncing immigration and refugees from Mexico and Syria have resonated with many Americans.

Although the movement toward a more egalitarian society is a conflicted one, *Talking American History* will focus its narrative upon a history from the bottom up that was embraced by many scholars during the 1960s and continues today within the academic focus upon issues of race, gender, and class. In other words, *Talking American History* will generally be aligned with the approach taken by Howard Zinn in his popular and influential *A People's History of the United States* (1980). There are some important differences, however, that distinguish *Talking American History* from Zinn's work. Making use of long quotations from primary documents, Zinn seeks to document the resistance of common Americans to capitalism, racism, sexism, territorial expansion, and mainstream political discourse. Thus, dissent emerges as a major theme in *A People's History*, and rebellion and resistance will also enjoy considerable emphasis in *Talking American History*. Yet, organizing *Talking American History* around a political narrative means that more traditional topics will also garner considerable attention.

For example, it will be difficult to discuss the colonization of North America without paying attention to the role played by religion—a topic often ignored by Zinn. Presidential administrations and politics will occupy an important place in the narrative. There is much to criticize in the leadership of Andrew Jackson and much to rejoice in having abolitionist Harriet Tubman eventually replace the slave-owning President on the twenty-dollar bill, but the Jackson Presidency is important and deserves attention. It is also difficult to ignore such Presidents as George Washington, Thomas Jefferson, Abraham Lincoln, Theodore Roosevelt, Franklin Roosevelt, Ronald Reagan, and Barack Obama. On the other hand, figures such as John Tyler, Franklin Pierce, Chester Arthur, and Benjamin Harrison do not merit major attention, while reformers and cultural influences such as Eugene V. Debs, Susan B. Anthony, W. E. B. Du Bois, Woody Guthrie, Betty Friedan, and Cesar Chavez deserve credit for their contributions to shaping the nation. A political orientation also does not mean that *Talking American History* will be organized around the topics of war and battles. Rather than concentrating upon military strategies, the focus will be upon how war has shaped American history, and the peacemakers should enjoy as much recognition as the generals. Explaining the factors that lead to conflict are really more important than the details of military strategy, but the horrors of those fighting and dying should never be forgotten.

Another problem for the political approach assumed by *Talking American History* is the danger of certain people and topics being downplayed or ignored. For example, women were not allowed to vote on the national level until passage of the Nineteenth Amendment and the Presidential election of 1920. This exclusion from the formal political process means that there is always the danger of history becoming simply his story, and *Talking American History* takes seriously the responsibility of including all citizens in its narrative. Whether it achieves this goal is another question and should be part of the conversation which this history seeks to foster.

Along with a sense of inclusion is the question of exclusion, for it is impossible to cover everything without ending up with Henry Ford's encyclopedic one damned thing after another. And perhaps no issue is more contentious than where do we begin the study of American history—a topic which will be discussed in the first chapter. So pull up a chair, perhaps have a cocktail or at least a little snack and let us talk about American history and see if we may employ the past to shed some light upon the contentious present. American history may not always be as exceptional as some would like to think, but it is always pretty damn interesting and important to understanding the world and who we are as a nation and a people. Maybe Henry Ford will join us, as he is part of the narrative as are we. Let us be passionate but civil, and please pass the dip!

1

Early English Settlement and Colonial Virginia

"Baptism of Pocahontas." 1904 photograph of a painting by John G. Chapman in U.S. capitol. Detroit Publishing Company Photograph Collection (Library of Congress). Painting embodies exploitation of Native women and efforts to eradicate Indigenous religion and culture.

Beginning a history of the United States with the first permanent English settlement at Jamestown in 1607 is a rather controversial choice. After all, it ignores the Spanish colonization of the Southwest and the diverse Native American civilizations that existed in the Americas before European contact. Commencing with Jamestown may even be challenged as a rather racist approach; for it seems to suggest that history begins when the white people take their place on the stage. And, indeed, much of American history seems to be the study of white people and their accomplishments. So why perpetuate this historical approach?

There are many answers given to this question, and most are simply rationalizations. It is certainly true that one cannot cover all of American history in a single volume, and some topics must be given less space or even omitted. The case for excluding pre-contact Native history and limiting the coverage of Spanish colonization usually concentrates upon the argument that English colonization was significant to the American Revolution and the drafting of such fundamental documents as the Declaration of Independence and Constitution that have influenced the course of American history. Spanish colonization is, thus, perceived as more important to the study of Latin American history. While somewhat simplistic, there is some validity to this argument, and traditional textbooks usually provide an introductory chapter on the contact between the Spanish colonizers and indigenous Native people and then cut to the English settlement, only to return to the Southwest with the Mexican War and Anglo settlement of the region. In the interest of time and space, *Talking American History* will essentially follow this conventional approach; although recognizing that important stories are being overlooked. But before focusing our attention on the English; it is essential to make some significant parallels, as well as some differences, between the Spanish and English experiences in the so-called New World.

It is also important to note that the Spanish conquest of the Southwest continues to cast a racial and cultural shadow despite the Chamber of Commerce claim in a state such as New Mexico that the Anglo, Hispanic, and Native cultures live in peace and harmony. Despite their conflicting territorial and colonial ambitions, the European powers of Spain and England (in addition to France in North America which will be discussed when examining the French and Indian Wars) shared a number of cultural, economic, and racial assumptions. The Europeans perceived themselves as bringing the benefits of Western civilization, including Christianity, to the indigenous people of the Americas. The English and Spanish also tried to enslave the Natives although they generally made poor agricultural laborers. These conquerors failed to respect indigenous religion and culture, implementing a policy of cultural and ethnic cleansing toward the Natives who found themselves vulnerable to the superior technological weapons of the Europeans. In addition, Natives displayed little resistance to European diseases such as smallpox that wiped out entire villages and quickly reduced the superior numbers of the indigenous population. The Europeans were motivated by the search for a trade route to China and the East Indies as well as a desire for land and gold which the Spanish found in the conquests of Mexico and Peru.

Spanish colonization in the Americas

Traditional texts often focus upon the stories of intrepid Spanish explorers such as Hernando Cortes, Hernando De Soto, Francisco Coronado, and Cabeza de Vaca. Father Junipero Serra, now recognized as a saint by the Catholic Church, is usually extolled for bringing the Native people of California into the Spanish mission system. Yet, many Native people opposed the canonization of Father Serra, viewing the priest as an example of cultural imperialism destructive of indigenous life and culture. The Spanish colonization also provoked Native resistance to which the Spanish responded with considerable cruelty. Following an uprising at Acoma Pueblo in 1598, Don Juan de Oñate responded with a military expedition that killed over 880 villagers with the remaining men, women, and children enslaved. Oñate also ordered that twenty-four male survivors would have a foot amputated. These reprisals along with efforts to destroy Native religion resulted in the Pueblo Revolt of 1680 led by Popé. The revolt was bloody with over four hundred Spanish colonizers killed and the Spanish driven out of what is today New Mexico. In 1692, however, Diego de Vargas led the re-conquest which brought the Spanish permanently back into the region.

The re-conquest, however, did not halt the conflict between the Spanish and Native population. The continuing legacy of conquest was evident in 1998 when a statue of Oñate in Alcade, New Mexico was defaced by having its right foot severed in memory of those who had suffered at Acoma. The Oñate statue incident indicates that despite a Spanish policy that encouraged intermarriage with the Native people, a practice which was forbidden in most English colonies through miscegenation laws, there remains a degree of cultural conflict in what is sometimes termed the Black Legend. According to Indian people, the Spanish conquest of the Southwest was an imperialist endeavor that attempted to destroy the Natives and their way of life through policies of rape, murder, and pillage that deprived Indians of their religion, wealth, liberty, and land. On the other hand, defenders of the Spanish settlement point out the benefits of the West brought by the Spanish such as the redemption of Christianity, new technology and agricultural techniques, education, medical advances, products such as wheat and rice, and even the introduction of horses which eventually became an integral part of Plains Indian culture. The emphasis in this refuting of the Black Legend is often upon intermarriage and intermingling of culture producing the mixed race mestizos of Latin America and the Southwest. Nevertheless, the cultural image of the Spanish conquistador remains influential as is evident by growing Native opposition to the official seal of the University of New Mexico that includes a proud Spanish conquistador. Native opponents of the seal observe that a more accurate template would have the conquistador standing upon the dead bodies of indigenous people. The University of New Mexico seal also features an armed frontiersman who might be interpreted as representing the Anglo expansion from England that would often exploit both the Native and Spanish populations of America.

Background to English colonization

This takes us to the question of how the tiny island nation of England became such a major player in the history of colonization. And the answer to this question is complicated and carries us well beyond English assumptions of racial superiority. Geography is always a good place to start, and the isolation of an island offered considerable protection from the religious warfare that often decimated continental Europe. While groups such as the Vikings did considerable damage with raiding parties, the last successful invasion of England was the Norman conquest of 1066, and the island nation was able to withstand the onslaughts of such European dictators as Napoleon and Hitler who were able to bring the rest of Europe under their control. Its position as an island also encouraged the development of an English maritime industry promoting trade with European neighbors and eventually more exotic destinations.

Religion also played a significant role in English expansion. While avoiding some of the massive destruction the wars of the Reformation brought to Europe, England was able to join the ranks of Protestant nations in a relatively bloodless coup organized by the English monarch Henry VIII against the Pope and Catholic Church. Seeking a male heir for his throne, Henry requested an annulment from his marriage to Catherine of Aragon in order to wed the young Anne Boleyn. When this request was denied by Pope Clement VII, Henry announced in 1533 that England was separating from the Catholic Church and would follow the Protestant faith by establishing a new state church, The Church of England, under the control of the English monarchy. This maneuver certainly freed up the King to pursue Boleyn and a male heir, but it also had the advantage of considerably increasing the power of the monarchy that would support colonization and expansion.

In addition, some scholars argue that the belief system of early Protestantism encouraged economic policies of expansion and colonization. Protestant theologians such as John Calvin emphasized the concept of predestination in which an omnipotent God knew from the beginning of time who was destined to achieve heaven or suffer in hell. Only God could know for sure who was chosen, but believers insisted that there were signs suggesting that an individual was probably one of God's elect. One could argue that he/she was of the elect by living a devout life of good works centered upon the church and its teachings. Also, if one were prosperous in business transactions, it was viewed by many as a sign of God's blessing—and certainly this is a perspective still promoted by many Christian evangelists. Thus, Protestantism in England was perceived as encouraging capitalism or the private accumulation of wealth.

Economic activity was also fostered by the enclosure movement and growth of manufacturing in England. Large property owners began to consolidate their holdings through the fencing of their land that often limited the access of smaller landowners to the village commons and their strips of land. While there were some peasant rebellions which were crushed by the mercenaries hired by the lords, most small landowners ended up selling or surrendering their property. Some stayed on the land as agricultural laborers, while others flocked to England's cities where they became a cheap source of labor for the industrial revolution and capitalist entrepreneurs who also exploited abundant English natural resources such as timber, iron ore, water, and coal. The surplus labor supply in the cities also included desperate people who were willing to become indentured servants and gamble upon the possibility of social mobility in the colonies. English capitalism, industry, and colonial enterprises were also encouraged by the development of new systems of business organization such as the joint stock company. Large scale enterprises were able to secure funding through the selling of stock shares. and due to the concept of limited liability an investor could only lose the money put into the enterprise.

England's expansion also brought the Protestant nation into conflict with Catholic Spain. Enjoying a considerable head start over the English in exploiting the Americas and Native people, Spain was sending home shiploads of gold and silver, while early English efforts at colonization were less successful in locating precious minerals. In response, English privateers such as Francis Drake, who were actually encouraged by Queen Elizabeth, attacked Spanish ships and sought to seize their precious cargos. Essentially, the Spanish were stealing from the Natives, and then the English were seizing the Spanish plunder. These acts of piracy, in addition to religious differences, convinced the Spanish monarch Phillip II to order a massive invasion of England. In 1588, the Spanish Armada moved into the English Channel. While outnumbered, the smaller English ships were more maneuverable in the Channel, and the Spanish fleet was also at the mercy of stormy weather, which many in England insisted upon calling the "Protestant wind." The surprising defeat of the Spanish Armada marked a significant turning point in the power politics of Europe and the world as England replaced Spain as the world's dominant nation; a position it retained into the early twentieth century.

Becoming a global power did not mean colonization would be a smooth road for England. Similar to contemporary space exploration, venturing into a new environment was not without its risks. For example, in 1587 Sir Walter Raleigh helped to establish the Roanoke Island colony off the coast of what is today North Carolina. When supply ships returned to the small settlement the approximately 120 inhabitants were missing with the word CROATOAN carved upon a tree. While no one is sure exactly what happened to the "lost colony," the best guess is that suffering from disease and starvation, the survivors were either attacked by or assimilated into the Native population with later accounts of blond-haired and blue-eyed Natives being sighted in the region. Also, explorers such as Sir Humphrey Gilbert perished on voyages of discovery, while others such as Martin Frobishner, searching for a northwest passage through North America to the Pacific and riches of Asia, were duped into overloading their ships with iron pyrite or "fool's gold."

Jamestown

This was the dangerous background to colonization when the Virginia Company, a joint stock company intent on earning profits, attempted to recruit colonists and investors for what would later become the Jamestown settlement. This enterprise was fraught with problems from the beginning as the Virginia Company, seeking to elicit support for the colony, was less than honest regarding the difficulties confronting the project. Ignoring the rights of Native Americans whose claims were not respected due to the fact that they were not Christians, the Virginia Company was granted a charter from the English monarchy. Potential settlers were not fully apprised of the potential problems with the Native inhabitants, and in addition the colonists were encouraged to believe that gold deposits would be found in the region. These misconceptions tended to attract too many so-called "gentlemen of leisure," who lacked many of the skills necessary to survive the challenges of a new environment. Many of these gentlemen were younger sons of the nobility who, due to the practice of primogeniture in which the eldest son inherited the family estate as his birthright, had no claims upon his father's lands in England.

But whether rich or poor, approximately two-thirds of the several hundred settlers perished during the "starving times" of 1607-1609. While the Natives were able to survive winter through storage of crops, fishing, and hunting, the English were poorly prepared. Time that might have been spent farming and preparing food was wasted in the vain pursuit of gold. Relations with the Confederacy of Chief Powhatan deteriorated, and the Natives were not eager to help the English colonists. The settlers were increasingly afraid to stray from their stockade, and this fear of the unknown contributed to the lack of substance. Thus, most of the colonists perished during the harsh winters, and there is evidence that some colonists may have resorted to cannibalism in order to survive the brutal conditions along the James River.

Until a relief expedition arrived, adventurer and soldier John Smith, along with a few followers, assumed control of the colony's meager supplies, asserting that colonists who did not contribute to the available rations would not be allowed to draw from the common storehouse. Smith is perhaps best known for the story that his execution by Powhatan was prevented by the chief's beautiful young daughter Pocahontas who had fallen in love with the handsome explorer. There is considerable doubt as to the validity of his tale as its chief source is Smith, and it is quite similar to a story he told about his capture by an Arab sultan during crusades into the Holy Land. Whether one believes Smith, the Jamestown colony was finally saved in 1609 when Lord De La Warr (namesake for the current state of Delaware) arrived with fresh supplies and colonists.

Life and labor in Colonial Virginia

From their base in Jamestown, the English settlers began to expand into Colonial Virginia. The Virginia Company, having failed to discover gold supplies to satisfy its investors, found a cash crop in tobacco, whose cultivation was introduced to colonists by John Rolfe who was married to Pocahontas to cement an alliance between the settlers and the Powhatan Confederacy. The story of Pocahontas does not exactly have a happy ending as when her husband brought Pocahontas to London, the young Native woman perished from tuberculosis. Meanwhile, tobacco, despite the opposition of King James II, became a popular product in England and Europe. In addition to smoking, tobacco placed in one's nostrils offered a far more pleasing smell than the stench of urban centers lacking sanitation and filled with people whose bathing habits were quite irregular.

Cultivating tobacco, however, required a labor supply, and the Virginia Company attempted to recruit colonists through the headright system in which one could receive fifty acres of land for every person brought to the colonies. The Virginia Company also tried to encourage population growth through the importation of young unmarried women who would provide brides for the predominantly male population of Virginia. Usually from poor families with limited prospects in England, these young women journeyed across the Atlantic and sought some form of social mobility on the American frontier. The encouragement of female immigration marked a settlement policy considerably different than that supported by the French and Spanish who fostered interracial relationships between male colonists and Native women. The English discouraged this racial mixing by importing white women to the colonies and passing miscegenation laws forbidding sexual relations and marriage across racial lines—a policy whose legacy was still apparent in the American South into the 1960s. The promotion of families produced workers and farmers that led to the expansion of English population and greater demands for land with ensuing conflicts between settlers and Natives.

The search for a labor supply in the tobacco fields also resulted in the importation of indentured servants. These servants were poor people, both men and women, who lacked the resources to book passage across the Atlantic. Thus, contracts were established in which Virginia landowners, and eventually masters in other colonies, would pay the passage of the indentured servant who would, then, owe their benefactor four to seven years of labor after which they might secure their own land. Under the contract, which enjoyed the force of law, the master agreed to provide such necessities as food and shelter, while the servant was expected to obey the master. Physical punishment to enforce obedience was allowed—beatings were allowed employing a stick that was not wider than the master's thumb (the rule of thumb). If a servant attempted to run away and was apprehended, additional years of service were added to the contract. On the other hand, if the demands of the master were excessive, the servant might bring suit against the master in court, although legal victories by the servants were exceedingly rare. Female servants were especially vulnerable to sexual exploitation and needed the permission of the master to marry as pregnancy might interfere with their labor obligations. During the early years of colonization, the death rate for indentured servants was high; however, as sanitation and general living conditions improved, more servants were completing their terms of service and making land claims. Thus, there was an increasing interest in some type of permanent labor supply. Similar to the Spanish, the English initially attempted to enslave the Native populations. This proved to be unsatisfactory for a number of reasons, including the fact that the Indians had little resistance to European diseases, and those living in close proximity with the whites suffered a significantly increased death rate. In addition, the fact that enslaved Natives lived near their families and geographical homelands made it easier to flee slavery and engage in uprisings against the practice. Many Native American cultures were also based upon hunting and gathering, and they proved to be poor farmers.

Introduction of slavery

A popular solution more fitting to the slave labor envisioned by many Virginia colonists was found in the black population of sub-Sahara Africa. Although the first Africans introduced into Virginia in 1619 were supposedly indentured servants, a system of racial slavery evolved with legislative slave codes carefully orchestrating the institution. The Africans offered numerous labor advantages as they proved more resistant to European diseases, and many laborers from West Africa were experienced farmers. In addition, separated from their native lands and people following the cruelty of the so-called Middle Passage across the Atlantic, in which the enslaved were packed like sardines into the dark holds of the slave ships, the Africans with diverse languages and cultures found it difficult to organize a resistance. The origin of African slavery also lies in the racism of English culture in which blackness was equated with evil and inferiority. The English also used

Christianity and the Bible to justify racial slavery, pointing to the passage in the book of Genesis where Noah's son Ham disobeys God by gazing upon his naked and intoxicated father. God decides to punish Ham and his descendants by casting them into darkness and slavery—establishing the origins of the African race and their status as slaves. While it is true that some Christians have also employed the Old Testament to support racial segregation and later opposition to the LGBTQ community, it is also important to note that other Christians found inspiration in the Bible to denounce slavery. People such as John Wesley, the founder of Methodism, opposed slavery, although many Southern Methodists later reconciled with the institution, and many abolitionists were influenced by scripture.

The slave codes which defined racial slavery as passing through the mother were enacted following Bacon's Rebellion in 1676. Nathanial Bacon was a landowner in the Piedmont section of Virginia where expanding white settlement came into conflict with the Indians. Bacon resented that the Tidewater aristocracy living along the coastline, and dominating the colonial assembly or House of Burgesses, failed to adequately support those living in the Piedmont or more mountainous frontier areas. Accordingly, he led a rebellion which occupied the capital of Williamsburg and convinced Governor William Berkeley to flee. Bacon, however, was unable to consolidate his control before his premature death—leading to various conspiracy theories that he was poisoned. Without Bacon's leadership, the movement deteriorated, and Governor Berkeley was able to reinstate more aristocratic control over the Virginia colony. Bacon's revolt was supported by a union of poor white and black indentured servants, and the interracial coalition proved a threat to aristocratic control. Accordingly, the House of Burgesses sought to drive a wedge in this coalition of the poor by enacting slave codes that essentially relegated black indentured servants to the status of slaves. This playing of the race card to assure the rule of the white plantation class by dividing the poor whites and blacks has cast a shadow upon the South which continues to influence the region.

Expansion of the Virginia colony

Although the local plantation class enjoyed some degree of self-determination through the House of Burgesses in which only wealthy white, property-owning males could vote and serve, Virginia was also a royal colony. While tobacco brought wealth to the coffers of the Virginia Company, the cost of defending the expanding colony in conflicts with the Indians, such as the Opechancanough War, severely cut into profits for the joint stock company. The company, therefore, returned control of the colony to the monarchy who appointed a royal governor who would share power with the House of Burgesses—a pattern of divided government that would cause considerable headaches for the crown.

From its humble beginnings at Jamestown and the starving times, Virginia was a thriving colony by the late seventeenth century, although there were relatively few large urban or market centers. The presence of numerous rivers navigable by ocean vessels made it possible for planters to create plantation docks through which they could directly load tobacco on ships returning to England. The geographical expansion of settlement was also due to the harsh impact of tobacco cultivation upon the soil. With so much available land, Virginia settlers gave little attention to ideas of soil conservation. Instead, the soil was often depleted in seven years, and a farmer would simply push westward to attain more land. This policy of constant expansion produced conflict with the indigenous population and fostered a culture of land use based upon the erroneous perception of infinite natural resources—a consumption rather than conservation ethic that has haunted the United States into the present day. The settlement of Colonial Virginia also introduced patterns that were repeated in other Southern colonies that will be developed in a subsequent chapter. The Southern colonies were primarily established for economic rather than religious motivations. They were based upon the extraction of agricultural products such as tobacco, rice, indigo, and later cotton, and African slaves were employed as a labor supply to cultivate these crops, while race was used to divide poor whites from blacks. This materialistic description is considerably different than the contemporary stereotype of the American South as the Bible belt, for the religious impulse in colonization was more significant in the settlement of the Pilgrims and Puritans in Massachusetts and New England.

Further Reading:

Andrews, Kenneth R. *Trade, Plunder, and Settlement: Maritime Enterprise and the Genesis of the British Empire, 1480–1630*. New York: Cambridge University Press, 1984.

Bridenbaugh, Carl. *Vexed and Troubled Englishmen, 1590–1642*. New York: Oxford University Press, 1968.

Crosby, Alfred. *The Columbian Exchange: Biological and Cultural Consequences of 1492*. Westport, CT: Greenwood, 1972.

Fagan, Brian M. *Kingdoms of Gold, Kingdoms of Jade: The Americas Before Columbus*. London: Thames & Hudson, 1991.

Gutierrez, Ramon A. *When Jesus Came, the Corn Mothers Went Away*. Stanford, CA: Stanford University Press, 1991.

Jordan, Winthrop. *White Over Black: American Attitudes Toward the Negro, 1550–1812*. Chapel Hill, NC: University of North Carolina Press, 1968.

Kelso, William M. *Jamestown: The Buried Truth*. Charlottesville, VA: University of Virginia Press, 2017.

Morgan, Edmund S. *American Slavery, American Freedom: The Ordeal of Colonial Virginia*. New York: W.W. Norton & Company, 1975.

Rice, James D. *Tales from a Revolution: Bacon's Rebellion and the Transformation of Early America*. New York: Oxford University Press, 2012.

Weber, David J. *The Spanish Frontier in North America*. New Haven, CT: Yale University Press, 1994.

2

Pilgrims and the Puritan City Upon a Hill

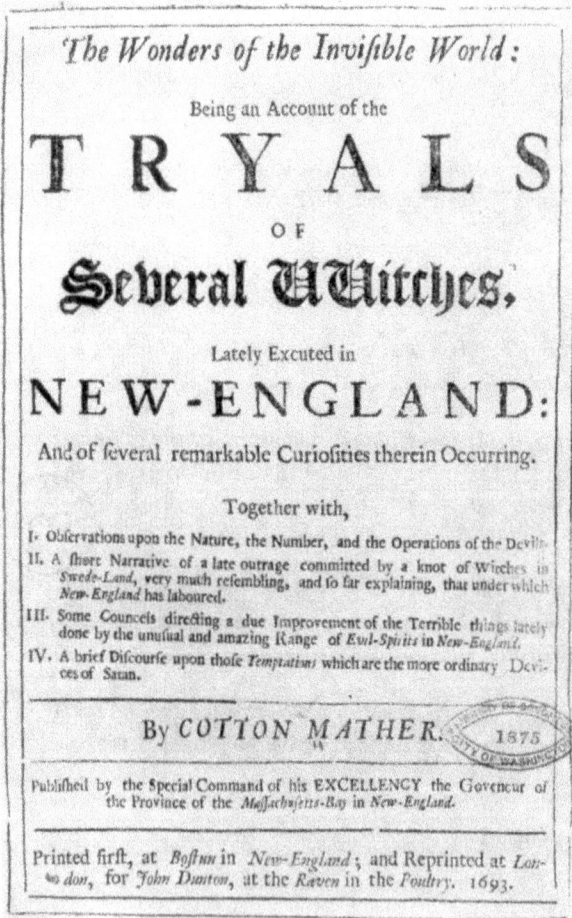

The Wonders of the Invisible World:

Being an Account of the

TRYALS

O F

Several Witches,

Lately Excuted in

NEW-ENGLAND:

And of several remarkable Curiosities therein Occurring.

Together with,

I. Observations upon the Nature, the Number, and the Operations of the Devil.

II. A short Narrative of a late outrage committed by a knot of Witches in Swede-Land, very much resembling, and so far explaining, that under which New-England has laboured.

III. Some Councels directing a due Improvement of the Terrible things lately done by the unusual and amazing Range of Evil-Spirits in New-England.

IV. A brief Discourse upon those Temptations which are the more ordinary Devices of Satan.

By COTTON MATHER.   1875

Published by the Special Command of his EXCELLENCY the Governour of the Province of the Massachusetts-Bay in New-England.

Printed first, at Boston in New-England; and Reprinted at London, for John Dunton, at the Raven in the Poultry. 1693.

Title page for *Wonders of the Invisible World* by Cotton Mather, published 1693. Library of Congress. The witchcraft trials in Salem, Massachusetts resulted in the executions of twenty people, primarily women, and solidified the power of the Puritan patriarchy.

Those who insist that America is a Christian nation often ignore the role of a joint stock enterprise such as the Virginia Company in the founding of America and focus upon the Pilgrims and Puritans of New England who celebrated the first Thanksgiving and perceived that the American colonies might become the shining city upon a hill that would serve as a beacon of religious and personal freedom to the world. This perception, however, fails to recognize a legacy of intolerance that was exhibited toward women in the witchcraft trials, Native Americans whose lands were taken in conflicts such as the Pequot War, and even fellow Christians such as the Quakers who were tortured on the streets of Boston. In addition, New England merchants were quite involved with the triangular trade that brought slaves from Africa into the Caribbean and American South. And the Puritans especially combined religious and commercial enterprises with the Massachusetts Bay Trading Company, and over time the economic ends seemed to take precedence over the religious goals.

The Pilgrims in Plymouth

The Pilgrims were an extreme English Protestant sect who perceived the Church of England as too Catholic in its sacraments and practices, making it impossible for them to swear an oath of allegiance to the church. Persecuted by the official state church, the Pilgrims were separatists who believed that there was little hope of reforming the Church of England. Emphasizing a sense of community and seeking not to draw undue attention upon the individual, the Pilgrims stressed simplicity in their daily lives and dress with black being the preferred color. The Pilgrims also perceived the ability to work as a gift from God, and they attempted to honor their Lord through hard work and a prosperous life that would provide proof that they were of the elect.

Facing persecution in England, the Pilgrims migrated to the Netherlands where religious toleration allowed them to practice their faith. The tolerance of Dutch society, however, proved to be too much for the Pilgrims who believed that their children were becoming corrupted by the lax Dutch culture. Accordingly, Pilgrim leaders made a deal with the Virginia Company that would take the religious group to North America. After a hazardous Atlantic voyage aboard the *Mayflower*, in November 1620 the Pilgrims landed on what is today Cape Cod. Not wanting to continue the voyage and well outside of the boundaries claimed by the Virginia

Company, the Pilgrims formed the *Mayflower* Compact in which they agreed to follow the democratic principle of majority rule. The *Mayflower* Compact is often perceived as a founding document of American democracy, but it was a document signed only by male members of the Pilgrim community, and certainly no attention was paid to the rights of Native Americans.

Regardless of the form of government, the Pilgrims confronted serious challenges to the survival of their Plymouth colony as chronicled in Governor William Bradford's *Of Plymouth Plantation*. Over half of the 102 who made the *Mayflower* voyage perished during the first harsh winter. The survivors were provided food and instructions for planting corn from the local Natives who did not initially see the starving Pilgrims as a major threat. The first Thanksgiving feast in which food was shared between the Natives and surviving Pilgrims was probably celebrated sometime in the fall of 1621 following the arrival of more Pilgrims and provisions from England. Unfortunately, in the long run the Native people of New England paid for their hospitality with the loss of their land, leading some communities to argue that Thanksgiving should be a day of fasting and declared Indigenous People's Day to mark the reality of the American experience for Native people.

Nevertheless, the growth of the Plymouth colony was extremely slow. The area near Cape Cod did not really provide a safe harbor for ocean vessels. In addition, the soil was rocky and not as fertile as Virginia had proved for the cultivation of tobacco. The Pilgrims did find a cash product in beaver pelts for which there was considerable demand in England. With little attention paid to conservation, the cash crop was soon trapped out in the region. Perhaps the greatest problem, however, for the Plymouth colony was that there were simply not enough separatists in England to provide an adequate population base for the colony. Thus, the Pilgrim Plymouth colony was eventually absorbed by the more prosperous and numerous Massachusetts Bay Puritans. In the larger history of the United States, the Puritans are far more influential than the Pilgrims, but due to the significance that the Thanksgiving holiday enjoys in American culture, the Pilgrims and images of Squanto teaching them the cultivation of corn is embodied in the national imagination as well as countless primary school pageants.

The Puritan city upon a hill

Although the Puritan legacy is a complex one, the term puritan has taken on a negative connotation in American culture perhaps best exemplified by the observation from the iconoclast journalist H. L. Mencken that a puritan was an American who was terrified that someone, somewhere, somehow, and with someone else might be having fun. Mencken's definition is probably a little harsh, but the Puritans certainly had little use for music or dance which they associated with the devil. On the other hand, there was little objection to tobacco or strong drink. During the cold New England winters, ample rations of warm rum were consumed in taverns, as the American colonies, both North and South, developed quite a reputation for their consumption of alcohol. As the New England practice of bundling and growing Puritan population well attest, sexuality was certainly part of the Puritan experience. Due to the sudden emergence of New England winter storms, it was sometimes necessary for a young man courting his potential bride to seek shelter in the girl's home. Spare bedrooms or beds were usually unavailable, so in the practice of bundling the potential bride and groom were placed in the same bed, and often the same bedroom as the parents, where they were bundled in tightly by blankets and often had a large board locked into place separating the couple. Nevertheless, the success of bundling in preventing premarital sexual activity was somewhat limited as the examination of marriage and birth records in Puritan New England indicates that it was not unusual for a couple's first child to be born after five to six months of marriage. There seemed to be no major problem as long as the couple married and there were no allegations of promiscuity. Thus, the Puritans certainly dealt with issues of sexuality still relevant to contemporary society, but they were, indeed, a serious people when it came to the subject of religion.

The Puritans shared many views similar to those of the Pilgrims, and they were also persecuted for failing to swear an oath of allegiance to the Church of England. However, the Puritans represented a more affluent class and were more numerous as they believed that the Church of England might be reformed through their efforts. In the Calvinist and Puritan perception of predestination, only God knew for sure who was destined for heaven, but it was possible for devout Puritan church members to essentially recognize those whom God had elected for salvation. The elect or "visible saints" would be accepted into the membership of a Puritan congregation through their good works and economic success that indicated one was blessed by God—a test that seems relevant today for some Protestant mega-churches. Thus, the Puritan church was controlled by the congregation who voted on issues such as the acceptance of members and selection of ministers. Puritan congregationalism is also often evoked in the origins of American democracy, but this was a limited democratic practice in which only male property-owning church members exercised decision-making power. While those elected to office were rarely ministers, for all intentional purposes the Puritan colony in Massachusetts functioned as a theocracy.

Puritans who grew despondent with reforming the church from within considered following the Pilgrim example and establishing a colony in North America. This course of action, however, presented a dilemma for the Puritans. How was it possible to leave England and at the same time continue the struggle to reform the Church of England from within? After considerable soul searching, Puritan John Winthrop, an attorney by profession who was later elected governor of the Massachusetts Bay colony, conceived the idea that the Puritan colony in New England would be like a bright shining light on a hill that would reform the Church of England by example. This concept developed by Winthrop has been employed by many believers in American exceptionalism, including President Ronald Reagan, as a metaphor to describe America's role in the world. Whether America has achieved this mission is subject to some of the historical debate that *Talking American History* seeks to spark.

While some Puritans refused to abandon the fight in England, others, posing as leaders of a business enterprise called the Massachusetts Bay Company, approached the monarchy for permission to establish a colony in Massachusetts and what is today Boston. Charles I realized that he was dealing with Puritans, but he welcomed the opportunity to rid England of religious dissenters. The Puritan migration was considerably different from that of the Pilgrims. Possessing greater wealth as well as knowledge of the dangers presented by colonization, the Puritans migrated in greater numbers and with ample provisions. In 1630, seventeen vessels with over a thousand colonists embarked on the first of numerous Puritan voyages to Massachusetts. The colony prospered as a haven for Puritans, and although elected leaders of the colony were not ministers, in many ways the Massachusetts Bay colony functioned as a theocracy. Non-Puritans were allowed to reside within the colony, but participation in the political process was limited to male property-owning members of the Puritan church, guaranteeing that control of the colony would remain in Puritan hands. The Puritan failure to provide a separation between church and state certainly provided a lesson for those drafting the Constitution and seeking to establish a division between religion and government; a tradition and legal boundary often challenged by the advocates for religious freedom laws that would allow for discrimination against members of the LGBTQ community.

Dissent in Massachusetts Bay

Religious control, however, did not prevent some deviant Puritans from challenging the religious orthodoxy of the colony's leadership. For example, minister Roger Williams argued for better relations with the colony's Indian neighbors, including respecting Native land claims in transactions. Williams also raised questions regarding the separation of church and state by suggesting that non-Puritan males with property be allowed to participate in the political process. Puritan leaders, such as Winthrop who was a friend to Williams, were concerned that such reforms would undermine the goal of constructing the city upon a hill. The threat posed by Williams led to calls for his execution, but Winthrop convinced the Puritan leadership to banish his friend from the colony. The harsh New England winter, however, did not result in the demise of Williams as he was taken in by his Indian friends. Eventually, Williams was able to secure a charter for his own colony, Rhode Island, which was a thorn in the side of the Puritans. Rhode Island welcomed religious dissenters and was the most tolerant of the English colonies.

Religious dissenter Anne Hutchinson, however, did not enjoy the same fate as Williams. A strong female character, Hutchinson challenged gender divisions by publicly enunciating her religious ideas that seemed to reflect the antinomian heresy that suggested it was impossible to ascertain whom God had destined for heaven. This line of thinking would make it more difficult to control the colony's residents, and she was called to appear before the General Court. If Hutchinson had humbled herself and apologized, she might have been spared punishment. Instead, she assumed the role of an "uppity woman" and questioned the authority of the male Puritan leadership. Hutchinson and her family were banished from the colony. When Puritan leaders later learned that Hutchinson and her family were killed during an Indian attack in the colony of New York, a day of thanksgiving was proclaimed in Massachusetts.

Hutchinson's name was also prominently mentioned in the witchcraft trials that plagued the Massachusetts colony, culminating with the 1692-1693 executions of twenty people in the village of Salem. There are many explanations put forth to shed some light on the hysteria that gripped the Puritans who, as revealed in the writings of ministers and Harvard founders Increase and Cotton Mather, believed that the devil was a real physical presence threatening God's divine plan for the city upon a hill. Historians have emphasized a degree of economic conflict in the accusations with some families gaining property and influence following the executions. Tied into these economic factors were elements of gender discrimination. While both males and females faced accusations, it was more likely for women, especially older females, to be found guilty and executed. These women were often singled out for being loud and unruly; in other words, they did not adhere to the traditional Puritan perception of women as obedient servants to their fathers and husbands who assumed the role of God within the family. In addition, many of these elderly women owned property and blocked the acquisition of land by males who then might be forced to leave the community in search of property. In the Puritan colony, and a practice followed in most of the English colonies, single or widowed women were allowed to own property, but upon marriage this property would belong to the husband. Thus, independent women were perceived as a threat to the patriarchal order.

Native response to Puritan expansion

Other scholars have perceived the insecurity of the Puritans as a reflection of the extreme violence that characterized the New England frontier as Natives resisted Puritan expansion. Many of the witchcraft accusers were servant girls who had lost family in the warfare, and in their testimony they might be perceived as using their condition to rebel against the gender expectations of their community. The religious impulse of the Puritan community was also evident as expansion was rarely the product of individual frontiersmen or families seeking new land. Instead, the Puritans tended to move as congregations under the guidance of ministers such as Thomas Hooker who moved his congregation into the rich farm land of the Connecticut River Valley. Puritan communities were, thus, established in what is today Connecticut, New Hampshire, Vermont, and Maine. Seeking to either convert or simply displace the Natives, the Puritans exhibited little respect for the land claims of the indigenous population, while differing perceptions of land and property made it difficult for the Europeans and Indians to establish any clear means of understanding one another. From the Native perspective, the land was a gift from God and could not be simply ceded to someone else. On the other hand, the Puritans emphasized the European concept of private property and interpreted any agreements as providing them with exclusive use and access. The fence and the concept of no trespassing, which Woody Guthrie denounced in "This Land Is Your Land," were at odds with the Native perception of land and resulted in considerable conflict between the expansionist Puritans and Native population. In the 1636 Pequot War, the Puritans accused the Pequot of murdering a merchant and launched a devastating assault that virtually annihilated the small Pequot nation. While the Pequot were massacred, in 1675, Metacom, called King Philip by the English, of the Wampanoga attempted to unify the New England tribes in resistance to the New England Confederation formed by the Puritan colonies. The New England frontier exploded in brutal warfare that saw massacres by both sides. In 1676, the Native resistance was finally put down with the burning of Native corn supplies, introducing the threat of starvation. The Narraganset nation was almost destroyed by the Puritans who drove the Indians into the mountains of western New Hampshire while enslaving captives and murdering Metacom who was drawn and quartered in addition to being beheaded and having his head placed on a pike for display among the celebrating Puritans.

Relationship between Massachusetts Bay and England

While the Puritan relationship with the Natives was bloody, relations with England were troubled but did not descend to the same level of violence. The New England Puritans were relatively free from strict English control from 1640 to 1660; a period sometimes referred to as salutary neglect. The conflict between English Puritans and supporters of the monarchy culminated in civil war, the execution of Charles I, and the virtual dictatorship of Oliver Cromwell. During Cromwell's rule, the New England Puritans were essentially free to pursue their policies without interference from the mother country. England grew weary of Cromwell's strict rule, and in 1660 the Restoration marked the ascendancy of Charles II to the English throne. After displacing Puritan rule in England, Charles II sought to establish his authority over the New England Puritans by imposing the Dominion of New England. The Massachusetts charter was revoked, and self-rule limited when Sir Edmond Andros was appointed as royal governor of the colony. In addition, the

New England tradition of town meetings was restricted, and the Anglican Church became the official church of the colony. In other words, the Puritan experiment of the city upon a hill was terminated. On an economic level, the English government would strictly enforce the Navigation Acts that asserted all colonial trade was to go through the mother country and only English ships were to be employed in transporting colonial products. Enforcement was targeted at the Puritan merchants who avoided trade with the mother country and fostered the lucrative triangular trade involving rum, sugar, and slaves. The Massachusetts Puritans were obviously unhappy with this effort at tightening England's control over the colony and seized the first opportunity to rebel.

English politics soon provided such an occasion during the so-called Glorious Revolution of 1688. Protestant leaders in Parliament were displeased when the elderly Catholic monarch James II apparently did the inconceivable and produced a male heir to the throne. Parliament moved to depose James and replace him with Mary, the daughter of his first wife, and her husband William of Orange. William and Mary assumed the throne but recognized the principle of Parliamentary supremacy which permanently altered English politics. Rebelling in the name of Parliament, the Massachusetts Puritans overthrew the Dominion of New England and placed Andros, who attempted to flee dressed as a women, under arrest. An effort to assert tighter English control over their North American colonies had failed; a pattern that eventually culminated in rebellion and independence.

The Puritan Legacy

As for the Puritans, they were unable to bring about a fundamental alteration of the Church of England. Nevertheless, the Puritan legacy remains influential. Drawing upon their belief in predestination, the Puritans were industrious and prospered in New England, although their commercial success tended to undermine their original religious impulse. The Puritans also emphasized the importance of working for the growth of the community, while their town meetings and congregationalism, limited to members of the Puritan faith, were early indications of inclinations toward some type of democratic self-rule. The Great Awakening also fostered a degree of democracy in the Puritan community during the 1730s and 1740s as evangelists such as George Whitefield emphasized individual religious conversion at the expense of the Puritan hierarchy. Education was another important contribution of the Puritans. Harvard University was created initially for the training of the Puritan ministry. While higher education was preserved for males, the Puritans believed that it was imperative that young women be taught the fundamentals of reading and writing, for later as mothers it would be necessary for them to provide religious instruction for their children. While education certainly focused upon religion, the Puritans cultivated an appreciation for literature such as sermons exemplified by the evangelistic minister Jonathan Edwards's "Sinners in the Hands of an Angry God." Michael Wigglesworth's epic poem "Day of Doom" also reveals some of the Puritan anxieties as Wigglesworth, recognizing that it was impossible to ascertain whether a child was destined for heaven, discusses infant damnation and describes children suffering in the fires of hell. With high infant mortality rates, these concerns about infant damnation certainly fostered Puritan angst. This uncertainty may have also contributed to the legacy of intolerance exhibited by the Puritans toward women branded as witches and servants of the devil, non-Puritan Christians such as the Quakers, Jews, Catholics, Native Americans, and enslaved Africans. Unfortunately, this legacy of intolerance plays a large role in American history and explains why the categories of race, gender, and class are so crucial to understanding the American experience.

Despite Puritan reservations about those who did not share their faith and culture, Puritan colonies allowed non-Puritan settlement; especially if they were wealthy and contributed to economic prosperity. Nevertheless, those not of the Puritan church were excluded from participating in the governance of the colony. This state of affairs led to the departure of some merchants who contributed to the Puritan economy. In addition, second and third generation Puritans who did not acknowledge a conversion experience were not allowed to participate in church affairs and governance. Concerned about the loss of important mercantile interests, the Puritans eventually compromised with the Half-Way Covenant of 1662 that opened church membership and the vote to second and third generation members of the community without a public conversion experience. This decision placed the Puritan community on a path that would eventually allow government participation by non-Puritan property-owning males. Thus, commercial interests seemed to overwhelm religious goals, and for all intentional purposes terminated the original Puritan experiment of reforming the Church of England by example. Proponents of American exceptionalism, however, maintain that metaphorically America remains as a city upon a hill and symbol of freedom for the world. *Talking American History* will raise some serious questions regarding this interpretation of the American experience beginning with the Puritans. The themes of commercialism, materialism, and pragmatism are also key concepts for understanding American history. American culture proves quite adept at commercializing dissent whether it is the Puritans or the counterculture of the 1960s, whose music, fashion, and politics were often commercialized with protest songs later used to sell products.

Although they may have succumbed to the lure of materialism, Puritan Massachusetts and New England demonstrate that religion played an important role in the formation of the English colonies. With Virginia and Massachusetts providing more detailed examples of English colonization in the south and north respectively, the next chapter will fill in the coastline by surveying the formation of the remaining colonies in Maryland, Pennsylvania, New York, New Jersey, the Carolinas, and Georgia in which economic motivation was dominant but religion remained significant. In addition, an English colonial culture began to develop with important regional differences amid conflicts with the Natives, Dutch, and French, culminating in an effort by the English monarchy to assert greater control over the transplanted English residents of North America.

Further Reading:

Barry, John. *Roger Williams and the Creation of the American Soul*. New York: Viking, 2012.

Cronon, William. *Changes in the Land: Indians, Colonists, and the Ecology of New England*. New York: Macmillan, 1983.

Demos, John. *The Unredeemed Captive: A Family Story from Early America*. New York: Random House, 1994.

Karlsen, Carol F. *The Devil in the Shape of a Woman: Witchcraft in Colonial New England*. New York: W.W. Norton & Company, 1987.

Lepore, Jill. *The Name of War: King Philip's War and the Origins of American Identity*. New York: Random House, 1999.

Lockridge, Kenneth. *A New England Town: The First Hundred Years*. New York: W.W. Norton & Company, 1970.

Morgan, Edmund S. *The Puritan Dilemma: The Story of John Winthrop*. Boston: Little, Brown and Company, 1958.

Norton, Mary Beth. *In the Devil's Snare: The Salem Witchcraft Trials of 1692*. New York: Knopf, 2007.

Stout, Harry. *The New England Soul: Preaching and Culture in Colonial New England*. New York: Oxford University Press, 1986.

Ulrich, Laurel T. *Good Wives: Image and Reality in the Lives of Women in Northern New England, 1650–1750*. New York: Random House, 1980.

3

Filling in the English Coastline

"William Penn's Treaty with the Indians, when he founded the province of Pennsylvania in North America, 1681." Painting by Benjamin West and engraving by John Hall, 1775. Library of Congress. The Quaker colony in Pennsylvania established by William Penn originally sought to foster a more respectful approach to relations with the Native population.

The English settlement of what is today North America was rather haphazard, with the English monarchy providing little in the way of central planning. The motivation for the establishment of these colonies was both economic and religious with the desire for wealth the primary driving force. The production of tobacco, rice, wheat, and indigo fostered the growth of an English colonial economy with New England merchants developing lucrative trade routes with the West Indies and mother country. Efforts by the English crown and colonial proprietors to exercise tighter control over this economic growth proved problematic as the availability of land made it difficult to enforce rules and regulations. If one's economic opportunities were being limited, it was simply possible to move west and acquire property beyond the reach of the crown or proprietors. This sense of independence and resistance to centralized control, of course, eventually culminated in the American Revolution. The story of an expanding English colonization, however, is not simply the tale of a march toward freedom and independence. The growth of the English colonies along the North American coastline was also based upon the exploitation of slave labor, natural resources, the Native population, and the unpaid labor of women and indentured servants. In addition to forging conflicts with the Native population, English expansion also resulted in warfare with other European powers such as the Dutch, Spanish, and French. A notable exception to this theme of exploitation and conflict was the colony of Pennsylvania in which the original Quaker settlers attempted to establish a peaceable kingdom based upon toleration and mutual respect, although the experiment proved to be short lived as commercial realities prevailed over Quaker idealism, and Pennsylvania followed the example of the other English colonies.

Maryland

Our brief discussion of the English colonies beyond Virginia and Puritan New England begins with the establishment of Maryland in 1634 by the family of George Calvert or Lord Baltimore. As a Catholic, Baltimore was concerned with the persecution of his co-religionists in Protestant England. Therefore, his colony was conceived as a haven for Catholic migrants, although to foster settlement and economic activity the migration of English Protestants was permitted. The Calvert family intended to establish a proprietary colony in which the inhabitants would pay rent and provide service to the lord who owned the property. Essentially, the idea was to transfer the European feudal model to North America. And building upon lessons learned from the settlement of Virginia, the Maryland colony enjoyed an element of success. Chesapeake Bay provided a degree of protection from harsh Atlantic storms, and a safe harbor for trade was established in the port city of Baltimore. The residents of the Maryland colony did not waste time in the futile pursuit of gold, but rather relied upon the cash cow of tobacco for which there was a strong European market. Maryland also followed the Virginia example of employing indentured servants and eventually slave labor from Africa to till the tobacco fields.

Nevertheless, the Calvert family struggled to maintain a degree of control over the Maryland colony. Concerned with the growing number of non-Catholics in the colony, a colonial assembly of land owners passed an act of religious toleration that would provide protection for the Catholic population that was in danger of becoming a minority. This act of religious toleration, however, was somewhat limited as it called for religious freedom to be extended to all Christians; in reality seeking to exclude Jews from the colony. The Calvert family enjoyed less success in maintaining economic control over the colony. The amount of available free land to be seized for farming encouraged settlers to ignore the rent payments required by the proprietors, moving west and setting up farms beyond the reach of the Calvert family. The expansion ignored the territorial claims of the Native population and contributed to considerable conflict along the Chesapeake frontier.

New York

While tobacco was being cultivated in the Chesapeake, the Dutch had established a lucrative mercantile colony in what is today New York. Dutch claims to the region were established in 1609 by explorer Henry Hudson when he sailed up the river that now bears his name, and fifteen years later New Amsterdam was founded as a trading post before becoming the capital of the New Netherlands. Although the Dutch are celebrated for their toleration, their colony in North America was governed by a more autocratic framework. The colony was under the control of the Dutch West India Company and the Director-General of the company with little provision for local governance. The company had little tolerance for the Native population, and a policy of exploitation is often remembered and symbolized in the story that the Dutch paid the Canarsee Indians approximately twenty-four dollars worth of trinkets for the rights to settle and develop Manhattan Island; today one of the most lucrative commercial properties on the planet. The Dutch West India Company also sought to encourage migration into the colony by offering patroonships along the Hudson River Valley to wealthy Dutch families who would settle fifty tenant families on the land they were allotted. This was another effort to introduce patterns of European feudalism into North America as the patroons would be granted considerable economic and political authority over their tenants. While it proved difficult for the patroons to attract tenants, the Roosevelt family, which provided two of America's Presidents, was the recipient of a patroonship.

The Dutch policy of expansion led to warfare with the Native population as well as European neighbors. Sweden established the colony of New Sweden in what is today the state of Delaware, but the area was conquered by the Dutch, although the Swedes are often credited with the introduction of what is considered to be an American icon—the log cabin. The continuation of the European conflicts to the North American continent resulted in the 1664 conquest of New Amsterdam by English forces under the leadership of the Duke of York, who later assumed the throne as James II. After the harsh rule of the Dutch Director-Generals such as William Kieft and Peter Stuyvesant, the English were essentially welcomed by the residents of the colony. Seeking to curry this favorable response, the English offered a degree of religious toleration and a limited representative assembly for the colony they called New York. The former Dutch colony, however, was not free from political and social discontent. Taking advantage of the political unrest following England's Glorious Revolution of 1688, a former Dutch soldier named Jacob Leisler seized power in New York. Playing upon the resentment of some middle-class Dutch merchants and artisans toward the new elite English rulers, Leisler freed imprisoned debtors, appointed artisans to official posts, and encouraged the political involvement of the lower class. When the crown appointed a new governor, Leisler was arrested and executed for treason—in large part due to his popularity among the city's artisans. New York City also witnessed racial unrest during the colonial period. Slavery was not confined to the agricultural endeavors of the Southern colonies, and Northern cities such as Boston and New York included large numbers of enslaved people. For example, it is estimated that by around 1700, over 40 percent of New York City households owned slaves. After taking control of the colony from the Dutch, the English expanded the importation of slaves and placed greater legal restrictions upon the enslaved population, resulting in a violent 1712 slave revolt that left nine whites dead. In response, seventy blacks were arrested, and twenty-one were convicted and executed by the colonial government. Oversight of both free and enslaved blacks was increased, although free blacks retained the right to own property. The New York colony was also subdivided when the Duke of York made a grant of what is today New Jersey to proprietors John Berkeley and George Carteret. Seeking to attract settlers, the New Jersey proprietors allowed for a representative assembly and cheap land sales, but with a poor coastline for trade, New Jersey remained subservient to New York as it is today.

The Carolinas

Both efforts to attain profits and engage in social engineering were evident in the southern Carolinas and Georgia. In 1662, Charles II bestowed upon several aristocratic families the right to establish a colony to the south of Virginia and Maryland which would be known as Carolina. Seeking to avoid the political and social conflicts that characterized England during the English Civil War (1642-1649), rule of Cromwell, and eventual restoration of the monarchy, the proprietors of the Carolina colony employed political philosopher John Locke, whose writing would be an important inspiration for Thomas Jefferson when drafting the Declaration of Independence, to write the Fundamental Constitution for the colony. Locke's document was a complicated framework that sought to restrict social conflict by providing for well-defined hierarchical class roles ranging from lords and freeholders to tenants, serfs, and slaves. Needless to say, the Carolina document appears a long way from Jefferson's phrase that "all men are created equal." But it proved impossible to construct the hierarchical society envisioned by Locke. Again the availability of land in the North American colonies made it difficult to transplant a version of structured European feudalism. Small farmers from Virginia and Maryland seeking new lands for their tobacco cultivation paid no attention to laws that would limit their expansion, while planters from Barbados and the West Indies were seeking a fresh start from depressed economic conditions in the islands. These planters from the West Indies brought the institution of slavery with them, and their efforts to enslave the Native peoples of the Carolina region assured considerable conflict for the Carolina frontier. Initial efforts to establish silkworm plantations to supply the fabric that fostered the search for a water way to Asian markets proved disastrous as the climate of the Carolina region was not advantageous to such an undertaking. Carolina, however, did provide a hospitable environment for the cultivation of tobacco and rice.

With the original designs of the aristocratic and feudalistic colony abandoned, in the 1720s the colony was divided into North Carolina and South Carolina. The economy of North Carolina was based upon the growing of tobacco and dominated by smaller family size farms rather than large plantations. While slavery was part of the labor supply in the colony, the typical slaveholder owned only a handful of slaves to work the family farm. The more mountainous terrain of North Carolina also seemed to attract dissenters and independent frontiersmen such as the French Huguenots who fled Catholic persecution and the Scotts-Irish who had little respect for neither Native nor English land claims. North Carolina regulators often fought against large landowners who sought to limit the expansion of small frontier farmers. As for South Carolina, it had some resemblance to the colony its founders originally envisioned. The Barbados planters were less refined than the aristocrats outlined by Locke, but they did establish lucrative rice plantations worked by the slave labor imported from the West Indies and Africa. To serve this trade in rice and slaves, the port of Charleston was constructed and assumed a significant role in the imperial English economy. Thus, slavery was essential to the development of South Carolina, and this trend would continue as the state economy moved from rice to cotton after the invention of the cotton gin. In fact, at the time of the American Civil War, South Carolina was the only majority black state, and it is not surprising that a war over slavery commenced with Fort Sumter in the harbor of Charleston. The historical evolution of the states of North and South Carolina owe much to their colonial histories, with North Carolina enjoying a more progressive reputation on racial issues than its more southern sister state.

Georgia

While the Carolina colony was perceived as an effort to perpetuate hierarchical order, Georgia was initially conceived as a refuge for the debtors languishing in English prisons. James Oglethorpe was a wealthy philanthropist and Member of Parliament who was concerned with the human waste represented by English debtors and their families. Sitting in jail made it almost impossible for one to pay off debts, so Oglethorpe proposed that these debtors be released from prison if they were willing to serve the goals of the British colonial empire in North America. The rice plantations in South Carolina were a valuable source of revenue for the English, but their profitability was threatened by the Seminole in Florida who often captured African slaves and incorporated them into their tribal structure, and the Spanish authorities, antagonistic toward the English, did little to halt these activities. Accordingly, Oglethorpe proposed that the colony of Georgia be established as a buffer zone between the lucrative rice plantations in South Carolina and Spanish Florida.

The debtors being dispatched to Georgia were not considered capable of self-government so a governing board of Twenty-One Trustees in England was entrusted with drafting a strict list of rules and regulations. In order to serve as a buffer against the Spanish and Natives in Florida, all male residents of the Georgia colony were required to provide military service with the colonial militia. To assure that there would be no mixed loyalties regarding Catholic Spain, debtors of the Catholic faith were forbidden to settle in the region. Since debtors were assumed to be incapable of governing their own affairs—a reflection of the concept that poverty is simply a matter of personal responsibility which resonates with many contemporary conservatives and libertarians—many of the colonial regulations were rather condescending. There would be no representative assembly, and efforts to mandate personal responsibility included curfews and limitations on alcohol. Land ownership was restricted, and slavery was prohibited. After all, if the debtor settlers had not been able to successfully oversee their personal affairs in England, how could they be entrusted with the supervision of enslaved people? The curbs on expansion were also expected to reduce conflict with the Native population of Georgia, so that the colonists might concentrate upon the threat posed by Spanish Florida. Needless to say, the policies of the Twenty-One Trustees proved quite unpopular with the Georgia colonists who refused to abide by the strict regulations. The proprietary colony of Georgia eventually reverted to the monarchy and demonstrated the difficulty of governing a colony from afar. Once again the availability of land, although fostering conflict with the Native population, emphasized that it was almost impossible to enforce strict rules and regulations upon the North American colonists.

The Quakers in Pennsylvania

This overview of the English colonies includes themes of exploitation as the settlers seized land from the Native Americans and introduced slave labor. One colony, however, at least briefly suggested that there might be another path. To settle an outstanding debt, Charles II granted permission for William Penn to establish a colony in the potentially fertile farming region between New York and Maryland. The colony would become called Penn's woods or Pennsylvania. As a merchant, Penn valued the economic possibilities of the colony, but he also sought a haven of religious toleration for his fellow Quakers (more precisely known as the Society of Friends). Penn had converted to what many in England perceived as a radical Christian sect that undermined a sense of order and hierarchy by emphasizing individual salvation. While the pejorative use of the word Quaker originated in the complaint that converts quaked when the spirit of God entered them, the real threat supposedly found in the faith was the concept of the inner light. The Quakers believed that the inner light of God burned within every individual, and the key to salvation was the discovery and cultivation of this flame. Potentially all could be saved and enter the kingdom of heaven. Such a belief system, for example, directly challenged the Puritan concept of predestination and visible saints. Quaker missionaries were banned and attacked by the Puritans in Massachusetts with Quakers tortured by mobs and marched naked through the streets of Boston.

The Quaker concept of the inner light also raised issues of equality as the faith assumed that Africans and Native Americans were also imbued with this eternal flame. Thus, Quakers became early opponents of slavery, finding it impossible to understand how it was morally proper to hold another child of God in chains. The Quakers also sought peaceable relations with their Native neighbors as Penn emphasized negotiation and the purchase of land in the establishment of the colony. While there was a strong initial effort within Pennsylvania to respect Native land rights, there was not necessarily a similar respect for Native culture as the Quakers hoped to save the souls of the Native people by converting them to Christianity. Nevertheless, the Quaker belief in pacifism brought a degree of peace to Indian-white relations in Pennsylvania that was not present in other colonies along the English coastline. The Quakers were opposed to military service as killing someone was the equivalent of destroying that person's inner light and a piece of God. In addition, Quakers opposed excessive taxation that would be used for military purposes. It is not surprising that during the 1960s the Quakers played a leading role in opposition to the Vietnam War and military draft. Although there remained a division of labor according to gender, the concept of the inner light also introduced elements of gender equality as the Quakers addressed men and women as equals. The construction of the Quaker meetinghouse also contributed to a degree of equality. The church pews faced one another, undermining a hierarchical order where all authority descended from the male minister and pulpit. And any member of the congregation, including women, could speak when the spirit moved them.

The Pennsylvania colony also enjoyed considerable economic success, although William Penn's personal fate in England was less fortuitous as he was saddled with large burdens of debt. The fertile soil of Pennsylvania provided bumper crops of wheat and corn which helped to feed the other English colonies, while the port of Philadelphia furthered maritime trade. Penn also carefully planned the growth and development of Philadelphia which emerged as one of the major cities of colonial America. Today the city remains well known for its organized street patterns, so different from the haphazard growth of many American cities. Religious toleration, at least for all Christians, was provided with the Great Law, and a colonial assembly in which all male property holders could vote guaranteed a degree of freedom for the colony's inhabitants. The tolerant spirit of the Pennsylvania colony was also evident in an immigration policy that welcomed non-Quakers as well as non-English migrants. The open immigration policy contributed to the diversity and economic vitality of the colony, but many of these immigrants failed to share the Quaker values regarding slavery, pacifism, and Native Americans, and the idealistic peaceable kingdom envisioned by the Quakers failed to survive. In 1763, Scotts-Irish frontiersmen known as the Paxton Boys attacked members of the Susquehannock tribe who had long lived in harmony with whites, massacring twenty-one of the Natives. Efforts to bring the Paxton Boys to justice were thwarted when a small army of approximately 250 frontiersmen marched on Philadelphia, and a governing delegation agreed to accept their petition and complaints about lack of support for settlers combatting Indians along the Pennsylvania frontier. As the Quaker influence in Pennsylvania waned, the themes of slavery and expansion at the expense of the Natives, so apparent in the history of English colonization in North America, was extended to Penn's woods as well.

Further reading:

Bonomi, Patricia. *A Fractious People: Politics and Society in Colonial New York.* New York: Columbia University Press, 1971.

Clemens, Paul G. E. *The Atlantic Economy and Colonial Maryland's Eastern Shore.* Ithaca, NY: Cornell University Press, 1980.

Dunn, Richard. *Sugar and Slaves: The Rise of the Planter Class in the English West Indies, 1624–1713.* Chapel Hill, NC: University of North Carolina Press, 1972.

Dunn, Richard and Mary, eds. *The World of William Penn.* Philadelphia: University of Pennsylvania Press, 1986.

Kars, Marjoleine. *Breaking Loose Together: The Regulator Rebellion in Pre-Revolutionary North Carolina.* Chapel Hill, NC: University of North Carolina Press, 2002.

Morgan, Philip D. *Slave Counterpoint: Black Culture in the Eighteenth-Century Chesapeake and Lowcountry.* Chapel Hill, NC: University of North Carolina Press, 1998.

Nash, Gary. *Quakers and Politics: Pennsylvania, 1681–1726.* Princeton, NJ: Princeton University Press, 1968.

———. *Red, White, and Black: The Peoples of Early America.* Englewood Cliffs, NJ: Prentice-Hall, 1974.

Richter, Daniel K. *Facing East from Indian Country: A Native History of Early America.* Cambridge, MA: Harvard University Press, 2001.

Wood, Peter. *Black Majority: Negroes in Colonial South Carolina from 1760 through the Stono Rebellion.* New York: W.W. Norton & Company, 1974.

4

Colonial Society and Economy

Portrait of Benjamin Franklin by Charles Wilson Peale. Photograph of painting at Pennsylvania Academy of Fine Art. Detroit Publishing Company Photograph Collection (Library of Congress). Benjamin Franklin's *Poor Richard's Almanack* celebrated the Colonial economy as providing opportunity for the self-made man, but this notion of social mobility was less applicable for women, indentured servants, Native people, and the enslaved population.

In fostering the development of colonies along the coastline of North America, the English monarchy was seeking to economically benefit the mother country with colonies supplying raw materials unavailable in England. As for those migrating to the colonies, they were seeking economic opportunities denied them in England. There was no room for expansion in the English countryside, but in North America land was available for the taking although there would be Native resistance to the land grab by the colonists. While they sought to improve their position in society often at the expense of dispossessing Natives and enslaving Africans, the colonists did not initially perceive themselves as forming a separate entity from England. The migrants considered themselves transplanted English citizens who would bring their culture to the New World. The American environment, however, made it difficult to simply transplant English culture. Distance and availability of land negated strict control by England over its colonial subjects as an American culture began to develop, although there were significant differences between the Northern and Southern colonies of North America. In addition, the English transplants seeking to rise in society began to perceive English mercantilist policy favoring the mother country as hindering their economic progress. Benjamin Franklin celebrated the American soil for fostering the self-made man, but there were limits to this social mobility that have persisted throughout the nation's history and challenged the American dream that through hard work everyone may rise in society. Nevertheless, the growing social and economic divisions between England and the North American colonists provided the foundation that culminated in the American Revolution.

Colonial governance

Perhaps one of the most obvious attempts to transplant an English model is the governance of the colonies. Based upon the English example of power sharing between the monarchy and Parliament, the governing structure of most colonies included a governor representing executive authority and a legislative assembly selected by the property-owning males of the colony. Just as in England, the power sharing arrangement sometimes led to political conflict. In the royal colonies, the governor was appointed by the king and served as the monarchy's personal representative. One might assume that with monarchial backing, the governor would enjoy considerable influence over the local assembly of propertied interests. To their long-term duress, however, the English monarchy squandered this advantage in colonial governance by insisting that the colonial assemblies pay the salaries of the governor. Through their control of the purse strings it was often possible for the assemblies to dominate and dictate to the royal representatives. In an effort to save money, the monarch surrendered considerable power and influence to the colonial assemblies.

These colonial representative bodies were not based upon democratic principles. Women, Natives, and slaves were denied a political voice, and participation in the political process was based upon property qualifications that varied somewhat from colony to colony. The idea was that a man of property was a stakeholder in the society and a concern for protecting his property and livelihood would assure his allegiance to the best interests of the community. Again, the system of voting was based upon the English example. With limitations to social mobility and the acquisition of land difficult, property qualifications in England were often rigid. The situation in the American colonies, however, was more fluid. It was certainly easier for a man in the colonies to attain property and to gain the suffrage than it was in England. Thus, even with the property qualifications, the American colonies were more democratic than the English homeland. Nonetheless, this fact did little to limit the influence of the most wealthy and aristocratic element upon colonial politics. Despite a relatively widespread suffrage, more modest property owners tended to defer to their social betters or most wealthy elements of society when selecting members of the local government. This concept of deference assumed that the most wealthy, educated, and aristocratic were successful and knew what was best for society. In places such as colonial Virginia where taverns often served as polling places, the aristocrats made their influence felt by the number of drinking rounds they purchased before and after the voting. While in contemporary America, we do attempt to close the bars and limit the influence of alcohol on election day, the idea of deference remains alive and well. While the United States has abandoned property qualifications for voting and holding office, the elected officials, especially at the state and national levels, hardly constitute a cross section of the population. It requires considerable financing to seek public office in the United States, and middle-class and working-class people have neither the time nor the money to serve. Notions of deference seemed to influence many voters to support Donald Trump in 2016. Despite his lack of political experience, voters deferred to Trump as a billionaire businessman who would run the country like his business and restore prosperity

Division between Northern and Southern colonies

Fundamental differences between England and the colonies were also apparent in the differing cultures of the Northern and Southern colonies—many of which persist into the present day. From the beginning, the Southern colonies were based primarily upon providing agricultural products such as tobacco and rice that could not be grown in England. For a labor supply, the large Southern plantations depended upon slaves imported from Africa. While the Northern colonies also allowed for slavery, slave labor was a more integral part of Southern culture. Northern merchants and shipping interests, however, played a crucial role in the Trans-Atlantic slave trade, which constituted a significant aspect of the Northern economy. With an emphasis upon shipping and trading, Northern civilization was more based upon urban centers and people loved in close proximity to one another. The South, on the other hand, was rural with settlement scattered on farms and plantations. From the urban/rural split flowed important differences in education and religion. The scattered settlement of the South made it nearly impossible to establish schools that would service the farming population. Thus, the lower class was often devoid of educational opportunities unless the parents were literate and able to teach their children. As for the upper-class planters, private tutors were employed to teach the children basic skills, and when older they might be dispatched to boarding schools in England or the North. This upper-class education in the Southern colonies was primarily for males, although some planters provided for the education of precocious daughters. Living in more urban communities, it was easier for the North to provide schools, and literacy was more prevalent in the Northern colonies although class differences in education were still significant. Higher education also spread in the North with the establishment of universities such as Harvard, Yale, and Brown whose lucrative endowments were based upon fortunes made from the international slave trade. These regional differences in education have persisted into contemporary America with the nation's most prestigious universities such as the Ivy League located in the North, while funding for public education continues to lag in many Southern states, contributing to and fostering racial inequality.

Religion also contributed to the colonial regional differences in education. Today the South is often described as the "Bible belt" of the United States, but the religious impulse for colonization was much stronger in the North with the Pilgrims, Puritans, and Quakers than in the South. The religious communities of the North were more concentrated in purpose and geographically, leading to the construction of churches with ordained ministers. The influence of these religious communities was also evident in governance as groups such as the Puritans sought to control behavior with strict Sabbath laws. The religious direction of the Northern colonies favored education so that all citizens could read the Bible and be aware of God's word. Thus, primary education for women was encouraged as they were the caretakers for children and would need to provide religious instruction for their young charges. Religion also fostered higher education in the Northern colonies with institutions such as Harvard founded for the training of ministers. On the other hand, the scattered settlement of the South was less conducive to building religious communities. In the backwoods of the South, isolated farming families married and produced children in relationships that were not formally consecrated until an iterant Methodist circuit rider clergyman arrived and blessed the union.

While Methodists were influential in the Southern backwoods, and even initially criticized slavery among the poor white population that owned few if any slaves, the traditional Anglican Church of England enjoyed an official standing in more aristocratic Virginia. Living much of their lives in rural isolation, white Southerners often viewed Sundays as an opportunity to socialize and pursue leisure activities such as gambling on horse races and cock fights. The rigidity of Puritan religious life was missing from the South, but plantation owners certainly introduced Christianity among their slaves to prevent rebellion. Slaves were instructed that if one obeyed his/her master and accepted a subservient status there would be a heavenly reward. Slaves, however, often adapted Christianity and the Bible for their own purposes, extolling the story of God delivering Moses and the Israelites from Egyptian bondage.

Class structure

The North/South dichotomy was also evident in the class structure of colonial America. While colonial society was often celebrated as offering an industrious individual the opportunity to rise in society and become the social equal of his peers, reality was far more complex. The upper class in the South consisted of aristocratic planters who owned hundreds of slaves on their tobacco and rice plantations. The planters constructed lavish homes where they entertained their guests like royalty but often treated their slaves with cruelty and contempt. The lifestyle of the Southern aristocratic planter is perhaps best exemplified in the diary of William Byrd of Virginia. While these planters were agrarian businessmen who governed vast estates, the prosperity of the planter families was clearly based upon the exploitation of slave labor. The upper class of the urban North was dominated by wealthy merchants whose fleet of ships linked the colonies with England and markets in the West Indies. While these merchants relied upon free labor to build and maintain their ships, these Northern masters of commerce were also heavily involved with the expanding slave economy for their ships carried cargos of enslaved people from the West Indies and Africa, earning huge profits for mercantile families.

The upper-class planters and merchants constituted only a small percentage of the colonial population, most of whom, whether living in the North or South, consisted of small family farmers. Life was hard for these middle-class commercial farmers who labored to feed themselves and produce a surplus for the market. Most commercial farmers could not afford slaves and were dependent upon family labor with wives and children often sharing labor in the fields. These farmers of wheat, corn, beans, and tobacco were the backbone of the colonial economy, but few were able to achieve the kind of success that would allow advancement into the upper class of planters and merchants, although the possibility of social mobility was greater in the North where commercial farmers had greater access to urban markets.

The colonial middle class also consisted of artisans who were located primarily in Northern cities where they would have access to customers. Among the significant skilled craftsmen of colonial America were gunsmiths, printers, silversmiths, coopers or barrel makers, carpenters, blacksmiths, tailors, cobblers, masons, weavers, and sail makers. There was a growing market for artisans in the North, and some lucky and industrious craftsmen were able to expand their business and enter the merchant class. Such a path for advancement was more difficult in the South as potential customers were scattered throughout the countryside. Large plantations also required the skilled craftsmanship of artisans, so sometimes slaves were trained as artisans. Although they served the plantations well, there was little opportunity for these enslaved black artisans to advance.

Social mobility among the lower class was also limited. Pioneers were subsistence farmers who lived on both the Northern and Southern frontiers between Native and white settlement. Their lives were difficult and dangerous, but the possibility of advancing in society was possible if the frontiersmen stayed on the land they occupied for some time and transitioned from subsistence to commercial farming. However, many of the pioneers valued their independence and eschewed living in the proximity of neighbors. They preferred growing their own food, hunting, and trading with the Natives, often relocating to wilderness as settlement and market forces caught up with them.

Sailors also played a significant role in the colonial economy. With shipping essential to the Northern economy, merchants required a steady supply of sailors to service their ships. The sailor's life was a difficult one and offered little stability for families. The pay was low and often compensation was available only after a successful voyage. One would be away from home for extended passages of time, and, indeed, some sailors established more than one family in numerous ports. Stereotypes of drunken sailors abound, but when one considers the excitement of shore after months at sea, such exuberance is hardly surprising. Danger was also a part of the sailor's life with pirates, storms, and shipwrecks always a possibility. The constant search for a labor supply meant that merchants and sea captains were willing to employ free men of color as sailors. Free blacks often struggled to find employment, and work as a sailor was sometimes the only available option. The sailor's challenging and unpredictable lifestyle provided little opportunity for social mobility, although on occasion a fortunate sailor might save his money from lucrative voyages and purchase a ship of his own.

Other lower-class professions offered more hope for advancement. For example, the apprentice system provided an avenue for young men to learn a trade and eventually rise to the status of a skilled craftsman. In the urban centers of the North, a poor family could apprentice a promising son, and this was almost exclusively a male privilege, to an artisan. The apprentice was to live with the artisan and work for him during a time specified by a contract. In exchange for the labor, the artisan was to provide food and shelter while training the apprentice in a trade. After the contract expired the apprentice would be able to establish his own shop as a skilled artisan. A good example of the mobility possible in an apprenticeship is the case of Benjamin Franklin whose family of meager means apprenticed their son to learn the trade of a printer. The resourceful Franklin became a successful publisher, author, inventor, and politician who amassed a small fortune, but few apprentices achieved the lofty status of Franklin.

Practiced throughout the English colonies, but especially prevalent in the South, indentured servitude was also expected to be a path for social mobility. Poor people, both men and women, could secure passage to the colonies if they would serve the master, who paid their passage, for four to seven years. After the contract expired, the former servant would be eligible to attain land and become a productive property holder. The system, however, proved to be less than a model path for advancement. In the early years of settlement, there was a high death rate for indentured servants, who were unable to make any land claims. As conditions improved, indentured servants were able to complete the terms of their contract and establish property claims. This, of course, limited land acquisition for the wealthy who turned to slavery for the provision of a more stable labor supply that would not be able to compete for land ownership. For social mobility was not part of the slave system in which the labor supply was controlled by the master. Some owners might allow their slaves to cultivate small plots of land and accumulate funds by selling produce and animals. In fact, a few slaves then used this money to purchase their freedom. The owners, however, had no legal obligation to allow slaves to purchase their freedom. Slaves were not persons with rights but rather the personal property of the master. A slave who tried to earn and save money could simply have these funds confiscated by the master. Slavery was an arbitrary system in which the laborer was totally at the mercy of the owner, and any sense of personal initiative and advancement could be abrogated by the master at any time.

Poor Richard's Almanack and the self-made man

Nevertheless, the colonial economy was celebrated as offering a haven for the self-made man of talent and ambition to rise in society. Ben Franklin's *Poor Richard's Almanack* was a popular publication that provided a formula for success in the bustling colonial economy. According to the proverbs and witticisms gathered by Franklin in a volume similar to contemporary self-help books, one could become wealthy through hard work and thrift. *Poor Richard's Almanack* included such common maxims as "neither a borrower nor a lender be," "early to bed and early to rise makes a man healthy, wealthy, and wise," and "a stitch in time saves nine." Franklin could also be a rather salty individual, suggesting that "he who lives on hope dies farting"—meaning that relying upon wishing for success rather than working for it was no more productive than passing gas. While Franklin did not always exactly practice what he preached in the *Almanack*, his ideas resonated in the belief that America is a land of opportunity where the individual may succeed by "pulling oneself up by his/her own bootstraps" and neither charity nor governmental assistance is needed. In fact, Social Darwinists, Presidents such as Herbert Hoover, and libertarian think tanks such as the Heritage Foundation argue that governmental assistance undermines independence and creates dependency. Thus, Franklin's ideology of the self-made individual has enjoyed considerable influence throughout American history even though the social mobility promise of American life has failed to reflect reality with the American dream often becoming a nightmare as racism, sexism, poverty, and xenophobia have placed considerable barriers in the path of class mobility. If one perceives the struggle for economic advancement as a race, then not everyone starts at the same place, and some have far more hurdles to clear than others. Most Americans remain in the social class into which they were born, but some do attain their dreams, and the myth of social mobility retains a considerable influence within the ideology of American exceptionalism.

And as for Franklin's colonial society, the clichés of *Poor Richard's Almanack* offered little succor for some groups. Although the growth of colonial America depended upon land belonging to the Native population, they were considered "the other" and the virtues described by Franklin were not extended to these non-Christians whose land was stolen, culture disrespected, and children murdered. Although the African slaves lived amongst the white population, Franklin's sermonizing offered little in the way of guidance. An enslaved person might work hard, obey the master, and embrace thrifty habits, but still have his or her family sold on the auction block. Slavery was an arbitrary system, and while some slaves were freed, this had little to do with Franklin's virtues. Rather, it was simply the luck of the draw regarding a master. With one's status as a slave inherited through the mother, the enslavement of Africans was developed to perpetuate a servile labor supply, not to provide for the social mobility of virtuous individuals.

Women were also excluded from Franklin's recipe for success. Viewed as the appendage of fathers, brothers, and husbands, white colonial women were excluded from most professions. While perceived as needing the protection of men, these colonial women were extremely resourceful, laboring alongside their male relatives in the fields and often operating farms and businesses when husbands were unavailable or deceased. Many widows were quite successful in maintaining taverns and boarding houses established by their former husbands. Yet when a woman married or remarried, the property over which she had previously exercised control was bestowed upon her new husband. Thus, George Washington became one of the wealthiest men in the colonies when he married the widow Martha Custis, whose property included a plantation and hundreds of slaves. In addition to being excluded from professions and commerce, colonial white women were denied an education beyond the primary grades, although some upper-class fathers might provide an extended private education to a favored daughter. Abigail Adams, as her letters indicate, was certainly the intellectual equal of John Adams, her Harvard educated attorney husband. While white colonial women made significant contributions to raising children and laboring alongside male relatives, they never received the financial rewards reserved for males, a problem that certainly continues to plague American society.

As for Native and enslaved women, they were not extended the patriarchal protection supposedly available for white women. Enslaved women labored in both the plantation homes and fields, contributing to the growing colonial economy. They were also wives and mothers, seeking to maintain the family bonds that slavery often tore apart. Yet in the arbitrary nature of slavery, these women were often subjected to rape by masters who respected no moral or family limits on the control of their property. Native women also suffered at the hands of white men. The matrilineal nature of some Native cultures was especially challenging to the English patriarchy, and, unlike the French and Spanish, the English colonial governments sought to ban miscegenation with Natives. On the isolated frontier where few white women were to be found, unions between white frontiersmen and Native women did, of course, take place. Nevertheless, the lack of respect for Native culture and rights fostered racist attitudes that encouraged rape and massacres. Natives, women, and Africans were not included in Franklin's version of the self-made man and a culture constructed on equal opportunity. It is a gap between myth and reality that has challenged the American experience into the present day.

Mercantilism and the colonial economy

The English monarchy and Parliament also viewed the colonization of North America as providing great promise for the mother country. As with most European governments, the English viewed colonization through the lens of mercantilism. In economic terms, the purpose of a colony was to benefit the mother country by producing goods that were unavailable on the home front, while serving as a market for items manufactured by the mother country. Thus, a colony was not expected to be in economic competition with the mother country, but there was a problem with the mercantilist theory when applied to the English colonies of North America. The Southern colonies of Virginia, Maryland, the Carolinas, and Georgia seemed to essentially fit the needs of England. For example, tobacco, rice, indigo, and later cotton were lucrative agricultural products that could not be grown in England and for which there was considerable demand. The English government, in fact, encouraged the production of crops such as indigo, a blue dye, by paying farmers a bounty for its planting and then, in turn, promising to purchase the crop after its harvesting. The paying of bounties made many Southern planters and farmers perceive English mercantile policy as beneficial to colonial growth and development. Thus, it is not surprising that when the American Revolution came, many planters were favorably disposed toward the mother country and joined the Loyalist cause.

The Northern colonies of New York, Pennsylvania, and Puritan New England were an entirely different matter. The problem for the English Northern colonies was one of a geography that was too much like the climate of the mother country. Vast forest lands and numerous ports encouraged the building of ships and created a merchant class that challenged the mercantile and fishing interests of England. In addition, the Northern colonies included rich deposits of raw materials such as iron ore that could provide the foundation for manufacturing. To assure that the Northern economy did not grow into a competition with England, Parliament passed a series of acts designed to restrict economic activity. The Industrial Acts such as the Iron Act and Hat Act sought to prohibit colonial manufacturing. The Iron Act legislated that iron ore would have to be shipped to England where it would be transformed into manufactured goods such as plows which would then be transported back to the colonies for purchase. Of course, the plows manufactured in England, with the additional cost of shipping across the Atlantic, were expensive for the colonists, but the goal of Parliament was to prevent the growth of colonial factories in competition with English manufacturing. The fur trade was a staple of the colonial economy in both the Northern and Southern colonies, but to prevent the manufacturing of beaver pelts into hats in Northern cities with large potential labor supplies, the Hat Act prohibited colonial production of beaver hats. The pelts would have to be dispatched to England where factories would produce beaver hats for the colonies. While there was colonial opposition to the Industrial Acts and illegal manufacturing developed in the Northern colonies, it was difficult to conceal factories from English inspectors, but defying England was easier for Northern merchants and shipping on the Atlantic Ocean.

Northern merchants were opposed to Parliament's Navigation Acts that asserted all colonial trade would have to go through England and employ English ships. The colonists were forbidden to trade directly with other nations or build their own ships. Enforcement of the Navigation Acts would essentially destroy the burgeoning Northern mercantile trade, and merchants responded by resorting to smuggling, producing the irony that the foundation of the American economy was based upon the Trans-Atlantic slave trade. Circumventing the English Navy and Navigation Acts, Northern merchants embraced the triangular trade in which slave ships from Northern ports sailed to the west coast of Africa where they traded rum for slaves captured by coastal nations and tribes. The slaves were then shipped to the West Indies sugar plantations to provide a labor supply for that precious sweet commodity. In the final leg of the trade, sugar was dispatched to the Northern colonies where it was employed in the production of rum. This brief overview of the triangular trade, however, hardly begins to describe the horrors of the middle passage in which captive men, women, and children were packed like sardines into the dark hold of slave ships. In the holocaust of the Trans-Atlantic slave trade, millions perished in the overloaded ships. Sharks were reported to follow slave ships as every day the bodies of dead captives were thrown overboard. When threatened by English ships, a smuggler might simply jettison an entire human cargo by throwing the chained-together captives overboard. Yet, out of this illegal and immoral trade huge fortunes were made.

The English colonies in North America were initially viewed as havens for transplanted English men and women who would benefit England by furnishing raw materials and serving as a market for the mother country. Things did not quite go as planned for the colonies began to develop a distinctive culture and economy that differed from what England had anticipated. Significant differences were also evident between the Northern and Southern colonies which continue to have ramifications for contemporary America. The seeds of the American Revolution were evident in resistance to efforts by England to establish strict controls over the colonial economy. But the story is much more complicated than simply the unfolding pageant of liberty that provided a beacon of freedom for the world. For the founding of America was based upon wresting lands from the Native people and a dependence upon slave labor that were essential elements in the French and Indian Wars and American Revolution that led to independence from England.

Further Reading:

Armitage, David. *Ideological Origins of the British Empire*. New York: Cambridge University Press, 2000.

Bailyn, Bernard. *Voyages to the West: A Passage in the Peopling of America on the Eve of the Revolution*. New York: Knopf, 1986.

Cremin, Lawrence. *American Education: The Colonial Experience, 1607–1783*. New York: Harper & Row, 1970.

Curtin, Philip D. *The African Slave Trade: A Census*. Madison, WI: University of Wisconsin Press, 1969.

Henretta, James. *The Evolution of American Society, 1700–1815* Lexington, MA: D.C. Heath, 1973.

Holifield, E. Brooks. *Era of Persuasion: American Thought and Culture, 1521–1680*. Boston: Twayne Publishers, 1989.

Kolp, John Gilman. *Gentlemen and Freeholders: Electoral Politics in Colonial Virginia*. Baltimore, MD: Johns Hopkins University Press, 1998.

Lockridge, Kenneth A. *The Diary and Life of William Byrd II of Virginia, 1674–1744*. Chapel Hill, NC: University of North Carolina, Press, 1987.

Menard, Russell. *Migrants, Servants and Slaves: Unfree Labor in Colonial British America*. New York: Routledge, 2001.

Rediker, Marcus. *Between the Devil and the Deep Blue Seas: Merchant Seamen, Pirates, and the Anglo-American Maritime World, 1700–1750*. New York: Cambridge University Press, 1987.

5

Expulsion of the French and the American Revolution

The Declaration of Independence painted by John Trumbull; engraved and printed by Illman Brothers. Library of Congress Prints and Photographs Division. This painting depicts the presentation of the Declaration to the Second Continental Congress. Jefferson's document declared that all men are created equal, but a denunciation of slavery was deleted from the final draft. The nation continues to struggle to achieve the ideas outlined by Jefferson.

The American Revolution is a pivotal moment in world history, but it lacked the social upheaval and class warfare of the French and Bolshevik Revolutions. It was not a revolt of the masses against an exploitative upper class, but instead the revolutionary leaders, such as George Washington, John Adams, and Thomas Jefferson, were well-educated and wealthy members of the colonial elite whose prospects were being circumscribed by an English government that perceived the colonies as only serving the purposes of the mother country. According to the Declaration of Independence, whose primary author was Jefferson, the colonists had no choice but to rebel as the English crown had violated the social contract by failing to protect their natural God-given rights of life, liberty, and the pursuit of happiness. Yet, there was a fundamental contradiction in the concept that all men are born free with inalienable rights of which they may not be deprived without just cause and due process. Many of the revolutionary leaders were slave owners who stole the labor of enslaved Africans while violently expropriating the lands of the Native population and simultaneously depriving women of fundamental social, economic, and political freedoms. The American Revolution may, thus, be viewed as a political confrontation between a colonial elite and the English government as to who would rule the American colonies. Nevertheless, this rather conservative political revolution served as an example for other colonial revolts and had a tremendous impact upon women, Natives, enslaved peoples, and common farmers and laborers. The American Revolution and Jefferson's rhetoric of inalienable rights unleashed a fervor regarding political freedoms and social equality that challenged the traditional modes of hierarchy in the post-revolutionary period and which continue to resonate today. Much of American history ranging from abolitionism to the Civil Rights Movement to women's rights and the struggles of the LGBTQ community are about extending the promises of the revolution to all Americans.

French and Indian War

To place the American Revolution within historical context, it is first necessary to consider the so-called French and Indian War, or Seven Years War (1756–1763) on the international stage, which paved the way for the colonial revolt against British rule. The term French and Indian War is somewhat of a misleading description as this conflict on the North American continent was part of a much larger struggle between the nations of France and England for world supremacy. In fact, some historians believe that the Seven Years War should be more accurately labeled as the First World War for French and English forces clashed in North America, Europe, India, and both the West and East Indies. In North America, this imperial rivalry focused upon the rich farm land of the Mississippi and Ohio River Valleys as well as the lucrative fur trade along the Great Lakes. English settlers had trapped out much of the beaver population east of the Appalachian Mountains, and English settlers were pouring into the Trans-Appalachian West in search of pelts and farm land. Contesting this new settlement were the French and their Native allies.

New France extended northward from Louisiana into Canada, with French claims reaching as far westward as the Rocky Mountains. These extensive territorial claims were supported by exploration, efforts by Jesuit priests to Christianize the Natives which often resulted in the decimation of the indigenous population by spreading European diseases, and a lucrative fur trade with the Natives. While there was some attention given to the establishment of farming communities, New France was dominated by fur trappers who lived somewhat in harmony with the Native way of life based upon hunting, fishing, and trading. The French did not encourage female migration to North America, so many of the French frontiersmen intermarried with Native women and adopted aspects of Native culture. The English, on the other hand, were a far greater threat to the Native population and way of life as their expanding farm communities desired Native land for permanent settlement. Essentially, the English sought to replace the Native people rather than live in harmony with them and the environment.

Posing less of a threat, the French initially enjoyed the support of numerous Native allies in the North American clash with the English. The English, however, were able to take advantage of inter-tribal rivalries to secure Indian allies of their own, and superior English trade goods played a pivotal role in securing agreements with the Iroquois Confederation in the north and powerful Cherokee in the south. The conflict along the Trans-Appalachian frontier was brutally exacerbated by the policy of both the French and British to reward their Indian allies by paying for scalps that assured the Natives were waging war along the frontier.

With the securing of some Native allies and a huge population advantage on the Atlantic seaboard with settlers spilling over the Appalachian Mountains, England appeared to have a significant edge over their French rivals. Nevertheless, a lack of unity among the colonists and conflict between England and its North American colonies considerably hampered efforts against the French, exposing divisions that have characterized much of American history. In addition to the major economic and cultural divisions among the Northern and Southern English colonists, various colonial governments such as Pennsylvania and Virginia issued conflicting claims on the rich farm lands west of the Appalachians. Also, many colonists chafed at English mercantile policies such as the Navigation and Industrial Acts that placed rules and regulations upon the developing colonial economy. This conflict between larger English imperial designs and local settlers desiring land was also evident in the failure of many colonists to respect agreements drafted between the British and Native American tribes. The problem of unity made it impossible to forge a common policy of colonial defense as was exhibited by the failure of the 1754 Albany Plan of Union proposed by Benjamin Franklin.

The final confrontation that resulted in the expulsion of the French from the North American continent began in 1754 when a young colonial military officer by the name of George Washington led a contingent of Virginia militiamen into the Ohio River Valley, testing French resolve and designs on the region. After constructing what he called Fort Necessity, near contemporary Pittsburgh where the Monongahela, Allegheny, and Ohio Rivers meet, Washington's men were opposed by a superior French force from Fort Duquesne, and the young officer withdrew his troops, having learned that the French seemed willing to fight for control of the Ohio River Valley. Washington returned to the region in 1755 as part of a larger British army under the command of General Edward Braddock whose mission was to capture Fort Duquesne. An overconfident Braddock marched his forces through the wilderness, and outside of Fort Duquesne (near contemporary Pittsburgh) Braddock's army was ambushed by a smaller number of French troops along with their Native allies. The French and Indians employed forest cover for their attack, while the English continued to emphasize traditional European military tactics of marching and fighting in fixed formations. In the battle. Braddock was killed and his junior officer George Washington wounded as the English withdrew.

1763 Treaty of Paris

The war, however, was hardly over. The English government and military reorganized for victory under the leadership of Prime Minister William Pitt who, despite suffering from seizures later identified as epilepsy, proved a brilliant strategist. While developing war plans that would lead England to global victory in the Seven Years War, Pitt directed that in North America the English adapt their tactics to fighting in the wilderness and making greater use of their Iroquois allies. The result of these altered tactics was that a British army under the command of Geoffrey Amherst captured Fort Duquesne which the English proceeded to name Pittsburgh in honor of the Prime Minister. Meanwhile, a force under General James Wolfe captured Quebec, the capital of New France, by scaling the rocky cliffs that guarded the city. The armies then clashed on the Plains of Abraham in which Wolfe was killed as well as his French counterpart, the Marquis de Montcalm. These English military victories paved the way for the 1763 Treaty of Paris in which the defeated French essentially withdrew from North America by ceding Canada and French territory between the Appalachian Mountains and Mississippi River to the English. Spain had supported the French cause and was punished by surrendering

Florida to the English, although the English did little to develop what they perceived as the swamplands of the territory, and Florida was eventually returned to Spanish control. To compensate Spain for its loss of Florida, France agreed that Spain would gain the Louisiana territory or French lands west of the Mississippi River. The French, however, would reclaim Louisiana with the rise of Napoleon Bonaparte and the Treaty of San Ildefonso (1803).

The 1763 Treaty of Paris was extremely significant to North American Indians. The territorial negotiations, of course, failed to consult Native leaders, and for the next century and a quarter considerable fighting was waged between the Native populations and the white governments of England, Canada, and the United States. The Canadian policy toward the Natives was no more enlightened than that of the United States, while England encountered the problem of controlling a colony whose European population was primarily French. England attempted to deal with their French-Canadian problem by forced evacuations to New Orleans and the Louisiana territory. The cost of relocating the large French-Canadian population proved too great, although those who were relocated to Louisiana introduced the Cajun culture to the region. The French population concentrated in the province of Quebec has remained a problem for Canada with some residents supporting separation from Canada and the creation of a French-speaking state. As for the United States, perhaps the greatest legacy of the 1763 treaty is that English policy following the French and Indian War contributed to the move toward independence and separation from England.

Proclamation Line of 1763 and Stamp Act

The French and Indian War was quite expensive for the English government, and the crown believed that the colonists, who benefitted from England's defense and expulsion of the French, should bear the brunt of the cost for the war. Tensions would grow between England and the colonists as the mother country moved to pay for the war by increasing taxation and enforcing mercantilist regulations such as the Navigation Acts. Conflict also arose when England attempted to impose the Proclamation Line of 1763 prohibiting settlement west of the Appalachians. The British government feared that further settlement would spark conflict with the Natives and add to the cost of defending the colonists. British concerns were confirmed when the Ottawa chief Pontiac organized a rebellion of tribes in the Northwest against the encroachment of colonists into lands that were recognized by the English as being preserved, at least for the present, for the Native population, many of whom had cooperated with the English in the fighting against the French. On the other hand, many colonists viewed the bloody French and Indian War as a struggle for the land beyond the Appalachian Mountains. The farm land of the Ohio and Tennessee River Valleys was assumed to be the just bounty for which the colonists had battled the French. By enacting the Proclamation Line of 1763 and not supporting them in the taking of Native lands, many colonists believed that the British government was betraying them and denying them the just rewards of their military sacrifice and victory. Colonists ignored the Parliamentary ban of westward expansion and poured across the Appalachian Mountains, promoting considerable conflict with the Natives along the Trans-Appalachian frontier.

Discontent was further exacerbated by Parliament's efforts to regulate colonial trade and forge new taxes to address English debt incurred by the French and Indian War. In the Sugar Act of 1764, Parliament placed a tax upon the importation of sugar from the West Indies, posing a threat to the lucrative triangular trade. After protest from colonial merchants, Parliament agreed to lower the tax, but in 1765 Parliament passed the Stamp Act, igniting even greater outrage among many colonists. The Stamp Act dictated that colonists would have to pay for a government seal or stamp that was required for bills of sale, playing cards, newspapers, pamphlets, and legal documents including diplomas and marriage licenses. Colonial opposition was more widespread than with the Sugar Act which some considered an external tax on trade that the mother country had the right to enact upon the colonies. The Stamp Act, on the other hand, was perceived as an internal tax that should not be imposed on colonists by Parliament. Instead, such internal taxation could only be enacted by colonial assemblies where the colonists were represented. The Stamp Act was denounced as taxation without representation as the colonists enjoyed no representation in the British Parliament. Members of Parliament appeared rather surprised by the colonial reaction as a stamp act was already implemented in England and had aroused little controversy. British officials responded to colonial complaints by observing that American colonists enjoyed virtual representation in Parliament as the legislative body represented all English citizens regardless of where they resided. The concept of virtual representation failed to appease the colonists, although England might have considered undermining the taxation without representation refrain by providing the colonies with a few representatives in Parliament.

Unable to quell the discontent, Parliament soon faced economic protest of the unpopular Stamp Act. Providing an early example of colonial unity, representatives from nine colonies met in Philadelphia to protest the tax and formed the Stamp Act Congress that called for placing pressure on England through the nonimportation or boycott of English trade goods. To provide some muscle for the boycott, artisans and workingmen met in taverns in major port cities such as Boston, New York, and Philadelphia and formed the Sons of Liberty. Merchants and consumers who violated the boycott and continued to import and purchase English goods were subject to physical intimidation and threats from the Sons of Liberty, demonstrating working-class discontent with the Stamp Act. The boycott impacted English merchants and manufacturers dependent upon the lucrative North American colonial markets, and these business interests began to demand that Parliament abandon the Stamp Act and restore trade with the American colonies. In response to the growing economic and political pressure, Parliament agreed to repeal the Stamp Act. England, however, was still in need of tax revenues, and many in Parliament resented the rebellious attitudes exhibited in the Stamp Act Congress and boycott. Accordingly, Parliament passed the Declaratory Act asserting that repeal of the Stamp Act should not be construed by the American colonists as establishing any precedent that England did not possess the right to tax her colonies. So once again in 1767, Parliament was back with a new revenue bill, the Townshend Act.

Townshend Act, Writs of Assistance, and Boston Massacre

Named after the English prime minister Charles Townshend, the Townshend Act sought to raise revenue for the crown by placing a tax on enumerated imports such as lead, paint, paper, and most importantly tea. Townshend believed that unlike the Stamp Act, which was an internal tax and colonists could plausibly argue should only be levied by colonial assemblies, the Townshend Act was an external tax on trade over which Parliament and England clearly exercised authority. Many colonists, however, disagreed, and the protest pattern established during the Stamp Act Congress was repeated, but with an even greater intensity in northern port cities such as Boston. In addition to pamphlets and broadsides again denouncing taxation without representation, colonial boycotts of English imports were re-introduced and enforced by the Sons of Liberty. Smuggling increased as colonists ignored British taxation and regulations, while consuming their tea from illicit sources. Tensions were increased when Parliament imposed the Writs of Assistance, which were essentially general search warrants that allowed British authorities and military personnel to search any home or place of business for smuggled goods such as tea. Among the most vocal opponents of the Writs was James Otis, who resigned as advocate general of the vice-admiralty court rather than enforce the despised search warrants. Arguing that the Writs deprived colonists of a natural right to privacy, Otis stated that a man's home was his castle and could not be invaded by the government without just cause. The reasoning of Otis was later recognized in the Bill of Rights with the Fourth Amendment's limits on governmental search and seizure, but in 1769 his effectiveness as an orator was silenced when he was struck in the head by a rifle butt wielded by a British soldier. The protest led by men such as Otis again placed pressure on Parliament to rescind the taxation and end the boycott of English goods. Wanting to restore trade but maintain some control over their increasingly rebellious American colonists, Parliament decided to lift the Townshend duties except for the tax on tea. Recognizing the dependence of colonists upon tea, often combined with rum, as a beverage of choice, the English authorities believed that the colonists would be unable to maintain their boycott. Once they caved and began to pay the tax on tea, the principle of Britain's right to raise revenue from the colonies would be established and other taxes could be enacted. However, to curtail the smuggling of tea it was necessary to send additional English soldiers to the colonies. Anger with the summoning of more troops to enforce the Writs and tax on tea helped precipitate violence such as the Boston Massacre.

On March 5, 1770 a crowd of approximately sixty colonists were harassing and throwing snowballs at a British patrol of ten soldiers on the streets of Boston. The soldiers responded by firing into the crowd, killing five and wounding another six. Among those killed was Crispus Attucks, a free man of color who appeared to be leading the protest. His death reflects the irony of the American Revolution in which the colonists revolted against England in the name of liberty but maintained a system of forced slave labor based upon race. The irony of a black man being the first to shed his blood in the American Revolution was not apparent to participants at the time, but many colonists were quick to describe the shooting as a massacre in which British soldiers fired indiscriminately into a crowd of innocent Boston residents. On the other hand, British authorities defended the soldiers as acting in self-defense for their safety was threatened by an unruly mob. These differing perceptions of the Boston violence are reminiscent of the killing of four students by the Ohio National Guard at Kent State University in May 1970 during campus protests over the American invasion of Cambodia. Unlike the Ohio National Guardsmen, the British soldiers faced trial for their actions in a Boston courtroom. While two of the soldiers were found guilty of manslaughter, the others were acquitted after a spirited defense by attorney John Adams. Although Adams was a frequent critic of British policies, he wanted to establish the principle that in the colonies the rule of law was followed. Nevertheless, for the rest of his life Adams was subject to criticism for his defense of the soldiers accused of murdering innocent Bostonians. To assure that news of events such as the Boston Massacre were made available throughout the widespread English colonies, Committees of Correspondence were formed, producing pamphlets and broadsides there were to be circulated throughout the colonies. Playing a key role in this propaganda effort was Sam Adams, the more radical cousin of John. An artisan brewer who lacked the education and financial success of his cousin who later served as the second President of the United States, Sam may be the better- known today for a popular beer product bearing his imprint.

Boston Tea Party and Intolerable Acts

The agitation encouraged by the Committees of Correspondence found a new cause in the Boston Tea Party which was repeated in other colonial port cities. Growing frustrated with the smuggling and opposition to paying the tax on tea, Parliament decided upon a new strategy to break the colonial boycott. The East India Company was given a monopoly over marketing tea to the colonies and proceeded to lower the price, assuming the colonists would pay the tax for the cheaper tea and the boycott would be broken. With the principle of England's right to tax imports recognized, the price could later be raised. Colonial leaders such as Sam Adams viewed the East India Company monopoly with alarm, and the Committees of Correspondence urged the Sons of Liberty to resist importation of the cheap tea. Large crowds gathered at the ports of New York City and Philadelphia to prevent the unloading of vessels from the East India Company, while in Annapolis, Maryland, an unruly mob boarded a ship and burned the cargo. The primary, focus, however, was again upon Boston where Governor Thomas Hutchinson declared that such illegal actions would not be tolerated. In defiance of Hutchinson, approximately one hundred Sons of Liberty, apparently after some time spent in local taverns, disguised themselves as Indians and boarded the English ships in Boston Harbor and dumped overboard more than 300 chests of tea.

The Committees of Correspondence trumpeted the so-called Boston Tea Party to the other colonies, and Parliament believed that it had no choice but to respond sternly to this breech of public order, passing a series of acts that would become known as the Intolerable Acts. These measures were known in England as the Coercive Acts, necessary to deal with increasingly rebellious colonists. Master propagandists such as Sam Adams and his Committees of Correspondence, however, succeeded in branding British actions with language such as the Boston Massacre and Intolerable Acts which continue to resonate in the history books down to the present day. The Port of Boston Act closed Boston Harbor until the perpetrators of the illegal tea dumping were identified and punished. In addition, restrictions were placed upon the New England tradition of the town meeting. Despite the principle of colonial fair trials demonstrated by John Adams in wake of the Boston Massacre, British officials and soldiers accused of committing crimes in the colonies would now be tried in England, making it extremely difficult for colonists to provide testimony. And a new Quartering Act asserted that citizens of Boston would be required to house some of the growing number of British soldiers in their homes. Widespread resistance to the Quartering Act eventually culminated in the Third Amendment to the Constitution. Colonists also lumped the separate Quebec Act into the Intolerable Acts. While the Quebec Act may appear relatively benign today, it antagonized many colonists by providing religious freedom for French Canadians and reserving for Quebec the rich farm lands of the Ohio River Valley. England perceived the act as rewarding the loyalty of the French-speaking population in Quebec, while colonists living along the eastern seaboard of colonial America viewed the legislation as a betrayal like the Proclamation Line of 1763. Also, the Quebec Act fostered the anti-Catholicism of many English Protestant settlers.

Lexington and Concord

Reaction to the Intolerable Acts encouraged a degree of colonial unity. For example, other colonies dispatched supplies overland to Boston whose port was closed by the British navy. To discuss the deteriorating political situation, a Continental Congress that included representatives from all the colonies, except for Georgia where distance made travel difficult, gathered in Philadelphia. Independence was not yet on the agenda, but the Congress did call for the abolition of all trade with the mother country until the differences between the colonies and England were resolved. It was during this tense time that fighting broke out in April 1775 at Lexington and Concord, a short distance from Boston. The altercation began when British General Thomas Gage decided that he would dispatch soldiers under his command from Boston to Lexington and Concord to confiscate guns and ammunition being stockpiled in the area as well as to arrest smugglers John Hancock and Sam Adams who were reportedly seeking refuge in the area. The British actions, however, were detected by the colonists, and a series of riders set out to warn the residents of Lexington and Concord. Among those seeking to spread the alarm was Paul Revere, a well-known Boston silversmith, who was captured before he could complete his ride. Yet, Revere became the most acclaimed of those warning the colonists, perhaps because his last name was excellent for the rhyming scheme of Henry Wadsworth Longfellow in his poem 'The Midnight Ride of Paul Revere." Learning that British soldiers were moving into the area, several hundred so-called Minutemen, who supposedly could gather their muskets within a minute and be prepared to resist British tyranny, blocked the English soldiers from crossing a bridge into Lexington. With military forces confronting one another, fighting soon broke out, and the British who had not anticipated armed resistance began to retreat toward Boston, pursued by the Minutemen who ambushed the retreating soldiers from stone fences and inflicted considerable casualties. Although there was no coordinated movement toward independence, fighting had now broken out between England and the North American colonies.

The confrontation at Lexington and Concord led to the formation of the Second Continental Congress which included representatives from all thirteen colonies. The delegates assembled in Philadelphia were still reluctant to declare independence for several excellent reasons. First, asserting independence from the mother country would constitute an act of treason for which the usual punishment was hanging. And the chances for success did not seem promising for the colonists who would be pitted against the powerful British Empire. Also, the colonists were hardly unified about independence with large numbers, perhaps a third of the population, opposed to any type of formal break with England. Accordingly, the Second Continental Congress initially proposed the Olive Branch Petition to advance negotiations between the crown and the colonies. George III, however, was in no mood to negotiate with the rebellious colonists who had fired upon his majesty's troops, and the Olive Branch Petition was rejected. Confronted with a growing number of soldiers dispatched to the colonies, the Second Continental Congress determined that for purposes of self-defense, but not yet independence, it would be necessary to form a colonial army. George Washington, who was attired in a military uniform, was selected as the commander of this army. The respected Washington was experienced as a military commander during the French and Indian War and hailed from the crucial state of Virginia.

Paine's *Common Sense* and Jefferson's *Declaration*

Circumstances propelled the reluctant Congress toward a declaration of independence as fighting began to erupt between the British and colonists in a number of locations, including Bunker Hill in Boston, Charleston, Brooklyn, and Canada. As the violence intensified, clever propagandists such as Tom Paine advocated for independence in popular publications such as *Common Sense*. The fifty-page pamphlet was published in January 1776, and over 200,000 copies were sold in the first three months of its release. Paine wrote in a straight-forward fashion that appealed to the common men and women of the colonies, declaring independence was simply common sense and reflected the natural order. The small island nation of England simply could not maintain control over the large North American continent. In the natural world the satellite was never greater than the primary planet, and the same was true for the relationship between England and its American colony. Asserting that in America the law and not hereditary monarchy should rule, the radical Paine called for the establishment of a republic in which power would reside in a virtuous citizenry. Unlike the more aristocratic revolutionary leaders such as Washington and Jefferson, Paine came from common roots. In England, Paine had taught school and served as a corset maker, but had a passion for politics and writing. He was encouraged to move to the colonies by Benjamin Franklin, who was impressed with Paine's potential. After arriving in the colonies, Paine was soon caught up in revolutionary politics. In addition to *Common Sense*, Paine would later write a series of pamphlets called *The American Crisis* encouraging the independence struggle against England. As a radical proponent of republicanism, Paine was somewhat of a professional revolutionary who sought to export the ideas of the American Revolution to England and France, where he was imprisoned for a year during the French Revolution. Paine also evoked considerable controversy with his *Age of Reason* (1795) in which he criticized traditional Christianity and championed the Enlightenment. Essentially, Paine embraced the Deist ideas that influenced the Founding Fathers. Deists believed that a supreme being had created the universe governed by natural laws. The supreme being also empowered humans with reason that allowed them to discover these natural laws and live accordingly. In a universe governed by natural law, there was no place for divine intervention, and *The Age of Reason* was denounced by traditional Christians. After his political activities in England and France, Paine returned to the United States and died in 1809. He played a prominent role in fostering the American Revolution, but his influence waned after the establishment of the American republic. Paine always seemed more comfortable in the role of an agitator advocating for liberty rather than exercising power.

Nevertheless, the ideas of Paine presented in *Common Sense*, along with the increased fighting between British and colonial forces, pushed the Continental Congress to act. Richard Henry Lee of Virginia, whose grandson Robert E. Lee later led the armies of the Confederacy, introduced a resolution calling for independence, and a committee that included Thomas Jefferson, Benjamin Franklin, and John Adams was formed to draft a document proclaiming independence. Most of the committee's work was done by Jefferson who was more comfortable as a writer than an orator. The document was formally adopted on July 4, 1776 by the Continental Congress after Jefferson's critique of the slave trade was removed. Jefferson based the Declaration of Independence upon the social contract theory of government developed by English philosopher John Locke in his *Second Treatise on Civil Government*. According to Locke and Jefferson, all men are created equal and are endowed with inalienable God-given natural rights such as life, liberty, and the pursuit of happiness. The purpose of government was to protect these natural rights. Locke argued that in a state of nature there was chaos in which the strong often preyed upon the weak and deprived them of freedom. Thus, governments were formed to protect natural rights. If the ruler protected the rights of the people, they were obligated to support the government. This was the social contract in which obedience was expected in exchange for protection. If the ruler failed to protect the natural rights of the subjects, however, they were then obligated to overthrow the existing authority and create a new form of government that would guarantee natural rights. In Locke's theory of revolution, it would be necessary to prove that the ruler had, indeed, failed to preserve the natural rights of the people. Thus, much of Jefferson's argument is an indictment of how the British monarchy violated the rights of the colonists, and they had no choice but to rebel and create a new form of government. Among the examples Jefferson offers of how George III violated the social contact are the suspending of colonial governments, imposing of taxation without the consent of the people, forbidding trade with other nations, forcing colonists to quarter troops, waging war against the colonists, and failing to hear their petitions for the redress of grievances. Jefferson concludes that these violations of the social contract left the colonists with no choice but to declare independence.

Application of natural rights

Yet, there appears to be a tremendous gap between Jefferson's rhetoric of natural rights and the reality of life in the colonies on the eve of the American Revolution. The most obvious disconnect is the phrase "all men are created equal" when the revolution failed to end the institution of slavery. To his credit, Jefferson, a slaveholder, recognized this inconsistency and censured the monarchy for introducing slavery into the American colonies. At the insistence of representatives from Georgia and South Carolina, however, the condemnation of slavery was removed from the Declaration. To maintain unity in the struggle against Britain, the natural rights of enslaved Africans were ignored, and patriots such as Patrick Henry of Virginia failed to acknowledge the irony in calling upon his fellow white Virginians to revolt and discard the chains of slavery imposed by the British. Enslaved Africans, nevertheless, recognized that the concept of natural rights should apply to them, and in 1774 a group of slaves appealed to Massachusetts Royal Governor Thomas Gage for their freedom as they had done nothing to forfeit their God-given natural rights. While Gage ignored the slave petition, Lord Dunsmore offered freedom to all slaves who deserted their masters and joined the British cause. Thousands of enslaved Africans flocked to the British side; however, many of these Africans were re-enslaved when the British deserted them following the military triumph of Washington and the revolutionary forces. Although approximately 5,000 former slaves gained their freedom while fighting in the revolutionary army, most blacks in the new American nation remained enslaved despite the revolutionary rhetoric of natural rights. It would take a bloody civil war to finally rid the United States of slavery

The revolutionary doctrine was also limited in its application to women and Native people. During the debates of the Second Continental Congress, Abigail Adams wrote her husband urging John and the other delegates to "not forget the ladies" when it came time to forge a new government. Adams mocked his wife's demands, asserting that the natural rights doctrine was, indeed, getting out of hand. Adams maintained this gender bias even though Abigail was the intellectual equal of her husband and demonstrated her abilities by maintaining the family household while John was absent for extended amounts of time engaging in political activities. The political rights championed by the revolution were not extended to women with the exception of New Jersey where property-owning women were briefly allowed to vote in local elections. It was assumed that men would represent the interests of their wives in the public and political sphere. Nevertheless, educated women such as Abigail Adams continued to speak out on public affairs, and many women who ran the homes, businesses, and farms while their husbands were absent gained a degree of independence during the revolution. In addition, revolutionary women played a key role in supporting the boycotts of English goods, and their sewing skills were essential for keeping the American soldiers clothed. Although a rather sexist idea by contemporary standards, women were viewed as having a greater degree of virtue through their exclusion from the corrupt world of politics and commerce, and thus these "republican mothers" were in the best position to inoculate the values of the revolution to a new generation, thus enhancing the status of women.

Native people were also excluded from revolutionary concepts of citizenship. In fact, Jefferson employed the Declaration to denounce Indians even though he often cited the virtues of Native leaders such as Logan of the Mingo people, who asserted that he was forced to resort to warfare when his family was killed by whites. Yet in the Declaration, Jefferson displays racial stereotypes when he denounces King George for encouraging insurrection against the colonists by "merciless Indian savages." These racist attitudes were certainly evident in the brutal conflict between Natives and American expansionists who often paid bounties for Indian scalps. Impressed by the power of Britain and the quality of their trade goods, the Iroquois led by Joseph Brant allied with the British, but lost much of their land when their English allies were defeated. In the 1784 Treaty of Fort Stanwix, the Iroquois were forced to surrender much of their land in New York and the Ohio territory. A similar fate met the Cherokee in the southeast with the Treaty of Hopewell. While the promises of the American Revolution were not extended to African slaves, women, and Natives, many artisans and small farmers were encouraged by the revolutionary ideology to engage in class conflict and challenge the prerogatives of wealthy merchants and aristocrats, a conflict that would continue after the revolution until the Constitution created a stronger central government to preserve order and protect property. While the revolution failed to usher in the more radical changes sought by many Americans, much of the nation's history is the story of reformers and activists striving to implement the vision proclaimed in Jefferson's Declaration of Independence.

In the more immediate sense, the declaring of independence provided tangible results such as providing the struggling colonists with a clear cause for which they were fighting. A formal declaration of independence from Britain also made it possible for the new nation to obtain support from other powers such as the French who were eager to take advantage of their British adversaries. In addition to these practical considerations, the Declaration of Independence served as an example to the world that it was possible for a colony to separate from its mother country and establish its own identity. Thus, the United States may be perceived as the first new nation and once again providing the example of a city upon a hill, proclaiming itself as a champion of self-determination and natural rights. Nevertheless, a policy of expansion at the expense of Native Americans, Mexicans, and the people of Latin America, Asia, Africa, and the Middle East, seeking to establish their own visions of self-determination, the American example of freedom has all too often degenerated into imperialism and conquest. Just as on the domestic level, the struggle in America's relationship with the world remains the gap between the myth and reality of America's founding document.

Revolutionary War

Before the consideration of America's place in the world, however, independence would have to be achieved against the armed might of the British Empire. The upstart Americans were dependent upon an army of volunteer farmer soldiers who often left the field to harvest a crop, while the British Empire was able to employ vast resources, a navy, and a professional army that included mercenaries such as the German Hessians. To have a chance, the Americans would need to wage a war of attrition that would eventually convince the British that it was not in their best interest to maintain the drain upon resources represented by a constant war footing. Thts was the same strategy adopted by the Vietnamese against the superior forces of the United States in the 1960s and 1970s. Vietnam was America's longest war since the American Revolution, but it has since been surpassed by the ongoing and seemingly interminable military intervention in Afghanistan following the

9/11 terrorist attacks. It would fall upon George Washington to apply his meager resources toward wearing the British down and attracting international support for the American cause.

The initial months of the war following the declaring of independence did not go well for the Americans with Washington's forces in retreat. Washington recognized that his troops needed a victory, and he saw his opportunity in December 1776, when British troops under the command of General William Howe occupied Trenton, New Jersey. On December 26, Howe's Hessian mercenaries were sleeping after Christmas Day drinking and partying, when Washington's army crossed the Delaware River and caught them by surprise. The British abandoned the city, and Washington had his first major victory of the Revolutionary War. Washington, however, lacked the resources to hold Trenton and withdrew a few days later, but he had earned an important psychological victory that kept the American army in the field.

Seeking to end the war in 1777, the British dispatched an army from Canada under the leadership of the dandy General "Gentleman Johnny" Burgoyne, whose purpose was to occupy the Hudson River Valley in New York and isolate the ardent revolutionaries in New England from the rest of the American colonies. Confronted with this threat to divide America, General Horatio Gates prepared to engage the British invasion in a traditional battle at Saratoga, New York. The Americans were fortunate that expected re-enforcements did not reach Burgoyne, and Gates was able to carry the day. The vain and arrogant American officer Benedict Arnold was angry that Washington did not give him more credit for the victory, and he would later betray the American cause. Regardless of who is given credit for the battle, Saratoga may be viewed as the turning point of the American Revolution. American diplomats led by Benjamin Franklin were able to convince the French to support the American rebellion. The French, of course, had little use for the English and hoped that they might be able to regain a footing on the North American continent from which they were expelled following the French and Indian War. The victory at Saratoga in a conventional battle convinced the French that with proper aid the Americans might have a chance to defeat the British. Although many American are reluctant to acknowledge the fact, the French alliance provided much needed troops and military supplies and was crucial to the success of the American Revolution. But to take advantage of this support, it was essential for the Americans to maintain an army in the field. Considerable credit must be given to Washington for his leadership during the difficult winter of 1777-1778. After being driven from Philadelphia by General Howe, Washington quartered his soldiers at Valley Forge. Short of food, shoes, and warm clothing, the American forces were on the verge of disintegrating, but with the example of Washington who shared the miseries of his men, they survived the winter, and under the training of Prussian Baron von Steuben emerged a more disciplined fighting force in the spring of 1778. With the arrival of French troops and naval support, the tide of the war began to change, and the British sought to at least retain their Southern colonies.

As war raged along the eastern seaboard, American settlers continued to covet the Trans-Appalachian West. With the Iroquois Confederation and Cherokee supporting their British allies, there was considerable bloody fighting along the frontier. While the Americans were intent upon asserting their freedom from England, there were few qualms expressed about employing the revolution as an opportunity to seize lands belonging to the Iroquois and Cherokee. In addition, frontiersman George Rogers Clark led forces into what is today the state of Illinois, capturing British forts and laying claim to Indian lands in the region. The revolution allowed Americans to move into the farm lands of the west that were reserved for Natives in the Proclamation Line of 1763, and there was little concern expressed for Native natural rights.

Yorktown and the 1783 Treaty of Paris

Meanwhile, the British hoped to at least retain their Southern colonies where Loyalist sympathies were stronger, and colonists had established more binding economic ties with the mother country. While encouraging Loyalist forces in Georgia, Britain landed an army in Charleston and sought to occupy the Carolinas and Virginia. The British, however, encountered more resistance than anticipated. In South Carolina, American forces under the command of Francis Marion, who became known as the "Swamp Fox," used what would later be known as guerrilla tactics, striking rapidly with his smaller numbers and then taking refuge in swampland where the British troops became bogged down. British advances in the Carolinas and Virginia were also contested by American General Nathaniel Greene who inflicted heavy casualties upon the British while slowly yielding ground in such battles as King's Mountain, Cowpens, and Guilford Courthouse. After having his superior numbers considerably reduced, British General Charles Cornwallis retreated to the Yorktown peninsula in Virginia located between the James and York Rivers where he could be resupplied by the British Navy. Instead, he was trapped when French ships blocked re-enforcement by sea, and a land retreat was thwarted by the armies of Washington and French troops under the command of Marquis de Lafayette. Under bombardment from both land and sea, on October 19, 1781 Cornwallis surrendered in what proved to be the last major battle of the revolution. The strategy of attrition had succeeded. After Yorktown, the British government simply determined that it was no longer worth the cost to maintain the conflict.

In the 1783 Treaty of Paris the English agreed to recognize the independence of the American colonies with the boundaries of the Mississippi River on the west, Florida to the south, the Atlantic Ocean on the east, and Canada and the Great Lakes on the north—although the Canadian boundary line would continue to be a point of dispute between the British and the Americans. The treaty was a great disappointment to the French as the wartime alliance between the French and Americans deteriorated with the French failing to reclaim a territorial foothold in North America. In fact, the French monarchy incurred considerable debt in supporting the American cause, and in the final analysis this debt played a significant role in the French Revolution and the end of monarchy in France. The provisions of the treaty led to disagreements that continued to plague the relationship between England and the new nation of the United States. The British insisted that the Americans agree to the principle of restitution for British Loyalists, many of whom fled to England to avoid persecution. It is difficult to estimate the number of Loyalists, although some historians place the figure at approximately 15 percent of the American white male population on the eve of the revolution. Although found in all regions and strata of society, Loyalist sympathies were strongest in the South and among the upper class whose prosperity was fostered by British policies and rule. Other Loyalists, however, were more motivated by a sense of dedication to king and country. With the advent of the revolution, Loyalists were viewed as traitors to the Patriot cause, and elements of class conflict were present in the persecution of Loyalists. Some Loyalists were attacked by mobs and hanged, while their homes were burned, and estates confiscated. The confiscation of Loyalist property appeared to offer an opportunity for fostering the redistribution of property and resources in the new nation; however, state governments usually awarded these estates to prominent property holders and military figures, furthering rather than reducing social inequality. Terrified Loyalists fled the country, with many seeking refuges in Canada and England. Britain attempted to redress their grievances in the treaty, but the new American nation lacked the resources to honor their pledge to compensate the Loyalists for their losses. And England was in no mood for a return to the battlefield over the issue of Loyalist property. The failure of the United States to provide Loyalist compensation, however, encouraged the English to abandon their pledge to withdraw from all forts, such as Detroit, in the northwest territories of the new American nation. The Americans lacked the military might to drive the British from the outposts, from which they could continue to trade with the Natives, and be able to reassert British influence if the struggling New American nation collapsed. These unresolved issues and attitudes encouraged continued conflicts between the British and Americans that culminated in the War of 1812 or what some have called the Second War for American Independence. After the revolution, however, most Americans were focused upon what type of government would be formed to oversee the United States and whether the vision outlined in Jefferson's Declaration of Independence would be realized.

Further Reading:

Anderson, Fred. *Crucible of War: The Seven Years War and the Fate of Empire in British North America, 1754–1766*. New York: Vintage Books, 2001.

Bailyn, Bernard. *Ideological Origins of the American Revolution*. Cambridge, MA: Harvard University Press, 1967.

Foner, Eric. *Tom Paine and Revolutionary America*. New York: Oxford University Press, 1976.

Frey, Sylvia R. *Water from the Rock: Black Resistance in a Revolutionary Age*. Princeton, NJ: Princeton University Press, 1991.

Holton, Woody. *Forced Founders: Indians, Debtors, Slaves, and the Making of the American Revolution in Virginia*. Chapel Hill, NC: University of North Carolina Press, 1999.

Kerber, Linda K. *Women of the Republic: Intellect and Ideology in Revolutionary America*. Chapel Hill: University of North Carolina Press, 1980.

Maier, Pauline. *American Scripture: The Making of the Declaration of Independence*. New York: Knopf, 1997.

Nash, Gary. *The Unknown American Revolution: The Unruly Birth of Democracy and the Struggle to Create America*. New York: Viking, 2005.

Raphael, Ray. *A People's History of the American Revolution*. New York: New Press, 2001.

Taylor, Alan. *American Revolutions: A Continental History, 1750–1804*. New York: W. W. Norton & Company, 2016.

6

Articles of Confederation and Constitution

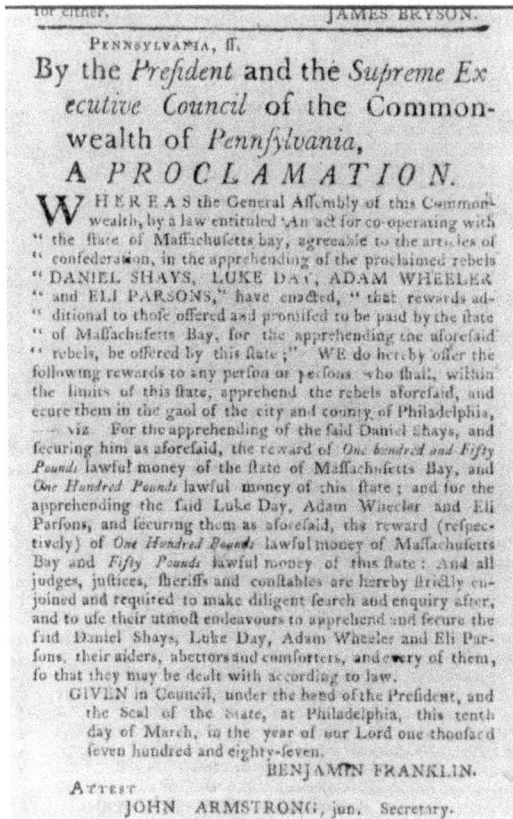

Proclamation by the State of Pennsylvania Offering Reward for Daniel Shays and Three Other Rebellion Ringleaders. Signed by Benjamin Franklin, May 19, 1787. Library of Congress Prints and Photographs Division. A rebellion of farmers in opposition to foreclosures and led by Revolutionary War veteran Daniel Shays terrified the creditor class, resulting in the replacement of the Articles of Confederation with a stronger central government in the Constitution.

Following the American Revolution, state governments tended to provide a foundation for democratization, but the situation on the national level proved more complicated. Based upon fears of a strong central government symbolized by the British monarchy against which the Americans rebelled, the new nation was governed initially by the Articles of Confederation in which greater power was concentrated in the states, serving as a model to which some contemporary conservatives seem to seek a return. Economic problems and political unrest under the Articles fostered demands for a stronger central government to protect property and the wealthy from too much democratization or what James Madison sometimes called the "mobocracy." Anti-Federalists perceived the Constitution as a counter-revolution by the forces of entrenched wealth such as the planters and merchants against the people, which was somewhat balanced by the inclusion of a Bill of Rights to protect individual liberties not mentioned in the founding document. Many Americans tend to treat the Constitution as if the document was drafted by Founding Fathers guided by divine providence. Instead, the Constitutional convention was a complicated governmental framework written by intelligent and wealthy politicians whose labors were perhaps more influenced by self-interest than divine intervention. Nevertheless, this rather conservative document, along with the Bill of Rights, has provided a framework through which Americans have been able to, through protest, amendment, and legislation, expand the promise of liberty for all as called for in the Declaration of Independence.

State constitutions

During and after the revolution, states drafted constitutions that protected fundamental freedoms or natural rights that would later be incorporated on the national level with the Bill of Rights. Among these fundamental rights were the freedom of speech, assembly, religion, petition, and press that the British sought to curtail as the colonists increasingly questioned their authority on the eve of revolution. These fundamental freedoms protected by the state constitutions were primarily abstract rights of political expression and failed to recognize individual economic rights such as the access to food, shelter, or health care described by President Franklin Roosevelt as the freedom from want during the Second World War. Considerable contemporary political debate is concentrated upon the issue of health care and whether access to doctors and health services is a basic human right which should be guaranteed by the government as part of the social contract or whether health care is a private matter outside of governmental intervention. This debate places the United States well out of step with other industrialized democracies which assure basic health care for their populations. Neither did the state constitutions guarantee access to education or the ballot. Ownership of property, tangible proof of one's stake in society, was still considered a prerogative for exercising the suffrage. However, the constitutions at the state level abolished once and for all the English law of primogeniture in which the eldest son as a matter of birthright was entitled to his father's lands. These property laws provided legal protection for large English landed estates and limited social mobility. With division of many large estates and tracts of land from which the Native population was displaced, property was more dispersed in the new nation and allowed for greater mobility as well as access to the ballot—at least for the male population.

Another important change written into the state constitutions was the disestablishment of religion, meaning that official state churches such as the Church of England were abolished. Thus, one could not be ordered to attend, take an oath, or be taxed in support of any official state church. This religious freedom would also later be recognized in the Bill of Rights, but some religious leaders maintain that America was founded as a Christian nation and argue that disestablishment and freedom of religion do not mean a separation of church and state. Instead, the Founders intended for America to be a Christian nation, although there would be no official state Christian church. This narrow perception fails to acknowledge the diversity of religious thought present in the new American nation as well as the influence of the Enlightenment and Deism upon that nation's founders who believed in freedom from religion as well as freedom to practice religion.

The rights and freedoms of the state documents did not extend to all inhabitants of the American nation. Although it may be argued that the American Revolution enhanced the status of women who were entrusted with indoctrinating the children into the virtues of republicanism, their legal status remained circumscribed with limits placed upon their access to voting, holding political office, property ownership, and divorce from abusive husbands. Only in New Jersey did women briefly exercise the suffrage after the revolution, and the founders did not remember the ladies as Abigail Adams requested. Native Americans remained outside of the legal structure and protections established by the states. In fact, the citizenship of the Native population would not be recognized until the 1924 Indian Citizenship Act. Meanwhile, the states and national government would continue to view the Natives and their tribal structures as a hindrance to western expansion and the bringing of civilization to the untamed wilderness. But perhaps the greatest challenge to the natural rights ideology of the revolution was the persistence of racial slavery. Many Americans understood the incompatibility of slavery with the ideas expressed by Jefferson in the Declaration of Independence. Accordingly, most Northern states with smaller slave populations began moves to abolish the institution although emancipation was often gradual with owners compensated for their slave property.

This limited abolition of slavery did not extend to the South where slave labor was still perceived as essential to the cultivation of rice, tobacco, and cotton. In addition, Northern merchants continued to reap profits from the Trans-Atlantic slave trade. The division and debates over slavery continued to plague the new nation.

Articles of Confederation

Under the Articles of Confederation, the states were recognized as harboring greater power than the national government. Americans were intent upon avoiding the centralization of sovereignty in the English monarch that had led to the American Revolution. Rather than power residing in a distant centralized government, the thirteen states of the new nation, located closer to the people, would exercise primary authority in the new government. The national government would consist of a unicameral legislature or congress in which each of the thirteen founding states, regardless of land size or population, would receive one vote. And to pass any legislation at the national level, two-thirds of the states would have to agree. This provision, of course, would make it difficult to enact legislation without a degree of consensus among the states. Included among the major powers assigned to the national government under the Articles of Confederation were the conduct of foreign affairs, the settlement of conflicts between the states as well as the admission of new states as settlement spread westward, the creation of a post office, and the borrowing of money. The ability to negotiate treaties and wage war involved not only the major European powers but perhaps more importantly the Native nations with whom the new government contested for control of the Trans-Appalachian West. Claims to the land in this region were also subject to conflict among the existing states, while land speculators and local politicians promoted the formation of new states as pioneers poured across the Appalachian Mountains. The settlement of the West is celebrated as one of the great achievements of the Articles, but this success was gained with considerable cost to the Native population. Another major accomplishment for the Articles was the creation of a national post office which played an essential role in unifying the new nation. With today's reliance upon the instantaneous nature of internet communication it is easy to overlook the significance of a post office in assuring communication through the expansive territory claimed by the new American nation. And the creation of a post office, surveying the west, and conducting war and peace required considerable funding.

While the national government under the Articles could borrow money, the Congress was denied the power to levy taxes upon the people. Remembering how revolutionary ardor was fueled by resistance to British taxation, under the Articles it was only possible for the national government to request funds from the states who could raise taxes to support the actions or borrowing of the Congress. Through control of the purse strings, the states, thus, exercised considerable influence over the conduct of the national government. Also, the economic powers of the new American nation were severely limited as the regulation of trade was reserved to the states. Again, the Articles were a reaction to colonial affairs when the centralized English government exercised control over trade through such measures as the Navigation Acts. However, the ability of states to place their own internal tariffs limited trade within the new nation, making the exchange of goods more expensive. And finally, there was no chief executive responsible for assuring that the laws of the new nation were administered uniformly.

The inability to raise funds quickly led to problems. To gain independence, the Americans secured financial aid from European nations who were eager to curry favor with them and punish the British for past transgressions. However, impatience with the Americans quickly grew as the United States could not repay the money they had borrowed to fund their revolution. While Americans enjoy thinking of themselves as a super power and express consternation with developing nations that are unable to meet their international financial obligations, it is worth recognizing that the United States was once an emerging nation struggling to pay its bills and gain international respect. In addition to being unable to pay foreign debts, the Articles moved to disband the revolutionary army and lacked the money to provide compensation which the soldiers were promised. Restless officers and soldiers threatened action against the unresponsive Congress, but influence of the well-respected George Washington prevented the type of military interference that has crushed the growth of democracy in many new nations.

Despite these many problems, the Articles are credited with providing for the orderly settlement of the West with legislation such as the Land Ordinance of 1785. Seeking to raise revenue through the selling of public lands, the legislation divided land into townships of six square miles, which in turn were subdivided into thirty-six sections of 640 acres each. The sixteenth section in each township was reserved for public education, but the legislation also benefitted speculators. While the price for an acre was only one dollar, one had to buy an entire section and thus needed $640. Land companies and speculators purchased the land at this low price and then subdivided the sections and charged settlers more than a dollar per acre. The law, however, provided for the rectangular grid system that characterizes much of the contemporary Midwestern United States. Settlement in the South was somewhat more haphazard, but pioneers and land speculations, such as Daniel Boone, helped pave the way for creation of new states such as Kentucky and Tennessee. In addition, the Northwest Ordinance of 1787 called for dividing the land of the old Northwest into five territories—Ohio, Indiana, Illinois, Michigan, and Wisconsin—that would be eligible for statehood after attaining 60,000 inhabitants, although the Native population was not considered in compiling this number. This significant legislation also asserted that slavery was to be banned from the Northwest territories and states, perpetuating the sectional division over slavery that eventually culminated in the Civil War. This settlement, however, came at the expense of Native people whose lands were diminished in imposed agreements such as the 1784 Treaty of Fort Stanwix in which the Iroquois Confederation was forced to cede Ohio to the whites.

Problems under the Articles and Shays's Rebellion

Despite the expansionist accomplishment of the Articles, the period after the revolution witnessed numerous problems for the new American nation. The weakness of the United States was evident in the difficulties the nation encountered in maintaining control of its borders. Although the British promised in the 1783 Treaty of Paris to vacate the Northwest posts on American soil, the United States lacked the military power to enforce the agreement, and the British remained. Meanwhile, relations with Spain deteriorated. The Mississippi River was an important trade route for the United States, but Spain controlled the port of New Orleans and by denying American merchants the right of deposit in the port city, Spain effectively limited American access to New Orleans. Spain entertained hopes that some western states would become frustrated with the situation and seek to gain use of New Orleans by joining the Spanish Empire. The United States was also beset by a post war depression after the British denied American merchants and farmers access to British markets in the West Indies. Although the American colonists often chafed under English regulation of trade, the colonies had established lucrative markets in the British West Indies. But since the Americans were no longer part of the British Empire, they were now restricted from these markets, setting off an economic depression as many American commercial farmers were unable to sell their surplus products.

The depressions exacerbated internal economic and class divisions within the new American nation. Debtor farmers who had borrowed from merchants and bankers were unable to sell their products and thus could not repay their creditors. Threatened with the loss of their farms, many debtors resisted foreclosures by taking up arms and putting pressure on state legislatures to enact stay laws that would protect farmers from eviction. The creditor class warned of anarchy and class warfare, and their worst fears seemed realized when Revolutionary War veteran Daniel Shays led a rebellion of farmers in western Massachusetts who took up arms to demand lower taxes and end of foreclosures. The rebellion was not particularly well organized and after a few skirmishes it was crushed by the established authorities. Although Shays's Rebellion was put down, it terrified the creditors and propertied class who feared that the next revolt might pose a more serious threat to the sanctity of wealth and private property. Accordingly, many within the upper class came to believe that the Articles of Confederation would need to be replaced with a stronger central government that would have the power to assure order and protect private property from the masses.

Constitutional Convention in Philadelphia

In 1786, the state of Virginia issued a call for a convention to reconsider the governmental structure of the new nation. When only five states sent representatives to Annapolis, Maryland, Alexander Hamilton of New York urged the states to try again and convene another convention the following year. On May 25, 1787 fifty-five delegates gathered in Philadelphia to consider revision of the Articles. The convention was legitimized through the participation of such respected figures as George Washington, Ben Franklin, James Madison, and Alexander Hamilton. However, other key revolutionary leaders were missing from the proceedings in Philadelphia. Men such as Thomas Jefferson, Sam Adams, John Hancock, Patrick Henry, and Tom Paine were suspicious of the convention, fearing that Philadelphia constituted an opportunity for the wealthy to create a counter-revolutionary document to thwart the democratic voice of the people. These men would later form the Anti-Federalist opposition to ratification of the Constitution. The Anti-Federalist perspective was given impetus as the Philadelphia delegates met in secret, with windows barred and closed during a hot and humid summer, and the delegates ignored their directive to amend the Articles and, instead, created an entirely new governmental framework.

The Constitution is today a revered document, leading some to conclude that the Philadelphia delegates were guided by the hand of God to create the ideal form of government, while a more secular perspective asserts that baseball, jazz, and the Constitution are America's greatest contributions to the world. Such perceptions of the Constitution, however, were challenged in 1913 by historian Charles Beard in the controversial *An Economic Interpretation of the Constitution*. Essentially, Beard argues that the Founders were guided more by their pocketbooks than the hand of God. The Founders desired a stronger central government that would assure the nation's stability by funding or paying off the national debt. Many bonds that were considered worthless were owned by widows and orphans of revolutionary soldiers, and speculators, many of them operating on the insider knowledge that the new government would honor these bonds in full, purchased the bonds for only a fraction of their worth. Thus, Beard maintains that many of the Founders were engaged in bond speculation and financially benefitted from the stronger central government created under the Constitution. While many scholars have challenged Beard's interpretation regarding the Founders personally benefitting from bond transactions, his overall argument that the Constitution was essentially a conservative document that favored the wealthy and property at the expense of the people seems to have some merit when one closely examines the document.

The delegates at Philadelphia appeared united in creating a stronger central government that enjoyed the power to create an army and employ state militias to suppress insurrections such as Shays's Rebellion. Beyond this consensus, there was considerable debate regarding the form this government would take and what checks might be placed upon it. The Constitution established a federal system in which power would be shared between the national and state governments, with the Constitution spelling out the powers belonging to the central government while all other governmental powers would be reserved to the states. Nevertheless, the powers belonging to the central government could be interpreted more broadly through provisions such as the necessary and proper clause. To place some limits on the national government, three branches of government were created to provide checks and balances on the centralization of power with a legislative branch to pass the laws, an executive branch to enforce the laws, and a judiciary to interpret the laws and allow a sense of justice. The checks and balances have often seemed to function quite well such as the Watergate crisis under President Richard Nixon during the 1970s, but the structure of the national government as created by the Founders also includes institutions that have limited democratic change and thwarted the voice of the people.

Creation of Congress

Much of the debate in Philadelphia concentrated upon how to constitute the legislative branch. The state of Virginia proposed a Congress in which representatives would be assigned according to the state's population. This so-called large state plan was opposed by New Jersey who called for all states to receive an equal number of votes in the legislative chamber. This impasse was eventually resolved by the Connecticut plan or great compromise that envisioned a bicameral legislative body. The House of Representatives was to be based upon population, while the Senate was to include two Senators from every state. To become a law, legislation would have to be passed through both branches and signed by the President. The Congress established by the Constitution enjoyed powers well beyond the unicameral legislative body under the Articles of Confederation. For example, the right to levy taxes and regulate trade denied the national government under the Articles was granted to the Congress by the Constitution. Among the other enumerated powers granted to Congress were naturalization laws, coining as well as borrowing of money, issuing patents and copyrights, creation of a post office, establishment of inferior federal courts below the Supreme Court, calling forth the state militias to maintain order, forming an army and navy, and declaring war. But perhaps the most significant privilege bestowed upon the Congress was the ability to enact legislation necessary to execute the enumerated powers. The so-called necessary and proper clause expanded the national government by suggesting that the Congress enjoyed implied powers if proposed legislation could be related to implementation of the enumerated powers listed in the Constitution. For example, Alexander Hamilton would later argue that the Constitution implied the need for a national bank by giving Congress the power to levy taxes, borrow funds, and coin money. Over the course of American history, the implied powers have been used to expand the reach of the national government, an outcome feared by the Anti-Federalists. Nevertheless, the structure of the Congress also limited the scope of democratic change.

The House of Representatives was the more democratic chamber with its membership elected directly by the people and apportioned according to state population. The House membership would remain close to the people through having to stand for election every two years. Furthermore, the Constitution set no property or financial qualifications for Representatives, although the states who established voting participation laws at the time continued to restrict suffrage through race, gender, and property requirements. Contemporary critics also maintain that the failure to include term limits encouraged the rise of professional politicians. But at the time the Constitution was written, the greatest controversy surrounding the creation of the House was over the institution of slavery. To assure political protection for slavery, Southern delegates at the Constitutional convention demanded that slaves be counted in the census to assure adequate representation in Congress. This would increase the clout of Southerners in the House who could protect slave property from emancipation. Many delegates from the North preferred some type of restrictions be placed upon slavery, but fears that Southerners might fail to support the Constitution led to the infamous three-fifths compromise which essentially made slavery an integral part of the original Constitution by allowing slaves to be counted as three-fifths of a person for purposes of apportionment. In addition, slavery was protected in the Constitution through the provision that fugitive slaves must be returned to their owners—in other words, enslaved people would be treated as property in the United States. Opponents of slavery were somewhat compensated with the provision that the importation of slaves would be abolished after 1808, but the Constitution placed no restrictions upon the nation's internal slave trade.

Minority slave interests and agricultural states were also protected by the structure of the Senate in which every state regardless of population was assigned two Senators. The Senate has traditionally functioned as a conservative check upon democratic change by protecting minority interests or property, reflecting the fact that the Constitution was enacted in opposition to the popular unrest of Shays's Rebellion. Popular influence over the Senate was limited by having Senators serve a six-year term, and Senators were to be selected by state legislatures rather than directly by the people—although direct election of Senators was introduced in the Seventeenth Amendment to the Constitution. This elite legislative body enjoys greater powers than its House counterpart, for in addition to passing legislation, the Senate must approve treaties negotiated by the executive branch and has the power of advice and consent over Presidential appointments and Supreme Court judge nominees.

Presidency and Supreme Court

The powers of Congress were to be checked by the executive branch as the President could veto legislation, although this veto may be overridden by a two-thirds vote. Alexander Hamilton envisioned a strong executive who would protect property and assure order as commander-in-chief of the nation's armed forces. Although Congress has the right to declare war, recent international events demonstrate the considerable power invested in the President as the country's chief diplomat and military commander. Thus, other founders worried about the chief executive assuming dictatorial power as a demagogue who might appeal to popular passions and abuse the office. The President would share appointment and treaty prerogatives with the Senate. If the President were to be abusive of his office, as some Founders feared that the office was too closely modeled after the English monarchy, Congress could impeach and remove the President from office if found guilty of high crimes and misdemeanors—although the meaning of this term remains a subject of considerable political debate. But perhaps the biggest check upon the Presidency was the Electoral College, an institution that has evolved over time but still remains a controversial example of what many Americans perceive as an undemocratic and dysfunctional method of selecting the country's leader. Founders such as James Madison were concerned that a President might secure election by appealing to the passions of what Madison termed "the mobocracy." To curtail a demagogue who might encourage anarchy and class warfare, the President would not be elected directly by the people. Instead, elite members of society, selected by the governors and legislatures of the states, would meet after the general election to cast the official votes of each state with the number of electoral votes apportioned according to the state's population. These electors would be free agents who could ratify the choice of the people, or if they believed that the people were misled by a demagogue the electors were able to overrule a popular vote that might threaten public order. Thus, the wealthy political elite had the final say in determining who occupied the Presidency. The Constitutional requirements for the office are minimal, describing that the President must be at least thirty-five years of age and born in the United States. While no property or wealth standards are outlined for the President whose four-year term initially included no limitations—which was altered by the Twenty-Second Amendment following the election of Franklin Roosevelt to four terms—the Electoral College assured that minority interests of wealth and property could block the popular will in regard to who exercised the powerful reins of the nation's commander-in-chief. The possibility of the Electoral College in which rural and often more conservative states may thwart the democratic goals of the majority was quite apparent in the Presidential elections of 2000 and 2016 in which George W. Bush and Donald Trump won a majority of the electoral votes but lost the popular vote.

Another check on the centralization of power as well as the will of the people was the creation of a judicial branch of the government headed by the Supreme

Court. The number of judges today on the highest court is limited to nine members, although the number is not written into the Constitution. The document lays out the jurisdiction of the court, although the power of judicial review on which the court may rule upon legal challenges to the Constitutionality of legislation was assumed by Chief Justice John Marshall in the case of *Marbury v. Madison* (1801). As with the President and Senators, the selection of federal judges was taken out of the people's hands. The President would appoint the judges subject to the confirmation of the Senate, and once confirmed the judges served for life. Many Anti-Federalists complained about these life appointments over which the people exercised no control, but Federalist supporters of the Constitution insisted that the anti-democratic provision was necessary to assure the independence of judges who could make their decisions without fear of public passion and re-election. Without the threat of being turned out of office for unpopular decisions, independent judges would follow the rule of law and insure that minority interests were protected from the tyranny of the majority. Today such minority interests are interpreted as referring to minority racial groups or members of the LGBTQ community, but to the Founders these minority interests were the wealthy and property threatened by the anarchy of popular uprisings such as Shays's Rebellion.

Ratification and Bill of Rights

For those who believe the document placed too much power in the hands of the elite and too often left the people out of the decision-making process, the Constitution included an amendment process. The Founders, however, made the amendment procedure a difficult one, and over the history of the United States only twenty-seven amendments to the Constitution have been ratified—and most of these were clumped around events such as the ratification struggle, Civil War, and Progressive period. To amend the Constitution, two-thirds of both houses of Congress or conventions called for by the state legislatures of two-thirds of the states may propose amendments that would be considered ratified when either three-quarters of state legislatures or conventions in three-quarters of the states approved the amendment. These stiff requirements certainly place restraints upon a democratic majority and have thwarted passage of popular Constitutional changes such as a proposed equal rights amendment supporting women's rights and barring gender discrimination. Incorporating the challenging amendment process, the Constitution was presented to the states and would replace the Articles of Confederation when nine state conventions ratified the document.

It is quite difficult for many Americans today who treat the Constitution as holy writ to comprehend the degree of controversy initially generated by the document as debate and sometimes violence divided the new nation. The Federalists, usually representing the wealthy planters and mercantile interests, insisted that ratification was essential for the formation of a government that would be able to assure order and protect property while fostering economic growth. The Anti-Federalists, on the other hand, perceived the Constitution as an effort by the wealthy elite to thwart popular rule, and they enjoyed support among the small farmers and artisan class although many of their leaders such as Jefferson were well-educated aristocrats. As the debate raged throughout the nation, the Federalists worked to gain the support of key states such as Virginia, New York, and Massachusetts. The large Southern state of Virginia was brought on board with the understanding that native son George Washington would become the first President under the Constitution. Although one of the wealthiest men in America, Washington was well respected for his military service during the revolution as well as lack of ambition to garner personal power. Federalists assured their opponents that Washington was a man they could trust. To address strong Anti-Federalist opposition in New York, Alexander Hamilton, John Jay, and James Madison wrote a series of newspaper articles, now known as the *Federalist Papers*, in support of the Constitution. These influential articles remain some of the best sources available for understanding the arguments of the Federalist Founders who insisted that while a stronger central government was necessary to assure order and prosperity, opponents had no need to fear their government whose influence would be limited through checks and balances assigned to the three branches of government.

Suspicions regarding the proposed Constitution were high in Massachusetts where revolutionary ardor fanned the flames of revolt against Britain and raised fears regarding another centralized government. The Anti-Federalists of Massachusetts were concerned that while the Constitution concentrated upon the powers of the new central government, there was little consideration given to protections for the natural rights of the people—the cause that had fueled the revolution in the first place. Although many Federalists believed that guarantee of natural rights was assumed in the document, James Madison, whose notes on the Constitutional convention are essential for understanding the proceedings in Philadelphia, recognized that Anti-Federalist concerns might be assuaged through a series of amendments specifically addressing the issue of natural rights guaranteed to the people. Accordingly, Madison, who is often acknowledged as the father of the Bill of Rights, lobbied for the adoption of the first ten amendments to the Constitution which guaranteed such natural rights as freedoom of religion, speech, press, assembly, and petition; freedom from cruel and unusual punishment; the right to a speedy trial; protection from self-incrimination, unreasonable searches, and the arbitrary quartering of soldiers in one's home; and the right to bear arms which it may be argued relates more to a well regulated militia than individual gun ownership. The Tenth Amendment concluded that all powers not delegated to the national government were reserved to the states. The inclusion of a Bill of Rights convinced Massachusetts and most Anti-Federalists to support the Constitution which was ratified on June 21, 1788 when New Hampshire became the ninth state to endorse the document. Rhode Island, with a tradition of political independence and dissent going back to Roger Williams, became the final of the original thirteen colonies to ratify in May 1790, a full year after the implementation of the new nation's government under the Constitution.

The formation of the Constitution, however, did not solve all the nation's problems. The first three Presidents of the country, George Washington, John Adams, and Thomas Jefferson, were confronted with establishing the economic foundation for the republic while carrying out a peaceful transfer of power—a test which many a new country has failed. Also unresolved was territorial expansion that continuously brought the republic into conflict with the Native population as well as the troublesome practice of slavery that stained the claim to be a city upon a hill and an example to the world. On the international stage, the legitimacy of the United States was challenged by the wars rising out of the French Revolution, and in 1812 the United States fought another war with Great Britain.

Further Reading:

Beard, Charles. *An Economic Interpretation of the Constitution.* New York: Macmillan, 1913.

Kaminski, John P., ed. *A Necessary Evil?: Slavery and the Debate over the Constitution.* Madison, WI: Madison House, 1995.

Kammen, Michael G. *A Machine That Would Go of Itself: The Constitution in American Culture.* New York: Knopf, 1986.

Kesler, Charles R., ed. *Saving the Revolution: The Federalist Papers and the American Founding.* New York: Free Press, 1987.

Levy, Leonard. *Original Intent and the Framers' Constitution.* New York: Macmillan, 1988.

Maier, Pauline. *Ratification: The People Debate the Constitution, 1787–1788.* New York: Simon & Schuster, 2010.

Main, Jackson T. *The Anti-federalists: Critics of the Constitution, 1781–1788.* New York: W.W. Norton & Company, 1974.

McDonald, Forrest. *We the People: The Economic Origins of the Constitution.* Chicago: University of Chicago Press, 1958.

Morris, Richard B. *The Forging of the Union, 1781–1787.* New York: Harper & Row, 1987.

Wood, Gordon. *The Creation of the American Republic, 1776–1787.* Chapel Hill, NC: University of North Carolina Press, 1969.

7

The Early Republic: Presidencies of Washington, Adams, and Jefferson

Portrait of Alexander Hamilton by John Trumbull. Detroit Publishing Company Photograph Collection (Library of Congress). As Secretary of the Treasury, Hamilton orchestrated a financial plan that promoted business and industry, while demonstrating the increased powers of the central government by crushing the Whiskey Rebellion of disgruntled farmers in western Pennsylvania.

Benjamin Franklin famously quipped that after the struggles for independence and the Constitution, the American people had a republic if they could keep it. The early republic under Presidents Washington, Adams, and Jefferson from 1789 to 1808 faced tremendous internal economic and political challenges as well as external threats to its existence. Washington was perceived as a unifying figure who might forge a sense of common purpose among the many divisions apparent during the revolution and drafting of a governmental framework, but political parties emerged during the presidencies of Adams and Jefferson and threatened the fragile new republic as it struggled to realize its promise.

Background of George Washington

For many Americans, Washington emerged as the indispensable man who provided a sense of unity by placing his country above personal ambition. Washington was primarily respected for his honesty and integrity rather than his intellect, but the myths about tossing a coin across the Potomac River and confessing to his father that he could not tell a lie after chopping down his parent's beloved cheery tree were created in popular children's stories by author Mason Locke "Parson" Weems following the first President's death. Born into a Virginia planter farming family of relatively modest means, Washington served as a surveyor before beginning a military career. Extremely tall for the time at six feet-two inches, Washington presented an imposing and commanding figure. While he was almost killed while accompanying British General Braddock into the frontier against the French and Indian forces, Washington emerged from the conflict with a respected military reputation. Thus, when the Continental Congress required a commander for the army they were forming to protect the colonies from the British troops, it is not surprising that they turned to Washington. In addition to his military background, the imposing young man from Virginia was one of the wealthiest individuals in the English colonies. His vast land holdings, which included the Mount Vernon plantation and numerous slaves, were based upon his marriage to the wealthy widow, Martha Custis, whose children from her first marriage never seemed to bond closely with their somewhat reserved stepfather. As for George and Martha, their union produced no children, leaving some to speculate whether the father of the country was sterile. His friendship with the young Alexander Hamilton seemed more affectionate than his relationship with the stepchildren. His Mount Vernon estate also made Washington a significant Virginia slaveholder, and he was reluctant to publicly question the institution. The respected leader, however, understood the inconsistency of slavery with the promise of the American Revolution. Privately, he often expressed his reservations regarding slavery, and in his will called for the emancipation of his slaves following the death of Martha, who outlived both of her husbands. Washington was such a revered figure that some believe that the history of the nation could have been altered and a civil war averted if he had publicly denounced slavery and emancipated his slaves following the revolution. Such an action might have placed pressure upon other plantation owners to follow his example. But, alas, Washington failed to publicly break with America's slave history, and an opportunity for emancipation was missed.

Continuing as a slaveholder, however, did not seriously undermine Washington's standing with his contemporaries. He was a military hero who inspired his troops during the difficult days at Valley Forge and led the American forces to victory at Trenton and Yorktown. After the victorious revolution, the modest Washington maintained the respect of the American people, denouncing personal ambition and retiring to his Mount Vernon estate. He re-entered politics during what he perceived as the threat of anarchy following Shays's Rebellion, serving in the Philadelphia Constitutional Convention and emerging as the consensus choice for President under the new Constitution. Washington was the unanimous choice of the Electoral College as the nation's first President, and his journey from Virginia to the capital in New York City—what was to later be Washington D.C. was a swampy marsh at the time—was celebrated by large crowds voicing their support for the leader whom many considered to be the indispensable man. As the nation's first President, the prudent Washington was quite aware that he was establishing significant precedents for the office. Displaying a reserved dignity which reflected his personality as well as his perception of the Presidency, Washington insisted that those wishing to consult with the President would need to visit him in his office rather than have the President compromise his position by calling upon others. There was also the matter of what to call the President. Revealing some nostalgia for the grandeur of monarchy, Alexander Hamilton and John Adams preferred titles such as "His Excellency," but Washington was uncomfortable with the trappings of monarchy and, instead, insisted upon the dignified but more republican, "Mr. President."

To allow for the more efficient functioning of a new government, Washington established cabinet level offices. This was an organizational approach followed by his successors as the range of governmental activities expanded. Initially, however, Washington created only three cabinet level offices, while the office of Attorney General, occupied by Edmund Randolph of Virginia, was only considered a part time position. With the continuing danger of conflict with the Native population and threats from European powers, a War Department was established under the direction of former revolutionary war general Henry Knox. To put the nation's finances in order, the Treasury Department was created under the direction of the brilliant young Alexander Hamilton, whose rather vain personal characteristics outraged many, but who remained a favorite of the President. The nation's diplomatic affairs, that included extensive treaty negotiations with Native nations as the United States embarked on a program of territorial expansion, were placed under the State Department headed by Thomas Jefferson. It was essential to bring the Virginian into the cabinet as Jefferson initially exhibited considerable reservations regarding the expanded powers of the central government under the Constitution. Expressing suspicion that the Constitution was written while he was absent representing the nation in France, Jefferson emerged as a leader of the Anti-Federalists, and Washington wanted his opposition within rather than outside the administration. Another key appointment for Washington was John Jay as the first Chief Justice of the Supreme Court

Hamilton's financial plan

.

The most influential and controversial member of the cabinet proved to be Hamilton, whose quarrels with Jefferson over economic policies and Constitutional principles provided the foundation for the country's first political party system. The talented but arrogant Hamilton was described by some of his political adversaries as literally and figuratively "a bastard," who was born out of wedlock in the British West Indies. Despite his humble origins, Hamilton rose quickly, reflecting the type of social mobility envisioned by Benjamin Franklin. After migrating to the New York colony, Hamilton became a successful lawyer and attached himself to the rising star of Washington, serving as the general's indispensable aide and secretary during the Revolutionary War. Hamilton's historical reputation has often been tainted by the anti-democratic tendencies of his policies for fostering a strong central government that favored the wealthy at the expense of the common people. On the other hand, Hamilton's standing has been resurrected with the popular and award-winning musical *Hamilton* in which composer Lin-Manuel Miranda of Puerto Rican descent portrays the West Indian native as a champion of diversity and the American dream in opposition to the slaveholding and aristocratic Jefferson. Following the success of the musical, discussion of removing Hamilton from the ten-dollar bill was dropped, and he has re-emerged as one of the best known of the Founding Fathers, although Miranda's positive depiction based upon Ron Chernow's *Hamilton* biography may be somewhat overly flattering.

The legislative centerpiece for the Washington administration was a financial plan designed by Hamilton. Although most Americans in the 1790s were small family farmers, the Treasury Secretary believed that the future of the American nation relied upon industry and commerce, not agriculture. To foster the transformation of America from an agricultural to an industrial nation would require a strong central government. The scale of economic activity advocated by

Hamilton would also entail considerable borrowing, and thus it was essential that the United States establish a solid credit rating which could only be obtained by paying off the considerable debt accrued during the American Revolution and under the Articles of Confederation. While some argued for canceling the debt, the first step in Hamilton's program was funding or paying off the debt in full to assert the status of the United States as a creditor rather than a debtor nation. Hamilton would also take on more debt by having the national government assume the debts of the states. This antagonized some states such as Virginia who had paid their obligation, but Hamilton argued that assumption of state debt assured the supremacy of the national government in directing American economic policy.

To raise the necessary money for funding this large debt, Hamilton proposed an excise tax on whiskey, a popular drink among Americans noted for their attraction to alcoholic beverages. To assure that consumers purchased their whiskey and paid the excise tax, it would be necessary for the government to curtail farmers from using their excess corn to manufacture whiskey which was often employed as a means of exchange on the frontier. Revenue would also be raised through the imposition of a tariff on the importation of European manufactured goods. In addition to providing revenue, a high protective tariff would help to safeguard fledgling American industries from foreign competition, fostering industrialization within the American nation. Finally, Hamilton argued that the large amount of money entering the nation's coffers would necessitate the creation of a National Bank to oversee America's finances.

Opposition to Hamilton's plan

Hamilton's proposals engendered considerable opposition in the Congress. Representatives from the South and agricultural districts lined up behind Secretary of State Thomas Jefferson, who opposed Hamilton's vision of an industrialized America. Jefferson was an advocate of agrarian democracy, believing that a nation of independent yeomen farmers owning their land assured a democratic foundation for the United States. On the other hand, cities with their overcrowding bred crime and corruption, while working for wages in a factory encouraged dependence rather than independence. Jefferson's republic of yeoman farmers seemed to offer little for Natives and blacks who were not represented by the Congressional forces coalescing around Jefferson's opposition to Hamilton's financial plan. Jefferson's home state of Virginia had paid its debt and was opposed to being taxed as part of a scheme to pay off the debts of less responsible state governments. Other opponents of Hamilton complained that funding of the debt would entail large payments to bond speculators who purchased debt from the original bondholders, many of whom were widows, orphans, and disabled veterans from the revolution. Many Jeffersonians desired to see the original bondholders compensated, but Hamilton insisted that the investors deserved compensation for the financial risk they had taken in purchasing the bonds. In addition, Hamilton maintained that the nation wanted to encourage these entrepreneurs who would, in turn, use their funds to invest in the creation of factories where many of the original bondholders would find employment. Thus, Hamilton may be perceived as an advocate for trickle down economics that Republicans such as Herbert Hoover began to articulate during the Great Depression. Southern farmers were especially concerned with the tariff that they perceived as subsidizing Northern manufacturing, while Southerners would be saddled with high prices for manufactured goods. Farmers in both the North and South were antagonized over the proposed excise tax which threatened their production and trading of whiskey.

Jefferson focused much of his criticism on the issue of the National Bank that the Secretary of State considered an un-Constitutional expansion of federal power. Concerned with quarreling in the cabinet, Washington asked Hamilton and Jefferson to set forth their arguments on the bank. Jefferson's position was based upon a strict construction of the Constitution. Since the creation of a bank was not listed among the enumerated powers entrusted to the Congress, it was simply forbidden for Congress to establish such an institution. Hamilton, however, proposed a broader reading of the Constitution grounded in the necessary and proper clause. He acknowledged that the power to create a bank was not expressly granted to Congress, but the Constitution did provide for the national government to coin money, borrow, and tax. To facilitate these economic activities, the creation of a bank was necessary and proper. Thus, Hamilton concluded that the Constitution provided the federal government with implied powers. As usual, Washington seemed to side with the arguments presented by his young Secretary of the Treasury and urged that a compromise be found to move the financial plan forward.

The bottom line is that the Congress finally agreed to enact Hamilton's economic program with one major concession to Jefferson. The financial plan would certainly create a stronger federal government which the Virginian abhorred; however, this more powerful government was to be located in the South where it would be more closely monitored by Southerners who favored a small governmental footprint. The compromise called for the creation of the nation's capital in Washington DC, at the time a swampy marsh that would be carved out of land provided by the states of Maryland and Virginia. In the final analysis, a beautiful capital was created out of this landscape that with its humidity and torrid heat retains some of its original geographical features. Hamilton, however, seemed to gain the better part of the bargain. He obtained a stronger federal government and a financial plan fostering trade and manufacturing, while the creation of a capital on Southern marshland did little to curtail the expanding power of the central government.

Hamilton was also provided with an opportunity to demonstrate the power of the federal government during the Whiskey Rebellion. Farmers in western Pennsylvania refused to pay the excise tax on whiskey and continued to manufacture their own corn-based whiskey, taking up arms against any government officials who attempted to halt their illegal production of the popular beverage. This began the long-running conflict between farmers producing "moonshine" and government agents seeking to shut down their activities. As for Hamilton, he welcomed the opportunity to assert the authority of the federal government that would not tolerate the anarchy and disorder of another Shays's Rebellion. The Secretary of the Treasury convinced Washington to take his uniform out of mothballs and lead a military expedition into western Pennsylvania to crush the rebellion and set an example for other potential rebels. Faced with an intimidating force assembled by Hamilton and Washington, the Whiskey Rebellion quickly collapsed, and its leaders were arrested.

Emergence of political parties

The ascendancy of the central government was established, but the divisions over the passage of Hamilton's financial plan hastened the formation of political parties, whose existence neither the Constitution nor Washington had anticipated. The Federalist Party coalesced under the leadership of Hamilton, while also enjoying the sponsorship of Washington and John Adams. The Federalists with the support of the upper class and mercantile interests favored a strong central government and a broad interpretation of the Constitution that would allow for the promotion of business and suppression of disorder. The Anti-Federalists, also known as the Democratic-Republicans, were followers of Jefferson and his chief lieutenant, James Madison. They found followers among artisans and small farmers. Seeking to establish a republic of virtue based upon independent producers and farmers, the Democratic-Republicans insisted upon a federal government whose powers would be limited through a strict constructionist reading of the Constitution. These political differences were exacerbated by the international unrest fomented by the French Revolution that culminated in a war between the major powers of England and France.

The English considered the French Revolution as a violent threat to monarchy and the established order in Europe, leading a coalition to stop the spread of a dangerous revolutionary ideology that all were created equal. Jefferson, who served as an American representative to the French government, was flattered that the French were influenced by the democratic ideas of the American Revolution and Declaration of Independence which many French soldiers spread in their own country after aiding the Americans in their fight for independence. Advocating a Francophile policy, Jefferson argued that the United States should be friendly to the French whose support was crucial to America obtaining its independence, but he acknowledged the extreme class violence that characterized the French Revolution. The Democratic-Republican leader believed that the best way to curb this extremism was for the United States to serve as a mediating influence with its French allies. Hamilton and the Federalists, on the other hand, insisted that the American nation owed no obligation to the French whose revolutionary fervor fostered the type of anarchy associated with Shays's Rebellion. Furthermore, it was in America's self-interest to align with the English, whose manufacturing base and mercantile interests made the British Empire an ideal trading partner for the new nation. In other words, economic self-interest dictated a closer relationship with the former mother country.

As the conflict between the French and English raged on the continent of Europe and the Atlantic Ocean, the two nations employed their navies to impose an embargo on trade with the enemy. This meant that American ships on the high seas were being seized with their cargos confiscated and their crews often impressed into service by their captors. With their larger navy, the British posed a greater threat to American trade than the French. Initially, the Washington administration issued a Neutrality Proclamation that did little to prevent the seizure of American ships.

Jay's Treaty and Washington's Farewell Address

Since the English were the primary culprits, Washington sought to negotiate an understanding by dispatching John Jay to London. Essentially, Jay was to assert that unless the English ceased the seizing of American ships and opened ports under their control to American trade, the United States would ally with the French against the British. The negotiating position, however, was somewhat of a bluff, and the Washington administration was not really prepared to follow through with this threat. The English seemed to recognize that the Americans were reluctant to follow through with this ultimatum, and there is some evidence to suggest that Hamilton may have communicated this policy to his English friends. Accordingly, Jay was unable to secure any concessions regarding British violations of American neutrality on the high seas. Jay, nevertheless, did secure an agreement to increase trade with the Americans and open British ports in the West Indies to American vessels. It was the type of treaty fostering trade that Hamilton favored, and after considerable debate in the Senate the treaty was ratified. While Pinckney's Treaty of 1793 was celebrated for gaining the United States the right of deposit for trade goods in Spanish New Orleans, many Americans believed that Jay's Treaty made the United States appear weak. The treaty was denounced by newspapers and politicians with mass torchlight parades held to demonstrate popular opposition. The thin-skinned Washington was the target for much of the condemnation, and the public uproar over Jay's Treaty convinced Washington not to seek a third term as President.

Washington, thus, established the two-term tradition followed by American Presidents until Franklin Roosevelt on the eve of American entrance into the Second World War was elected to a third term in 1940. In reaction to Roosevelt's popularity, Republicans passed the Twenty-Second Amendment limiting the President to two elected terms. Washington also commenced the tradition of a Farewell Address presented before leaving office, but few have risen to the level of the final comments of the first President. Seizing the opportunity to warn his country of what he considered the beginning of dangerous trends, Washington pointed out the pitfalls of faction and sectionalism. The President was not pleased with the growth of political parties which he deplored, believing that it would lead American politicians and citizens to place loyalty to party above their allegiance to the nation. In addition, Washington was concerned with sectionalism that encouraged Americans to place regional loyalties above national concerns. Finally, the arguments of whether the United States owed treaty obligations to the French convinced Washington that Americans should maintain freedom of action by avoiding entangling alliances. Washington's concerns were largely ignored, although national independence from entangling alliances was essentially followed until the post-World War II North Atlantic Treaty Organization was formed to thwart the expansion of the Soviet Union. The failure to heed Washington's warnings about sectionalism culminated, of course, in the bloodshed and destruction of civil war, while the factionalism of political parties was well under way by the time Washington left the Presidency and appears to dominate contemporary political discourse.

John Adams prepares for war with France

In the Presidential election of 1796, John Adams supported by the Federalist Party was opposed by Jefferson and the Democratic-Republicans. With the endorsement of the still generally popular Washington, Adams was elected President with Jefferson as his Vice President—for in the original wording of the Constitution, which did not account for the divisiveness of political parties, the candidate with the second greatest number of electoral votes assumed the Vice-Presidency. Adams was a Harvard-educated attorney whose service in the Continental Congress and as Vice President under Washington provided him with considerable governmental experience. It is also worth noting that among America's first five Presidents, Adams was the only non-slaveholder. While he did not champion equality for women during his political career, in private life his assumptions regarding gender were often challenged by his articulate and politically astute wife, Abigail. In public life, his support for democratic principles was questioned by Democratic-Republicans, many of whom remembered the legal defense he provided for the British soldiers accused of murder during the Boston Massacre. As he assumed the Presidency, Adams and the Untied States remained caught between the super powers of England and France as the conflict unleashed by the French Revolution continued to engulf the Atlantic world.

With Jay's Treaty, the Washington administration had attempted to address the English violation of American neutrality, so Adams sought to address concerns with the French by dispatching a diplomatic mission to Paris. The American delegation led by John Marshall, who was later appointed by Adams as Chief Justice of the Supreme Court, was upset when they received a series of notes from French representatives identified as X, Y, and Z, asserting that before the Americans could be officially received and begin negotiations, they would need to pay a fee or bribe of $250,000. Although this was a somewhat accepted custom and other nations paid the demanded sum, the proud American delegation refused and withdrew. The Adams administration backed its diplomats, while Federalists in Congress asserted they would provide millions for defense, but not one penny for tribute. In fact, the Federalist-dominated Congress began to prepare for war with France by increasing appropriations for defense, including the expansion of the Navy and creation of what would later be known as the Marine Corps.

Alien and Sedition Acts

Many Democratic-Republicans expressed reservations regarding this military buildup, so the Federalists moved to block dissent and criticism of President Adams by passing the Alien and Sedition Acts, which may be compared with the Patriot Act enacted after 9/11 to expand the powers of the government to limit dissent under the guise of patriotism. With the Alien and Sedition Acts, the naturalization period for immigrants was expanded from five to fourteen years. During this extended naturalization period, the immigrants, many of whom were drawn to Democratic-Republican principles, were to remain aliens subject to deportation if they openly criticized the President and war preparations. American citizens were not subject to deportation, but under the Sedition Act they could be arrested if their criticisms of the President were deemed sedition or treasonous speech by a Federalist-dominated judiciary. A number of Democratic-Republican newspaper editors were imprisoned under the act, which some, including Alexander Hamilton, believed might ensnare Vice President Jefferson.

In response to this assault upon free speech, Jefferson and James Madison wrote the Virginia and Kentucky Resolutions which they convinced the legislatures of the two states to adopt rather than risk detention by issuing the statements under their names. The Virginia and Kentucky Resolutions announced that since the Alien and Sedition Acts were in violation of Constitutional guarantees regarding freedom of speech, they were null and void and would not be enforced in the two states. Many Federalists asserted that Virginia and Kentucky were in rebellion against the national government and called for military intervention to enforce the law. Recognizing that the American nation was in danger of disintegrating into civil war, President Adams sought to defuse the situation by placing his country above political partisanship. First, Adams moved to reopen negotiations with the French government. In the Convention of 1800, the Americans and French agreed to avert war, and the alliance between the United States and France going back to the American Revolution was formally terminated with the acknowledgement that the United States had no formal obligations toward the French nation—although issues regarding French seizure of American ships intent upon trading with English ports was not addressed. With the removal of war clouds over France, the Federalist efforts to limit dissent during wartime were no longer necessary, and the Alien and Sedition Acts were allowed to expire although the issues of war, patriotism, and dissent were hardly resolved.

Election of 1800

Partisanship remained part of the political landscape as the nation approached the Presidential election of 1800 in which the two leading candidates were again Adams and Jefferson. Under the Constitution, the candidate receiving a majority of the electoral votes is declared President. In 1800, however, there was a tie between Jefferson and his running mate New Yorker Aaron Burr. Due to a technicality, Democratic-Republican electors cast their votes for both men as the Constitution failed to anticipate the existence of political parties. With no candidate, thus, receiving a majority, the winner, as the Constitution provides, was to be determined by the House of Representatives. Many Federalists who still controlled the Congress disliked Jefferson and considered casting their votes for Burr, who antagonized many Jefferson supporters by not more strenuously denouncing his claim to the Presidency. Hamilton, who had little use for Jefferson but disliked his fellow New Yorker Burr even more, urged Federalists to vote for Jefferson, who eventually emerged as the winner. The disputed election of 1800 marked a key moment for American democracy as it constituted the first peaceful transfer of power from one party to another. It is a test which many new nations fail and of which Americans should justly be proud. In the so-called Revolution of 1800, Adams surrendered power to Jefferson who called for unity, asserting that we are all Federalists and Democratic-Republicans—a line later employed by George W. Bush following the disputed election of 2000.

In a significant footnote to the election of 1800, the Twelfth Amendment to the Constitution essentially recognized political parties by having Presidential candidates designate a running mate. As for Burr, since he finished second before the Constitutional change, the New Yorker assumed the Vice-Presidency under Jefferson who distrusted Burr and gave him few responsibilities. Burr resented Hamilton and blamed his New York rival for his political demise. The simmering feud between the two men culminated in an 1804 New Jersey duel in which Hamilton was fatally wounded. Facing possible legal action for dueling, Burr eventually fled to the West where he was later accused of treason for encouraging Western states to leave the union and align with Spain. Although Burr was never convicted of treason or killing Hamilton, his political career was over.

Jefferson and the Federalist judiciary

Meanwhile, Jefferson assumed the Presidency and was reelected four years later, but the gifted and controversial American left the office a frustrated individual. Jefferson's immense talents were acknowledged by President John Kennedy when he told a crowd of assembled artists that they were the most talent gathered at the White House since Thomas Jefferson dined alone. Jefferson was a naturalist, scientist, architect with his beautiful Monticello plantation, violinist, inventor with a prototype for the dumb waiter and writing machine to make copes of his extensive correspondence, politician, and writer whose most enduring legacy is the Declaration of Independence. Jefferson was also a lover of books and reading, who when faced with debt sold his extensive book collection to the government and founded the Library of Congress. Despite his many achievements, Jefferson's legacy is clouded by his association with slavery. Although he often denounced slavery, Jefferson's Monticello plantation depended upon slave labor, opening him to accusations of hypocrisy. Jefferson's explanation that he failed to free his slaves because he wanted to protect them from prejudice and poor treatment accorded free blacks in Virginia rings hollow. And there is also the matter of Sally Hemings, a young slave woman with whom the widower Jefferson fathered several children. Jefferson's political opponents criticized him for the relationship with a slave woman, pointing out that her children had red hair similar to that of Jefferson. While Jefferson never directly addressed these accusations, his relatives denied the charges and asserted that the Hemings children were fathered by other members of the extended Jefferson family. Sally Hemings, however, informed her children that Thomas Jefferson was their father, and when the former President died the only slaves he freed in his will were Sally and her children. Despite denials by some family members and Jefferson advocates, contemporary scientific evidence supports that Jefferson was the father of Sally's children. What are we to make of this fact! Was Jefferson a racist who forced himself upon the much younger enslaved woman? Were they two lovers who could not publicly celebrate their relationship due to slavery and racism? We have no letters to document the relationship as Sally Hemings was illiterate for the slaveholders refused to educate their slaves. But what the Jefferson and Hemings relationship does illustrate is the frequent inter-racial sexual activity fostered by slavery and the shadow that slavery cast upon the ideas Jefferson expressed in the Declaration of Independence.

As President, Jefferson failed to tackle the slavery issue, but he did confront the judiciary where the Federalists with life terms continued to enjoy considerable influence. Democratic-Republicans in Congress brought impeachment proceedings against Supreme Court Justice Samuel Chase, denouncing Chase for public drunkenness although political motivations were paramount. After fierce political debate, Chase was not removed from office, and the principle of an independent judiciary was maintained. In fact, Chief Justice John Marshall and a Federalist significantly enhanced the powers of the court by establishing the doctrine of judicial review in the case of *Marbury v. Madison* (1801). As he left office, President Adams conferred what his opponents called "midnight appointments" of Federalist judges. William Marbury failed to receive his appointment and sued Secretary of State James Madison to deliver his nomination. In a complicated and masterful decision, Marshall ruled against Marbury, providing an apparent victory for Jefferson and the Democratic-Republicans. Marshall argued that while Madison should have delivered the appointment, he did not have to do so as the court lacked the authority to compel the Secretary of State because the Judiciary Act of 1789 conveying such power was un-Constitutional. Thus, the Federalist Party lost a judge, but gained or usurped the right of the Supreme Court, a Federalist stronghold at the time, to rule on the Constitutionality of Congressional actions.

Louisiana Purchase

While Jefferson was somewhat outflanked by Marshall in the *Marbury v. Madison* decision, his most significant action as President was the Louisiana Purchase, a transaction that provided the United States with a claim to the Louisiana territory that extended from the Mississippi River westward to the Oregon territory and Spanish southwest including California. Louisiana was ceded by the French to Spain in the 1763 Treaty of Paris, but following Napoleon's conquest of Spain, the Iberian nation was forced to restore Louisiana to French control. Napoleon harbored ambitions of establishing a French empire in North America, but these designs were thwarted by the successful slave rebellion in Santo Domingo or Haiti that Napoleon had anticipated using as a base from which to launch his plans for North America. American Minister to France Robert Livingston approached Napoleon's government about purchasing New Orleans for approximately $10 million to safeguard American trade on the Mississippi and guarantee access to the port. Napoleon shocked the American diplomat by offering to sale the entire Louisiana territory for $15 million, and Livingston quickly agreed to the deal. Jefferson had Constitutional scruples as to whether the Constitution bestowed the power upon the President to undertake such a huge territorial acquisition, but he was finally convinced that the French offer was simply too good to refuse. As for the Haitians, they were betrayed by both the French and Americans. Napoleon invited revolutionary leader Toussaint L'Ouverture to France where he was arrested and imprisoned. The United States, fearing that Haiti might inspire American slaves to fight for their freedom, attempted to isolate the new nation economically and diplomatically, assuring that Haiti remained the poorest nation in the Western Hemisphere.

While isolating Haiti, Jefferson sought to follow up the Louisiana Purchase, over 800,000 square miles costing about three cents an acre, with an expedition led by Jefferson's secretary Meriwether Lewis and frontiersman William Clark, whose extensive journals described the land and people brought under American control. The celebration of the Shoshoni woman Sacajawea as a guide for Lewis and Clark often obscures that the expedition was also about conquest. The Natives encountered by Lewis and Clark were informed that they were under the jurisdiction of the American President in Washington to whom they now owed fealty. There was certainly no effort to ascertain whether the Natives wanted to become part of the American empire. The expedition lasted over two and a half years with Lewis and Clark crossing the Rocky Mountains and traveling down the Columbia River to the Pacific Ocean, providing the United States with a claim to the Oregon territory also coveted by the British in Canada. While the Lewis and Clark expedition provided considerable information and expanded the territorial ambitions of the United States, for the Native people living west of the Mississippi it marked the beginning of a conquest that would nearly destroy the Native people and culture. The legacy of Lewis and Clark is certainly a mixed one.

Impressment and the Embargo Act

The Jefferson Presidency was also confronted with numerous foreign policy issues. The Barbary pirates concentrated in Tripoli or contemporary Libya preyed upon European and American shipping in the Mediterranean, demanding that bribes and ransoms be paid for cargos and prisoners. Jefferson resented these payments and dispatched the Marines to attack the pirates and rescue American hostages. While Jefferson was assertive with the Tripoli pirates, he was less successful with the French and British who continued to violate American neutrality on the high seas. This was especially true of the powerful British Navy attempting to block trade with ports under French control. The British Navy, with a reputation for harsh discipline, was certainly in need of additional sailors, boarding American ships and claiming that American seamen were deserters and impressing them into service on British ships. These boardings and impressment or kidnapping of American sailors insulted national honor and interfered with trade, although some of the sailors may have been British deserters who sometimes climbed into baby cribs in ports such as Boston so that witnesses might swear that they knew the man since he was in the cradle. A public example of impressment occurred when an American ship the *Chesapeake* left the post of Baltimore. Still within sight of the shore, the *Chesapeake* was confronted by a British warship the *Leopard*, whose commander insisted upon boarding the American vessel. When the *Chesapeake* refused, it was fired upon by the *Leopard* and followed by a boarding party in which several American sailors were impressed into British service.

Stung by these provocations, Jefferson and the Democratic-Republicans in Congress implemented the Non-Importation Act in which the Americans would refuse to import French and British goods, returning to the boycott used so effectively during the revolutionary period. However, the nation was now far more dependent upon trade, and non-importation failed to stop the seizure of American ships and crews. In response, the Jefferson administration supported a far more radical piece of legislation called the Embargo Act. Under the Embargo Act, the United States simply withdrew from international trade and closed its ports. Shutting down trade altogether certainly prevented the seizure of American ships, but the measure proved highly unpopular as it contributed to a depression for a country increasingly dependent upon trade. In the long run, however, the Embargo Act stimulated the economy by encouraging domestic manufacturing. Since the Americans could not access European goods, they would have to produce their own products such as textiles and plows. While it was certainly not his goal, Jefferson, the champion of agrarian democracy, may have done more to foster manufacturing with the Embargo Act than Hamilton with his financial plan. Even from beyond the grave, Hamilton seemed to dominate his Virginian nemesis.

The unpopular Embargo Act was eventually replaced by the Non-Intercourse Act which restored trade with both France and England, but if either power promised to relinquish the policy of interfering with American trade, then the United States would agree to cease trade with the other great power. Unable to resolve the problems arising from the seizure of American ships and crews, a frustrated Jefferson left the Presidency after two terms and retreated to Monticello, leaving the issue to his successor James Madison, who would lead the nation into the War of 1812 with Great Britain.

Further Reading:

Ambrose, Stephen. *Undaunted Courage: Merewether Lewis, Thomas Jefferson, and Opening of the American West*. New York: Simon & Schuster, 1996.

Appleby, Joyce. *Capitalism and a New Social Order: The Republican Vision of the 1790s*. New York: New York University Press, 1984.

Chernow, Ron. *Alexander Hamilton*. New York: Penguin Press, 2004.

DeConde, Alexander. *Entangling Alliance: Politics and Diplomacy Under George Washington*. Durham, NC: Duke University Press, 1958.

Elkins, Stanley and Eric McKitrick. *The Age of Federalism: The Early American Republic, 1788-1800*. New York: Oxford University Press, 1993.

Flexner, James T. *George Washington and the New Nation, 1783-1789*. Boston: Little, Brown and Company, 1970.

Levy, Leonard. *Legacy of Suppression: Freedom of Speech and Press in Early American History*. Cambridge, MA: Harvard University Press, 1960.

Peterson, Merrill. *Thomas Jefferson and the New Nation*. New York: Oxford University Press, 1970.

Sharp, James Roger. *American Politics in the Early Republic: The New Nation in Crisis*. New Haven, CT: Yale University Press, 1993.

Slaughter, Thomas P. *The Whiskey Rebellion: Frontier Epilogue to the American Revolution*. New York: Oxford University Press, 1986.

8

War of 1812 and Post War Nationalism

Tecumseh. Halftone reproduction of watercolor drawing by Mathias Noheimer. Library of Congress Prints and Photographs Division. Shawnee patriot chief Tecumseh sought to unify Native nations of the Ohio River Valley in opposition to westward expansion by the new American nation, playing a significant role in the War of 1812 between the United States and Great Britain.

American unity was seriously challenged during the War of 1812 in which the United States again clashed with Britain in what many consider to be America's second war for independence. For those who exalt American military might, the war was a draw at best and witnessed the burning of Washington DC. Nevertheless, the victory of American forces under the leadership of Andrew Jackson at the Battle of New Orleans—actually fought after a peace treaty was signed—convinced many Americans that they had won the war and ushered in a period of post war nationalism characterized by the growth of internal improvements tying the nation together. The forces of sectionalism, however, proved divisive, and territorial expansion fostered conflict with the Natives as well as internal strife over the institution of slavery.

War Hawks

In 1809, James Madison—yet another Virginia slaveholder—was elected President. He served as Jefferson's chief lieutenant in the Democratic-Republican Party and is credited with fostering ratification of the Constitution by incorporating the Bill of Rights into the document. Upon assuming the Presidency, Madison was confronted by a younger group of politicians from the South and West favoring a policy of territorial expansion that they believed was threatened by the British who often supported Native resistance to the American state. The War Hawks were a younger generation who had missed the Revolutionary War, but they wanted to make their contribution to American nationalism. They thrived on stories of courage displayed during battle but tended to ignore the devastation brought by war. Among the Congressional leaders of the War Hawks were Henry Clay of Kentucky and John C. Calhoun of South Carolina whose political careers played a large role on the national stage during the first half of the nineteenth century. Many of the War Hawks envisioned an expansionist American nation that would dominate North America with the acquisition of Spanish Florida and Canada from the British.

But blocking these grand designs were the Natives determined to fight for their land. Following the military victories of General "Mad" Anthony Wayne, settlers were pouring into the upper Midwest. Seeking to halt this assault upon Native life, land, and culture, the Shawnee chieftain Tecumseh and his brother, known to white Americans as the Prophet, fostered a strong resistance by stressing a religious revitalization movement and a unity among the Native nations of the Ohio River Valley. This resistance was also encouraged by the British in Canada who supplied Tecumseh with munitions and made the Native leader an honorary officer in the British Army. From a British perspective, the threat posed by Tecumseh would focus American military action upon the Natives in the interior and prevent the United States from entering a conflict with the British who were still preying upon American shipping and impressing sailors as the Napoleonic wars with France continued. In addition to British support for Tecumseh, the seizing of American ships was having an economic impact upon Southern and Western farmers whose products were not reaching international markets. While few families in the South or West were directly impacted by the impressment of American sailors, there was a strong sense of national honor in the regions which made an injury to one American an injury to all.

Thus, the War Hawks pressed for Congress to issue a declaration of war aimed at the British, but mercantile interests in New England were opposed to the war measure. New England merchants were losing ships and crews, but they continued to reap profits by charging more for their services threatened by the British Navy. Also, residents of New England feared that war with England would result in assaults upon the Eastern seaboard that would bring considerable destruction to the region. Eastern interests and the Federalist Party, however, proved unable to block the declaration of war which passed the Senate by the slim margin of nineteen to thirteen, and the United States was divided as it entered the War of 1812. Modern communications would likely have prevented this conflict as while the American Congress was approving a war measure, the British decided to abandon their Orders in Council which authorized the seizure of American ships. By the time the United States learned of the English policy change, war was already declared and military operations under way.

Military aspects of the conflict

The conflict did not initially go well for the United States. Assumptions that Canadians were anxious to join the United States were naïve at best, and efforts to invade Canada were repulsed. Counter fears that the British in Canada might be able to occupy American cities were relieved when naval forces under the command of Oliver Hazard Perry retained control of the Great Lakes. The war was essentially a stand-off along the American and Canadian border, while the powerful British Navy dominated the Atlantic. Nevertheless, the *U.S.S. Constitution* salvaged some pride with victories over British warships. A symbol of American nationalism, the *Constitution* is docked in Boston harbor and attracts numerous tourists, leading the government to fear that the ship might become a terrorist target in the wake of 9/11.

As the British suspected, much of the American focus in the war was upon the threat posed by Tecumseh to western expansion. A large army under the command of William Henry Harrison was dispatched to deal with Tecumseh, and in the battles of Kithtippecanoe—later simply referred to as Tippecanoe in Harrison's 1840 Presidential campaign—and the Thames near Detroit, Tecumseh's confederation was defeated. When Tecumseh was killed at the Thames, his brother supposedly laid a curse upon Harrison that was later referred to as the "zero factor" in American politics. It seems that every President, beginning with Harrison in 1840, who was elected in a year ending with zero died in office. The streak was broken with Ronald Reagan elected in 1980, who survived an assassin's bullet to the chest. While the British failed to equip Tecumseh with all the promised weapons and support, the Shawnee leader had certainly fulfilled the strategy of forcing American attention upon the western frontier, while American cities along the Atlantic remained vulnerable to British attack.

In August 1814, British forces assaulted and destroyed much of Washington DC, and in the process, they almost succeeded in capturing President Madison. The President's wife, Dolly demonstrated her courage by running into the burning White House to rescue a portrait of George Washington. Americans were embarrassed by the destruction of the nation's capital that was followed by an assault upon Baltimore. The entrance into the Baltimore harbor was blocked by Fort McHenry which the British relentlessly bombarded on the evening of September 13, 1814. When the sun rose the next morning, the American flag still waved over Fort McHenry, and the British fleet withdrew. Francis Scott Key, a Baltimore attorney, was on board one of the English ships attempting to gain the release of a captured American citizen, and he was so inspired by the defense of Fort McHenry that he composed a poem entitled "The Spangled Banner" that would eventually be selected as the National Anthem.

Battle of New Orleans, Treaty of Ghent, and Hartford Convention

The British planned a third assault against the crucial trading center of New Orleans. The invading force, however, was betrayed by a break in a heavy fog which left the British soldiers exposed to the fire of an American army under the command of Andrew Jackson who had previously earned fame for defeating the Creek Indians blocking expansion into Alabama and Mississippi. The Battle of New Orleans, which helped to establish Jackson as a national hero, was really more of a massacre as British soldiers were gunned down by American frontiersmen firing behind bales of cotton. The British had over two thousand soldiers killed or wounded, while American losses were approximately seventy men, many of whom perished when an overheated cannon exploded. The victory was later memorialized by folksinger Johnnie Horton with the popular "Ballad of New Orleans" (1961).

Many Americans learned of the Battle of New Orleans and the Treaty of Ghent simultaneously and assumed that the British surrendered due to Jackson's overwhelming victory. In reality, the Battle of New Orleans was fought on January 8, 1815, while the peace treaty was signed two weeks earlier on Christmas Eve in Ghent, Belgium. Lack of modern communications meant that the combatants at New Orleans had no idea that the war was over. The British troops died in vain, and even if they had prevailed in the assault, under the terms of the treaty the British were committed to restoring the port to American control. Nevertheless, the American people were convinced that the Battle of New Orleans was a historic victory over the British Empire, ushering in a sense of extreme nationalism following the war. Discounting New Orleans, the War of 1812 was at best a draw. The invasion of Canada was a failure, while Washington DC was burned. The major American victories were against Native resistance that was encouraged by territorial aggression and British promises of support that were often unfulfilled.

The Treaty of Ghent was negotiated by Henry Clay of Kentucky and John Quincy Adams, the well-educated son of John and Abigail Adams. Clay was a man who enjoyed his alcohol and social life, while the more fastidious Adams preferred to concentrate upon the task at hand. When the two men were finally able to meet at the same time, the provisions of the treaty were rather simple. The British impressment and interference with trade were not even mentioned in the treaty as with the defeat of Napoleon, there was no longer any reason for the British Navy to interdict American shipping. With the issue of impressment off the table, the two sides simply agreed to end the conflict and asserted that there would be no territorial gains from the war. The Treaty of Ghent ended the War of 1812 and ushered in a period of intense American nationalism.

Before learning of Ghent and New Orleans, the Federalist Party held a meeting in Hartford, Connecticut to express discontent with the war and seek change in the Constitution that would protect the New England region where the party was concentrated. Many in New England believed that they bore the brunt of the fighting and wanted to assure that future wars would require a two-thirds vote in Congress. The Federalists also sought abolition of the notorious three-fifths compromise that increased Southern representation in Congress. The timing of the Federalists, however, proved to be terrible as when word arrived of the peace conference and victory at New Orleans, their criticisms of the war made them appear to be unpatriotic. The Hartford Convention was disbanded, but the damage was done. The discredited Federalist Party continued to exercise influence in New England, but its existence as a national party was over, and the United States following the War of 1812 was ruled by Jefferson's party, the Democratic-Republicans.

Literary declaration of independence

The political nationalism following the war was also displayed in a cultural or literary declaration of independence. Although the United States formally separated from England during the Revolutionary War, educated Americans continued to rely upon England for its reading material. This dependence was challenged following the War of 1812 as American authors began to produce books on national subjects. For example, Washington Irving drew upon the folklore of his native New York state to write his *Knickerbocker Tales* (1809) and *Sketch Book* (1819–1821) that included such famous stories as "Rip Van Winkle" and "Legend of Sleepy Hollow" that continue to resonate with Americans. In many ways James Fenimore Cooper was the father of American Westerns with his *Leather Stocking Tales* that featured frontiersman Natty Bumppo. In books such as *The Deerslayer* (1841) and *Last of the Mohicans* (1826), Bumppo was the hero who bridged the gap between nature and civilization, introducing themes of the Western genre in literature and later film. To emphasize the independence of American speech from its British origins, Noah Webster introduced a dictionary concentrating upon American usage of the English language.

Nationalist agendas pursued by the Congress and Supreme Court

On a more political level, a nationalist agenda was enacted by Congress following the War of 1812. With the discredited Federalist Party in disarray, the Democratic-Republicans dominated Congress, but, ironically, they now pursued a more Federalist agenda that would strengthen the national government and promote business. For example, Congress re-chartered Hamilton's National Bank and approved the 1816 tariff which increased taxation upon imports and thus subsidized Northern manufacturing. Although President Madison voiced his opposition by vetoing legislation such as the Maysville Road Bill, Congress supported internal improvements by increasing appropriations for projects such as roads and bridges that would further commerce and unite the nation.

A similar agenda was pursued by the Supreme Court under the direction of Chief Justice John Marshall for with life-time appointments the federal judiciary remained packed with Federalists. The powers of the federal government were expanded in the landmark case of *McCulloch v. Maryland* (1814) in which a Maryland law that taxed transactions of the National Bank within the state was declared null and void. The state of Maryland sought to employ the tax to destroy the bank within the state, but Marshall argued that the power to destroy implies the power to create which the state of Maryland did not possess in regard to the bank. The Marshall court, however, went beyond declaring the Maryland law un-Constitutional, for the court recognized the existence of implied powers within the Constitution by ruling that Congress did enjoy the power to create a bank. In the case of *Cohens v. Virginia* (1821), Marshall expanded the reach of the federal judiciary over the states. The Cohens protested the right of Virginia to regulate a lottery the family was operating. The Marshall court ruled in favor of the state, but Virginia was not pleased as the case established the precedent that the federal courts could extend the principle of judicial review to laws and actions taken by state governments and legislatures.

The Marshall decisions also enhanced the power of business by recognizing the sanctity of contracts. In the case of *Fletcher v. Peck* (1810), the state legislature in Georgia had bestowed land grants that were purchased by bribes and political favors. After a political uproar in the state, a new legislature moved to void the initial land grants. The Marshall court acknowledged the degree of corruption involved with the original land grants but ruled that the sanctity of contracts was essential for commerce. Therefore, the court would not void the land transactions in Georgia. A similar precedent was established in *Dartmouth College v. Woodward* (1819) as the democratic state legislature of New Hampshire sought to make changes in the original college charter granted under George III. Again Marshall ruled in favor of the sanctity of contracts, setting a precedent that would be interpreted as treating corporations as individuals whose rights could not be abridged by legislation. This line of reasoning continues to influence the courts up to the present day with decisions such as *Citizens United* (2012) in which powerful and wealthy corporations are perceived as enjoying rights which cannot be regulated by democratic legislative bodies in the public interest.

Adams-Onis Treaty and Monroe Doctrine

Nationalist sentiment and expansion were also evident in American foreign policy following the War of 1812. Southern states such as Georgia, Alabama, and South Carolina complained of Seminole Indian raids from Spanish Florida in which Natives freed slaves and incorporated them into the tribe. To punish the Seminoles whom the Spanish could not seem to control, President James Monroe and Secretary of State John Quincy Adams authorized a punitive expedition into Florida under the leadership of Andrew Jackson. The headstrong Jackson, however, exceeded his original orders by pushing deeper into Florida, attacking both the Spanish and Seminole while hanging some British citizens who were selling guns to the Seminole. Jackson's actions provoked international protest over the American violation of the Spanish border, and Monroe was prepared to recall Jackson. However, Secretary of State Adams, who was no admirer of Jackson, counseled that the United States might be able to take advantage of the situation and acquire Spanish Florida.

Accordingly, the Monroe administration backed Jackson and opened negotiations with Spain for the purchase of Florida. The United States was essentially telling the Spanish government if they would not sell Florida, Jackson would simply occupy the territory and seize it by force. Spain relented, and in the Adams-Onis Treaty, Florida was purchased by the United States, while Spain denounced any claims to the Oregon territory and the United States made a similar pledge regarding Texas— although this promise was certainly abandoned with the annexation of Texas and Mexican War.

American policy appeared somewhat more benevolent with the issuance of the Monroe Doctrine in 1823. The Spanish monarchy, however, which had supported the American cause during the Revolutionary War was eventually rewarded with loss of territory to the expanding American state. The Napoleonic wars in which the French ruler assumed power in Spain offered the opportunity for many Spanish colonies in Latin America, including Mexico, to declare their independence. Following the defeat of Napoleon, the victorious European powers at the Congress of Vienna sought to restore the old order and vowed to help Spain regain its empire in the Western Hemisphere. For economic and political reasons, the United States was opposed to the reassertion of a great European power into the Western Hemisphere. The United States had established trading relationships with many of the newly independent Latin American republics, and the restoration of a Spanish empire would interfere with this commerce. In addition, the United States perceived the new republics as posing little threat to American expansion. A major European power on the border might block expansion and present a security threat. In response, President Monroe in 1823 issued a proclamation, actually written by Secretary of State Adams, that would become a bulwark of American foreign policy during the nineteenth and twentieth centuries. The Monroe Doctrine announced the Western Hemisphere was closed to further European colonization. European powers could retain their current colonies in the region, but the United States would oppose any further colonizing ventures. The United States agreed to reciprocate by adopting a policy of nonintervention in European affairs. This was a rather bold statement, as the United States lacked the military might to threaten the European powers, but nevertheless the Europeans respected the Monroe Doctrine and failed to challenge American policy primarily because it was understood that the British Navy supported the American position. England had established commercial relations with new Latin American republics and believed that a restoration of Spanish control would undermine this commerce. As for the Latin American republics, they initially welcomed the Monroe Doctrine and credited the United States for fostering the growth of democracy and self-government in the Western Hemisphere. This perception of the Monroe Doctrine, however, disappeared following the Mexican War and numerous military interventions by the United States in Latin America during the twentieth century. It seemed that the United States wanted the Europeans out of their way so that they might prey upon their neighbors to the south.

Sectionalism with the Panic of 1819 and Missouri Compromise

The surge of nationalism following the War of 1812 is often referred to as the Era of Good Feelings in which unity was emphasized over the discord of political division, seemingly fulfilling the vision of Washington's Farewell Address. The nation was governed by one political party, and Democratic-Republican James Monroe was essentially unopposed for the Presidency in 1816 and 1820. Monroe continued the legacy of slave-owning Presidents from the state of Virginia, but behind this façade of national unity there were serious issues of sectionalism that would eventually explode into civil war. Western expansion was fueled by cheap land prices and liberal lending policies. Such practices lead to an overextension of credit, and when the Bank of the United States began to curtail loans, many farmers and debtors could not meet their financial obligations as foreclosures rose. Known as the Panic of 1819, this drop in Western land values caused widespread economic distress among Western farmers who blamed the Bank of the United States located in the East for their plight, fostering a sectional grievance that would help propel Andrew Jackson to the White House. Perhaps a brief note regarding language is in order here. An economic crisis in the nineteenth and early twentieth centuries was referred to as a panic, accurately reflecting what capitalistic business cycles actually meant to ordinary Americans. The term panic, which suggested a relatively short-term crisis, was replaced in the 1930s with depression as the capitalist order struggled to regain some type of balance. In the second half of the twentieth century, economists employed the term recession to suggest that we were only suffering a recess or temporary break from prosperity. These ideas were tested by the economic crisis of 2008, indicating that perhaps we should return to the more realistic nineteenth-century description of a panic.

The greatest threat to American unity, however, was not economic conflict between the East and West, but rather the differences between the North and South with the spread of slave labor. By 1820, the balance between free and slave states was threatened by the admission of Missouri to the union. Slavery existed within the territory, but the Talmadge Amendment proposed in Congress sought to admit Missouri without slavery, setting off a tumultuous debate in Congress and throughout the country. Politicians such as Henry Clay attempted to alleviate the divisions over slavery by passing the Missouri Compromise in which Missouri would be admitted as a slave state, but this would be balanced with the free labor state of Maine which had been considered part of Massachusetts. To forestall future division and debates over slavery, states seeking to enter the union from the Louisiana Purchase would be relegated according to the boundary line of 36-36, the southern boundary of Missouri. Henceforth, states above this line, with the exception of Missouri, would be free states, while those below would allow slavery. Since this agreement pertained only to the Louisiana Purchase territory, the North would in the long run attain more states, but geography seemed to dictate that it would be impossible to extend the lucrative cotton market to the Great Plains and Rocky Mountains. In addition, this compromise would assure that slavery would not be part of the political debate as the nation expanded, and Congress adopted gag orders to prevent further debate regarding the divisive issue of slavery. This compromise, however, was shattered when the United States expanded to include the Southwest and California following the Mexican War, reinvigorating the slavery debate that culminated in the Civil War.

While the Missouri Compromise curtailed the Congressional discussion of slavery for almost thirty years, it did little to address the plight of enslaved blacks who continued to suffer under the plantation lash. The War of 1812 and a resurgent nationalism following the conflict proved unable to alleviate the regional, class, and racial divisions plaguing the new nation. Andrew Jackson would lead a popular uprising of male workers and farmers excluded from the political process. While Jacksonian Democracy abolished many economic restrictions placed upon poor whites from exercising the suffrage, the rise of the common white man was based upon the exploitation of women, Irish immigrants, Hispanics, Indians, and black slaves.

Further Reading:

Ammon, Harry. *James Monroe: The Quest for National Identity*. New York: McGraw-Hill, 1971.

Brown, Roger H. *The Republic in Peril, 1812*. New York: Columbia University Press, 1964.

Dowd, Gregory Evans. *A Spirited Resistance: The North American Indian Struggle for Unity, 1775–1815*. Baltimore, MD: Johns Hopkins University Press, 1992.

Hickey, Donald R. *The War of 1812: A Forgotten Conflict*. Urbana, IL: University of Illinois Press, 2012.

Kerber, Linda. *Federalists in Dissent: Imagery and Ideology in Jeffersonian America*. Ithaca, NY: Cornell University Press, 1970.

Perkins, Dexter. *A History of the Monroe Doctrine*. Boston: Little, Brown and Company, 1963.

Smith, Jean Edward. *John Marshall: Definer of a Nation*. New York: Henry Holt and Company, 1996.

Stagg, J. C. A. *Mr. Madison's War: Politics, Diplomacy and Warfare in the Early American Republic*. Princeton, NJ: Princeton University Press, 1983.

Watts, Steven. *The Republic Reborn: War and the Making of Liberal America, 1790–1820*. Baltimore, MD: Johns Hopkins University Press, 1987.

Wiebe, Robert H. *Opening of American Society: From the Adoption of the Constitution to the Eve of Disunion*. New York: Knopf, 1984.

9

Jacksonian Democracy, 1824–1840

Andrew Jackson portrait. Library of Congress Prints and Photographs Division. Jackson was portrayed as the father of Jacksonian democracy and the rise of the common man. But in reality, it was the rise of the common white man on the backs of enslaved African labor in the South, the exploitation of children, women, and Irish immigrants in Northern factories, and territorial expansion to the West at the expense of Natives and Mexico.

Although Andrew Jackson only served as President for two terms, 1828–1836, he both literally and symbolically dominated American politics for almost three decades, lending his name to the democratization of American politics in which barriers to participation by common white men were shattered. Jackson's reputation as populist champion of the common people was embraced by President Donald Trump, who has otherwise demonstrated little interest in American history. Surrounding himself in the White House with portraits and sculptures of Jackson, Trump seems to admire the combative nature of the President in championing the common people of America, but President Trump seems unaware of Jackson's extreme partisanship, persecution of Native Americans, and defense of slavery as a plantation owner—all of which contributed to the divisiveness of the United States under Jackson and the controversial nature of his historical reputation.

Background of Andrew Jackson

In his background, Jackson was, indeed, a symbol of the rising common man denoted by the concept of Jacksonian democracy. Born in the Carolinas, Jackson was orphaned at a young age and received little in the way of a formal education. He migrated to Tennessee and became a social climber in the more open society of that Western state. The aggressive young man began to acquire property and practiced law when little formal training was required for that profession. Jackson also gained a reputation for being somewhat of a frontier ruffian, who was more than willing to settle disputes by resorting to physical confrontations in which formal rules of restraint were often abandoned. This reputation for violence also served Jackson well as a military figure who was celebrated for subduing the Creek nation, defeating the British at New Orleans, and expanding the United States into Florida. Jackson's rise in Tennessee culminated in a political career and acquisition of his Hermitage Plantation, on which Jackson oversaw the labor of hundreds of slaves. This social mobility, however, was not without its tragic personal side. Jackson had fallen in love with and married a widow, Rachel Robards. His political opponents discovered that Rachel's first husband was still alive, and an annulment, divorce, and remarriage were hastily arranged. Rachel was subject to considerable censure from her husband's political enemies, and Jackson blamed her premature death on the intense criticism she often received. For Jackson, much of the intense partisanship during his political career was personally motivated, and he never remarried after Rachel's death.

John Quincy Adams and the "Corrupt Bargain" of 1824

After serving as a Senator from Tennessee, Jackson sought the Presidency in 1824 when Monroe decided to follow Washington's two term tradition. Although America remained essentially a one-party system under the direction of the Democratic-Republicans, various regional candidates for the Presidency emerged. The four major candidates were Jackson, John Quincy Adams of Massachusetts, Henry Clay of Kentucky, and William Crawford of Georgia. Jackson received a plurality of both the popular and electoral votes, but to achieve the Presidency one must attain a majority of electoral votes. As the Constitution provides, the House of Representative would select the winner from the top three candidates. After finishing fourth in the balloting, Clay's name was eliminated, but as Speaker of the House, Clay still exercised considerable influence over the proceedings. The House elected Adams as President, who then appointed Clay as Secretary of State. Jackson's supporters cried foul, termed the selection of Adams as "the corrupt bargain of 1824," and immediately began campaigning for the 1828 election.

Like the only other Presidential son to gain the White House, George W. Bush after the disputed election of 2000, Adams began his Presidency under a cloud that questioned the legitimacy of his election. With the guidance of his politically astute parents, Harvard education, international travel, and political experience, Adams was well qualified for the Presidency, but he was out of step with the times. During the rise of the common man, Adams was perceived as an aristocrat who did not reflect the populist virtues of the era. Many in the South distrusted Adams who was the first non-slaveholder President since his father held the office. During a period when sectionalism was being reasserted within the national political framework, he also embraced the American system of Henry Clay, calling for such nationalist policies as a protective tariff and federal support for internal improvement such as roads and canals. Adams advocated for a national observatory to promote science and a national university where the best and brightest of the nation would be educated at government expense. To Jackson's populist supporters, such measures smacked of elitism. Economic conflict between the North and South was exacerbated by Congressional actions increasing the tariff in 1824 and 1828, the latter of which was labeled by many Southerners as the "tariff of abomination." Southerners perceived the tariff as economically benefitting Northern manufacturers who were protected from foreign competition by tariffs that made the factory goods purchased by Southerners more expensive. Some Southerners also believed that Northern politicians who enacted a tariff might be able to pass legislation that could threaten the institution of slavery. Thus, the 1828 tariff, just as many Jacksonians expected, only increased the unpopularity of Adams.

Jackson inauguration and spoils system

In 1828, Jackson campaigned vigorously against Adams, maintaining that the President had stolen the previous election. This rhetoric resonated with the people, and Jackson won easily with both the popular and electoral votes. To celebrate the people's victory, Jackson eschewed a traditional and formal inauguration. Instead, he invited the common people who had stood behind him to the White House to celebrate his victory. The Jackson inauguration proved to be quite a party, with thousands from the countryside pouring into Washington and taking advantage of the readily available alcohol. In the process, considerable damage was done to the White House, leading Jackson to take refuge in a nearby hotel, while some have suggested that it was cheaper to rebuild the White House after the British burning than the clean up after Jackson's inaugural. Jackson also pleased his followers by announcing that he was implementing the spoils system in which governmental appointments were based upon loyalty to the President and his policies. Sounding much like President Trump's pledge to drain the political swamp in Washington, Jackson claimed the democracy would be furthered through removing appointments made by his predecessor and replacing them with representatives selected from the more common ranks of Jacksonian supporters. While there is some validity to this argument, the problem was that many of Jackson's appointees lacked formal education and political experience, culminating in examples of corruption such as Samuel Swartwout who after several months collecting the tariff at the port of New York fled to England with millions of tax dollars.

Peggy O'Neal "affair" and Nullification Crisis

Jackson also allowed his personal feelings to influence his political decisions. Secretary of War William Eaton was the subject of gossip regarding his relationship with the beautiful Peggy O'Neal, who along with her mother operated a boarding house where the bachelor politician resided. Eaton responded to rumors of impropriety by marrying Peggy. Vice President John C. Calhoun and his socially-prominent wife insisted that Eaton should resign. Instead, Jackson, remembering how his wife had been the target of gossip, championed Peggy in White House social circles, outraging Calhoun who eventually resigned and returned to South Carolina, where after being elected to the Senate by the state legislature, emerged as one of the President's major political opponents. Sensing the changing political wind, the crafty Secretary of State Martin Van Buren also championed Peggy's cause and emerged as a Jackson political favorite who gained the Democratic President nomination in 1836. The Peggy O'Neal affair, however, was much more than a sex scandal as it exacerbated the growing political divisions between Jackson and Calhoun over the tariff and powers of the national government.

South Carolina responded to the tariff issue by adopting a resolution of nullification that rendered the "Tariff of Abomination" null and void in the state. In other words, the state of South Carolina refused to recognize the authority of the federal government to collect the tariff within its borders. Calhoun embraced the nullification ordinance, and Jackson considered South Carolina's action as a direct challenge to his authority and a threat to the union similar to that presented by the Alien and Sedition Acts and the Virginia and Kentucky Resolutions in the 1790s. The case against nullification in the Congress was carried by the oratory of Massachusetts Senator Daniel Webster who declared that union and liberty were inseparable and could not be dissolved by the states negating federal law. Jackson's oratory, however, was less flowery, and he threatened to invade South Carolina and hang the nullifiers. Cooler heads prevailed in Congress, and a political deal was brokered to end the crisis. In the Compromise Tariff of 1833 the extreme rates of 1828 were somewhat reduced, and Calhoun could declare victory and have the nullification ordinance withdrawn. Jackson was to be pacified with the Force Bill which asserted that the President enjoyed the power to invade the states if necessary to enforce obedience to the laws of the national government. The issue of state rights was hardly resolved for after the election of Republican Abraham Lincoln in 1860, South Carolina was the first state to pass a motion of secession from the United States. It is interesting to note that the Force Act was to later be used by President Dwight Eisenhower in the 1950s to enforce Southern adherence to the *Brown v. Board of Education* Supreme Court decision mandating desegregation of public schools.

Jackson and the National Bank

While Jackson was a champion of nationalism during the nullification crisis, his economic policies were more opposed to the exercise of federal power and eventually culminated in the Panic of 1837. Jackson detested the Bank of the United States, perceiving Hamilton's creation as a monopoly that fostered control over the economy by an elite Eastern financial institution discriminating against state banks located in the West and South. Thus, Jackson welcomed the opportunity to veto an extension of the National Bank engineered by Henry Clay's supporters in Congress, who believed that a renewal of the bank's charter would provide Clay with a campaign issue for the 1832 election. Jackson's decision to veto the bank extension, however, proved popular with his followers, and the President easily won re-election over Clay. The veto, however, did prove to have serious economic repercussions. The Bank of the United States had several years left on its previous

Congressional authorization, and the bank's President Nicholas Biddle sought to strike back at Jackson and his followers by calling in loans that had been extended for the purchase of land in the West. Biddle's policy of liquidating the bank's Western holdings negatively impacted land purchases in the region, and Jackson sought to stabilize land prices by employing his authority as President to withdraw government funds from the Bank of the United States and deposit them in Western regional financial institutions. The problem with Jackson's action was that the banks selected as depositories for federal funds were often controlled by associates of the President. Many of these so-called "pet banks" were more interested in land speculation than solid financial investments to support long term growth. Accordingly, Jackson's pet banks contributed to a financial crisis in the West characterized by corruption and unsecured loans leading to inflated land prices. To bring this inflation under control, the Jackson administration finally issued the Specie Circular which stated that all government lands would have to be purchased through specie or cash. The Specie Circular did help to bring down the price of Western lands, but the legislation also paved the way for the financial Panic of 1837 after Jackson departed the White House. The champion of the common man left the nation in a difficult economic situation

Trail of tears

Yet, Jackson remained a popular figure as his policies encouraged expansion and reflected the popular prejudices of the day. The hunger of white settlers for land was fed by a policy of Indian removal in which the United States government pressured Native nations to move westward and surrender traditional lands to the whites. After years of resistance and loss of land, Native nations in the southeastern United States hoped to avoid this fate by a policy of accommodation in which they adopted elements of white culture and attempted to live in peace with their Anglo neighbors. Thus, the Seminole, Creek, Chickasaw, Choctaw, and Cherokee were referred to as "the five civilized tribes" by many whites in the South. The Cherokee even went so far as to create their own written alphabet and print newspapers while educating their children in schools established by the tribe. Some Cherokee even adopted the Southern practice of enslaving blacks while cultivating cotton. This accommodation and assimilation, however, failed to protect the Native people when gold was discovered on their land in Georgia and South Carolina, leading to white demands for the land of the Indians. Congress responded with the Indian Removal Act of 1830 that proposed to move the "civilized" tribes from their traditional lands and relocate them westward away from white settlement in the Indian territory later known as Oklahoma. Rather that resorting to war, the Cherokee attempted to fight the government in a civilized manner by appealing to the court system. The Supreme Court under Justice Marshall sided with the Cherokee, arguing that the national government could not unilaterally abrogate a treaty. President Jackson, however, ignored the Supreme Court and pointed out that Marshall lacked the powers which Jackson enjoyed as commander-in-chief. Jackson ordered the military to forcibly remove the Natives in what became known as the "trail of tears."

Although there was armed resistance by the Seminole under Osceola, over 100,000 Natives were uprooted and removed from their eastern homes and marched to Oklahoma, with thousands perishing during the treacherous crossing of the Mississippi River. There was no movement to impeach President Jackson for violating the order of the Supreme Court as Jackson's action in moving the Natives across the Mississippi simply reflected the popular prejudice of the day. Yet in some ways, the transplanted five tribes would be able to gain some economic advantage over the whites who had exiled them to Oklahoma. The Native people initially struggled in their new home on the treeless plains as the five tribes were woodlands Indians who had to adjust culturally to a new environment. But Jackson and his administration were unaware that they had placed the five tribes upon oil deposits that would enrich Oklahoma and some descendants of the trail of tears in the twentieth century.

Texas Revolution and slavery expansion

Jackson's appetite for slavery expansion was also apparent in his interest at adding the Mexican territory of Texas to the United States. After Mexico obtained its independence from Spain, the new republic encountered considerable difficulty with exercising control over the northern province of Teas which was dominated by the Comanche nation. Mexican efforts to assert influence over Texas resulted in a land grant policy that encouraged the immigration of settlers such as Stephen Austin from the United States. After fierce fighting, the Comanche were somewhat neutralized with the influx of settlers from the American republic. Most of these migrants were from the South and brought their slaves into the Mexican territory. The migrants maintained an allegiance to the United States and made their desire to join their former homeland quite apparent to the Mexican authorities. Mexico responded by attempting to centralize its control over Texas. Further immigration from the United States was forbidden, residents were required to convert to Catholicism, and slavery was abolished. Although these restrictions were often disregarded by the settlers in Texas, most of whom were Anglo, the Texans in 1836 declared independence from Mexico, insisting that the Mexican government had violated their natural rights. Such rhetoric ignored the inconsistency that the Texans were rebelling for the natural right to hold black people in bondage while violating their inalienable rights to life, liberty, and the pursuit of happiness.

Mexican President and General Antonio Lopez de Santa Anna responded to the rebellion by leading an army of over 5,000 conscripts across the Rio Grande. As

Santa Anna advanced into Texas, he encountered approximately 200 Texans near San Antonio in the Alamo, a Spanish mission converted to a fort. Santa Anna might have bypassed the fort, but he was uncomfortable with the possibility of the Texans interfering with his supply lines. Accordingly, he laid siege to the Alamo whose defenders put up a more spirited resistance than anticipated. After a thirteen-day battle the Alamo fell and all its defenders perished, including Tejanos of Mexican descent and such well-known Anglo American figures as William Travis, Jim Bowie, and Davy Crockett. A former member of Congress from Tennessee and prominent political opponent of Jackson, Crockett's death especially gained the attention of the press in the United States. In the 1950s, Walt Disney further enhanced the myth of the Alamo in American popular culture with a series of films highlighting the career of Crockett and fostering the fad of coonskin cap-wearing youth in homage to the "king of the wild frontier." Some historians have argued that Texas native son President Lyndon Johnson was influenced by the example of Crockett and other defenders of the Alamo in his stubborn commitment to the Vietnam War which during the 1960s got many of Disney's former young Crockett admirers killed. Mexican sources, however, question the heroic image of Crockett and suggest that he attempted to surrender before being executed by Santa Anna. Regardless of historical realities, the myth of the Alamo continues to resonate in American culture.

At the time, the defense of the Alamo did seem to provide an opportunity for Sam Houston to organize an army of defense for the Texas Revolution. As Santa Anna advanced further into Texas, Houston and his army retreated until they were able to surprise the Mexicans at the Battle of San Jacinto near present day Houston. Many of the exhausted Mexican forces where sleeping when the Texans attacked, and Mexican soldiers attempting to surrender were slaughtered by Texans shouting, "Remember the Alamo." Amid the chaos, Santa Anna was captured in his sleeping clothes. When confronted with the threat of execution, the Mexican leader agreed to withdraw his troops and recognize the independence of Texas from Mexico. Following his release and return to Mexico City, Santa Anna reneged upon the agreement that was signed under duress.

Meanwhile, Sam Houston, selected as the President of the Republic of Texas, petitioned his old Tennessee friend Jackson to support the annexation of Texas into the United States. While Jackson was an expansionist who had no problems with slavery, the annexation of Texas posed major problems for Jackson as he prepared to leave the Presidency after two turbulent terms. The addition of Texas as a slave state would upset the Congressional balance between free and slave states and overturn the Missouri Compromise that had curtailed Congressional debate over slavery. Reluctantly, Jackson failed to support annexation, but he did extend diplomatic recognition to the Republic of Texas, although Mexico still officially claimed the territory.

Rise of the Whigs

Jackson's final years in office were also marked by the rise of an opposition party, the Whigs. Rather than characterized by the ideological divisions between Hamilton and Jefferson that influenced the first party system, the second party system centered around the personality of Jackson as the unifying factor for the Whigs was their opposition to the Jackson Presidency. The Whig leadership included such figures as Senators Daniel Webster, Henry Clay, and John C. Calhoun whose policies often contradicted one another. Thus, the Whigs included adherents of Clay's American system extolling the virtues of a national government promoting internal improvements, Northern manufacturers in favor of a protective tariff, and Southern planters opposed to a strong central government that could threaten South Carolina with invasion. In the election of 1836, the Whigs could not agree upon a candidate to face Jackson's Democratic favorite Martin Van Buren who had served as Secretary of State and Vice President under Jackson. With Jackson's endorsement and working-class support in his native state of New York, Van Buren was able to defeat of group of Whig regional "favorite son" candidates. While the popular vote was close, Van Buren enjoyed a substantial advantage in the Electoral College. The Van Buren Presidency, however, proved to be unpopular. The New Yorker lacked the populist touch that Jackson employed to enlist the support of the common man in the South and West. In addition, Van Buren was saddled with the Panic of 1837 that was fostered by Jackson as he battled with the Bank of the United States. Unable to get out from under this economic burden, Van Buren was turned out of office in 1840 by the Whigs who coalesced around the candidacy of William Henry Harrison of Indiana. Chanting "Van's a used-up man," the Whigs sought to present Harrison as the champion of the common people, even though he was from an aristocratic slave-owning Virginia family. Instead, the Whigs portrayed Harrison as a military hero similar to Jackson, celebrating Harrison's victory over Tecumseh with the slogan of "Tippecanoe and Tyler too." The "Hard Cider and Log Cabin" campaign of the Whigs in 1840 joined the Democrats in embracing the rise of the common man in American politics.

Legacy of Jacksonian democracy

Jacksonian democracy abolished property qualifications for voting and ushered in universal suffrage for white men, although political participation beyond this core group was not part of the Jackson agenda. Rather than have a caucus of party leaders select candidates for office, nominating conventions in which the common man might participate were introduced into the political process. This democratization, however, exacerbated other problems. The belief that any man could hold public office tended to depreciate experience and education as prerequisites for office holders, and the Jacksonian era witnessed a rise in political corruption. The intense partisanship of the Jacksonian period also fostered maneuvers such as gerrymandering in which politicians establish electoral districts based upon partisan advantage rather than democratic principles, a practice which continues to dominate contemporary American politics.

The corruption of Jacksonian society was coupled with opportunity according to the French nobleman Alexis de Tocqueville who toured American in the 1830s and published his findings in *Democracy in America*. While celebrating Jacksonian society in offering opportunity for the common man, the French author also observed a growing degree of class conflict within the rising republic. According to de Tocqueville, a fundamental conflict existed between American beliefs in both equality and freedom which tend to conflict. Americans try to get around this dichotomy by emphasizing equality of opportunity, a classless concept that does not reflect the reality of class divisions within American society. The economy of the Jacksonian period was characterized by growth. European immigration from nations such as Germany and Ireland poured into a country also experiencing a natural population increase. A mercantile economy based upon urbanization and industrialization developed in the North, while in the South cotton and slavery expanded. To promote this economic growth, roads, bridges, canals, and railroads were constructed. But the expansion of the Jacksonian economy was based upon exploitation. The common white man was rising on the backs of others. Industrial growth in the North was based upon the labor of poorly paid factory women and Irish laborers. Southern cotton culture was grounded in the enslavement of black men and women in the cotton fields, while Western expansion was achieved at the expense of Native and Mexican people being dispossessed of their land. The materialism of Jacksonian society, however, also drew the criticism of reformers, abolitionists, and utopians who recognized that the reformation of society required more than just the political rise of the common white man.

Further Reading:

Benson, Lee. *The Concept of Jacksonian Democracy: New York as a Test Case.* Princeton, NJ: Princeton University Press, 1961.

Freehling, William W. *Prelude to Civil War: The Nullification Controversy in South Carolina, 1816–1836.* New York: Harper & Row, 1966.

Holt, Michael F. *The Rise and Fall of the American Whig* Party: *Jacksonian Politics and the Onset of the Civil War.* New York: Oxford University Press, 1978.

Pessen, Edward. *Jacksonian America: Society, Personality, and Politics.* Homewood, IL: Dorsey Press, 1978.

Peterson, Merrill D. *The Great Triumvirate: Webster, Clay, and Calhoun.* New York: Oxford University Press, 1987.

Remini, Robert V. *Andrew Jackson and the Course of American Democracy.* Baltimore, MD: Johns Hopkins University Press, 1991.

Schlesinger Jr., Arthur M. *The Age of Jackson.* Boston: Little, Brown and Company, 1945.

Sellers, Charles. *The Market Revolution: Jacksonian America, 1815–1846.* New York: Oxford University Press, 1991.

Wallace, Anthony. *The Long Bitter Trail: Andrew Jackson and the Indians.* New York: Hill and Wang, 1993.

Wilentz, Sean. *The Rise of American Democracy: Jefferson to Lincoln.* New York: W.W. Norton & Company, 2005.

10

American Society, 1830–1860: Factories, Slavery, and Reform Movements

Frederick Douglass. Reproduction of a portrait by George Kendall Warren. Liljenquist Family Collection of Civil War Photographs (Library of Congress). After escaping from slavery, Frederick Douglass became a significant orator and writer for the abolitionist cause, while also embracing other reform issues such as women's suffrage. Northern reformers challenged the materialism of American society based upon slavery and the factory system.

The thirty years before the American Civil War were a tremendous era of economic development based upon the cultivation of fertile farmland in the Midwest, the rise of a factory system in the Northeast, and the expansion of cotton culture and slavery in the South. While the prosperity of both the Northern and Southern economies were based upon the exploitation of women, immigrants, and people of color, there was a fundamental difference between the two regions. The Northern economy was based upon free labor, and despite often horrendous working conditions in the factories there was at least the possibility of social mobility. The slave economy of the South, on the other hand, was a closed system in which black Americans were subjected to bondage based upon a social caste system that also offered little opportunity for poor whites. These exploitive and materialistic economies produced reform movements, primarily in the North, that sought to curb the excesses of the unfettered Jacksonian market economy. These reforms ranged from women's rights to public education to utopian socialism to religious revivalism and to abolitionism. While these reform endeavors were successful in providing some relief to the laboring class and addressing some of the excesses found in American capitalism, they were not in the final analysis able to eradicate concepts of manifest destiny based upon racist notions of American exceptionalism or prevent a war over free and slave labor. Abolitionism was a noble attempt to address the scourge of American slavery, but it would take a bloody civil war to abolish slavery, and we continue to grapple with the legacy of racial slavery for American life.

The Old Northwest and free labor

For a nation to industrialize, there must be a solid agricultural foundation on which to feed a labor supply leaving the countryside to find employment in urban factories. The Midwest, or the Old Northwest as it was often called in the 1830s and 1840s, provided this function for the new American nation. States such as Iowa, Indiana, Ohio, Michigan, Illinois, and Minnesota served as the breadbasket for the country, producing the corn and wheat to feed the growing population. The cultivation of these rich wheat and corn fields, however, was not based upon the employment of slave labor. Instead, farmers of the Old Northwest increasingly relied upon the introduction of innovative agricultural technology such as the mechanized harvester and reaper developed by Cyrus McCormick of Chicago, establishing an enterprise that eventually developed into the globally influential corporation, International Harvester. Working the wheat fields was still strenuous labor, but the introduction of automated machinery to the fields required a smaller labor supply than in the South where, for example, cotton continued to be picked by hand well into the twentieth century.

The Old Northwest, in which slavery was banned and innovation was seemingly encouraged, was also politically and economically tied to the Northeast through the building of the Erie Canal. Major trading centers, such as Cleveland, Chicago, and Buffalo, emerged along the Great Lakes as hubs for the agricultural commerce of the Old Northwest. The construction of the Erie Canal, stretching approximately 360 miles across the state of New York, linked Buffalo to Albany and the Hudson River. Goods could, then, be dispatched down the Hudson River to the harbor of New York City, opening to national and international markets. While the pace of mules pulling the barges along the canal was rather slow—but providing the inspiration for folksongs such as "Fifteen Miles on the Erie Canal" still sung in the schools—transportation rates were reduced, and the economy of western New York boomed. The success of the Erie Canal set off an enthusiasm for canal building in the United States, although by the 1830s and 1840s railroads were challenging the dominance of the canals.

The economic and transportation link between the Old Northwest and the Northeast also helped to forge an ideological link between the two regions that proved influential during the Civil War. It was in the Old Northwest, home to Abraham Lincoln, that the concept of free labor, free soil, and free men nourished and developed. This concept was essentially a white nationalist ideology that endorsed both antislavery and anti-black sentiments. Thus, the Old Northwest was perceived as a region for white social mobility. White workers could migrate to the region and, with the promise of free labor, they could earn good wages that would allow them to save money and eventually purchase land where they could raise a family. The ownership of land would provide these former wage workers with independence and a stake in society. The expansion of slavery, however, posed a threat to this dream of white social mobility. Slave labor would drive down wages, and white workers in the western territories would suffer the degradation of poor Southern whites. White free labor could not compete with slave labor. Thus, slavery expansion was opposed not because of the terrible conditions under which black Americans lived and labored, but rather because slavery posed a threat to white people. The Old Northwest was, accordingly, often both antislavery and anti-black, explaining why many states in the region passed laws to prevent the immigration of blacks into the area. And it is worth remembering that while Lincoln's views on slavery and racial equality evolved, his early political observations on slavery often reflected the prejudices of his region.

Emergence of the factory system

While the Old Northwest exercised considerable economic and ideological influence upon Northern society, the population of the United States was centered in the Northeast where the industrial system envisioned by Alexander Hamilton was taking hold. The Jacksonian society of the Northeast was characterized by the rise of merchants, cities, factories, opportunity—at least for white men—and materialism. The foundation for this materialism was the factory system based upon the model of the industrial revolution in England. A key figure in this industrial system was Samuel Slater who is credited with memorizing the plans for spinning cotton into thread on a mass production level and bringing them to the United States, thwarting British efforts to maintain a monopoly in the textile industry. A Yankee inventor Eli Whitney, who revolutionized Southern culture with the cotton gin, also helped to pioneer the concept of interchangeable parts that allowed for the factory model of the assembly line. And reflecting the tremendous influence that a gun culture continues to exercise over American society, it seems most fitting that Whitney's contribution focused upon the manufacture of firearms. Before the emergence of mass production, guns were less prominent in American life than many might imagine for they were crafted by skilled gunsmiths. The weapons were well made, but the drawback was that they were quite expensive and if broken they were difficult to replace. Mass production of guns on an assembly line, however, provided for interchangeable parts and drove prices down, making guns more readily available. This concept, of course, was applicable to the production of numerous items, especially textiles for which there was considerable demand.

For this mass production, factory owners sought a cheap labor supply, relying upon the exploitation of female and child labor. The assumption was that they could be paid less, for unlike men they were not the major breadwinners of a family—a concept that still seems to govern the practices of some employers. Factory owners also believed that it would be easier to control and intimidate women and children, who would be less likely to form labor organizations—although many employers would be surprised by the organizing efforts of their female workers. Women were also perceived as bringing their sewing skills to the job as factories replaced the domestic putting out system in which farm women earned extra money by sewing at home for merchants. Children were also perceived as easy to control and subject to lower pay. Their small stature also meant that employers could spend less money on workspaces or mine shafts. With families desperate for additional money and the lack of public schools with compulsory attendance laws, child labor was a significant element in American industrialization.

Many of the women and children relegated to the factories were immigrants fleeing poverty and political unrest in Europe. This was especially true of the Irish as millions starved in their native land due to the potato blight and English laws limiting the importation of grain that would have saved Irish lives. Those who escaped Ireland were desperate for work and had little choice but to accept low wages and dangerous working conditions. The deplorable overcrowding and filth in which many Irish families were forced to live re-enforced English stereotypes of the Irish as an inferior people. The Irish who immigrated to the United States faced considerable discrimination and economic misery, but they enjoyed better prospects for social mobility than their African brothers and sisters in the American South.

Immigrant laborers from nations such as Ireland confronted terrible working condition in the factories. Work days ranged from twelve to fourteen hours with a short break for lunch and to relieve oneself. Lunch was usually consumed alongside a sewing machine or work station. To make sure that they did not wander, children were often chained to machines, and many accidents occurred as exhausted young children dozed off during the long work day. In addition to being subject to the sexual harassment of factory managers, women with long hair were sometimes literally "scalped" when their hair became entangled in a machine which they were operating. Female workers were also expected to return to their jobs shortly after giving birth—there was no such policy as family or maternal leave. Those who had just given birth were often drenched by the breast milk that could not be consumed by babies entrusted to the care of other siblings who were mere children themselves. To prevent the starving babies from crying all day and exhausting themselves to the point of death, the infants were often given rags soaked in whiskey to suck upon and produce a stupor that might allow them to survive until mother returned from the factory and was able to provide nourishment.

Early efforts at labor reform

Worker compensation was not a factor in the laissez-faire economy as employers asserted that laborers willingly accepted the dangerous conditions of the workplace. If they did not like the conditions or pay, they could always quit for there was another immigrant eager to take their place. As for those injured on the job, there was always another worker willing to accept the dangers of the position. A desperate workforce put little pressure on employers, but there were some efforts at worker organization during the Jacksonian era. Fledgling workingmen's political parties were put forth in cities such as Philadelphia and New York, while a National Trade Union failed to establish a foothold among the American working class. The crowded and desperate labor market made it difficult for workers to organize and demand their rights, while businessmen in cahoots with government strongly suppressed any efforts by workers to unionize. In addition to suppression, it has been difficult to organize American workers due to the persistence of Ben Franklin's self-made man and the mythology of the American dream. While the concept of class holds greater sway in Europe, Americans cling to the notion of social mobility and individualism. Why should they combine with other workers to establish better conditions and higher pay, when through hard work and perseverance they may end up owning the factory some day? This lack of class consciousness has made the United States a difficult environment for union organization from the Jacksonian period into the twenty-first century.

One of the few labor achievements from the Jacksonian era was the establishment of a ten-hour day for the federal government whose presence in the workforce was quite limited during the 1830s and 1840s. Nevertheless, the excesses of industrialization did result in calls for reform; although many of these movements focused upon larger social and cultural issues while ignoring the gruesome details of labor in the factories, reflecting the generally middle-class origins of reformers who had little direct knowledge of working conditions. One notable effort at labor reform, however, was pursued at the textile mills in Waltham, Massachusetts. Reflecting the concern of some employers regarding hiring and managing immigrant workers, the Waltham experiment proposed the hiring of young women from rural areas in Massachusetts to work in the mills. It was not easy to recruit these native workers as factory employment was perceived as lower-class work and a danger to the morals of young women. To address these concerns, the factory owners of Waltham proposed hiring the young daughters of farmers by assuring their parents that the young women would be properly chaperoned and supervised. The women fresh from the farms would be housed and fed in dormitories located next to the mills, and they would be supervised by matrons who would see to the religious instruction and moral behavior of their charges. With their reputations thus protected, the "Waltham girls" would be able to earn money for their families and arrange suitable marriages when they departed the workforce. But the Waltham experiment did not quite work out as planned. The young women chafed at these efforts to control their lives and protested to gain greater freedom and compensation. In addition, young male suitors were not always available for the "Waltham girls," who had perhaps gained too much independence. Thus, many of the mill operators returned to the exploitation of immigrant labor.

Ralph Waldo Emerson and Henry David Thoreau

Other efforts to address the materialism of Jacksonian society were less concentrated upon working conditions. Philosopher and lyceum lecturer Ralph Waldo Emerson of Concord, Massachusetts criticized the materialism and consumerism of Jacksonian America, writing, "Things are in the saddle and ride mankind." Emerson embraced individualism and challenged orthodoxy, arguing that consistency was the "hobgoblin" of small minds and that to be great one must be a nonconformist. One of Emerson's major disciples was Henry David Thoreau, the son of a relatively wealthy Concord family who owned a pencil factory. Seeking to implement Emerson's ideas regarding nature and independence, Thoreau endeavored to live simply on his own at Walden Pond, just outside of Concord. Thoreau recorded his experience in *Walden* (1854) which remains a staple of environmental literature. While residing at Walden, Thoreau was arrested for failure to pay his taxes in protest of the Mexican War and the American government's association with slavery. Although Thoreau's stay in jail was short as a relative stepped in and paid his taxes, the young philosopher seized upon the experience of his incarceration to pen *The Essay on Civil Disobedience*. Thoreau's argument that the individual must march to his/her own drummer and follow the higher law or conscience over man-made law influenced contemporaries such as abolitionist John Brown and has been associated with the civil disobedience of figures such as Gandhi and Martin Luther King Jr.

Dorothea Dix and Horace Mann

Dorothea Dix and Horace Mann were residents of Massachusetts who attempted to reform the market society critiqued by Emerson and Thoreau. The daughter of a New England minister, Dix investigated how those suffering from mental illness were treated in Massachusetts. To her horror, Dix discovered that those suffering from mental illness were often treated as common criminals or were "skeletons in the closet," hidden by their families from public view in attics and cellars. Demonstrating an expanded role for educated women, Dix testified before the Massachusetts state legislature, arguing that the measure of a society is how it treats the underprivileged such as the mentally ill. Dix was instrumental in convincing the state of Massachusetts to provide asylums for the care and treatment of the mentally ill. While mental hospitals today are all too often underfunded and overcrowded, they represented an improvement over the deplorable conditions that Dix discovered in the attics, cellars, and basements of Massachusetts.

As Secretary of the Massachusetts Board of Education, Horace Mann sought to broaden the focus of reform to include all children. While the wealthy educated their children with private tutors and schools, the children of the poor were denied an education and forced into the factories. Mann proposed to address this class division through the institution of public schools funded by taxation, insisting that the education of all children is an investment that benefits society and all social classes. Mann's vision of universal public education is an avenue through which to provide the social mobility celebrated in the American dream, but the discrepancy in funding for schools, often based upon local property taxes, has prevented public education from achieving the goals envisioned by Mann.

Other reformers perceived alcohol, a mainstay of the American economy since colonial times, as an impediment to social mobility. Although the experiment with prohibition under the Eighteenth Amendment during the 1920s has largely discredited the idea of a societal ban on alcohol, many reformers in the Jacksonian era argued that demon rum was a threat to the American family and nation. While the movement was only successful in enacting prohibition at the state level in Maine during the antebellum period, women were especially drawn to the idea of abolishing alcohol, for, just as today, it was the fuel for domestic abuse of women by their husbands. Thus, the prohibition crusade was part of a growing women's rights movement within Jacksonian society

Seneca Falls and the women's movement

In July 1848, a small group of men and women gathered in Seneca Falls, New York to consider the status of women in Jacksonian America. Led by Elizabeth Cady Stanton and her younger protégé, Susan B. Anthony, the Seneca Falls Conference produced a document called the Declaration of Sentiments with its structure based upon Jefferson's Declaration of Independence. Making the case for gender equality, the document called for female suffrage and a married woman's property law to assure that women remained independent and did not simply become wards of their husbands. The Declaration of Sentiments also called for expanded educational opportunities for women, which would, in turn, allow women to enter such professions as the medical, legal, and theological fields. Reform of divorce laws was also required as in most states only a man could institute divorce proceedings with the primary grounds being infidelity on the part of a wife. The double standard of sexual expectations did not extend similar limitations upon husbands. And since divorced women were perceived as morally suspect, the courts rewarded fathers with the custody of children. Reflecting the middle-class origins of the Seneca Falls Conference, the conditions of women laboring in the factories were not addressed in the Declaration of Sentiments. Nevertheless, Stanton and Anthony remained advocates for women's rights throughout their lives, although neither lived to see the adoption of the Nineteenth Amendment to the Constitution, providing female suffrage on the national level.

Seneca Falls challenged the concept of separate spheres which many men in the nineteenth century employed to justify gender inequality. A bit more sophisticated than sexist notions that women were inferior to men and their talents were best used in the kitchen and bedroom, the separate spheres concept maintained that women were morally superior to men who were degraded by their participation in the world of commerce and politics. According to this ideology, any good that men accomplished in the world was due to the influence of their mothers. While men were dominant in the environment outside the home, women were superior on the domestic front. Women were able to exercise this superiority and provide moral guidance to their children because they were not compromised by involvement with business and politics. Thus, it was essential to maintain the separate spheres. Stanton, on the other hand, argued that since women enjoyed a proclivity toward moral judgment, then they should use these abilities to clean up the mess men had made in politics and business with war, violence, and corruption.

Religion and reform

The reform cause was also fostered by religious revivalism, especially in western New York which become known as the burned-over district due to the fires of religious enthusiasm which swept the region. Western New York experienced a significant economic boom in the early nineteenth century following construction of the Erie Canal; however, with the competition of railroads nationally by the 1830s and 1840s, the region underwent a major economic decline. Seeking an explanation for this rapid reversal of fortune, many residents sought solace in religion, and the religious revivalism of the Second Great Awakening swept through the region. Many perceived the trials and tribulations as a sign that the Biblical end of times was nigh. To prepare oneself for the millennium and return of Jesus, it was essential to abandon materialism and purify oneself. An example of this religious enthusiasm was the Millerites led by evangelist William Miller who claimed that his study of scripture indicated that Jesus would return to greet his followers in 1843. Miller's teachings garnered a considerable following in western New York, and preparations were made to greet the messiah, who failed to appear on two occasions predicted by the Millerites. After this disappointment, the movement tended to collapse, but the enthusiasm and despair with which many embraced Miller's teachings and predictions reveal much about the fragile condition of many Americans in the nineteenth century as well as today when many cling to millennial visions to provide a sense of hope in their lives.

The Shakers, who would shake when the spirit of God entered them, were also millennials who believed in the imminent return of Jesus, but they did not believe it was possible to predict the exact timing. Therefore, it was necessary for them to purify themselves as Jesus might return at any moment. The Shakers had originated in England, but they enjoyed their greatest popularity in the United States between 1820 and 1860. Emphasizing a simplistic, communal lifestyle, the Shakers practiced a degree of gender equality and sought to purify themselves by abstaining from alcohol and practicing celibacy—not a formula for sustaining a religious movement if the millennium is not soon nigh. While not self-sustaining in the long run, the Shakers were able to subsist with new converts and the adoption of children, while becoming respected for their skilled craftsmanship such as furniture making.

Religious fervor and belief in the supernatural were apparent in the popularity of spiritualism, especially among the more affluent classes who believed that direct communication with spirits as well as the dead was possible. Spiritualism was also associated with women's rights as well as other reform movements as females, such as sisters Kate and Margaret Fox, were perceived as medians who enjoyed unique God-given powers to communicate with spirits. Opposed by the mainstream Protestant churches, many viewed spiritualism as a fraud or part of the occult, and the movement never gained a major following.

One major world religion, however, did emerge from the Second Great Awakening and religious fervor of the burned-over district. Mormonism was born in western New York when Joseph Smith proclaimed that an angel had appeared into him, revealing buried golden tablets on which the *Book of Mormon* was written, revealing the ministry of Jesus in the Americas and calling for believers to restore the original principles of Christianity. Rooted within an environment of religious enthusiasm, Smith's teachings soon attracted a following. Emphasizing family values and a community of believers, the Mormons often antagonized their neighbors with their economic success based upon a strong sense of supporting the church and other Mormons. Also, controversy centered upon the practice of polygamy which allowed Mormon men to have more than one wife—and certainly a better plan for fostering a religion than the celibacy of the Shakers—that was often defended as a means through which to protect women. Opposition to the Mormons or the Church of Jesus Christ of Latter-Day Saints led to violence, and in 1844 Smith was murdered at the hands of a lynch mob in Nauvoo, Illinois. Such persecution, as well as internal divisions, led Brigham Young to seek refuge for the group in the wilderness of Utah. While the Utah frontier appeared a hostile environment for the Mormon settlers, they made the desert bloom and found prosperity in Utah. While the history of the Mormons in Utah is shrouded with controversy such as the Mountain Meadows Massacre in September 1857, the Mormon War with the United States government, and treatment of people of African descent, there is no denying the continuing world impact of the religion that arose out of the burned-over district and Second Great Awakening.

Utopian communities

But not all reformers sought a heavenly reward to address the economic and social conditions of Jacksonian society. During the antebellum period, the United States witnessed a number of utopian settlements, many of them based upon European socialist models, that sought to provide heaven on earth and change capitalist society by example—in many ways these utopian settlements of the 1830s and 1840s were similar to the communes of the 1960s that endeavored to present a countercultural alternative to mainstream American society. For example, Welsh industrialist and social reformer Robert Owen attempted to establish a society based upon socialist principles in New Harmony, Indiana. The experiment lasted only a few years, beset by poor leadership, internal divisions, and competition from neighboring communities who adhered to a different set of values. New Harmony, nevertheless, deserves some credit for challenging practices of child labor by calling for the public education of both male and female children within the community.

A better-known example of the Jacksonian utopian communities is Brook Farm established in 1840 just outside of Boston. The settlement was created by George Ripley and was based upon the ideas of French socialist Charles Fourier and the transcendentalist movement popularized by Emerson and Thoreau. The transcendentalists believed in the redemptive powers of nature transcending the materialistic values of a consumer society. Seeking to blend the individuality of Emerson's "self-reliance" with the communal aspects of socialism, Brook Farm attempted to promote an environment in which the community would benefit from sharing the bounty of each member pursuing his/her interests and talents. One of the problems for Brook Farm, as was the case for many of the communes during the 1960s, is that the experimental farm attracted more idealistic intellectuals rather than practical and skilled farmers and laborers. The community produced an outstanding literary magazine, but Brook Farm was less successful in cultivating agricultural produce that might provide a financial foundation for the community. Struggling to survive financially, Brook Farm never recovered from a fire in 1847.

Women played an important role in many of the utopian communities. Margaret Fuller was an independent female reformer and writer who was associated with transcendentalism and Brook Farm. She edited the transcendentalist journal *The Dial* and advocated for women's rights while writing for American newspapers. While serving as a foreign correspondent for the *New York Tribune*, Fuller became involved with an Italian revolutionary and the movement to establish an Italian state. When returning to the United States, she perished in a tragic shipwreck. Even more scandalous to mainstream Americans was the Scottish reformer Frances Wright who established the short-lived utopian experiment of Nashoba in Tennessee. After touring the country in 1824 with the Marquis de Lafayette, Wright decided to settle in the United States. Enthusiastic about her adopted homeland, Wright in 1828 delivered what was probably the first public Fourth of July oration by a woman in which she argued that American patriotism should be measured by adherence to the principles of freedom enunciated in the Declaration of Independence. Wright tested the boundaries of American freedom in the 1830s and1840s with her antislavery views, as well as advocating for the sexual and political independence of women. She attempted to implement her antislavery views at Nashoba in Tennessee where she would purchase slaves and emancipate them. The former slaves would be educated and provide labor on the farm, demonstrating the capabilities of free black labor, before being returned to Africa. While advocating racial equality, the administration of Nashoba was rather condescending, and the community was constantly strapped for cash as the purchasing of slaves to emancipate was a major expense. In addition, the antislavery experiment earned the ire of Nashoba's white neighbors who accused Wright of promoting interracial sexual relationships, including taking on black lovers of her own. Nashoba collapsed after only three years.

Allegations of free love also helped to derail the Oneida community in western New York. The Oneida community was established in 1848 by George Humphrey Noyes and based upon communal principles in which all possessions and labor were to be shared. Noyes also preached a form of free love or complex marriage in which older members of the community were to initiate the youth into sexual activity. This free sexual association eventually led to internal discord at Oneida as well as bringing down the condemnation of New York civil authorities upon the community. The original commune founded by Noyes disintegrated, but the remnants of the community produced the lucrative Oneida silverware company. The utopian communities of the Jacksonian era sought to challenge the materialism and exploitation of the factories and slavery by offering an alternative model of organizing society along more egalitarian and communal values. They wanted to change society by example, but failed due to a variety of factors, including opposition from the dominant culture and economy, lack of funds, difficulty in attracting members with suitable skills, and internal division over sharing labor and possessions as well as "free love." These are essentially the same reasons that many of the communes from the 1960s, designed to challenge the conformity and shallow consumerism of post-World War II America, were not more successful. Yet, the utopian experiments of both the 1960s and Jacksonian period share a rather traditional American belief dating back to the Puritan concept of the "city upon a hill" that the world may be reformed through example.

Origins of abolitionism

The most notable and noble reform effort of the antebellum period was the struggle to abolish slavery. Abolitionism was a diverse movement that often led antislavery advocates into extreme danger. The first abolitionists in America were the Quakers whose belief that all people carried within them God's inner light encouraged them to oppose slavery. The Quakers eventually lost control of the Pennsylvania colony, and the Society of Friends became less influential within American religious life. Methodism was popular among many less affluent Southern farmers and expressed opposition to slaveholding, but eventually leaders of the church abandoned their denunciation of slavery, removing a source of class conflict in the back country of the American South.

In the early nineteenth century, antislavery sentiments often focused upon the American Colonization Society which proposed to end slavery by compensating slave owners for their property and returning the freed blacks to their African homeland. While opposed to slavery, supporters of the Colonization Society did not believe that whites and blacks could exist upon an equal footing in the United States, and colonization would solve the problem of what to do with the emancipated slaves. The Colonization Society succeeded in returning thousands of slaves to Africa, helping to establish the nation of Liberia with its capital of Monrovia, where the descendants of American slaves continue to play a significant role. Influential Americans such as Henry Clay and a young Abraham Lincoln supported the Colonization Society, but there were many problems with this approach to ending slavery. Arranging compensation to slave owners and providing transportation to Africa were expensive undertakings, and the Colonization Society was constantly short of funds and concentrated much of its time and energy on fund raising. It never occurred to the Colonization Society that it was perhaps the enslaved people and not slave owners who deserved compensation, as contemporary concerns with reparations for slavery suggest. In addition, not all emancipated slaves were eager to be relocated to Africa. By the 1830s, many slave families had lived in the United States for generations and their ties to their home continent primarily were perpetuated through African American culture rather than direct experience. The desire for many enslaved people was to be freed and take their place as equal citizens of America as constituted in Jefferson's Declaration. Although the Constitution called for the end of slave importation from Africa in 1808, the expansion of cotton culture led to an increase of the slave population, and colonization was neither a practical nor a moral alternative.

Colonization was, nevertheless, popular with many Southern adherents to the antislavery movement. James G. Birney was a Southern slaveholder from Kentucky who freed his slaves and became a supporter of the Colonization Society. As his opposition to slavery intensified, Birney's life in the South was increasingly uncomfortable, and, like many Southern abolitionists, he moved to the North, where he became increasingly involved in abolitionist politics. In 1844, Birney was the Presidential candidate of the Liberty Party opposed to slave expansion. Cassius Marcellus Clay, after whom heavyweight boxing champion Mohammad Ali was originally named, was another Kentucky abolitionist—a state with a relatively small enslaved population. Unlike Birney, Clay decided to remain in the South, and after freeing the slaves that he inherited from his father, Clay took up the cause of abolition. Clay's politics antagonized many of his associates who made several attempts upon his life.

The diversity of abolitionism

Many in the North, however, grew impatient with the gradual emancipation advocated by Southern abolitionists and the Colonization Society. Radicals such as William Lloyd Garrison, who published the antislavery paper *The Liberator* in Boston, called for the immediate emancipation of all slaves. For Garrison, slavery was a moral issue, and one did not compromise or equivocate with evil. He denounced the Constitution for recognizing slavery and publicly destroyed a copy of the document. His radicalism provoked fears, among some Massachusetts mill operators and workers, that the agitation over slavery might disrupt the supply of cotton to the mills and threaten jobs. A lynch mob assailed Garrison, and he was nearly lynched from a lamp post in Boston. But such actions failed to silence Garrison, who founded the American Anti-Slavery Society and championed other reforms, including temperance, world peace, and women's rights.

Many female reformers such as Lucy Stone and Lucretia Mott embraced both the cause of antislavery and women's rights. Among the women who recognized the connection between the conditions of slaves and women of all races denied their natural rights was Angelina Grimké. Angelina and her sister Sarah were the daughters of a prominent South Carolina slaveholding family. The Grimké sisters eventually moved to the North, converted to Quakerism, and joined the abolitionist movement. In 1836, the articulate Angelina braved a mob in Philadelphia to address an antislavery meeting. She made the case for connecting the struggles of the enslaved and women's rights, calling for Americans to embrace the promise of natural rights contained in Jefferson's Declaration. An anti-abolitionist mob was unable to intimidate Angelina, but her voice was eventually silenced as her husband, the prominent abolitionist minister Theodore Weld, was uncomfortable with his wife assuming such a public role. Women such as Stanton and Anthony were also disappointed following the Civil War when male abolitionists urged them not to endanger the prospects for black suffrage by also insisting that women be awarded the vote. The women reformers were admonished to remember that this was the "Negro's hour."

With the emergence of the Second Great Awakening, religion continued to play a major role in the abolition movement, although Christianity was also employed in the South to defend the institution of slavery as ordained by the Bible. A belief in millennialism was connected to the antislavery cause as it would be necessary for the nation to purge itself of the sin of slavery in preparation for the return of Christ. Among the more important religious figures in the antislavery movement was evangelist Theodore Weld, whose book *Slavery As It Is* (1839), based upon slavery testimony gathered while he was visiting and ministering in the South, was one of the most influential antislavery tracts. Weld's work is credited with inspiring Harriet Beecher Stowe to write the novel *Uncle Tom's Cabin* (1852). The novel became a best-seller in the North, and some argue that the book played a pivotal role in causing the Civil War—although the story that Lincoln once greeted Stowe by stating that she was the lady who started this great war is likely apocryphal. Stowe's novel certainly denounced slavery, but it was overly sentimental and with its embrace of the redemptive power of love it was as concerned with saving the souls of white slave owners as it was in freeing enslaved blacks.

Abolitionism was not simply the crusade of moral whites to free the slaves, for black abolitionists played a significant role in the movement. Perhaps the most influential of the black abolitionists was Frederick Douglass, who was born into slavery. Raised in the border state of Maryland, Douglass—which he employed to replace his slave name of Bailey—was taught to read and write by one of his white mistresses in violation of Southern law forbidding the education of slaves. His education did not prevent Douglass from being relegated to field labor, but he was able to use his skills to forge a pass and purchase a railroad ticket from Baltimore to free soil in the North. Douglass employed his freedom to forge a career in the antislavery movement, proving to be a gifted orator and writer whose mere presence challenged assumptions of racial inferiority. His notoriety raised concerns that he could become a target for slave catchers, so Douglass was dispatched to England on a fund-raising mission while his friends arranged for the purchase of his freedom. Douglass returned to the United States and continued to support abolition in his antislavery newspaper *The North Star* and influential autobiography. He also became a good friend of Abraham Lincoln and is credited with broadening the President's views on racial equality. A strong advocate for women's rights, as well as racial equality, Douglass was a fixture in Republican politics following the Civil War.

Abolitionism was a diverse movement that challenged the racial assumptions of many white Americans and endangered the powerful Southern institution of slavery. While Southern states passed legislation to ban abolitionist publications and imprisoned antislavery agitators, abolitionists were hardly safe in the North. Anti-abolitionist mobs attacked antislavery advocates in both the North and South. One of the most notorious incidents of violence against abolitionists was the 1837 murder of antislavery newspaper editor Elijah Lovejoy in Alton, Illinois. In addition to racial prejudice, many in the North feared that abolitionist agitation might threaten the economy and textile industry. Mill operators and workers believed that Southern cotton producers might abandon their Northern markets and ship their cotton to English textile mills. However, as cotton culture and slavery threatened to expand into the western territories that were supposedly reserved for white social mobility, many workers in the North began to alter their opinions on abolitionism, perceiving slavery as a threat to free labor.

The cotton gin and expansion of slavery

While slavery was important to the cultivation of tobacco and rice in colonial America and the early republic, cotton remained a relatively minor product due to the time and labor required to separate the fiber from the seeds and husks. Slaves could pick cotton from the plants rather quickly, but the separation of the fiber was a laborious and expensive process when undertaken by hand. With these limitations on cotton production in the South, some apologists for slavery asserted that the institution would eventually die out of its own accord, and there was little need for abolitionist agitation. Everything changed, however, when the Northern inventor Eli Whitney was working as a tutor on a Southern plantation and produced a prototype for what would become the cotton gin—a large machine with metal blades that could separate the cotton. This invention changed the game as the cotton gin could process the valuable fibers as quickly as they could be picked in the fields. The cotton gin required an increased number of field hands, and Southern planters sought to meet this demand by increasing their dependence upon slave labor. However, there was a problem as the Constitution prohibited slave importation after 1808 in the hopes that the institution might eventually die out. While there was smuggling of slaves into the country, there were no restrictions on the internal slave trade. Therefore, many enslaved people were sold from the upper South to the cotton culture of the lower South in states such as Alabama, Mississippi, and Louisiana—where the working conditions and climate were more difficult for slave labor. The selling of slaves became a lucrative business with some plantations serving as crude breeding grounds to guarantee a steady supply of slave labor. Slave women with broad hips who could provide many children were stripped and sold for top dollar on the auction block. Thus, the slave population was increasing. With a market for cotton in the textile mills of the North as well as England and Europe, cotton cultivation and slavery expanded westward. The Southern economy was increasingly concentrated upon cotton and dependent upon slave labor.

Positive defense of slavery and class structure of the South

Before the cotton boom, many whites in the South had apologized for slavery and defended the institution as an economic measure that would eventually die out. The geographical expansion of king cotton convinced many white Southerners to abandon such assumptions and instead embrace slavery as an institution that demonstrated the highest qualities of Southern civilization. The positive defense of slavery is perhaps best demonstrated in the book *Cannibals All!* (1857) by Southern planter George Fitzhugh. According to Fitzhugh, slavery demonstrated the civilizing mission of planters who saved Africans, at least those fortunate enough to be enslaved, from the barbarism of life in Africa. As far as Fitzhugh was concerned, there was no civilized life for Africans as he dismissed the cultural contributions of the continent and its people. Rescued from barbarism, enslaved Africans were provided with decent clothing instead of decadent nakedness and taught how to cultivate the earth rather than roam as nomads. But the greatest gift bestowed upon the enslaved was an introduction to Christianity which offered the promise of everlasting life for believers. Africans who were not captured and brought to America, and converted to Christianity, were destined to live their lives in ignorance and would burn in hell for eternity as they never enjoyed the opportunity to accept Jesus Christ as their personal savior.

Fitzhugh also proclaimed the superiority of Southern slavery over Northern factory work in which poor Irish families labored and lived in squalor. Slaves, on the other hand, were taken care of and provided for from the cradle to the grave in one of the greatest systems ever designed by God. Newborns were provided with shelter, food, and clothing in slave quarters, and child care was provided by older slaves who could no longer labor in the fields. After childhood, slaves were provided with jobs in the fields or as domestics. In contrast to the Irish in the North who had to stress about securing a job—slavery provided for full employment. And when one could no longer work in the fields, a sense of purpose was still available in caring for the children and helping in the preparation of meals. When death came, one was buried in the slave quarters, secure of ever-lasting life in the hands of a Christian God. Of course, the reality of slave labor was hardly the ideal experience described by Fitzhugh, who ignored the separation of families and other coercive aspects of slavery. While Irish workers and families lived in terrible conditions among the factories and tenements of Jacksonian society in the North, they would not exchange places with the enslaved of the South. Slavery was a closed system that offered no opportunity for advancement no matter how hard one labored, and while mobility was limited in the North, it was at least possible for the children of factory workers to improve their lot in life. While *Cannibals All!* was a work of propaganda, one may concede that Fitzhugh did have a point that the North often failed to acknowledge its role in the international slave trade that enriched merchant families on the eastern seaboard during the colonial era.

There is often considerable misunderstanding regarding the class structure of the slave South touted by Fitzhugh. Although the slave population of the region grew considerably following implementation of the cotton gin, enslaved people did not constitute a majority of the Southern population—with the exception of South Carolina where the Civil War would begin in 1861. Although slavery and cotton production dominated the Southern economy, most Southern whites did not own slaves. The poor Southern whites simply could not afford them. Of the white population who did own slaves, most had fewer than ten slaves who labored on the small farms of the region. In 1850, there were about 1,700 families that possessed more than 100 slaves each, and this group of planters dominated the Southern economy and politics. Since Bacon's Rebellion in 1676, the planter class employed race to divide poor white and black workers and families who constituted a majority of the Southern population. Even with the achievements of the Civil Rights Movement, this manipulation of race continues to plague political life in the American South.

The planter class also created a mythology of slavery that persists today, in which grateful and happy slaves worked for benevolent owners who provided and cared for those placed under their supervision. It was an idealistic way of life in which different races and classes lived together in a hierarchal harmony reflected by relationships that were more important than the crass commerce of the marketplace. The agrarian lifestyle of the antebellum South moved slowly and in harmony with nature—unlike the hustle and bustle of urban life in the North where human needs and desires were subordinated to the pursuit of money. However, this ideal way of life described by George Fitzhugh in *Cannibals All!* and romanticized by Margaret Mitchell in *Gone With the Wind* (1939) was destroyed by the Civil War, and Confederate statues were erected to commemorate the Lost Cause and war fought to preserve this ideal and lost world.

Exploitation of slave labor

Of course, nothing could be further from the truth. The Southern way of life extolled by romantics and slave apologists was based upon a brutal class, racial, and sexual exploitation and oppression that fueled the Southern and American economy during the Jacksonian era. The goal of Southern racial slavery was to produce a subservient labor supply for the white masters. However, this dream of creating a sambo population grateful for the work, food, shelter, and clothing with which they were provided by the paternalistic white masters was never achieved, as the enslaved resisted their masters and struggled to develop and maintain their own African American culture.

Most slaves in the South were employed as field hands in the cultivation of the lucrative and ever-expanding westward cotton fields. Labor in the cotton fields was brutal as this author can testify from experience picking and chopping cotton during my youth in rural West Texas of the 1950s and early 1960s. In the slave South women and men worked in the fields from dawn until sunset six days a week. In the spring, seeds were planted by hand, and during the late spring and early summer, slaves labored in the hot sun chopping cotton, employing a hoe to chop down the weeds and grass that competed with cotton for nutrients and moisture in the soil. In the late summertime and early fall, slaves endured the back-breaking work of picking the cotton. Slaves, including children, moved down the long rows of cotton, bent over at the waist, snapping off the sharp cotton husks and placing them in bags, often weighing 50 to a 100 pounds when filled with cotton and rubbing sores on their shoulders as they dragged their burdens down the long rows of cotton—all this labor during temperatures exceeding 100 degrees in the humid South. This work, conducted under the supervision of overseers who would not spare the lash, was oppressive, and the life expectancy of field hands was short. Nor did the winter season bring great relief to the laborers. While some were busy making repairs for the next cotton season, other slaves were loaned out to work in the cities and factories of the South. There were strict contracts negotiated for the slaves loaned out to the cities and factories. Owners would be compensated for the labor of their slaves, and while the enslaved were not paid, they were to be fed and sheltered. The contracts also called for the slave workers to be returned in good condition, ready to again commence their work in the cotton fields.

On the plantations, there was a division of labor between field hands and domestics, whose legacy to the African-American community was addressed by Malcolm X. Domestic slaves were selected to do chores for the masters such as caring for and nursing children, driving coaches, preparing meals, and serving as butlers and maids. In fact, one of the ironies regarding slavery is that so many masters entrusted the wet nursing and care of their infants to black women considered as inferiors by the ideology of racial slavery. Domestic positions were usually considered preferable to working in the fields but being in proximity to the changing moods of the masters was not always a pleasant task. Since the domestics tended to spend more time around the whites, they were usually handed somewhat better clothing, and skin tone seemed to play a significant role in their selection. The white masters preferred that the slaves around whom they would spend more time be pleasing in their appearance—in other words, the domestic slaves were usually of lighter skin complexion, and many were likely the sons and daughters of masters who raped enslaved women. Some domestics tended to look down upon the darker field hands, and Malcolm X argued that this division persisted into the mid-twentieth century with efforts by some blacks to employ skin creams and conking—or hair straightening—to make their appearance more like white people. In the arena of American popular culture, blacks with lighter skins have often enjoyed wider public acceptance as models, actors, singers, and celebrities. Malcolm X and the Black Power Movement challenged this popular attitude and legacy of slavery by emphasizing that black is beautiful. Some slaves also attempted to curry favor with the masters by serving as overseers who aided in the supervision of other slaves. While it is certainly true that serving as an overseer may be perceived as betraying one's people, some slaves resorted to this collaboration in order to obtain some benefits from their masters such as protection for wives and children as sexual exploitation was a significant factor in American slavery.

Slave women were at the mercy of their male masters, and rape was a common occurrence. Although masters often encouraged slave marriages, this did not prevent the owners from insisting that married enslaved women be available for the sexual pleasure of the masters. And the plantations were full of mixed race children whose parentage was not usually acknowledged by the whites in public. Although the mistress of the plantation was often aware of this sexual exploitation, it was tolerated as this rape often protected white women from the lust and violence of their husbands. Also, there was a double standard in play, and sexual liaisons between enslaved men and a white mistress was intolerable and subject to harsh punishment. As far as the male masters were concerned, rape was simply the right to do with their property as they saw fit, and, of course, pregnancies simply increased the supply of valuable slave property. The degree to which interracial sexual activity was part and parcel of slavery is found in the crude Southern saying regarding white families, "There's a 'nigger' in the woodpile somewhere"—a recognition borne out by DNA testing proving the existence of slaves in the genealogy of prominent plantation families.

Coercive aspects of the slave system

This sexual exploitation and the control of black labor was enforced through a regime of violence and intimidation directed at the enslaved population. The most common type of punishment was a public lashing that also intimidated other slaves, and plantations contained prominent whipping posts—although these are often not featured on contemporary tours of Southern plantations. Lashings were painful, but they usually stopped short of permanent injuries. In addition, the scars from a lashing could serve as warning to other slaves. However, a slave whose back was too lined with the evidence of lashings could indicate a rebellious slave and thus reduce the potential value of the property. Better to sell the slave rather than continuously engage in the discipline of the lash. The value and labor of a slave usually prevented owners from punishments such as amputations or mutilations. But the branding of enslaved people was a rather common practice as the advertisements in Southern newspapers for runaway slaves well attest. So that these markings were apparent to casual white observers, who believed that all blacks looked similar, they were usually placed upon the hand, shoulder, neck, or face. Further proof that many owners viewed their slaves as chattel was the employment of slave collars in which the slaves were chained like dogs were often treated.

Perhaps even more horrendous was the breaking up of slave families. Masters encouraged the formation of slave marriages and families as this provided another means through which to control the enslaved who would be less inclined to run away if it meant deserting their families. In addition, slaves entrusted to run errands would return to the plantation to rejoin their families. Promises that slave owners made pledging that they would not destroy a family, however, were often broken, and, of course, there was no way to enforce such an agreement. And even if owners intended to honor a pledge about an enslaved family, debts and the death of an owner could lead to the breakup of a family as slavery was an arbitrary system. Thus, it was a common sight for infants and children to be torn away from weeping slave parents.

To control the movement of slaves within the Southern countryside, slave patrols were formed to monitor the roads and streams. Any black walking down a road and encountered by a slave patrol would have to produce a pass signed by the master or be subjected to immediate arrest. This monitoring also sometimes led to the seizure and enslavement of free blacks who lacked proper documentation. Concerned that slaves might forge a pass, most Southern states enacted laws that prohibited masters from educating their slaves. This legislation, however, was sometimes violated as owners found slaves that could read and write to be valuable for running errands or conducting some business. But the bottom line is that slavery was a brutal and cruel institution that was a closed system for enslaved people, offering no path out of bondage. While it was technically against the law to murder a slave, there was little legal protection for slaves as only white people had standing in court. Thus, if a master were to be held accountable for killing a slave, another white man would have to initiate a criminal proceeding. The best protection for an enslaved person was their value within the capitalist marketplace.

Slave resistance

Accordingly, it is not surprising that there was widespread resistance to the slave system. This resistance is often dismissed because there were not more widespread slave revolts. A revolt, however, required coordination and organization that was considerably difficult with the isolated nature of slaves living in the Southern countryside of scattered plantations and small farms. But resistance was frequent as Southern slave owners complained daily in their journals and diaries about the incompetence of their slaves which may be read as acts of sabotage. For example, their racism led many masters to expect little of their slaves; therefore, enslaved people took advantage of these low expectations by "puttin' on ole massa." In other words, play upon racist assumption by acting stupid. Masters, exasperated by the incompetence and stupidity of their slaves, were often shocked after emancipation to observe the skills and abilities of the slaves they once deemed to be incapable of completing simple tasks. Enslaved people undermined the slave regime on a daily basis by manipulating racist assumption, but some acts of sabotage took on a more deadly and dangerous tone. For example, some slave cooks poisoned their masters, but there was often swift retribution by the ruling class as slaves preparing food were often suspected in the sudden death of their owners. Also, many "accidents" on the plantations were questionable, with stock suddenly dying and farm buildings burned down by overturned lamps. The extreme measures to which slavery drove some of the enslaved are incidents of infanticide in which slave mothers killed their babies to save their children the degradation of slavery and deprive the masters— who sometimes fathered the children—of a valuable property. Infanticide which usually involved the smothering of babies was also difficult for suspicious owners to prove.

A more common act of disobedience for slaves was to run away and attempt to reach the North—although fugitive slaves were pursued into the North by slave catchers, and the safest destination was Canada which opposed the return of fugitive slaves. It is difficult to determine the number of slaves who attempted to escape and perished while seeking freedom, but scholars estimate that approximately 100,000 escaped slaves reached Northern free soil. Fugitive slaves were often aided along their way by conductors on the underground railroad. Courageous free blacks and sympathetic whites, often Quakers or Methodists working from a religious motivation, provided safe havens or shelter for runaway slaves making their way north. Usually traveling at night, conductors along the allegorical railroad moved the runaways from one safe destination to the next—sometimes designated by quilt patterns not understood by the general population. One of the best known of these conductors was Harriet Tubman; a woman who escaped from slavery and then returned to the South to help other runaways flee the slave system.

Fugitive slaves were certainly more common than revolts, but Southern whites were terrified of slave rebellions, fearing that they might suffer the violent fate of slave owners in Santo Domingo or Haiti, where a slave population gained its freedom in bloody revolt. The most violent Southern slave rebellion occurred in 1831 among the small tobacco farms of Southampton County, Virginia. The revolt was led by slave preacher Nat Turner, whose preaching activity was originally supported by the slave owners in the region. Other slave revolts such as those led by Gabriel Prosser in Virginia and Denmark Vesey in Charleston, South Carolina were discovered in advance and violently crushed by the Southern authorities, but Turner's revolt reached fruition. Turner and his followers killed approximately sixty whites before being subdued by the local militia. In retaliation, white vigilantes executed hundreds of slaves, most of whom had nothing to do with the revolt, and severed heads were placed on fenceposts as warnings to other blacks, both free and slave, in the region. After hiding in a cave for several weeks, Turner was captured and placed on trial for murder—Virginia had turned to a judicial process after some slave owners initiated legal action to receive compensation for valuable slaves arbitrarily killed by white mobs. Before his execution, Turner provided a confession to his white attorney Thomas Gray that was reprinted in many Southern newspapers. The confession seemed to place the blame for the revolt upon Nat's religious fanaticism rather than the institution of slavery, but the numerous laws passed after the revolt to suppress abolitionist activity and exercise tighter control over the movement of both free and enslaved backs provide ample evidence that white Southerners did not rest easy after Turner's revolt and feared the fire next time.

While it would take the violence of the Civil War to finally end slavery, to survive the daily degradation of the institution, enslaved people developed and nourished an African-American culture focused upon the family that passed down a rich tradition of music, folktales, language, food, religion, and love. When presented with Christian religion, the enslaved seized upon the story of Moses and the Israelites which they related to the struggle for freedom which permeated African American culture, and the black church would become a focal point for the Civil Rights Movement. Meanwhile, whites in the South increasingly focused upon defending slavery. While the plantation class was becoming enriched through the spread of cotton cultivation, poorer whites were encouraged to support slavery as a system of racial control. Emancipation would be a threat to their social status or what we might today term white privilege. Thus, the region rallied around the institution of slavery, and the South became a closed society opposed to debate upon issues such as slavery. On the national stage, the Missouri Compromise had supposedly ended within the halls of Congress discussion of slave expansion. However, the ideology of manifest destiny, westward expansion, and the Mexican War which added potential new slave territory to the nation reopened the slave debate and pushed the country on the road to a civil war that the reformers of the Jacksonian era were unable to avoid.

Further Reading:

Cochran, Thomas C. *Frontiers of Change: Early Industrialism in America*. New York: Oxford University Press, 1981.

Dublin, Thomas. *Women at Work: The Transformation of Work and Community in Lowell, Massachusetts, 1826–1860*. New York: Columbia University Press, 1979.

Foner, Eric. *Free Soil, Free Labor, Free Men: The Ideology of the Republican Party Before the Civil War*. New York: Oxford University Press, 1970.

Fredrickson, George. *The Black Image in the White Mind: The Debate on Afro-American Character and Destiny, 1817–1914*. New York: Harper & Row, 1971.

Genovese, Eugene. *Roll, Jordan, Roll: The World the Slaves Made*. New York: Random House, 1974.

Gutman, Herbert. *The Black Family in Slavery and Freedom, 1750–1925*. New York: Pantheon Books, 1976.

Levine, Lawrence. *Black Culture and Black Consciousness: Afro-American Folk Thought from Slavery to Freedom*. New York: Oxford University Press, 1977.

McMillen, Sally Gregory. *Seneca Falls and the Origins of the Women's Rights Movement*. New York: Oxford University Press, 2008.

Miller, Kerby A. *Emigrants and Exiles: Ireland and the Irish Exodus to North America*. New York: Oxford University Press, 1985.

Nye, Russel B. *Society and Culture in America, 1830–1860*. New York: HarperCollins, 1974.

11

Manifest Destiny and the Mexican War

PLUCKED:

THE MEXICAN EAGLE BEFORE THE WAR!   THE MEXICAN EAGLE AFTER THE WAR!

"Plucked or, the Mexican eagle before the war! The Mexican eagle after the war!" Library of Congress. Manifest Destiny justified a war of aggression against Mexico that garnered the Southwest for the United States. However, the war fostered distrust of the United States in Latin America and reopened the issue of slavery expansion, culminating in the Civil War.

The United States of America was established upon a foundation of territorial expansion at the expense of Native people who were denied the natural rights proclaimed in the nation's founding documents. In the 1840s, this westward expansion was captured in the phrase manifest destiny, supposedly coined by journalist John O'Sullivan, editor of the *Democratic Review*. In a rather jingoistic fashion, manifest destiny rhetoric extolled the territorial expansion of the United States as a civilizing mission ordained by God. In other words, the United States was chosen by God to spread the benefits of its superior democratic ideas and economic system into the West which was left undeveloped during its occupation by Native people and the Mexican government. The United States, thus, had an obligation to bring the benefits of its superior civilization to the West and make the region bloom. The irony that the expansion of democracy included spreading the ideology of slavery and justified the seizure of Native lands and the destruction of their culture was lost upon many Americans who embraced the racism of manifest destiny without raising questions. In many ways, manifest destiny was similar to the "white man's burden" later proclaimed by British writer Rudyard Kipling to support British imperialism in India and Africa. Expansion was perceived as a civilizing mission that might entail short-term conflict and sacrifice but assure long-range progress for all people brought within the orbit of the American nation.

In the 1840s, manifest destiny justified a war of aggression against Mexico that concluded with the acquisition of Texas, California, and the American Southwest. This territorial aggrandizement, however, reopened the slavery issue in American politics, and the politicians were unable to put this genie back in the bottle. Territorial expansion with slavery at its core fostered a civil conflict that almost destroyed the American nation, and manifest destiny was a phrase that fell out of common usage. Nevertheless, the expansionist ideology upon which the nation was founded continued to be at the forefront of American politics, contradicting the principles of Jefferson's Declaration. Following the Civil War, the Indian Wars in the West crushed Native resistance to the taking of their lands. American leaders also encouraged business investments in Latin America and Asia, seeking cheap labor and markets for American goods. In 1898, America officially became an imperial power with the acquisition of Guam, Puerto Rico, and the Philippines from Spain, while establishing a virtual protectorate over Cuba. Today, the economic and political hegemony of the United States extends over the globe with nearly 800 military bases in more than 70 countries and territories abroad. The contradictions between this military presence and democratic principles is usually defended by appealing to national security and the concept of American exceptionalism. Accordingly, when America becomes involved in the affairs of other nations and governments, it is not imperialism because the United States is different as a unique nation consecrated by God to spread its democratic and civilizing mission to the less fortunate people of the world. The manifest destiny of the 1840s justified territorial expansion that would take the United States from the Atlantic to the Pacific Oceans, while contemporary American exceptionalism excuses a global domination that contradicts the nation's adherence to democratic principles. The failure of many Americans to recognize how this history of expansionism is negatively perceived by people around the globe is a tragedy of American history.

John Tyler and the annexation of Texas

The crisis of expansionism and manifest destiny during the 1840s focused upon Texas which existed as an independent republic following the defeat of Mexico at the Battle of San Jacinto. There was sentiment in both Texas and the United States for the annexation of the republic following its declared independence from Mexico. However, there were significant political and diplomatic obstacles to annexing Texas. When the Mexican leader Santa Anna returned to Mexico following his defeat at San Jacinto, he reneged upon his promise to recognize the independence of Texas. With Mexico still claiming that Texas was part of its territory, the annexation of the republic might provoke war between the United States and Mexico. In addition, Texas was a slave territory, and its absorption into the nation would reignite the slavery debate in Congress that was stilled by the Missouri Compromise in 1820. Despite these obstacles, American President John Tyler decided to pursue annexation.

Tyler's Presidency was a troubled one. In 1840, Tyler, a former Virginia Democrat, agreed to run for Vice President alongside the Whig Presidential candidate, William Henry Harrison; the hero of the Tippecanoe battle against Tecumseh and, thus, the political slogan of "Tippecanoe and Tyler too." Although coming from an aristocratic Virginia family, Harrison campaigned as a commoner while extolling images of "hard cider and a log cabin," defeating the unpopular Martin Van Buren who was saddled with blame for the Panic of 1837. The Harrison Presidency, however, proved to be short-lived. Following the delivery of his inaugural address during a Washington blizzard, Harrison died after only a month in office. Referred to as "his accidency" by his political opponents, Tyler became the first Vice President to assume the office of the Presidency following the death of his successor. The former Democrat almost immediately began to quarrel with Whig leaders in Congress. An advocate for state rights, Tyler vetoed bills increasing the power of the federal government that were sponsored by Henry Clay, the Congressional leader of the Whigs. This conflict led to Clay, rather than Tyler, being selected as the Whig Party's Presidential candidate in 1844.

Tyler, accordingly, had little to show for his Presidency, but he hoped to achieve a lasting legacy for his administration by securing the annexation of Texas through a joint resolution of Congress. Fearing that Texas might decide to join either the British or French empires then flirting with the republic, Tyler offered provisions that would make Texas a rather unique state. Texas would retain control of all its public lands, and it reserved the right to divide into five states if it should desire. This would seemingly provide Texas with incredible potential political power in an institution such as the Senate, but such a scenario assumes a degree of unity not always found within the geographically diverse state of Texas. Tyler succeeded in getting his resolution through in the final days of his administration, but it would be up to the next President to implement the legislation.

Election of 1844 and the Oregon question

The annexation of Texas and the spread of slave territory became a major issue in the 1844 Presidential election. Van Buren hoped to once again be selected by the Democrats; however, the party nominated instead the first so-called "dark horse" candidate, James K. Polk of Tennessee who had served in the House of Representatives and as Governor of the state. Polk enthusiastically endorsed a platform of manifest destiny, expressing his support for annexing Texas with its border along the Rio Grande River as opposed to the more northern boundary of the Nueces River claimed by Mexico. In addition, Polk expressed his interest in obtaining California from Mexico, and the Democratic nominee insisted that he would fight for the most northern boundary of the Oregon territory in negotiations with the British. The Whig Party selected Henry Clay as their candidate, and he proceeded to waffle on the Texas issue, concerned about antagonizing the antislavery wing of his party. A clear alternative on the Texas issue was offered by the Liberty Party and its Presidential candidate James G. Birney who opposed the annexation of Texas and slavery expansion. The election was extremely close and came down to the state of New York, where the Liberty Party appeared to take votes from Clay and provide the Democrats with a narrow margin for Polk.

As President, Polk intended to deliver on his campaign promises, but he disappointed some of his followers by compromising on the Oregon question. The Oregon territory was claimed at various times by Great Britain, Spain, and Russia, with the United States making its case following the Lewis and Clark expedition that paved the way for white farm settlement in the Northwest. By the mid-1840s, the two primary powers in the region were the United States and Britain, whose claims were bolstered by the activities of the Hudson Bay Company trading and trapping in the region. Of course, these conflicting claims and discussions between the British and Americans tended to ignore the Native presence and rights in the region. Strong advocates of manifest destiny, cognizant of growing American settlement in Oregon, proclaimed "54-40 or fight," vowing war if the United States was not awarded what is today British Columbia in Canada. Polk, however, disappointed these extreme nationalists by abandoning the "54-40" position and compromising by essentially extending the 49th parallel dividing Canada and the United States, as confirmed in the 1842 Webster-Ashburton Treaty, into the Pacific Northwest. The Polk administration made this deal with the British as the President feared a war with the powerful British Empire at the time he was contemplating a military conflict with Mexico over Texas and California.

Polk prepares for war with Mexico

In terms of California, Polk, in this period before the gold rush, was primarily interested in San Francisco, which offered a deep-water port to pursue Asian markets in China and Japan. Thus, Polk approached the Mexican government about purchasing California. The Mexicans, however, rebuffed the mission of American diplomat John Slidell who was authorized to offer $25 million for California. The Mexicans were not disposed to deal with the Americans whom they perceived as exhibiting attitudes of racial superiority in negotiations dealing with the financial claims of American citizens against the Mexican government for failing to protect their property and investments. Also, the Mexicans were not in a mood to negotiate as the United States maneuvered to annex Texas which the Mexican government claimed as its territory. Since he was unable to gain California through diplomatic means, Polk moved toward instigating a war with Mexico that would allow the President to realize his manifest destiny ambitions for California and the Southwest.

Having secured his northern flank by reaching a settlement with the British over the Oregon territory, Polk attempted to provoke the Mexicans by ordering American troops under the command of General Zachary Taylor to take up a position along the disputed Rio Grande boundary, for Mexico claimed the Nueces River, approximately 150 miles to the north, as the proper border between Mexico and Texas. Polk intentionally placed American troops in territory claimed by Mexico, hoping to provoke an attack. Polk's strategy worked as in April 1846, Taylor's command came under attack from Mexican forces. Taylor was able to repulse the Mexican assault, but more important to Polk is that he now had grounds to approach Congress for a declaration of war against Mexico. Not bothering to explain that American forces were occupying territory claimed by the Mexicans, Polk proclaimed that "American blood was shed upon American soil." Polk got his declaration of war, but many in Congress, including a young Whig Congressman from Illinois named Abraham Lincoln, eventually came to believe that the President duped Congress in order to get his war and expand the American slave territory. Polk's misleading case for war against Mexico may be compared to the American invasion of Iraq in 2003. There is considerable evidence that the Bush administration manipulated intelligence reports to bolster claims that the invasion was necessary because the Iraqi dictator Saddam Hussein possessed weapons of mass destruction. After the U. S. military occupation of Iraq, these reports were proven false, but by that time it was difficult to politically or militarily disengage American troops. The same was true for the Mexican War as Polk moved aggressively against Mexico before opposition to the conflict could crystallize.

Mexican War

Taking advantage of advanced planning for the anticipated conflict, the Polk administration quickly seized New Mexico and California. Although sparsely populated, New Mexico contained the valuable Santa Fe Trail trade route, and an American army under the command of Stephen Watts Kearny was dispatched to occupy the region. Hoping to dispel resistance by a predominantly Hispanic population to an Anglo invasion, Kearney issued a proclamation declaring that the property rights and land grants of the original Hispanic settlers would be respected. While there was some resistance, the occupation of New Mexico was largely peaceful, but the history of the territory and state bears witness to a steady deterioration of Hispanic land grants being replaced by Anglo business interests, negating the promises made by Kearney and later affirmed in the Treaty of Guadalupe Hidalgo. After establishing a temporary civil government in New Mexico under American control, Kearney moved his forces toward California, where American agents had already maneuvered to foster a revolt against Mexican authorities. In preparation for war and an opportunity to seize California which Mexico had refused to sell, the Polk administration entrusted agents such as naval officer Robert Stockton and military commander John C. Frémont to foment a revolt which overthrew the Mexican authorities and established the Bear Flag Republic of California, which then appealed to the United States for annexation. Rather than a rebellion by the people of California against Mexican control, the revolt in California was more like a military coup engineered by the United States.

After these initial moves to seize New Mexico and California, the Polk administration was prepared to make a peace agreement if Mexico would recognize American acquisition of the two territories. The proud Mexican government, whose confidence in its military proved to be misplaced, refused to acquiesce in the American occupation. Accordingly, Polk ordered General Taylor's army to invade Mexico and march upon Mexico City. Although the Mexicans put up a fierce resistance, Taylor's forces steadily advanced in a series of engagements such as the Battle of Buena Vista in which a numerically superior Mexican army was decimated by American artillery. Taylor's advance through Mexico was marked by numerous atrocities committed against the Mexican people, including the execution of priests and the rape of nuns. These atrocities were especially offensive to American soldiers of Irish descent who resented the treatment of their fellow Catholics. This led some of these Irish solders to desert and join the Mexican forces, forming the San Patricio (St. Patrick) Battalion that fought the American toops. The record of the regular American army was generally good in Mexico, and many of the atrocities were carried out by Texas volunteers. Eventually, Taylor, unable to control the racism of the volunteers who claimed they were seeking revenge for the Alamo, sent the Texas volunteers, including the heralded Texas Rangers, home. Taylor's victories on the road to Mexico City made the general a national hero, and Polk became concerned about the political ambitions of the military leader who was known to be a member of the Whig Party. Accordingly, Polk decided to halt Taylor's advance on Mexico City. Instead, the capture of the Mexican capital would be assigned to another force under the command of General Winfield Scott, who would attack the port city of Vera Cruz and then advance upon Mexico City.

Scott, who also proved to harbor political ambitions after the war, was able to capture the capital after fierce resistance exemplified by the defense of Chapultepec Castle by young Mexican cadets who wrapped themselves in the national flag and plunged to their death rather than entertain disgrace and capture by the American forces. As the capital fell, Santa Anna moved to make peace with the invaders. Anticipating this opportunity, the Polk administration had dispatched diplomatic representative Nicholas Trist to accompany Scott and negotiate an end to the war. While Trist and Scott often argued over lines of authority, Trist was able to conclude a deal which was eventually ratified as the Treaty of Guadalupe Hidalgo. Polk, however, was initially displeased with the negotiations in which Trist failed to push for the acquisition of Baja California. In fact, Trist was fired by Polk but refused to leave his post and completed the negotiations, returning to Washington with the Treaty of Guadalupe Hidalgo. Polk believed that Trist could have gained more territory for the United States, but faced with growing antislavery opposition to the war, the President decided that rather than continue talks with Mexico the prudent thing to do was submit Trist's treaty to the Senate for ratification.

Treaty of Guadalupe Hidalgo

The Treaty of Guadalupe Hidalgo brought an end to the Mexican War, and the Mexican government agreed to recognize Texas as part of the United States with the border along the Rio Grande, acknowledging the larger Texas desired by the United States. In addition, under the Mexican Cession the United States would pay Mexico approximately $15 million and settle the claims of American citizens against Mexico in exchange for ceding California and the New Mexico territory to the United States—an area of approximately 530,000 square miles that today encompasses the states of Arizona, New Mexico, Colorado, Nevada, Utah, and parts of Wyoming. The treaty also acknowledged that the largely Hispanic residents of the region would have little choice as to their incorporation into the United States. If they wanted to remain Mexican citizens, they would have to move out of the American Southwest. After one year, anyone residing in the Mexican Cession would be under the jurisdiction of the American government. Reflecting the fact that many Hispanics were residents of the Southwest for generations, approximately 90 percent stayed on their family lands. To induce the Mexican citizens to stay and become part of the United States, the Treaty of Guadalupe Hidalgo asserted that Spanish and Mexican land grants would be respected by the new American government. However, the course of Southwestern history has witnessed the steady accumulation of these original grants by Anglo business interests and Hispanics who sought to cooperate with the invaders. What happened in the Mexican War and treaty is that in a war of aggression, the United States acquired the Southwest, and the border crossed many families who were divided by political events over which they had little control. While some American politicians call for the construction of walls and strict regulation of the borders, many residents of the Southwest recognize the arbitrary nature of the border with Mexico and assert their right to freely move across the border which crossed over their families in 1848 through a war of territorial expansion and manifest destiny.

Despite the vast territorial gains of the Mexican War, some Senatorial critics of the Treaty of Guadalupe Hidalgo believed that the treaty did not acquire enough territory. Polk was disappointed that the negotiations did not include Baja California, while other opponents of the treaty believed that with an American army occupying Mexico City the United States should annex all of Mexico. In fact, some Southern slave owners perceived Mexico and Central America as logical targets for manifest destiny and the extension of cotton culture. A policy which some Southerners, such as William Walker, sought to implement with filibustering expeditions into Nicaragua and other Central American nations. It is ironic, however, that racist assumptions on the part of many Senators thwarted the goal of annexing greater Mexico. While advocates of manifest destiny coveted Mexican land, there was the problem of the Mexican people deemed as racially inferior due to the mixture of Spanish and Native blood lines. In addition to being racially inferior and, thus, unable to assimilate into American society, the Mexican people were also predominantly Catholic, which in the eyes of many Anglo Protestant Americans made them unfit for citizenship. Thus, racism and religious prejudice influenced many Senators to support the taking of Mexican land that was sparsely populated, while opposing the acquisition of territory with more Mexican inhabitants. Ironically, racial prejudice placed some check on the appetite of manifest destiny.

Legacy of manifest destiny and the Mexican War

While the legacy of the Mexican War and Treaty of Guadalupe Hidalgo continue to cast a troubling shadow on relations between the United States and Mexico, the immediate aftermath of the conflict exacerbated sectional tensions over slavery expansion and damaged relations between the Untied States and Latin America as the region increasingly perceived the colossus of the North as a threat. Opponents of the war and treaty maintained that the Polk administration manipulated the nation into a war of aggression against Mexico in order to expand the economic, territorial, and political influence of the slavocracy. Whig Senator Thomas Corwin of Ohio argued that the United Stats betrayed its principles in provoking war with Mexico as a pretense to stealing the land of another people and nation. Corwin also bemoaned that Mexico was invaded in order to extend the reach of American slavery, predicting that the legacy of the war with Mexico would be a sectional conflict in the United States between North and South. And Corwin was correct that slavery extension became a focal point of Congressional debate. Congressman David Wilmot of Pennsylvania introduced a proviso that would forbid the expansion of slavery into any territory gained in the Mexican War. The measure passed the House of Representatives but was not enacted in the Senate where the South exercised greater political power. Although the proviso did not become law, sectional debate over the slavery issue was joined, and during the 1850s the crisis over slavery intensified, culminating in war. The Mexican War played a significant role in placing the United States upon the road to civil war.

The implications of manifest destiny explicit in the Mexican War and Treaty of Guadalupe Hidalgo were apparent to the rest of the world, especially Latin America. The proclamation of the Monroe Doctrine in 1823 was initially greeted with enthusiasm by the independent nations of Latin America. The United States announced that it would oppose efforts by the European powers to impose further colonization in the Western Hemisphere. The Americans were perceived in Latin America as defending democracy and national self-determination. This perception, however, changed with the Mexican War. The United States had initiated a war with its Latin neighbor in order to seize its land, leading to the refrain, "poor little Mexico, so far from God and so near the United States." The Americans had seemingly told the Europeans to stay out so that the colossus of the north might expand and take advantage of its Latin American neighbors to the south. Southern filibusters and rhetoric about spreading slavery into Latin America also bolstered regional fears about the designs of the United States. Following the Mexican War, Latin American nations viewed the United States and Monroe Doctrine with suspicion—concerns that were certainly confirmed with American business, political, and military expansion into the region during the twentieth century.

The manifest destiny of the 1840s was celebrated as serving the nation's civilizing mission by wresting control of the Southwest and California from Mexico. And the idea that the United States was a special nation governed by God's destiny was evident in the fact that shortly after American acquisition gold was discovered in California, setting off a rush to settle and develop the state's resources. Yet, this expansion was at the expense of Natives and Hispanics whose lands were stolen, and culture endangered. Latin American nations also recognized the danger inherent in the ideology of manifest destiny and expansion as practiced by the United States—an awareness that would become more global in the twentieth century. In the short run, the manifest destiny pursued by the Polk administration provoked a war that led to the expansion of slave territory and reignited the debate over slavery—an issue that culminated in civil war and almost destroyed the nation.

Further Reading:

Brack, Gene M. *Mexico Views Manifest Destiny, 1821–1846.* Albuquerque, NM: University of New Mexico Press, 1976.

Dusinberre, William. *Slavemaster President: The Double Career of James K. Polk.* New York: Oxford University Press, 2003.

Horsman, Reginald. *Race and Manifest Destiny: The Origins of American Racial Anglo-Saxonism.* Cambridge, MA: Harvard University Press, 1981.

Johannsen, Robert W. *To the Halls of the Montezumas: The Mexican War in the American Imagination.* New York: Oxford University Press, 1985.

May, Robert E. *Manifest Destiny's Underworld: Filibustering in Antebellum America.* Chapel Hill, NC: University of North Carolina Press, 2002.

Merk, Frederick. *Manifest Destiny and Mission in American History.* New York: Knopf, 1963.

Pletcher, David M. *The Diplomacy of the Annexation of Texas, Oregon, and the Mexican War.* Columbia, MO: University of Missouri Press, 1973.

Schroeder, John H. *Mr. Polk's War: American Opposition and Dissent, 1846–1848.* Madison, WI: University of Wisconsin Press, 1973.

Weber, David. *The Mexican Frontier, 1821–1846: The American Southwest under Mexico.* Albuquerque, NM: University of New Mexico Press, 1982.

Winders, Richard Bruce. *Crisis in the Southwest: The United States, Mexico, and the Struggle over Texas.* Wilmington, DE: SR Books, 2002.

12

Political Breakdown
and the Road to Civil War

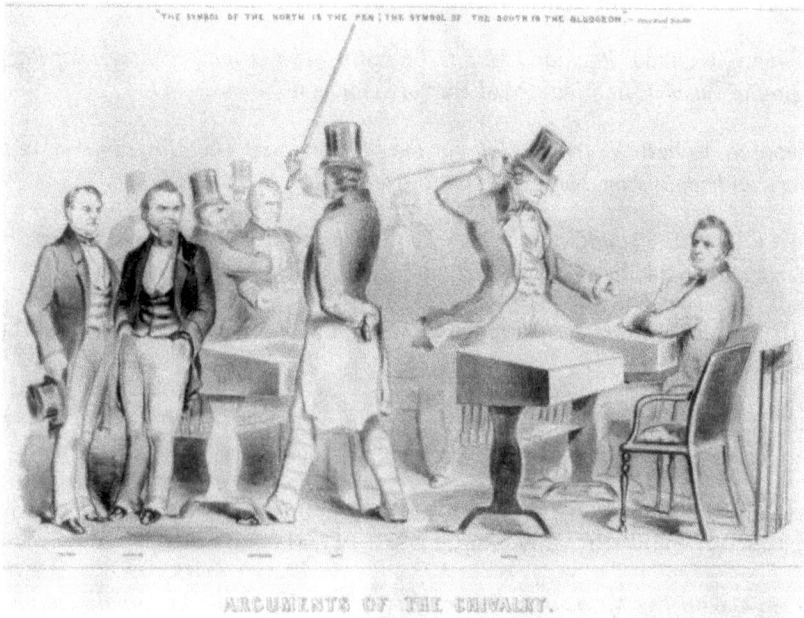

"Argument of the Chivalry." John Henry Bufford and Winslow Homer. Library of Congress Prints and Photographs Division. This print depicts the May 22, 1856 caning of Massachusetts Senator Charles Sumner by South Carolina Congressman Preston Brooks after Sumner delivered a speech blaming the Southern slaveocracy for "Bleeding Kansas." Sumner was seriously injured and was absent from the Senate for an extended amount of time, while Brooks was reelected and sent more canes from his constituents. The Sumner-Brooks affair offered further proof that it would be difficult to reach any type of compromise regarding the slave issue.

Many Americans continue to believe that the nation's Civil War was fought over states' rights or economic issues such as the tariff. However, the centrality of slavery as the explanation for the conflict is quite evident from the Southern state Ordinances of Succession in which the protection of slavery was the paramount concern. In addition, the questions regarding states' rights and economic development also focus upon the cotton culture and institution of slavery that the South sought to expand and defend. Thus, this narrative of the events leading to the Civil War will concentrate upon the issue of slavery, and the failure of the American political system to resolve this moral question which contradicted the founding principles of the nation and continues to cast a long shadow over American life.

James Polk, a slaveholder, delivered on his platform of manifest destiny, expanding the United States into California, Texas, Oregon, and the Southwest. In achieving these goals, Polk essentially worked himself to death, and suffering from dysentery, he died in 1849. Other politicians would have to deal with the issues of slave expansion exacerbated by Mr. Polk's war. Yet, the major political parties tried to ignore the moral issues raised by American slavery. In 1848, the Whig Party nominated General Zachary Taylor, who emerged from the Mexican War as a national hero. Although a slaveholder from Louisiana, Taylor in his campaign sought to avoid the controversial slave issue and focus upon his war record. The Democratic nominee for President was Senator Lewis Cass of Michigan who offered a solution to the slavery question that was seemingly based upon fundamental principles of American democracy. Cass proposed the doctrine of popular sovereignty in which the white male settlers of a territory would vote on whether slavery should be extended into the region. Needless to say, the enslaved would play no role in this decision, and popular sovereignty with its limited concept of majority rule paid no attention to the moral aspects of the slavery debate. Although Cass's idea gained some traction among American politicians and voters, Taylor's appeal as a war hero was a dominant factor in the election, and Taylor assumed the Presidency.

Compromise of 1850

Concerned about the divisive impact of slave expansion, Senators such as Henry Clay of Kentucky and Daniel Webster of Massachusetts sought some type of grand compromise upon the issue. Others, such as Senator John C. Calhoun of South Carolina were opposed to any type of political deal concerning slavery. For Calhoun, slavery was a positive institution as exemplified in the work of such slavery apologists as George Fitzhugh. Although ill and spitting up blood on the Senate floor, Calhoun adamantly asserted that the holding of slaves was a natural right protected by the Constitution, and the national government had no business interfering with how an individual dealt with private property such as slaves. President Taylor essentially sided with Calhoun and did not pursue compromise on the slavery issue. The political deadlock, however, was altered by the unexpected death of Taylor in 1850, and the elevation of the former New York Whig Congressman and Vice President Millard Fillmore to the Presidency. Some Southerners saw an abolitionist conspiracy in Taylor's sudden death and maintained that the President was poisoned. The Taylor family agreed to the exhuming of the body, and this myth was finally put to rest in the 1980s. It is more likely that Taylor died when he anchored himself under a shade tree on a muggy Washington summer day and consumed several pounds of cherries along with raw vegetables. Although Fillmore is trivialized for introducing the first bathtub in the White House—one in which William Howard Taft was ostensibly later stuck—he played a pivotal role in implementing the Compromise of 1850 and pushing the legislation through Congress along with Clay and Webster.

The major issues addressed in the Compromise of 1850 were the status of slavery in the territories gained from the Mexican War and Southern interest in a strict fugitive slave law. Due to the discovery of gold at Sutter's Mill, there was a sudden influx of population into the territory of California which rapidly qualified for statehood. While the colder temperatures of northern California were not conducive to cotton cultivation, the southern part of the state appeared to offer a climate in which cotton and its slave labor supply might thrive. After heated debate, California was added to the union as a free state. The less populated territories of Utah and New Mexico were possible sites for cotton cultivation, to which the legislation applied the principle of popular sovereignty, although neither territory in the final analysis adopted slavery. The Compromise of 1850 also attempted to address the claims of Texas upon parts of the New Mexico territory to the east of the Rio Grande River. This extended border would increase the size of slaveholding Texas, whose government had dispatched a military expedition to occupy the disputed area. Texas, however, was convinced to give up its claim in exchange for a $10 million payment from the federal government. In addition, antislavery advocates were appalled by the trading of slaves within the nation's capital, with auctions taking place on the steps of the Capitol Building. Many foreign visitors and diplomats were especially critical of this public display involving the buying and selling of human beings. As part of the compromise package, the slave trade in Washington DC was abolished, but enslaved people would continue to suffer the indignity of the auction block in the adjacent states of Maryland and Virginia. In exchange for these concessions, the South would receive a strict fugitive slave law. Although the Constitution called for the return of runaway slaves to their Southern owners, this provision was not always followed by the Northern states. Under the new legislation, Northern states were compelled to return fugitive slaves, and furthermore anyone aiding an escaped slave was subject to legal action. In the Compromise of 1850, the South seemed to be trading territory—although the addition of Texas as a slave state considerably expanded the reach of slavery—in exchange for a strict fugitive slave law. Many Southerners, however, criticized the North and antislavery politicians for bargaining in bad faith, as many Northern states enacted personal liberty laws that sought to prevent state officials from cooperating in the capture and return of escaped slaves. Many in the North resented slave hunters disrupting their communities by capturing blacks who, in many cases, had resided in the area for years. Also, the threat that whites who aided runaways could be incarcerated raised the ire of many Northern states. Rather than having slavery relegated to the South, the power of Southern slave owners now extended into Northern communities. Passage of the Fugitive Slave Law increased abolitionist sentiment in the North.

Presidency of Franklin Pierce and Ostend Manifesto

The Compromise of 1850 failed to solve the slave issue, and in some ways exacerbated sectional antagonism. Fillmore's support of the legislation made him suspect to many Southern Whigs, and the Presidential nomination of the party in 1852 was, instead, awarded to Winfield Scott, another general from the Mexican War whose military record was prioritized in the campaign. The Democrats emulated the Whigs and nominated Franklin Pierce who had served under Scott. Pierce, who represented New Hampshire in Congress, was in many ways an ideal candidate as he was a Northerner with Southern sympathies who perceived the abolitionist movement as a threat to national unity. After winning the Presidential campaign of 1852, the Pierce administration pursued a policy of slave expansion that alarmed many in the North and convinced them that the abolitionists were correct in their assessment that slave expansion was a threat to white social mobility and free labor in the territories.

In the Ostend Manifesto, diplomats representing the Pierce administration met with Spanish officials in Ostend, Belgium about possibly purchasing the Spanish colony of Cuba. The negotiations did not lead to American acquisition; however, the press learned about the talks and reported on the American interest in Cuba, setting off alarms among many in the Northern United States about the dangers of slave expansion into Latin America. While the slave labor in the sugar cane plantations of Cuba was not incorporated as an American territory, the Pierce administration was successful in advancing Southern and slave interests on other fronts. Seeking the best possible route for a proposed Southern transcontinental railroad, Pierce instructed Ambassador to Mexico William Gadsden to purchase 30,000 acres in what is today southwestern New Mexico and southern Arizona, including the city of Tucson. Wanting to avoid further conflict with the United States, Mexico agreed to the transaction for $30 million.

Kansas-Nebraska Act and Bleeding Kansas

The decision of the Pierce administration to support the Kansas-Nebraska Act provoked even greater concern about the possibilities of slave expansion. The legislation proposed to implement the policy of popular sovereignty to determine whether slavery was to be allowed in the Kansas and Nebraska territories, thus overturning the Missouri Compromise which outlawed the introduction of slavery into the region. Democratic Senator Stephen A. Douglas of Illinois agreed to introduce the controversial piece of legislation, erroneously believing that it would further his Presidential ambitions. Douglas anticipated that popular sovereignty would provide a compromise solution in which both sections could claim victory—Nebraska would reject slavery as the territory was simply too cold for cotton cultivation, while parts of Kansas could support cotton and its slave labor and, thus, the expansion of slavery into the state would be approved. What Douglas failed to recognize was the degree of alarm and distrust unleashed in the North by abandoning the Missouri Compromise and potentially expanding slavery into territory that had been preserved for free white labor. The support for abolitionists in the North increased as their warnings about a conspiracy to expand slave labor and threaten white social mobility nationally seemed to have merit. With the backing of President Pierce, the Kansas-Nebraska bill, nevertheless, narrowly passed through the Congress. The bill also led to the disintegration of the Whig Party and the establishment of a new political party. The Republican Party, formed by former Whigs, Free-Soilers, and antislavery advocates, quickly gained support in the North for its opposition to slave labor as a threat to free labor and economic modernization.

The Kansas-Nebraska legislation increased rather than reduced sectional animosity as popular sovereignty failed miserably in Kansas. Rather than a peaceful exercise at the ballot box, pro and anti-slavery forces quickly moved into Kansas and established armed camps, leading to violence and what became known as "Bleeding Kansas." Lawrence, where the University of Kansas is now located, was established by antislavery settlers from Massachusetts who hoped to make Kansas a free state. In 1856, the settlement was attacked by proslavery forces who ransacked the town and destroyed antislavery newspapers. The sacking of Lawrence set off a guerilla war in Kansas which lead to a second far bloodier assault on Lawrence led by Southern guerillas, including Frank and Jesse James, under the command of William Quantrill in 1863. The violence in Kansas convinced abolitionist John Brown to leave Massachusetts and come to the aid of antislavery settlers, including members of his own family, in Kansas. Brown, who fathered twenty children with two wives, was an abolitionist who believed that slavery was an affront to God and that it was the duty of Christians to oppose the evils of slavery. There could be no compromise with evil and the human suffering perpetuated by slavery, and Brown called for immediate action. After leaving his struggling woolen business in Massachusetts for Kansas following the first sacking of Lawrence, Brown and a group of followers, including several of his sons, conducted a raid upon a small slave settlement in Pottawatomie Creek, freeing the slaves and killing four male slave owners. Brown was involved in several other Kansas skirmishes and was wanted for murder. Seeking to avoid federal prosecution, Brown returned to Massachusetts, where he was greeted as a hero by many abolitionists. Henry David Thoreau lauded Brown for following the higher law of God and conscience extolled in the *Essay on Civil Disobedience*. Most white Southerners, however, simply viewed Brown as a murderer. These extreme positions on Brown certainly indicated that it would be difficult to find a peaceful resolution to the issue of slavery. The brutality and violence of slavery provoked a response in kind that would finally destroy slavery, and the nation had not heard the last of John Brown. As for Kansas, the proslavery Lecompton Constitution was eventually rejected, and Kansas entered the union as a free state.

Sumner-Brooks affair and Election of 1856

In reaction to the instability and chaos in Kansas, Massachusetts Republican Senator Charles Sumner gave a speech in the Senate entitled "The Crime Against Kansas," in which he blamed the violence upon the South. South Carolina Congressman Preston Brooks objected to Sumner's remarks, especially those critical of South Carolina Senator Pierce Butler who was related to Brooks. Seeking to defend regional and family honor, on May 22, 1856, Brooks approached Sumner while the Senator was seated at his desk in the Senate and proceeded to severely beat the Senator with his cane which was shattered in the savage assault. Sumner was seriously injured in the attack and was unable to resume his Senatorial career for nearly three years, but he would emerge as an important voice for racial equality following the Civil War. As for Brooks, he was arrested and fined for his action, serving no prison time. He refused to apologize for the assault, although he resigned and was overwhelmingly re-elected to Congress with the approval of his constituents, who also showered the Congressman with new canes to replace the one he had shattered over Sumner's head. This violence on the Senate floor and aftermath of approval was further evidence that it would be difficult to find a political solution to slavery and the sectional divide.

In the Presidential election of 1856, the Democrats denied Pierce a second term due to the controversy and unrest unleashed by the Kansas-Nebraska Act. Instead, they nominated James Buchanan of Pennsylvania, a former Secretary of State and Ambassador to Great Britain who is the only bachelor to ever occupy the White House. While attempting to downplay the slavery issue, Buchanan believed that the antislavery expansion platform of the Republican Party was a threat to national unity, and later as President, he supported the proslavery Lecompton

Constitution for Kansas as well as the infamous Supreme Court decision in the Dred Scott case. Buchanan easily defeated the Republican candidate John C. Frémont, renowned as an explorer and military figure. While quickly establishing itself in the North, the Republicans were not yet on the ballot in every state. A third party, officially called the American Party but better known as the Know Nothings for their origins as a secret society, gained almost 20 percent of the popular vote and carried the state of Maryland with former President Millard Fillmore as its nominee. The Know Nothings believed that there was a far greater threat to the United States than the expansion of slavery. Concerned about a Catholic conspiracy to undermine American democracy and place the nation's future under the control of the Papacy, the Know Nothings were a xenophobic movement opposed to immigration. Of special concern to the movement was the rising number of Catholic families entering the nation from Ireland, who became the victim of mob violence such as the burning of a convent in Charleston, Massachusetts. Thus, nativism is nothing new in American history, raising its ugly head periodically in moments of uncertainty such as the 1850s, 1920s, and 2016. The nativist rhetoric of Donald Trump is the continuation of a disturbing element in American history.

Dred Scott Decision

For most Americans in the 1850s, however, the slavery debate took precedence over the immigration issue. While politicians in the White House and Congress failed to resolve the slavery issue, the Supreme Court sought to end agitation over the slavery question with the Dred Scott Decision (1857). Dred Scott was a slave whose owners had taken the slave into free states and territories, leading abolitionists to support Scott's petition for freedom. Although Scott died from natural causes before the court rendered its decision, Chief Justice Roger Taney, supported by President Buchanan, wanted to fashion a verdict that might quell national unrest over the slave question. In a seven to two decision authored by Taney, the Supreme Court ruled that Scott had no grounds upon which to approach the court for relief as, reflecting the history of racial slavery, blacks were not American citizens. Thus, citizenship was to be defined along racial lines, but the court went ever further to protect slavery, declaring the Missouri Compromise of 1820 to be un-Constitutional. According to Taney's reasoning, since slaves were not citizens, they were simply property, and under the Constitution it was unlawful for Congress to enact legislation depriving citizens of the right to dispose of their property as they saw fit. Congress, accordingly, could not prevent slaveholders from taking their slave property into any state or territory. The Dred Scott Decision ruled that there could be no limitations placed upon slavery, and the entire nation was now potential slave territory. While many white Southerners welcomed the decision and argued that it was the final word on the slave controversy, there was outrage against the Dred Scott Decision throughout the North. Both abolitionists and advocates of popular sovereignty refused to follow the decision, asserting that it was merely an opinion. The Dred Scott Decision strengthened the abolitionists and Republican Party, fostering the belief that slavery was indeed a national threat to free labor and social mobility. The political institutions seemed unable to deal with the crisis, lending support to the voice of John Brown and others that more extreme measures would be required to deal with the evil of slavery. The Dred Scott Decision is sometimes compared with the 1973 *Roe v. Wade* ruling that recognized abortion as a right protected under the Constitution. The losing side in both cases refused to accept a court ruling which they believed to be in violation of their moral principles. The Right to Life movement insists that the rulings are similar in that *Scott* failed to protect black Americans while *Roe v. Wade* ignored the rights of the unborn. In addition to downplaying the horrors of slavery, such an analogy fails to consider the right of women to exercise control over their own bodies and reproductive rights.

Lincoln-Douglas debates

As the nation struggled with the moral and political implications of the Dred Scott Decision, attention turned to a Senatorial contest in Illinois in which both candidates were perceived as contenders for the Presidency in 1860. Incumbent Democratic Senator Stephen Douglas was a proponent of popular sovereignty, while his opponent Abraham Lincoln was a former Whig who had joined the Republican Party and emerged as a leading opponent of slavery expansion. In addition, the two men were personal rivals who competed for the affection of Mary Todd, who eventually married Lincoln. In a series of seven debates around the state, large boisterous crowds supported their favorite with torchlight parades and heckling of his opponent. The atmosphere was more akin to the entertainment of a modern-day professional wrestling event rather than the bland discourse of contemporary political debate. With intelligence and quick wits, Lincoln and Douglas were able to both entertain and educate their audiences without resorting to name calling and personal insults. Douglas argued that he was neither for nor against slavery, it was simply an issue that the white men of each territory would need to settle through the democratic tradition of the ballot box. On the other hand, Douglas sought to appeal to the racial prejudice of many voters. While Illinois was a free state, it bordered slaveholding states such as Kentucky and Missouri, and many of its residents hailed from the South. The Democrat attempted to place his opponent on the defensive by insisting that Lincoln favored racial equality and that his opposition to slavery would result in more free blacks residing within Illinois.

Lincoln's response to Douglas was nuanced. The Republican was consistent in his opposition to slave expansion as a threat to white social mobility, and he put forth his life story as exemplifying the virtues of free labor. Lincoln was born February 12, 1809 in Kentucky to a poor farm family that moved to Indiana and

Illinois. He labored on the family farm in his youth, but Lincoln did not particularly care for farm work. He gravitated toward books and was largely self-educated, spending many evenings reading by the light of the family fireplace. After failing in his efforts to run a country store, Lincoln read for the law and entered politics. Although he had little formal education, Lincoln's intelligence and oratorical skills furthered both his political and legal careers. Lincoln credited his success to the free labor environment of Illinois in which a man of modest means could rise through education and hard work—essentially the self-made man championed by Benjamin Franklin. The expansion of slavery, however, would drive down wages and threaten the existence of territories as places where poor whites could relocate and rise in society.

Thus, Lincoln was opposed to the institution of slavery and its expansion; nevertheless, he stated that he did not propose threatening slavery in the Southern states where it already existed. Lincoln's vision, however, was perceived as hostile to Southern slavery when he announced that the United States could not permanently exist as a house divided over the slavery question. Thus, limiting the extension of slavery territory would place the institution on the road to its eventual extinction, although Lincoln would not dare to predict how long this process might take. In many ways, Lincoln's thinking anticipated the containment policy later developed by George Kennan as a Cold War strategy to contain the Soviet Union and communism in the post-World War II period.

While Lincoln was consistent in denouncing slavery, especially as a threat to white social mobility, he hedged in his response to Douglas's accusations that he was a champion of racial equality. Bowing to the prejudice of his time and place, Lincoln asserted that both he and Douglas were in favor of the race to which they belonged maintaining the superior and privileged position in society. Thus, Abe Lincoln did embrace white supremacy in the Lincoln-Douglas debates, but to his credit Lincoln was a man whose views on race were capable of evolving, and by the time of his assassination, the Republican leader was moving toward embracing equal rights for the freedmen after the Civil War. Lincoln's compromising efforts to denounce slavery but support white supremacy, however, did not convince the Illinois state legislature to elevate him to the Senate, and Senator Douglas was returned to Washington. The Lincoln-Douglas debates, nevertheless, made Lincoln a national figure, and many in the North believed the Illinois politician would be the Republican nominee for President in 1860.

John Brown and Harpers Ferry

Abolitionists such as John Brown resented Lincoln's compromising stand on slavery. Lincoln's policy of opposing slavery expansion would indefinitely perpetuate the horrors and brutality of slavery, and even after slavery's destruction, the Illinois politician failed to envision a racial future in which the principles of equality enunciated in the Declaration of Independence would be realized. Thus, Brown insisted that the only morally defensible position on slavery was to work, by any means necessary, for its immediate extinction. Believing that there was no compromising with evil, Brown began to gather supporters for an October 1859 strike against slavery. Brown proposed an assault upon the government armory in Harpers Ferry, Virginia. The plan was to then arm the slaves in the region as a first step in a more widespread slave insurrection. The raid, however, was poorly executed as most slaves in the area knew nothing about the raid. Instead of slaves flocking to gather arms, Brown's raiders were attacked by troops under the command of Robert E. Lee. After several days of fierce fighting, the surviving raiders, including a wounded Brown, surrendered. Brown was put on trial for insurrection and was sentenced to be hanged. A defiant Brown refused to apologize for his actions; instead, the abolitionist asserted that he followed the higher law and struck a blow for freedom against the tyranny of slavery. To many in the North, Brown was a martyr and Christ figure who was willing to sacrifice his life in the pursuit of liberty for the enslaved. Many white Southerners, however, simply dismissed Brown as a fanatic and murderer whose execution for treason was well deserved. These polarizing reactions to Brown and the raid on Harpers Ferry provide further proof that the nation was teetering on the edge of civil war. And Brown remains a polarizing figure. He is often dismissed as a religious fanatic or depicted in popular culture as a madman and terrorist who fostered violence and murder. Yet, it is also worthwhile remembering that Brown was willing to sacrifice his own life—and admittedly others—in the cause of abolishing the atrocity that was American slavery and restoring the nation to its founding principles. Mere persuasion seems to have fallen on deaf ears.

The election of Lincoln and Southern secession

The straw that broke the camel's back for many Southern firebrands was the election of Republican Abraham Lincoln to the Presidency in 1860. The Democratic Party splintered over the slavery issue with Northern Democrats nominating Stephen Douglas and endorsing popular sovereignty. Southern Democrats, however, refused to accept any restrictions upon slavery extension and endorsed the candidacy of Vice President John C. Breckenridge from Kentucky. Although abolitionists preferred William Seward of New York, the Republicans nominated Lincoln, who was considered a compromise choice for opposing the extension of slavery but allowing the institution to stand in states where it already existed. The Republican platform also supported a policy of fostering economic growth through a protective tariff, subsidies for a transcontinental railroad, and homesteads in the West. The Constitutional Union Party, made up primarily of former Whigs who opposed dissolution of the union over the slavery issue, nominated John Bell of

Tennessee for President and urged compromise. In a bitterly contested election, Lincoln received only about 40 percent of the popular vote, but the Republican emerged with a majority in the Electoral College, although all of Lincoln's electoral votes were from Northern states.

As a sectional candidate, Lincoln attempted to address Southern fears by reiterating that he had no intension of interfering with slavery where it already existed, but the South was in no mood to compromise. Beginning with South Carolina, eleven Southern slave states eventually seceded from the Union and formed the Confederate States of America with Jefferson Davis of Mississippi as their President. Border states such as Maryland, Delaware, Kentucky, and Missouri with fewer slaves, however, remained in the Union, and Lincoln sought to maintain their allegiance by making no moves against slavery. In many ways, secession was an unreasonable action for with the Supreme Court and the Senate, slaveholding states retained the political clout to protect the institution, but they seemed to agree with Lincoln that preventing the spread of slavery would place the institution on the road to extinction. As the Southern states moved toward secession and seized federal forts within their states, President Buchanan refused to take any action against the rebellion. Lincoln was elected in November, but under the Constitution the new President did not take office until March—although the long interregnum was changed to January with the Twentieth Amendment to the Constitution. By the time Lincoln assumed the Presidency, eleven Southern states had left the Union and only one fort in the region remained in the hands of federal forces—Fort Sumter which guarded the entrance to the harbor in Charleston, South Carolina.

Fort Sumter

Lincoln refused to recognize secession and insisted that the Southern states were still part of the Union, and he was their President. Yet, he understood that it would likely take an application of force to convince the seceding Southern states of this fact. Accordingly, Lincoln began to carefully maneuver the Confederacy into firing the first shot, so that the President might label them as rebels who had attacked the flag. Lincoln proclaimed that he would not surrender Fort Sumter to South Carolina; however, he countered that he did not want to provoke a military confrontation. The President would, therefore, send provisions to maintain the Union troops holding Fort Sumter, but he would not dispatch additional soldiers to defend the fort. The proud South Carolinians considered Lincoln's refusal to abandon the fort a provocation, and on April 12, 1861, they fired upon Fort Sumter in what proved to be the first military action of a bloody war. The shelling of Fort Sumter, however, did not result in the loss of life—with the exception of a horse struck by a cannon ball. Nevertheless, Lincoln now ordered the surrender of the fort, as its location made it difficult to provision or re-enforce. For Lincoln, Fort Sumter had served its purpose. He could now appear before Congress and request 75,000 troops to deal with the rebellion as the Confederates had committed treason by firing upon the flag of the United States.

The slavery issue had taken the nation to the brink of war although Lincoln would initially emphasize the union as the cause of the conflict. But as the body counts rose, the war was to become a struggle to end slavery and culminated in the Emancipation Proclamation and Thirteenth Amendment outlawing slavery. America's original sin of slavery cost the nation dearly with over 750,000 dead in four years of fighting—although it is estimated that the holocaust of the Trans-Atlantic slave trade resulted in the death of over two million Africans. The Civil War would ostensibly settle the issues of slavery and secession, but the conflict left unresolved whether the promises of the Declaration would be extended to all Americans after the abolishment of slavery—a struggle which continues to the present day.

Further Reading:

Donald, David H. *Charles Sumner and the Coming of the Civil War*. New York: Knopf, 1960.

Etcheson, Nicole. *Bleeding Kansas: Contested Liberty in the Civil War Era*. Lawrence, KS: University Press of Kentucky, 2004.

Fehrenbacher, Don E. *The Dred Scott Case: Its Significance in American Law and Politics*. New York: Oxford University Press, 1978.

Foner, Eric. *The Fiery Trial: Abraham Lincoln and American Slavery*. New York: W.W. Norton & Company, 2010.

Freehling, William. *Road to the Disunion: Secessionists at Bay, 1776–1854*. New York: Oxford University Press, 1990.

Levine, Bruce. *Half Slave and Half Free: The Roots of the Civil War*. New York: Hill and Wang, 1990.

Potter, David M. *The Impending Crisis, 1848–1861* (1976).

Reynolds, David S. *John Brown, Abolitionist: The Man who Killed Slavery, Sparked the Civil War, and Seeded Civil Rights*. New York: Knopf, 2006.

Richards, Leonard L. *The Slave Power: The Free North and Southern Domination, 1780–1860*. Baton Rouge, LA: Louisiana State University Press, 2000.

Stampp, Kenneth M. *America in 1857: A Nation on the Brink*. New York: Oxford University Press, 1990.

13

The American Civil War

243.   On the Battlefield at Gettysburg.
[FOR DESCRIPTION OF THIS VIEW SEE THE OTHER SIDE OF THIS CARD.]

"The Battlefield at Gettysburg." Photograph by James F. Gibson, 1863. Brady's National Photographic Portrait Galleries (Library of Congress). Photography shows the bloated bodies of Union soldiers killed on July 1, 1863. Over 51,000 Confederate and Union soldiers died during the Battle of Gettysburg in a war started by Southern secession to protect racial slavery and cotton production upon which the region was dependent.

The American Civil War that raged from 1861 to 1865 was the bloodiest conflict in the nation's history with approximately 750,000 deaths. It remains the most studied and written about topic in American history, with much of this attention concentrated upon the battlefield exploits of the Northern and Southern armies and leaders. This emphasis upon the military aspects of the conflict is also apparent in the popularity of Civil War re-enactments along with parks and memorials, such as the Gettysburg battlefield site, that attract thousands of visitors every year. Many of these commemorative sites are located in the South where the myth of the Lost Cause continues to exert considerable influence. In this mythology, the war is viewed as a gallant effort to preserve an ideal agrarian way of life in which people, both black and white, lived in harmony with nature and one another until consumed by the destructive forces of modernization brought on by the Northern victory. This perception ignores the brutal reality of American slavery and is perpetuated by Confederate memorials and statues. Most of the Confederate statues, whose removal is so fiercely resisted in some places such as Charlottesville, Virginia, were constructed either during the emergence of the Jim Crow era following the premature end of Reconstruction or as a reaction to the emergence of the Civil Rights Movement in the 1950s and 1960s. The statues are a reminder of a government and society constructed to preserve racial slavery and perpetuate the mythology of the Lost Cause. Accordingly, this account of the Civil War will endeavor to keep the bigger picture of race and slavery in focus without becoming bogged down in the details of military engagements already subjected to considerable detailed study.

Overview of the war

As the war began, many on both sides were enthusiastic and assumed the conflict would be of a short duration. This initial excitement was replaced with the crushing burden of total war that led to disillusionment within both the Northern and Southern populations. In addition, a longer war favored the North with its superior resources and manpower. The South, however, believed that they enjoyed the advantage of fighting on their own soil where they would enjoy popular support and knowledge of the terrain. The goal of the Confederacy was simply to withdraw from the Union and preserve the institution of slavery. It would not be necessary to invade the North to achieve their ends if Lincoln would only agree to their departure. Lincoln had no intention of allowing secession and the dissolution of the American nation. He pointed out that the country was created by we the people and not we the states, and political differences were to be resolved under the Constitution. Lincoln recognized, however, that the seceding states were unwilling to compromise and peacefully reassume their status within the nation, Therefore, it would be necessary to invade the Confederacy and force these states to reassume their rightful position within the country. The war was to be fought primarily in the South with the resulting destruction of Southern infrastructure, including transportation, agriculture, cities, factories, and the slave labor system. The South might have taken advantage of the situation by employing the tactics of guerrilla warfare, disrupting Union supply lines and extending a conflict which the North might eventually despair of pursuing. In many ways, this strategy worked for the Americans in the Revolutionary War, and it has been employed against the United States by the Vietnamese and the Taliban in Afghanistan.

Confederate military leaders, however, were reluctant to pursue such a strategy, as it clashed with perceptions of Southern manhood. Instead, the South continued to employ the military tactics of the Napoleonic era with their large casualty rates as the technology of death and destruction increased. The failure to embrace a policy of guerrilla warfare, which was followed in some locations such as Missouri, would have allowed the South with its lack of manpower to prolong the war. The military leadership of Confederate generals such as Robert E. Lee and Thomas "Stonewall" Jackson, nevertheless, is often extolled and credited with almost leading the South to victory in the war. Jackson was a popular instructor at the Virginia Military Institute, and the slaveowner supported Virginia's decision to leave the Union. He was celebrated as a commander who urged his soldiers to never retreat and stand firm like a stone wall. During the battle of Chancellorsville in 1863, Jackson was accidentally shot by a Confederate sentry and died after his wounded arm was amputated. Some considered Jackson's death to be a turning point in the conflict, but the South still enjoyed the leadership of Lee. A wealthy Virginia plantation owner, Lee was a respected Union commander who is usually described as reluctantly following Virginia's decision to secede. As commander of the Southern forces in Virginia, Lee was lauded as a brilliant military strategist. Yet, his emphasis upon stubbornly attacking superior Union forces at Antietam and Gettysburg resulted in major Southern losses; soldiers that would be needed later in the conflict. While the tactics of Lee are subject to considerable criticism, Southerners such as Jackson and Lee represented a strong regional military attachment which is still present in the American armed forces. And outnumbered Southern forces, despite a lack of supplies, often fought quite well. This Southern affinity for arms and soldiering may be found in the rural nature of the region. While many in the North resided in cities and could call upon a police force for protection, Southerners often lived miles from their neighbors and would have to defend themselves. Also, hunting was an important supplement in feeding one's family. The Southern military tradition may, thus, be found in a culture where hunting, guns, and violence were often common, but the fighting habit was not enough to lead the South to victory in the Civil War.

Confederate resources and governmental structure

Resources were a major problem for the South, who believed that they might be saved by "king cotton." Southern diplomats entertained the hope that English dependence upon Southern cotton to supply its textile mills would convince the British government to recognize and support the Confederacy. These hopes were misplaced as the English labor force had little sympathy for the American slaveowners, and the English developed important sources of cotton from within their empire in Egypt and South Africa. Thus, the English ended up being more dependent on supplies of wheat and corn from the American Midwest to feed their population than cotton to supply their mills. King grain trumped king cotton. The South also lacked a strong transportation and factory system to support an extended conflict with the North. While the South had some factories, such as ironworks in Richmond, the region was essentially an agricultural economy dependent upon industrial products from the North and England. In terms of infrastructure for war, the Confederacy not only lacked guns and ammunition for an army, but factories to produce the supplies and uniforms, especially shoes, necessary to sustain a fighting force. In fact, many Southern soldiers entered battle in their bare feet, and the clash in Gettysburg was fostered, in part, by Southern efforts to capture a shoe factory to equip the troops with boots. For internal transportation, the South was primarily dependent upon rivers and had failed to develop an extensive railroad network. In addition, the South relied upon Northern merchants whose ships provided for the transportation of slaves before 1808 and carried cotton to Northern and European markets. The failure to develop railroad and shipping facilities hindered the South's deployment of troops and made it difficult to resist a Union blockade of Southern ports.

The South's ability to wage war was also limited by the governmental structure of the Confederacy. Deploring what was perceived as the tyranny of a strong central government under the Constitution, the Confederacy was modeled upon the Articles of Confederation, and power was to reside with the states. The central government would request taxes and troops from the states to facilitate the war effort. In addition to leaving the Confederate government constantly short of funds, states were unable to muster the expected volunteers to defend slavery. The Confederate Congress responded to this manpower crisis by enacting a conscription act that violated the concept of states' rights and exacerbated class conflict in the South. The draft law eventually covered all white men between the ages of 18 and 45; however, an exemption was provided for planters who would be required on the home front to control the slave labor supply during a crisis that might foster unrest. The exemption for slave owners antagonized poor Southern whites who could not afford slaves. These poor whites resented being drafted to fight for slavery and the planters; a fact evident in that the Ordinances of Secession in some Southern states were narrowly approved. Opposition to secession in the Appalachian region of Virginia by small farmers led to the creation of West Virginia that remained loyal to the Union and defiant of the Tidewater aristocracy. Resentment toward conscription was also apparent in the high rates of desertion experienced by the Confederate forces who had to expend considerable time and energy in hunting down and in many cases executing poor whites who left the army to return to their farms and families. In the state of Mississippi, Confederate deserters formed the Free State of Jones in defiance of the planter class and a war fought to preserve slavery. Nevertheless, playing upon poor whites' racial fears, the planters were able to maintain their political power. This history of class conflict within the South is obscured by the mythology of the Lost Cause and Confederate monuments, but it certainly impeded the Southern military effort.

Northern resources and manpower

The Union would also have issues of race and class, but the North possessed the resources to support a more sustained conflict. The Northern infrastructure was deemed strong by European investors and bankers who were prepared to provide loans to the government. While borrowing was the major source for funding the war effort, the Union relied upon an income tax that was discontinued following the conflict, the issuing of greenbacks or paper money that had the drawback of increasing inflation, and the tariff—a means of funding to which the South was normally opposed but turned toward in desperation during the war. The Northern factory system could be converted to producing armaments and supplies for the troops, even fostering industries such as the meat packing plants of the Swift and Armour families in Chicago to feed the soldiers—but not without a few cases of contaminated products that poisoned some recruits. The manufacturing base was enhanced by a railroad network that allowed for the efficient movement of troops and supplies. The Northern superiority in shipping fostered international trade as well as contributing to a strong naval force that blockaded Southern ports during the war. While cotton exports were curtailed, grain from the Midwest flowed into European markets, guaranteeing the ascendancy of grain over cotton.

The Southern armies often fought well against superior odds, but the greater manpower reserves of the North usually prevailed. Immigration from Europe, especially the Irish fleeing starvation and the famine, seemed to provide the Union with an endless supply of troops. Just as with the South, however, volunteers did not always flock to the colors as causality rates rose. Therefore, the North also turned to conscription with a class bias. The draft law enacted by Congress included a provision that allowed wealthy individuals to avoid conscription by hiring a substitute for the sum of $300. Affluent Americans such as the budding industrialist John D. Rockefeller paid the fee, but Irish immigrants could not, causing considerable resentment that culminated in the New York City Draft Riots of July 13-16, 1863. Mobs, dominated by poor Irish immigrants, roamed the streets of New York City attacking the wealthy and scapegoating blacks upon whom they blamed the war. Hundreds were killed, as free blacks were tortured, raped, and lynched from lampposts, while buildings such as the Colored Orphan Asylum were torched. Troops had to be withdrawn from the battlefield to restore order in the city, and thousands of men, women, and children may have died as the soldiers mercilessly subdued the mob and took few prisoners. The New York City Draft Riots undermined the war effort, while demonstrating the racial and class divisions within Northern society.

Use of black troops

Black Americans wanted to fight for their freedom, and free blacks and escaped slaves would provide another important source of manpower for the Union war effort. Lincoln, however, also recognized the racial prejudice of many white Northerners toward serving with black troops. Lobbied by Frederick Douglass and other abolitionists, Lincoln eventually agreed to the formation of separate black regiments under the command of white officers—a military and racial arrangement that was not abandoned until President Harry Truman's desegregation of the armed forces following World War II. Although many Northern soldiers made racist claims that blacks would not make good soldiers, the black regiments fought quite bravely. For example, the 54th Massachusetts (Colored) Volunteers Regiment suffered heavy casualties during an assault upon Fort Wagner in South Carolina—an event depicted in the Hollywood film *Glory* (1989). By the end of the war, it is estimated that approximately 10 percent of the Union army was comprised of black soldiers. The South, however, refused to accept black belligerents, and the Confederate Congress passed a law that any black troops fighting for the Union would be treated as if they were escaped slaves. This policy led to the massacre of black troops such as at Fort Pillow in Tennessee when Confederate forces under the command of General Nathan Bedford Forrest, who played a pivotal role in the establishment of the Ku Klux Klan following the Civil War, massacred several hundred captured black soldiers. Although suffering from a dire manpower shortage, the racism on display at Fort Pillow stopped the South from employing black troops. Arming the slaves and placing them in the field alongside white troops would sanction a degree of racial equality that would have destroyed the slave system and the Confederacy's reason for existence. And there is no evidence that armed slaves would have fought for the South, but plenty of slaves flocked to the Union lines and were willing to join the fight against slavery. The claims of some Southern slave apologists that enslaved men fought for the Confederacy seem to have little merit, although slaves were used to construct fortifications and provide some support tasks.

Lincoln's goals in the conflict

The racist attitudes of many in the North prevented Lincoln from initially endorsing the war as a struggle to destroy slavery. Instead, Lincoln emphasized the conflict as a patriotic fight to preserve the Union and save the Constitution. The Confederacy was a rebellion against the United States and would have to be crushed if a government of the people, by the people, and for the people were to persist. In addition, Lincoln was concerned that denunciations of slavery might drive the slaveholding border states into the arms of the Confederacy. Any initial actions toward slavery, therefore, were justified as military measures against rebel forces dependent upon a slave labor system. Lincoln was only willing to expand the war aims of the North toward destroying slavery as Union forces triumphed on the battlefield. Lincoln moved slowly and employed military necessity to justify the Emancipation Proclamation and Thirteenth Amendment to expand the war from defending the Union to a crusade to end slavery.

Lincoln outlined a military strategy that would cripple the South economically and force the Confederacy to capitulate. Following the firing upon Fort Sumter, Lincoln did not wait for a Congressional declaration of war to order a naval blockade of Southern ports. The blockade would prevent the South from raising much needed funds through the selling of its cotton on international markets. Instead, the valuable cotton crop was left in Southern warehouses until confiscated by invading Union forces. While Southern blockade runners were successful in exporting some cotton, overall the blockade was quite effective, and European powers were not willing to challenge the Union's naval forces. The North also sought to isolate the western Confederacy, especially Texas, from the eastern front in Virginia where most of the fighting was taking place. When the North gained control over the Mississippi River following the capture of Vicksburg, the western Confederacy was separated, isolating Texas from the conflict in the east, while Texan efforts to expand into New Mexico were thwarted at the Battle of Glorieta Pass. In a similar divide and conquer strategy, the upper South was isolated from the lower South following William T. Sherman's march across Georgia and South Carolina. The final triumph of the North would be assured by the capture of the Southern capital in Richmond, which was approximately ninety miles from Washington, and much of the war's fighting took place in the area between the two capitals. The Confederate capital was originally placed in Montgomery, Alabama, but the strategical and financial importance of Virginia to the Southern cause led to the relocation of the capital.

Bull Run and the Peninsula Campaign

The Northern goals were finally realized in April 1865, but only after far more difficulty than anyone anticipated. Both sides were overly confident and believed that a show of force would be enough to convince the other side to abandon the conflict. The first real battle of the Civil War was fought in July 1861 at Bull Run or Manassas, a Virginia railroad junction located between Richmond and Washington. The Union soldiers were so confident that some families followed the troops in a rather festive mood, assuming that after the battle there would be an opportunity to celebrate the crushing of the rebellion. Instead, the Southern troops failed to collapse when fired upon, and it was the Northern army that beat a steady retreat to Washington, often running past the onlookers who had gathered to observe the battle. The undisciplined retreat of the Union army left Washington vulnerable, but the South failed to capitalize on this victory in the First Battle of Bull Run. They erroneously believed that the North and Lincoln would now agree to their secession. The South underestimated the tenacity of Lincoln, and the war bogged down into a far more destructive and deadly conflict than anyone had anticipated.

After Bull Run, Lincoln acknowledged that the Union army required greater discipline and training, assigning this task to General George McClellan—a West Point dandy who fancied himself the Napoleon of the West. McClellan did seem to instill order within the Northern forces, and he began to plan a military operation against the Northern capital of Richmond. In the Peninsula Campaign the Army of the Potomac would advance along the James and York Rivers to capture Richmond. McClellan's reorganization of the Union forces appears to have significantly increased morale, but Lincoln was impatient with McClellan's reluctance to employ his superior numbers against the Confederate capital. Finally, in March 1862, McClellan unleashed his offensive; however, when met with heavy resistance outside Richmond, McClellan was hesitant to risk his reorganized forces in a full assault, withdrawing the Army of the Potomac and failing to capture his goal, and frustrating his commander-in-chief with a lack of aggression.

Antietam

Following the failure of the Peninsula Campaign, Lee retaliated with an offensive of his own into the border state of Maryland, hoping to detach the slave border state from the Union. McClellan had no choice but to fight this time as Lee's advance constituted a major threat to the Union. The armies of Lee and McClellan clashed at Antietam Creek on September 17, 1862 in a battle that witnessed nearly 23,000 casualties. While McClellan's army suffered greater losses, Lee was forced to withdraw back into Virginia. At this point, McClellan might have been able to employ his superior forces in pursuit of Lee and crush the Confederate army. Instead, the cautious McClellan decided to rest his soldiers and care for the wounded. This proved to be the last straw for Lincoln, and McClellan was removed from his command. The war would not come to a quick end, and certainly Antietam demonstrated the destructive possibilities of the conflict. The horrific nature of the fighting during the Civil War is evident in the estimated 60,000 amputations carried out in field hospitals where doctors labored away with dull blades on patients, often without sanitary measures or anesthesia, who in many cases bled to death. Infections from bullet wounds to the leg or arm usually resulted in amputations, and piles of discarded limbs were often piled outside of operating tents. Wounded soldiers were often better off left on the battlefield where maggots might devour the infected flesh, and soldiers would sometimes stick their hands into a wound to remove the maggots before they began to feed on the healthy flesh. The medical challenges of the Civil War required the assistance of nurses who in the North were organized into the Sanitary Commission headed by reformer Dorothea Dix and the American Red Cross founded by Clara Barton.

The Battle of Antietam also had significant political implications. The Northern victory convinced European powers that the Confederacy could not win the war, and there would be no diplomatic recognition extended to the Confederate States of America. Also, Lincoln had been seeking a military victory that would provide him an opportunity to strike a blow against slavery and extend the purpose of the war beyond saving the Union. Thus, on January 1, 1863 Lincoln issued the Emancipation Proclamation, whose cautionary nature is often misunderstood. Still concerned about public opinion in the slaveholding border states, Lincoln's proclamation declared that slaves residing in states that had rebelled against the government of the United States were now free, and many Southern slaves flocked to the invading Union armies. Lincoln justified his actions under his authority as commander-in-chief for the end of slavery would strike a blow against the Southern economy. Abolitionists complained that Lincoln had emancipated the slaves in the region where his authority was not recognized, while ignoring the plight of the enslaved within the border states. Nevertheless, the purpose of the war was expanded, and a Union victory now seemed to assure the destruction of the slave system—although the Emancipation Proclamation failed to consider what would be the status of the formerly enslaved within the American nation.

Vicksburg and Gettysburg

Meanwhile, on the western front Lincoln discovered a fighting general in Ulysses S. Grant whose victories at Shiloh and Vicksburg provided the Union with control of the Mississippi River and divided the Confederacy. The capture of Vicksburg, Mississippi on July 4, 1863 ended a siege of forty days in which the Confederate forces and civilians suffered from starvation and were reduced to capturing and eating rats. As Vicksburg fell, the largest battle of the war was taking place in Gettysburg, Pennsylvania. With an army of 70,000 men, Lee launched another invasion of the North in an effort to take the pressure off battle-scarred northern Virginia, gain provisions such as food and shoes for his army, and convince Northern peace politicians that the cost of prolonging the war was too dear. Opposing Lee's advance was a Northern force of over 100,000 men under the command of George Meade. Lee sought a decisive victory at Gettysburg, but he was at a disadvantage in that Union forces occupied the higher ground overlooking the small Pennsylvania town. Over three days of heavy fighting, July1-3, 1863, Lee attempted to drive the Union troops from Cemetery Ridge. Lee's decision to engage in a frontal assault on the entrenched Northern forces resulted in heavy losses; exemplified by the courageous but ill-advised charge led by Major General George Pickett in which 12,500 Confederates rushed three-quarters of a mile uphill against the Northern soldiers. The Southerners were slaughtered with over 50 percent casualties, and Lee was forced to retreat. In three days of fighting at Gettysburg, the two sides suffered approximately 50,000 casualties. Gettysburg is usually viewed as the turning point of the war as the Confederates were never able to mount another offensive threat. While Lee is often viewed as a great strategist, his assault upon Northern forces occupying higher ground wasted many soldiers who might have helped to defend Virginia against Union invaders.

On November 19, 1863, Lincoln delivered his Gettysburg Address to dedicate the cemetery at Gettysburg that contained the bodies of both Union and Confederate soldiers. The keynote speaker that day was noted orator Edward Everett who provided a two-hour address. As President, Lincoln was also asked to deliver some remarks. Speaking for only about two minutes, Lincoln evoked American democracy as a great experiment that was being tested by war, but the sacrifices of those who perished in the fields of Gettysburg must be honored by the living whose mission it was to guarantee that the founding principles of the nation were carried forth in the future. Lincoln's remarks may certainly be interpreted as endorsing the expansion of American democracy and liberties in the abstract, but he avoided any specific mention as to whether these principles would be extended to black Americans—an issue that divided Americans during the Civil War and afterwards.

Sherman's march and the Wilderness Campaign

After Vicksburg and Gettysburg, the war became increasingly difficult for the South. Union forces under the command of Grant drove Confederates from Chattanooga, Tennessee, and in September 1864 William T. Sherman captured Atlanta. After torching the Georgia city, Grant authorized Sherman to march across the state to the coast city of Savannah. To move rapidly, Sherman's army of 60,000 would live off the land, seizing provisions from plantations, farms, towns, and white Southerners who stood in their way. Sherman followed a scorched-earth policy, burning everything in a fifty-mile wide path across the state. Southern infrastructure was devastated as Sherman's army destroyed railroads by heating the iron rails and wrapping them around trees—described as "Sherman's neckties." While the invasion helped to free many slaves, there were also atrocities that resulted in the killing of many civilians. Sherman and his march are still reviled by many white Southerners. Stating that "war was hell," Sherman recognized that the march was brutal, but he defended his tactics by observing that the march undermined Southern morale and the ability to continue the war. And, indeed, Southern desertions increased as soldiers returned home to safeguard their families. Sherman essentially argued that his brutality was necessary to shorten the war, and in the long run his actions would save both Northern and Southern lives. This is quite similar to the justification President Harry Truman employed to explain the dropping of atomic bombs on Hiroshima and Nagasaki to end World War II—a topic that will be addressed later in this volume. Unfortunately, all too often America is a rather militaristic nation that tends to honor warriors above peacemakers, perpetuating the idea that peace in some distant future may be best achieved through warfare and violence. Following the capture of Savannah, Sherman's army continued to ransack the Southern countryside as they moved into South Carolina and burned the capital of Columbia.

While Sherman marched through Georgia and South Carolina, the hell of war continued on the eastern front. To capture Richmond, Lincoln assigned his fighting general Grant to lead the Wilderness Campaign in which Union troops would advance the approximately ninety miles between Washington and the Confederate capital. In battles such as Cold Harbor, Grant employed his superior numbers to push back the stubborn but outnumbered Confederate defenders. Grant's aggressive tactics led to Union advances, and casualty rates encouraged critics to complain of "Grant, the butcher." Recognizing the high death rate, many of Grant's soldiers went into battle with farewell letters to their families penned on their chests. This carnage certainly bothered Grant and only exacerbated his difficulties with alcohol. Lincoln admired Grant, and the President would sometimes dispatch the General's wife to the front in order to comfort her husband on the eve of major battles. The push against Richmond finally culminated in the fall of the city to Grant's forces in April 1865. Lee's retreating army was pursued to Appomattox Courthouse where Lee surrendered his sword and army to the victorious Union forces—a process that was swiftly followed by other Southern commanders. Grant was magnanimous in victory, releasing Lee and his soldiers to return to their homes and families where they would resume their lives as residents of the United States. But the aftermath of the Civil War was hardly that simple as the country struggled with what to do about the former rebels and determining the status of black Americans freed from the crucible of slavery.

Leadership of Lincoln

Lincoln, whose leadership played a decisive role in the Union victory, was confronted with tremendous challenges in reconstructing the country after the destruction of the war, but he had demonstrated growth on issues of racial equality that might allow the United States to attain the promise of its founding documents as outlined in the Gettysburg Address. Convinced that a Union victory in the Civil War was the only possible way to achieve the country's democratic principles, Lincoln did not worry about Constitutional scruples. Essentially, Lincoln believed that in order to save the Constitution, it might be necessary to suspend some freedoms as temporary war measures—a dangerous precedent to which incarcerated Japanese Americans during World War II may well attest. Citing his authority as commander-in-chief, Lincoln responded to the attack on Fort Sumter by ordering a naval blockade of the South, essentially an act of war, and increasing the size of the nation's armed forces without Congressional authorization. In addition, Lincoln used the war emergency to justify the suppression of newspapers the President deemed as undermining the war effort. Along with some violations of the Constitution dealing with the freedom of speech and press, Lincoln temporarily suspended the writ of habeas corpus which allowed the government to arrest American citizens without having to produce any evidence to support its actions. Perhaps the most notorious case regarding wartime suppression of free speech in the North was the case of Clement Vallandigham, a Democratic Congressman from Ohio. Vallandigham was a prominent leader of Northern Democrats opposed to the war, whom Republican critics labeled as Copperheads—a clever use of propaganda as the copperhead is one of the most poisonous snakes indigenous to North America. Lincoln considered the Copperheads to be traitors, and he was especially critical of Vallandigham, approving of his arrest and expulsion from the United States by a military tribunal. The politician was initially sent to the South, where he was briefly incarcerated before being released. Vallandigham's racist attitudes make him a rather unattractive figure, but his case again raises dangerous precedents of trading liberty for security.

Nevertheless, it is worth remembering that Lincoln, who has achieved virtual sainthood among American politicians, seemed quite vulnerable politically in 1864, and some advisers even questioned the viability of conducting an election amid a war that was not going particularly well for the North. While some abolitionists still opposed Lincoln, the President easily received the Republican nomination, but he decided to reach out to Democrats by selecting Andrew Johnson of Tennessee, a war Democrat who had not followed his state into secession, as his Vice-Presidential running mate. Meanwhile, the Northern Democrats selected as their candidate Lincoln's nemesis General George McClellan, whom Lincoln had fired after the Battle of Antietam. McClellan ran as a peace candidate, reflecting Northern discontent with the war effort. As the fortunes of war tilted toward the Union with victories at Vicksburg and Gettysburg, however, antiwar sentiment began to dissipate, and Lincoln was re-elected in a relatively easy fashion—although the

President sought to guarantee his electoral success by garnering the soldiers' vote through furloughs and appeals to Union commanders.

After securing re-election, Lincoln relentlessly prosecuted the war to its conclusion with the unconditional surrender of the South, and he skillfully guided Congress into approving the Thirteenth Amendment outlawing slavery in the United States. The bloody Civil War had settled the issues of slavery and secession, but whether the promises of equality suggested by Jefferson and Lincoln would be extended to the formerly enslaved black Americans was another question that the conflict had not resolved. Reconstruction was in many ways even a greater challenge than the war itself. We will never know if Lincoln, whose views on race had evolved toward equality, would have been able to lead the country toward racial reconciliation, for Lincoln's post war plans were cut short by an assassin's bullet.

Further Reading:

Cox, LaWanda. *Lincoln and Black Freedom: A Study in Presidential Leadership.* Columbia, SC: University of South Carolina Press, 1981.

Fahs, Alice and Joan Waugh, eds. *The Memory of the Civil War in American Culture.* Chapel Hill, NC: University of North Carolina Press, 2004.

Foote, Shelby. *The Civil War*, 3 vols. New York: Random House, 1958-1974

McPherson, James M. *Battle Cry of Freedom: The Civil War Era.* New York: Oxford University Press, 1988.

Mitchell, Reid. *The Vacant Chair: The Northern Soldier Leaves Home.* New York: Oxford University Press, 1993.

Nevins, Allan. *Ordeal of the Union*, 8 vols. New York: Scribners, 1947-1971.

Paludan, Phillip Shaw. *"A People's Contest": The Union and the Civil War, 1861–1865.* New York: Harper & Row, 1988.

Royster, Charles B. *The Destructive War: William Tecumseh Sherman, Stonewall Jackson, and the Americans.* New York: Knopf, 1991.

Vorenberg, Michael. *Final Freedom: The Civil War, the Abolition of Slavery, and the Thirteenth Amendment.* New York: Cambridge University Press, 2001.

Williams, David. *Rich Man's War: Class, Caste, and Confederate Defeat in the Lower Chattahoochee Valley.* Athens, GA: University of Georgia Press, 1998.

14

The Reconstruction Experiment
and Its Premature End

THE UNION AS IT WAS.
THIS IS A WHITE
MANS GOVERNMENT

THE LOST CAUSE

WORSE THAN SLAVERY.

WHITE LEAGUE

K.K.

SCHOOL HOUSE.

How easily wicked and treasonable organizations may gain the control over the peaceable and the industrious members of society has always been signally apparent at the South. A

Tennessee, venture even to denounce the murderers or the violators of the laws; or if any Northern journal, roused to a proper indignation by the wrongs inflicted upon peaceable settlers

"The Union as It Was: The Lost Cause Worse than Slavery." Thomas Nast drawing from *Harper's Weekly*, 1874. Library of Congress. Nast's drawing depicts the rise of the Ku Klux Klan and betrayal of the South's black population during Reconstruction when the promise of citizenship was denied.

The Reconstruction of the South following the Civil War is one of the most misunderstood aspects of American history, and the perception that white Southerners were the victims of persecution by Northern Republicans and their black allies is perpetuated in American history textbooks and popular culture. Thus, the South may be viewed as having lost the war and won the peace as the myth of the Lost Cause continues to exercise considerable influence in American culture. The reality of Reconstruction is that it was a noble experiment to honor the principles of democracy and equality celebrated by Jefferson and Lincoln. The Reconstruction of the South sought to address the legacy of slavery by providing for the education and employment of the former enslaved blacks. In addition, democracy was brought into the region with the Fourteenth and Fifteenth Amendments to the Constitution providing for equality before the law and black suffrage—at least for black men. Introducing political and social democracy after several hundred years of American racial slavery would take time, but many Northern Republicans tired of pursuing this democratic experiment. Reflecting the racial prejudice that was also present in the North, Republicans became focused upon fostering industrialization and the ensuing corruption, while lacking the resolve to resist the emergence of terrorist organizations such as the Ku Klux Klan and the restoration of white rule in the Jim Crow South. Reconstruction prematurely ended with the disputed Presidential election of 1876 and Compromise of 1877 that withdrew federal troops from the South. The freedmen of the South were abandoned by their former Northern Republican allies and left to battle alone against their former white masters. If Reconstruction had not been betrayed, the United States would not have required a second reconstruction in the Civil Rights Movement. Many Americans paid a tremendous price in the 1950s and 1960s for the nation's abandonment of the freedmen in 1877

Reconstruction mythology

Despite the best efforts of contemporary historians such as Eric Foner to document Reconstruction as a noble effort to redress the wrongs of slavery and embrace the promise of American democracy, many Americans continue to believe in the mythology put forth by early twentieth-century scholars such as Woodrow Wilson of Princeton and William Dunning of Columbia University that

Reconstruction was an ill-conceived attempt by Radical Republicans to humiliate and economically exploit the South by fostering black rule. This outdated perception, however, is still perpetuated in many American history textbooks and taught in the nation's high schools. This myth of Reconstruction is also the product of American popular culture and two influential films. In 1915, D. W. Griffith released *The Birth of a Nation,* based upon Thomas Dixon's novel *The Clansman*, to large receptive American audiences. The three-hour silent film was a masterful bit of filmmaking for the era, but *The Birth of a Nation* also demonstrated the intense racism of early twentieth-century America. Griffith's depiction of freed blacks assaulting white women who personify the purity and innocence of Southern civilization encouraged racial violence and the lynching of black Americans by white mobs—although Griffith's sex-crazed African Americans are not blacks, but rather whites in black face. In Griffith's scenario, this threat to Southern womanhood and civilization was thwarted by the Ku Klux Klan, who are portrayed as romantic knights riding to the rescue. The film concludes by endorsing the violent suppression of the Fifteenth Amendment, while celebrating the reconciliation of white Northern and Southern families once the threat of black sexual and political dominance is removed. Many of these same themes were echoed in the Hollywood blockbuster *Gone with the Wind* (1939) based upon the Margaret Mitchell novel. The film employed black performers, and Hattie McDaniel portraying "Mammy" became the first black actor to earn an Academy Award, but *Gone with the Wind* encourages black stereotypes and depicts Reconstruction as an assault upon the Southern way of life. In its portrayal of the Civil War and its aftermath, the film embraces the mythology of the Lost Cause with heroine Scarlett O'Hara serving as a symbol of the South. An idealistic slave system in which the races lived in harmony is swept away by the Civil War, and Scarlet loses her plantation, Tara. But like the South, Scarlett will rise again for tomorrow is another day.

Gone with the Wind e ssentially depicts Reconstruction as the rape of the South for Scarlett is attacked by free blacks, Carpetbaggers, and Scalawags, and she must struggle to maintain her honor. The word rape here is not used lightly for fears of miscegenation and black men raping white women was used to justify lynching and the violence perpetuated by organizations such as the Klan. The sexual boundaries between black and white were frequently crossed during slavery as white masters raped enslaved women, but when threatened by black freedom during Reconstruction, the former masters employed sexual race purity as a means through which to resist black political and social equality. In the final analysis, Scarlett and Southern civilization are saved from the corrupt Reconstruction governments through the intervention of the Klan and courageous Southern white men reasserting their rights.

A more realistic depiction of Carpetbaggers and Scalawags

Although the mythology of *Gone with the Wind* and the Lost Cause still exert considerable influence within American culture, contemporary historians paint a considerably different portrait of Reconstruction. For example, Carpetbaggers are stereotypically depicted as Northerners who went into the South with their empty carpetbags or suitcases and returned to the North with their bags full of resources and money which they stole from the prostrate white Southerners. This robbery of the South was ostensibly carried out by Northern Republicans who manipulated the freed blacks and Scalawags, the poor white trash of the region, to assist in the exploitation of the plantation South. In reality, the Carpetbaggers were primarily Northern businessmen who perceived the South as a region ripe for investment after the destruction of the Civil War. These Northern Carpetbaggers, many of whom had experienced the favorable climate of the South while serving in the Union army, wanted to get in on the ground floor of Southern rebuilding, and their investments played a major role in the rise of Southern business and industry such as iron and steel production in Birmingham, Alabama. The Scalawags were Southern whites who cooperated with the Carpetbaggers but were hardly the poor whites of the region. While some whites in the South perceived the Scalawags as traitors, in reality they were Southern businessmen who wanted to play a role in the economic reconstruction of the region. The war, however, had resulted in their financial ruin, and they lacked the funds for investment. Thus, they offered their business knowledge of the South in exchange for the capital provided by Northern Carpetbaggers, and the Scalawags expressed little concern with poor Southern whites except as a source of cheap labor.

Black Americans in the Reconstruction South

Although primarily interested in business expansion, the Carpetbaggers and Scalawags did join with freedmen in the formation of Reconstruction governments. Efforts to enforce the Fifteenth Amendment and black suffrage, of course, resulted in black governmental participation, but blacks did not dominate the Reconstruction governments as depicted in the racist *Birth of a Nation*, where black legislators are shown eating watermelons and gambling. Only the state of South Carolina had a black majority, but blacks were represented in Southern governments for the first time. Many Southern whites employed racist arguments to insist that blacks were incapable of self-government; however, the history of Reconstruction demonstrates that black legislators and officials represented their states well. For example, Mississippi, with a significant black population, elected two black men, H. R. Revels and Blanche Kelso, to the U.S. Senate, and both served with distinction. Despite this positive legacy, no black has been elected to the Senate from Mississippi since Reconstruction. The corruption of Reconstruction governments was also cited as evidence for the incompetence of black legislators. It is true that the Southern Reconstruction governments surpassed the spending habits of previous administrations, but it is also worth pointing out that the Reconstruction governments were investing in the infrastructure of transportation and education that had been neglected in the past. And allegations of corruption raised regarding Southern Reconstruction legislatures often pale in comparison with the scandals that plagued Congress on the national level following the Civil War.

Most former slaves in the South, however, were not involved in governmental service. Instead, they were interested in attempting to re-unite with their families and find work outside of the slave labor system, providing little substance to Southern white fears of rape, violence, and retaliation. Following the end of slavery, observers were amazed with the multitude of blacks roaming the roads of the rural South in search of family members who were separated from their parents, children, spouses, and siblings due to the tyranny of slavery in which families were not respected. Many were never able to find their lost relatives, but it is astounding how many slave families retained knowledge of their departed members and were able to find one another. After this period of family reconciliation, there was still a need to find work. Although the Republican Congress initiated programs for the education and re-training of the formerly enslaved population, most black Southerners were used to tilling the soil and picking cotton. Thus, many blacks drifted back to their former plantations and were willing to work in the fields for pay rather than as slave labor. Following the destruction of the Southern currency, most planters, however, lacked the funds to pay field hands.

But they did have work and land which led to the sharecropping system in which the laborers would work the plantation owner's land in exchange for a share of the harvested crop. In practice, this often worked out to a third for the land owner, a third for the family working the land, and a third for the store owner who supplied necessary seeds and tools to work the land. Ideally, the laborers should have been able to save a little money each harvest and finally purchase the land which they were cultivating. The reality of sharecropping, however, was considerably different. Due to problems with drought, flooding, hailstorms, or infestations of insects, sharecroppers could not always produce a crop to share. During the lean years and harvests, sharecropping families fell into debt with sharecropping evolving to become a system of peonage. Falling further into debt each year, sharecroppers were increasingly unable to leave the land, and planters once again enjoyed a subservient labor supply that was expanded to also include poor Southern whites—again exhibiting a common economic bond going back to Bacon's Rebellion in 1676. Confronted with a lack of economic opportunity and rising Klan violence, one wonders why more blacks did not leave the South, and some did move west and take advantage of the Homestead Act. Most families that had survived the slave system, however, lacked the necessary funds to relocate, and they were not exactly welcome in the North where many states passed legislation to prohibit black immigration.

Birth of the Klan

Central to the mythology of Reconstruction perpetuated by films such as *The Birth of a Nation* is the idea of the Klan as a heroic organization formed to save Southern civilization and white women from the tyranny of black rule. To put it quite bluntly, the Klan was and remains a terrorist organization. Led by former Confederate General Nathan Bedford Forrest, whose troops were responsible for the infamous Fort Pillow Massacre of black Union soldiers, the Klan was comprised largely of Confederate veterans dedicated to the employment of violence to maintain and enforce an ideology of white supremacy. The targets of Klan violence and murder were blacks and their white allies in the Republican Reconstruction state governments of the South. Through the intimidation of black voters, the Klan sought to block implementation of the Fifteenth Amendment and black suffrage. The hoods and robes were ostensibly to convince the former slaves that the Klan were ghosts of Confederate soldiers who had perished in the war, but in reality it was necessary for the Klansmen to conceal their identity as they pursued their lawless agenda. Klan violence eventually led Congress to crack down on terrorists with the Ku Klux Klan Act of 1871, but by this time much of the damage was done with the Reconstruction governments in retreat, and white rule was being restored in the South. The Klan, however, would rise again in the 1920s and extend its influence on the national stage with nativist denunciations of immigrants and anti-Catholicism, and in the 1950s and 1960s the Klan engaged in a violent resistance to the integrationist goals of the Civil Rights Movement. The continuing appeal of the Klan's origins in *The Birth of a Nation* and *Gone with the Wind* mythology of Reconstruction, nevertheless, may be found in the Klan propagandist depictions on the internet of Southern whites in the era suffering mistreatment at the hand of blacks urged on by treacherous white Carpetbaggers and Scalawags. The ideology of white supremacy and nationalism extolled by the Klan, unfortunately, retains a national audience which embraces the myths of Reconstruction and the Lost Cause.

Lincoln's Plan for Reconstruction

Political Reconstruction in the South was initially in the hands of Lincoln who proposed the rather moderate 10 percent plan. Lincoln wanted to restore the Southern states to the Union as quickly as possible, and his plan asserted that the states of the former Confederacy would rejoin the Union as soon as 10 percent of their voters swore an oath of allegiance to the government of the United States and agreed to the Thirteenth Amendment. Lincoln also called for a generous amnesty that would allow most Confederates to participate in the political process despite having taken up arms against the American government. Radical Republicans in Congress viewed

Lincoln's proposal as too generous to the South and passed the Wade-Davis Bill, establishing a 50 percent threshold for the readmission of a Southern state. Lincoln refused to sign the legislation, and there was a stalemate between the President and Congress regarding Reconstruction policy. This impasse was shattered, however, with the assassination of Lincoln by Southern actor John Wilks Booth on April 14, 1865. The assassination was a plot by Booth and other Southern sympathizers to punish Lincoln and his administration for what the conspirators considered to be war atrocities committed against the Confederacy and its people. The plans of the plotters called for attacks upon other members of Lincoln's cabinet, but most of these assaults were not implemented, although Secretary of State William Seward was stabbed in his home. While Lincoln was attending the theater, he was shot in the back of the head by Booth, who leaped from a balcony, breaking his ankle, and shouted death to tyrants before making his escape amid the chaos. Booth was hunted down and killed by federal troops, while the other conspirators were placed on trial for treason and executed, including Mary Surratt at whose boarding house the plotters met. The conspirators, however, failed to advance Southern interests as with the death of Lincoln, Republicans in Congress were able to pursue a more stringent policy toward the South and attempt to implement legislation promoting racial justice.

Reconstruction under Andrew Johnson

Initially, however, the Republican agenda was blocked by Andrew Johnson who ascended to the Presidency following Lincoln's assassination. Johnson was a Democratic politician from Tennessee who stayed loyal to the Union and was awarded with the Vice-Presidential slot alongside Lincoln in a union ticket emphasizing sectional reconciliation. The former Senator from Tennessee was also a poor Southern white who had little use for the planter class upon whom he placed blame for the devastation of the Civil War. He had little formal education, and before entering politics he labored as a tailor. Johnson also shared the prejudice of many in his social class toward black Americans, and as President he was not interested in pursuing legislation and policies that would promote the interests of the freedmen. Accordingly, Johnson essentially embraced the 10 percent plan proposed by Lincoln with one major exception: his disdain for the planter class was evident in a far more limited amnesty that would disqualify wealthy Southern property owners from political participation. Despite the limitations placed upon the planters, most Southern states sought readmission to the Union under what they considered the fairly lenient provisions outlined by the President. Many Republicans in Congress, however, were opposed to the generous terms offered by Lincoln and Johnson. For example, Thad Stevens, who represented Pennsylvania in the House of Representatives and whose family's factories were damaged in the fighting, insisted that the South should be treated as a conquered province under the supervision of the Union army. Charles Sumner of Massachusetts, who had reassumed his Senate seat following the beating by Preston Brooks, agreed with Stevens, believing that military occupation might provide the opportunity for Congress to push an agenda of racial equality in the South. And Sumner was no hypocrite as he battled for racial justice in Massachusetts and throughout the nation. Ben Wade of Ohio also called for a more extended period of Southern supervision by Congress that would provide time to establish the Republican Party in the region as well as foster the economic growth of manufacturing and business within the South.

While the Republican Congress called for a more stringent Reconstruction policy, the Southern states moved toward readmission by following the Presidential plan of Johnson. The North, however, reacted unfavorably to the application of Presidential Reconstruction. The Southern states were conducting elections in which blacks were not allowed to vote, and many former Confederate leaders, such as Alexander Stephens of Georgia who served as Vice President of the Confederacy, were elevated to office. In addition, the former Confederate states were enacting Black Codes that would restrict the freedoms of their black populations. Under the Black Codes, Southern courts sought to assure a black labor supply by restricting freedom of movement for blacks and using flimsy charges such as vagrancy to sentence former slaves to plantation labor—in many cases assigning them to forced labor on plantations where they were once enslaved. For all intentional purposes, the Black Codes provided a means through which the former Confederate states could reinstitute racial slavery, and many Northern politicians and citizens wondered why they had fought the Civil War.

Congressional Reconstruction

Therefore, Congressional Republicans reacted to the election of ex-Confederates and the imposition of Black Codes by taking Reconstruction out of the hands of Johnson and placing it under control of the Congress. Under Congressional Reconstruction, policy would be guided by the report from the Joint Congressional Committee on Reconstruction that found the policy of Johnson to be unacceptable. Much of the legislation passed by the Republican Congress was vetoed by Johnson, but the Congress, without the presence of the ex-Confederate states, had the necessary two-thirds majority to overrule the President's objections. Congressional Reconstruction is often perceived as a radical agenda attempting to alter the Southern way of life, but the Republicans in Congress passed on an opportunity to fundamentally restructure the Southern economy and legacy of slavery. During the Civil War, Congress passed confiscation acts as war measures that would allow Union commanders to confiscate the property, including plantations and slaves, of Confederate rebels, and Union commanders such as William T. Sherman implemented these measures, sometimes allowing freed slaves to occupy former plantation land.

These acts encouraged blacks to believe that Reconstruction agencies such as the Freedmen's Bureau might provide Southern blacks with compensation, in terms of land grants from the division of plantations, for the value of their labor which was stolen under the slave system. Expectations that the families of the freedmen would be awarded forty acres and a mule to provide them an economic foundation in a reconstructed South free from racial slavery, however, were not realized as Northern Republicans in Congress were not prepared to abandon the notion of a market economy and producer capitalism providing for social mobility. Therefore, the Civil War and Reconstruction failed to provide a fundamental restructuring of the Southern economy that would have altered the racial power structure of the region.

The Freedmen's Bureau attempted to provide governmental assistance to freed blacks, but the agency did not introduce the radical change feared by Southern whites. Johnson opposed government aid to blacks and vetoed an extension of the agency, but the veto was overridden by Congress. The Freedmen's Bureau was to provide education, job training, legal advice, and welfare services such as reuniting families. But rather than introducing the breakdown of the plantation system by fostering independent black farmers, the lawyers of the Freedmen's Bureau helped black laborers and white plantation owners negotiate contracts that guaranteed a steady labor supply for the cultivation of Southern staples such as cotton. Nevertheless, many white Southerners resented the Freedmen's Bureau as well as passage of the 1866 Civil Rights Act that provided equal protection of the laws to all American citizens, including those of African descent once enslaved in the South. Two years later these protections were incorporated into the Fourteenth Amendment. In response, the teachers, both male and female, who migrated to the South to fulfill the educational mission of the Freedmen's Bureau were often the targets of violence perpetuated by organizations such as the Klan opposed to black education and citizenship.

President Johnson resented Congress taking charge of Reconstruction policy, and in the Congressional elections of 1866 he actively campaigned against the so-called Radical Republicans. With the readmission of Southern states blocked by the Republican Congress, Johnson campaigned throughout the North for Democratic Congressional candidates. Johnson's vitriolic speeches embraced racial prejudice, and his opponents accused the President of public drunkenness during the bitter electoral contest for control of the Congress. Reacting negatively toward Johnson and growing violence in the South, Republican candidates did exceedingly well in the election and pursued a more aggressive Reconstruction policy. In 1867, Congress enacted the Military Reconstruction Act which divided the former Confederate states—except for Tennessee which had already ratified the Fourteenth Amendment—into five military districts that would be governed by Union commanders. To restore civilian control and assure the removal of the federal troops, the Southern states were required to ratify the Thirteenth, Fourteenth, and Fifteenth Amendments to the Constitution. Most white Southerners now recognized that slavery would not be coming back, but many whites in the South were opposed to the Fourteenth and Fifteenth Amendments that provided for black citizenship and suffrage. The Fifteenth Amendment was considered particularly threatening as black suffrage posed the specter of black political power, leading to violent confrontations between Union troops and white supremacists of the Klan.

Impeachment and trial of Andrew Johnson

Amid this violence, the Republican Congress began impeachment proceedings against Johnson, enacting a law that the President was almost assured of violating. The Tenure of Office Act proclaimed that the President could not remove a member of his cabinet without Congressional authorization—a measure that was later declared un-Constitutional for violating the separation of powers. Congress passed the legislation to both provoke Johnson and protect the Secretary of War Edwin Stanton, who was allied politically with the Radical Republicans. When Stanton refused to implement orders from the President, he was fired by Johnson. Stanton, however, ignored that order as well and had to be forcibly removed from his office. The House then voted for articles of impeachment against Johnson, and the President faced trial in the Senate where a two-thirds vote is required to remove the President from office. The conventional political wisdom was that the Republicans had the necessary votes to remove the President; however, three Republican Senators defied party discipline and voted for Johnson's acquittal, saving him by one vote. The antipathy with which popular culture has traditionally viewed the Radical Republicans and favored the racist Johnson is evident in John F. Kennedy's Pulitzer Prize-winning *Profiles in Courage* (1957)—ghost written by Kennedy speechwriter Ted Sorenson—that praises Kansas Republican Senator Edmund G. Ross for his courageous not guilty vote. The public was less forgiving as the three Republican Senators who voted not guilty were never again elected to public office. As for Johnson, the President remained in office, although he was ineffective in opposing the will of Congress that consistently enacted Reconstruction legislation over the President's veto.

Grant Presidency

The Democrats had little interest in nominating the unpopular Johnson in 1868 and selected New York Governor Horatio Seymour as their candidate. The Republicans tapped Civil War hero U. S. Grant as their nominee who urged Northern voters to "vote as they shot," depicting the Democrats as traitors and "waving the bloody shirt" to politically exploit the war's legacy. Grant also did well with black voters who appreciated his support for Congressional Reconstruction as well as his military record of welcoming escaped slaves into Union lines and application of the confiscation acts. Although a popular war hero, Grant's Presidency was more complex. While he was committed to the enforcement of the Fourteenth and Fifteenth Amendments, the Grant Presidency was marred by political scandals in which the President was not involved personally. Nevertheless, many of his friends and appointees to office were associated with corruption, and Grant's character judgments were not always the best and perhaps exacerbated by his problems with alcohol.

Among the scandals that did not reflect well on the Grant administration was the attempt by speculators Jay Gould and Jim Fisk to corner the gold market through advance knowledge of government gold sales gained through members of the Grant family. The scheme was foiled when Grant authorized the unleashing of additional gold reserves and prevented the speculators from cornering the gold market. The post-Civil War period also saw a boom in railroad construction encouraged by the Congress. The Credit Mobilier was a government-chartered railroad construction company that earned excessive profits by overcharging the Union Pacific Railroad in the building of a transcontinental railroad. It was later revealed that many Congressmen, including Schuyler Colfax of New York who served as Grant's Vice President, garnered considerable profits from Credit Mobilier stock. The Grant administration, however, was credited with settling the *Alabama* claims for the damages inflicted upon Northern shipping by Confederate commerce raiders, such as the *Alabama*, constructed in English shipyards. The settling of these claims fostered a close political and economic relationship between the Americans and British following the American Civil War. Grant also supported Congressional passage of the 1871 Ku Klux Klan Act that expanded the Union military response to the violence carried out in the South by the terrorist organization. The application of force did help to drive the Klan underground, but by this time considerable damage was done to the Reconstruction governments, and the North was growing weary of the sustained effort that would be required to address the legacy of slavery.

Despite the scandals and waning support for Reconstruction, Grant remained personally popular and was easily nominated for a second term. Nevertheless, the Liberal Republicans, who opposed the corruption of the Grant administration, refused to endorse the President and, instead, nominated crusading newspaper editor Horace Greeley of the *New York Tribune* for the Presidency. The Democrats, who were desperate to win a national election, followed suit and endorsed the candidacy of Greeley. Widely admired in the North, Grant was returned to the White House, and the nation avoided a Constitutional crisis when Greeley suddenly died after the voting. During his second term, the Grant Presidency continued to be plagued by scandal, although in fairness it should be noted that corruption after the sacrifices of the Civil War was hardly limited to one administration or political party. In New York City, the Democratic political machine of Tammany Hall under the direction of William M. "Boss" Tweed, who eventually ended his political career in prison, was notorious for the fixing of elections and demands for the payment of "kickbacks" from politicians and businessmen. Grant, however, could not escape the accusations of corruption regarding his friends and associates. Secretary of War William Belknap faced impeachment charges for his mismanagement of trading posts as the government forced the Plains Indians on to reservations. Several members of the Grant administration, including his personal secretary General Orville Babcock, were accused of personally profiting from the taxation levied on alcohol in a scandal that became known as the "Whiskey Ring." Grant's second term was also marred by the Panic of 1873 that was fostered by inflation, speculative investments in railroads that led to the collapse of Jay Cooke and Company, and the government's decision to forego the purchase of silver to back the money supply. The Panic was a world depression that lasted until the late 1870s and struggling working-class people in the North began to lose interest in the plight of their black brethren in the South.

Disputed election of 1876

Grant entertained hopes for a third term, but reformers in the Republican Party were tired of scandal, and the 1876 nomination was bestowed upon Ohio Governor Rutherford B. Hayes, who served under Grant during the war and had established a positive reputation as a reformer and defender of civil rights. The Democrats selected New York Governor Samuel Tilden who promised reform and an end to Reconstruction. Tilden won a majority of the popular vote, but there was a problem with disputed electoral votes from the Southern states of Louisiana, Florida, and South Carolina. While most of the former Confederacy was readmitted to the Union with white "redeemer" governments overthrowing the Republican Reconstruction state administrations, these three Southern states were in the midst of power struggles for political control with Democratic "redeemer" forces and a more diverse Republican coalition both claiming to constitute the legitimate government. Thus, the Congress was presented with two sets of electoral votes from each of the three Southern states. To decide how the disputed electoral votes were to be counted, the Congress authorized a fifteen-man Electoral Commission consisting of five Supreme Court judges, five House members, and five Senators. After considerable political maneuvering, the Republican Party emerged with an eight to seven majority on the Electoral Commission, which was prepared to award Hayes the Presidency with the disputed electoral votes. Claiming that the election was stolen, some Southern Democrats were again talking secession and war. Cooler heads prevailed, and party leaders convened at the Wormley Hotel, only blocks from the White House, and negotiated the Compromise of 1877 that betrayed Southern blacks, assigning them to almost a century of second-class citizenship.

Compromise of 1877

In the compromise, the Republicans retained the Presidency, although Hayes promised that he would not be a candidate for re-election in 1880. In exchange for surrendering the vast powers of the Presidency, Congressional Republicans made significant concessions to Southern Democrats. Congress would provide funds for internal improvements in the South such as roads, bridges, and railroads, while federal patronage positions would be awarded to Democrats, ending the Republican lock upon federal political offices in the region. The most important agenda item for the South was the withdrawal of Union forces; for all intentional purposes ending the Republican commitment to Reconstruction and equality before the law for black citizens in the South. This process was already well underway throughout the former Confederate states, but the Compromise of 1877 provided an official acknowledgement that Reconstruction was over. Without the protection of federal troops, Southern blacks were at the mercy of white racists and planters who sought to control the black population and their labor through a Jim Crow system of racial apartheid enforced through the law as well as by extralegal violence and lynch mobs. Reconstruction was not the rape of the South by blacks, Scalawags, and Carpetbaggers as popular culture and high school history courses might suggest. Instead, it was a noble experiment in reconstructing race relations that was prematurely ended. As the nation turned its back on the former slaves of the South, attention turned to accumulating vast amounts of money through the rapid industrialization of the country. Exploitation, nevertheless, was still the name of the game as robber baron industrialists garnered huge fortunes in what Mark Twain called the Gilded Age. Taking advantage of a corrupt political system, the robber baron industrialists exploited natural resources, removed the Plains Indians to reservations, took advantage of desperate immigrant workers, and in the search for markets made the United States into an imperial power.

Further Reading:

Benedict, Michael L. *The Impeachment and Trial of Andrew Johnson*. New York: W.W. Norton & Company, 1973.

Blight, David W. *Race and Reunion: The Civil War in American Memory*. Cambridge, MA: Harvard University Press, 2001.

Chernow, Ron. *Grant*. New York: Penguin Books, 2017.

Current, Richard N. *Those Terrible Carpetbaggers*. New York: Oxford University Press, 1988.

Donald, David H., Jean H. Baker, and Michael F. Holt. *The Civil War and Reconstruction*. New York: W.W. Norton & Company, 2001.

Foner, Eric. *Reconstruction: America's Unfinished Revolution, 1863–1877*. New York: Harper & Row, 1988.

Litwack, Leon. *Been in the Storm So Long: The Aftermath of Slavery*. New York: Knopf, 1979.

McPherson, James M. *Ordeal by Fire: The Civil War and Reconstruction*. New York: Knopf, 1982.

Morris, Roy Jr. *Fraud of the Century: Rutherford B. Hayes, Samuel Tilden, and the Stolen Election of 1876*. New York: Simon & Schuster, 2003.

Nieman, Donald. *To Set the Law in Motion: The Freedman's Bureau and the Legal Rights of Blacks, 1865–1868*. Millwood, NY: KTO Press, 1979.

Richardson, Heather Cox. *The Death of Reconstruction: Race, Labor, and Politics in the Post-Civil War North, 1865–1901*. Cambridge, MA: Harvard University Press, 2001.

15

Emergence of Big Business, 1865–1900

John D. Rockefeller. Portrait 1909. Library of Congress. Following the Civil War, the United States became the leading industrial power in the world. This growth was accompanied by the exploitation of factory workers and the influence of monopoly capitalism. best symbolized by John D. Rockefeller and the Standard Oil Company.

Between the Civil War and the beginning of the twentieth century, the United States emerged as the world's leading industrial nation. This tremendous growth is usually attributed to multiple factors, including: the Civil War, government fostering of business development, vast natural resources, technological innovation, an expanding population to provide a cheap labor supply and markets, capital formation, business leadership, and societal belief in change and progress. These factors tend to celebrate the triumph of free enterprise and capitalism, but there was a considerable price to be paid for these economic gains that were hardly equitably distributed among the population. To foster economic growth, the Plains Indians were forcibly placed on reservations, immigrant workers labored long hours under harsh and dangerous conditions, exploitation of resources took precedence over conservation, and nations such as the Philippines were annexed in the search for markets without the consent of indigenous populations. In addition, the expansion of the railroads, America's take-off industry, was encouraged by government subsidies amid an orgy of corruption and scandals. The growth of big business in America was hardly the product of laissez-faire economics as government policies subsidized industrial expansion in exchange for campaign contributions, forming an alliance between business and politicians that continues to dominate the American economy and political system. Despite oratory lauding free enterprise and competition, the rise of American business was characterized by the development of monopolies in industries such as steel and oil. Monopoly was often justified by the bastardization of scientific evolution called Social Darwinism which argued that poverty was the fault of the poor and there should be no restrictions placed upon the wealthy who earned their dominant position within the society through hard work. Thus, the tradition of corporate welfare being justified as investment was established, while subsidies for the poor are denounced as fostering dependency and "welfare queens." The rise of big business also produced the countervailing resistance of class conflict and the union movement, conservation and environmentalism, armed opposition by Native Americans and Filipinos, and reform movements such as Populism and Progressivism. The rise of big business presented major challenges to the democratic ideas of Jefferson's Declaration, and that struggle continues into the present day.

The myth of laissez-faire

The Civil War on one level represented a conflict over who would control the government and guide the economic future of the nation. Would America be primarily an agrarian nation with slave labor or an industrial country with free labor? The industrial North won the war, and business leaders lobbied the government to pursue policies that would benefit the rise of business. In terms of subsidies, the Republican Congress expanded tariffs to protect American industries, such as rising iron and steel production, from foreign competition and allow them to charge higher prices—as a developing industrial nation, the United States favored large protective tariffs, but as the economy matured during the twentieth century, free trade became the favored policy. Following the Civil War, the settlement of the West was promoted through the Morrill Act and promotion of land grant colleges as well as the Homestead Act that awarded 160 acres of land to a family that would spend five years working and improving the homestead. Congress also encouraged the opening of the West through direct subsidies paid to foster the building of a transcontinental railroad. In addition, railroad expansion into undeveloped areas was promoted through land grants bestowed for every mile of track constructed. To pave the way out West for the railroads and farmers, the government employed the army to force the Plains Indians on to the reservations. The coercive power of the government was also apparent in late nineteenth-century labor disputes. Government was not an umpire between labor and capital as troops were dispatched to quell labor unrest such as the railway strike of 1877. And the American military helped to spread business interests abroad with the Spanish-American War and suppression of the Filipino insurrection against American annexation.

Business growth was also encouraged through low taxation. Relying upon tariffs, excise taxes on goods such as alcohol, and taxation of land to fund the government, the large profits garnered by American business leaders were largely exempt from taxation until passage of the Sixteenth Amendment that provided for the income tax as part of the early twentieth-century Progressive reform movement. Corporations were also protected from government regulation through such Supreme Court rulings as *Santa Clara County v. Southern Pacific Railroad Company* (1886) which concluded that the equal protection of the law provisions of the Fourteenth Amendment applied to corporations as well as individuals. The concept of treating corporations as people has continued into the twenty-first century with the *Citizens United v. Federal Election Commission* (2010) decision in which the justices asserted that the free speech rights of corporations could not be limited through legislation restricting campaign contributions. The persistent close connection between government and business is evident on the state and local levels in subsidies offered to lure business relocations. Among the subsidies dangled before businesses are tax incentives, transportation infrastructure to connect business with roads and waterways, provision of public utilities, and grants of land upon which to construct a plant or factory. Such generous concessions to business at taxpayer expense are usually justified as investments that will help to create jobs in the area. Whether such subsidies are a valid investment is a debatable question, and businesses often relocate when another community offers a better financial package. The contemporary competition among cities to create an investment package to attract a business such as Amazon is intensive, indicating that the nineteenth-century alliance between business and government remains alive and well. Nevertheless, the myth of laissez-faire economics persists and exercises considerable influence upon American politics and culture, denouncing government aid to the poor while ignoring the subsidies extended to influential business interests.

Exploitation of natural resources

The industrialization of the United States also benefitted from ample natural resources, although it is worth remembering that many of these resources originally belonged to the Native people or Hispanic settlers in the Southwest who were deprived of their assets through the territorial expansion of the United States. Many Europeans were initially attracted to the fertile soil for farming available in the so-called "new world." An abundance of forest land for shelter and water for crops and industry furthered expansion. Industrialization was fueled by rich deposits of coal in states such as Pennsylvania and West Virginia, while the development of the iron and steel industry was based upon extensive iron ore deposits in Michigan and Minnesota's Mesabi Range. Westward expansion into Arizona, New Mexico, and Montana uncovered extensive cooper deposits, while the nation's wealth and monetary supply was enhanced by the discovery of silver in the Comstock Lode of Nevada and gold strikes in California, Montana, Colorado, Alaska, and the Black Hills of South Dakota. In the late nineteenth and early twentieth centuries, oil challenged coal as the driving energy source for industrialization with significant oil booms in Pennsylvania, Ohio, Texas, Oklahoma, and California. Ample rainfall, vast forests, and good farmland also brought settlers and the timber industry into the Pacific Northwest.

Admittedly, as settlers moved westward, water did become somewhat of an issue, but this did not stop farming in the Great Plains. Over plowing and cultivation of the region culminated in the man-made disaster of the Dust Bowl in the 1930s that drove many families off the land. In fact, the Dust Bowl and ensuing trek to California by many displaced "Okies," so well depicted by John Steinbeck in *The Grapes of Wrath*, well demonstrates the lack of a conservation ethic in American expansionism and the rise of industry. Going back to the cultivation of tobacco in colonial Virginia, the vast resources of North America have convinced Americans that there is little need to be concerned about the conservation of natural resources. This attitude has contributed to pollution and waste with the clearcutting of forests, dumping of chemicals into rivers, deteriorating air quality, and landfills based upon disposable products. In addition to pollution, industries such as coal mining have proven to be quite dangerous to workers and miners. In more recent decades, the United States has attempted to redress the environmental damage of the industrial revolution with agencies and legislation such as the Environmental Protection

Agency, Endangered Species Act, and Clean Water Act. Concerns about unfettered expansion and consumption have encouraged recycling and a conservation ethic promising new renewable energy sources such as wind and solar power which pose less danger to the environment. Evidence that traditional American attitudes toward the environment must change is provided by the scientific consensus that man-made global warming is producing climate change with devastating implications for human and animal life on the planet. The warnings of the scientific community, however, are challenged by representatives of the fossil fuel industry who want to continue energy dependence upon oil and coal and have found an appreciative audience in the administration of President Donald Trump where the extractive policies of American industry in the period following the Civil War continue to find a champion.

Technological innovation

Optimists insist that the crisis of global warming will be addressed through technological innovation, and certainly Americans, from the rise of industry in the late nineteenth century to the cutting edge of computers and the internet, have placed considerable faith in technology. Believing that building a better mousetrap will improve society as well as enhance the finances of the inventor, Americans embrace capitalism and entrepreneurship as a means through which to improve the quality of life, although many technological innovations are also double-edged swords and produce unanticipated consequences. Seeking to cash in on their innovations, American inventors in the late nineteenth century flooded the U.S. Patent Office with their plans, and some were able to accumulate vast fortunes from their ideas. The Bessemer process was pioneered by English industrialist Henry Bessemer, allowing for the mass production of steel from molten iron ore by removing the impurities from the iron through oxidation. This innovation allowed for industrialists such as Andrew Carnegie to take advantage of America's rich iron ore deposits and make Pittsburgh a focal point of world steel production. Modern communication was introduced with Alexander Graham Bell's invention of the telephone. Basing his research into hearing devices upon his concern with deafness in his family, Bell was awarded a patent for the first telephone in 1876. Finding a receptive audience for his invention, Bell founded the American Telephone and Telegraph Company (AT& T). The many innovations and functions that we now associate with mobile telephones, however, were blocked by the monopoly exercised by AT&T until the communications behemoth was broken up under the Sherman Anti-trust Act in the 1980s. The telephone also expanded the participation of women in the workforce who were recruited to serve as switchboard operators. Female employment in American business was also fostered by the invention of the typewriter that was patented in 1868 by newspaper editor Christopher Latham Sholes. The genius of Sholes is evident with the keyboard that is still present with the personal computer that far exceeds the original communication purposes of Sholes. In fact, a time traveler from the nineteenth century might take one look at a computer and through the keyboard have a good clue as to the purpose of the technology. Along with the telephone, the invention of the typewriter and its adoption by most American businesses brought educated mostly white, middle-class women into the workplace as typists and secretaries. Although initially these positions were perceived as temporary jobs, preferable to factory work with its negative class connotations, for young women until they married, women settled into secretarial jobs as a profession and were able to exercise influence within the business office environment where management remained primarily a male prerogative.

The best-known American inventor of the late nineteenth and early twentieth centuries was Thomas Alva Edison. From his laboratory in Menlo Park, New Jersey, Edison registered over a thousand patents; although he is best known for his invention of the electric light bulb, the phonograph, and motion picture camera— all of which fostered major industries and transformed American life. Edison was also a businessman who embraced the monopolistic practices of contemporaries such as Andrew Carnegie and John D. Rockefeller. Seeking to maintain control over the fledgling motion picture industry, Edison formed the Motion Pictures Patent Company which was eventually disbanded as an illegal restraint of trade under the Sherman Anti-trust Act. Among Edison's contemporaries, Henry Ford along with Orville and Wilber Wright were able to take advantage of the invention of the internal combustion engine to transform American transportation in the early twentieth century with the mass production of automobiles and aircraft.

Belief in progress

The popular adoption of the technological innovations in the late nineteenth and early twentieth centuries associated with the rise of American industry and big business indicate a societal belief that these modern inventions would improve the quality of American life. This belief in progress makes Americans especially susceptible to technological innovations that are assumed to promote social mobility although most American remain within the social class into which they were born. While there is evidence to suggest that the industrial revolution somewhat enhanced the status of families over generations, technological change has proven to be a mixed blessing. New products such as telephones, typewriters, and automobiles increased consumer demand, but longer working hours were required to pursue the American dream. To participate in a rising standard of living, many working-class Americans are forced into holding down multiple jobs. One spends so much time working that it becomes increasingly difficult to enjoy the fruit of one's labors. Even household innovations such as the washing machine or vacuum cleaner failed to fulfill their promise of reducing domestic drudgery as with these inventions working and cleaning tend to become daily chores rather than being reserved for a particular day of the week such as relegating Mondays for laundry. Overworked Americans find it difficult to take vacations or time away from work to the consternation of many contemporary European nations where the concept of a four to six-week holiday annually is common. The industrial revolution also facilitated a factory system and culture built around subservience to the clock and factory whistle apparent in the organization of American daily life and the school system. Rather than living in harmony with nature as with the rhythm of the seasons, inventions such as Edison's light bulb allowed for evening factory shifts. Supposedly the introduction of modern technology and communication has freed Americans from the tyranny of the factory and clock. However, the ability to work out of the home afforded by modern computers has actually increased labor intensity as the division between home and work is blurred, and one may now work all the time, including while on vacation. Modern technology has enhanced our ability to connect with a more diverse population, but this innovation has rendered many Americans dependent upon technology and reduced our interpersonal connections with friends, family, colleagues, and the environment. As we become isolated in our daily contacts and slaves to pursuing the latest technological innovation, there is considerable evidence that the love affair with technology and progress is a double-edged sword.

Labor supply

To create the technology that fueled the rise of industry and business following the Civil War, entrepreneurs required an abundant supply of cheap labor that would mine the coal, cut the timber, and work in the factories. As American farmers increased their production of surplus food supplies, their children were increasingly freed to leave the country and seek to improve their lot in growing cities such as Chicago and New York. The greatest source of the cheap labor supply that fostered urbanization and industrialization was immigration from Europe. Political unrest, war and conscription, and discrimination such as the pogroms aimed at the Jewish population of Tsarist Russia convinced millions from Eastern and Southern Europe to seek opportunity in the growing economy of the United States. These immigrants poured into New York harbor where they were processed at Ellis Island. Some were turned away by government inspectors who were concerned that these new immigrants from Southern and Eastern Europe might be bringing with them infectious diseases, but most were allowed into the country. Despite some nativist concerns, this relatively open immigration well served business interests who could pay lower wages in the crowded labor market. On the Pacific coast, immigration was primarily from Japan, the Philippines, and China. Desperate economic conditions in China fostered unrestricted immigration of "coolie" labor. Paid little and considered expendable, Chinese labor was essential for the construction of the Central Pacific Railroad through the Sierra Nevada Mountains where many of these laborers perished amid dangerous working conditions. Following construction of the transcontinental railroads, there was a racist reaction and persecution in the West toward the Chinese immigrants who were considered a threat to white workers. While there is extensive contemporary political debate regarding immigration from Mexico, during the late nineteenth and early twentieth centuries the border in the Southwest was fluid as Mexican workers crossed freely across the border providing labor for factories and agricultural workers to harvest the farm produce of the region. Unrestricted immigration and the resulting low wages were key factors in the industrialization of America, and the surplus value of this labor, which industrialists used to expand their businesses, proved to be crucial to the excess capital required for the rise of American big business—which was also facilitated by European bankers who found the American economy an attractive source of investment. In the search for the American dream, many discovered the nightmare of American working conditions, yet many immigrant families did find some improvement in status over the generations.

Horatio Alger myth

Government assistance, technology, natural resources, and immigrant labor were exploited by business leaders who were extolled as Horatio Alger types who exemplified the rags to riches mythology made popular by Ben Franklin or denounced as robber barons whose success was due to their ruthless and unscrupulous business practices. Horatio Alger was a Harvard-educated Unitarian minister whose best-selling books of the late nineteenth century celebrated the rise of poor boys to great wealth through hard work and perseverance, although a great deal of luck also seemed to be involved. In a typical Alger scenario, an impoverished youth might sell match boxes and pine for the beautiful daughter of the factory owner. Then, as luck would have it, the young man seized upon his opportunity to rescue the young woman from a fire, and she fell in love with her rescuer who was awarded with a management position in the family business. This formula proved quite successful for Alger in a score of books beginning with *Ragged Dick* (1868), and Alger's name became synonymous with the mythology that American businessmen of the late nineteenth century were examples of poor boys making good—although allegations of sexual misconduct by Alger with young boys are less well known and dissolved the author's relationship with the Unitarian church.

Carnegie and steel

An American industrialist who appears to fit the Horatio Alger type is Andrew Carnegie whose poor family migrated to the United States from Scotland in 1848. Finding employment as a telegraph operator, Carnegie went to work for Thomas A. Scott of the Pennsylvania Railroad. Demonstrating frugality and a strong work ethic, Carnegie made sound investments that allowed him to advance in the railroad business and move into the steel industry. Carnegie made his fortune in steel where he developed the monopolistic practice of vertical integration that allowed him to control every aspect of the burgeoning industry and avoid making payments to the "middleman" or other businessmen. For example, the Carnegie Steel Company gained control of iron ore and coal deposits which were then transported on railroads owned by Carnegie to the smelters and steel plants of the Pittsburgh area, producing almost 2,000 tons of steel per day in the 1880s that played an essential role in the industrialization of the United States. In 1901, Carnegie sold his business to Wall Street banker J. P. Morgan who paid over $400 million for what became the U.S. Steel Corporation. Carnegie devoted his final years to philanthropy, dispensing as much as $350 million to public libraries, foundations, charities, and educational institutions—firmly establishing his reputation as a Horatio Alger figure who earned his wealth through perseverance and hard work, while using his wealth to enhance the quality of life for all Americans. Carnegie's workers, however, did not find the steel magnate to be so generous, and efforts by the Carnegie Steel Company to reduce wages produced a violent confrontation between striking steel workers and Pinkerton detectives brought in by the company to break the Homestead Strike in 1892. Carnegie was also associated with the Johnstown Flood of 1889 in which over two thousand people perished following the collapse of the South Fork Dam about fourteen miles upstream from Johnstown, Pennsylvania. The structural integrity of the dam was undermined by the creation of the South Fork Fishing and Hunting Club of which Carnegie and his business associates were members. While some blamed the exclusive private club for the disaster, Carnegie was still perceived by many as a hero for donating money to the victims of the flood.

Rockefeller and Standard Oil

Although he also established a reputation for philanthropy and described his wealth as a blessing from God, John D. Rockefeller was a businessman and monopolist who earned more of a reputation as a robber baron due to his practices of "cutthroat competition" which financially destroyed many of his business competitors. Growing up in a middle-class family, Rockefeller was influenced by his deeply religious mother, while his father was a salesman and somewhat of a con-artist in his business enterprises. After serving as a bookkeeper in Cleveland, Rockefeller got in on the ground floor of the oil industry in Ohio and Pennsylvania. Not wanting the Civil War to interfere with his budding business career, Rockefeller paid for a substitute to avoid conscription and military service. After establishing the Standard Oil Company in 1870, Rockefeller dominated the oil business in the Eastern United States, but new discoveries of oil in areas such as Texas, Oklahoma, and California threatened his monopoly. Accordingly, Rockefeller would increase prices in the East to cover his losses in the West, where he would charge lower prices until he crushed the competition, buying them out and restoring higher prices for refining the oil after re-establishing monopoly control. He also pushed the railroads to extend rebates to Standard Oil for the lucrative business of the corporation—a volume of business that other companies could not provide. By the end of the century, Standard Oil controlled approximately 95 percent of the oil refineries in the United States. In 1911, the Standard Oil Company was broken up by the government under the Sherman Anti-trust Act for restraint of trade, but companies such as ExxonMobil carved out of Standard Oil continue to dominate the fossil fuel industry. In his old age, Rockefeller became a notable philanthropist who sought to defend his aggressive business tactics by citing both God's blessing and "survival of the fittest" as justification for his monopolistic practices as well as opposition to organized labor that was evident in the violent suppression of strikers against Rockefeller's Colorado Fuel and Iron Company in the 1914 Ludlow Massacre.

Railroads and corruption

While the oil and steel industries dominated the American economy in the twentieth century, the take-off industry for American business following the Civil War was the railroads—an industry that exemplified the close alliance between business and government, exposing the myth of a laissez-faire economy and revealing a degree of corruption that characterized many industrialists as robber barons. The transcontinental railroad was the dream of Abraham Lincoln, and many Republicans in Congress asserted that government support for the railroads would honor the slain President's memory and unify the nation following the sectional conflict. Accordingly, Congress authorized loans to the Union Pacific and Central Pacific Railroads to begin construction of tracks into isolated regions populated primarily by Native Americans who would have to be driven off the land in preparation for white settlement. The federal government also promoted railroad construction with generous grants of land for every mile of track constructed—land grants to the railroads from the national government amounted to over 150,000,000 acres, while millions of additional acres were given away by state and local governments to entice the railroads to build in their states and cities. The railroads were then able to sell these valuable tracts near a transportation route the same way that riverfront property or locations alongside a major highway increase in value. Thus, the railroads were responsible for the rapid settlement of the West as Natives were displaced, while Irish and Chinese laborers were recruited for the rapid and dangerous building of the transcontinental railroad. Numerous Chinese lives were lost as the Central Pacific, under the control of Leland Stanford and Collis P. Huntington, dynamited its way through the Sierra Nevada Mountains. In addition to fostering settlement of the West, the railroads provided what economists refer to as a multiplier effect for the expanding country, encouraging the growth of other industries such as coal, timber, and steel that were required to keep the railroads rolling. This activity culminated in the May 10, 1869 driving of the golden spike at Ogden, Utah, symbolizing the completion of the first transcontinental railroad uniting the Union Pacific and Central Pacific Railroads. This first transcontinental railroad was soon joined by the Northern Pacific, Southern Pacific, and Great Northern rail lines. This orgy of railroad construction contributed to considerable corruption on the local, state, and national levels as lobbyists competed to gain favor with the railroads. To gain the patronage of a large shipper such as Standard Oil, railroads would provide rebates that were unavailable to other customers. Speculators were also eager to cash in on the public's desire to invest in the railroad boom. This speculative frenzy led to watered or worthless stock—a terminology based upon pumping cattle full of water to increase their weight and then selling them for an inflated price—in an unregulated stock and bonds market. Potential investors were often fleeced by unscrupulous businessmen selling stocks in nonexistent railroad enterprises.

Perhaps the most celebrated case regarding worthless stock concerns Cornelius Vanderbilt and his acquisition of the Erie Railroad in New York state. After amassing a fortune in steamship lines, Vanderbilt turned his attention to the railroads and was convinced that the Erie Railroad represented a solid investment. Vanderbilt purchased the railroad from Daniel Drew, who stayed on as treasurer of the corporation. Drew then conspired with speculators Jay Gould and Jim Fisk to defraud Vanderbilt by selling the industrialist additional worthless shares of stock in the Erie Railroad between 1866 and 1868, costing Vanderbilt an additional seven million dollars. Under the legal protection of Tammany Hall, Gould and Fisk proceeded to again manipulate the stock price, and Drew became the victim of a bankruptcy that destroyed his financial career. As for Fisk, he was murdered in 1872 by a romantic rival, and Gould lost control of the Erie Railroad following financial losses in the Panic of 1873. The manipulations and antics of men such as Drew, Fisk, and Gould entertained the public who perceived them as celebrities, but these con-artists also exemplified the corrupt influence of big business such as railroads in the rise of American industry.

Monopoly and Social Darwinism

Big business was also characterized by a drive toward monopoly that culminated in approximately 10 percent of industries controlling over 80 percent of the nation's capital by 1905. The desire to eliminate competition and create monopolistic control over an industry reveal the reality of the late nineteenth and early twentieth-century American economy that bore little resemblance to the myth of an economy guided by the invisible hand of the market. Instead, businesses of the era conspired with government to create a corrupt system in which competition was crushed in favor of monopoly—that is until the government finally recognized that the monopoly industrialists were intent upon destroying the democratic principles upon which the American nation was founded, and reform efforts were made to address the worst abuses of monopoly capitalism. To foster monopoly, industrialists introduced pools and trusts, often justifying these policies by appealing to Social Darwinism. In forming pools, some businesses sought to limit competition and create an oligopoly by fixing prices and dividing the market among themselves. The informal pool agreements were often difficult to enforce, and some monopolists found the formation of a trust to be more dependable. In a trust, competition is eliminated by having the corporations in a given industry place control of their stock in a common board of trustees who will then establish common business practices for the industry. The power of these trusts emerged as threats to capitalism and promoted reforms such as the Sherman Anti-trust Act. Business leaders such as John D. Rockefeller justified their monopolistic practices by appealing to Social Darwinism, an ideology that owed its origins to the classical liberalism of David Ricardo and Thomas Malthus, Charles Darwin's scientific theories of evolution, English philosopher Herbert Spencer, and the writings of Yale sociologist William Graham Sumner who championed laissez-faire economics and argued that government intervention on behalf of the poor or unfit in society would threaten American prosperity. In many ways, the term Social Darwinism was a misnomer as Spencer coined the phrase "survival of the fittest" before publication of Darwin's theories, and while Darwin emphasized natural selection, most philosophers and economists associated with Social Darwinism believed in a fixed natural order with which they feared that government might interfere. Poverty was thus the fault of the poor, while the wealthy enjoyed their privileged position due to thrift and hard work. Private philanthropy was admirable, but government action on behalf of the working class would destroy the natural order of things. Although few conservatives today would refer to themselves as Social Darwinists, they still maintain allegiance to the idea that the poor are shiftless and lazy, while government welfare policies undermine individualism and foster dependence.

Yet these same advocates of free enterprise and laissez-faire capitalism seem to have no problem with government intervention in the economy on behalf of big business. The next chapter will examine in some detail how the alliance between politics and big business was forged in the late nineteenth century, culminating in challenges to the monopolistic capitalist system by reformers such as the Populists and Progressives, as well as more radical alternatives to the existing order with anarchism, socialism, syndicalism, and communism.

Further Reading:

Chandler, Alfred D. Jr. *The Visible Hand: The Managerial Revolution in American Business*. Cambridge, MA: Harvard University Press, 1978.

Chernow, Ron. *Titan: The Life of John D. Rockefeller Sr.* New York: Random House, 1988.

Hays, Samuel P. *The Response to Industrialism, 1885–1914*. Chicago: University of Chicago Press, 1957.

Hofstadter, Richard. *Social Darwinism in American Thought*. Boston: Beacon Press, 1955.

Josephson, Matthew. *The Robber Barons: The Great American Capitalists, 1861-1901*. New York: Harcourt, Brace and Company, 1934.

Lamoreaux, Naomi. *The Great Merger Movement in American Business, 1895–1904* (1985).

Perrow, Charles. *Organizing America: Wealth, Power, and the Origins of Corporate Capitalism*. New York: Cambridge University Press, 2002.

Rodgers, Daniel T. *The Work Ethic in Industrial America, 1850–1920*. Chicago: University of Chicago Press, 1978.

White, Richard. *Railroaded: The Transcontinentals and the Making of Modern America*. New York: W.W. Norton & Company, 2011.

Zunz, Olivier. *Making America Corporate, 1870–1920*. Chicago: University of Chicago Press, 1990.

16

Late Nineteenth Century
Politics and Populism

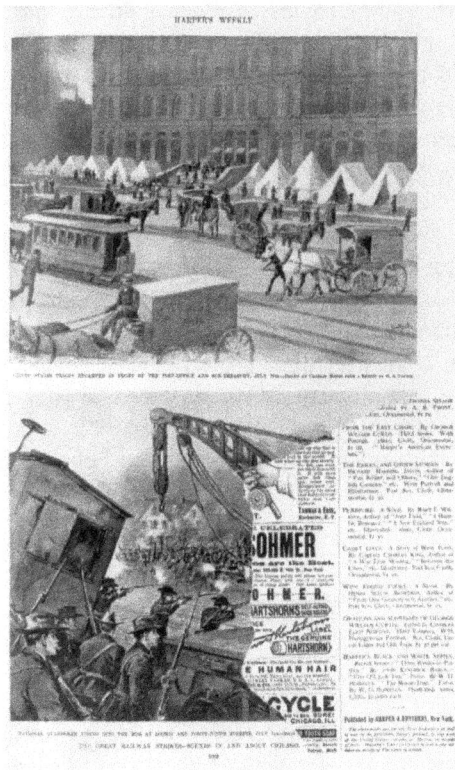

"The Great Railway Strikes. Scenes in and about Chicago." Drawing by Charles Mente in *Harper's Weekly*, 1894. Library of Congress. The rise of monopoly capitalism in the late nineteenth century led to numerous clashes between labor and capital. The drawing from *Harper's Weekly* depicts the Panic of 1893 that led to the Pullman Strike over which Eugene Debs and the American Railway Union exercised leadership before being crushed by government military intervention.

American politics in the late nineteenth century are often ignored in favor of the Populist and Progressive reform movements, but the period between 1876 and 1900 was crucial in shaping modern America. The bearded Presidents of the era are not well known today, but they presided over the close alliance between business and politics which characterizes the American political system. While the Republican Party usually prevailed at the Presidential level, there was strong party competition for control of the Congress. Following the overthrow of Reconstruction associated with the Republicans, the white "redeemers" of the South established Jim Crow segregation and aligned with the Democratic Party which dominated Southern politics until Lyndon Johnson pushed the Civil Rights Act of 1964 through Congress and Republican leaders such as Richard Nixon responded with a Southern strategy that characterizes regional politics today. The Republican Party, with its strength primarily in the Northeast and Midwest, was also divided between Stalwarts, who tended to place party above country and formed the core of the party, and reformers who were referred to in the pejorative sense with the terms "Mugwumps" and "Half-breeds"—reflecting the racism of the period. The alliance between business and politics that promoted big business and industry produced a political reaction in rural America that marked the final protest of Jeffersonian agrarian democracy in opposition to the Hamiltonian industrial order. While there is a tendency today to dismiss the politics of rural and small-town America as reactionary, it is worth remembering the democratic potential of the Populist insurgency that was circumvented with the election of William McKinley in 1896.

Hayes Presidency

The Presidency of Rutherford B. Hayes was clouded by the disputed election of 1876 and the premature abandonment of Reconstruction despite the President's personal commitment to civil rights. In his campaign, Hayes promised that he would restore integrity to the government after eight years of the Grant administration mired in scandal. Symbolically, this cleaning up of the White House was conducted by Mrs. Rutherford Hayes, referred to as "Lemonade Lucy" for her efforts to banish alcohol from Presidential functions. Her husband attempted to honor his reform pledge by removing Chester A. Arthur as Collector at the Port of New York which placed Arthur in charge of collecting the revenue from the high tariffs placed on imports passing through the port of New York City. In this official capacity, Arthur insured that the coffers of the Republican Party received a significant share of the taxes collected at the port. The firing of Arthur angered the Stalwart faction of the party and Arthur's patron, New York Senator Roscoe B. Conkling. For his party service, and not his honesty, Arthur was rewarded in 1880 with the Republican Vice-Presidential nomination. On the other hand, the Hayes administration employed federal troops to crush the strike that began in 1877 when the Baltimore and Ohio Railroad cut wages and prompted a labor stoppage that spread to other Eastern and Midwestern rail lines. Over one hundred workers were killed in the ensuing violence that characterized the growing class struggle in America as workers unionized in resistance to the growing power of big business in American life.

The Stalwart faction of the Republican Party, nevertheless, refused to support Hayes for another term, and the 1880 Presidential nomination was bestowed upon Ohio Congressman James Garfield as a compromise choice between the rival factions of the party. Garfield was viewed by some in the Stalwart faction as a reformer, so Senator Conkling insisted that Chester Arthur be nominated for Vice President. The Democrats selected Winfield Scott Hancock who had a distinguished record as a Union commander during the Civil War. Hancock could depend upon support from the solid Democratic South, and the party hoped that his war record would entice Northern voters. Democratic opposition to the tariff, however, limited the Northern support for Hancock's candidacy.

Garfield assassination and civil service reform

After winning the Presidency in a relatively close election, Garfield was besieged by office seekers, indicative of the considerable patronage powers of the Chief Executive. On July 2, 1881, Garfield was shot at a train station in Washington DC by a dissatisfied office seeker, Charles J. Guiteau. Garfield did not immediately succumb to his wounds, but there is evidence that the lack of attention paid to sanitation by the physician in charge of caring for the President's wounds led to an infection which eventually resulted in Garfield's death on September 19, 1881. Suffering from his wounds, Garfield was unable to attend to the duties of his office, and it is likely that he would have been forced to step down from the Presidency under the disability provisions of the Twenty-fifth Amendment passed in the wake of the John Kennedy assassination. Guiteau's attorney attempted to use the poor work by Garfield's attending physician to save his client's life, but Guiteau was executed for the murder of the President.

With the death of Garfield, Vice President Arthur ascended to the Presidency. Although the new President was associated with the Stalwart faction and had a reputation for corruption, Arthur became a champion for reform when he signed the

Pendleton or Civil Service Reform Act into law over the opposition of the Stalwarts. The legislation passed by Congress in response to the Garfield assassination sought to limit patronage pressures on the President by expanding the number of government positions that would be awarded by competitive merit-based civil service examination rather than political appointment to the highest bidder. The act was lauded for making competence rather than political influence the criterion for government office. This reform, however, had the unintended consequence of making political parties even more dependent upon contributions from business to finance campaigns. Before civil service reform, the political parties solicited contributions or "kickbacks" for political appointments—on one level selling the offices in the belief that "to the victor belong the spoils." With this avenue of revenue somewhat limited by civil service reform, politicians increasingly sought large contributions from business interests who were motivated by securing legislative and regulatory favors, forging an alliance between business and politicians that continues to plague the American political system and provide large contributors with influence beyond the reach of most Americans—posing significant challenges to implementing the democratic principles enunciated by Jefferson and Lincoln.

Mongrel tariff and Chinese exclusion

Reform, however, was not the top priority of Congress during the Arthur administration. Initially presented as an effort to adjust excessive tariff rates, the Tariff Act of 1883, instead, raised the rate on many imported goods and became referred to pejoratively as the "Mongrel Tariff." This legislation filled the coffers of the U.S. Treasury, and the United States confronted a surplus rather than a deficit problem. Congress responded to the surplus issue by increasing spending on projects that many critics labeled as "pork barrel legislation," contributing to the corruption and scandal of the era. In 1882, Congress enacted a nefarious piece of discriminatory legislation in the Chinese Exclusion Act, which was the first Congressional action to single out a specific nationality or ethnic group to be forbidden from entering the United States which normally welcomed the cheap labor supply provided by immigration. Chinese labor was initially contracted to play a crucial role in the building of railroads such as the Central Pacific. After the construction of the transcontinental railroad, however, there were concerns that the growing Chinese population in the West posed a threat to white jobs and social mobility. The Chinese were depicted as reducing the standard of living by their willingness to accept lower wages and live in abysmal conditions that decent Americans would find unacceptable. Politicians and self-proclaimed reformers also accused the Chinese of debasing American culture through the introduction of opium dens into Western cities, ignoring the history of the Opium Wars in which the British foisted opium from India upon the Chinese. In response to this derogatory propaganda, the Chinese population in the West was subjected to the type of discrimination, lynch mobs, and violence that plagued black Americans in the South. Many Western states also enacted discriminatory legislation limiting Chinese ownership of land. The Chinese Exclusion Act was not repealed until 1943 when China was the ally of the United States against Japan during the Second World War

Election of 1884 and Cleveland Presidency

Despite continuing high tariffs and the signing of the Chinese Exclusion Act, Arthur's reputation among the Stalwarts was soiled by his support for civil service reform. Accordingly, in 1884, the Republicans ignored Arthur and selected as their Presidential nominee James G. Blaine, "the man from Maine," who served as Secretary of State under Garfield and was admired by the Stalwart faction. Angered by the nomination of Blaine with his reputation for corruption, the Mugwumps or reform Republicans refused to support the party's nominee, with many voting for the Democratic candidate, Grover Cleveland. A former Governor of New York, Cleveland embraced the idea that the role of the national government in the economy was limited—although he would later approve the use of troops to crush the Pullman Strike in 1894. Much of the campaign focused upon personal issues with Blaine tainted by the "Mulligan letters," in which as a Congressman, Blaine allegedly admitted to accepting bribes from business interests. Cleveland, on the other hand, was accused of fathering a child out of wedlock while serving as Mayor of Buffalo. The bachelor candidate acknowledged the relationship and accepted financial responsibility for the child. Blaine supporters sought to discredit Cleveland by chanting, "Ma, ma, where's my pa," to which the Democrats replied, "Gone to the White House, ha, ha, ha." Cleveland survived the scandal, and Blaine suffered greater political damage when a New York Protestant minister, speaking on behalf of the Republican candidate, denounced the Democrats as a party of "Rum, Romanism, and Rebellion." Cleveland received a slight plurality in New York which provided the necessary electoral votes for his narrow victory. With New York and the South in his column, Cleveland became the first Democrat to be elected President since the Civil War, essentially putting to an end to the Republican tradition of "waving the bloody shirt" in national elections.

Cleveland enjoyed a reputation for honesty, and in support of his philosophy of limited government, the President opposed the tariff and subsidies to businesses as well as compensation for veterans and farmers seeking relief from drought conditions. Believing that Reconstruction was a failure, Cleveland expressed little interest in supporting enforcement of the Fourteenth and Fifteenth Amendments in the South. More attention was paid by the public to his personal life when the President married twenty-one-year-old Francis Folsom, the daughter of his former law partner. Despite the considerable age difference between the President and his young bride, there was little public criticism of the marriage, and the birth of their first child, Ruth was widely celebrated—with the candy bar "Baby Ruth" named after Cleveland's daughter and not the baseball star Babe Ruth as many assume.

Tariffs, Jim Crow, and restrictions on democracy

In 1888, Cleveland easily won re-nomination by the Democrats and was opposed by Benjamin Harrison, the Republican Senator from Indiana and grandson of former President and military hero, William Henry Harrison. Again, the election was extremely close, and Cleveland won the popular vote, but the Democrat suffered defeat in the Electoral College when Harrison gained all of the electoral votes from New York after winning the state by approximately 15,000 votes. Seeking business support, Harrison campaigned on a platform endorsing high protective tariffs, and as President he signed into law the McKinley Tariff—guided to Congressional passage by Ohio Representative William McKinley who ascended to the Presidency in 1896—that enacted the highest average tariff rates in American history. The protective tariff again produced a surplus and stimulated the spending of the Fifty-first Congress, known as the "Billion Dollar Congress," and once again contributing to the graft and corruption of the era promoting business expansion. While the tariffs and spending bills dominated the Harrison administration, the President did express concern about Southern violations of the Fifteenth Amendment, and Congress considered a force act that would have re-introduced federal troops into the region. Alarmed by this potential legislation, Southern states began to pass laws to protect Jim Crow segregation and the disenfranchisement of black voters. To limit black suffrage, Southern states enacted literacy tests which could be administered in a racially discriminatory fashion, property qualifications, and a poll tax one paid to vote. Some Southern states sought to protect the ballot for poor Southern whites through a grandfather clause that would allow one the franchise if that right was extended to the voter's grandfather—a provision that would disenfranchise blacks whose ancestors were enslaved. Some states in the region also proposed white primary laws that designated political parties as private organizations that could establish their own rules for participation. Thus, it would be legal for the Democratic Party to ban blacks from voting in the party's primary elections. Blacks, however, would be allowed to vote in the general election, and the Fifteenth Amendment would, thus, be protected. The catch was that by the late nineteenth century the Republican Party had virtually disappeared in most Southern states, and the Republicans often did not even field candidates in the general election. Accordingly, elections were decided in the Democratic primary in which blacks were not allowed to participate. Many of these discriminatory provisions remained in effect until challenged by the Civil Rights Movement.

While Congress and the Presidents of the era focused upon business subsidies such as the tariff and ignored the plight of black Americans, the democratic promise of America was still denied to half of the nation's population. Thwarted in their effort to incorporate female suffrage into the Fifteenth Amendment, suffragettes Elizabeth Cady Stanton and Susan B. Anthony continued the struggle for women's rights and votes throughout the late nineteenth century and into the early twentieth century, although the Nineteenth Amendment providing for women's suffrage was not ratified until after the death of both women. In her later years, Stanton was a divisive figure in the women's movement with publication of *The Woman's Bible* (1895) in which she criticized the sexism of orthodox Christianity. Anthony maintained her concentration on the suffrage issue, insisting that the Fourteenth Amendment, with its provision that all persons born or naturalized in the United States were citizens and entitled to the full rights of citizenship, implicitly provided for female suffrage as women were citizens. After appealing to this interpretation of the Constitution, Anthony was arrested in Rochester, New York for attempting to vote in the 1872 Presidential election. She was found guilty but refused to pay the fine as she continued her crusade for the ballot which was finally realized in 1920.

Challenges confronting American farmers

Despite the best efforts of Anthony and other suffragettes, the nation's political focus in the nineteenth century centered upon an agrarian challenge to the emerging industrial order that culminated in the Populist Party. Farmers were suffering from a political system that bestowed favors upon business and industry in exchange for campaign contributions and financial support. For example, high protective tariffs upon industrial products insured that farmers paid high prices for items such as plows that were protected from foreign competition. The price for agricultural goods, on the other hand, was established by the market and not subject to tariff protection. For the transportation of these products, farmers were increasingly dependent upon the railroads which often exercised monopolistic control over shipping rates, and farmers were not extended the rebates often provided for big business. Farmers also required more generous credit provisions from the banking system as the nature of agricultural production meant that farmers needed to borrow money that would carry them until harvest and the selling of their crop. Without money coming in on a regular basis as it did for other occupations, farmers were dependent upon long term credit. In addition, farmers were subject to high taxes from local and state governments who depended upon property taxes, while many businesses paid little in the way of taxes for there were no corporate or income taxes. And farmers, working individually to maximize production and hopefully earn some profits, failed to recognize that their very success contributed to overproduction and falling market prices.

The Grange and anti-monopoly sentiment

The first major farmer political organization to challenge the inequities of the industrial order was the Grange formed by Oliver H. Kelly in the Midwest. The Grange initially functioned as a fraternal organization for isolated farmers and their families. As they gathered for fellowship, the attention of farmers turned toward how the political system was stacked against them, and the Grange embraced politics, electing members to the state legislatures in the Midwest. A series of Granger laws were enacted providing for state regulation of the excessive rates charged by the railroads in the region. Railroad operators took umbrage to this political revolt and sought relief in the courts to protect their monopolistic control. In the 1886 *Wabash* Case, the Supreme Court of the United States overturned the Granger laws passed in the Midwest, ruling that under the Constitution states did not enjoy the power to regulate interstate commerce such as the railroads. Following this defeat in the Supreme Court, the Grange retreated from political protest and assumed a more social and educational role in the lives of farmers.

The political activity of the Grange, however, did have repercussions on the national level as the *Wabash* ruling acknowledged that the Congress did have the power to regulate the interstate commerce of the railroads. Accordingly, in 1877 Congress passed the Interstate Commerce Act that provided for an Interstate Commerce Commission to assure that railroad rates be "reasonable and just." The Commission, however, was not given the power to fix railroad rates. Rather, the focus was upon the publication of railroad rates, forbidding rebates, and abandoning the discriminatory long haul/short haul practice that allowed railroads to charge more for shipping goods a short distance. While preferring no governmental regulation, railroad operators favored national legislation as opposed to combatting various state laws, with one uniform system providing greater efficiency. In addition, railroad operators and other businesses lobbied to assure that their representatives, who claimed knowledge of the industry, be placed on regulatory boards such as the Interstate Commerce Commission—in effect, limiting public oversight by allowing business to regulate itself. The rising political protest against monopoly also convinced Congress to enact the Sherman Anti-trust Act in 1890 that allowed the government to break up trusts or monopolies in restraint of trade. The legislation was vaguely worded and inconsistently applied, with the act often employed in its early years to prohibit the formation of trade unions.

These rather tepid forms of regulation on the national level did not stop the growing protest and concern over monopoly and the alliance between business and politics that guided the new industrial order. Anti-monopoly sentiment was fueled by the writings of Henry George and Edward Bellamy. George was a journalist who addressed the increase in poverty within the United States just as the overall economy and technology were registering sustained progress. In his influential work *Progress and Poverty* (1879), George proposed the single tax as a solution for this economic and social enigma. According to George, the propertied class profited from the pressures of a growing population upon a fixed supply of land. A single tax of 100 percent upon the windfall profits from land ownership would eliminate the inequity that characterized the monopolistic American capitalistic system. The anti-monopoly ideas of George were also echoed in the best-selling novel *Looking Backward* (1889) by Bellamy. In the novel, the protagonist falls into a deep sleep and awakens in the year 2000 to discover that the inequalities of late nineteenth-century America have been addressed through the nationalization of big business and natural resources to serve the public interest. This utopian socialist solution to the nation's ills found a following among reformers and Bellamy Clubs joined with Single Tax Clubs to discuss solutions for the challenge to American democracy posed by the trusts.

Populist Party Platform

Perhaps the most powerful manifestation of this political discontent was the Populist Party which began as the Farmers' Alliance in the Midwest and South. While the Populists have been denounced as reactionaries for anti-Semitic attacks upon Jewish bankers and supporting Jim Crow in the South, the Populist Party was also a democratic response to the centralization of economic and political power in the new industrial order. The Populist farmers made common cause with single tax reformers, organized labor, and even black voters and Republicans in some Southern states such as North Carolina. Enjoying considerable political influence in Midwestern states such as Kansas, the Populists initially appeared as a real threat to the two-party system, and in 1892 the Populists nominated Iowa Congressman James Weaver for the Presidency and endorsed a political platform that would have significant long-range impact upon the American political system. Seeking to address the power of monopoly, the Populist platform called for governmental control and regulation of monopolies and the railroads. To assure that industrialists paid their fair share of taxes, the Populists advocated a graduated income tax. The platform also endorsed the Australian or secret ballot for American elections to prevent the political intimidation of farmers by lenders and banks. To provide for a more democratic political system, the Populists insisted that the Constitution be amended so that Senators were elected by the people rather than the state legislatures. This reform would eliminate the control maintained by big business over state legislatures who were bribed to make the Senate what critics called a "millionaires club." Calling for the abolition of private banks, the Populist platform advocated the establishment of a federal loan system to insure farmers the long-term credit that their vocation required. Farmers would also be able to exercise some control over agricultural prices through federal storage facilities for their crops. An appeal was made to organized labor with the endorsement of an eight-hour day as well as call for the abolishment of employing detectives from organizations such as the Pinkerton Agency to serve as strike breakers in labor disputes. The Populists also created controversy with their demand for the free coinage of silver which would add to inflation by making silver as well as gold the basis for the nation's money supply. As debtors, farmers believed that cheap money would make it easier to pay off their debts and farm mortgages, although many workers worried more about rising rents and prices.

The Populist platform, nevertheless, had considerable appeal to many American voters, and in the Presidential election of 1892 James Weaver garnered the electoral votes of four states. The new party did well in the Midwest and West where Mary Elizabeth Lease, a suffragette and supporter of Henry George, urged farmers to "grow less corn and raise more hell." Although concerned about the rise of a third party, the Democrats and Republicans continued to dominate the national political stage. President Harrison and the Republican Party were criticized for the protectionist McKinley Tariff and subsequent rising prices, while the Democrats again turned to the personally popular Cleveland, who advocated lowering the tariff and opposed government interference in the American economy. In a three-party race, Cleveland received a plurality of the popular vote and attained the required majority in the Electoral College. Cleveland remains the only President to be elected to a non-consecutive term in office.

Panic of 1893 and Coxey's Army

During his second term, Cleveland was confronted with an economic crisis in the Panic of 1893. The Panic was caused by an international banking crisis in Argentina that prompted European investors to make a run on gold reserves in the U.S. Treasury, eroding the confidence of American businesses who contracted and laid off many workers. Prices declined, and farmers were increasingly concerned about losing their land. Cleveland tended to blame the crisis upon the Sherman Silver Purchase Act of 1890 that had renewed limited government purchase of silver—a policy favored by Western mining interests. Accordingly, Cleveland convinced Congress to repeal the Sherman Silver Purchase Act, but this did little to alleviate the economic Panic engulfing the nation. Led by Ohio businessman Jacob Coxey, the unemployed of Coxey's Army marched on the nation's capital, demanding that the President and Congress revive the economy with a $500 million federal works program. Only a few hundred of Coxey's followers completed the march to Washington, where they were ignored by Cleveland, who rejected any tope of governmental intervention on behalf of the unemployed and insisted that the nation stay on the gold standard.

The unrest exemplified by Coxey's Army is often interpreted as influencing L. Frank Baum to pen *The Wonderful Wizard of Oz*—the first in a series of Oz books that was published in 1900. Although Baum denied that this tale was meant to be a political parable, he was a close observer of the Populist insurgency in the Midwest, and the parallels with the political climate of the 1890s are striking. The cyclone from Kansas that carried Dorothy Gale into Oz may be equated with the Populist Party. In Oz, Dorothy becomes the champion of the munchkins or the common little people. She is dispatched on a journey to seek relief for the common people by appealing to the all-powerful wizard who lives in the capital city of Oz, symbolic of Cleveland and Washington DC. On her march to Oz, Dorothy is joined by the Scarecrow and Tin Man who seem to reflect the union of farmers and workers seeking government relief. This trio is joined by the Cowardly Lion who may represent Coxey or the 1896 Presidential candidate of the Populists, William Jennings Bryan. When they reach Oz, Dorothy and her friends find that the Wizard is not all-powerful and can do little for them—just as Cleveland declined to address the grievances of Coxey's Army. Dorothy and her associates were instructed to follow the yellow brick road or gold standard embraced by Cleveland which brought them little relief. Instead, the answer to their quest lies in the magic of Dorothy's silver slippers which corresponds nicely to the Populist crusade for free silver. The historical analogy does not work out quite as well for the 1939 film as Dorothy acquires ruby slippers which looked better in the color format of the film.

Election of 1896

Unable to simply click their silver slippers together, the Populists, farmers, workers, and unemployed of the mid-1890s suffered greatly from the Panic and Cleveland's failure to act—although he intervened with the military to suppress the Pullman Strike. The Presidential election of 1896, however, offered another political opportunity to address their plight. While continuing to support industrial subsidies such as the tariff, the Republicans nominated Ohio Governor and former Congressman William McKinley, who agreed with Cleveland that the country should stay on the gold standard and not support measures such as the purchase of silver that would inflate the economy. McKinley's candidacy was promoted by wealthy industrialist Marcus Hanna who was caricatured as the candidate's puppet master. Fearing that McKinley might make a mistake on the campaign trail, Hanna managed a front-porch campaign in which delegations journeyed to McKinley's Ohio home to meet with the candidate in a political environment controlled by Hanna. The Democrats in 1896 moved in a considerably different direction. After repudiating Cleveland for his handling of the economic crisis, the Democrats selected William Jennings Bryan, a thirty-six-year old Congressman from Nebraska, who had electrified the party convention with his "Cross of Gold" speech, denouncing big business for crucifying common workers and farmers on a cross of gold by refusing to abandon the gold standard. With Bryan as their standard bearer, the Democrats essentially endorsed or stole the Populist platform. Bryan campaigned for the free coinage of silver, a graduated or progressive income tax, and greater government regulation of business. Meeting a few months later, the Populist Party reluctantly concluded that they had no choice but to endorse the candidacy of Bryan who was running on the Populist platform, although they tried to demonstrate some independence by selecting their own candidate for Vice President with Congressman Tom Watson of Georgia. The dilemma of the Populist Party in 1896 well illustrates the problems confronting a third party in the American political system. If a third party such as the Populists emerge with strong popular support, the two main parties will simply embrace their ideas and coopt their platform as the Democrats did with the Populists in 1896. Although this may be changing somewhat in contemporary politics, the Democratic and Republican Parties have essentially been non-ideological organizations more intent upon winning elections than enforcing ideological orthodoxy. Thus, most of the provisions outlined by the Populists in their 1892 platform were implemented at a later date by the Democratic and Republican Parties.

Enjoying the support of both Democrats and Populists, many expected Bryan, with his oratorical skills and vigorous campaigning, to prevail over McKinley who stayed on his Ohio front porch. However, a number of factors propelled McKinley to victory in both the popular and electoral vote. First and foremost, the McKinley campaign with the support of Hanna and other wealthy industrialists had access to far greater financial resources than the Democrats could muster. Bryan also had to deal with the fact that many voters blamed the Democrats and Grover Cleveland for the Panic of 1893. In addition, the issue of free silver and an inflated money supply had a rather limited appeal. Inflation was attractive to many farmers who were heavily in debt and preferred to pay off their obligations and mortgages with cheaper money. Factory workers, on the other hand, did not own their homes and feared that inflation would diminish their wages with higher rents and prices. Business owners played on these fears by telling their workers that if Bryan was elected, they would have no choice but to close the factory gates and shut down the business. Notices to this effect were placed in the pay envelopes of many workers. In the final analysis, Bryan did well in the South and West, but he was unable to prevail in the industrialized states of the Northeast.

Legacy of Populism

To many commentators and historians, the election of 1896 marked the final battle between Jeffersonian agrarianism and the Hamiltonian industrial order. The future of the nation once and for all belonged to business and industry as the Populist Party declined after the 1896 Bryan campaign and was essentially absorbed into the Democratic Party. In the South, Democrats used racial divisions to thwart fusion between Populists and Republicans, culminating in a Wilmington, North Carolina race riot directed at black political participation. But reform was hardly dead in the United States. The predatory policies of big business and the harsh factory conditions produced working-class resistance with labor unrest and a growing socialist movement, while the insecurities of the urban middle class produced the Progressive reform movement. Before examining these insurgencies against the industrial order, it is worth taking some time to consider the resistance of Natives, especially the Plains Indians, to the expansion of business into the American West. The politics of the late nineteenth century established a close alignment between big business and politics that endangered the democratic promise of America, but resistance to this system remains an essential element of American history and the country's egalitarian principles.

Further Reading:

Cherny, Robert W. *American Politics in the Gilded Age, 1868–1900*. Wheeling, IL: Harlan Davidson, 1997.

Edwards, Rebecca. *New Spirits: Americans in the Gilded Age, 1865–1905*. New York: Oxford University Press, 2006.

Faulkner, Harold U. *Politics, Reform, and Expansion, 1890–1900*. New York: Harper & Row, 1959.

Glad, Paul W. *McKinley, Bryan and the People*. Philadelphia: Lippincott, 1964.

Goodwyn, Lawrence. *Democratic Promise: The Populist Moment in America*. New York: Oxford University Press, 1976.

Kazin, Michael. *The Populist Persuasion: An American History*. New York: Basic Books, 1995.

Kleppner, Paul. *The Third Electoral System, 1853–1892: Parties, Voters, and Political Cultures*. Chapel Hill, NC: University of North Carolina Press, 1979.

McMath, Robert C. *American Populism: A Social History, 1877–1898*. New York: Hill and Wang, 1993.

Millard, Candice. *Destiny of the Republic: A Tale of Madness, Medicine, and the Murder of a President*. New York: Doubleday, 2011.

Morgan, Wayne H. *From Hayes to McKinley: National Party Politics, 1877-1896*. Syracuse, NY: Syracuse University Press, 1969.

17

The American West: Anglo Settlement and Native American Response

GENERAL CUSTER'S DEATH STRUGGLE.
The Battle of the Little Big Horn.

"General Custer's Death Struggle: The Battle of the Little Big Horn." Painting by H. Steinegger and published by The Pacific Art Company of San Francisco, 1878. Prints and Photographs Division, Library of Congress. On June 25-26, 1876, Sioux, Cheyenne, and Arapaho warriors under the leadership of Crazy Horse and Sitting Bull defeated George Armstrong Custer and the Seventh Cavalry at the Battle of Littlebig Horn. This greatest Native victory in the Indian Wars led the United States government to pursue a policy of conquest that eventually forced the Sioux onto the Pine Ridge Reservation.

As big business consolidated its control of the American economy and politics following the Civil War, white settlers poured into the Great Plains and Rocky Mountains. With the exception of the Mormons in Utah, this region was considered inhospitable to Anglo settlement and farming, allowing the Plains Indians to pursue the buffalo in a nomadic lifestyle that existed in harmony with the climate and geography of the Great Plains. For many farmers, expansion was halted along the 98th parallel due to a lack of rainfall. The discovery of gold in California and the rich farmland of the Oregon territory enticed settlers to pass over the Great Plains and Rocky Mountains, but after the Civil War, the continuing demand for land induced farmers and business into a region described in many older maps as the Great American Desert. It was not the best farm land to say the least, and it was occupied by a Native population that resisted the Anglo assault upon their land and way of life. Although hardly the virgin land celebrated by many of its promoters, the American West of the Great Plains represented the largest remaining territory in the United States not penetrated by white settlement. The railroad expansion of the post-Civil War era helped to lure settlers westward, and the government encouraged this growth through land grants to the railroads, passage of the Homestead Act, and military removal of the Plains Indians on to reservations. The Trans-Mississippi West between 1865 and 1900 is often celebrated as the triumph of American democracy and individualism; a perspective developed by scholars such as Frederick Jackson Turner and William Prescott Webb as well as in the popular culture of the dime novels and that most American of film genres—the Western. The American cowboy has become a symbol of the cult of rugged individualism, but the settlement of the West was much more diverse than the cowboy stereotype. The story of the Trans-Mississippi West involves the role played by women, farmers, miners, ranchers, Hispanics already living in the region, African Americans, Natives, and immigrants from China and around the world. The government promoted the development of the region through a series of frontiers focusing upon mining, ranching, and farming in which big business played a far more significant role than is generally acknowledged. This development was destructive of the environment with mining and logging industries placing profits above conservation and future generations. In addition, the exploitive nature of these extractive industries fostered considerable labor conflict in the West. The American West lacked adequate water resources to support the sustained economic development of the region. Over cultivation of the Great Plains with limited rainfall contributed to one of the greatest environmental disasters of American history with the Dust Bowl of the 1930s. But perhaps the greatest tragedy of the American West was the destruction of the Plains Indian culture through the slaughter of the buffalo and a series of bloody wars that assigned proud nations such as the Sioux or Lakota people to some of the worst land and living conditions in the nation.

Mining Frontier

Major discoveries of precious metals such as gold, silver, and copper attracted prospectors into the West in search of making it rich and attaining the American dream. The strikes were widespread throughout the West with productive mines established in Colorado, Nevada, Montana, Idaho, and the Black Hills of South Dakota. The independent prospectors initially attracted by these discoveries came from throughout the United States and the world, including many who had journeyed unsuccessfully to California in search of gold but now hoped to change their luck in the Rocky Mountains. Of course, the vast majority of these prospectors never made significant claims, but the story of impoverished Irish immigrant John MacKay who gained control of the rich silver deposits in Nevada's Comstock Lode kept the hope of gaining a fortune alive just as Americans continue to pursue the long shot of winning the lottery. These prospectors were usually males who had left their families in pursuit of finding a fortune. They searched for gold and silver with a pick axe and shovel, while employing placer mining to look for precious metals in stream beds. Their possessions and equipment were usually carried on a couple of mules, and these independent prospectors lived isolated and lonely lives. The individual prospectors, however, sometimes did make discoveries and filed claims for the metals they uncovered. The problem for these prospectors was that they lacked the capital to extract the valuable gold and silver which was usually embedded in rock deposits deep beneath the ground. To excavate these mines required considerable capital and labor, and the prospectors did not possess these types of resources. Accordingly, the prospector would sell his claim to big business interests who could provide the funds for developing the mines. The rugged individualism of the prospector was quickly replaced by the power of monopolists such as John D. Rockefeller who invested heavily in Western mining and recruited laborers for the drudgery as well as the dangerous work required for extracting the mineral wealth.

The lure of riches drew many men to the West, and the mining industry was characterized by a boom and bust psychology. After a vein was discovered, many businesses were attracted to provide laborers and prospectors with needed supplies. Mining communities required general stores to equip the miners—and it is worth noting that Levi Strauss got its start providing jeans or work clothes in the mining fields of California. With money flowing, banks were often one of the first businesses opened, along with bars and bordellos to provide pleasure for the miners. In fact, the three b's of bordello, bar, and bank were often established under one roof or tent in the early days of the mining camps. Prostitutes were recruited to provide the miners with sexual favors. The women were exploited by pimps and the miners, but there were few avenues of advancement for poor women in the American West. Occupations such as mining were closed to female labor, and prostitution offered at least a possibility of advancement for women who were able to use the sex industry in the West to attain a degree of social mobility through marriage or owning their own bordello. Although many mining communities went through the boom and bust cycle of the extractive industries, some stabilized over time and attracted families and more permanent businesses. But typical of the mining industry concentration upon immediate profits and depleting mineral deposits was the rise of a ghost town such as Shakespeare, Arizona where once a thriving community had existed. Another good example of this overexpansion was the city of Bisbee, Arizona which was once the largest Western city between St. Louis and San Francisco, but today Bisbee is primarily an art colony with tourists visiting abandoned copper mines. While at the local level the mining industry was extremely volatile, fostering labor unrest and paying little attention to environmental constraints, on the national level the gold and silver discoveries in the West contributed to an increased money supply that fueled the nation's industrialization as well as political division over the free silver issue.

Cattle drives and cowboys

While the mining industry was significant to the development of the American economy, the Western industry that has most captured the public imagination is the ranching frontier and the cowboy. The ranching frontier began in Texas following the Civil War. With the collapse of Confederate currency, Texans had little money, but there were plenty of longhorn cattle that freely roamed the state's grasslands. The cattle were a tremendous source of potential wealth as with population growth throughout the country, and especially in the Northeast, there was a demand for beef. The problem was that the railroads which could get the cattle to slaughterhouses in Chicago and then to Eastern markets did not go through Texas. The transcontinental railroads that connected the nation ran through Kansas and Missouri. To tap the Texas cattle market, Joseph McCoy of the Kansas Pacific Railroad announced that his rail line would make Abilene, Kansas a shipping point for Texas cattle. He would pay top dollar for Texas beef, leading ranchers such as Charles Goodnight to form cattle drives that would take the cattle from their Texas homes to the railheads in Kansas and Missouri.

While an important Western industry that refilled the coffers of Texas ranchers and profited the railways and packing plants of Chicago, the cattle drive also helped to form the iconic American image of the cowboy as an independent and courageous figure who tamed the frontier—although the Spanish influence of the vaquero and Mexican ranching traditions are rarely acknowledged in the popular culture and advertising industry that established the cowboy as a romantic figure. For example, the cigarette industry employed the rugged individual image of the cowboy to sell their products, but in reality the actor portraying "the Marlboro man" ended up a cancer victim. The life of a cowboy on the cattle drives was more boring and dangerous than romantic. Also, viewers of the Western genre on film and television might be surprised to learn that many cowboys in the exploitive ranching industry were African Americans.

The cattle drives were long with the famous Chisholm Trail extending over a thousand miles. The drives moved slowly, averaging approximately fifteen miles per day as the cattle needed to graze on the open range so that they would not lose weight on the journey and be able to fetch a top price when arriving at the railhead. Ten to twelve cowboys were employed to guide the herds of sometimes several thousand head of cattle. The drives would last for months with the cowboys working everyday to keep the cattle moving, and payday would not come until the herd was sold at the railhead. While sleeping out under the stars every night might sound romantic, cowboys had little shelter from the elements when exposed to rain and thunderstorms. In addition, the stench of several thousand head of cattle, not to mention the dust raised by the animals, hardly makes for a glamorous lifestyle—and the odor of the cowboys was probably not much better than the animals they tended. Nor was the food particularly appealing for the drives which usually included a cook and chuck wagon. The cowboys existed on a steady diet of beans, biscuits, and coffee. Despite the abundance of beef, it was rare for the cowboys to slaughter any of the cattle for barbeque as that would cut into the profits of the drives. The monotony of this daily existence was often shattered by dangers. A stampede often caused by thunderstorms could threaten the very lifeblood of the drive as running and frightened cattle might follow one another right off a cliff. It was the job of cowboys to use their guns and try to turn the herd, but such efforts were not always successful, and many cowboys perished in stampedes. Cowboys and cattle drives also fell prey to Natives and rustlers. For some reason, the Natives objected to thousands of head of cattle being moved through their traditional hunting lands as overgrazing deprived buffalo herds of needed nourishment. Especially as the drives neared the market, cattle rustlers might ambush the cowboys and attempt to collect the payday for completing the drive. Cowboys also feared that they might be exposed to diseases such as anthrax or Texas fever transmitted by cattle.

For the cowboys who survived the drive, there was a payday when they reached the railhead in cattle towns such as Abilene and Dodge City, Kansas. These cattle towns earned a reputation for violence and lawlessness as cowboys who were finally paid after months of constant work sought solace with a bath, alcohol, and female companionship. The cowboys were in many ways like sailors. It would be possible to save one's money from several drives or voyages and then purchase one's own ranch or ship, but the human psychology of making up for long periods of deprivation by spending one's money in celebration was usually too tempting. The cowboy life of the cattle drive was hardly the formula for social mobility, as in the words of musician Willie Nelson, you "ended up spending all your money and calling everybody honey." The cattle towns were violent, and gunfighter lawmen such as Wyatt Earp, James Butler "Wild Bill" Hickock, and Bat Masterson gained reputations for taming these towns—although the number of killings did not exceed the violence of Eastern cities in the era. The popular culture of the Western film genre is misleading in regard to the typical cowboy and use of the six-shooter revolver. The handguns employed in the 1860s and 1870s were heavy and often inaccurate pieces of hardware that cowboys primarily used for herding cattle rather than gunplay on the streets. There were, of course, gunfighters or shootists who gained reputations as killers, but the Western film genre perpetuates the notion that such gunplay was common in the post-Civil War West. In addition, cattle towns usually only served as railheads for five to ten years as the railroads moved into Texas and there was less need for the long drives. Yet, the popular Western television series *Gunsmoke* had Marshal Matt Dillon policing the cattle town of Dodge City for over thirty years.

Adjustments on the ranching frontier

The cattle drives, however, paved the way for ranching and cattle to emerge as a significant Western industry in the 1870s and 1880s. In fact, the open range policy in the West allowed cattle to roam freely in search of water and grass, and the territory from Texas into Wyoming eventually became one giant well-stocked cattle range. For this to happen, the Native population was resettled in a series of Indian wars to be discussed later in this chapter. As part of a strategy to force the Plains Indians onto reservations and deprive cattle of their major competitors for grazing land, the vast herds of buffalo in the West were slaughtered and nearly made extinct. Hunting was often conducted on railroad car platforms for fun, but there was a demand for hides supplied by buffalo skinners who left tens of thousands of buffalo carcasses in their wake. There was little demand for buffalo meat—which has become quite fashionable today as the buffalo has made a comeback from near extinction—as it was considered Indian food and thus not acceptable for consumption by civilized Americans. The demand for beef, however, increased as the American population grew. Beef on the table for every meal was a sign of prosperity, and there were few health concerns expressed with consuming large amounts of red meat. And the expansion of the railroads allowed for the speedy dispatch of cattle to the Chicago slaughterhouses and Eastern markets. While the ranching boom was celebrated as the product of American enterprise and rugged individualism, it is ironic to note that the cattle industry was also the product of capital provided by European investors and bankers. In fact, the XIT ranch, the largest in Texas, was owned by British bankers, but managed on a daily basis by Texans more knowledgeable with the industry.

The cattle bubble, however, burst somewhat in the late 1880s as the Western ranges were overstocked, and cattle often searched in vain for supplies of grass and water. The crisis on the Western range was exacerbated by the disastrous blizzard of 1887 in which it is estimated that nearly 90 percent of free-grazing cattle perished. Ranchers who survived the winter readjusted to accommodate changing conditions by growing forage such as hay that would provide food for their cattle during extreme winters. Ranchers began to focus upon the quality of their stock, emphasizing scientific breeding and sending their children to the state agricultural colleges.

Homestead Act

But perhaps the greatest challenge to traditional ranching practices was the movement of farmers into the West promoted by the Homestead Act. The farmers were a threat to the open range as they constructed fences to protect their crops from wandering cattle. Ranchers opposed fencing that might restrict cattle from freely roaming in search of water and grass, tearing down fences and provoking violence that resulted in range wars along the Western frontier. Among the most famous of these conflicts was the Johnson County War in Wyoming during which ranchers hired gunmen to assault farmers whom the ranchers accused of being cattle thieves. The ensuing violence convinced President Benjamin Harrison to dispatch federal troops in an effort to restore the peace. The Johnson Country War served as an inspiration for such Western films as *Shane* (1953) and *Heaven's Gate* (1980), examining class conflict in the American West. The growing number of farmers eventually overwhelmed the ranching frontier, and ranchers adjusted to changing economic realities by constructing their own fences to protect the access of their cattle to water and grass.

The triumph of the farmers' frontier in the West was promoted by governmental policies that fostered settlement and cultivation of the land. The Homestead Act of 1862 was a crucial piece of Congressional legislation that offered farm families 160 acres of land free if they would live on the land and farm it for five years. The act is praised for bringing civilization to the "virgin land" of the West; a concept that ignores the fact that this settlement was achieved through the destruction of the Plains Indian culture. Perhaps the greatest intellectual champion of the Homestead Act was historian Frederick Jackson Turner whose 1893 essay "The Significance of the Frontier in American History" lauded the frontier and settlement of the West as essential attributes of American democracy. Turner's safety valve theory maintained that the frontier explains why the United States was able to avoid the class conflict and violence of events such as the French Revolution that have plagued other nations and societies. According to Turner, Americans could escape urban poverty by moving to the frontier where available land through laws such as the Homestead Act provided an opportunity for the impoverished to begin anew and achieve the American dream of social mobility. Societies without the social pressure relief valve of a frontier often exploded with political violence. Turner also argued that the frontier furthered American democracy by offering a laboratory in which democratic experiments such as female suffrage could be tested on the local and state levels before being enacted on the national stage. Turner's frontier thesis, however, fails to consider the less than democratic treatment of blacks, Natives, Chinese, and Hispanics in the West, and there is considerable evidence to suggest that the Homestead Act failed to provide the safety value depicted by the historian.

Many working-class families simply lacked the means to take advantage of the free land available in the West. Historians estimate that a family would require at least $500 for the expenses of relocation that would include transportation, seeds and farming equipment, oxen to pull a plow, and money to survive upon until the first crop was harvested. Rather than alleviating poverty, the Homestead Act offered an avenue through which the middle class might be able to improve their lot in life, leaving most of the working class in the factories to form unions and embrace doctrines such as socialism to combat the inequities of the economic system. And those who did muster the funds to file for a homestead still often found the American dream unattainable. The lack of rainfall in the Great Plains contributed to a 50 percent failure rate as farmers abandoned their homesteads before the allotted five years that would have allowed them to secure their own land. Many farmers perished in pursuit of their homesteads, and life was especially difficult for farm women who lived isolated lives on the farming frontier. Men would take a crop to market, leaving their wives in charge of the farm and taking care of the children. Despite the challenges of isolation, which sometimes led to madness, sustainable homesteads owed much to the labor of prairie women. The Homestead Act was also plagued by corruption. The original purpose of the legislation was to promote settlement of the Great Plains, but speculators schemed to fool government inspectors through portable shacks they moved from one homestead to another, claiming that the land was being lived upon and improved. Witnesses and government inspectors were bribed by unscrupulous businessmen to falsely authenticate claims of settlement. In addition, homesteads near water were often secured by ranchers who charged their neighbors considerable fees for use of the scarce water supply.

Farming on the Great Plains

While many farmers succumbed to the elements and abandoned their homesteads, those that survived had to make significant adjustments to farming on the Great Plains. In the East, farmers had to clear the land of timber which they then used for constructing homes and fences. The Great Plains offered no forests for building supplies, and initially many of the homesteaders lived in cellars they dug out of the prairie soil. Eventually farmers discovered that shelters could be constructed from the thick prairie grasslands, providing decent insulation but vulnerable to the thunderstorms and rains which sometimes visited the region. The sod house frontier also owes its origins to the adobe mudbricks employed in the Southwest by Spanish settlers in another region short of trees and water. For fencing material, farmers initially used wire strung between fence posts, but cattle often pushed right through these fences in search of food and water. To address this problem, Joseph Glidden in 1874 received a patent for the manufacture of barbed wire which added sharp edges or points to the traditional metal wire fencing, allowing for the cattle to become entangled in the wire and, thus, unable to uproot the fences, while cowboys were given the thankless task of untangling the distressed cattle. Barbed wire played a crucial role in halting the open grazing of cattle in the West.

The major challenge to farmers on the Great Plains was the lack of rainfall. The West, however, had plenty of wind and dust storms as well as underground water supplies or aquifers that could be pumped to the surface by windmills, which became a feature of the Great Plains landscape. Dependence upon the underground sources of water has encouraged the urbanization and overgrowth of the West based upon a water supply that is not sustainable in the long run. Business and government, nevertheless, have continued to promote Western development. A homestead of 160 acres in the East was a sustainable farm, but in the West with a lack of rainfall and less productive soil this small farm was insufficient acreage. The government, accordingly, pursued additional legislation that would allow farmers to acquire more land and adjust to the conditions of the West. In the Timber Culture Act of 1873, farmers could acquire an additional 160 acres by planting trees on a fourth of their homestead. The Desert Land Act of 1877 allowed farmers implementing irrigation projects to attain additional land, although many legal disputes over water rights would grow out of the irrigation projects encouraged by the government. Water remains a scarce resource in the West, but this fact has hardly deterred the consumption ethic that has governed American history at the expense of conservation.

The final farming frontier to be opened for settlement was Oklahoma. The Oklahoma territory was initially preserved as land for the Cherokee and other tribes forced out of the Southeast by President Jackson in the Trail of Tears. As the demand for land grew, the Congress decided to open some of the best farmland in Oklahoma to white settlement with the Oklahoma land rush of 1889. Approximately 50,000 people lined up to stake their claims to the two million acres opened to settlement, although corruption was again rampant with "sooners" moving into the region and staking claims in advance of the land rush—providing the name for the University of Oklahoma athletic teams. The frenzy of the land rush exemplifies the land hunger of many Americans in the late nineteenth century, but the Homestead Act did not provide the path for social mobility envisioned by Frederick Jackson Turner. Working-class families lacked the money and in many cases the agricultural experience and acumen that would allow them to take advantage of the law. And those who acquired the funds to move West often encountered failure in their quest for advancement. The Homestead Act, nevertheless, may have served an important psychological role in keeping the American dream alive for many impoverished working-class families. Even if reality prevented most poor factory workers from relocating to the West, the idea that somehow, someway they might be able to gain a homestead and move up in American society kept hope alive. While many workers would turn to more radical remedies, others continued to have faith in the mythology of the American dream and Franklin's self-made man.

Indian Wars in the West

This dream of Westward expansion and mobility was also kept alive through a series of wars conducted to displace the Native population of the region. The Plains Indian nations of the Blackfeet, Arapaho, Cheyenne, Crow, Kiowa, and Lakota shared a nomadic culture based upon hunting, warfare, and mastery of the horse which had been introduced into the region by the Spanish. The buffalo were essential to the Plains Indians' way of life as the animals were a major food supply, while their bones provided tools and skins were a source of clothing and shelter. Thus, the path for white settlement of the West was constructed upon the destruction of buffalo herds and Plains Indian culture. Without the buffalo, the Plains Indians would lose their independence and be forced onto reservations where they would become wards of the government providing the blankets and foods that Natives once attained for themselves through hunting. The wholesale slaughter of the buffalo, thus, was intended to destroy the independence of the Plains Indians against which nations such as the Sioux waged a fierce resistance.

The assault on the Plains Indians commenced with the 1851 Treaty of Fort Laramie that essentially recognized tribal claims to most of the Great Plains as long as settlers were allowed safe passage through the region on routes such as the Oregon Trail that would allow them to reach the gold fields and farmlands of California and the Pacific Northwest. The Native rights to territories in which white settlers were not interested was acknowledged in the treaty that was supposed to bring "a lasting peace" to the West, but the discovery of gold in areas such as Colorado rather quickly abrogated the territorial provisions of the treaty. Gold fever induced prospectors and settlers to move onto Native lands, provoking attacks from Native nations followed by demands that the American government dispatch troops into the region to protect white settlement. The frontier soon erupted into violence with atrocities and mutilation of bodies all too common in what was essentially a racial conflict in which the enemy was demonized and treated as the "other" stripped of a common humanity. It was the type of savage war without mercy that characterized World War II in the Pacific and the Vietnam War. On November 29, 1864, Cheyenne Indians under Chief Black Kettle were encamped at Sand Creek, Colorado where they were promised protection from attack by U.S. forces. Although the encampment of approximately 500 Natives was composed primarily of women, children, and old men constituting no threat, they were attacked by Colorado militia under the command of U.S. Army Colonel John Chivington. Black Kettle immediately raised a white flag, but he could not prevent the slaughter of over 100 Native people whose bodies were mutilated in the aftermath of the massacre. Corpses were scalped, while male genitalia and women's breasts were removed from the bodies and proudly displayed as trophies that were sometimes made into tobacco pouches. There was criticism of the massacre which is now a historical site administered by the National Park Service, but Chivington was not disciplined for the atrocity. The Cheyenne, however, retaliated with numerous raids on white settlers.

Meanwhile, fighting continued to rage throughout the region, and on December 21, 1866 the U.S. Army suffered a significant defeat near Fort Phil Kearny in Wyoming as part of a conflict known as Red Cloud's War against the Lakota, Cheyenne, and Arapaho nations. In the Fetterman Massacre or Battle of the Hundred-in-the-Hands, a small group of warriors under Lakota Chief Crazy Horse—who later gained fame at the Battle of Little Bighorn—lured eighty soldiers under the command of Captain William Fetterman outside of the fort, where they were attacked by a larger group of Native warriors, and all of the troopers were killed. This defeat shocked the American government who put additional forces into the West, including the Buffalo Soldiers—black regiments from the Civil War who were now assigned to the frontier and Indian Wars in a classic example of pitting minority groups against one another. In fact, Native resistance had benefitted from the focus of the national government upon the sectional crisis and Civil War, but with the defeat of the Confederacy additional resources and troops could be dispatched to the Western frontier.

Second Treaty of Fort Laramie and Battle of Little Bighorn

In 1867, accordingly, the Second Treaty of Fort Laramie was negotiated in which Native territorial rights were considerably reduced and much of the Great Plains and Rocky Mountains opened to white settlement. The Lakota nation reserve included their sacred burial grounds in the Black Hills; a region that was deemed unsuitable for white settlement and cultivation. The American government promised the Lakota that they would prevent white intrusion into the Black Hills, but that agreement fell apart in 1874 when gold was discovered in the region. Soldiers were unable to stop the surge of white prospectors and settlers, and when they were attacked by the Lakota there was a demand that troops be sent to the Black Hills to protect the besieged whites. In what became known as the Great Sioux War, the Seventh Cavalry under the command of Lieutenant Colonel George Armstrong Custer was dispatched into the region to restore order and subdue the Lakota. Custer was a controversial figure. After graduating last in his West Point class, Custer rose to the rank of general during the Civil War, earning his reputation as a Union commander who was willing to take chances. After the Civil War, Custer continued his military career in the Western Indian Wars although his rank was reduced. He was recognized as an Indian fighter in the 1868 Battle of Washita River against the Cheyenne for which Custer and his troops were criticized for the unnecessary murder of Native women and children.

After arriving in the Black Hills, Custer divided his command in half; a disastrous move which his critics insist was motivated by his political ambitions. He wanted to find and subdue the Lakota quickly before reinforcements arrived so that he could gain full credit for the victory. This tactic, however, backfired as Custer and approximately 250 troopers came under attack by thousands of Lakota and Cheyenne warriors under the leadership of Chiefs Crazy Horse and Sitting Bull. At the Battle of Little Bighorn in the Montana territory, Custer and his men were caught in the open and were forced to use their horses for cover. After several attacks, Custer and his entire command were killed; although Lakota oral tradition contends that before the final Native assault the remaining soldiers used their last bullets to take their own lives rather than face capture and possible torture. Custer's defeat alarmed the American public who could not believe that the soldiers of a great technological civilization could be subdued by primitive savages. Many blamed Custer for the defeat; however, his reputation was saved by the lobbying efforts of his widow, Elizabeth Bacon Custer, extolling the heroic image of "Custer's Last Stand" until the 1960s when some balance was restored by examining Custer through a Native lens. In the 1870s, Custer had to be revenged and national pride restored through the devastation of the Lakota Nation who achieved the greatest Native victory of the Indian Wars. Seeking to make an example of the Lakota, American forces under the command of General Alfred Terry relentlessly pursued the Native warriors.

Wounded Knee

Crazy Horse was captured and died while in the custody of American forces. Sitting Bull retreated to Canada, although eventually returning to the United States and surrendering after the passions generated by Little Bighorn had cooled. With the Lakota relegated to the Pine Ridge Reservation in South Dakota, Sitting Bull appeared to be less of a threat, and he was invited to participate in the Western nostalgic experience of the Buffalo Bill Cody Wild West Shows. He eventually returned to the reservation, and Sitting Bull was killed while allegedly resisting arrest by government agents concerned about his participation in the Ghost Dance revitalization movement. After being placed on the desolate Pine Ridge Reservation, the Lakota were experiencing a cultural renaissance with the Ghost Dance. This spiritual movement recalled the independent lifestyle of hunting the buffalo, alarming government agents on the reservation who outlawed the Ghost Dance. The Lakota persisted with the spiritual revitalization, and additional forces were sent to police the reservation. On December 29, 1890 near Wounded Knee Creek on the Pine Ridge Reservation, American soldiers armed with artillery and Gatling guns attempted to disarm an encampment of Lakota associated with the banned dance. When the soldiers believed the Sioux were resisting their orders, they opened fire on the encampment and killed over 150 Lakota, including women and children. The Wounded Knee Massacre is often described as the last battle of the Indian Wars, and it became a symbolic location for Native resistance in the 1970s with the American Indian Movement (AIM).

Native resistance in the Southwest and Northwest

The Indian Wars of the late nineteenth century were not limited to the Sioux or Great Plains. In the Southwest, Geronimo was an Apache warrior and raider who escaped from the Apache reservation in Arizona, leading assaults on American and Mexican settlements. After his capture in 1886, the American government treated Geronimo as a prisoner of war and exiled him to Florida. Despite becoming somewhat of a celebrity and even appearing at the 1904 World's Fair in St. Louis, Geronimo was never allowed to return to Arizona and died in 1809 at Fort Sill, Oklahoma. Chief Joseph of the Nez Perce also gained national attention when he refused to accept relocation from the Nez Perce homeland in Oregon to a reservation in the Idaho territory. After several violent encounters with American forces, Chief Joseph led approximately 700 members of the Nez Perce nation on a journey to find refuge in Canada. They were pursued relentlessly by troops under the command of General Oliver Howard until in October 1877 when they were cornered in the Montana territory, and Chief Joseph negotiated a surrender which he believed would result in his people being returned to the tribal reservation in Idaho. Instead, Joseph was imprisoned in various forts until he was finally assigned to the Colville Indian Reservation in Washington state where he died in 1904. Chief Joseph's courage and eloquence in fighting for his people's self-determination garnered the respect of many white Americans, but their admiration did not translate into his being allowed to live and die in the traditional homeland of the Nez Perce.

Dawes Act

The example of Native leaders such as Chief Joseph, who followed his promise "to fight no more forever," convinced reformers that a change in Indian policy was required. Helen Hunt Jackson was born in Amherst, Massachusetts, but relocated to Colorado where she remained following the death of her first husband and two children. While living in Colorado, she became interested in the plight of the American Indian. In 1881, Jackson wrote *A Century of Dishonor* criticizing American Indian policy and sent a copy of the volume to every member of Congress. Jackson argued that the American government had followed an aggressive policy employing violence and broken treaties to seize Native lands. It was impossible to change the past, but in the future Natives should be treated with respect while being Christianized and prepared to assume their roles as American citizens. The assimilationist goals advocated by Jackson were embedded by Congress in the 1887 Dawes Act or General Allotment Act in which tribal lands were to be divided into individual homesteads for Indian families. The purpose of the legislation was cultural genocide in which the tribes were to be destroyed and the Native people transformed into individual farmers participating in the marketplace similar to their white brethren. This assault upon Native culture was coupled with the practice of educating Native children at Indian Boarding Schools where they were forced to practice Christianity and forbidden to speak their Native languages. Boys were forced to cut their hair, and both genders were unable to follow traditional habits of dressing and eating. For those who resisted this cruel assimilation, beatings were a common means of discipline administered by the Christians running the boarding schools. Nevertheless, there was widespread resistance to the assimilationist policies with many Natives refusing to send their children to the boarding schools or accept their individual allotments—although the overall impact of the Dawes Act was the considerable loss of Native land.

Twentieth-century Indian policy

Despite the assault upon traditional Native culture and government, the tribes survived, and in the Indian Reorganization Act of 1934, President Franklin Roosevelt and his Commissioner of Indian Affairs, John Collier introduced the Indian New Deal that encouraged Native self-determination. But advocates of assimilation regained the upper hand in Indian policy during the 1950s, and the Dwight Eisenhower administration introduced a termination policy that sought to end federal recognition of tribal entities as sovereign governments. In the late 1960s, the American Indian Movement—an organization that will be more fully developed in a chapter on civil rights and social protest in the 1960s—fought for cultural renewal and the restoration of tribal governments which was eventually supported by President Lyndon Johnson and Congress. Since the 1960s, the authority of tribal governments and treaty rights have also received the support of federal courts, and some tribes have used this sovereignty to enhance their wealth through the construction of casinos beyond the reach of state laws on gambling. While these casinos have brought an infusion of cash into Indian country, the distribution of the gambling funds is often a cause for concern, and widespread Native American poverty persists—a legacy of the nineteenth century Western expansion that attempted to destroy the culture of the Plains Indians and introduced settlement that continues to strain the resources of the region. While big business and industry attempted to subdue the American West, the opposition of labor and workers to exploitation in the factories, mines, and fields fostered an indigenous radical resistance whose legacy is all too often ignored in American history and politics.

Further Reading:

Brown, Dee. *Bury My Heart at Wounded Knee: An Indian History of the American West*. New York: Holt, Rinehart & Winston, 1970.

Deloria Jr., Vine. *Custer Died for Your Sins: An Indian Manifesto*. New York: Macmillan, 1969.

Drinnon, Richard. *Facing West: The Metaphysics of Indian Hating and Empire Building*. Minneapolis, MN: University of Minnesota Press, 1980.

Dykstra, Robert. *The Cattle Towns*. New York: Knopf, 1968.

Greene, Jerome A., ed. *Lakota and Cheyenne Indian Views of the Great Sioux Wars, 1876–1877*. Norman, OK: University of Oklahoma Press, 1994.

Limerick, Patricia Nelson. *The Legacy of Conquest: The Unbroken Past of the American West*. New York: W.W. Norton & Company, 1987.

Pisani, Donald J. *From the Family Farm to Agribusiness: The Irrigation Crusade in California and the West, 1850–1931*. Berkeley, CA: University of California Press, 1984.

Riley, Glenda. *The Female Frontier: A Comparative View of Women on the Prairie and Plains*. Lawrence, KS: University Press of Kansas, 1950.

Smith, Henry Nash. *Virgin Land: The American West as Symbol and Myth*. Cambridge, MA: Harvard University Press, 1950.

Utley, Robert. *The Indian Frontier of the American West, 1846–1890*. Albuquerque, NM: University of New Mexico Press, 1984.

Webb, Walter Prescott. *The Great Plains*. Boston: Ginn and Company, 1931.

White, Richard. *"It's Your Misfortune and None of My Own": A New History of the American West*. Norman, OK: University of Oklahoma Press, 1991.

Worster, Donald. *Rivers of Empire: Water, Aridity, and the Growth of the American West*. New York: Pantheon Books, 1985.

18

Indigenous Radicalism and Labor's Response to Industrialization

"Now for a Round-Up." Drawing by W. A. Rogers. *New York Herald*, May 9, 1918. Cabinet of American Illustrations, Library of Congress. This drawing depicts the government employing the Sedition Act of 1918 to arrest and incarcerate labor leaders by accusing them of treason. The war was used as an excuse to crush a growing radicalism in the United States. The Industrial Workers of the World and Socialist Party would never again be so influential in American politics, and in 1920 Eugene Debs would run for the Presidency from his prison cell in a federal penitentiary.

Reasons for unionization of the labor force

The exploitation of workers exacerbated the rapid industrialization of the United States in the late nineteenth century and precipitated the rise of a countervailing economic power with the union movement and an indigenous radicalism that embraced elements of European socialism and communism. The union of big business and government that characterized American capitalism created monopolies, subjugated the American West and the region's Native population, promoted expansionism into foreign markets, and offered low pay to factory laborers amid miserable and dangerous working conditions. Just as Natives resisted Westward expansion, American workers, many of them recent immigrants, fought for their rights against the powers of big business. The exploitive potential of American capitalism in the late nineteenth century was nothing new, but the rise of large corporations whose tentacles and influence spread throughout the national economy was something different. Before the rise of corporations, workers on the local level could at least directly confront their employers regarding labor conditions. While certainly such protests were not always successful, at least the workers enjoyed the psychological satisfaction of expressing their discontent. The corporation offered no avenue for the individual to express one's anger within the workplace. Corporate policies were often established at offices located far from the factory floor, and the local manager might simply inform a disgruntled worker that he was following company policies dictated from corporate headquarters. If the worker disagreed, he or she could simply quit. Within the larger corporate structure, the voice of a single worker carried little weight. On the other hand, if the workers in a corporation could be organized into a large industrial union, employers would be forced to listen. The game changed when a union leader explained to a Rockefeller or a Carnegie that if the businessmen refused to listen to complaints or negotiate a contract with the union representative, then hundreds of thousands of workers would walk off the job. The worker was not alone, and there was strength in the union and numbers.

Thus, the rise of big business necessitated the countervailing power of big labor. This fact was difficult for many Americans to accept as it went against the grain of rugged individualism and the mythology of the self-made man extolled by Benjamin Franklin and Horatio Alger. Within a capitalist American system, nevertheless, a community of workers could attain through organization and solidarity the wages and benefits that were contained in the elusive concept of the American dream. Big business certainly recognized the threat that unions posed to their power and profits, and their opposition to the organization of labor produced considerable class conflict in late nineteenth and early twentieth-century America. During the crisis atmosphere of the Great Depression and World War II, labor enjoyed considerable success, but in the post war environment, issues of communism and radicalism were used to discredit the labor movement. In contemporary America only about 10 percent of the workforce is unionized, and economists often complain that wages fail to rise within a competitive labor market without acknowledging that the countervailing power of the union movement is missing from the economic equation.

While supporting the union movement in the late nineteenth century, other working-class leaders such as Eugene V. Debs believed that more fundamental transformation of the capitalist system was required. Thus, socialism, anarchism, and communism found support among intellectuals as well as working families. This indigenous radicalism was attacked as un-American and anti-patriotic during World War I and the Cold War hysteria of McCarthyism. Although socialism enjoyed considerable support in many American cities and even the Oklahoma countryside before World War I, democratic socialism has been dismissed as an alien ideology repugnant to American individualism. However, the 2016 Presidential campaign of democratic socialist Bernie Sanders suggests that many Americans, especially a younger generation, are willing to move beyond the reactionary politics of post-World War I and II fears. Unfettered capitalism has denied many Americans the health care and family leave protection taken for granted in other industrialized nations. An examination of labor organization and indigenous radicalism in the late nineteenth and early twentieth centuries, as well as the fierce opposition to these movements, indicates that these ideas are part of American history and not simply alien ideologies. Community and collaboration may offer a path toward achieving the promise of American life outlined in the nation's founding principles.

Knights of Labor

As big business made its imprint on American society following the Civil War, the Knights of Labor were founded as a countervailing force to the power and influence of corporate capitalism. Headed by the Grand Master Workman Terence V. Powderly, the Knights of Labor advocated for a union that would encompass all workers including women and blacks. In the West, however, the organization often supported discrimination toward Chinese labor, and members of the Knights were involved with the 1885 Rock Springs Massacre in Wyoming in which a mob attacked the local Chinese community for allegedly supplying strikebreakers. While suggesting that cooperatives could reduce costs for the working class, the Knights were essentially willing to function within the capitalist system, advocating such reforms as the eight-hour day, abolishing child labor, and adopting a graduated income tax in which the wealthy would face greater taxation on their incomes. Due to state legal restrictions on labor organizing as well as business intimidating workers for union membership, the Knights of Labor were initially a secret society. Once the Knights successfully infiltrated certain industries such as the railroads, the secrecy was abandoned as were many of the rituals that made the organization appear to be more of a fraternal organization than a union. Secrecy, however, allowed the Knights to take some employers by surprise; such as the notorious Jay Gould who operated the Wabash Railroad. In 1885, the Knights initiated a strike for which Gould was ill prepared and negotiated a favorable settlement with the railroad. Workers throughout the nation were impressed with the Wabash strike, and membership in the Knights expanded to over 800,000 laborers.

After the initial surge, membership declined as businesses began to take a strong stand against the Knights, taking advantage of the Knights support for a unified labor front by sowing seeds of discord and promoting the division of workers along gender, racial, and ethnic lines. Business leaders also informed skilled workers that they would be able to earn better wages if they were not associated with an organization that also represented unskilled labor. Seeking to separate the working class, corporate America would not again be taken by surprise and planned to antagonize white workers by employing blacks as strikebreakers

Haymarket bombing

The Knights were also discredited by their association with the Haymarket Square bombing in Chicago on May 4, 1886. The Knights and other labor groups sponsored demonstrations throughout the nation around the May Day celebration calling for reforms such as the eight-hour day. The protest in Chicago was relatively peaceful until someone tossed a bomb that killed seven policeman and four civilians, while at least another dozen bystanders were injured. No one could identify who threw the bomb, but the authorities used the explosion as an excuse to arrest prominent anarchists and leaders of the Knights for conspiracy in calling for demonstrations that culminated in violence—in some ways resembling the conspiracy charges filed against the Chicago Seven for the protests in 1968 during the Democratic National Convention that led to fighting in the streets. Eight defendants were placed on trial after the Haymarket bombing, and seven sentenced to death following a courtroom ordeal that often focused upon the radical political ideas of the accused. For example, Albert Parsons of Texas was interrogated about his anarchist writings and his marriage to black activist, Lucy Parsons. Four of the convicted, including Parsons, were hanged by the state, while another cheated the hangman by committing suicide. Illinois Governor John Peter Altgeld, who was elected after the Haymarket affair, commuted the sentences of the two remaining Haymarket martyrs. But the damage was done. The Knights of Labor were discredited and associated with political violence as membership in the organization rapidly declined. Haymarket, nevertheless, continued to resonate as a symbol of labor resistance associated with May Day celebrations, and in the 1960s, the Weather faction of the Students for a Democratic Society twice bombed the Haymarket Martyrs Monument which only honored the fallen policemen. The original monument has today been replaced with a more suitable memorial that honors all of those who perished at Haymarket.

Samuel Gompers and the AFL

Not wanting to end up on the gallows like the Haymarket defendants, skilled workers, representing crafts such as bricklayers and carpenters, formed the American Federation of Labor (AFL). Essentially following the business rhetoric propagated against the Knights of Labor, the AFL maintained that separated from the unskilled labor of blacks, women, and the Chinese, it would be possible for skilled workers to use their expertise to obtain better wages and working conditions. Abandoning class solidarity, the AFL supported bread and butter unionism within the capitalist system. In other words, the skilled workers wanted their fair share of the capitalist pie, demanding higher wages, shorter hours, and better working conditions. Although the AFL is today associated with the Democratic Party, the labor organization initially eschewed any type of political entanglements, fearing that union leaders could become the victim of political persecution as suffered by the Haymarket martyrs. The AFL was also blessed with the stable leadership of Samuel Gompers, an English immigrant who was a skilled cigar roller and served as president of the labor organization from 1886 to 1924 except for a two-year term in the 1890s. Gompers was a champion of the eight-hour day which he asserted would provide workers with eight hours of labor, eight hours of rest, and eight hours of leisure during which they could improve their minds. However, this did work out exactly as envisioned by Gompers as today many workers have to labor more than eight hours a day at multiple jobs to support a family as the minimum wage fails to keep up with the cost of living. The policy of the AFL to work within the system made Gompers an acceptable labor leader to most mainstream American politicians, and he was praised for denouncing socialism and supporting America's entrance into the First World War. In addition, Gompers supported Labor Day as a national holiday on the first Monday in September that would separate the federal holiday from the more radical May Day celebrations often associated with the Haymarket affair.

Homestead Strike

But the AFL represented only an elite minority of the American workforce, while other industrialized workers engaged in more violent confrontations with business during the late nineteenth century. One of the deadliest labor struggles was in 1892 at the Homestead mills of Carnegie's Pennsylvania steel mills. Carnegie and his Homestead plant manager, Henry Clay Frick, decided to cut wages as a pretext to break the Amalgamated Association of Iron & Steel Workers (AA). After the workers went on strike, Carnegie and Frick conspired to bring strikebreakers into the plant. Hundreds of Pinkerton detectives were hired to provide security for the strikebreakers or "scabs" who were to be dispatched via boats across the Monongahela River to occupy the plant. On the evening of July 5, Carnegie and Frick attempted to implement their plan, but the striking workers were warned of the plot. When the boatloads of Pinkertons and strikebreakers approached the plant, the armed strikers resisted their landing. In the ensuing fighting, three Pinkertons and seven strikers were killed, while dozens were wounded. Citing civil unrest, the Governor of Pennsylvania dispatched the state militia to Homestead. The striking steel workers initially welcomed the troops whom they perceived as common folk like themselves who would protect the workers and their families from further aggression at the hands of the Pinkerton "thugs" hired by Carnegie and Frick. Instead, the militia sided with the company and offered protection for the strikebreakers. With this intervention on behalf of the company by the state, the strike was broken, and the AA was effectively destroyed as a union presence in the steel plants. In this ruthless union busting, Carnegie allowed Frick to be the public face of the company and assume some blame for the ensuing violence. In the aftermath of the strike, anarchist Alexander Berkman posed as a journalist and gained access to Frick's office where he shot and stabbed the steel operator, but Frick survived the assassination attempt and even seemed to gain some public sympathy after the assault.

Panic of 1893 and Pullman Strike

Broader labor unrest and class conflict was apparent in the Pullman Strike that occurred as the Panic of 1893 deprived many workers and their families of jobs and livelihood. The strike began on May 11, 1894 at the Pullman company on the South Side of Chicago. Industrialist George Pullman had created a company town where workers manufactured Pullman sleeping cars for the railroads. The workers at Pullman were required to live in company housing where utilities were provided. Residents were expected to purchase their supplies from stores associated with the company. The structure of Pullman's company town was paternalistic with city governance appointed by the company rather than democratically elected by the residents, reflecting the attitude that workers were not capable of self-governance. In response to lower demand for railroad sleeping cars during the Panic of 1893, Pullman decided to reduce wages and lay off workers, although there was no corresponding decrease in rents, prices, and utilities that workers were expected to pay. Although the Pullman workers were forbidden to form a union, an unauthorized "wildcat" strike began at the plant, and the American Railway Union (ARU) under the leadership of Eugene V. Debs agreed to assume primary responsibility for conducting the strike and representing the Pullman workers. When Pullman would not negotiate with the ARU, Debs proposed to put pressure on the company by having his railway workers refuse to handle Pullman cars. This boycott would often be implemented by separating or unlinking the Pullman cars from other railroad traffic, tying up railroad operations throughout the country. By eschewing violence, Debs hoped to avoid the government intervention that crushed the Homestead Strike. Nevertheless, the effort to disconnect Pullman cars from the trains often provoked confrontations resulting in violence and deaths, negating the nonviolent strategy pursued by the ARU. President Grover Cleveland opposed the strike and directed his Attorney General Richard Olney, a former attorney for the railroad operators, to provide a legal justification for government intervention to terminate the strike. Claiming that the activities of the ARU interfered with the speedy delivery of mail transported by the railroads, Olney convinced a federal court to issue an injunction against Debs and the union. When Debs refused to obey the injunction, he was arrested, and troops were dispatched to end the strike, crushing the ARU. As for Debs, his experience convinced him that a more radical transformation of American capitalism was required to prevent the military intervention that ended the Homestead and Pullman Strikes. After spending jail time studying the works of Karl Marx and other socialist thinkers, the labor leader became one of the founders of the American Socialist Party in 1901.

Eugene V. Debs and American socialism

The platform of the American Socialist Party denounced the monopolistic control of the American economy and government by corporations and big business, calling for the collective ownership of transportation and communication facilities, the banking system, and natural resources for the benefit of all citizens. Unemployment would be addressed through public works, and the platform advocated abolishing child labor, fostering government supervision of working conditions, and establishing the eight-hour day. The Socialists also called for such democratic reforms as women's suffrage, a graduated income tax, and abolition of the Electoral College in favor of direct election of the President by the people. In the early twentieth century, the Socialist Party enjoyed some political success, electing two members of Congress, Myer London from New York and Victor

Berger from Wisconsin, over seventy mayors, and numerous city councilors and state legislators. The party found support among German, Jewish, and Scandinavian immigrants in the cities of the Northeast and Midwest, but the party also resonated with farmers in areas such as Oklahoma, where it was assumed that there was no fundamental conflict between Marx and Jesus. Socialism would implement the Christian socialist principles preached by Jesus in "The Sermon on the Mount" and drive the moneychangers from the temple. On the national level, Debs, who was born in Indiana, proved to be a popular figure, earning the Socialist Party nomination for President five times, and in 1912, the Socialist candidate earned 6 percent of the popular vote. In 1920, Debs ran for President from his jail cell in an Atlanta penitentiary, where he was incarcerated under sedition charges for opposing conscription and American entrance into the First World War. Despite his imprisonment, Debs was still able to garner over 900,000 votes. Opposition to World War I, however, allowed threatened Democratic and Republican politicians to denounce Socialists as un-American and unpatriotic despite the popular support for the party and Debs before the war.

Anarchism and Emma Goldman

During the late nineteenth century, anarchism also gained a foothold in America. While anarchism was influenced by European philosophers such as Peter Kropotkin and Pierre-Joseph Proudhon and was popular among immigrants from Southern and Eastern Europe, the movement in the United States also owed its genesis to American individualism and writers such as Henry David Thoreau. Nevertheless, many Americans dismiss anarchism as an alien ideology advocating violence. While some anarchists did embrace violence and political assassination in what was termed the "propaganda of the deed," philosophical anarchism is more complicated and resonates with American principles of liberty and self-determination. Seeking to maximize the freedom of the individual from the restrictive powers of the state and other social institutions, anarchists advocate freedom of association in which non-hierarchical societies are self-governing bodies without recourse to force or compulsion. The collectivist and cooperative emphasis within anarchism also encourages support for the labor movement and what is sometimes termed anarcho-communism. Perhaps the most prominent American advocate for anarchism was the feminist and labor organizer Emma Goldman.

Goldman was born in 1867 and grew up in Lithuania within the Russian Empire. Seeking to escape the tyranny of her father and anti-Semitic pogroms, Goldman immigrated to the United States, where she joined her sister in Rochester, New York. After a disillusioning early marriage and work experience in the garment industry, the intellectually inclined young woman became a writer and speaker advocating labor organization, women's rights, and anarchism. The fiery Goldman was also associated with the propaganda of the deed when her lover Alexander Berkman attempted to assassinate industrialist Henry Clay Frick following the suppression of the 1882 Homestead Strike. Goldman was arrested, but the authorities could find no evidence to link her with Berkman's deed for which the anarchist received a twenty-year prison sentence. In 1901, another anarchist admirer of Goldman's, Leon Czolgosz shot and killed President William McKinley. Law enforcement incarcerated Goldman, but once again they were unable to link the anarchist to the assassination. Goldman, nevertheless, continued to voice support for Czolgosz until the assassin's execution. But there was more to Goldman than this association with political violence.

Along with Margaret Sanger, the founder of Planned Parenthood, Goldman recognized that working-class women were in desperate need of birth control information as they labored in the tenements under the burdens of poverty and large families with continuous pregnancies. Under the Comstock Laws proposed by Postal Inspector Anthony Comstock and passed by Congress in 1873, birth control information or devices were considered pornographic and could not be discussed in public or disseminated through the mails. Upper and middle-class women could receive birth control information through private consultation with their physicians; however, poor women lacked the funds to solicit a doctor. Goldman challenged the class divide by giving public lectures in which she instructed working-class women on ways to avoid an unwanted pregnancy; a violation of the Comstock Laws that often subjected the anarchist to arrest. Goldman also shocked many Americans by attacking the institution of marriage as a manifestation of capitalism in which women were simply treated as the property of their husbands. Instead, Goldman advocated "free love" in which a woman could freely select her sexual partners without interference from the state. Although she was known for accepting many lovers, Goldman had no problem with monogamy if that is what one desired. She simply opposed the state dictating her sexuality.

As a labor agitator, Goldman was also arrested numerous times for what the authorities claimed was inciting workers to riot. The anarchist, nevertheless, was able to avoid long-term incarceration until 1917 when she and Berkman, who had been released from prison, were convicted of violating the Espionage Act by urging young men to avoid conscription during the First World War. During the anticommunist hysteria that swept over America following World War I and the Bolshevik Revolution in Russia, Goldman was denied her political rights and deported to the Soviet Union. While Goldman initially welcomed the Bolshevik Revolution, she soon became a thorn in the side of the Bolshevik leadership whom she criticized for suppressing dissent. Lenin responded to Goldman's critique by expelling her from the Soviet Union. Banished from both the United States and Soviet Union, Goldman lived in France and Canada while continuing to be an advocate for anarchism until her death in 1940.

Industrial Workers of the World

An even greater threat to the American capitalist order was the formation of the Industrial Workers of the World (IWW or Wobblies) in 1905. Meeting in Chicago, the founders of the IWW included anarchist Lucy Parsons, union organizer Mary Harris "Mother Jones," Eugene Debs representing the Socialist Party, and Big Bill Haywood who headed the Western Federation of Miners (WFM). Opposed to the narrow craft unionism embraced by Gompers and the AFL, the IWW advanced an industrial unionism that would include all workers in one big union "where an injury to one is an injury to all." The IWW sought to appeal to women, unskilled labor, and workers of color who were generally excluded from the AFL, calling for a form of syndicalism in which workers would engage in self-management through controlling the means of production and distribution. While eschewing armed revolution, the IWW asserted that capitalism would eventually be overthrown through direct action such as boycotts and the general strike. The anti-capitalist agenda of the IWW was a threat to corporate America who reacted with considerable violence to the emergence of the Wobblies.

Under the leadership of Haywood, a product of the labor wars on the Western mining frontier, the IWW assumed an aggressive stance that also demonstrated the union leader's mastery of propaganda. Haywood's name was also associated with violence as he and other associates from the WFM were indicted for the 1905 assassination of former Idaho Governor Frank Steunenberg who antagonized union leaders when he declared martial law and requested federal troops to quell labor unrest. Represented by attorney Clarence Darrow, who gained considerable fame as a lawyer for the downtrodden, labor, and free speech advocates, Haywood was acquitted and free to pursue his expansionist plans for the IWW. In addition to the organizing of miners, the IWW made significant inroads in the West with loggers and migrant laborers—workers long ignored by other unions. In the East, the IWW assumed a leading role in the 1912 Lawrence, Massachusetts strike of predominantly female immigrant textile workers, many of them Italian, in response to plant reductions of pay. Seeking to prove that the IWW could organize a diverse coalition of immigrant labor, Haywood and his associate Elizabeth Gurley Flynn seized upon the strategy of dispatching the children of striking workers to live with sympathetic families in New York and New Jersey where they were fed and cared for during the bitter labor dispute. This tactic gained considerable favorable coverage in the press, and textile mill operators were perceived as villains when the police intervened to prevent another exodus of children. Responding to growing criticism, mill operators offered to settle the so-called "Bread and Roses" strike by increasing wages in the Lawrence mills. The IWW, however, failed to consolidate the gains made in Lawrence, and in 1913 Haywood led a strike of Paterson, New Jersey silk workers that suffered defeat when automation or advanced technology was used to replace striking workers. However, a Madison Square Garden pageant organized by Haywood and the IWW gained considerable funding and publicity for the Paterson strike.

Despite the failure of the Paterson strike, the popular appeal of the IWW was furthered through the songs of Joe Hill, who often supplied radical lyrics to traditional tunes familiar to workers and their families. Born Joel Emmanuel Hagglund in Sweden, he immigrated to the United States and worked as a common laborer while writing songs and drawing cartoons for the IWW. Among the songs attributed to Hill are "There Is Power in a Union," "Casey Jones—the Union Scab," "Rebel Girl," and "The Preacher and the Slave" in which the songwriter indicts preachers for promising "pie in the sky" to workers who will not criticize their capitalist bosses. In November 1915, Hill's voice was silenced when he was executed by a Utah firing squad for his involvement in a Salt Lake City grocery store robbery and murder. Hill's alibi involved a woman whose honor he would not besmirch by bringing her name into the court proceedings. Before his execution, Hill wrote a letter to Haywood urging the IWW leader not to mourn his death but rather to continue his efforts at union organizing, and the martyr's ashes were supposedly scattered around the world by his followers.

Calumet and Ludlow Massacres

The organizing activities of the IWW produced considerable backlash beyond Hill's execution. The IWW was involved with the Michigan copper strike of 1913 seeking union recognition, higher wages, and better working conditions in the mines. On Christmas Eve of 1913, union leaders organized a holiday party for the families of striking workers at Italian Hall in Calumet, Michigan. Someone disrupted the festivities by shouting fire, and the occupants of a crowded ballroom attempted to exit Italian Hall down a steep staircase, where many of those fleeing the supposed fire were trapped and crushed. Seventy-five people, most of them children, were killed, and many witnesses insist that the doors of Italian Hall, which opened onto the street, were barred by company "thugs and strikebreakers." An investigation of the "Calumet Massacre of 1913" produced no indictments, and the strike in Michigan's copper country was eventually abandoned—although Woody Guthrie's composition "1913 Massacre" has immortalized the tragedy.

Class conflict was also evident in the 1914 Ludlow Massacre and violence in Colorado's coal fields. The United Mine Workers (UMW) and WFM led workers at the Colorado Fuel & Iron Company, owned by John D. Rockefeller, out on strike demanding the eight-hour day, better pay, union recognition, and abolition of payment in scrip that could only be used in company stores. The workers were evicted from company housing and living in a tent city near Ludlow, Colorado, when on April 20, 1914 they were attacked by company guards and the Colorado National Guard armed with machine guns. Approximately twenty-five people were killed in the ensuing chaos, most of them children placed in a trench where it was thought they would be safe from harm. Instead, eleven children were trapped under a burning tent and suffocated. Armed miners sought revenge for the Ludlow Massacre, and for the next ten days fighting raged in Colorado, leaving at least fifty dead before President Woodrow Wilson sent federal troops to end the class warfare. The strike collapsed, but in response to the criticism he earned for the violence at Ludlow, Rockefeller improved condition in the company town organized by the Colorado Fuel & Iron Company and authorized a company union. The workers continued to be treated in a patronizing manner until the UMW enjoyed some organizing success in the Colorado coal fields during the 1930s.

Wartime persecution of radicals

Radical unions such as the IWW were perceived as a significant threat to the capitalist order with hundreds of thousands of workers represented by the union—although the exact number of IWW members, who included migrant workers, is difficult to ascertain. However, the opposition to the First World War expressed by many IWW leaders provided the government and business an opportunity to attack the union, just as they had moved against the Socialist Party, in the name of patriotism. IWW leaders such as Haywood perceived World War I as a conflict destined to benefit capitalists and munition makers by pitting American workers against German laborers. Emphasizing class solidarity above more narrow nationalism, many Wobblies—although the union issued an official statement that was more neutral—believed the youth of America should not be conscripted to fight young German workers. The government indicted Haywood and other IWW leaders for violating the Espionage Act, and Wobbly literature and newspapers were confiscated and banned from the mails. The harsh wartime response of the federal government also encouraged vigilante leaders on the local level to act against the IWW. In Butte, Montana, Frank Little, a Wobbly organizer who opposed the war, was seized by a mob and hanged from a railroad trestle after being tortured. In Bisbee, Arizona, approximately 1,300 striking copper miners associated with the IWW were arrested and deported from the area on July 17, 1917. The Phelps Dodge Corporation provided local authorities and deputized vigilantes with a list of names they wanted removed from Bisbee. The miners and their families were then shipped on cattle cars to western New Mexico and threatened with execution if they returned to Bisbee. The corporation defended its actions by describing the deportation as a patriotic measure to rid Bisbee of dangerous radical agitators who were imperiling the war effort by striking against the copper industry. The federal government denounced the deportation, but no legal measures were taken against those responsible for the vigilante activity in Bisbee.

Meanwhile, the federal government placed Haywood and 100 other IWW members on trial for conspiring to hinder the draft, encourage desertion, and undermine the war effort through work stoppages. The trial was presided over by federal judge Kenesaw Mountain Landis whose stern manner with labor radicals convinced baseball owners that he should become the first Commissioner of Baseball and deal with the threat posed to the sport by the "Black Sox" scandal in which members of the Chicago White Sox conspired with gamblers to fix the 1919 World Series. Haywood and his co-defendants were found guilty, and while out of jail appealing his twenty-year prison sentence, the labor leader sought refuge in the Soviet Union where he died in 1926. The prosecution of Haywood and other union officials did not destroy the IWW which continues to function as a contemporary labor organization. The IWW, however, never regained the influence and membership it enjoyed in the period before World War I. The persecution of perceived radicals and threats such as the IWW, anarchists like Emma Goldman, and the Socialist Party during and following World War I provided the corporate capitalist order with an opportunity to suppress collectivist alternatives under the guise of patriotism. During the First Red Scare following World War I—which will be discussed in greater detail as part of the nativist reaction to the New Immigration in the 1920s—indigenous radicals were described as un-American, while socialism, communism, and anarchism were condemned as alien ideologies; a process that was repeated in the post-World War II Cold War environment and hysteria of McCarthyism. The suppression of indigenous radicalism and the labor movement in the late nineteenth and early twentieth centuries succeeded in marginalizing radical alternatives to American capitalism, and the history of American radicalism has largely been removed from the history books and national consciousness. Yet, these radical alternatives and class conflict played a significant role in American history, threatening middle-class Americans who responded by supporting the progressive reform movement between 1900 and 1917 that attempted to prevent revolution by propping up the system through addressing some of the worst abuses of capitalism. Indigenous radicalism and labor organizing in the late nineteenth and early twentieth centuries, nevertheless, expanded the possibilities of American democracy.

Further Reading:

Bissett, Jim. *Agrarian Socialism in America: Marx, Jefferson, and Jesus in the Oklahoma Countryside, 1904–1920*. Norman, OK: University of Oklahoma Press, 1999.

Buhle, Paul. *Taking Care of Business: Samuel Gompers, George Meany, Lane Kirkland, and the Tragedy of American Labor*. New York: Monthly Review Press, 1999.

Dubofsky, Melvyn. *We Shall Be All: A History of the Industrial Workers of the World*. Chicago: Quadrangle Books, 1969.

Falk, Candace. *Love, Anarchy, and Emma Goldman*. New York: Holt, Rinehart, and Winston, 1984.

Fink, Leon. *Workingmen's Democracy: The Knights of Labor and American Politics*. Urbana, IL: University of Illinois Press, 1983.

Green, James. *Death in the Haymarket: A Story of Chicago, the First Labor Movement, and the Bombing that Divided Gilded Age America*. New York: Pantheon Books, 2006.

Gutman, Herbert. *Work, Culture, and Society in Industrializing America*. New York: Random House, 1976.

Kessler-Harris, Alice. *Out to Work: A History of Wage-Earning Women in the United States*. New York: Oxford University Press, 1982.

Krause, Paul. *The Battle for Homestead, 1880–1892: Politics, Culture, and Steel*. Pittsburgh, PA: University of Pittsburgh Press, 1992.

Martelle, Scott. *Blood Passion: The Ludlow Massacre and Class War in the American West*. New Brunswick, NJ: Rutgers University Press, 2007.

Montgomery, David. *The Fall of the House of Labor: The Workplace, the State, and American Labor Activism, 1865–1925*. New York: Cambridge University Press, 1982.

Salvatore, Nick. *Eugene V. Debs: Citizen and Socialist*. Urbana, IL: University of Illinois Press, 1982.

19

The Progressive Movement, 1900–1917

Elizabeth Cady Stanton, seated, and Susan B. Anthony, standing, 1890. Prints and Photographs Division, Library of Congress. Stanton and Anthony fought for women's suffrage throughout the nineteenth century, but both were deceased before passage of the Nineteenth Amendment in 1920 as part of the progressive reform movement.

The class conflict that beset the United States in the late nineteenth and early twentieth centuries especially alarmed middle-class Americans who feared that they might be destroyed in a struggle between monopolistic capitalism and working-class revolution. Concerned about their endangered status, urban middle-class American professionals and small business owners embraced the progressive reform movement that they hoped would mitigate the worst excesses of capitalism and prevent a revolutionary class struggle. Working on the city, state, and national levels, the progressive reformers embraced a contradictory political agenda that both endorsed democratic reforms and placed restrictions upon the immigrants from Southern and Eastern Europe crowding into American cities. The ambiguous progressive agenda included the reform administrations of Presidents Theodore Roosevelt, William Howard Taft, and Woodrow Wilson as well as passage of the Sixteenth, Seventeenth, Eighteenth, and Nineteenth Amendments to the Constitution, but offered little for African Americans and was brought to a halt by the First World War and re-consolidation of big business influence over the government and nation.

Middle-class concerns regarding monopoly and revolution

The growth of big business and monopolies were a threat to small middle-class businesses. Local retailers found it difficult to compete with national chain stores whose large volume made it easier for them to charge lower prices for their merchandise. These stores—such as F. W. Woolworth, Montgomery Ward, and Sears, Roebuck and Company which began as a mail order catalog company—destroyed local businesses that could simply not compete with the discounted prices offered by the chains. On the retail level, these chains were the equivalent of monopolists such as Rockefeller and Carnegie who controlled natural resources in oil and steel. The process of retail consolidation beginning in the late nineteenth century has continued into the present day with even larger retail corporations such as Walmart who have captured the trade once going to F. W. Woolworth, Montgomery Ward, and Sears. Walmart often locates its stores in small towns, and a local business culture is destroyed along with the downtown community. Services once provided by local merchants are now housed under one roof with Walmart, and money flows out of America's small towns. A similar process is taking place with the online retailing of Amazon replacing actual brick and mortar stores. Even in dealing with the necessity of food, chain restaurants have often replaced authentic local cuisine. Today, as in the late nineteenth century, many owners of small businesses fear that they will be driven out of the middle class and into low paying jobs or poverty. They simply cannot compete with the political and economic clout of corporate America.

In addition to their concerns about monopoly and the power of big business, the middle class feared revolution from below as a threat to their way of life. Rising class conflict in America convinced many in the urban middle class that the United States was hardly immune to the violence and chaos of the French Revolution that also seemed to engulf Imperial Russia in the early twentieth century. The desperate living conditions of many immigrants in American cities were apparent to urban residents who often rubbed shoulders with the poor in cities that were less segregated than today. The plight of the urban poor in New York City was also brought home to middle-class Americans through the work of Danish-born journalist Jacob Riis. His books *How the Other Half Lives* (1890)—which included extensive documentary photography of New York City's overcrowded tenements—and *The Battle with the Slums* (1902) examined the horrible living and working conditions in the slums that made it difficult for the immigrants pouring in from Southern and Eastern Europe to escape the cycle of poverty and attain social mobility. Riis worried that failure to address the problem of the slums would lead to the destruction of the American democratic experiment. He called for reform to prevent revolution, although some critics perceived reform and welfare as attempts by the middle class to orchestrate a safety net or stake in the system for the poor that would forestall a more radical transformation of American capitalism. The concerns of the working poor were also brought home to middle-class Americans through the violence of the Ludlow Massacre in Colorado and textile strikes in Lawrence, Massachusetts and Paterson, New Jersey. The horrible and dangerous working conditions experienced daily by many American laborers was also dramatized by the 1911 New York City Triangle Shirtwaist Factory Fire during which 146 garment workers—123 women and 23 men—perished. The fire was in the eighth, ninth, and tenth floors of the factory building, and the exits were locked to prevent employees from leaving without being inspected to assure that they were not departing with any garment or clothing fragments. Unable to escape from the burning building, many women plunged to their deaths after leaping from windows. Revealing the greed of some capitalists, the Triangle Fire encouraged the growth of the International Ladies' Garment Workers Union, while progressive reformers called for improved safety conditions in the factories, fearing that such dangerous workplaces might contribute to further class conflict.

Contradictions within progressive reform

Afraid of being squeezed between the monopolies from above and revolution from below, the middle class sought to preserve their status through contradictory reforms calling for both greater democracy as well as social control over the new immigrants. Progressives advocated for democratic changes that they viewed as primarily benefitting the middle class. Greater economic democracy was envisioned with the Sixteenth Amendment providing for a progressive income tax that would assure the upper class paid its fair share of taxes and relieve some of the financial burden placed on the middle class. Progressives were also concerned about political corruption and believed that the direct election of U.S. Senators by the people, enacted in the Seventeenth Amendment, would lessen the influence of corporate interests on the selection of Senators by state legislatures. Middle-class voters would select honest men and rid the Senate of its reputation as a club for millionaires representing corporate America. Democracy would also be furthered through extending the suffrage to middle-class women who could realize Elizabeth Cady Stanton's dream of harnessing their superior morality to the reforming of the American political system. Of course, a problem with this expansion of democracy was the lower class, many of whom lacked the education and moral discipline of the middle class.

Thus, it was necessary to place some social controls upon the working class and immigrants who were not quite ready to receive the mantle of American democracy. The middle- class professionals believed in the superiority of a well-educated class who would rise above the corruption of the marketplace. On the city level, professional urban planners could be appointed to operate the cities and would not be susceptible to the bribes and corruption of political bosses elected by the urban masses. To assure honest and efficient regulation of large corporations, university experts could be appointed to state regulatory boards, assuring fair and unbiased professional governance. In addition, prohibition of alcohol, realized in the Eighteenth Amendment, was justified by many middle-class progressives as a way to gain some social control over the immigrant urban masses who culturally and temperamentally could not exercise self-control over their drinking habits. The prohibition of alcohol would provide for a more productive workforce, and drunken working men would no longer be a physical threat to their wives and families. Democracy would be improved as alcohol could no longer be employed to purchase the vote of working men. Through prohibition, progressives believed that they could improve the quality of life for the poor immigrant working class. Another major example of progressive social control reform was the creation of professional organizations. Concerned that many immigrants were encroaching upon middle-class professions, progressives sought to establish standards that would control admission to fields such as law or medicine. Higher educational qualifications and examinations administered by state boards would control admission into a profession, and by keeping standards high and the number of professionals limited, higher fees could be charged for professional services. Thus, it is not surprising that organizations such as the American Bar Association, American Medical Association, American Dental Association, and even the American Historical Association were founded in the early twentieth century. These professional organizations were able to establish quotas and keep expertise largely in the hands of a white middle-class elite.

Muckrakers and novelists

Awareness of the threats posed to the middle class from both the monopolists and working class was promoted through the work of progressive journalists whom Theodore Roosevelt labeled as "muckrakers" who dragged American society through the mire of corruption threatening the nation. Somewhat of a pejorative term, these muckrakers might be better described today as investigative journalists or whistle blowers seeking to expose corruption in the American political system. Writing to educate the middle-class readers of such magazines as *McClure's*, *Collier's*, and *Munsey's*, these muckrakers provided exposés that were often expanded into book-length manuscripts. Building upon the work of Jacob Riis, journalist Lincoln Steffens investigated political corruption in cities such as St. Louis and New York City which was published as *Shame of the Cities* (1904). While urging democratic reforms to limit the role of crooked mayors, Steffens lost faith in gradual change and embraced the Bolshevik Revolution. Other prominent muckrakers included Ray Stannard Baker, Charles Edward Russell, and Ida Tarbell. In a series of *McClure's* articles that were eventually published as *A History of the Standard Oil Company* (1904), Tarbell developed a devastating critique of Rockefeller that contributed to the government's anti-trust action against Standard Oil. Rockefeller associates provided Tarbell with access to company policies, assuming that the female writer was planning a favorable tribute to a male industrialist.

In addition to devouring the muckraking accounts in America's expanding magazine industry, middle-class readers sought both entertainment and political education from novelists sometimes referred to as naturalists who attempted to expose the problems of American society in a realistic and unsentimental fashion. Frank Norris, although not well known today, was an excellent popular example of the naturalist novelist whose writing was also often associated with progressive reform. In his novels, Norris examined greed as a motivating factor in human behavior, and his most famous work, *The Octopus* (1901) was based upon the undue influence exercised by the Southern Pacific Railroad upon the politics and economy of California, with the rails like the tentacles of an octopus engulfing the farmers of the state. Better known today are the novels of Jack London such as *Call of the Wild* (1903) and *White Fang* (1906) based upon the author's experience in the Klondike gold rush. London was also a member of the Socialist Party, and in *The Iron Heel* (1908) he alarmed many of his middle-class readers by depicting how monopolistic capitalism might provoke class warfare. In his reporting on black heavyweight boxing champion Jack Johnson, London also revealed the racial stereotypes embraced by many progressives. While Norris and London were popular novelists, perhaps the best example of literature's impact on progressivism was Upon Sinclair's *The Jungle* (1906). Sinclair hoped that his novel depicting the prejudice and horrible working conditions in the meatpacking plants of Chicago confronting a family of Lithuanian immigrants might inspire Americans to desert capitalism in favor of socialism. Aiming at the hearts of his readers, Sinclair seems to have, instead, hit their stomachs by describing the unsanitary conditions that prevailed in the meatpacking plants. Rather than becoming converts to socialism, the readers of Sinclair's novel, including President Theodore Roosevelt, supported progressive reforms that would insure government regulation and inspection of the meat industry.

Government reform on the city level

The middle class, who pursued literature and magazines for pleasure and knowledge in the era before television, were educated by muckrakers and novelists who exposed the threats confronting the middle class and offered reform agendas through which to address the crisis in American democracy and capitalism. Much of the reform on the local level focused upon corruption and how political bosses in cities such as Chicago and New York City manipulated the barely literate immigrant voters into supporting political machines that provided some constituent services, including alcohol and Christmas turkeys, in exchange for votes. While their campaign rhetoric suggested that the political machines were concerned with living and working conditions of the poor, in reality the urban political bosses often worked in cooperation with business leaders to advance the corporate agenda. To reduce the corrupt influence of urban political machines, progressives proposed the city manager form of government in which the chief executive of the city would be appointed rather than elected. The city manager selected by the city council was to be an educated professional urban planner who would be above politics. As a professional appointee, the city manager would be less susceptible to bribery by business interests and would not have to make campaign promises to please the masses who often placed unqualified individuals in office. Replacing an elected mayor with a city manager reflected the progressive values of honesty, professionalism, and efficiency, but the city manager form of government also epitomized the elitism and anti-democratic values of many progressives who did not trust the people, especially newly arrived immigrants, to support good government. The elitist preference of many progressives for experts, who knew little about the people for whom they were making decisions, led to a political backlash, and many cities that had replaced mayors with city managers returned to the more democratic practice of electing mayors to preside over the urban environment.

Jane Addams and Hull House

Cities were also concerned with how to meet the educational and social needs of immigrants flocking to America, but in the late nineteenth century social welfare was considered to be the responsibility of charities and the churches, and not the state. Into this breech stepped women such as Jane Addams who in 1889 established Hull House in Chicago as a settlement house to provide much needed services for immigrant families. Coming from a well-educated rural Illinois family, Addams found social work to be a rewarding avenue for her professional and philanthropic ambitions. In raising funds for administering Hull House, Addams certainly expanded the public role for professional women, although the caretaking role of social workers fit well into the traditional sphere of women's activities. Hull House provided a variety of services for immigrant families; including shelter, food, clothing, health care, hygiene, childcare, and an employment bureau. The settlement house also offered a variety of educational activities such as art classes, drama clubs, English language instruction, cooking classes, evening classes for workers, recreational facilities such as a gym, and job training. While Addams's concern and compassion for immigrant families were sincere, it is a fact that the goals of many activities at Hull House were assimilationist with a focus upon helping immigrants adjust to American society. The celebration of ethnic diversity was not part of the melting pot agenda pursued at Hull House. Besides expanding the scope of social work and philanthropy for women, Addams was an advocate for women's suffrage and world peace for which she was awarded the Nobel Peace Prize in 1931. Despite the nation's lack of tolerance for same-sex couples in the early twentieth century, Addams shared a forty-year relationship with Mary Rozel Smith, one of her financial benefactors.

Women and progressive reform

Women were also active in progressive reform on the state level where the four Constitutional amendments adopted during the progressive era required ratification by three-quarters of the states. The Women's Christian Temperance Union maintained that prohibition was necessary to protect women from domestic abuse at the hands of intoxicated husbands. Middle-class white women often embraced prohibition as providing a means of social control over the New Immigration from Southern and Eastern Europe. whose cultures were perceived as fostering strong drink and excess rather than the discipline of Anglo Saxon America. World War I also played a significant role in the final adoption of the Eighteenth Amendment as prohibition advocates argued that wheat and barley used in the production of beer were needed in the war effort to feed American soldiers and starving European allies. Women also played a crucial role in passage of the Nineteenth Amendment, convincing male politicians to ratify women's suffrage. Cassie Chapman Catt headed the mainstream National American Woman Suffrage Association (NAWSA) that emphasized traditional political techniques such as lobbying Congress and state legislatures to endorse the amendment. The National Women's Party (NWP), led by Alice Paul, demanded more direct action to achieve the vote, and these activists were arrested for protest activities such as picketing the White House. While incarcerated, some NWP members, known as the Silent Sentinels, engaged in hunger strikes and were force fed by the authorities. Following ratification of the Nineteenth Amendment, the NWA pursued passage of an Equal Rights Amendment to the Constitution, while the NAWSA evolved into the League of Women Voters. Women's suffrage became the law of the land when Tennessee ratified the amendment on August 26, 1920. The Tennessee ratification struggle, however, reveals a disturbing element about the women's suffrage movement. Black women such as journalist Ida Wells played a significant role in the struggle, but black suffragettes were discouraged from lobbying Tennessee legislators who were concerned that the Nineteenth Amendment would expand Negro suffrage by allowing black women to vote. The face of female suffrage remained white, as did most of progressive reform.

An expanded role for women, at least white women, was evident in the progressive effort to enact a Constitutional amendment prohibiting child labor of persons under eighteen years of age that fell one state short of ratification. Progressive advocates of child labor turned to the states as did supporters of legislation to improve the conditions of women in the workplace. The legislative efforts, however, sometimes backfired as in New York state where a minimum wage for women and maximum hours for female labor were used as an excuse by employers to discharge women in favor of male workers whose wages and hours were not subject to legislative protection. Concern for protecting women and legislating morality were also part of the progressive agenda that culminated in the Mann Act passed by Congress in 1910. Frustrated by their efforts to deal with prostitution on the local and state levels, this piece of progressive legislation made it a federal crime to take a woman across state lines for illicit sexual purposes. Reflecting the racial politics of the movement, progressives worried about what they called "white slavery" in which innocent young white women were forced into prostitution by pimps who were often men of color. While many immigrants and women of color were exploited and forced into prostitution, the progressives were less focused on their plight, assuming a more sexual nature for these women. Many progressives sought to dictate morality by using the Mann Act to punish sexual activity out of wedlock, but the racial nature of progressive morality was certainly apparent in the case of black heavyweight boxing champion Jack Johnson. When no "white hope" could be found to defeat Johnson in the ring, he was arrested for violating the Mann Act by traveling across state lines with his white female companion.

Reform at the state level

Progressives at the state level were more effective in achieving political reforms such as the initiative, referendum, and recall that provided for more direct democracy. These reforms were concerned with circumventing the corrupt control that lobbyists for big business often exercised over state legislatures. Corporate interests often prevented passage of state laws to regulate business, so the initiative allowed voters to petition for a measure to be placed on the ballot and enacted into law directly by the people without having to be passed by the legislature and signed by the governor. On the other hand, if the legislature enacted a measure opposed by the people, the referendum offered a means through which citizens might petition for a vote to remove the offensive law. Concern about corrupt politicians not following the will of the people was provided for by the recall in which the people could petition and vote to remove an official before the term of office expired. These attempts at direct democracy somewhat contradict the progressive emphasis upon professional experts and are still used today in states such as California.

A number of progressive governors were elected, but perhaps the most significant was Robert M. LaFollette of Wisconsin whose state was perceived as a laboratory for progressive reform. Among the legislative actions supported by the LaFollette administration were taxation of corporate profits, regulation of business lobbying activities with state legislators, minimum wages, a workers' compensation system, and the employment of university professors as professional experts to serve on state regulatory commissions. Another pioneering reform endorsed by LaFollette was the idea of the open primary that allowed the voters rather than party officials or conventions to select the candidate for state elections. A Republican insurgent, LaFollette was elected in 1905 to the Senate where he engaged with three progressive Presidents during his twenty-year tenure.

Rise of Theodore Roosevelt

The first President to openly identify himself as a progressive was the popular and often controversial Theodore Roosevelt. Born into a prominent New York family, Roosevelt was a rather sickly young boy who turned to intellectual pursuits, although as an adult he attempted to compensate for missing a rough and tumble boyhood. Roosevelt attended Harvard and gained a reputation as a historian for his naval history of the War of 1812. After graduation, he entered politics and was elected as a Republican to the New York State Assembly. On February 14, 1884, Roosevelt's life was shattered by tragedy when his mother and first wife died on the same day, just two days after the birth of his daughter, Alice Lee Roosevelt. A distraught Roosevelt left his daughter with relatives and sought refuge in the West, where he pursued ranching in the Dakota territory. He returned to the East and his daughter after two years, but Roosevelt's Western sojourn allowed him to mourn as well as assume the masculine identity of a cowboy. Back home in the East, Roosevelt remarried and resumed his political career, garnering an appointment as New York City Police Commissioner and earning a reputation for honest and enthusiastic involvement with policing activities. A strong believer in naval power and American expansion on the world stage, Roosevelt was appointed Assistant Secretary of the Navy by President McKinley in 1897. Following the 1898 declaration of war against Spain, Roosevelt resigned his position and formed a voluntary cavalry regiment called the Rough Riders, recruiting cowboys from areas such as New Mexico. Although suffering from poor eyesight, Roosevelt gained fame as a war hero for leading a successful assault upon San Juan Hill in Cuba. After returning from Cuba, Roosevelt was elected Governor of New York, but he antagonized mainstream Republicans by embracing such progressive causes as civil service reform and regulation of business. He also supported American imperialism as is evident in his 1899 address entitled "In Praise of the Strenuous Life," in which Roosevelt asserted that Americans must accept the responsibility of world leadership thrust upon them by the Spanish-American War. Appealing to notions of muscular Christian masculinity, Anglo Saxon superiority, militarism, and Social Darwinism, Roosevelt exclaimed that Americans must not shrink from its responsibilities as only through strife and struggle could the nation realize its destiny and greatness.

Although Roosevelt's imperialism clashed with many of the nation's founding principles, his war record, identification with progressive reform, and outgoing personality made him a popular figure with the public. Republican leaders, however, were exasperated with Roosevelt and decided that elevation to the Vice Presidency might get Roosevelt out of the public eye and New York politics. Accordingly, Roosevelt was offered the position of McKinley's running mate in 1900 as the President sought re-election. The McKinley-Roosevelt ticket prevailed, but in September 1901 McKinley was assassinated while attending the Pan-American Exposition in Buffalo, and in the words of McKinley's campaign manager Marcus Hanna, "that damned cowboy is President." At age forty-two, Roosevelt was the youngest man to become President, and he moved quickly to establish his control over the office and allegiance to progressive principles.

Roosevelt's progressive agenda

Roosevelt gained a reputation for being a progressive trust buster in the Northern Securities Case (1902) in which the administration employed the Sherman Anti-trust Act to break up the Northern Securities Company organized by banking titan J. P. Morgan and railroad entrepreneur James G. Hill to attain a railroad monopoly in the Northwest. While Roosevelt did not break up as many trusts as his successor William Howard Taft, he was a master of self-promotion and made sure that the newspapers highlighted his trust-busting activities. In fact, Roosevelt perceived big business as efficient and important to the economy, but he believed government regulation, and the more extreme measure of breaking up trusts, were necessary to maintain a degree of authority and control over big business. Roosevelt also aspired to take a more progressive stance toward labor. Previous administrations sided with business and used federal troops to crush strikes, but Roosevelt asserted that he favored a "square deal" in which the government would assume a more neutral role in conflicts between labor and capital. The Anthracite Coal Strike of 1902 in the coalfields of Pennsylvania threatened the nation's economy and offered Roosevelt the opportunity to implement the "square deal." Coal operators finally agreed to accept arbitration after the President threatened to dispatch federal troops and seize the coal mines. The arbitration commission called for the striking miners to receive higher pay and reduced hours, but labor's power was limited when the coal operators were not required to recognize the United Mine Workers as the bargaining agent for the miners.

As an avid hunter who loved the Western environment and outdoors, Roosevelt's greatest progressive contribution was perhaps the creation of national parks and an emphasis upon the conservation of natural resources which he publicized by convening a White House conference on conservation. In fact, during one of his Presidential hunting expeditions, he supposedly refused to shoot a bear that was chained to a tree. A political cartoon depicting the event inspired the creation of the "teddy bear," playing upon the popularity of the President. Rather than a strict preservationist regarding the wilderness, Roosevelt believed in the planned use and renewal of resources for future generations that was certainly an improvement over the consumption ethic that guided America since the colonial era. Roosevelt appointed Gifford Pinchot as the first Chief of the United States Forest Service, angering Western timber interests who preferred the unfettered harvesting of the forests. Roosevelt also signed into law the creation of five national parks, and under the 1906 Antiquities Act the President proclaimed eighteen new national monuments.

Roosevelt easily won re-election in 1904 and continued to pursue a progressive agenda during his second term. In addition to expanding the forest acreage set aside for future use, the Roosevelt administration pushed Congress to enact such reform legislation as the Hepburn Act which called for the Interstate Commerce Commission to impose "just and reasonable" rates for the railroads and the Pure Food and Drug Act of 1906 that established government regulation to prevent the adulteration and mislabeling of foods and pharmaceuticals. Supposedly, after perusing Sinclair's *The Jungle* as part of his extended early morning reading and consuming one of his hearty sausage breakfasts, Roosevelt decided to support passage of the 1906 Meat Inspection Act. Still relatively young and popular with many Americans, Roosevelt could have sought another Presidential term in 1908, but essentially pleased with his progressive achievements and seeking new adventures, he turned down the

Republican nomination and supported his Secretary of War, William Howard Taft as the Republican candidate. With the popular Roosevelt's backing, Taft received the Republican nomination and easily defeated the Democratic nominee, William Jennings Bryan who was the party's standard bearer for the third time. Satisfied with the electoral outcome, Roosevelt believed that the country and progressive movement were in good hands, and he set off for an African hunting expedition.

William Howard Taft and a split in the progressive ranks

Taft, however, was very different from Roosevelt in background and temperament. A rather large man, Taft lacked the hyper activity of his predecessor in the Presidency. Rather than wanting to be a hunter or cowboy, Taft enjoyed golfing and watching boat races from the comfort of a hammock. Coming from a family where his father was a judge, Taft was deliberate and contemplative in contrast with the extroverted character of Roosevelt. After graduating from Yale, Taft entered the legal profession and secured a judicial appointment. In 1901, McKinley appointed him as the Governor-General of the Philippines which the United States acquired following the Spanish-American War, and three years later Roosevelt tapped Taft to serve in his cabinet as Secretary of War. Although Taft was a progressive who busted more trusts than Roosevelt and set aside considerable acreage for conservation, he lacked the self-promotion talent of Roosevelt and was perceived as betraying the progressive legacy of his predecessor. Taft had promised tariff reform and called a special session of Congress to enact reduced rates; however, the Payne-Aldrich Tariff that passed the Congress failed to provide the expected relief. Confronted with a divided Republican Party, Taft reluctantly signed the legislation, angering progressives. Taft was also denounced for abandoning progressive conservation principles in the Ballinger-Pinchot Controversy. Progressives were disappointed when Taft replaced Roosevelt's Secretary of the Interior James Rudolph Garfield with Richard Ballinger, a former mayor of Seattle. Ballinger exacerbated the situation by opening some Western public lands to business development; an action that was criticized by Roosevelt's friend Chief Forester Gifford Pinchot. Taft supported Ballinger, and Pinchot was dismissed for insubordination, leading many progressives to accuse the President of breaking with the Roosevelt progressive legacy.

Election of 1912

The split within the progressive ranks of the Republican Party convinced Roosevelt that it was time for his return to the United States. Overcoming reservations about serving a third term, Roosevelt challenged Taft for the Republican Presidential nomination in 1912. Roosevelt did well in the primaries, but Taft now controlled the political machinery of the party and narrowly gained the nomination at a raucous convention. A disgruntled Roosevelt decided to mount a third-party challenge to Taft and accepted the nomination of the Progressive Party, often referred to as the Bull Moose Party, after the exuberant Roosevelt replied to a reporter's question about his health that he felt like a bull moose. On the campaign trail, Roosevelt articulated the philosophy of the New Nationalism in which the former President embraced the efficiency of big business but insisted that the regulatory powers of the government must be expanded to police the behavior of "bad" trusts who abused their economic power. Although the Bull Moose platform also endorsed women's suffrage and social welfare policies such as a minimum wage, critics worried that the centralization of power inherent in the New Nationalism was a threat to American democracy.

Sensing an opportunity to take advantage of the split within the Republican ranks, the Democrats nominated New Jersey Governor Woodrow Wilson as their Presidential candidate. Wilson was a Southerner from Virginia who grew up in South Carolina and Georgia under the tutelage of his strict Presbyterian minister father whose influence was apparent in his son's moralistic approach to politics and diplomacy as President. Rather than joining the ministry, Wilson was a history and political science scholar who earned a doctorate from Johns Hopkins University. In his scholarship and politics, Wilson reflected the prejudices of his Southern heritage, embracing the mythology of the Lost Cause, denouncing the tyranny of Reconstruction, and supporting racial segregation. After serving as President of Princeton University, Wilson was elected Governor of New Jersey, where he pursued a progressive reform agenda. As a Presidential candidate in 1912, Wilson developed the New Freedom as an alternative to the New Nationalism proposed by Roosevelt. The New Freedom platform called for the regulation and breaking up of big business in order to restore the economic and political freedom of the common people. Freed from the control of the trusts, free competition, Wilson argued, would allow resourceful workers and small businesses to reach their full potential. Although Wilson and his New Freedom agenda garnered only about 40 percent of the popular vote, the Democratic candidate won an overwhelming Electoral College victory in an election where the Republican vote was split with Roosevelt finishing ahead of Taft—although Taft would later be appointed to the Supreme Court by President Warren G. Harding. Progressivism appeared to be the big winner in the Election of 1912 with Wilson, Taft, and Roosevelt running as Progressives; although some Americans still believed in more fundamental transformation of the economy with Socialist Party candidate Debs garnering over 900,000 votes and approximately 6 percent of the electorate.

Woodrow Wilson's New Freedom

After assuming office, Wilson worked to implement his New Freedom agenda with the Democratic-controlled Congress. To increase competition and reduce subsidies to big business, Congress enacted the Underwood-Simmons Tariff and substantially lowered rates. The Federal Reserve Act was proposed as a means through which to reduce the power of Wall Street bankers over the American economy. A Federal Reserve Board appointed by the President was to supervise a national system of twelve regional banks overseeing the private banks as members of the Federal Reserve System. Flexibility in the nation's monetary system was to be assured through the board's control over the nation's money supply by expansion during deflation and reduction in periods of inflation—a system today in which the board exercises regulatory control by establishing interest rates for its member banks. Competition was also to be increased through the establishment of the Federal Trade Commission to monitor unfair trade practices such as false advertising, price fixing, and anticompetitive business activities. The Clayton Anti-trust Act was also passed to increase the powers of the government to regulate the trusts, but the legislation was also proclaimed by Samuel Gompers of the AFL as the "Magna Carts for labor," as it exempted unions from the anti-trust laws. Wilson also gained labor support with his appointment of progressive activist attorney Louis Brandies to the Supreme Court. The selection encountered considerable opposition from Republicans and business interests, but Brandies was narrowly confirmed and became the first Jewish member of the nation's highest court.

Although Wilson won praise for enacting his New Freedom agenda and was reelected in 1916, his attention was increasingly focused upon the Great War in Europe, and progressive reform was downplayed. Middle-class adherents of progressive reform wanted to address the abuses of capitalism and circumvent more radical change. Some progressives feared that continued governmental regulation of business might lead the nation in the direction of socialism and, thus, believed that progressive reform had achieved its goals. In addition, when the United States entered the First World War in April 1917, the war superseded reform as a national priority. Business leaders and corporations who were censured by progressives for their monopolistic practices were now perceived as possessing the talent and organizational skills necessary to achieve a military victory for the United States. The war effort required centralized management and planning, not the busting of trusts, and big business reasserted its dominant position in the American economy; a position that it would assume in the 1920s until the crisis of capitalism with the onset of the Great Depression in 1929.

Progressivism and black Americans

While progressive reform claimed to represent the common people of America, the predominantly white middle-class reformers were condescending, at best, to the New Immigration and essentially ignored the black community while failing to mount a challenge to racial segregation. The progressive Presidents displayed little interest in the plight of black Americans, and it was left to black leaders to design strategies for addressing racial inequality. Although Roosevelt initially invited the conservative black educator, Booker T. Washington to dinner at the White House, he retreated after fierce opposition was expressed to having a black man to dinner at the people's White House. Spokesmen for the President insisted that the visit was just an informal lunch and not a dinner with the Presidential family, and Roosevelt failed to issue another invitation to the black spokesman. Perhaps a better indication of Roosevelt's racial attitudes was how he handled the Brownsville Affair in 1906. Residents of Brownsville, Texas were unhappy with the stationing of Buffalo Soldiers to the region. When a white man was killed, the townspeople placed the blame upon the black soldiers, although there was little evidence to confirm their suspicions. President Roosevelt, nevertheless, accepted the recommendation of the Army's Inspector General and dishonorably discharged 167 troopers who were no longer able to receive military pensions. In 1972, the Army revisited the case, and the soldiers were found innocent with their dishonorable discharges overturned. In addition to the Brownsville Affair, Roosevelt embraced manifest destiny and the superiority of Anglo Saxon civilization, expressing concern about miscegenation and the mongrelizing of the white race while endorsing the eugenics movement. Wilson, who was the first Southerner to reside in the White House since Zachary Taylor, believed in the racial inferiority of blacks and brought the Jim Crow segregation of the South into the daily operations of the federal government. As a scholar, Wilson denounced Reconstruction efforts to enforce the Fourteenth and Fifteenth Amendments, preferring instead the racist propaganda of *The Birth of a Nation* which was screened at the White House and praised by the President. With progressive leaders ignoring racial segregation and violent lynching, it was incumbent upon black leaders to formulate their own strategies for confronting American racism. A conflicting black response was offered in the contrasting ideologies of Booker T. Washington and W. E. B. DuBois that remained influential into the Civil Rights Movement of the 1950s and 1960s.

Booker T. Washington and W. E. B. DuBois

Washington was born into slavery on a Virginia farm in 1856. After emancipation, he was interested in obtaining an education, and Washington enrolled at Hampton Institute, where he worked as a custodian to pay for tuition. Establishing himself as a teacher, Washington was selected in 1881 to head Tuskegee Institute in Alabama. Under the leadership of Washington, Tuskegee became one of the leading black colleges in the South, and the educator became an important spokesman for black Americans. In 1895, Washington was invited to explain his philosophy of education and race relations before a largely white audience at the Atlanta Exposition. In his so-called Atlanta Compromise, the educator advocated a gradual approach to racial progress. Rather than immediately expecting to achieve racial and political equality, Washington urged blacks to learn a trade and pursue vocational education that would provide an economic foundation for the black community. Washington asserted that in social and political matters, blacks and whites could be as separate as the fingers, but when it came to economics they could be as one with the hand. The temporary acceptance of segregation would earn the respect of whites who were largely supportive of Washington as a black leader.

While Washington had a large following, other black leaders rejected the educator's compromise and demanded that America honor its commitment to equal rights for all citizens. This position was well articulated by W. E. B. DuBois who emerged as the predominant black intellectual of the twentieth century. Coming from a very different background than Washington, DuBois grew up in the relatively integrated community of Great Barrington, Massachusetts. He studied at Fisk University in Atlanta and earned a doctorate from Harvard, accepting a professorship in history at Atlanta University. As a scholar, DuBois offered a more positive interpretation of Reconstruction, and in the seminal *The Souls of Black Folks* (1903), he analyzed the dual consciousness of his race as blacks and Americans. Refusing to accept segregation, DuBois joined with other black activists and sympathetic whites to form The National Association for the Advancement of Colored People (NAACP), serving as the editor of the organization's newspaper *The Crisis* from 1910 to 1934. DuBois was also a critic of Washington's educational philosophy, arguing that rather than concentrating upon vocational education, the black community should emphasize gaining the best education possible for the talented tenth of the community who would lead black Americans to achieve equality and full citizenship. In many ways, the life and career of Martin Luther King Jr. fulfilled the DuBois vision of the talented tenth. A critic of American racism and capitalism, DuBois eventually tired of the struggle and spent his final years in Africa. Supposedly when King was on the podium about to deliver his "I Have a Dream" speech on August 28, 1963, he was informed that the "old man" had died in Africa, and King insisted that the spirit of DuBois guided him in the inspirational address.

Legacy of progressivism

The progressive movement brought considerable political and economic reform to the United States, but for many black Americans and members of the working class, life had not changed that much, and big business regained much of its power and influence during the First World War. The struggle of the common people to achieve the promise of American life would continue into the 1920s as nativism again raised its ugly head during that turbulent decade.

Territorial expansion has been an integral part of American history since Jamestown and the Pilgrims and Puritans of the New England frontier. This expansion was justified with the concept of manifest destiny which envisioned the United States expanding its superior civilization from the Atlantic to the Pacific at the expense of Natives and, in the Southwest, Hispanics. In the period between 1865 and 1920, the United States extended its reach beyond North America, becoming an imperialist power with territorial possessions around the world. The rise of big business following the Civil War brought with it the rise of monopoly capitalism, an alliance between business and politics, the subjugation of the American West, and the creation of an American empire. There was considerable resistance, however, to the rise of the corporate order from Natives, working men and women, racial minorities, immigrants, indigenous radicals, Populist farmers, middle-class progressive reformers, and colonized people opposed to the imposition of an American empire. As the United States expanded its presence on the world stage between 1865 and 1920, often justifying empire with the rhetoric of American exceptionalism, there was also a countervailing resistance of anti-imperialism, arguing that the nation was betraying its democratic vision in the reach for empire and an American world order.

Further Reading:

Coletta, Paolo. *The Presidency of William Howard Taft*. Lawrence, KS: University Press of Kansas, 1973.

Chambers, John W. *The Tyranny of Change: America in the Progressive Era, 1900–1917*. New York: St. Martin's Press, 1980.

Davis, Allen. *Spearheads for Reform: The Social Settlements & The Progressive Movement, 1890–1914*. New York: Oxford University Press, 1967.

Hays, Samuel P. *Conservation and the Gospel of Efficiency: The Progressive Conservation Movement, 1890–1920*. Cambridge, MA: Harvard University Press, 1989.

Kolko, Gabriel. *The Triumph of Conservatism: A Reinterpretation of American History, 1900–1916*. New York: Free Press, 1963.

Lewis, David Levering. *W. E. B. DuBois: A Biography, 1868–1963*. New York: Holt, 2009.

McGerr, Michael. *A Fierce Discontent: The Rise and Fall of the Progressive Movement in America, 1870–1920*. New York: Free Press, 2003.

Morris, Edmund. *Theodore Rex*. New York: Random House, 2001.

Muncy, Robyn. *Creating a Female Dominion in American Reform, 1890–1935*. New York: Oxford University Press, 1994.

Stromquist, Shelton. *Reinventing "The People": The Progressive Movement, the Class Problem, and the Origins of American Liberalism*. Urbana, IL: University of Illinois Press, 2006.

Thelen, David. *The New Citizenship: Origins of Progressivism in Wisconsin, 1885–1900*. Columbia, MO: University of Missouri Press, 1972.

Wiebe, Robert. *The Search for Order, 1877–1920*. New York: Hill and Wang, 1967.

20

America on the World Stage, 1865–1920

"Trench at Bud Dajo." Prints and Photographs Division, Library of Congress. The Spanish-American War made the United States an imperial power. The nation's democratic principles were betrayed in the Philippine-American War in which as many as one million Filipinos were killed in a failed insurrection to attain self-government. In the ensuing Moro Rebellion, over a thousand fighters and Muslim civilians were killed by U.S. troops during the Battle of Bud Dajo, depicted in the photograph, in March 1906.

During the late nineteenth and early twentieth centuries, the United States transitioned from a continental expansionist power based upon manifest destiny to a global imperial nation motivated to a great extent by the capitalist search for resources and markets. This global expansion led to conflicts with other imperial nations and indigenous populations, promoting military interventions in Cuba, Haiti, Dominican Republic, Panama, Mexico, Hawaii, Russia, Philippines, and World War I. Anti-imperialists complained that in this global military and economic expansion the United States was betraying its founding principles that all men and women are created equal—although Native Americans might beg to differ with this interpretation of American history and continental expansion.

Nevertheless, by 1920 the United States had emerged as a major world power. Presidents Woodrow Wilson and Teddy Roosevelt offered contrasting visions for America's growing presence on the world stage that have often been embraced by their predecessors who prefer to ignore economic motivations such as securing oil reserves. Believing in the superior moral values of the United States, Wilson insisted that American power must be employed to promote national values such as democracy. Roosevelt considered himself a realist and rejected the Wilsonian moralizing, arguing that military power, or as he sometimes called it "the big stick," must be used to protect national interests and assure America's predominant position on the world stage. Whether one adheres to the approaches of Wilson or Roosevelt, since the Civil War the United States has embarked upon a course of empire bringing the nation into numerous conflicts which raise serious questions about the democratic principles upon which America was supposedly founded.

Reasons for global expansion

Many justifications were offered for America's expansion on the world stage following the Civil War. The rhetoric of manifest destiny, although originally designed to support continental expansion and the Mexican War, celebrated American exceptionalism and duty to impart on a civilizing world mission. In the early twentieth century, the religious implications of manifest destiny were often downplayed in favor of Social Darwinism, supposedly grounded in a more scientific understanding of the world. Employing concepts like survival of the fittest, imperialists such as Roosevelt argued that if America did not move forward to acquire territory and resources, other nations would, and this would undermine

America's position in the world. This rationalization was also related to scientific theories of racism that created racial hierarchies with Anglo Saxons on the top rung of the ladder. To maintain world order, it was the responsibility of civilized nations such as the United States to combat barbarism. Intellectuals such as Frederick Jackson Turner also insisted that the frontier was crucial as a safety valve for the survival of democracy, but the American frontier was supposedly closed in 1893. Advocates who agreed with Turner's frontier thesis, such as the Christian imperialist Josiah Strong, speculated as to why the frontier had to stop at the California shores of the Pacific Ocean. The civilizing and democratic mission of the frontier experience could be continued beyond American shores in Latin America, Africa, and Asia.

On a more concrete level, Naval officer Alfred T. Mahan argued that the study of history provided evidence that the nations with powerful navies who could control, and secure strategic global trading locations were best prepared to assume global leadership and dominance. In his significant work *The Influence of Sea Power Upon History* (1890), Mahan maintained that control of strategic sites such as the Strait of Gibraltar, Suez Canal, Pacific coaling stations, and Panama as the possible location of a canal across Central America would provide security for world trade as well as naval dominance on the high seas. Mahan's work certainly impressed Roosevelt who, as Assistant Secretary of the Navy, labored to implement the Naval officer's strategy. This naval expansion also promoted the search for international markets and resources pursued by American business interests. The Panics of 1873, 1893, and 1907 concerned American business leaders who worried that these economic depressions were the result of overexpansion, and domestic markets could not supply the necessary demand for growing factories and production. Therefore, it was the responsibility of the American government to promote and support, with military power if required, the expansion of business into the world market. An ever-expanding world marketplace was necessary to prevent depressions and domestic political unrest. Although often cloaked in the rhetoric of manifest destiny or American exceptionalism, the growth of American imperialism might be best understood by examining the search for markets and resources to support the capitalist corporate order.

Acquisitions of Alaska and Hawaii

The first major expansionist move following the Civil War was in 1867 during the Presidency of Andrew Johnson. Hoping to tap the natural resources of Alaska and take the nation's mind off the Civil War and Reconstruction, Johnson's Secretary of State William Seward purchased the territory from Imperial Russia. Seward was also concerned that the British in Canada might acquire Alaska, so he negotiated a treaty in which the United States paid $7.2 million for the region which the Russians had been unable to develop. Critics denounced the treaty, calling the proposed purchase "Seward's folly" and arguing that the price was too expensive for an isolated wilderness. Russia was also accused of bribing Senators to approve the purchase treaty, but Seward's vision appeared to be redeemed in 1896 when gold was discovered in Alaska. The region was found to include other valuable resources such as oil, and in 1959 Alaska was admitted to the union as a state. Today, there is considerable debate over the impact of development such as oil pipelines upon the Alaskan environment and indigenous people—who were certainly not consulted during the purchase negotiations between the Russians and Americans.

A similar disregard for indigenous rights was apparent in the approach of the United States to Hawaii. Although Hawaii was an independent kingdom from 1810 to 1893, the Native population was decimated by disease brought in by the Europeans and Chinese laborers. In the 1820s, American missionaries sought to Christianize the inhabitants of the Hawaiian Islands, and the religious community was soon followed by American businessmen who sought to promote a lucrative sugar trade between Hawaii and the United States. There were strong commercial ties with the United States as Hawaiian sugar was imported duty free, however, due to the political pressure from domestic sugar growers in Louisiana, the McKinley Tariff of 1890 removed Hawaiian sugar from the duty-free list. The tariff disrupted the sugar industry on the islands, but it occurred to American businessmen that annexation by the United States would restore their access to the American market. Accordingly, American businessmen, led by attorney and planter Samuel Dole, formed a Committee for Public Safety and planned a coup in January 1893 to overthrow the monarchy of Queen Lili'uokalani with the support of John L. Stevens, the American Minister to the Kingdom of Hawaii, who arranged for American Marines to be on hand to protect American property. With the acquiescence of Stevens, the Queen was placed under house arrest and forced to recognize the Republic of Hawaii with Dole as President. The American sugar planters assumed that annexation by the United States would follow the coup, but President Grover Cleveland was an anti-imperialist and refused to recognize the coup which did not enjoy the support of the Hawaiian people. The Republic of Hawaii formed by the planters remained in power until 1898 when the Spanish-American War provided a new opportunity for American annexation.

Origins of the Spanish-American War

The Spanish-American War was a conflict that elevated the United States to an imperial power, and whose significance to American history is all too often understated. The conflict originated with the desire of Cubans to break free from the yoke of Spanish colonialism. Americans were generally sympathetic to the Cuban struggle as it was associated with memories of the American Revolution and independence from British rule as well as the Monroe Doctrine of 1823 declaring that the United States opposed further European colonization in the Western Hemisphere. In addition, the late nineteenth century witnessed the growth of considerable trade between the United States and Cuba, whose appreciation for American culture was notable in the island's enthusiasm for American baseball over Spanish bull fighting. Opposition to the policies of Spanish General Valeriano Weyler, who employed concentration camps to control the restive Cuban population, was fanned by the yellow journalism of newspaper editors Joseph Pulitzer of the *New York World* and William Randolph Hearst of the *New York Journal* who were locked in newspaper circulation wars. Believing that sex and violence sold newspapers, the editors were convinced that a war with Spain might be good for business. Hearst encouraged reporters in Cuba to concentrate upon alleged atrocities committed by Spanish forces, and he claimed credit for starting the war, allegedly telling artist Frederick Remington whom the editor dispatched to Cuba, "You furnish the pictures, and I'll furnish the war." Hearst exaggerated his role in starting the war, but he did inflame the American public with his newspaper coverage of events in Cuba and publication of the de Lôme letter. Cuban rebels intercepted a communication between Enrique Dupuy de Lôme, the Spanish Ambassador to the United States, and the Foreign Minister of Spain, providing the letter to Hearst who published it in the *Journal*. The letter was critical of McKinley's leadership, and Hearst denounced de Lôme whose comments were intended for private consumption.

The growing concern regarding events in Cuba convinced McKinley to send the battleship *Maine* to Havana. While anchored in the Cuban harbor, the battleship exploded on February 15, 1898 with the loss of 260 sailors. Without any hard evidence, many American newspapers and politicians immediately blamed Spain for the explosion. A Hearst headline proclaimed, "Remember the *Maine*! To Hell with Spain!" It was not until the 1970s that an official Naval board of inquiry accepted the conclusion that the explosion was the result of internal combustion in a powder magazine as Spain had claimed at the time. Congress and the McKinley administration responded to the national uproar with a declaration of war against Spain, and Hearst set out to Cuba with the American troops to personally cover the war. To forestall criticism that the war represented an excursion into imperialism, Congress passed the Teller Amendment, introduced by Colorado Senator Henry Teller, asserting that the United States had no territorial designs on the island of Cuba—although in the aftermath of a victorious war these anti-imperialist sentiments were largely abandoned. As for the yellow journalists, Pulitzer expressed regret for his actions and used his fortune to establish prizes for journalistic excellence that are still honored today, while Hearst pursued a political career that failed to fulfill his Presidential ambitions and whose ambiguity was captured in the Orson Welles film, *Citizen Kane* (1941).

Spanish-American War and 1898 Treaty of Paris

The Spanish-American War was a resounding military success for the United States. American forces quickly drove the Spanish from Cuba and occupied the island of Puerto Rico. Approximately 400 Americans died during the Cuban campaign, in which Roosevelt emerged as a hero, while over 5,000 soldiers died due to poisoned canned meat, malaria, and yellow fever—in fact, the research conducted by Doctor Walter Reed into yellow fever during the campaign later played a key role in allowing the United States to conquer the deadly disease and construct the Panama Canal. Meanwhile, before leaving his position as Assistant Secretary of the Navy and joining the Rough Riders, Roosevelt dispatched a fleet under the command of Admiral George Dewey to attack the Spanish Naval squadron at Manila Bay in the Spanish Philippines colony. Taken by surprise, the Spanish ships, many of them wooden vessels, were no match for the modern American Navy which scored an overwhelming victory. Dewey then joined with Filipino troops under the command of Emilio Aguinaldo to force the Spanish from the islands. With an American fleet in the Philippines, the United States reconsidered its position on the acquisition of Hawaii as the islands could now serve as a coaling station for ships on the way to the Philippines, and Hawaii was annexed in July 1898. A similar rationale was used to acquire American Samoa and the port of Pago-Pago in the South Pacific in an 1899 agreement.

Overwhelmed militarily, Spain sued for an armistice, and the war was officially ended by the December 1898 Treaty of Paris in which the United States emerged as an imperial power. Cuban independence was recognized by the treaty, but the U.S. Congress no longer felt bound by the anti-imperialist principles of the Teller Resolution. In the Platt Amendment, the United States established a virtual military protectorate over Cuba, asserting the right to militarily intervene on the island in the event of political instability or Cuba falling into the hands of a government or foreign power opposed to the United States. Cuba was also forced to accept the construction of an American Naval installation on Cuban soil which became the Guantánamo Bay base—an installation which provided Fidel Castro with plenty of ammunition to denounce American imperialism and during the so-called war on terrorism emerged as a symbol of torture and disregard for international standards of justice. After paying Spain $20 million for the Philippines, the United States annexed the former Spanish colonies of Puerto Rico, the Philippines, and the island of Guam in the north Pacific. The United States was now an imperial power with colonial possessions that were annexed without the consent of the indigenous populations, and anti-imperialists charged that the United States betrayed its founding principles in the jungles of the Philippines.

Anti-imperialism

The American Anti-Imperialist League was formed to resist annexation of the Philippines, and included such prominent Americans as Jane Addams, Republican Senator George Frisbie Hoar of Massachusetts, educator John Dewey, former President Grover Cleveland, and authors Henry James and Mark Twain. As a brilliant satirist, Twain composed an updated version of "The Battle Hymn of the Republic," in which greed rather than truth is marching on. Although unable to prevent annexation of the Philippines, anti-imperialists endorsed the 1900 Presidential candidacy of Democrat William Jennings Bryan who denounced the imperialistic policies of the McKinley administration. Many pundits perceived the election of 1900 as a referendum on American empire, interpreting McKinley's victory as a popular mandate for American imperialism. However, that may be reading too much into the electoral results, as by 1900 the American economy was finally recovering from the devastating Panic of 1893, and incumbents such as McKinley usually benefit electorally from a growing economy. So paychecks rather than imperialism may have been uppermost in the minds of voters.

Resistance to American imperialism, however, was paramount to many residents of Puerto Rico and the Philippines. In Puerto Rico, poet and statesman José De Diego urged cultural and political resistance to the island's control by the United States without the consent of the governed. In 1897, Spain had granted broad powers of self-government to Puerto Rico, but these rights were dissolved by the occupying Americans. Today, Puerto Rico is a commonwealth of the United States, which exempts Puerto Ricans from paying federal income taxes and provides for residents to freely enter the United States without passports or visas. Puerto Ricans, nevertheless, do not enjoy the full political rights of American citizens. Residents of the island may elect their own governor and legislature, but they are not represented in Congress except for an observer status that does not include a vote for the territory whose population exceeds that of twenty-one American states. In addition, Puerto Rico is not included in the Electoral College, and its residents are denied the right to vote for President. This political disenfranchisement is often costly as is evident in the tardy federal response to Hurricane Maria that devastated Puerto Rico in 2017 in contrast with the more immediate aid dispatched to hurricane victims in Texas and Florida. Puerto Ricans have been divided in their political reaction to the relationship with the United States: some preferring statehood, others content with maintaining a commonwealth status, and still others advocating an independent nation—a movement that has resulted in violent political confrontations and what the United States government has deemed terrorist acts.

Philippine-American War

The people of the Philippines initially welcomed Americans as liberators who would help them overthrow the yoke of Spanish imperialism. Instead, the United States ignored the will of the Filipino people, determining that their "little brown brothers"—to employ the racist political language of the Congressional debate—lacked the qualities for self-government and would benefit from the civilizing mission of American democracy, not to mention that annexation opened Filipino markets and resources to American corporations. Responding to what they perceived as a political betrayal by the United States, Filipino forces under the leadership of President Emilio Aguinaldo resisted the imposition of American rule in the Philippine-American War that raged from 1899 to 1902. Although little known to many Americans, this brutal jungle conflict witnessed the type of atrocities that later characterized the Vietnam War. American soldiers were frustrated by the guerrilla tactics employed by the Filipinos and complained that they could not distinguish combatants from civilians who supported the insurgents. To deny the guerrilla army popular assistance, the Americans destroyed crops, forced village populations into concentration or internment camps, and used torture tactics such as waterboarding. These savage practices resulted in the death of perhaps a million Filipinos who perished in the fighting and starvation promoted by the American strategy of total war. Approximately 5,000 American soldiers were killed in the war which officially ended in 1902 with the capture of Aguinaldo who called upon his people to give up the struggle. Resistance in more remote areas continued among groups such as the Moro people until their defeat at the Battle of Bud Bagsak in June 1913 when American forces under the command of General John J. Pershing, who later led American troops to victory in World War I, annihilated almost 5,000 fighters and civilians who had retreated to a remote mountain outpost. The Moro people of the Philippines, who are predominantly Muslim, have provided some support for Islamic militants as the legacy of American imperialism continues to cast a shadow upon the region. The Philippines finally received their independence after World War II in which Filipinos joined with Americans to resist the invasion of Japanese imperialists, although the presence of American military installations in the independent nation and support for dictators such as the Marcos family continued to cause friction between the two nations.

Open door in China

The creation of an American colony in the Philippines fostered additional interest in tapping the potential lucrative Asian markets, leading to the acquisition of American Samoa and Hawaii. American corporate interests were especially intrigued by the possibilities of the China market with its large population, although most of the Chinese people lacked the resources to purchase American products. Another problem for American business penetration of China was that the leading European powers had already carved a weakened China into spheres of influence or protectorates. Arriving on the imperialistic scene a little late, the United States pursued a strategy that would open these spheres of influence in China to American trade. McKinley's Secretary of State John Hay dispatched diplomatic notes in 1899 to Russia, England, Germany, France, Italy, and Japan, asserting the right of an open door to American trade within their respective Chinese spheres of influence. The replies to these so-called open-door notes were essentially diplomatic and non-committal in tone. Hay, however, seized upon this ambiguity to proclaim that the major powers had agreed in principle to the American demand for an open door in China. Of course, the question remained as to whether the United States was prepared to employ force in pursuit of this trade policy. An opportunity for the United States to back up its open door presented itself with the 1900 Boxer Rebellion in China. The Boxers were a nationalistic movement opposed to the foreign cultural and political domination of China. Prepared to drive foreigners from China, the Boxers laid siege to the large international community in the capital city of Peking or Beijing as it is called today. When Chinese authorities proved unable to protect the foreign enclave in Peking, an international military force, which included American troops, was organized to conduct a rescue mission. Despite the opposition of the Chinese imperial government, the international force intervened and crushed the rebellion which was a threat to American, European, and Japanese investments. The invading forces committed atrocities upon any Chinese associated with the Boxers, and the Chinese government was forced to pay a large indemnity that also included funds designated for the United States. With the defeat of the Boxer Rebellion, the United States demonstrated its commitment to the open-door policy that would have major ramifications for America and the world. With a policy of expansion in Asia and the Pacific, the United States was on a collision course with Japan, who following the 1868 Meiji Restoration was devoted to policies of industrialization and expansion that rivaled the imperial ambitions of the major European powers and challenged the racial assumptions of both Americans and Europeans. In the 1930s, Japan invaded China and announced that they were terminating the open door in China; actions that culminated in World War II in the Pacific.

Roosevelt Corollary and Panama Canal

A strong supporter of American expansion in Asia, President Theodore Roosevelt also extended American political and economic influence within the Caribbean and Latin America. In his 1904 State of the Union message, the President issued what is known as the Roosevelt Corollary to the Monroe Doctrine in response to the Venezuela Crisis of 1902-1903 during which European powers threatened a military intervention to collect debts. Roosevelt expressed his support for the Monroe Doctrine and the principle of opposing European intervention into the Western Hemisphere. He did, however, acknowledge that the European nations did have a point regarding the political instability in Latin America that could lead to an international crisis. Therefore, if a European power had a legitimate claim against a Latin nation which refused to honor its obligations, the United States reserved the right to intervene and settle the dispute. In other words, Roosevelt decreed that the United States would henceforth serve as the police force of Latin America—a policy that was unilaterally declared by the United States without the consultation of the Latin American republics. The Monroe Doctrine which was initially perceived as offering protection for the fledgling democracies of Latin America was now viewed as a tool through which the United States justified intervention into the internal affairs of these republics. In 1904, Roosevelt ordered two warships to the Dominican Republic and demanded that collection of duties at the port of Santa Domingo be turned over to the United States. The action was taken in response to claims of corruption in the Dominican Republic and to forestall a threatened invasion by Germany to collect debts from the troubled nation. The United States would now efficiently operate the customs house and assure that the Dominicans honored their obligations. The Roosevelt Corollary established a precedent for intervention embraced by Roosevelt's successors in Cuba (1906–1909), Nicaragua (1909–1910, 1912–1925), Haiti (1915–1934), and the Dominican Republic (1916–1924).

The aggression of Roosevelt toward America's Latin neighbors was perhaps most notable in the acquisition of the Panama Canal. With the seizure of an American empire in the Pacific, there was an increased demand by merchants and Naval officers for the building of a canal through Central America that would allow for shipping and Naval vessels to rapidly move from the Atlantic to the Pacific without having to travel around South America. Initial efforts to build a canal focused upon Nicaragua, but volcanic activity in that nation led to the abandonment of a Nicaraguan route. Attention turned toward Panama where the French were forced by an outbreak of yellow fever to forego their efforts to complete a canal project. Under the Clayton-Bulwer Treaty of 1850, the United States and England were pledged to jointly construct a canal accessible to the shipping of both nations. In 1901, Britain, bogged down by the burdens of empire with the Boer War in South Africa, informally recognized Latin America as a sphere of influence under the domination of the United States and negotiated the Hay-Pauncefote Treaty in which the British abandoned joint construction of a Central American canal. Freed from British constraints, the United States turned its attention to Panama and negotiating a treaty with Colombia who exercised sovereignty over Panama. After agreeing to pay French business interests represented by Philippe-Jean Bunau-Varilla $40 million to complete the canal French engineers had started, the United States negotiated the Hay-Herrán Treaty with Colombia in which the United States agreed to pay Colombia $10 million plus an annual payment of $250,000 to construct and operate a canal on a six-mile wide strip of land across the isthmus of Panama. The Colombian Senate, however, rejected the treaty, believing that the terms should be more financially favorable to the South American nation. Roosevelt was furious and believed that the Colombians had negotiated in bad faith, exacerbating the President's condescending view of the Latin American people. Thus, Roosevelt agreed to a plot orchestrated by Bunau-Varilla for a Panamanian revolution supported by the United States. When the Panamanians revolted, Roosevelt dispatched troops and American Naval vessels to prevent the Colombians from crushing the uprising. The United States then immediately recognized the independence of Panama and negotiated a new canal treaty with Varilla who was appointed Foreign Minister of the Panamanian government. The terms of the Hay-Varilla Treaty were essentially the same as the Hay-Herrán Treaty with the exception that the American Canal Zone was now ten rather than six miles wide, and Colombia received no compensation. The completion of the new agreement also insured that Varilla received the $40 million for surrendering the French rights. The aggressive tactics Roosevelt employed to gain the canal were denounced throughout Latin America, but the President paid little attention to such criticism, ostensibly telling reporters that he had "stolen the canal fair and square." During the Warren G. Harding administration, the United States did agree to pay Colombia $25 million in compensation, and Colombia officially recognized the independence of Panama. Nevertheless, the Panama Canal remained a symbol of American imperialism, leading Presidents Gerald Ford and Jimmy Carter to pursue negotiations culminating in Panama gaining control of the canal on December 31, 1999, although the United States reserved the right to militarily intervene if the neutrality of the canal was compromised.

Taft's dollar diplomacy

Although less prone to military adventures than his predecessor, William Howard Taft supported American expansionism with his "dollar diplomacy" generally replacing Roosevelt's "big stick" diplomacy. Taft and his Secretary of State, corporate lawyer Philander Knox, believed that promoting international stability through guaranteeing loans to American corporations and friendly foreign governments would provide access to international capitalist markets and promote American influence in the world. The idea was that the United States could exercise soft power control over international markets and governments through promoting investment to insure stability and economic growth. The dollar diplomacy of the Taft administration was especially interested in fostering business expansion into Central America and the Far East. Roosevelt was awarded the Nobel Peace Prize for negotiating an end to the Russo-Japanese War of 1905, and the Taft administration sought to extend American influence into Manchuria by encouraging the railroad investments of American bankers. Taft supported the United Fruit Company which exercised considerable political and economic influence within Central America, but the investments of the corporation earned profits for stockholders rather than improving the living conditions of indigenous people in the region. Thus, the dollar diplomacy endorsed by Taft was unable to prevent revolutionary unrest from challenging the capitalist order. In the final analysis, the Taft administration was often forced to employ bayonets in support of American dollars.

Wilsonian idealism and the Mexican Revolution

Woodrow Wilson found both the militarism of Roosevelt and the dollar diplomacy of Taft to be unacceptable. Assuming a moralistic perspective, Wilson believed that to fulfill the vision of America's founders, it was imperative that the foreign policy of the United States promote not business and empire, but rather export democracy. Wilsonian idealism tended to ignore the fact that American history was deficient in bringing democracy and equality before the law to all citizens of the nation. Indeed, Wilson's racism blinded him to the imperfections of the democracy he hoped to export. Wilsonian moralism may actually be responsible for more wars and deaths than the traditional imperialism of a Teddy Roosevelt as the struggle to make the world safe for democracy embraces a crusading attitude in support of military interventions.

The Mexican Revolution offered Wilson an opportunity to assert this democratic ideology. In 1910, the Mexican people overthrew the thirty-five-year dictatorship of Porfirio Diaz that enriched foreign investors and the Mexican elite. The leader of the revolutionary forces in Mexico was Francisco Madero, a scholar who supported many of Wilson's ideas. Madero, however, was betrayed and murdered by General Victoriano Huerta who assumed power in Mexico. Outraged by this immoral assumption of power, Wilson allegedly remarked that he "would teach Mexico to elect good men." Taking advantage of an incident in Tampico, Mexico, where American sailors were arrested and released by Mexican authorities who refused to acknowledge the American Navy with a twenty-one-gun salute, Wilson invaded Vera Cruz and sought to prevent munition shipments to Huerta, who was eventually forced from power. Venustiano Carranza, who fought against Huerta but opposed Wilson's military intervention, assumed power in Mexico, but the country remained in turmoil. On March 9, 1916, Pancho Villa, a revolutionary leader and bandit opposed to Carranza, raided the border town of Columbus, New Mexico, and nineteen civilians were killed. While it was difficult to ascertain Villa's motives for the attack, Wilson responded by sending an expeditionary force under the command of General Pershing to invade Mexico over the objections of Carranza. The invaders clashed with Carranza's forces, but were unable to find Villa. The American troops were withdrawn as the United States turned its attention to the war in Europe, but young officers such as Dwight Eisenhower, George Patton, and Douglas MacArthur gained military experience they would later apply in World Wars I and II. Wilson's efforts to instruct the Mexican people in democracy resulted in two American invasions that violated the democratic principles of self-determination.

The United States enters World War One

While the Wilson administration also employed democratic rhetoric to justify the dispatching of troops to Haiti in 1916 to prevent political violence and assure the stability of American investments, the President's attention was increasingly drawn toward the conflict in Europe between the Triple Alliance of Germany, Austria-Hungary, and Italy and the Triple Entente of England, France, and Russia. As the war on the Western front became bogged down in the savagery of trench warfare, Americans wanted to avoid this carnage, and the Wilson administration announced a policy of neutrality. In the Presidential election of 1916, Wilson defeated the Republican nominee Supreme Court Chief Justice Charles Evans Hughes, relying upon the slogan, "he kept us out of war." Within months of his second inauguration, however, the United States entered the conflict on the side of the Triple Entente. It was difficult to maintain a neutral stance, as numerous factors inclined the United States to side with the British. Ancestral ties encouraged many Americans to favor aiding the British, while a common language made it easier for the English to influence the American public with stories of German atrocities such as the massacre of civilians in the invasion of neutral Belgium. The most essential tie to the British Empire, however, proved to be the lucrative trade between the United States and their British cousins, and Wall Street was concerned about repayment of extensive loans provided to the British side. Wilson, nevertheless, was uncomfortable with relying upon monetary arguments, and instead chided the Germans for employing what the President considered to be an immoral weapon, the submarine whose sinking of vessels without warning was considered by Wilson to be a violation of international law. Unable to break the stalemate on the Western front, Germany attempted to defeat England by using unrestricted submarine warfare to blockade the island nation. Wilson was incensed when on May 7, 1915, a German submarine sank the English ocean liner *Lusitania* off the coast of Ireland with the loss of 1,198 people, including 128 Americans. Germany responded to the outcry over the sinking by observing that it had warned Americans not to sail on the ship which sank quickly due to explosions from munitions which the British were attempting to sneak across the Atlantic on a civilian ocean liner. The British vehemently denied that they were storing munitions on the *Lusitania*, but subsequent investigations have supported the German claim. Faced with protest over the sinking of other ships as well, the Germans pledged to abandon submarine warfare. Wilson's protest over the *Lusitania* was strong enough to convince the more pacifist-leaning William Jennings Bryan to resign as Wilson's Secretary of State to be replaced by Robert Lansing, who urged Wilson to take a stronger stance against German aggression.

The Germans did temporarily refrain from submarine warfare, but in January 1917, they resumed the policy. Deadlocked on the Western front with dwindling resources and troops, the Germans gambled that a submarine blockade might drive England out of the war before the United States could train and dispatch soldiers to the trenches of France. The gamble failed as the United States was able to mobilize more quickly and efficiently than Germany had anticipated. The move to war was also exacerbated by the Zimmerman Telegram which British intelligence intercepted and publicly revealed. The communication from the German Foreign Office to the Mexican government proposed an alliance between the two nations if the United States entered the war against Germany. Hoping to keep American troops tied down in North America, Germany promised to help Mexico regain the Southwestern territory they lost to the United States in the Mexican War. Devastated by the Mexican Revolution, Mexico was in no position to make such an alliance, no matter how much resentment was still felt toward the colossus of the North for the aggression of the 1840s, but the Zimmerman Telegram fulfilled its propaganda purposes for the British. In April 1917, President Wilson asked Congress for a declaration of war against Germany, stating the American war aims in the messianic rhetoric of Wilsonian idealism. Wilson declared that the crusade in Europe would be "the war to end all wars" and that America's goal was not territory or wealth, but rather to make "the world safe for democracy." The irony of militarily imposing democracy remained lost on Wilson, and the idealism of Wilson's rhetoric was soon overwhelmed by nationalistic excess.

World War I on the home front and battlefield

One of the first casualties of the war was free speech. Shortly after approving a declaration of war, Congress enacted the Espionage Act that prohibited interference with military operations and the conscription of American civilians. In *Schenck v. United States* (1919), the Supreme Court unanimously ruled that free speech did not apply to draft resistance which constituted "a clear and present danger" to American security, underscoring a trend in which during times of crisis, the United States has sacrificed liberty on the altar of security. Under the Espionage Act, dissident Americans such as Victor Berger, Eugene Debs, and Emma Goldman were arrested and imprisoned, preparing the ground for the wholescale violation of civil liberties during the First Red Scare which followed World War I. The intolerant tone set by the federal government was followed by state and local authorities as well as vigilante mobs. The Committee on Public Information headed by journalist George Creel promoted a propaganda campaign on behalf of the war effort that stigmatized German Americans, some of whom changed their sir names from Schmidt to Smith for self-preservation. German language classes were discontinued in many high schools and universities, while sauerkraut became "liberty cabbage" and hamburger "liberty steak." Mobs attacked German Americans and radicals, killing a German socialist in Illinois and lynching IWW organizer Frank Little in Montana.

Meanwhile, American forces acquitted themselves well on the battlefield. Under the overall command of General Pershing, who had seen action during the American military interventions in the Philippines and Mexico, American fighting men played a significant role in stopping a German offensive at Belleau Wood in France, and with the fresh troops from the United States, the German were being pushed back on the Western front. With Germany on the defensive, Wilson issued his peace plans which he called the Fourteen Points. Wilson extolled the peace plans as promoting a new international order that would prevent future wars, and he believed that his pledge to assure peace without victory would bring Germany to the negotiating table. Among the Fourteen Points were open diplomacy targeting secret treaties and territorial agreements that promoted conflict, reduction of armaments, freedom of trade and navigation on the high seas, self-determination—although this embracing of democracy was somewhat limited as Wilson believed that colonized people of color were not yet ready for self-government—,and a League of Nations that would provide for an international body to oversee the treaty and prevent future wars. In November 1918, the Germans agreed to an armistice based on the principles of the Fourteen Points, but at the peace conference in Versailles they were treated as a defeated nation.

Treaty of Versailles

Wilson enjoyed considerable prestige after the war and confidently prepared to head the American delegation to Versailles, where he assumed that his plans for a new international order would be enacted. But Wilson discovered that the world and peace process were not so easily managed. A challenge to Wilson's capitalist international order emerged in Russia with the Bolshevik Revolution. Wilson perceived revolutionary change, whether in Russia or Mexico, as a threat to stability and free trade that would be guaranteed by a League of Nations. Concerned with the ideology of communism as well as what he considered the treachery of the Bolsheviks abandoning treaty obligations to their British and French allies by reaching a separate agreement with the Germans, Wilson committed American troops to an international force that briefly intervened in the Russian civil war following the Bolshevik seizure of power. However, there was little enthusiasm for a more extended intervention from a war-weary nation. Wilson also assumed that problems emanating from the Bolshevik Revolution could be addressed through the liberal world order to be ratified at Versailles, although the Bolshevik government was not invited to the peace conference.

Wilson's contemporaries in France and England did not share his vision of peace without victory, insisting that Germany should be censured for its aggressive policies that led to war in 1914 and the deaths of so many French and British soldiers. The Treaty of Versailles, accordingly, was hardly peace without victory. The terms were dictated to Germany who was forced to accept a war guilt clause and assigned $32 billion in reparations. Paying off this enormous war debt was made even more difficult when the Germans were forced to surrender territory such as the

Saar coalfields, Sudetenland, and Danzig Corridor. Wilson recognized the inequities of the treaty, but he believed that the problems could be addressed by the League of Nations after the passions generated by the war had cooled. Essentially, Wilson was willing to compromise everything but the League, and his judgment may have been impaired by a stroke suffered during the negotiations.

Senate ratification struggle

After so many compromises at Versailles, Wilson was not in a mood to deal with Senate Republicans opposed to the treaty. Wilson got off to an awkward footing with Senate Republicans when he neglected to appoint any leaders of the opposition party to the Versailles delegation. As Chairman of the Senate Foreign Relations Committee, Henry Cabot Lodge of Massachusetts led the opposition to the treaty, insisting that his reservations be addressed through revisions of the Versailles agreement. Lodge was especially concerned with Article X which the Senator interpreted as committing the United States to militarily defending the treaty and the international status quo, undermining the nation's independence and the power of Congress to declare war. Another group of approximately a dozen Senators were called Irreconcilables and opposed ratification of the treaty under any circumstances. Led by William Borah of Idaho, Robert LaFollette of Wisconsin, and George Norris of Nebraska, the Irreconcilables included both Republicans and Democrats, primarily from the West and Midwest.

Wilson, however, was not prepared to negotiate with either group, deciding that he would go over the heads of the Senators and appeal directly to the American people, launching an ambitious national speaking tour on behalf of the treaty. In late September 1919, Wilson collapsed shortly before a speaking engagement in Pueblo, Colorado, and his train returned immediately to Washington, where the President suffered a massive stroke on October 2 that left him paralyzed on one side of his body and barely able to speak. The extent of Wilson's health crisis was not made apparent to the American public as access to the President was limited to his wife and personal physician. Today, the Twenty-fifth Amendment to the Constitution would provide for the Vice President to temporarily assume the Presidency in such a scenario, but Wilson was certainly not willing to resign. Instead with the President isolated in the White House, all communications were conducted through his wife Edith Bolling Galt Wilson, and for all intentional purposes the United States had its first female chief executive. Speaking for her husband, Mrs. Wilson made it clear to Senate Democratic leaders that they were to make no amendments or accept reservations to the treaty, and the Treaty of Versailles failed to obtain the required two-thirds Senate vote for ratification.

Myth of isolationism

Following the final rejection of the treaty in March 1920, many historians argue that the United States entered a period of isolationism, but this term is often misconstrued. There was certainly a period of disillusionment after the moral crusade proclaimed by Wilson resulted in over 116,000 American fatalities without achieving the League of Nations that the President promised would provide the means to prevent future conflicts. In rejecting the treaty and other international organizations such as the World Court, the United States was taking a unilateralist, but not isolationist, approach to international relations. The United States might be going it alone politically, but after the creation of an American empire business interests were hardly prepared to retreat from the search for global markets. During the 1920s, the United States continued intervention in Central American nations such as Nicaragua in support of American corporations. The emergence of the United States as a world power did not necessarily usher in a period of peace and prosperity. Republican Senators George Norris of Nebraska and Robert LaFollette of Wisconsin voted against expansion and American entrance into World War I, arguing that the war would primarily benefit munition makers and Wall Street bankers as America betrayed its traditional democratic values in pursuit of wealth and empire. Rather than the roaring 1920s of good times after the sacrifices of wartime, the decade was characterized by uncertainty and cultural conflicts with the suppression of dissent, xenophobia and the emergence of the Second Ku Klux Klan, along with class and racial conflict that climaxed in the Great Depression and crisis of capitalism.

Further Reading:

Beisner, Robert L. *Twelve Against Empire: The Anti-Imperialists, 1898–1900*. New York: McGraw-Hill, 1968.

Collin, Richard H. *Theodore Roosevelt's Caribbean: The Panama Canal, the Monroe Doctrine, and the Latin American Context*. Baton Rouge, LA: Louisiana State University Press, 1990.

Drake, Richard. *The Education of an Anti-Imperialist: Robert LaFollette and U.S. Expansion*. Madison, WI: University of Wisconsin Press, 2013.

Jacobson, Matthew Fyre. *Barbarian Virtues: The United States Encounters Foreign Peoples at Home and Abroad, 1876–1917*. New York: Hill and Wang, 2000.

Kazin, Michael. *War Against War: The American Fight for Peace, 1914–1918*. New York: Simon & Schuster, 2017.

Kennedy, David M. *Over Here: The First World War and American Society*. New York: Oxford University Press, 1980.

Kinzer, Stephen. *The True Flag: Theodore Roosevelt, Mark Twain, and the Birth of American Empire*. New York: Henry Holt and Company, 2017.

LaFeber, Walter. *The American Search for Opportunity, 1865–1913*. New York: Cambridge University Press, 1993.

Levin, N. Gordon Jr. *Woodrow Wilson and World Politics: America's Response to War and Revolution*. New York: Oxford University Press, 1968.

O'Toole, Patricia. *The Moralist: Woodrow Wilson and the World He Made*. New York: Simon & Schuster, 2018.

Thomas, Evan. *The War Lovers: Roosevelt, Lodge, Hearst, and the Road to Empire, 1898*. New York: Little, Brown and Company, 2010.

Williams, William Appleman. *The Tragedy of American Diplomacy*. New York: Dell, 1972.

21

The 1920s

"Ku Klux Klan Parade, Washington, DC, September 13, 1926." Prints and Photographs Division, Library of Congress. The 1920s were an era of xenophobia and nativism as Congress passed the Immigration Act of 1924 limiting the "New Immigration" from Southern and Eastern Europe. The Ku Klux Klan expanded its anti-black focus to include discrimination toward Jews, Catholics, and immigrants from Southern and Eastern Europe, gaining a national following that was apparent in a Washington, DC march down Pennsylvania Avenue in front of the White House.

The Roaring Twenties. In American popular culture the decade of the 1920s is often described as an era of prosperity populated by gangsters, flappers, bathtub gin, jazz, speakeasies, and dancing the Charleston—the America described by F. Scott Fitzgerald in *The Great Gatsby* (1925). Beneath this stereotype of gaiety were social, racial, ethnic, cultural, and financial concerns that reflected a society and nation undergoing the stress and strain of modernization and change. As sociologists Robert Staughton and Helen Lynd documented in *Middletown: A Study in Contemporary American Culture* (1929), based upon Muncie, Indiana, white Americans in small towns were challenged by what they perceived as threats to traditional values and the morals of the youth symbolized by the loss of community in the anonymity of emerging urbanization, constituting a cultural and political conflict between rural and urban Americans that continues to reflect divisions within the country.

This uncertainty was due to myriad factors. The United States lost over 116,000 soldiers in World War I, but even more devastating was the influenza pandemic that went through the global community in 1918 and 1919, killing perhaps as many as 100 million people. In the United States the death toll is estimated as high as 675,000, with over 30 percent of the nation's population having been infected. Although the United States prevailed on the battlefield, the casualties from war and disease hardly provided the nation with a sense of confidence entering a new decade. The traditional white Americans of *Middletown* feared social and political change: labor unrest, a Bolshevik revolution in the United States, the New Immigration from Southern and Eastern Europe, the mass migration of black Americans from the rural South to the cities of the North, the rise of the Ku Klux Klan, prohibition and gangsters, and modernism and the questioning of fundamentalist Christianity.

Flappers and the new woman

But perhaps the greatest concern to many traditional Americans was the emergence of flappers, young women who challenged the conventional values of their parents. Although some traditionalists blamed the appearance of the flappers upon the Nineteenth Amendment and women's participation in politics, the flappers who emerged in the United States and Western Europe following the First World

War were more interested in social rather than political change. Seeking new job opportunities and moving out of their parents' homes and supervision, the flappers wanted to challenge the conventions of Victorian society that culminated in the death and destruction of World War I. The flappers bobbed or cut their hair short, wore shorter skirts, were more open in regard to sexuality, and were comfortable with smoking and drinking in public. They were also drawn to dancing and jazz music which their parents often dismissed as "Negro music," with their daughters moving to primitive jungle rhythms and perhaps dancing with black men. While contemporary teens tend to view jazz music as rather tame, they should note that parental objections to jazz in the 1920s were quite similar to the condemnation of rock and roll in the 1950s and 1960s and hip-hop from the 1990s to the present day. While popular music has proven to break down social and racial barriers, technology has also exercised considerable influence upon youthful freedom. The emergence of the automobile changed courtship patterns in the United States as parents found it increasingly difficult to exercise control over their mobile offspring. Essentially courtship moved from the front parlor or porch to the backseat of an automobile far removed from parental supervision. It is hardly surprising that births out of wedlock rose with the growth of an automobile culture. More open attitudes in urban areas toward sexuality were also evident in the growing acceptance of the writings of Sigmund Freud, as well as in the fledgling film industry where starlet Clara Bow was celebrated as the "it" girl who displayed sex appeal on the silver screen. While the flapper drew the attention of the media and concerned parents, most Americans, nevertheless, still adhered to traditional habits of life and labor, just as the hippies of the 1960s provoked consternation and debate while most people still followed their daily routines of work and family.

The flapper image became less prominent during the difficult days of the Great Depression as survival trumped freedom of expression for many young women. And behind much of the cultural conflict during the 1920s was economic insecurity as rural areas throughout the decade struggled with an agricultural depression as well as significant downturns in such industries as textile mills and coal mining. Most Americans did not share in the prosperity of the stock market and feared that the forces of modernism and automation posed a threat to their way of life. The Republican Presidents of the era, Warren Harding, Calvin Coolidge, and Herbert Hoover, did little to address these concerns, with the cultural and economic conflicts of the 1920s culminating in the Great Depression that exposed the shortcomings of American capitalism.

New Immigration

Immigration has always played an important role in the United States but beginning in the 1890s the primary source of that immigrant population was changing. Many of the early migrants to the country came from the British Isles and Western Europe, reinforcing ideas of racial superiority and assimilation into America's melting pot from which blacks, Hispanics, and Asians were generally excluded. This pattern began to change around 1890 with growing economic and political instability, along with religious persecution, in Southern and Eastern Europe resulting in the increasing entry into the United States of immigrants from countries such as Poland, Russia, Greece, Turkey, Italy, and the Austro-Hungarian Empire. Many Americans of Western European ancestry expressed concern that this New Immigration posed a threat to American greatness that was based upon the achievements of the Nordic race. These racist perceptions were popularized through the writings of amateur anthropologist Madison Grant in such best-selling books as *The Passing of the Great Race* (1916). Grant expressed alarm regarding the "mongrelization" or pollution of the pure Nordic Americans through intermarriage with inferior racial stock, advocating miscegenation laws and supporting an American eugenics movement that later inspired racial policies in Nazi Germany. According to Grant, the inferior racial population of Southern and Eastern Europe simply lacked the intelligence that would allow them to assimilate into the United States. Instead, their growing presence in American cities would drag the entire nation down to their primitive level of existence.

Acclimated to a low standard of living, the New Immigration would accept lower wages and jobs unfit for decent Americans, leading to the demise of the nation's economy. On the other hand, the inferior European stock was depicted as shiftless and lazy people who would be a burden upon hard-working Nordic Americans. This contradictory economic argument regarding immigration continues to influence contemporary debate. Immigrants are described as both lazy and too willing to work long hours at low wages, suggesting a perplexing false racial and ethnic stereotype of hard-working lazy bums. The anti-immigration rhetoric of the 1920s also focused upon America as a white Christian nation whose mission as the city upon a hill would be compromised through an immigrant population consisting of Jews, Catholics, Greek Orthodox, Slavs, and even Muslims. In addition, the New Immigration came from countries lacking strong democratic traditions where radical ideologies such as anarchism and communism thrived. This inferior racial stock was depicted as lacking the intelligence necessary for voting and participating in politics as democratic citizens.

Postwar labor unrest

These economic, religious, and political fears were exacerbated by the labor unrest following World War I. Responding to a post war recession, steel workers went out on strike in September 1919. The steel operators played upon popular prejudices to discredit the strike, pointing out that many steel workers came from

Southern and Eastern Europe and exposing that strike leader William Foster was a radical and former Wobblie—a disillusioned Foster would eventually join the Communist Party after the steel strike of 1919 was defeated. The strike was also hampered by a lack of labor unity between the American Federation of Labor and Amalgamated Association of Iron, Steel, and Tin Workers. Authorities took advantage of this disunity by importing black and Mexican strikebreakers, and in Gary, Indiana the National Guard was employed to crush the strike. Concern about revolution coming to America was also exacerbated during the Seattle General Strike which shut down the city from February 6-11, 1916. Over 65,000 workers went out on strike in support of a shipyard labor dispute. While critics insisted that the strike would usher in anarchy, the strike committee maintained essential services and order in the streets that prevented violence. The strike was broken by the threats of a military retaliation from Mayor Ole Hanson who was assembling a force to prevent what he referred to as a Bolshevik Revolution in America. Also, national union leaders from organization such as the American Federation of Labor feared being associated with radicalism and urged an end to the strike. While resolve to continue the strike collapsed, the Seattle General Strike demonstrated the ability of workers to run a major city and struck fear into the capitalist order.

Post-war class conflict was also evident in the coal fields of West Virginia as Appalachian coal miners struggled for higher wages, better safety conditions, and union recognition. On May 19, 1920 in the town of Matewan, West Virginia, representatives from the Baldwin-Felts Detective Agency attempted to evict the families of striking miners from company housing. Resistance to the evictions was led by Police Chief Sid Hatfield and deputized miners. In the ensuing gun battle, often referred to as the Matewan Massacre, seven detectives and three miners were killed. Hatfield was a hero to many miners, and his murder on August 1, 1921, while unarmed and attending a court date, increased the tension between the miners and coal operators that turned into open warfare in the West Virginia coal fields of Logan and Mingo counties. In late August 1921, thousands of miners and a large private army funded by the coal operators fought the Battle of Blair Mountain. After days of fighting in which over a hundred men perished, President Harding ordered the intervention of federal troops which ended the battle. In the aftermath of the fighting, hundreds of union leaders were arrested, and United Mine Workers membership declined, but a foundation of resistance was created that fostered greater success during the 1930s.

First Red Scare and executions of Sacco and Vanzetti

The context of class conflict amid fears that the immigrants from Southern and Eastern Europe were exporting Bolshevism and anarchism to the United States contributed to the violation of civil liberties that characterized the First Red Scare.

During the First World War, the American government used the Espionage Act as a means through which to discredit and destroy radical and labor opposition to the corporate capitalist order. In response to the arrest of anarchist and socialist leaders, many of whose ethnicity also made their loyalty suspect to authorities, a series of letter and package bombs were mailed to prominent business and government figures in April and June 1919, including one that damaged the home of Attorney General A. Mitchell Palmer. Accompanying the bombs were political flyers denouncing capitalism and embracing anarchist principles, leading the federal authorities to place blame upon the followers of Italian anarchist Luigi Galleani. Attorney General Palmer took these threats personally, and incidentally attempted to promote his political ambitions, by initiating raids upon alien radicals and urging their deportation. In addition, Palmer promoted a young J. Edgar Hoover to head the Justice Department's Bureau of Investigation and identify the members of radical groups. Hoover would use this position to create the powerful Federal Bureau of Investigation (FBI), a personal fiefdom from which he sought to limit freedom of speech and dissent into the 1970s. The hysteria of the country regarding the threat of radicalism was enhanced by a September 16, 1920 bombing on Wall Street in which 100 people were injured and thirty-eight killed. Although the case was never solved, suspicion was again directed against Italian anarchists associated with Galleani. Thousands were arrested, and over 500 noncitizens were deported as threats to the United States. The Palmer Raids also led to the incarceration of accused radicals for their political beliefs or affiliations, violating Constitutional guarantees of free speech and freedom of association. In addition, thousands were mistakenly arrested and assumed to be politically suspect due to their ethnicity. This mass violation of civil liberties did provoke political pushback as Roger Baldwin, a conscientious objector during the First World War, formed the American Civil Liberties Union in 1920 to provide legal assistance to those rounded up in the Palmer Raids. Within the Wilson Administration, Assistant Secretary of Labor Louis Freeland Post headed the Bureau of Immigration and refused to sign deportation orders for thousands whom he believed were illegally detained by Palmer, leading Hoover to open a security file on Post. These efforts to halt the mass incarceration of suspected violent foreign radicals based on insufficient evidence, however, did little for Italian anarchists Nicola Sacco and Bartolomeo Vanzetti.

On April 15, 1920, the robbery of a shoe factory payroll in South Braintree, Massachusetts resulted in the murders of a paymaster and security guard. The authorities charged Italian immigrants and anarchists Nicola Sacco, a shoemaker, and Bartolomeo Vanzetti, a fish merchant, with the crime. Although the two men proclaimed their innocence, Sacco and Vanzetti were convicted and executed by the state of Massachusetts on August 23, 1927. Much of the case focused upon the political beliefs of the defendants, who were depicted as followers of the violent anarchist Galleani and denounced for fleeing to Mexico to avoid conscription during World War I. Presiding Judge Webster Thayer, from a well-established New England family, reportedly remarked that he was going to "fry those anarchist bastards," and many observers of the trial perceived the convictions as proof of the prejudice against anarchists and the New Immigration that characterized the American political scene during the post-World War I Red Scare. Appeals from intellectuals in the United States and around the world, as well as global protests by workers, failed to halt the executions. In 1977, however, on the fiftieth anniversary of their deaths, Massachusetts Governor Michael Dukakis, citing the prejudicial atmosphere in which the trial was conducted, signed legislation exonerating Sacco and Vanzetti.

Immigration Act of 1924

While the prosecution of alleged radicals in the Palmer Raids and executions of Sacco and Vanzetti supposedly ridded the country of undesirable alien radicals, the larger issue of what to do about the threat to American culture ostensibly represented by the New Immigration was left to Congress. The Immigration Act of 1924 altered the liberal immigration policy of the United States, although not applied to non-whites such as the Chinese, endorsed by big business to assure a cheap labor supply. The legislation provided for national quotas of two percent of the number of foreign-born persons of each nationality residing in the United States in 1890. The key provision to understanding this piece of legislation is that the quota system was based upon the census of 1890 before significant arrivals from Southern and Eastern Europe, thus making the Immigration Act of 1924 discriminatory toward the New Immigration, while quotas for those of Western European ancestry remained relatively high. The effort to preserve a more homogeneous and "white" society essentially prevailed until the Immigration Act of 1965 signed by Lyndon Johnson abolished the national origins formula and opened the United States to a more diverse immigrant population.

Great Migration and race riots

The insecurity of many traditional white Americans was also apparent in the reaction to the Great Migration of black Americans from the South to the North in pursuit of employment opportunities during the First World War. Between 1916 and 1930, it is estimated that approximately 1.6 million black Americans migrated from the rural South and agricultural labor to live and work in the urban North, sparking fear among white Americans as the races competed for jobs and housing in the post-World War I period. White veterans complained that they returned from the war to find their jobs taken by blacks who would work for cheaper wages, and the post war era was marred by race riots which usually consisted of white mobs attacking black communities. The summer of 1919 became known as "red summer" due to the amount of bloodshed from racial conflicts in more than a dozen cities. In Chicago, thirty-eight people, twenty-three of whom were blacks, died amid tensions arising as blacks moved into traditional Irish neighborhoods on the South Side of Chicago. A black youth was killed for swimming in an area designated for whites only, and when the police refused to make an arrest, fighting broke out, and soon white mobs were attacking the black community. The rioting lasted almost a week and only ended when the National Guard was deployed, but by that time many black businesses and homes were destroyed.

While considerable national attention was concentrated upon racial conflict in places such as Chicago and Washington DC, perhaps the bloodies riot of the early 1920s was in Tulsa, Oklahoma where estimates of those killed range from approximately fifty to several hundred, with most of the victims being black. In addition, the prosperous African American business and residential district of Greenwood, which antagonized many whites in Tulsa, was destroyed by fire. The Tulsa race riot began on May 31, 1921 when a young black man was accused of touching a white female elevator operator in downtown Tulsa. When armed blacks gathered at the courthouse to avert a lynching, whites used this supposed threat of a black uprising to launch an assault upon the black community that destroyed Greenwood and left almost 10,000 blacks homeless. Some witnesses reported the existence of a Klan air force that dropped sticks of dynamite from planes flying over the Greenwood district. National Guard troops were dispatched to the city and proceeded to place hundreds of blacks under arrest. The Great Migration may have provoked a white backlash, but this movement was also responsible for the growth of black communities in Northern cities that fostered major achievements in intellectual and artistic life. Perhaps the best known of these intellectual and artistic developments is the Harlem Renaissance which contributed such major writers and poets as Langston Hughes, Claude McKay, and Zora Neale Hurston to American arts and letters. The white resistance to the African diaspora convinced Marcus Garvey, who was born in Jamaica, to form the Universal Negro Improvement Association and advocate for the return of black Americans to their African roots. The appeal of the popular Garvey in the urban North was perceived as a threat to the black labor supply, and Garvey was harassed by the government and eventually convicted of mail fraud.

Ku Klux Klan in the 1920s

Nevertheless, many white Americans viewed the artistic and political ambitions of black Americans as a threat, and the racial violence in the nation reflected the rise of the Second Ku Klux Klan in the 1920s. The initial Klan had achieved its purpose of encouraging Southern white resistance to Reconstruction and was largely defunct by the early 1870s. The premiere of *The Birth of a Nation* in Atlanta convinced William J. Simmons to resurrect the Klan at Stone Mountain, Georgia in November 1915. The Second Klan found a national audience in the 1920s with membership peaking at perhaps four million. The Klan appealed to a white Protestant America that perceived its status and values under assault from the Great Migration, communism, labor unrest, modernism and changing values, and the New Immigration that increased the nation's population of Jews, Catholics, and Southeastern Europeans who could not be assimilated into the United States. These national threats moved beyond the South, and the Second Klan enjoyed support in the Midwest, West, and East with considerable influence in such states as Indiana, Oregon, and Pennsylvania. An effort to denounce the Klan bitterly divided the national Democratic Party in 1924. The Klan continued to use violence and intimidation against those it deemed as challenging the existence of the United States as a white Anglo-Saxon nation. With its robes, elaborate rituals, and even women's auxiliaries, the Klan also provided a sense of security for Americans who perceived themselves and their values under assault from modernism. The Klan seemed to reach the zenith of its influence in August 1925 when perhaps as many as 50,000 Klansmen marched through the streets of the nation's capital. After achieving this public manifestation of its power, the Second Klan began to decline, primarily due to internal scandals. Many white Americans, as well as black, Jewish, labor, and Catholic organizations, maintained a strong opposition to the Klan, while efforts of the hooded empire to milk even more money from its constituents through raising memberships rates and expensive regalia began to backfire with many Klan members of modest means. In addition, the arrest of prominent Indiana Klan leader David Stephenson for the rape and murder of a white school teacher exposed the mission of the Klan to defend white womanhood as the rankest hypocrisy. With the enactment of legislation such as the Immigration Act of 1924 and the crushing of labor unrest, the Second Klan achieved part of its agenda, and when the nation descended into the Great Depression, there was little money available to spend upon such frivolous expenses as Klan regalia.

Prohibition

The Klan was also involved in the national experiment with prohibition during the 1920s, associating the Eighteenth Amendment with the attempt to control the immigrant population by depriving them of demon drink. Perceiving prohibition as a means through which to preserve traditional Protestant values, the Klan joined with progressive reformers, women's groups such as the Anti-Saloon League, anti-immigration groups concerned about German breweries, and advocates for preserving grain for the war effort to finally enact the amendment in 1920. Congress passed the Volstead Act as enabling legislation for the amendment, focusing upon banning the manufacturing and selling of alcoholic beverages, but allowing some exceptions such as the use of wine in religious ceremonies. The Volstead Act also included beer and wine as beverages that were banned under the amendment, although some critics believed that exempting beer and wine from the legislation might have allowed the noble experiment to succeed. While federal agents and vigilante groups such as the Klan attempted to enforce the amendment, there was widespread violations of prohibition with the emergence of such 1920s stereotypes as illegal speakeasies and homemade bathtub gin. Much of this illegal alcohol was provided through organized crime syndicates, many of them representatives of the New Immigration whose rise in American society through legal means was limited by discrimination. Thus, Irish, Jewish, and Italian criminal gangs often battled for control of the illicit alcohol trade. In Chicago, Italian gangster Al Capone emerged as a crime boss and was eventually convicted for income tax evasion, but who, nevertheless, enjoyed some popularity due to his charitable contributions to the city. In 1931, the Wickersham Commission headed by former Attorney General George W. Wickersham and appointed by President Herbert Hoover wrote a report urging more federal resources be applied to the enforcement of prohibition as the large circulation of illegal alcohol was undermining respect of Americans for the law and legal authorities. By that time many Americans had grown tired of the prohibition experiment, and President Franklin Roosevelt endorsed repeal of prohibition with the Twenty-first Amendment. The failure of prohibition has encouraged efforts to change the nation's drug laws and legalize the use of marijuana, although there is evidence that alcohol consumption did decline during the 1920s, but the question remains as to at what cost for society and individuals incarcerated during the reign of prohibition.

Scopes Trial

Traditional religious values also seemed under attack from modernism and science such as the theory of evolution based upon natural selection rather than divine intervention. Many fundamentalist Christians perceived evolution as a repudiation of the Bible, believing in a literal reading of the religious text that the world was created in six twenty-four-hour day periods and objecting to the idea of Christian modernists that the Bible could be symbolic with a geological period standing for one of the days mentioned in the Bible. To protect the school children of Tennessee from the evil influence of Darwin's teachings, the state of Tennessee passed the Butler Act that prohibited the teaching of evolution in the state's public schools. Biology teacher John Scopes of Dayton, Tennessee agreed to test the validity of the law and enjoyed the support of the American Civil Liberties Union who provided for the teacher's legal defense with the renowned criminal defense attorney Clarence Darrow whose agnostic views were well established. To counteract Darrow, the state of Tennessee appointed William Jennings Bryan as a special prosecutor. Bryan was a three-time Democratic nominee for the Presidency who championed the common people and urged the reform of monopolistic capitalism, but he also illuminated the dark side of populism that insisted upon a conformity of thought. By 1925, when Scopes challenged the Butler Act, Bryan was more of an evangelist for fundamentalist Christianity than a political reformer challenging the status quo. The entrance of Darrow and Bryan into the trial guaranteed that the proceedings would receive national attention which included live radio broadcasts from the warm summertime Dayton courtroom. Darrow was frustrated with the court's ruling that he could not provide expert scientific witnesses on behalf of evolution, so he seized upon the strategy of calling his adversary Bryan as an expert witness upon the Bible. Although an irregular courtroom procedure, Bryan agreed to assume the witness stand, where Darrow questioned and sometimes confused the witness on accounts of Biblical miracles. Although many believed that Darrow outwitted Bryan, Scopes was found guilty and fined a $100. While many modernists were convinced that Darrow carried the day and discredited fundamentalism, many states in the South passed laws similar to the Butler Act in Tennessee, and opposition to the teaching of evolution remained strong in the hinterland. Today, the issues raised by the Scopes Trial remain relevant as some politicians continue to oppose the accepted scientific theory of evolution and insist that the pseudo-science of creationism be incorporated into the school curriculum

American literature in the 1920s

The battles between traditional values and modernism were also apparent in the literature of the 1920s. Leading writers of the era claimed to represent a lost generation of young Americans who went off to fight in the trenches of France, only to return to an America in which Klansmen paraded on the streets and they could not even legally enjoy an alcoholic drink. This disillusioned generation was represented by writers such as Ernest Hemingway, F. Scott Fitzgerald, and Sinclair Lewis. Hemingway, who served as an ambulance driver during the First World War, captured the lost generation in his *The Sun Also Rises* (1926) about disillusioned young Americans in Europe following the war. Fitzgerald and his wife Zelda appeared to epitomize the glamourous lifestyle of the Roaring Twenties, but in the epic *The Great Gatsby* (1925), the author interrogated the materialism of the age. Lewis, from the small town of Sauk Centre, Minnesota, was the first American writer to be awarded the Nobel Prize in Literature, providing a devastating critique of American conformity and materialism during the 1920s with such novels as *Main Street* (1920), *Babbitt* (1922), and *Elmer Gantry* (1927). These writers of the lost generation are still taught in many high school and college literature courses, but the best-selling author of the decade appealed to more traditional values. Zane Grey was the author of several dozen Western novels that were also made into films, making him one of the most popular writers in American history. The popular culture of the 1920s was also epitomized by the rise of mass spectator sports at both the collegiate and professional levels, along with the emergence of sporting heroes such as college football player Red Grange, boxer Jack Dempsey, and Babe Ruth of the New York Yankees.

Economy of the 1920s

The hoopla over American sport in the 1920s provided a respite from cultural conflicts of the era. The clash of values between urban and rural America over such issues as immigration, race, prohibition, and religion were manifestations of deeper economic insecurities. While the cities appeared to be booming in the 1920s and beckoning young Americans with job opportunities and cultural freedoms, the rural areas and small towns of America were suffering from economic hardships. Americans on main street, much as today, did not share in the rising prosperity of the stock market that benefitted Wall Street. During the First World War, American farmers were encouraged to grow more crops to feed the troops and citizens of war-devastated Europe. As grain prices rose, farmers borrowed money to increase their acreage. This debt burden destroyed many family farmers as after the war world grain prices dropped with surplus production from the United States and European farmers who were able to resume their labors. Faced with foreclosures and declining markets, American farmers responded by increasing production, which only exacerbated their problems and contributed to the depletion of the soil, culminating in the Dust Bowl of the 1930s. The depression came to American farmers about a decade before enveloping the rest of the nation. Small towns also suffered economically during the 1920s from a decline in the production of textile mills and coal mining. Seeking cheaper labor with the rise of unions in the North, many textile mills switched their operations to the South. But by the 1920s many of these textile jobs were being lost to automation and even cheaper sources of labor outside the United States. Meanwhile, coal which had powered the industrial revolution was being replaced by oil as the lubricant of the American economy. Oil production was booming in Oklahoma, Texas, and California with little thought given to dependence upon another finite energy source. Construction of an oil rig was relatively inexpensive, and oil companies were not dependent upon a large labor supply as were the coal operators. The replacement of coal with oil contributed to growing unemployment in many parts of rural America, and the decline of coal remains an economic, environmental, and social issue on the American political scene.

Warren G. Harding and normalcy

These economic problems, however, received relatively little attention from the Republican Presidents of the era who believed that intervention into the economy on behalf of common Americans might undermine individual initiative. In 1920, Americans appeared weary of progressive reform and Democrat Woodrow Wilson's missionary diplomacy that did not seem to make the world safe for democracy. The voters rejected Ohio Governor James Cox and his running mate young Franklin Roosevelt in favor of Republican Ohio Senator Warren Harding, a small-town newspaper editor whose affable manner made him a favorite among Republican Senatorial colleagues. Harding asserted that the country was tired of reform and wanted to get back to "normalcy," a word invented by Harding that seemed to imply big business could resume its influence over the American economy free from governmental interference. As President, Harding sponsored the Washington Naval Conference that limited naval construction temporarily but was certainly unable to halt the movement toward war in the late 1930s.

The Harding administration, however, was best known for a series of political scandals, although his frequent sexual dalliances outside of marriage were not generally known by the public. Charges of corruption were lodged against Attorney General Harry Daughtery along with allegations of mismanagement in the Veterans Bureau, but the major scandal of the Harding administration was Teapot Dome, which was not fully revealed until after the death of the President. Teapot Dome was a bribery scandal involving Secretary of the Interior Albert Fall of New Mexico. A Senate investigation revealed that Fall had leased navy oil reserves at Teapot Dome in Wyoming and Elk Hills in California to Harry F. Sinclair of Mammouth Oil and Edward L. Doherty of Pan American Petroleum. The generous leasing rights were bestowed without competitive bidding, and it was revealed that the oil executives rewarded the Secretary of the Interior with no interest loans and cash gifts to remodel and expand his New Mexico ranch. Fall was convicted of accepting bribes and became the first former cabinet officer sentenced to prison. Confronted with growing scandals, Harding sought to escape Washington on a speaking tour that took him to Alaska, Canada, and California. While in San Francisco, Harding collapsed from an apparent heart attack and died on August 2, 1923.

Silent Cal and the election of 1924

Vice President Calvin Coolidge from New England assumed the Presidency. Born in Vermont, Coolidge pursued a political career in Massachusetts, and as Mayor of Boston his strong opposition to union recognition in the Boston Police Strike of 1919 helped him to gain the 1920 Republican Vice-Presidential nomination. His dour personality earned him the description "Silent Cal," but Coolidge had little patience for the corruption surrounding Harding, restoring a reputation for honesty to the Presidency. Coolidge was popular with conservatives and business, proclaiming that "the business of America is business" and advocating a small role for government. Since there was little for the President to do, Coolidge insisted upon a daily nap, and his philosophy and approach to government later made him a favorite of President Ronald Reagan who also enjoyed his napping. Coolidge sought to balance the budget by reducing government spending, but at the same time he proposed to cut taxes—believing as Reagan did later with supply side economics that reduced taxation would encourage economic activity and produce greater revenue; a theory that has not been vindicated by history. Thus, Coolidge signed into law the Revenue Act of 1924 proposed by Secretary of the Treasury Andrew Mellon, one of the wealthiest men in America, that drastically reduced federal income taxation, especially for the wealthiest in the highest tax bracket. Despite the continuing farm depression, Coolidge refused to support agricultural relief and vetoed the McNary-Haugen Bill that would have provided subsidies for the nation's suffering farmers. Coolidge's conservatism earned him the Presidential nomination of the Republican Party, urging Americans to stay "cool with Coolidge."

The 1924 Democratic Presidential campaign revealed the fissures within the party and nation. The two major candidates seemed to demonstrate the differing perspectives of an urban and rural/small town America; a division which continues to characterize American politics. William Gibbs McAdoo, the son-in-law of former President Wilson, enjoyed a reputation for progressive reform, but much of his political support in 1924 was from Southern Democrats. Thus, he refused to support a denunciation of the Klan that divided the Democrats during their 1924 convention at Madison Square Garden in New York City. McAdoo also drew rural support as a "dry," who urged continued adherence to the prohibition crusade. On the other hand, McAdoo's chief competitor was Al Smith, Governor of New York. Smith was born in New York City and was a Catholic from an Irish-American family. He denounced the bigotry of the Klan and was a "wet" who perceived prohibition as an overreach by the government. His background and policies made Smith a favorite of the New Immigrants residing in Northern and Midwestern cities, but his Catholic faith made Smith an anathema to many of McAdoo's backers. After 102 ballots—a two-thirds majority was required for nomination by the Democrats at the time—the Democrats could not agree on a candidate and were in danger of being evicted from Madison Square Garden in favor of a circus. On the 103rd ballot, finally, the convention agreed to nominate West Virginia Congressman John W. Davis as a compromise choice.

The divided Democrats proved no match for Coolidge and the Republicans who cruised to an easy victory. However, there was a third political party involved in the national campaign. Wisconsin Senator Robert LaFollette accepted the nomination of the Progressive Party, denouncing Coolidge for his opposition to unions, failure to aid the nation's farmers, and subservience to big business. LaFollette supported expanded trust-busting, increased taxation upon the wealthy, collective bargaining rights for labor, and nationalization of essential industries such as the railroads. The Progressive candidate carried his home state of Wisconsin and earned over 16 percent of the popular vote, a strong showing for a third party in American politics, indicating that even during the Republican ascendancy of the 1920s, critics of monopoly capitalism maintained a following in the United States upon which reformers and radicals might draw during the crisis of the Great Depression.

Herbert Hoover and the self-made man

Coolidge remained popular with American business interests during his first full elected term, but declined to seek re-election, and his Secretary of Commerce Herbert Hoover gained the Republican nomination in 1928. Hoover's background epitomized the rise of the self-made man. Coming from a poor family and orphaned at a young age, Hoover worked his way through Stanford University. After earning an engineering degree, the young mining engineer earned a fortune by discovering important mineral deposits around the world. During the First World War, Hoover's reputation was enhanced by his service as head of the U.S. Food Administration and organizing relief for starving European families. During the administrations of Harding and Coolidge, Hoover served as Commerce Secretary, promoting efficiency and the expansion of American business. Dedicated to continuing the policies of Coolidge, Hoover was easily elected in 1928 over the Democratic nominee, Al Smith. Hoover even made inroads into the solid Democratic South, as there was considerable regional opposition to Smith's Catholicism. In 1960, John Kennedy would have to address similar prejudices that a Catholic would be under the control of the Pope and abrogate the American separation of church and state. Smith, however, did well in many urban areas and suggested a more progressive electoral constituency that was later tapped by his fellow New Yorker, Franklin Roosevelt and his New Deal.

A confident Hoover assumed that he would preside over the continuing prosperity of American capitalism on both the national and international stages; however, only a year into his Presidency, Hoover was confronted with an economic crisis that challenged his political principles and culminated in a global depression. The capitalist order was under assault, and its preservation and reform required changes beyond the capacity of Hoover's orthodoxy of rugged individualism. The Roaring Twenties of flappers, bathtub gin, speakeasies, jazz, gangsters, and mass culture overshadowed an economic conflict that separated Americans during the decade on ethnic, racial, regional, and class lines. But the Great Depression ushered in a degree of equality in which Americans of various backgrounds were forced to interrogate the fundamental principles of American democracy and capitalism.

Further Reading:

Allen, Frederick Lewis. *Only Yesterday: An Informal History of the 1920s*. New York: Harper & Brothers, 1931.

Bernstein, Irving. *The Lean Years: A History of the American Worker, 1926–1933*. Boston: Houghton Mifflin, 1960.

Burner, David. *The Politics of Provincialism: The Democratic Party in Transition, 1918–1932*. Westport, CT: Greenwood Press, 1967.

Chiles, Robert. *The Revolution of '28: Al Smith, American Progressivism, and the Coming of the New Deal*. Ithaca, NY: Cornell University Press, 2018.

Gordon, Linda. *The Second Coming of the KKK: The Ku Klux Klan of the 1920s and the American Political Tradition*. New York: W.W. Norton & Company, 2017.

Larson, Edward J. *Summer for the Gods: The Scopes Trial and America's Continuing Debate over Science and Religion*. New York: Basic Books, 1997.

Mackrell, Judith. *Flappers: Six Women of a Dangerous Generation*. New York: Farrar, Straus and Giroux, 2014.

McWhirter, Cameron. *Red Summer: The Summer of 1919 and the Awakening of Black America*. New York: Henry Holt & Company, 2011.

Miller, Nathan. *New World Coming: The 1920s and the Making of Modern America*. New York: Scribner, 2003.

Murray, Robert K. *The Harding Era: Warren G. Harding and His Administration*. Minneapolis, MN: University of Minnesota Press, 1969.

Noggle, Burl. *Into the Twenties: The United States from Armistice to Normalcy*. Urbana, IL: University of Illinois Press, 1969.

Okrent, Daniel. *Last Call: The Rise and Fall of Prohibition*. New York: Scribner, 2010.

22

The Great Depression and the New Deal

"Destitute Pea Pickers in California. Mother of seven children, age 32." Photography by Dorothea Lange, near Nipomo, California, February 1936. Prints and Photographs Division, Library of Congress. The photographs of Dorothea Lange for the Farm Securities Administration, along with the music of Woody Guthrie and John Steinbeck's *Grapes of Wrath*, documented and dramatized the plight of dust bowl migrants fleeing the Great Plains for California.

The economic malaise that many American farmers were suffering during the 1920s was brought home to the rest of the nation with the Great Depression. Although there were many underlying structural problems with the economy, the Great Depression within the United States is often considered as beginning with Black Tuesday, October 29, 1929, when the stock market lost billions in value and thousands of Americans lost their saving which they had invested in the market. The crash was part of a world depression in the industrialized nations who responded to the crisis by tariffs and curtailing trade. Within the United States between 1929 and 1932, the gross national product fell by over 15 percent, and the national unemployment rate rose to over 25 percent. Some Americans faced starvation, and families were separated as husbands and older children rode the rails in search of work. This crisis of capitalism fostered the growth of fascism and communism within the industrialized West. The United States witnessed the rise of demagogues such as Huey Long, and one historian described the 1930s as the heyday of American communism.

President Hoover responded to the collapse by urging his fellow Americans to stay the course with the rugged individualism that awarded Ben Franklin and Horatio Alger but had deserted so many Americans—although Hoover would somewhat compromise his views as the depression worsened. Patrician-born Franklin Roosevelt feared a political collapse and revolution, proposing a New Deal that fostered unions and expanded the role of government in the American economy. While some conservative critics perceive the New Deal as an abandonment of the economic and political system that had propelled American exceptionalism, the Roosevelt administration was committed to the reform, not destruction, of American capitalism. Critics on the left believe that the New Deal and Roosevelt missed an opportunity to fundamentally restructure the economy of the United States in favor of a superficial reform that retained corporate control over the nation. In the final analysis, it would take the Second World War to finally restore full employment and put Americans back to work in a national security state that continued into the post-war world.

Causes of the Great Depression

While the stock market crash in October 1929 is often depicted in popular culture as causing the Great Depression, there were serious structural problems with the American economy that made recovery from the unregulated stock market collapse difficult. Most Americans were not investors on Wall Street and, thus, were not directly impacted by the declining value of stocks. If the basic structure of the economy was sound, the nation could have bounced back from Black Tuesday. Many economists believe that the depression of the 1930s was a crisis of consumption rather than production. During the relatively affluent 1920s, the wealthiest 1 percent of Americans saw their incomes rise by over 75 percent, while for the rest of the nation's population this growth was a modest 9 percent. This maldistribution of wealth and income, a problem which continues to plague the United States, contributed to a lack of purchasing power in the system. No matter how much money they possessed, the small percentage of wealthy Americans simply could not purchase enough automobiles, homes, clothing, and consumer goods to keep factory workers employed. And as factories shut down and laid off their workers, the gap between rich and poor spiraled. The poor corporate structure of American business also exacerbated the situation. In a generally unregulated economy, many banks placed their money in holding companies which produced nothing but existed primarily to hold stock in other holding companies. When the factories and productive industries closed their gates, these interlocking holding companies collapsed like a house of cards. The international trade of the 1920s was also constructed upon a flimsy foundation. During the First World War, American bankers made extensive loans to allies such as France and England. To repay these loans, France and Britain were dependent upon the reparations assigned Germany in the Treaty of Versailles. When the Weimar Republic struggled to make these reparation payments, American bankers again stepped into the void and extended loans, with profitable rates of interest, to jump start production in Europe and stimulate trade among the industrialized nations of the West. This structure of trade and investment, however, was endangered by the financial collapse of 1929, and the governmental response to these economic challenges only made the situation worse. In the United States, the Hoover administration and Congress enacted the Hawley-Smoot Tariff that sought to protect American companies through substantial tariff protection; in some cases, increasing rates by as much as 40 percent. This protectionist policy angered European trading partners who retaliated with their own high tariffs, and international trade came to a virtual standstill. Policies of economic nationalism only increased the impact of the depression, fostering the rise of totalitarian governments believing that increased military budgets and territorial expansion in search of scarce natural resources might bring some relief to their people.

Impact of the depression upon the American family

In the United States, those who lost their savings in the stock market crash or the collapse of the banking system joined many rural Americans who had not shared in the prosperity of the 1920s. Farmers who responded to the slogan of "food will win the war" by expanding production were confronted by a post war price decline that persisted throughout the 1920s. Seeking to pay their mortgages, farmers continued to increase production, contributing to the environmental disaster of the dust bowl. Meanwhile, textile mills and coal mining which provided the economic foundation for many small towns were in decline and increased the number of unemployed. While it is possible to marshal considerable statistical evidence in support of the depression's impact on the American people, the personal suffering fostered by the Great Depression is perhaps best expressed in the documentary photography of Dorothy Lange, the dust bowl ballads of Woody Guthrie, and John Steinbeck's *The Grapes of Wrath* chronicling the travails of farmers from the Great Plains who were forced off their land and became migrants in their own country. These cultural accounts, however, tend to focus upon poor rural whites and ignore how the depression impacted blacks, Natives, Hispanics, and other minorities who were often the last hired and the first fired.

But no matter one's racial or ethnic background, the depression shattered many families and scarred the psyche of Americans for the rest of their lives—and this was especially true for Hispanics in California and the Southwest as the government stepped up deportation procedures that separated families, and in some cases American citizens were dispatched to Mexico if unable to document their citizenship. Confronted with lost jobs, savings, and homes, many males struggled with the destruction of their traditional function as the breadwinner of the family. Many husbands and fathers deserted their families out of shame and headed out on the rails in search of work, leading to that depression-era expression "write if you get work." But many families never heard again from their husbands and fathers. Most mothers did not have this option as they could not desert the family for they were the primary caregivers for the children. The poor families of the depression were kept together through the strength and determination of the women as exemplified by Ma Joad in *The Grapes of Wrath*. Women who could not find jobs outside the home provided childcare for those who did have jobs. To survive and support their families, they rented out bedrooms and provided room and board, took in washing and ironing, planted gardens, raised chickens and sold eggs, and in some extreme cases served as sex workers.

Woody Guthrie and cultural radicalism

These strong depression-era women were celebrated in the music of Woody Guthrie in songs such as "Union Maid" (1940). In his wanderings from the dust bowl of Oklahoma and Texas to the green pastures of California and finally the sidewalks of New York City, Guthrie chronicled the experience of dust bowl refugees and drew upon the indigenous radicalism of American history to champion the common people and challenge capitalism. He composed his best-known song "This Land Is Your Land" in response to what he considered to be the mindless American exceptionalism of Irving Berlin's "God Bless America," although the radical verses by Guthrie questioning private property are often ignored today. In his music and political activities, Guthrie embraced the union movement as the best tool for improving the lot of America's working class. Joining the anti-fascist politics of the Popular Front, the folksinger denounced Jim Crow as an example of American fascism. Guthrie perceived the Second World War as a struggle in which the common people of America and around the world would destroy fascism. He ran around New York City with the slogan "this machine kills fascists" etched on his guitar and eventually joined the Merchant Marine during the conflict. The native of Oklahoma was disappointed with post war McCarthyism and the Cold War, while his voice was stilled after being diagnosed with Huntington's disease. Guthrie was accused of being a member of the Communist Party, and he even wrote a column called "Woody Sez" for the communist newspaper, *The Daily Worker*. The FBI maintained surveillance of the musician but was never able to establish his party membership. Guthrie, nevertheless, admired the Communist Party during the 1930s for supporting the union idea and fighting against big business and Jim Crow. Woody Guthrie represented the tradition of indigenous radicalism established by the IWW, agrarian populism, Christian socialism, Eugene Debs, and the Socialist Party which was popular in the Oklahoma countryside before the First World War.

Hoover responds to the depression

The crisis of capitalism fostered a proletarian popular culture found in the music of Guthrie, but President Hoover had no intention of acknowledging this tradition of protest in American history. Instead, the President remained a prisoner of his background as an orphan who had worked his way through Stanford University and accumulated a fortune as a mining engineer, maintaining his faith in what Hoover termed the rugged individualism of American capitalism. Hoover had escaped poverty through hard work and determination, and he failed to see why unemployed Americans in the early 1930s could not follow his example. The President opposed Congressional legislation to provide direct government relief to the starving and unemployed as such programs would undermine American individualism and create a sense of dependency upon government. Hoover insisted that enterprising Americans could sell apples on the street corners of the nation, but he failed to recognize the depths into which the depression had plunged the American people. Who had the funds to purchase the apples? The economic situation in which Hoover completed his rise from rags to riches was different from the crisis atmosphere of the late 1920s and early 1930s.

The President and his supporters believed that the stock market crash was only a temporary market adjustment similar to the panics of the nineteenth century. Thus, he sought to restore the confidence of the American people in a series of speeches in which he proclaimed that the foundation of the American economic system was fundamentally sound. Hoover also signed legislation reducing taxes, believing that such a measure would restore purchasing power by placing more money in the pockets of working Americans. Many Americans, however, were unemployed and paid no income tax, so tax relief failed to provide them with greater purchasing power. As these measures failed to alleviate the crisis, Hoover only made matters worse by supporting the Hawley-Smoot Tariff which contributed to the collapse of world trade. An increasingly troubled Hoover was finally convinced to make some alterations in his philosophy of rugged individualism. He supported passage of the Reconstruction Finance Corporation (RFC) which created an independent government corporation to provide loans to banks and businesses with generous repayment provisions. The recipients of the loans could then expand and hire the unemployed without workers becoming dependent upon government subsidies. This is often referred to as the "trickle down" approach in which government promotes prosperity by stimulating business which then passes along these benefits to the people through job growth. This type of corporate welfare is perceived as not violating the fundamental tenets of American capitalism as opposed to direct intervention of the government on behalf of working families. Hoover's RFC did make numerous loans, but this compromise measure failed to bring the nation out of the depression. In the crisis of the early 1930s, more than the allocated two billion dollars was needed, and many of the businesses who accepted the loans used the money to consolidate existing debt, lacking the confidence to undertake expansion in the midst of the depression.

Hoover also alienated many Americans by the way he handled the Bonus March. In 1924, Congress agreed to pay a bonus for veterans of World War I which they would receive some time in the 1940s when many would be reaching retirement from the labor force—and it is worth remembering that this legislation was enacted before the passage of Social Security. With the onset of the depression, however, many veterans were unemployed and needed their bonuses honored early so that they might feed their families. Veterans marched on Washington, demanding that Hoover and Congress fund the bonus early to aid veterans and their families. Hoover was alarmed by the encampment of bonus marchers near the White House and erroneously proclaimed that many of the bonus marchers were communists who had never served in the military. Instead of meeting with representatives from the "Bonus Expeditionary Army," Hoover ordered General Douglas MacArthur to employ tanks, tear gas, and troops with bayonets to drive the bonus marchers and their families from an encampment near the White House. The assault upon American veterans and their families further discredited Hoover during the 1932 Presidential campaign when many Americans had lost their homes and were living in shanty towns popularly referred to as "Hoovervilles."

Election of 1932 and the Roosevelts

In the Presidential election of 1932, Hoover was overwhelmingly defeated by the Democratic candidate New York Governor Franklin Delano Roosevelt. It is likely that any Democrat could have defeated Hoover in 1932, but the patrician Roosevelt appeared to convey a special concern for the plight of common Americans. Born into a wealthy upstate New York family of Dutch ancestry and a cousin of Theodore Roosevelt, Franklin was an only child and raised primarily by his mother Sara who was considerably younger than her husband. The young Roosevelt was somewhat of a "momma's boy," and Sara kept her son in curls and dresses for his youngest years. A son of privilege, Roosevelt attended the elite Groton School before moving on to Harvard and law school at Columbia. Preferring social life over academics, Roosevelt considered himself a well-rounded student, striving for the "gentleman's C" academic average. After graduation, Roosevelt had little interest in practicing law, moving to the family estate at Hyde Park where he followed his father into the Democratic Party and was elected to the New York State Assembly. After supporting Woodrow Wilson for the Presidency, Roosevelt was awarded with an appointment as Assistant Secretary of the Navy, a position held formerly by cousin Theodore. In 1920, the Democrats selected the ambitious young man as their Vice-Presidential candidate alongside Ohio Governor James Cox. While Harding won the election, Roosevelt appeared to have a sold political future that was nearly derailed by marital difficulties and health concerns.

The handsome and social Roosevelt surprised many of his friends when he decided to marry his distant cousin, Eleanor. Franklin's mother opposed the marriage but was unable to dissuade her son, although she did insist upon living with Eleanor and Franklin. Obviously attracted to her intelligence, Franklin seemed to believe that Eleanor's sage counsel would help promote his political career. And Eleanor was certainly the more liberal of the two, expanding her husband's horizons on issues of race, class, and gender. In 1918, she discovered that Franklin was having an affair with her social secretary, Lucy Mercer. Sara Roosevelt intervened and prevented a divorce which she feared might destroy her son's political career. Franklin promised that he would stop seeing Lucy, but later the couple resumed their relationship, and Lucy was with the President when he died in 1945. Franklin was also rumored to have numerous other relationships, including his secretary Missy LeHand and Crown Princess Martha of Norway who was a resident of the White House during the Second World War—although these relationships were not generally reported by the press or known by the public. The marriage produced six children, and Eleanor and Franklin remained a formidable political pair, but the couple were evidently no longer intimate during the White House years. Her private letters indicate that Eleanor pursued a loving and intimate relationship with reporter Lorena Hickok.

Nevertheless, Eleanor stayed beside her husband when he was stricken by polio in 1921. Franklin survived the disease that left him with paralysis in both legs, and he was unable to walk and stand without the aid of crutches. During the entirely of his Presidency, Roosevelt was confined to a wheelchair, although this was not known by all Americans, and the press agreed to not photograph the President being carried on to planes and trains. On the other hand, many of Roosevelt's biographers believe that his bout with polio fostered his compassion for downtrodden Americans. Eleanor also encouraged her husband to re-enter politics, and during his Presidency, she often served as Franklin's legs, visiting work sites and natural disasters inaccessible to her husband. In 1928, Franklin was elected Governor of New York, describing himself as a progressive and supporting government assistance to farmers along with a program of old age assistance.

New Deal and the 100 Days

Four years later, Roosevelt proclaimed that the American people deserved a New Deal, but the meaning of that slogan was unclear and ambivalent. Roosevelt recognized that the nation was in crisis and that the rugged individualism of the Hoover administration was not working. It was imperative that the government take action or face revolution and a turn toward fascism or communism. But there was uncertainty as to what these policies should be, leading to a degree of inconsistency in Roosevelt's approach to combating the depression. The New Deal often seemed improvised with an approach of "ready, fire, aim" in which advocates of differing solutions were thrown into a room together and told to come up with a program or solution for implementing the so-called three r's of relief, recovery, and reform. For example, the "brain trust" of academic advisers Adolf Berle, Raymond Moley, and Rexford Tugwell from Columbia University urged the President to pursue more centralized planning for the economy, but legislation would have to be passed through a Congress dominated by the seniority of Southern Democrats who feared that too much change might disrupt racial segregation. While Roosevelt was prepared to adopt the deficit spending advocated by British economist John Maynard Keynes, he was uncomfortable with Keynesian economics and hoped to restore a balanced budget as soon as possible. Nevertheless, the New Deal played an essential role in creating modern America by expanding the role of government, although leftist critics of the New Deal believe an opportunity to more fundamentally alter the American economy and address issues of inequality was missed.

Guided by a sense of urgency, Roosevelt assumed office in March 1933 with a flurry of activity and legislation known as the 100 Days. Roosevelt had first to deal with the banking crisis which saw the collapse of financial institutions around the country with bank runs and customers withdrawing deposits that the banks could not cover. The result was that many Americans lost their life savings, leading to a distrust of banks that led some to keep their money stuffed in mattresses or buried in the back yard. Roosevelt declared a banking holiday and assured Americans that

that under the Emergency Banking Act, the financial institutions would only resume operations after the government assured that they were financially sound. This was a guarantee which the Roosevelt administration could not really enforce, but it seemed that most Americans were reassured by the President. When the banks reopened, the panic had subsided as the bank runs were largely over. Roosevelt had proven to be a great communicator whose eloquence and compassion during the banking crisis was institutionalized by the fireside chats in which the President utilized the radio to develop a sense of rapport and direct communication with constituents who felt as if the President were a welcome guest in their home. Confidence in the banking system was also provided through the Glass-Steagall Act that introduced greater regulation of the industry by separating commercial and investment banking, while also creating the Federal Deposit Insurance Corporation (FDIC) to guarantee deposits of up to $2,500. That figure has been raised many times since 1933, and the FDIC remains a cornerstone of the banking system that was tested during the savings and loan crisis of the 1980s. In addition to the regulation of banking, the New Deal provided for government supervision of the stock market and Wall Street through the Securities and Exchange Commission (SEC), initially headed by Joseph Kennedy, whose son was later elected President. Kennedy and other wealthy Americans were able to purchase devalued stock for extremely low prices and benefit financially from the recovery of a regulated stock market that restored confidence for investors.

Repeal of prohibition and direct relief for the unemployed

The Roosevelt administration also moved to repeal the Volstead Act and enact the Twenty-first Amendment abandoning the national experiment with prohibition. In addition to fitting with the Roosevelt slogan that "happy days are here again," repeal of prohibition was pursued for a number of reasons. Taxation on alcohol was viewed as a means through which to increase government revenues— with similar arguments offered today for the legalization of marijuana. In addition, there was continuing concern about prohibition contributing to a growing sense of lawlessness in the land. However, the exploits of outlaws such as John Dillinger, "Baby Face" Nelson, "Pretty Boy" Floyd, and Bonnie and Clyde were probably due more to the depression context rather than prohibition as these outlaws were viewed as somewhat of Robin Hood figures by the common folk of the Midwest and Southwest. J. Edgar Hoover also employed these outlaws to extend the power of the FBI, which continued to maintain files on anyone, including Woody Guthrie, who was deemed as critical of the capitalist system.

Meanwhile, President Roosevelt and Congress sought to address the discontent fostered by the depression by authorizing funds for the states to provide direct relief to the starving and destitute through the Federal Emergency Relief Administration (FERA). This direct assistance to the poor was unpopular with some Americans as it challenged the self-made man ideology that hard work would be rewarded with wages and advancement in the American system. Direct relief undermined these assumptions and exposed the harsh reality of the American dream. From Roosevelt to Bill Clinton, who signed legislation that terminated the federal government's involvement with the welfare system, direct relief by the national government was never adequately funded and represented only a small percentage of the federal budget, although often denounced by conservative politicians as a major contributor to the deficit.

Putting Americans to work—CCC, PWA, and WPA

Roosevelt was much more comfortable with work programs such as the Civilian Conservation Corps (CCC). The CCC was designed to deal with the problem of youth unemployment in the urban areas of the nation which sometimes exceeded 50 percent and was believed to be a major factor promoting criminal activity. The youth of the CCC were to be assigned to camps in the wilderness areas of the West, where they would plant trees and make trails while addressing the environmental damage wrought by the dust bowl and lack of conservation. Since the youth in the CCC would have little use for money in their remote encampments, some of the funds they were allotted for their labor went directly to the parents. Initially, the CCC was only a program for young men, but Eleanor Roosevelt complained about this gender inequality, prevailing upon her husband and the Congress to expand the CCC to include young women. The CCC contributed to preserving the nation's resources, and many of the CCC camps and trails are still used today, but the program was abandoned as the nation moved to a war footing in 1941.

Work requirements were essential to the Public Works Administration (PWA) administered by the Secretary of the Interior Harold Ickes. The PWA sought to address unemployment and stimulate the economy through major construction projects such as roads, dams, bridges, hospitals, schools, and government buildings such as post offices. Between 1933 and 1939, the PWA spent over $7 billion on over 34,000 projects, providing much of the nation's infrastructure for the twentieth century, and many insist that a new PWA is required to address the deteriorating infrastructure of the United States. Among the most notable of the PWA projects were the Lincoln Tunnel in New York City, the Grand Coulee Dam in Washington state, and Bonneville Dam in Oregon. Unskilled workers found job opportunities with the Works Progress Administration (WPA) administered by social worker Harry Hopkins. The WPA put unemployed and unskilled workers on projects such as roads, public housing, and parks. Between 1935 and 1943, the agency employed 3.5 million people, providing unskilled laborers with meaningful work. The WPA also included a special program for unemployed young workers, the National Youth Administration (NYA)—an organization which a young Lyndon Johnson administered in Texas during the 1930s and attempted to resurrect in the 1960s as part of the Great Society. The most controversial aspect of the WPA was the effort to provide work for unemployed musicians, artists, writers, directors, and actors with art, theatrical, and literary projects. Under the auspices of the WPA, murals were painted and plays produced that were made available to common workers who usually lacked access to the arts. Writers for the WPA interviewed former enslaved people and provided guidebooks for each state that made historical and cultural knowledge available for the general public. Conservative critics, however, maintained that government funds for programs such as the Federal Theatre Project (FTP) were used to finance plays critical of American capitalism and race relations. Art for the masses seemed threatening to many in Congress, and the FTP was disbanded in 1937.

Restructuring the economy—AAA, NRA, and TVA

The New Deal also sought to address the plight of American farmers who had been mired in an agricultural depression throughout the 1920s. With the Agricultural Adjustment Administration (AAA), the New Deal attempted to subsidize farm prices by paying farmers to reduce their acreage, thus encouraging conservation through providing financial incentives aimed at the problem of overproduction. When the AAA was passed by Congress, many crops were already planted, and during a time of scarcity crops were plowed under and destroyed so that the farm crisis could be addressed by immediate application of the farm bill. In addition, pigs and cattle were destroyed and buried in mass graves while Americans were starving. In 1936, the Supreme Court overturned the AAA, declaring that funding the program through a tax on companies processing agricultural products was un-Constitutional. The Roosevelt administration and Congress responded to the court's reservations with the Soil Conservation and Domestic Allotment Act which continued the policy of reducing productivity by allowing farmers to receive subsidies for planting soil-conserving crops such as soybeans or letting some of their land lay fallow. The AAA provided relief to many farmers who benefitted by taking land out of production, but sharecropper tenants did not share in this prosperity as they were forced off the lands that were now left fallow or placed in the soil bank. The legislation pleased many Congressional Southern Democrats who owned farmland, but poor white and black sharecroppers often suffered under the AAA. There was an effort to provide assistance for dislocated tenant farmers with the Resettlement Administration under the auspices of the Farm Securities Administration (FSA), but these relief camps, praised by Steinbeck in *The Grapes of Wrath*, and resettlement communities were never adequately funded as many in Congress complained about these programs for migrants promoting socialism—a concern not usually expressed regarding the AAA which worked more for large scale farmers.

While the New Deal moved to aid farmers and rural America with the AAA, industrial recovery was addressed with the ambitious National Recovery Administration (NRA). Under the NRA, representatives from industry and government were to draw up fair codes of competition that would reduce the waste and destruction of cut-throat competition under unregulated capitalism. The codes of competition for over 200 industries ranging from big businesses such as oil companies to more local concerns such as barbershops also sought to include the voice of labor as the NRA recognized the formation of unions by promoting collective bargaining. The New Deal believed that the inclusion of labor would prevent costly strikes and raise wages, thus helping to provide the purchasing power that might allow Americans to consume their way out of the depression. The codes of competition were essentially to be enforced by what we might today call peer group pressure. Citizens were encouraged to not patronize any business that failed to display the NRA symbol of the Blue Eagle, signifying that the company or establishment was adhering to the code of competition negotiated for that enterprise. Parades were organized, and armbands handed out to encourage popular enthusiasm, while some critics maintained that the NRA and Blue Eagle reminded them of the symbols and propaganda employed by the Nazi Party in Germany. The NRA, nevertheless, initially enjoyed popular support as the New Deal sought to confront the crisis of the Great Depression, but as conditions improved somewhat under the leadership of Roosevelt, it became increasingly difficult to enforce the codes of competition, as businesses maneuvered to gain a competitive advantage. In 1935, the Supreme Court struck down the NRA, arguing in the *Schechter* or "sick chicken" decision that the codes of competition, regulating even local businesses such as a chicken farm in New York. were an un-Constitutional application of executive authority and the commerce clause. Roosevelt denounced the decision and later supported the Wagner Act to restore support for collective bargaining.

With the Tennessee Valley Authority (TVA), the New Deal promoted a policy of regional planning that, through a series of dams constructed on the Tennessee River, would prevent destructive flooding, expand employment, and provide cheap public power to rural areas lacking electrification. Similar programs were planned for other regions such as the Bonneville Power Administration (BPA) in the Pacific Northwest. The TVA provoked some complaints regarding its environmental impact and the dislocation of residents in the region, but the chief opposition to the concepts of government power and planning embodied by the TVA came from private utility companies, whose profits were endangered by the expanding government public power on behalf of the people. While expansion of regional planning envisioned by the New Deal was limited by influential utility companies bemoaning the promotion of socialism, the TVA continues to function today as an important site for the generation of electricity and is expanding into alternative energy sources such as wind and solar, although its ambitious program of nuclear power has been curtailed by safety considerations.

Opposition to the New Deal

The expansive powers of the New Deal such as the TVA provoked considerable opposition to the Roosevelt administration. The Liberty League was a group of prominent business leaders who opposed the New Deal as a threat to American individual liberties—or perhaps it was simply a drain on their profits— and considered Roosevelt to be a traitor to his class. Politically, however, Roosevelt recognized that the Liberty League did not constitute a major threat as the depression had discredited business leaders and bankers who were now the villains in many Hollywood films. Roosevelt was more concerned about populist threats and demagogues maintaining that the New Deal had not accomplished enough to relieve the plight of common Americans. Working as a Catholic priest out of the National Shrine of the Little Flower Church in Detroit, Father Charles Coughlin gained a popular following with his national radio broadcasts that included considerable political commentary. Coughlin was initially a supporter of Roosevelt and the New Deal, but he believed the President's programs failed to provide for adequate regulation of the banking system that the radio priest insisted was controlled by Jewish interests. Coughlin began referring to the President as "Rosenfeld" and filled his broadcasts with anti-Semitic messages. The appeal of these broadcasts reflected an anti-Semitic element in the United States for whom Hitler's rhetoric and policies toward the Jews resonated and encouraged immigration restrictions against European Jews attempting to flee fascism. The radio priest expressed his admiration for the fascist policies pursued by Adolph Hitler and Benito Mussolini, which he assured his listeners would provide social justice for the common people. Roosevelt perceived Coughlin and his National Union for Social Justice organization as a threat to the New Deal, and the President put pressure upon the Catholic hierarchy to remove Coughlin from the air waves. Although he remained as a priest, the church eventually withdrew support for Coughlin's radio program, and Roosevelt repaid the debt by refusing to support the legitimate Spanish Republic that was opposed by the Catholic Church and overthrown by Fascist General Francisco Franco in the bloody Spanish Civil War.

Roosevelt was also concerned with California physician Frances Townsend, who was not personally seeking political power, and his Old-Age Revolving Pension Plan which was organized throughout the country. Townsend was focused upon the plight of the elderly in depression America, and the doctor endorsed a program in which retired Americans over sixty years of age would receive $200 a month from the government which they would be obligated to spend in thirty days as stimulus for the economy. The plan would be financed through a national sales tax. Roosevelt worried about the financing of the plan and the political implications of a national organization opposing the New Deal agenda. He would eventually steal the thunder from Townsend's organization by supporting Congressional passage of the Social Security Act.

Huey Long

Roosevelt, however, was convinced that his greatest political threat was from Huey P. Long of Louisiana; hailed by some as the "Messiah of the Rednecks." As Governor of Louisiana from 1928 to 1932, Long opposed the economic power of the large oil companies that had blocked progressive economic change in the state, providing free textbooks for school children and spending increased tax revenues on building roads, bridges, hospitals, and schools for the common people. Long accomplished these goals without playing the race card employed by many Southern populists. Black residents of Louisiana benefitted from Long's programs, and when he once called the Grand Dragon of the Louisiana Klan "a son of a bitch," Long insisted that rather than being profane, he was simply referring to the circumstances of his birth. Long's critics, however, maintained that the Governor's accomplishments were gained through political intimidation, and his methods were a threat to American democracy.

In 1932, Long brought his politics to the national stage when he was elected to the Senate. The Senator did not believe that the New Deal was doing enough to alleviate the suffering of common Americans. To end the depression, Long advocated his Share the Wealth program that would place a floor and ceiling for individual incomes, addressing the nation's economic inequality. Long proclaimed that under his plan every American family would be able to own a car, a home worth $5,000, and a radio so that they could listen to the "Kingfish," as Long often liked to call himself. The Senator from Louisiana maintained that his plan was hardly communism as there would still be an economic gap between the top and bottom, but a common-sense redistribution of the nation's wealth would provide economic security for all Americans. Roosevelt was concerned that Long would challenge him for the 1936 Democratic Presidential bid, and the President was even having Long investigated for possible income tax evasion. Long's political ambitions, however, were cut short when he was assassinated in 1935 on the steps of the Louisiana State Capital. Conspiracy theorists like to believe that Roosevelt was somehow involved with the assassination, but Long was shot by a physician upset over the impeachment of his father-in-law as a judge. Long's enigmatic political career is considered by many to be the inspiration for Robert Penn Warren's novel *All the King's Men* (1946).

FDR moves the New Deal to the left—Social Security and the Wagner Act

To forestall the appeal of another populist demagogue such as Long, Roosevelt decided to move the New Deal to the political left before the 1936 election. Roosevelt implored Congress to raise taxes on the wealthy and railed against those whom he termed "economic royalists," although the actual tax hikes were not as steep as the Presidential rhetoric might have suggested. The President also decided to endorse the Social Security Act languishing in Congress. With Roosevelt's backing, one of the most significant pieces of legislation in American history passed the Congress. The Social Security Act provided for a national insurance system that would assure a safety net of government protection and payments for the unemployed, disabled, widows and orphans, as well as old age pensions to be financed out of payroll taxes. Although the allotted amounts were small and remain so, the Social Security bill placed the United States in line with the social welfare policies of other industrialized nations, although the act did not cover health care—an omission and problem which continues to plague the United States. While conservatives still complain about Social Security, it is one of the most popular of government programs in the United States.

Roosevelt also backed the Wagner Act that would restore government support of collective bargaining after the NRA was declared un-Constitutional. Under the Wagner Act, the National Labor Relations Board was established to supervise elections in which workers petitioned to have union representation. With the backing of the Roosevelt administration, union membership grew in the 1930s, but not without considerable division in labor's ranks. The American Federation of Labor (AFL) was the nation's most influential union and was composed of skilled workers organized along craft lines. The AFL was reluctant to lend its full support to industrial unionism, leading John L. Lewis, leader of the United Mine Workers, to form the rival Congress of Industrial Organization (CI0)—although the two labor organizations would unify in the 1950s to form the AFL-CIO. The CIO concentrated upon unorganized assembly line workers long ignored by the AFL, and the new labor organization also advocated for greater participation of workers in management decisions as well as the inclusion of black workers in the union; practices which led critics of the CIO to brand the union as being influenced by communist organizers and ideas. The CIO efforts at industrial unionism were met with considerable violence, extending from the coal mines of Harlan County in Kentucky to the shooting and killing of over twenty striking steel workers at the Republic Steel Mill in Chicago. At the so-called Battle of the Overpass near the River Rouge Plant in Dearborn, Michigan, Walter Reuther of the United Auto Workers (UAW) was severely beaten by security guards from the Ford Motor Company. In Flint, Michigan, the UAW organized sit-down strikes against General Motors as auto workers occupied the plants and means of production. Security guards beat women who attempted to provide supplies for the strikers, but the women and strikers persevered as a violent attack upon the strikers risked destruction of the plants. When the smoke cleared by the late 1930s, the CIO had made tremendous gains organizing steel and auto workers.

Election of 1936 and Roosevelt coalition

Thus, labor became a key constituency in the Roosevelt coalition that propelled the President to reelection in 1936. The Republicans nominated Governor Alf Landon of Kansas, who essentially proposed following the Hoover strategy of condemning excessive New Deal intervention in the markets and economy—differing general perspectives which continue to guide the two major political parties into the present day. Many pundits believed that Landon might win the election. For example, a poll by the influential *Literary Digest* found that a majority of Americans favored the Republican candidate. On election day, however, Landon only carried the states of Maine and Vermont. It seems that the magazine poll relied upon telephone calls, while the majority of Americans who rallied to Roosevelt and the New Deal could not afford the extravagance of a private telephone. The Democratic coalition formed by Roosevelt dominated American politics into the 1970s with government programs attracting various constituencies. Older Americans were enthusiastic about Social Security, while the Wagner Act rallied labor support, and the AAA provided benefits for farmers. Although there were few specific New Deal initiatives aimed at black Americans, in 1936 the black population completed its abandonment of the party of Lincoln which had freed the slaves. The depression hit the black community especially hard with reduced wages and an unemployment rate of 50 percent. Although programs such as the AAA were often discriminatory, the welfare and work programs sponsored by the New Deal did bring relief to the nation's black population. The Communist Party also made some inroads with black Americans by opposing segregation and defending the Scottsboro boys, who were accused of raping two young white women on a freight train in Alabama. Despite efforts to reduce female workforce participation in favor of husbands as the breadwinner of a family, women were attracted to Roosevelt and the New Deal through the activism of First Lady Eleanor Roosevelt and Secretary of Labor Francis Perkins, who was the first woman to serve as a cabinet officer.

Court packing plan

Moving into his second term, Roosevelt was frustrated that the momentum of the New Deal was being undermined by what the President called an old-fashioned "horse and buggy" Supreme Court that declared such legislation as the NRA and AAA un-Constitutional. To address the issue of reforming the court, Roosevelt proposed the Judicial Procedures Reform Bill which his opponents insisted upon calling the "court packing plan." The proposed legislation would allow the President to appoint an additional judge to the Supreme Court for every member of the judicial body over seventy years of age. Six of the judges in 1937 were over seventy, and Roosevelt's bill would allow the President to enlarge the court to fifteen members. Congressional advocates of Roosevelt's plan argued that it would bring greater efficiency to the court and the Constitution did not specify the number of Supreme Court justices. Opponents denounced the plan as violating the principle of checks and balances by making the President an autocrat who would now control the judicial branch. The court bill provided Congressional adversaries of Roosevelt an opportunity to defy the President without appearing to vote against legislation to help the people, and the court bill marked Roosevelt's first major legislative defeat. The court, however, did seem to be influenced by the Congressional debate, and with a shift in the voting pattern of Justice Owen Roberts, New Deal legislation such as the Wagner Act was confirmed by the court. Other justices eventually resigned or died, and Roosevelt was able to appoint more liberal justices such as Hugo Black, Stanley Reed, Felix Frankfurter, William O. Douglas, and Frank Murphy during the President's second term. Roosevelt, however, may have won the battle and lost the war as during the court battle a legislative coalition of Southern Democrats and Northern Republicans formed that was largely resistant to additional New Deal bills and programs.

Thus, Roosevelt during his second term enjoyed fewer legislative victories, although one significant bill that gained passage through the conservative coalition was the Fair Labor Standards Act of 1938 which embraced a forty-hour work week with provisions for overtime pay. The bill also established the principle of a national minimum wage—with major exemptions for restaurants and agricultural labor—originally set at forty cents per hour. As of this writing, the national minimum wage remains a rather paltry $7.25 per hour, hardly an adequate sum to support a family or escape poverty. Also, Roosevelt remained somewhat of an economic conservative who was uncomfortable with the unbalanced budgets of his Presidency. In 1937, he attempted to abandon Keynesian economics and reduced federal spending. This action resulted in a recession, and the President returned to priming the economic pump with additional government spending.

Legacy of the New Deal

During his second term, Roosevelt was also increasingly focused upon the international scene with the rise of militarism and totalitarian regimes which seemed to herald the possibility of another world war. And it would take World War II to finally end the Great Depression and bring full employment to the United States. Americans seem to have few problems with deficits and spending when it involves the military and may be described as necessary for national defense, but they cannot seem to perceive unemployment or health care as constituting a similar degree of national emergency. Thus, the impact of the New Deal upon American history remains somewhat ambivalent. Many conservatives insist that by intervening in the marketplace, the New Deal prolonged the depression and the natural corrective provided by the market's invisible hand. But market corrections do not necessarily feed crying babies, so in the New Deal, Roosevelt sought to save capitalism by instituting regulatory reform and government programs such as Social Security that would provide a modest safety net for those suffering under the excesses of capitalism. The reforms of the New Deal, however, may be viewed as missing an opportunity for enacting more fundamental changes such as guaranteed health coverage for all, subsidized child care, paid paternity leave, mass transit, equal access to education, and gender and racial equality in the workplace—reforms that one might find in a democratic socialist system. The New Deal offered an opportunity for the country to achieve its democratic promise and foster the American dream, but reform gave way to the war against fascism or in the words of Roosevelt, "Dr. Win the War replaced Dr. New Deal."

Further Reading:

Brands, H. W. *Traitor to His Class: The Privileged Life and Radical Presidency of Franklin Delano Roosevelt*. New York: Doubleday, 2008.

Brinkley, Alan. *Voices of Protest: Huey Long, Father Coughlin, and the Great Depression*. New York: Knopf, 1982.

Cook, Blanche Wiesen. *Eleanor Roosevelt: Volume 2, The Defining Years, 1933-1938*. New York: Penguin, 1999.

Galbraith, John Kenneth. *The Great Crash, 1929*. Boston: Houghton Mifflin, 1955.

Gregory, James N. *American Exodus: The Dust Bowl Migration and Okie Culture in California*. New York: Oxford University Press, 1989.

Leuchtenburg, William. *Franklin Roosevelt and the New Deal, 1932–1940*. New York: Harper & Row, 1963.

McElvaine, Robert. *The Great Depression: America 1929–1941*. New York: Times Books, 1984.

Pells, Richard H. *Radial Visions and American Dreams: Culture and Social Thought in the Depression Years*. New York: Harper & Row, 1973.

Schlesinger Jr., Arthur M. *The Crisis of the Old Order, 1919–1933*. Boston: Houghton Mifflin, 1957.

Terkel, Studs. *Hard Times: An Oral History of the Great Depression*. New York: Pantheon Books, 1970.

Ware, Susan. *Beyond Suffrage: Women in the New Deal*. Cambridge, MA: Harvard University Press, 1981.

Weiss, Nancy J. *Farewell to the Party of Lincoln: Black Politics in the Age of FDR*. Princeton, NJ: Princeton University Press, 1983.

23

The United States in World War II

"I've Found the Job Where I Fit Best." Office of War Information, 1943. Prints and Photographs Division, Library of Congress. During the Second World War, the government encouraged women to enter the workforce to replace men drafted into military service. The women did an excellent job in the factories, but they were forced out of these jobs after the war as men returned from the battlefield.

For better or worse, the Second World War transformed the United States into a world power that led a global crusade against fascism. Yet, the legacy of what many Americans still call "the good war" is mixed with the development of the atomic bomb, a dangerous Cold War between the United States and Soviet Union, and the growth of a military-industrial complex projecting American military and economic power globally in a Pax Americana that has brought little peace to the world. Domestically, the war helped bring a halt to the reforms of the New Deal, but massive spending on the military and conscription finally brought fill employment and the end of the depression without adequately addressing the causes of inequality in American life. anti-Semitism, racism, and gender discrimination remained rampant during the war years, but expanding employment opportunities helped to provide the economic foundation for post war feminism and the Civil Rights Movement. The G.I. Bill was also a crucial factor in promoting an expanding post war middle class, yet poverty remained a fact of life for many Americans. There was also considerable irony in the fact that while the so-called "greatest generation" made tremendous sacrifices during the war in the struggle for freedom, the post war political atmosphere in the United States witnessed the emergence of McCarthyism and efforts to silence dissent. New Dealers, labor leaders, women demanding their rights, and advocates for civil rights were denounced as communists and their causes dismissed during a reactionary period of conformity. The ambiguous legacy of the Second World War would be addressed by the baby boomer children of the "greatest generation" in the Civil Rights Movement and protest against the Vietnam War.

After assuming the Presidency in 1933, the Roosevelt administration certainly concentrated upon domestic issues and implementing the New Deal, but the new President was unable to ignore an international situation in which the world was seemingly drifting toward another global conflict. In 1933, the United States became the last major industrial nation to diplomatically recognize the Soviet Union. Roosevelt's critics accused the President of appeasing communism, but he was simply acknowledging the reality of Soviet power, hoping to promote some trade, and perhaps enlist Stalin in limiting the expansionism of Germany, Italy, and Japan. Roosevelt also sought to establish better relations with Latin American nations who were upset with United States military interventions dating back to the Panama Canal and Roosevelt Corollary of Franklin's Republican cousin, Theodore. Withdrawing American troops from Haiti, Roosevelt introduced the Good Neighbor Policy with Latin America, promoting trade and fostering hemispheric cooperation that paid off during World War II.

On the other hand, more isolationist tendencies were evident in Roosevelt's failure to engage with the 1933 London Economic Conference attended by sixty-six nations. The President was wary of an international agreement that might restrict his domestic policies toward addressing the depression. The collapse of the London Conference, however, exacerbated the economic nationalism exemplified by the Hawley-Smoot Tariff. Isolationist sentiment was also strong among many Americans disillusioned regarding the aftermath of World War I. The sacrifices endured in the crusade to "make the world safe for democracy" failed to render World War I "the war to end all wars" as President Wilson had proclaimed. Instead, by the 1930s the world was plagued with depression, the rise of totalitarianism, and a drift toward war. The antiwar beliefs of many Americans were evident in the popularity of the 1930 film version of Erich Maria Remarque's novel *All Quiet on the Western Front* (1929) exposing the futility of war.

Nye Committee and neutrality legislation

These sentiments were also exemplified by the Special Committee on Investigation of the Munitions Industry, usually referred to as the Nye Committee chaired by Republican Senator Gerald P. Nye of North Dakota. The Congressional committee concluded that the munitions industry and bankers manipulated the United States into entering the First World War so that they could earn greater profits and secure repayment of their international loans. While reflecting a genuine disillusionment with war, the Nye Committee also preyed upon anti-Semitic stereotypes in the denunciation of international bankers—a pattern that was repeated in Senator Nye's investigation of the Hollywood film industry. The Nye Committee encouraged Congressional passage of neutrality legislation that might prevent American entrance into another world war by forbidding Americans to trade with or make loans to belligerent nations in conflicts recognized by the government of the United States. Drawing upon submarine warfare which propelled the Wilson administration into war, Americans were forbidden to sail on the vessels of belligerent nations. The neutrality laws also prevented the United States from aiding Ethiopia and the Republican government in Spain when they were subject to fascist aggression.

Focusing upon the internal politics of the New Deal, Roosevelt initially paid little attention to the neutrality laws, but as the international situation worsened, the President began to change his mind. Perceiving the expansionist policies of Japan, and especially Germany, as a threat to the United States, Roosevelt began to seek revision of the neutrality laws. While the President had to respond simultaneously to international tensions in both Europe and Asia, for purposes of clarification we will engage in separate discussions of Roosevelt's diplomacy and how he responded to the crises of the Atlantic and Pacific. Fascists in Europe and militarists in Japan reacted to the world depression by moving toward totalitarian governments that endorsed war and seizure of regional resources. The general will of the people would be embodied in a dictator restoring national greatness through war and demanding obedience.

Roosevelt seeks to amend neutrality legislation

On the European continent the rise of fascism was exemplified by the regimes of Hitler in Germany, Mussolini in Italy, and Franco in Spain. The mass appeal of fascism extended beyond these dictators with fascist politicians and movements threatening such established democracies as England and France. Totalitarianism was also embodied in the Soviet dictatorship of Joseph Stalin who consolidated his hold on power through a purge of his former Bolshevik comrades. Roosevelt was increasingly concerned by the expansion of Nazi Germany which had the potential to cut the United States off from European markets as well as the colonial economies of European powers. The President was also worried about the anti-Semitic ideology of the Nazis, although these reservations were not initially expressed publicly due to domestic political considerations, and many European Jews seeking to flee the Nazi regime were blocked from entering the United States.

In 1939, Roosevelt convinced Congress to amend the neutrality laws by providing a cash and carry exemption that would allow a belligerent nation to purchase arms from the United States as long as the country would pay for the American supplies with cash and use their own vessels to ship the goods. This exception was designed to benefit England which with its superior naval resources would be in good position to take advantage of cash and carry. The amended Neutrality Act of 1939 was passed after the 1938 Munich crisis and Hitler's annexation of Austria and Czechoslovakia. Hitler's invasion of Poland in September 1939 provoked a European war, and Roosevelt wanted to bolster resistance to the Nazi leader from England and France. The situation was even more dire in September 1940 when Roosevelt agreed to transfer fifty U.S. Navy destroyers to the British in exchange for the right of American forces to use British bases in Newfoundland and the Caribbean; an exchange that would allow the United States to better defend the Western Hemisphere against aggression. Roosevelt was concerned about the British being able to hold out against Nazi Germany which had defeated France and occupied much of Europe. In the Battle of Britain, the Germans were subjecting London and England to heavy bombing which many feared was the prelude to an invasion. Roosevelt hoped that the destroyers would help the cash-strapped British resist an invasion. The President concluded the deal with Britain through an executive agreement as it was not likely that a divided Congress would have approved such a transaction.

Political divisions and a third term for FDR

Americans were uncertain as to how their nation might avoid the conflict in Europe as the 1940 Presidential election approached. An isolationist position was championed by the America First Committee which included such prominent Americans as industrialist Henry Ford and aviator Charles Lindbergh, who expressed some sympathy for the anti-Semitic policies of Hitler and feared that Jewish bankers might drag America into the conflict. According to America First, the Atlantic and Pacific Oceans provided a buttress against foreign attack, while the United States enjoyed friendly neighbors in Mexico and Canada. Thus, there was no reason for the Untied States to become involved in the disputes of European nations. The technological and military developments of the Second World War destroyed many of these arguments for geographical isolationism, while Philip Roth's novel *The Plot Against America* (2005) has exposed the racist assumption of the America First movement. Supporters of Roosevelt formed an alternative organization called the Committee to Defend America by Aiding the Allies, perceiving Nazi Germany as a threat to American ideas and security. The best way to avoid war would be through supporting the resistance of nations such as Great Britain to German aggression.

As the election of 1940 approached, Roosevelt was convinced that the United States would eventually need to enter the war against Germany, but in the meantime, it was imperative for the United States to aid Britain. He recognized, however, that the American people were not yet prepared for such a bold move, but Roosevelt believed that he was the indispensable man who might be able to persuade his fellow citizens that war against Germany was in their best interest. Roosevelt, thus, decided that it was necessary to violate the tradition established by George Washington that the President would only serve two terms in office. He managed for the Democratic National convention to essentially draft him for a third term, while the Republicans selected businessman Wendell Willkie, who denounced Roosevelt for seeking a third term. The Republican criticized the New Deal for waste and inefficiency, while supporting an internationalist approach to foreign affairs opposed by the isolationist wing of his party. Meanwhile, Roosevelt was rather deceptive in his campaign, pledging that under his leadership American boys would not be sent to fight and die in foreign lands, while personally believing that it would eventually be necessary for the United States to ally with Britain against Germany. Willkie's candidacy saw increased Republican support in the Midwest, and some Americans were concerned about abandoning the two-term tradition, but the popular Roosevelt won re-election rather handily.

Lend-Lease

Roosevelt immediately moved toward fostering greater support for the British by proposing the Lend-Lease bill. Under this piece of legislation, the United States identified the Axis powers of Germany, Italy, and Japan, who formed an alliance with the Tripartite Pact in 1940, as a threat to national security, and the United States was prepared to lend or lease American supplies to nations fighting the Axis powers. This American aid went primarily to Britain, China, the Free French, and later the Soviet Union after they were invaded by Nazi Germany in June 1941. These allied nations were in no position to pay for these American supplies, and some in Congress complained about the lack of compensation. In response, Roosevelt articulated what reporters called the garden hose analogy. The President suggested that if your neighbor's house were on fire and you were afraid that your own home might be destroyed by the flames, you would not negotiate with your neighbor when he requested to borrow your garden hose in order to put out the fire. Instead, you would immediately loan them your hose and worry about repayment or the condition of the hose later after the danger had passed. Congress agreed with Roosevelt's arguments, and the Lend-Lease bill was enacted into law, essentially placing the United States on a war footing. Recognizing that the British could not spare the ships to transport the Lend-Lease supplies, Roosevelt provided for American vessels to convey the materials. Germany announced that her submarines would attack American merchant vessels carrying Lend-Lease supplies, and Roosevelt was convinced that German sinking of American merchant ships would bring the United States into the war like the unrestricted submarine warfare of the Germans in the First World War.

Japan challenges the open door in China

Before this happened, however, the United States was brought into the global conflict by Japan through what some called "the back door to war." Although Roosevelt believed Nazi Germany to be the greater threat, the United States and Japan had been on somewhat of a collision course throughout the 1930s. In 1931, Japan, in search of natural resources such as iron ore and coal, seized Manchuria from China, creating the puppet state of Manchukuo under Japanese control. Six years later, clashes between Japanese and Chinese forces led to war and a Japanese invasion of China. These aggressive expansionist policies were attributed to Japanese militarists under the command of Hideki Tojo who served as Prime Minister from 1941 to 1944. While Emperor Hirohito was often perceived as a moderating influence upon the militarists, many historians assign him greater responsibility for Japanese military and foreign policy during the 1930s and World War II. The Hoover administration responded to the Japanese invasion and acquisition of Manchuria by instituting what Secretary of State Henry Stimson termed a policy of non-recognition; the United States would not extend diplomatic recognition to territorial changes brought about by war or force. While this policy did little to halt Japanese aggression, it did keep the United States out of an Asian war, and the Roosevelt administration, primarily focused upon domestic concerns, inherited the so-called Stimson Doctrine of non-recognition.

When conflict between Japan and China resumed, Roosevelt considered taking a stronger stand against Japan. In an October 5, 1937 speech in Chicago, Roosevelt suggested that the United States should "quarantine" or economically isolate nations who pursued aggressive policies in violation of international agreements and organizations such as the League of Nations—of which the United States was not a member. Although specific nations were not mentioned, the speech was understood to be a reference toward Japan, Germany, and Italy. When the quarantine idea floated by Roosevelt met with considerable resistance, the President backed away from confronting Japanese expansionism. The degree of anti-war sentiment in the nation was well exemplified by the Ludlow Amendment proposed by Democratic Congressman Louis Ludlow of Indiana. Under this proposed amendment to the Constitution, the people of the United States would have to ratify a Congressional declaration of war unless the nation was under direct attack. The amendment garnered considerable popular support with opinion polls indicating that nearly three-quarter of Americans were favorable. When legislation came up for a House vote in 1938, however, it was defeated in a relatively close vote.

Thus, Roosevelt moved cautiously in his policy toward Japan. The President was reluctant to impose an American embargo on the Japanese for fear that cutting off scarce resources such as oil would simply encourage the militarists to pursue even more aggressive actions to acquire resources that were in short supply. Continued Japanese aggression appeared to force the hand of the President who was increasingly concerned with Japanese expansion as a threat to American economic interests in Asia and the Pacific. As the Japanese extended their territorial control over China, they declared that the American open door policy for China was no longer valid, proposing instead a new order in Asia with the Greater East Asia Co-Prosperity Sphere; a coalition of Asian nations organized by Japan in opposition to the colonization by Western powers that had dominated the region. While nations such as the Philippines were opposed to American and European imperialism, they were suspicious that the Japanese were attempting to impose a colonial empire of their own. Roosevelt responded by imposing a partial embargo that would deny the Japanese military access to American aircraft parts and other military supplies that the President deemed essential to the national defense of the United States. This embargo, however, failed to deter the Japanese from moving into Indochina in July 1941. After its defeat and occupation by Germany, the French regime in Vichy was in no position to defend its Indochinese colonial possessions, and the Japanese sought to avail themselves of resources such as the rubber tree plantations in Vietnam. The United States retaliated by freezing all Japanese assets held by

American banks; an action that made it virtually impossible for Japan to purchase American oil reserves. The Roosevelt administration asserted that sanctions would be lifted if the Japanese were to withdraw from Indochina as well as the territory seized from China, whose plight was sympathetically viewed by Americans through the lens of Christian missionaries despite a legacy of discrimination toward the Chinese community in the United States.

Pearl Harbor

The Japanese military machine was dependent upon American oil supplies; however, Japan was not prepared to abandon the expansionist policy pursued throughout the 1930s. It would be imperative for Japan to find another source to fuel Imperial ambitions. In consultation with the Emperor, the military identified the Dutch East Indies, today Indonesia, as a region that could provide the required petroleum supplies. While occupied by the Germans, it would be impossible for the Dutch to defend their valuable colony. The Japanese government, nonetheless, recognized that the United States would likely employ its military resources in the Pacific to resist an invasion of the Dutch East Indies. Therefore, it would first be necessary to neutralize the United States by attacking the American Navy at Pearl Harbor in Hawaii and Army forces stationed in the Philippines. Japan, meanwhile, moved to resolve the crisis by dispatching a negotiating team to the United States. When no agreement was reached by November 25, 1941, the Japanese military machine secretly moved toward Hawaii and the Philippines; although as a diplomatic cover for these military maneuvers, the negotiations in Washington continued.

On December 7, 1941, the Japanese government sent a long message to Washington terminating diplomatic relations with the United States; however, the bombs were already falling on Pearly Harbor before the message was translated and delivered to an angry Secretary of State Cordell Hull. The Japanese aerial assault from aircraft carriers caught the Americans by surprise. In approximately ninety minutes, the attack sank four battleships and damaged four more in addition to numerous other vessels docked at Pearl Harbor. Over 160 aircraft were destroyed, and approximately 2,400 Americans killed. The greatest loss of life occurred on the *USS Arizona* where 1,177 Naval officers and sailors perished after a Japanese bomb hit a powder magazine; many of those killed were sleeping below deck after a Saturday night in Honolulu. Pearl Harbor, however, was hardly an unqualified success for the Imperial Japanese Navy. The three American aircraft carriers that the Japanese assumed would be docked at Pearl Harbor were designated for other missions and escaped damage on December 7th—leading Japanese Admiral Isoroku Yamamoto to despair about the attack and conclude that the Japanese had only succeeded in waking a sleeping giant.

In response to the attack, President Roosevelt appeared before a joint session of Congress, asking for a declaration of war against the Japanese Empire and proclaiming December 7, 1941 as a day that would live in infamy. Roosevelt was concerned that the Congress might not declare war against Germany who had not attacked the United States. However, Hitler and Mussolini alleviated these concerns when Germany and Italy, in support of their Japanese allies, issued declarations of war against the United States which reciprocated, and the United States was finally drawn into the Second World War.

The fact that the United States was caught so unprepared at Pearl Harbor has provoked conspiracy theories that President Roosevelt knew of the attack and allowed it to happen in order to get the Untied States into the war, while the aircraft carriers were not present at Pearl Harbor so that they would remain available for the reconquest of the Pacific. Congress appointed a commission to investigate Pearl Harbor, but while the investigative body found that plenty of mistakes were made, there was no evidence of a conspiracy. The United States had broken the Japanese codes and knew that an attack was imminent, but the intelligence community was divided as to the site of a Japanese assault, sending warnings to such possible targets as the Panama Canal in addition to Pearl Harbor. The military commanders at Pearl Harbor, General Walter Short and Admiral Husband Kimmel, misinterpreted the warning, assuming that the Japanese Navy was incapable of launching an aerial assault on Pearl Harbor from aircraft carriers. Instead, they believed that American military installations in Hawaii were most vulnerable to sabotage from the large Japanese population of the islands. The commanders, accordingly, placed American aircraft wing tip to wing tip in the middle of airfields where they could be protected by soldiers from sabotage. Of course, the massed aircraft proved to make perfect targets for the Japanese aviators. Overconfidence and misjudgment were based upon assumptions of racial superiority and were far more to blame for the disaster at Pearl Harbor than conspiracy.

Bataan

A similar surprise assault struck the American forces on the Philippines under the command of General Douglas MacArthur, whose preparations for an attack again focused upon sabotage. Unlike Hawaii, the Japanese attack on the Philippines included a full-scale invasion. While the Filipino people had a troubled history with the American occupation of the islands, they did not welcome the Japanese as liberators and joined with the Americans in resistance against the invaders. Caught by surprise, American and Filipino forces on the island of Luzon retreated to the Bataan peninsula where they made a stand against superior numbers of Japanese troops. The "battling bastards of Bataan" were told that no rescue would be forthcoming. It was their job to hold off the Japanese as long as possible and buy time for the United

States to get on a full wartime footing. A submarine was dispatched to bring General MacArthur and his family to Australia where the United States and its allies planned to organize an offensive that would push the Japanese back and return Americans to the Philippines, but in the meantime the soldiers and sailors of Bataan knew that they had no choice but to continue the struggle. After three long months of fighting and running out of ammunition, approximately 60,000 exhausted, ill, and starving American and Filipino troops surrendered. The Japanese then marched the prisoners approximately ninety miles to a railhead where they would be sent to prisoner of war camps. In what became known as the Bataan Death March, exhausted soldiers who collapsed were bayonetted by the Japanese, and some were even beheaded by officers with Samurai swords. Filipino women and children who attempted to aid the prisoners by providing food and water were also attacked. In the forced march, it is estimated that as many as 18,000 Filipinos and 650 Americans perished. The Bataan Death March was termed a war crime at the Tokyo War Crimes Tribunal, but there remains some dispute as to whether the Death March, like the Japanese atrocities committed during the "rape of Nanking" in China, were premeditated by Japanese authorities or the actions of undisciplined soldiers and officers in the field.

Internment of Japanese Americans

The American reaction to Pearl Harbor and Bataan was severe for Japanese Americans. Surrendering to racial prejudice that Americans of Japanese ancestry could not be trusted and would support a Japanese invasion of the West Coast, in February 1942 Roosevelt issued Executive Order 9066 that allowed military commanders to designate the West Coast as a "military area" from which all persons of Japanese ancestry were to be removed as a war measure, although in reality there was no proof that the Japanese Americans were a security risk. Nevertheless, approximately 120,000 people of Japanese ancestry, of whom over 60 percent were citizens of the United States, were relocated to concentration camps in isolated regions of the American West where they were incarcerated in many cases for the duration of the war. Families were required to report to detention centers on short notice, and professions and schooling were interrupted. Living in the primitive camp conditions disrupted family life within the crowded dormitory-like facilities. Many packed so quickly that they neglected to bring property deeds with them, and following the closure of the camps, many Japanese Americans returned to find their homes and businesses taken over by Anglo Americans whose occupancy was often supported by local authorities. The camps were surrounded by barbed wire and armed soldiers who daily reminded the Japanese that they were not to be treated as American citizens. Young Japanese males in the camps, however, were still subject to military conscription, and draft notices produced riots in some of the camps. But most of the Japanese were eager to prove their loyalty to the United States, and the 442nd Regiment Combat Team, sometimes referred to as the Nisei Division, was one of the most decorated combat units in the American military, although they were assigned to the European theater as there remained concern about whether they could be trusted to fight against Imperial Japan. And the courts provided little protection for Japanese Americans as in the infamous 1944 *Korematsu* Decision the Supreme Court upheld Executive Order 9066 as a legitimate exercise of the President's wartime authority as Commander-in-Chief, establishing a terrible and dangerous precedent that has never officially been overturned. However, under Presidents Reagan and George H. W. Bush apologies and some compensation were provided for the Japanese American community, but the precedent of Japanese internment during the Second World War is something of which all Americans should be wary.

Germany first and the North African campaign

While the American people were eager to exact retribution for Pearl Harbor, Roosevelt perceived Germany as the greater threat and made the war in Europe a priority as he feared the possibility that German scientists might provide the Nazi regime with rockets and weapons of mass destruction that would provide the foundation for Hitler's victory. Although Germany was not quite as advanced on an atomic weapon to mount on their rockets as Roosevelt feared, the scientific knowledge advanced by German physicists played a key role in America's eventual development of an atomic weapon, and some pundits maintain that in the Cold War the German scientists coopted by the United States defeated the former German scientists recruited by the Soviets. While fighting was occurring simultaneously in both the European and Pacific theaters, defeating Germany remained a priority, and for purposes of organization this account will also concentrate upon a Europe first strategy.

While the war initially resulted in German domination of the European continent, an emerging alliance among the United States, Great Britain, and Soviet Union began to change the tide of the war in late 1942. American long-range bombers based in Britain were able to begin bombing missions against German factories as well as civilians, bringing the war home to the German people for the first time. World War II was a savage conflict in which aerial assaults from both the Axis and Allies targeted civilian populations to destroy morale on the home front, creating an environment of total war. Meanwhile, a German advance across North Africa toward the Suez Canal and oilfields of Iran—and which was designed to eventually link up with their Japanese allies in India—was halted by the British at the Battle of El Alamein in Egypt. Perhaps Hitler's greatest strategical error in the war was the invasion of the Soviet Union in 1941. The unprepared Soviet forces were initially pushed back by the German invaders after Hitler betrayed his alliance with Stalin; however, the Soviet dictator rallied his nation by appealing to patriotism rather than communism, stopping the German advance at the siege of Leningrad and Battle of Stalingrad, that lasted from November 1942 to February 1943 in which nearly two million were killed, wounded, or captured in the fierce fighting. Hitler refused to disengage and lost military personnel that could have later been employed to defend the German homeland. Following Stalingrad, the Soviets began to push the Germans back on the Eastern Front where the heaviest fighting of the war took place, and Americans tend to forget that the Soviets did the brunt of the fighting against Nazi Germany during the Second World War.

Stalin wanted the United States to launch an invasion of France that would create a second front and take pressure off the Soviet Red Army. Roosevelt, however, did not believe that the inexperienced American Army was prepared to deal with the heavily defended beaches of France. Instead, the United States proposed a military operation in North Africa that would join with the British to drive the Africa Corps under the command of General Erwin Rommel out of the region. The reservations of Roosevelt regarding American military preparedness were borne out in February 1943 at the Battle of Kasserine Pass in Tunisia. American forces initially fought poorly and were pushed back approximately fifty miles before regrouping and assuming the offensive. Joining with their British allies, the Americans were able to force the Germans out of North Africa in May 1943.

Casablanca Conference and invasion of Italy

Once the American troops were seasoned with combat experience, Stalin assumed that the United States and Britain were prepared to open a second front in France. But perhaps Stalin should have attended the January 1943 Casablanca Conference in French Morocco between Roosevelt and British Prime Minister Winston Churchill. The conference is famous for the decision by the allied leaders to declare that they would accept only unconditional surrender from the Axis powers. While some critics complain that this stance lengthened the war by offering no incentives for negotiating or overthrowing dictators such as Hitler, it also committed the United States to the total destruction of fascism—although post war fears regarding communism made the accomplishment of this goal somewhat ambiguous in places such as Spain. While Stalin stayed away from Casablanca, insisting that he was needed to direct the Battle of Stalingrad, Roosevelt and Churchill made the decision that their next major objective was the invasion of fascist Italy. Churchill persuaded Roosevelt that the Italians would not put up a spirited resistance and represented the soft underbelly of Europe. The British Prime Minister was also concerned with the growth of communism in post war Eastern Europe as many of the partisans fighting against the fascists were communists. Thus, Churchill sough to promote a strong British presence in the region following the war.

Accordingly, in August 1943, the Allies invaded the island of Sicily which they wanted as a base from which to launch the assault upon Italy. Churchill was right as the Italians had lost their appetite for fascism, overthrowing Mussolini and seeking peace with the Allies. The surrender of the Italians, however, hardly ended the fighting as the large contingent of German troops continued to resist the Allied invasion. The Anzio amphibious operation eventually resulted in the capture of Rome in June 1944 after fierce German resistance, but the progress of the Allied forces up the Italian boot was extremely slow, and American troops were still bogged down in Italy at the war's conclusion.

The second front and invasion of Normandy

The Italian campaign and failure to open a second front in France led to rumors that Stalin might make a separate peace with Hitler. Seeking to appease the angry Soviets, Roosevelt, Stalin, and Churchill met in November 1943 at the Teheran Conference in Iran. Essentially, Roosevelt and Churchill came to Stalin as the Soviet leader continued to assert that he could not be far away from the battlefields where his Red Army was doing most of the fighting against Nazi Germany. In his first meeting with the Soviet leader, Roosevelt relied upon his personal charm and believed that he made a personal connection that would benefit the United States in future negotiations. The major outcome of the meetings was Stalin's promise that he would continue his offensive in the East and make no separate agreements with Hitler in exchange for the opening of an Allied second front in France by May 1944.

On June 6, 1944, Allied soldiers from the United States, Britain, Canada, and the Free French under the command of American General Dwight David Eisenhower launched the largest amphibious operation in history with landings on five beaches in Normandy, located on the northern coast of France. Behind the Atlantic Wall of coastal defenses, the Germans were expecting an invasion, but their forces were somewhat depleted by the transfer of forces to the fierce fighting on the Eastern front. Nevertheless, the resistance was strong, and 29,000 Americans died before the Allies were able to break through the German lines. Under the command of General George Patton, American tanks and troops moved rapidly across the French countryside, reaching Paris in August 1944, where they were greeted as liberators—an image of cheering crowds which more recent military actions by the Untied States have been unable to replicate.

As the German troops were being pushed back toward their homeland, Roosevelt had to deal with the Presidential election of 1944. Although some expressed concern about the President's health after twelve years on the job, Roosevelt believed that it was unwise to change leaders in the middle of a global conflict, and he accepted the Democratic nomination for a fourth term. Conservative

Democrats, however, expressed reservations regarding his Vice President Henry Wallace of Iowa, who had also served the President as Secretary of Agriculture. Wallace was a liberal who viewed the defeat of fascism as a victory of the common man and perceived the post war environment as offering an opportunity for international cooperation. Roosevelt reluctantly agreed to dump Wallace, and the convention selected Senator Harry Truman of Missouri, who gained publicity by chairing a Senate committee investigating waste within wartime industries, as his running mate. Truman had little experience in international affairs, and one wonders if the post war world might have been different if Wallace rather than Truman had replaced Roosevelt. With the war in Europe demonstrating progress, the popular Roosevelt was elected to a fourth term over the young Republican nominee, forty-two-year old New York Governor Thomas Dewey.

In December 1944, a desperate Hitler launched a counterattack, relying upon the conscription of young boys and older men, in the Ardennes Forest of Belgium that the Germans hoped would split the Allied forces and convince them to negotiate a peace allowing Hitler to concentrate upon the Soviets. The Allies were caught by surprise and initially pushed back in what became known as the Battle of the Bulge, but the Americans made a determined stand at Bastogne, and the German advance halted. As fog lifted and Allied aircraft were able to dominate the skies, the Germans retreated, and the war's end was near. In this final major battle of the European war, over 19,000 Americans were killed.

Yalta Conference

As the end for Nazi Germany became more apparent, Roosevelt, Churchill, and Stalin met in February 1945 at Yalta on the Crimean Peninsula to discuss the design of post war Europe. The Yalta Conference remains controversial today with some extreme anticommunists accusing the President of treason and selling out to the Soviets, while others defend Roosevelt by asserting that his decisions were impacted by his declining health. On the other hand, it may be argued that considering the military situation in Europe and the continuing war against Japan, Roosevelt achieved the best deal possible at Yalta. In exchange for Stalin's agreement to seek membership in the proposed United Nations to replace the collapsed League of Nations and join the war against Japan three months after the surrender of Germany, the Soviets would be allowed to occupy the Kuril Islands and the southern half of Sakhalin Island from the Japanese. In addition, the Soviets agreed to demands from the United States that free elections be held to determine the post war future of Poland. The elections, however, would be conducted under the supervision of the Soviets. Accordingly, the communists dominated the Polish elections, establishing a precedent that would be followed in other Eastern European nations liberated and occupied by the Red Army. Defenders of Roosevelt point out that while still sustaining considerable losses in the war against Japan, the United States was in no position to wage a conflict with the Soviets to dislodge them from Eastern Europe which they viewed as an important buffer zone to prevent another invasion of Mother Russia. Also, the territorial concessions to the Soviets in the Far East would place some limits on Stalin's ambitions. It is also essential to remember that at the time of the Yalta Conference, the atomic bomb had not yet been tested, and the conventional wisdom was that the seasoned Red Army would be needed for the anticipated bloody invasion of Japan. Roosevelt also remained convinced that he had forged a positive personal relationship with Stalin, and that Soviet concessions in Eastern Europe might be obtained through the United Nations after the passions of the war were somewhat cooled.

Death of FDR and collapse of Nazi Germany

Following the Yalta Conference and depletion of resources in the Battle of the Bulge, the German military rapidly collapsed under the weight of a two-front offensive with the Russians pushing on Berlin from the East and the Allied forces from the West. In March 1945, American troops crossed the Rhine River into Germany, but in April 1945, Eisenhower halted the American advance at the Elba River, allowing the Russians to first enter Berlin. This decision was made in recognition of the sacrifices made by the Red Army in taking on the brunt of the fighting against the Nazis as well as the atrocities which the German invaders had perpetuated upon the Russian people. There was considerable revenge taken on the Germans by the Soviets, and many German soldiers desperately searched for Americans to whom they were eager to surrender. In the midst of the Nazi collapse, Roosevelt suffered a cerebral hemorrhage on April 12, 1945 at his Warm Springs, Georgia retreat where he was accompanied by Lucy Mercer and his daughter, Anna Roosevelt Boettiger. Mercer left the premises before Eleanor was informed of her husband's death and began making funeral preparations. The entire nation was shocked as many Americans had never experienced another President during their adult lives, but perhaps the most unprepared for Roosevelt's death was Vice President Truman, who was not taken into the President's confidence and knew nothing about the Manhattan Project to develop the atomic bomb.

As Truman attempted to adjust to the demands of the Presidency, Hitler committed suicide on April 30, 1945, shortly after marrying his long-term mistress, Eva Braun. There has been speculation that someway Hitler was able to flee before the fall of Berlin, but his body was burned, and dental records have established that the Fuhrer was unable to escape the destruction of the Third Reich. A week later on May 7, 1945, the Allies accepted the unconditional surrender of the German government. While some German scientists who had served the Nazis were allowed to escape punishment and switch allegiance to the victorious powers, the Allies were determined to place Nazi leaders on trial in Nuremburg, where Hitler conducted massive Nazi Party rallies, for crimes against humanity. Americans and the world were stunned by the liberation of the Nazi concentration camps and discovery of the Holocaust in which the Nazi regime systematically murdered six million European Jews and millions of others who were considered racially inferior or enemies of the state, including Gypsies, Slavs, Jehovah's Witnesses, homosexuals, and the disabled and mentally ill. While the American public may have been unaware of the genocide pursued by the Nazi regime, the Allies were in possession of intelligence regarding the extermination camps, and leaders such as Roosevelt and Churchill have been condemned for not taking military action against the camps to halt the human slaughter. Churchill retorted that the best way to aid those in the camps was to defeat Nazi Germany as quickly as possible and not divert resources to the halting of trains with human cargo to the camps. Many wonder, nevertheless, whether the concern would have been greater if so many of the victims had not been Jews. This perception certainly contributed to the creation of Israel to provide a Jewish homeland, but this solution failed to take into consideration the wishes of the Palestinian people, creating new international tensions.

The first Nuremberg trial resulted in the death sentence for twelve Nazi leaders, although Hitler's lieutenant Hermann Goring cheated the hangman by swallowing a cyanide pill the night before his scheduled execution. The Nuremberg trials established the precedent that genocide and crimes against humanity could be punished in international courts and the argument that one was simply following orders was an inadequate defense for immoral actions that violated moral principles and established codes of conduct. A precedent was established that many legal experts believe could have been applied against the United States for its conduct of the war in Vietnam, but these abstract principles of justice do not seem to apply to the victors.

The United States goes on the offensive in the Pacific

While the United States pursued it policy of Europe first, the Pacific War persisted. After the initial victories of the Japanese at Pearl Harbor, the Philippines, China, Burma, Singapore, and the Dutch East Indies, the Americans and Allies relied upon Australia as a base of operations from which to launch the reconquest of the Pacific. This essential supply line was kept open in the Battle of the Coral Sea in May 1942 as American and Australian naval forces employed aircraft carriers to block a Japanese advance into the region. Many historians view the Battle of Midway on June 3-6, 1942 as the turning point for the Pacific War. The Imperial Japanese Navy hoped to draw the American aircraft carriers into a decisive engagement by occupying the island of Midway as the first step in a campaign that would eventually include an assault upon Hawaii. Breaking the Japanese codes, the Americans were prepared for the attack on Midway, and in a decisive battle relying upon planes launched from carriers, the United States destroyed four Japanese aircraft carriers that had played a key role in the Pearl Harbor operation, while losing one carrier, the *Yorktown*. The Japanese Navy never quite recovered from the significant losses as the Americans moved on the offensive.

In August 1942, the United States launched an invasion of the Japanese-held island of Guadalcanal in the Solomon Islands as part of a campaign in which General MacArthur would advance along the coast of New Guinea from which an eventual invasion of the Philippines might be launched. After months of savage fighting on Guadalcanal, the Marines achieved their first major land victory in the Pacific, although at the cost of over 7,000 dead Americans. Meanwhile, MacArthur launched his offensive against the heavily fortified Japanese positions in New Guinea. While the New Guinea campaign eventually succeeded in neutralizing such key objectives as Port Moresby and Rabaul, the progress of MacArthur was extremely slow, leading the Navy and Admiral Chester Nimitz to propose the island-hopping strategy across the Central Pacific in which Marines would invade a large island in an archipelago and build an airbase from which they could isolate Japanese forces on other islands in the chain and begin a bombing campaign against the next archipelago. This concept, somewhat borrowed from the Army's campaign in New Guinea, meant that the Japanese would not have to be driven from every island, and the plan would eventually place bombers close enough to the Japanese home islands for attacks against Tokyo.

MacArthur opposed the leap-frogging approach across the Central Pacific as he feared that it would divert resources from the liberation of the Philippines to which the General had pledged to return following his rescue from Bataan. Seeking to appease inter-service rivalry, Roosevelt and George C. Marshall, the Army's Chief of Staff in Washington, decided to pursue both strategies. With this green light for its island-hopping plans, the Marines invaded Tarawa in the Gilbert Islands on November 20, 1943. After securing Tarawa and neutralizing Japanese forces in the Gilberts, in February 1944 the Marines attacked the islands of Kwajalein and Eniwetok in the Marshall Islands. Again, the Japanese resistance was fierce, but the Marshall Islands provided a foundation from which to launch assaults against the Mariana Islands, placing the American forces within heavy bomber distance of the Japanese home islands. As the American troops moved closer to the Japanese homeland, the resistance to the Marines was even more intense. Following the successful campaign in July 1944 on the islands of Guam and Saipan, American bombers launched regular missions against Japan.

Although the Navy insisted that their rapid movement across the Central Pacific could allow the United States to bypass the Philippines, MacArthur insisted that he be allowed to lead an invasion force to liberate the American colony, and for symbolic and political considerations, Roosevelt agreed. In October 1944 MacArthur's pledge "I shall return" was redeemed, although the General enjoyed a little help from his friends. At the Battle of Leyte Gulf, the Japanese Navy suffered a devastating defeat in which they lost twenty-six warships, and what was left of the Japanese fleet retreated to the home islands.

Iwo Jima and Okinawa

As the Americans closed in on Japan, two of the bloodiest battles in the Pacific War were fought on Iwo Jima and Okinawa. The small volcanic island of Iwo Jima between the Marianas and Japan was viewed as a site for airbases from which American fighter escorts could support the bombing missions launching from Guam and Saipan. The battle for Iwo Jima raged from February 19 to March 26, 1945. Rather than pursuing frontal attacks to drive the Americans from the beach, the Japanese constructed an elaborate network of caves on the island from which they stubbornly resisted the invasion. Over 20,000 Japanese perished in the battle with only slightly over 200 taken prisoner. The Japanese were determined to fight to the last man, and the Marines, who suffered over 26,000 casualties, were not too interested in taking prisoners. The Battle of Iwo Jima is immortalized in the photograph of six Marines raising the American flag over Mount Suribachi. Ironically, one of the Marines photographed hoisting the flag was Ira Hayes, a Pima Indian from Arizona, who after the war battled with alcoholism and died from exposure after a drinking bout—embodying the nation's use and abuse of its Native people.

Located only 340 miles from the Japanese home islands, the large island of Okinawa was viewed as a base from which to stage the invasion of Japan. The assault on Okinawa began on April 1 and lasted until June 22, 1945. The death toll in the battle was astounding with 75,000 Allied casualties and over 100,000 estimated Japanese dead, in addition to perhaps 150,000 Okinawan civilians killed, some of whom leaped to their death from cliffs in fear of the American invaders. The American Navy also suffered considerable damage from Japanese Kamikaze or suicide missions as Japanese pilots crashed their planes into American ships. The Kamikaze attacks have created an impression of the Japanese as fanatics who cared little for human life, but it is worth noting that the Japanese did not resort to such desperate attacks until the latter stages of the war when they were considerably short of aviation fuel and bombs. The Japanese resistance encountered at Iwo Jima and Okinawa convinced American war planners that an invasion of Japan would be an extremely bloody affair, and Russian assistance would be welcome. However, the successful testing of the atomic bomb in New Mexico altered that conclusion.

Potsdam Conference

Shortly after the conclusion of fighting on Okinawa, President Truman, Churchill, and Stalin met in Potsdam, Germany from July 17 to August 2, 1945—although Churchill was replaced by Labor Party leader Clement Atlee after the British electorate decided that Labor rather than the Conservatives was the preferred party to guide Britain's post war reconstruction. Truman, with a considerably different background than Roosevelt, was suspicious of Stalin and his motives. The President had little international experience and was from a relatively poor family. He was not a college graduate and after service in World War I failed in several business ventures. Truman, however, forged a political career under the sponsorship of Kansas City political boss Tom Pendergast that elevated the Missourian to the Senate. During the course of the deliberations at Potsdam, Truman was pleased to learn that American scientists, under the direction of physicist J. Robert Oppenheimer in remote Los Alamos, New Mexico, had successfully tested the atomic bomb. With this new weapon at his disposal, Truman was less willing to compromise with the Soviets and believed that he no longer needed the Red Army for an invasion of Japan; although Stalin assured him that the Soviets were fully prepared to honor their pledge to enter the war against Japan. Truman proudly informed Stalin about America's new weapon of mass destruction, but through his espionage resources which reached into New Mexico, the Soviet leader was already aware of the breakthrough by the American scientists. At Potsdam, the Americans, British, and Soviets agreed to divide defeated Germany into four zones of occupation—with the fourth zone going to the French, although a chagrined French leader Charles De Gaulle was not extended an invitation to the conference. But a difference was beginning to emerge between how the United States and Soviets viewed a post war Germany. The Soviets preferred harsh penalties and reparations that would essentially de-industrialize Germany and render them incapable of ever again invading the Soviet homeland. On the other hand, the United States was beginning to view a de-Nazified but strong Germany as a political barrier or even ally against Soviet expansion. The Potsdam Conference concluded with the United States issuing stern objections to the Soviets consolidating control over the Eastern European nations that they had liberated from Nazi occupation. The United States also issued the Potsdam Declaration, warning the Japanese if they did not immediately agree to an unconditional surrender they would be subject to "prompt and utter destruction."

Hiroshima and Nagasaki

When the Japanese did not respond to the Potsdam Declaration, Truman moved ahead with his plan to employ the new weapon. Scientists led by Oppenheimer urged the President to move slowly, asserting that neither the President nor the Japanese leaders understood the force of the bomb which they had developed. The scientists suggested that a demonstration explosion be arranged under the auspices of a neutral nation or organization so that the Japanese could perceive the destructive power of the new weapon. The Truman administration rejected this idea, asserting that with only two bombs available it would be too risky to stage a demonstration. Many military planners believed that the atomic bomb might end the war without suffering the casualties that an invasion of Japan would entail, but others asserted that a weakened Japan was short of resources and no longer constituted an offensive threat, advocating that a Naval blockade could eventually bring about Japan's surrender. Truman, however, was convinced that the American people were ready to end the war as soon as possible, and in his memoirs, the President insisted that he had no reservations about using the atomic bomb which he claimed in the long run saved both Japanese and American lives. Meanwhile, the firebombing of Tokyo on March 9-10, 1945 killed an estimated 100,000 civilians, and advisers to the President suggested that he take the next logical step with the atomic bomb whose construction cost Americans an estimated two billion dollars.

Accordingly, on August 6, 1945 the first atomic bomb was dropped on the Japanese city of Hiroshima; a so-called virgin target that was spared in earlier bombings. This would allow the United States to better gauge the impact of the bomb which proved to be considerable, destroying almost 70 percent of the city's buildings and immediately killing approximately 70,000 people with a death toll that rose to well over 100,000 by the end of the year with radiation poisoning. The bomb severed all communications and isolated Hiroshima, yet three days later the second atomic bomb was dropped upon Nagasaki, giving the Japanese little time to assess what had happened to them. In many ways, the detonation of the second bomb in Nagasaki was even more controversial than Hiroshima. Why was Truman in such a hurry? Revisionist historians suggest that the explanation may lie in the fact that on August 8, Stalin honored his pledge to enter the war against Japan, and the United States wanted to end the war as quickly as possible before the Soviet military was able to liberate or seize territory in the Far East. Further evidence for this explanation is provided by the abandonment of unconditional surrender. When the Japanese failed to surrender following Nagasaki, the Truman administration agreed to allow Emperor Hirohito to maintain his status in post war Japan. Thus, the Emperor was spared from the Tokyo War Crimes Tribunal which followed Japan's surrender on August 14. The Emperor remained an important symbol of national identity under an American occupation which sought to remake Japan in a more Western and American model. General MacArthur presided over the drafting of a constitution with a parliamentary democracy and women's suffrage that placed considerable limitations upon Japanese militarism. In fact, during the American occupation, Samurai films were banned for fear they would promote militarism.

Legacy of World War II

World War II transformed America and the world, but after the great victory over fascism, many Americans were insecure as is exemplified culturally by the popularity in post war Hollywood of film noir in which the future was shrouded in shadow and ambiguity. The American people sacrificed a great deal during the Second World War, postponing consumption, investing their savings into war bonds, and suffering over 400,000 Americans killed in action. The burden of so many deaths and wounded weighed heavily on the survivors, and Americans feared another depression when the soldiers were demobilized. In addition, the depravity of humankind was demonstrated to Americans and the world with the horrors of the Holocaust. The G.I. Bill, on the other hand, offered an avenue for many veterans to attain an education, own a home, and move into the middle class, but discriminatory policies such as redlining by banks and mortgage companies limited the progress of black Americans. Despite such prejudice, the war did provide increased economic opportunity for women, blacks, and Hispanics. On the international scene, creation of the United Nations offered hope for world peace, and many credit the organization for helping to avoid a third world war.

The Manhattan Project, nevertheless, unleashed a Frankenstein monster of nuclear weapons with the potential to destroy the world, and this nuclear nightmare continues to threaten our future. While the United States and the Soviet Union were able to cooperate against a common enemy in Hitler, the capitalist and communist states were unable to reach agreement on the shape of the post war world, ushering in the Cold War complete with nuclear arsenals and surrogate wars in Korea, Vietnam, and Afghanistan. Even with the demise of the Cold War, the threat of nuclear war or terrorist possession of nuclear weapons continues to plague Americans and the world, although as of this writing, the United States remains the only power to have employed the weapon against a civilian or military target. The United States was also in a unique position following the war as the only industrial nation not to have suffered extensive damage to its factories and was, thus, able to promote and benefit from free trade policies fostered by the Bretton Woods Agreement establishing an international post war monetary order. This Pax Americana was also propped up by an American military presence around the globe, but the American industrial sector was challenged in the 1970s by nations such as Germany and Japan who constructed new modern factory systems. The Cold War also dominated American politics with anticommunism used to prevent progressive change, labeling New Dealers, feminists, civil rights advocates, and labor unions as associated with the ideology of communism. This political culture created a sense of conformity in which middle-class whites hunkered down in the suburbs, consuming the latest products and gadgets while seeking to ignore issues of race, gender, and class in American society.

Women on the home front during World War II

For women, the war offered significant employment opportunities. With so many men away at war, factories began to hire women, and this practice was promoted by the government with images of Rosie the Riveter. Women proved quite capable of handling the industrial jobs once reserved for men, and nearly 400,000 women served in the military during the war, although usually removed from combat situations. Many women enjoyed the freedom, responsibility, and higher pay of factory work—although a gender wage gap was certainly apparent. Also, government promises of childcare facilities were not realized, and working women were often blamed for the rising rate of juvenile delinquency. When the war ended, many working women preferred to stay in their factory jobs; however, an alliance of government, business, and labor, afraid that returning veterans might not be able to find employment, maneuvered to provide former male workers with seniority for military service, laying off their female employees. Women were forced out of the factories and higher paying jobs after the Second World War, but a few years later more women than ever were working outside the home. Many of these women, however, were from the middle class and were only working part time in retail and clerical positions to enhance the family's consumption of consumer goods. Opportunities for women in the professions and better paying factory jobs were still limited, and it would be the daughters and granddaughters of Rosie the Riveter who would make some significant dents in the glass ceiling in the 1960s and 1970s in Second-Wave Feminism that broadened the topic of gender equality beyond suffrage and property rights. The baby boom following the war as soldiers returned home to pursue families greatly influenced post war America. These children, who grew up in the shadow of the atomic bomb and enjoyed relatively greater prosperity than their parents, would later challenge the emphasis of the older generation upon security and consumption, contributing to the Civil Rights Movement, protest against the Vietnam War, and the development of a counterculture.

Impact of the war upon blacks, Hispanics, and Native Americans

Racial minorities were also impacted by the war as employment opportunities grew. Black civil rights and labor leader A Philip Randolph, who organized the first predominantly black union with the Brotherhood of Sleeping Car Porters, threatened President Roosevelt with a march on Washington protesting racial discrimination in defense industries. The President convinced Randolph to call off the march by issuing Executive Order 8802 in 1941 that outlawed racial discrimination in defense industries, although the order was certainly not always enforced. Randolph also advocated for the racial integration of American military forces, but the termination of racial segregation in the armed forces did not come until 1948 when President Truman issued an executive order ending the racial segregation that had governed the American military since the Civil War. As job opportunities for black workers increased, there was racial backlash from white workers. In Detroit, black and white workers, many of whom had migrated from the South to the North in search of employment, competed for jobs and housing as the population of the city expanded with auto plants converting to become the arsenal of democracy. This arsenal of democracy, however, was shut down in June 1943 for almost a week as the overcrowding and promotion of some black workers resulted in a riot that left thirty-four people dead, twenty-five of them black, and required the deployment of National Guard units to quell. Despite the racial animosity that continued during the war, over one million black Americans served in the segregated World War II military, and black troops recognized the irony of fighting the racism of Nazi Germany, while the United States continued to practice Jim Crow. Following the war, many of these black veterans, such as baseball's Jackie Robinson, returned to the United States and played key roles in the emerging Civil Rights Movement. In addition, the war, despite economic discrimination, increased the financial resources of the black community, establishing an economic foundation to fund many of the legal challenges that would eventually topple Jim Crow.

The Latino/a community experienced a similar transformation as a result of the Second World War, but they were considered as whites by the military establishment and not subject to racial segregation—although discrimination for such offenses as speaking Spanish was a common practice. It is estimated that 500,000 Hispanics served in the military during the Second World War, but this level of patriotism failed to halt the violence of the Zoot Suit Riots perpetrated upon young Latino men during the summer of 1943 in San Diego, Los Angeles, and Oakland. Sailors attacked young Mexican men wearing the flashy and popular Zoot Suits which were considered unpatriotic due to the excess material required to make these outfits during a time when fabric was in short supply for the war effort. Resentment by the sailors was also fueled by the popularity of the zoot suiters with young females, as well as the fact that the Latinos were not in military uniform as many were from Mexico and thus not subject to conscription. Local officials did little to halt the attacks as popular prejudice associated Mexican American young men with gang violence; an image perpetuated by the highly publicized 1942 Sleepy Lagoon murder case in Los Angeles. Nine young Mexican American men were found guilty of murder in the case, although their convictions were later overturned. The military and shore patrol eventually intervened to stop the riots as Washington was concerned that the violence might endanger the Bracero Program in which laborers were imported from Mexico to harvest and pick the produce of California's agricultural industry. The World War II experience also produced Hispanic organizations such as the G.I. Forum to challenge racial discrimination and increase economic opportunity for Hispanic veterans.

The war also changed life for Native Americans, challenging the isolation of the reservations as Natives were conscripted or volunteered for military service, while others sought employment in defense industries. Following the war, the income of Native Americans increased somewhat, and the number of Natives living in urban areas rose from 5 to 20 percent. This transformation, nevertheless, still left many Natives in poverty and disrupted Native culture. In addition, Washington seized Native lands for use in the war effort, ranging from isolated bombing ranges to the ironic use of Native land for Japanese American internment camps. While approximately 25,000 Natives served in the military during the war, the best-known contribution of Native warriors is the Navajo Code Talkers who used their language to prevent Japanese penetration of American communications, although the government kept the project a secret until the late 1970s.

The Four Freedoms

In his 1941 State of the Union Message, President Roosevelt laid out his vision for the fundamental freedoms that all people of the world should enjoy. Although the United States had not yet entered the Second World War at the time of the speech, the Four Freedoms discussed by the President became the idealistic goals for which Americans sacrificed so much during the Second World War. Roosevelt's Four Freedoms called for freedom of speech and expression, freedom of worship, freedom from want, and freedom from fear—incorporating both economic and political ideas for the post war world. These idealistic goals coincide well with the principles outlined by Winthrop's city upon a hill and Jefferson's Declaration of Independence, even if these visions did not always reflect the reality of the American experience. Roosevelt rallied the American people to the defeat of international fascism, but this victory failed to usher in freedom from want and fear. Post war America witnessed the expansion of the middle class, but many Americans remained in poverty, while economically powerful corporations successfully limited the influence of organized labor. Women and minorities, especially black Americans, remained second-class citizens. The atomic bomb and Cold War fed the flames of fear and insecurity which produced the paranoia of McCarthyism and constituted a fundamental threat to American liberty and the freedoms outlined by President Roosevelt.

Further Reading:

Alperovitz, Gar. *The Decision to Use the Atomic Bomb and the Architecture of an American Myth.* New York: Knopf, 1995.

Burns, James MacGregor. *Roosevelt: The Soldier of Freedom (1940–1945).* New York: Harcourt Brace and Jovanovich, 1970.

Chafe, William H. *The American Woman: Her Changing Social, Economic, and Political Roles, 1920–1970.* New York: Oxford University Press, 1972.

Dallek, Robert. *Franklin D. Roosevelt and American Foreign Policy, 1932–1945.* New York: Oxford University Press, 1995.

Goodwin, Doris Kearns. *No Ordinary Time: Franklin and Eleanor Roosevelt: The Home Front in World War II.* New York: Simon & Schuster, 1994.

Irons, Peter. *Justice at War: The Story of the Japanese-American Internment Cases.* New York: Oxford University Press, 1983

Kolko, Gabriel. *The Politics of War: The World and United States Foreign Policy, 1943–1945.* New York: Random House, 1968.

O'Neill, William L. *A Democracy at War: America's Fight at Home and Abroad in World War II.* New York: Free Press, 1993.

Prange, Gordon W. *At Dawn We Slept: The Untold Story of Pearl Harbor.* New York: McGraw-Hill, 1981.

Smith, Gaddis. *American Diplomacy During the Second World War.* New York: Wiley, 1968.

Takaki, Ronald. *Double Victory: A Multicultural History of America in World War II.* Boston: Little, Brown and Company, 2000.

Weinberg, Gerhard L. *A World at Arms: A Global History of World War II.* New York: Cambridge University Press, 1994.

24

Origins of the Cold War and Truman and Eisenhower Administrations

"Julius and Ethel Rosenberg Separated by Heavy Wire as They Leave U.S. Court House after Being Found Guilty by Jury." Photograph by Roger Higgin, 1951, *New York World Telegram*. *New York World Telegram & Sun* Newspaper Photograph Collection (Library of Congress). The Cold War and Red Scare led to the imprisonment and blacklisting of Americans accused of supporting communism, culminating in the conviction and execution of Julius and Ethel Rosenberg, the parents of two young boys, for espionage and delivering plans for the atomic bomb to the Soviets. They maintained their innocence, while others such as Ethel's brother David Greenglass had their lives spared when they cooperated with the government. Soviet archives seem to suggest that Julius was working for the Soviets, but the evidence against Ethel remains more problematic.

Television became a fixture in most American homes during the 1950s, and popular family shows such as *The Adventures of Ozzie and Harriet* (1952–1966), *Leave It to Beaver* (1957–1963), and *Father Knows Best* (1954–1960) depicted a nation of healthy white families residing in the affluent suburbs with a stay at home mom and father who commuted to his office job in the city. The most serious problem confronting the family might be the Beaver having a "crush" on his grade school teacher. In this idyllic world there are no black or minority faces, and even working-class whites—except for Jackie Gleason's *The Honeymooners* (1955–1956)—were excluded. The white picket fences of suburbia reflected the political ideology of the post-World War II liberal consensus in which all could attain middle-class status if they adhered to the American creed of hard work and consumption. There was no need for dissent or protest as an expanding capitalism would bring prosperity to all who were willing to work for it. Prejudice and racism were wrong, but these problems would be erased over time by economic growth and expansion of the middle class. The only threat to this future of prosperity was the alien ideology of communism, and it was essential that all Americans adhere to the ideology of anticommunism. Democrats and Republicans might disagree upon the means to assure security and prosperity, but within the consensus of capitalism and anticommunism there was no room for compromise.

Post World War II liberal consensus

In addition to adhering to capitalism and anticommunism, the ideology of the liberal consensus assumed that all real Americans were heterosexuals, believed in the sanctity of marriage and the traditional family, and were faithful to the Judeo-Christian religious faith upon which the nation was supposedly founded. To be an atheist, agnostic, Muslim, Buddhist, gay, lesbian, or transgender was simply un-American, and the suburbs became prisons of conformity in which families sought to demonstrate their fealty to the consensus through consuming the latest "new and improved" product. Social gatherings such as backyard barbeques provided residents with an opportunity to demonstrate the latest acquired gadget and adherence to consensus values. Conformity was praised and individuality suspect in the middle-class suburbs. In *The Organization Man* (1956), sociologist William Whyte argued that successful businessmen embodied the values of the organization for which they worked and incorporated these values into their daily lives. This conformity of thought, behavior, and appearance was also addressed in the novel *The Man in the Grey Flannel Suit* (1955) by Sloan Wilson. Sociologist David Riesman described the change in American culture as one from the inner-directed to the outer-directed personality. In *The Lonely Crowd* (1950), Riesman asserted that previously Americans were motivated by an internal drive to satisfy individual needs, desires, and ambitions. These individualistic objectives were now subservient to outer-directed goals in which one sought to achieve the approval of the group, society, or business organization by displaying allegiance to consensus values. The nineteenth-century idea of treating corporations as people now seemed realized in a society where individuals increasingly followed the corporate line and consumption of corporate goods was the ultimate form of patriotism as outlined by Vance Packard's *The Hidden Persuaders* (1957), describing the power of advertising to influence buying habits and instill the waste of built-in obsolescence. The irony of this group think based on the ideology of anticommunism was well noted in the clever science-fiction film *Invasion of the Body Snatchers* (1956). The liberal consensus and the conformity of the suburbs were based upon post war fears rather than confidence in the future. Americans who had sacrificed so much during the Great Depression and Second World War were grasping for security, fearing another depression or global war. Little Beaver Cleaver was brought up under the insecurities of the Cold War and atomic bomb, practicing duck and cover drills that would have proven futile in the event of a nuclear war. The myths of suburbia and the liberal consensus did not reflect the reality of many Americans.

Practices such as redlining, in which services like banking and insurance were denied to black Americans and other racial minorities, assured that that an expanding capitalism would not serve all Americans. Economic opportunity was also thwarted by racial segregation that limited access to education. To make the promise of American life a reality for a diverse nation, it would require a Civil Rights Movement to challenge racial discrimination. Working-class Americans also saw their ability to be represented by labor unions under attack in the guise of anticommunism from which American labor has never fully recovered. Furthermore, many middle-class women viewed themselves as virtual prisoners in the suburbs, forced to abandon any pursuit of personal and professional goals in the service of their husbands and children. The discontent of these women, who sometimes sought solace in valium and alcohol, was well documented in Betty Friedan's *The Feminine Mystique* (1963). Many young people found the consumerism of their parents to be shallow, and in the emerging culture of rock and roll music, they discovered a common bond that often-transcended race with a white Elvis Presley sounding to many like a black musician. The failure of the liberal consensus to address the reality of post-World War II America exploded in the generational, class, gender, and racial conflicts of the 1960s and 1970s.

Origins of the Cold War

Perhaps the most overwhelming factor in post war America was the Cold War and atomic bomb which threatened to destroy human society. The baby boomers born in the immediate years following the war had the looming shadow of the Cold War cast upon their lives for over forty years and continuing international conflict over nuclear proliferation suggests that perhaps the genie of nuclear war will never be put back in the bottle. The Cold War was a global political, military, nuclear, space exploration, economic, technological, and ideological conflict between the capitalist United States and communist Soviet Union that dominated the world from 1945 until the collapse of the Soviet Union in 1991. The term Cold War is employed to suggest that the United States and Soviets had to avoid a direct confrontation or war that might destroy the world, but the Cold War was plenty hot as in their search for allies and influence, the United States and their Soviet adversaries fostered numerous global conflicts, including wars in Korea, Vietnam, and Afghanistan.

The Americans and Soviets worked together as allies to bring about the defeat of Nazi Germany, but their conflicting ideologies and ambitions were evident from the origins of the Soviet state when President Wilson dispatched troops to Russia in 1917 in opposition to the Bolshevik Revolution. Although extending diplomatic recognition to the Soviets in 1933, the United States remained wary of the communist state. Americans perceived the post-World War II period as offering a unique opportunity to promote free elections and markets, allowing the American nation that had escaped the destruction of its industrial base to economically dominate world markets and avoid another depression. The Soviet experience in World War II was considerably different, and Stalin sought to provide the Soviet state with a sense of security. The Soviet Union was invaded in both world wars by German troops moving through Poland, and these military invasions entailed considerable loss of life and property to the Soviet homeland; in fact, both Soviet civilian and military deaths in World War II are estimated to total over twenty million people. To forestall future attacks, the Soviets wanted to guarantee the existence of friendly and allied neighboring states. Thus, Stalin installed communist governments in the Eastern European nations liberated by the Red Army, although this was usually done under the guise of free elections supervised by the Soviets. These guarantees of Soviet security, thus, included the spread of communism, although the extent to which Stalin was motivated by ideological considerations is open to debate. The Soviet Union was also devastated economically and forced to relocate its factories east of the Ural Mountains during the Nazi occupation. As the Soviets attempted to re-establish their industrial base, they were in no position to compete on an equal footing in the free market. Instead, the Soviets essentially acquired satellite states that would provide guaranteed markets for their goods and products as well as access to resources. It may, thus, be argued that the development of a Soviet Empire in Eastern Europe was as much about military and economic security as the extension of communism as an ideology.

The differences between the American and Soviet perspectives of the post war world were borne out in the major meetings of the victorious leaders as Nazi Germany collapsed. At the Yalta Conference in February 1945, the Americans. with the support of Churchill and the British, reluctantly agreed to allow Stalin a free hand in Poland in exchange for a pledge to enter the war against Japan after the surrender of Germany. At the Potsdam Conference in July 1945, Truman replaced the deceased Roosevelt, and following news of the successful Trinity bomb test in New Mexico, the new President proceeded to take a hard line with Stalin, believing that the Americans no longer required Soviet assistance to subdue Japan. Although he was not prepared to go to war with Stalin, Truman vehemently asserted his displeasure with the Soviet designs upon Eastern Europe. While agreeing to four occupation zones for defeated Germany, the United States began to envision a democratic and strong post war German state as a buffer zone against further Soviet expansion. With the atomic bomb now in his possession, Truman believed that he needed to make few concessions to the Soviets, and Potsdam revealed considerably antagonistic perspectives of the post war world.

Post war uncertainty

After the surrender of Japan following the deployment of atomic bombs on Hiroshima and Nagasaki, along with concessions to the Japanese on the post war status of the Emperor, the relationship between the United States and Soviet Union entered a period of uncertainty in 1946. The United States concluded the war with an armed force of over twelve million men and women scattered around the globe. Some anticommunists such as General George Patton believed that this military presence should be employed to intimidate the Soviets and dictate the structure of the post war world. American service personnel and their families disagreed, demanding that the troops be brought home immediately. They had fulfilled their mission of defeating fascism, and restive soldiers began to stage "we wanna go home" demonstrations. The United States government listened to these demands, and by 1947 the size of the United States military force shrank to about 1,500,000.

While the number of troops were quickly reduced, the United States still enjoyed a monopoly of nuclear weapons. As Soviet scientists worked on the development of their own nuclear weapon, the United States had a short window in which the nation would not risk nuclear retaliation, but the American people were simply not prepared to use a weapon of mass destruction against the Russian people. There was little public outcry against employing the atomic bomb on the Japanese people. In addition to the element of racial prejudice which placed Japanese Americans and not German Americans in concentration camps, the attacks on Pearl Harbor and Bataan, along with four long years of fighting and a propaganda campaign of films, cartoons, comic books, and newsreels, had well-conditioned the American public to perceive the Japanese as less than human. The same was not true of the Russian people. American and Soviet soldiers had celebrated together following the defeat of Nazi Germany. In addition, American popular culture presented their Russian allies during the war in a positive light in Warner Brothers cartoons such as *Gremlins from the Kremlin* (1944) and Hollywood films such as *The North Star* (1943) and *Song of Russia* (1944). Warner Brothers also released *Mission to Moscow* (1943) based upon the memoirs of former Ambassador to the Soviet Union, businessman Joseph E. Davies, presenting a favorable depiction of Stalin and his purges. While Russian exile and novelist Ayn Rand described these films as evidence that Hollywood was under the control of the Communist Party, these films may be better understood as efforts to foster cooperation with an essential wartime ally. Thus, the American people were hardly prepared to drop an atomic bomb upon the Russians who were also white; however, after the development of Cold War popular culture portraying the Russians as evil villains in comics, films, cartoons, pulp fiction, and government propaganda, the employment of the atomic bomb against them no longer seemed so outlandish—but by that time the Soviets also possessed nuclear weapons.

Baruch Plan and firing of Commerce Secretary Henry Wallace

The Truman administration sought to take advantage of its temporary nuclear monopoly with the Baruch Plan drafted by American businessman Bernard Baruch. Under this plan, the United States would place control of its nuclear weapons and research under the United Nations Atomic Energy Commission (UNAEC), who would then oversee and monitor all nuclear research and development. The United States earned considerable international acclaim for its willingness to share its knowledge. The Baruch Plan also placed the Soviets in a difficult position. They were near to completing their own bomb but agreeing to the Baruch Plan would place the Soviet nuclear industry under the control and supervision of the United Nations, an organization which the Soviets perceived as being dominated by the United States and its allies. Thus, the Soviet Union rejected the Baruch Plan and pursued its own independent nuclear development, which culminated in the production of a weapon in 1949, but the United States achieved a major public relations coup for offering to share its nuclear research.

Meanwhile, the political stalemate between the United States and Soviet Union hardened. On March 5, 1946, Churchill received an honorary degree from Westminster College in Fulton, Missouri. The former Prime Minister used the occasion to denounce the Soviet Union for imposing an iron curtain over Eastern Europe that denied the people freedom and opportunity, while forcing them to accept Soviet domination. Churchill's rhetoric was welcomed by the Truman administration that took an increasingly anti-Soviet posture, and the term "iron curtain" would become an essential image of Cold War propaganda. As Truman embraced a policy of confronting the Soviet Union, he was increasingly intolerant of dissent within his own ranks. In September 1946, he dismissed former Vice President Henry Wallace as Secretary of Commerce. To appease the liberal wing of the Democratic Party, Truman was forced to accept Wallace in his cabinet. However, when Wallace publicly criticized the President for provoking the Soviets, arguing for a more conciliatory position recognizing the contributions made by the Soviets to the defeat of fascism, Truman removed Wallace from the cabinet. The firing of Wallace was an early indication that dissent from anticommunist politics would not be tolerated during the Cold War, and free speech became a casualty of the conflict.

Development of containment policy

As relations between the United States and Soviet Union deteriorated, the United States searched for a strategic plan to guide their opposition to the Soviets. The development of the containment doctrine to oppose the Soviet Union is usually attributed to diplomat George Kennan, who outlined his views in the so-called 1946 long cable from the American embassy in Moscow and a 1947 article in *Foreign Affairs*, published under the pseudonym of "X." Kennan asserted that the Soviet Union was a communist state dedicated to the territorial and political expansion of its ideology. Assuming a monolithic interpretation of international communism guided by the Soviet Union, Kennan advocated a foreign policy that involved the United States in numerous global conflicts, often ignoring regional and national contexts. Kennan, however, insisted that the United States would have to recognize, at least for the time being, communism in the Soviet Union and satellite states where it already existed. A war to rollback communism in the Soviet Union and Eastern Europe would be too costly. Since the life of Soviet communism, however, was dependent upon territorial expansion, the Soviets could be resisted through a policy of containment using economic, political, and military means to thwart Soviet expansion. Denied the ability to grow, the Soviet Union and communism would eventually collapse due to internal contradictions. Kennan asserted that the struggle to contain Soviet expansion would take time and resources, but he was convinced that in the long term the United States and capitalism would prevail. In many ways, the containment strategy is reminiscent of Lincoln's "House Divided" speech in which the President maintained that if slavery expansion were curtailed, then the institution would eventually collapse. Critics of containment countered that the strategy would involve the United States in wars around the world in which the enemy would select the location of conflicts and dictate the terms of engagement. While Kennan replied that the United States would have to pick and choose the time and place where it was necessary to intervene against the Soviets, containment in practice resulted in global American military actions, often in support of dictatorial regimes who touted their anticommunist credentials.

Truman Doctrine and Marshall Plan

To implement the containment strategy, Truman seized upon the crisis in Greece, introducing what would become known as the Truman Doctrine. Following the end of Nazi occupation, a civil war raged in Greece between royalist and communist forces. The royalist government was backed by the British in a region where they exercised a sphere of influence. But by early 1948, the British lacked the resources to continue supporting the royalist regime and informed Truman that Greece would fall to the communists unless the United States intervened in the civil war. After telling his new political ally Republican Senator Arthur Vandenberg from Michigan, who had shifted from an isolationist to a supporter of international anticommunism, that it would be necessary to scare the hell out of the American people, the President delivered an address to Congress, asserting that military aid must be extended to Greece and its rival nation of Turkey to prevent the spread of Soviet communism which posed a clear and present danger to American security. In fact, Truman's description of the situation was rather misleading for Stalin's lack of support played a crucial role in the Greek communists suffering defeat in another civil war marked by atrocities. Honoring a wartime agreement with Churchill that following the war Greece would be a British sphere of influence while the Soviets would be given a free hand in Bulgaria and Romania, Stalin had cut off supplies to the Greek communists and put pressure on Tito in the more independent communist state of Yugoslavia to follow a similar policy. With American military assistance, the royalist forces, who were hardly democratic, triumphed, and an important precedent was established. Under the Truman Doctrine, the United States agreed to provide military aid to any state or government threatened with communist subversion. Accordingly, it became common practice for many authoritarian governments to describe their democratic opposition as under the influence of communists, garnering American military support to suppress opposition parties and movements. Under the guise of the Truman Doctrine, the United States bolstered anticommunist dictators and authoritarian governments around the world, including the Somoza family in Nicaragua, Augusto Pinochet in Chile, Ferdinand Marcos in the Philippines, Joseph-Désiré in the Congo, Mohammed Reza Pahlavi in Iran, and Suharto in Indonesia, who murdered over a half-million of his people in an anticommunist purge. This support for anticommunist authoritarian regimes around the globe led many to questions America's commitment to democratic principles.

Truman was also concerned a devastated Western Europe was susceptible to communist infiltration. Except in this case the United States was not worried about the troops and tanks of the Red Army. Instead, the fear was that the communists in Western Europe might take power through the ballot box, offering Marxist solutions to the rebuilding of devastated nations whose citizens were desperate for food and shelter. In states such as Italy and France, the communists had also earned considerable respect for their wartime opposition to the Nazis as partisans or members of the French underground. The Central Intelligence Agency (CIA), which had been created from the World War II Office of Strategic Services (OSS) under the National Security Act of 1947, took an active interest in the post war elections of Western Europe, intervening with bribes and the manipulation of vote totals to assure the election of anticommunist parties and candidates. On a more strategic level, the Congress in April 1948 authorized the Marshall Plan, named after General George Marshall who also served as Secretary of State under Truman, which provided thirteen billion dollars for the economic reconstruction of Western Europe. The goal of this spending was to prevent the spread of communism and support American business by restoring the number one trading partner of the United States. The Marshall Plan played a pivotal role in restoring European capitalist economies and American markets for the region. Assistance was also offered to Eastern Europe, but the Soviets recognized that extension of the Marshall Plan would lead to American economic dominance of the region and undermine Russian recovery.

Berlin airlift and formation of NATO

Stalin tested the resolve of the United States to pursue the policy of containment with a Soviet blockade of Berlin in June 1948. The Americans, French, and British had zones of occupation in Berlin, but the city was located within the Russian occupation zone of eastern Germany. Stalin ordered rail and road routes from western Germany to Berlin be blocked by Soviet troops. Recognizing that a military response to the Soviet provocation might bring about war, the United States and its allies organized an airlift to keep the western zones of Berlin supplied with food and fuel. From June 1948 to May 1949, approximately 200,000 sorties were flown, providing Berliners in the Western zones with nearly 13,000 tons of supplies per day. Although some planes crashed, and pilots died flying in bad weather, the Soviets essentially decided to not oppose the airlift. Having tested the resolve of the Truman administration, Stalin lifted the blockade in May 1949, and the Cold War lines of demarcation in Europe hardened during that pivotal year.

In April 1949, the North Atlantic Treaty Organization (NATO) was formed with twelve nations establishing a mutual defense pact aimed at blocking Soviet expansion into Western Europe. The signatories, including the United States and Canada, would consider an attack upon one as an attack upon all. This peacetime alliance violated Washington's Farewell Address warning against entangling alliances, placing Cold War America on a wartime footing which included implementation of a "peacetime" draft. The decision to incorporate a re-militarized West Germany into NATO in 1955 also led to the formation of the Warsaw Pact, committing the Soviet Union and seven of its Eastern European satellite states, including East Germany, to a mutual defense pact in opposition to NATO. The collapse of the Soviet Union led to the end of the Warsaw Pact, and today some former Soviet republics and allies are members of the NATO alliance, raising the question of whether the primary purpose of the organization remains a check on Russian expansion. The mutual defense pact, however, was invoked to support military action by the United States against Afghanistan following the 9/11 attacks upon the United States.

Rosenberg case

NATO, however, failed to provide much reassurance for Americans when the Soviets announced the successful test of an atomic bomb on August 29, 1949. Insecurities were only increased when Americans learned that the Soviets, whose scientists had been working on the bomb, were helped along by spies who had penetrated the security of Los Alamos. Although allied with the Soviet Union, the United States made the decision to not share its atomic bomb research with the Soviets as they had with their British allies. The Soviets, accordingly, pursued a path of espionage to penetrate the Manhattan Project and Los Alamos. British physicist Klaus Fuch was a scientist working at Los Alamos and conspired to provide the Soviets with information on the bomb, believing that an American monopoly on the weapon was dangerous to the world, and that if the Soviets also had the nuclear device, there would be a check upon American use of the weapon again. Fuch turned his research over to a young Army officer, David Greenglass, who traveled from Los Alamos to Albuquerque, New Mexico, where the plans were given to Soviet agents Martin Sobel and Harry Gold who passed along the information to the Soviet Union. When the FBI investigated the spy ring, Greenglass claimed that he was recruited by his brother-in-law Julius Rosenberg. Julius and his wife Ethel hardly fit the popular romantic image of spies. Although leftist in their political orientation, the Rosenbergs lived modestly and were hardly part of some liberal elite. Julius and Ethel were the parents of two young boys, and the family lived in a small Brooklyn apartment above the appliance repair shop maintained by Julius. The Jewish couple also demonstrated allegiance to traditional American institutions with their prison letters containing numerous references to baseball, Jackie Robinson, and the Brooklyn Dodgers. While insisting upon their innocence, the Rosenbergs were placed on trial for treason. Although much evidence against the couple was difficult to corroborate due to national security concerns, the Rosenbergs were found guilty, and Judge Irving Kaufman sentenced both to die in the electric chair. Some believe that Kaufman, who was Jewish, imposed the death penalty to demonstrate Jewish loyalty as the Rosenberg case contributed to a rising anti-Semitism and red scare that associated American Jews with communism. Other defendants in the atomic bomb spy ring case cooperated with the FBI and received reduced prison sentences. Only the Rosenbergs maintained their innocence and refused to share information with the government. Some argue that the FBI did not believe Ethel was guilty, but

J. Edgar Hoover assumed that her prosecution would eventually bring about Julius's cooperation, so she could raise the couple's children. Julius, however, refused to break, and the Rosenbergs were executed on June 19, 1953.

The innocence of the Rosenbergs was a tenet of faith on the American left, and the Rosenberg children campaigned in adulthood to overturn the conviction of their parents. The collapse of the Soviet Union and opening of the Soviet archives such as the Verona Cables, however, have provided evidence that Julius was, indeed, a Soviet agent, although the status of Ethel remains more problematic. While the material given to the Soviets may have allowed them to produce their bomb a year ahead of schedule, the death penalty seems harsh and emblematic of the hysteria and fear that was beginning to dominate American life. If a nice working-class Jewish couple with young children could be atomic bomb spies, then anyone could be a communist, and patriotic Americans should be suspicious of teachers, ministers, politicians, friends, and neighbors who dissented from the orthodoxy of the American consensus.

Arms race and rise of Communist China

In addition, Soviet possession of the atomic bomb propelled an arms race which became a critical component of the Cold War. American scientists such as physicist Edward Teller pushed for the development of a more powerful hydrogen bomb as a deterrent to the Soviets. Teller also played a significant role in Oppenheimer, who was less supportive of an expanded nuclear weapons arsenal, losing his security clearance due to his somewhat leftist political views and associates. The expanding arms race also produced a Soviet hydrogen weapon, and little security was provided by the idea of mutually assured destruction satirized so beautifully by Stanley Kubrick in *Dr. Strangelove* (1964).

If the arms race and spy networks were not enough, the political situation in the Far East contributed to American fears that communism was on the march with the triumph of Mao Zedong in the Chinese civil war. During the Second World War, Mao and his communist forces allied with Chiang Kai-shek and his Nationalist government against the Japanese invaders, although Chiang often seemed more concerned with the threat posed by his communist allies. Following the surrender of the Japanese, fighting broke out between the communists and Chiang's Kuomintang forces. After four years of bitter fighting, Mao triumphed on the mainland of China with Chiang and his Nationalist government retreating to the island of Taiwan. Americans were shocked by millions of Chinese waving Mao's *Little Red Book*, and some Republican politicians blamed Truman for losing China and not dispatching adequate military supplies to the Nationalist cause. A study of the situation by the State Department produced a White Paper asserting that the triumph of Mao was due to support for the communists by the peasant population of China who resented the corruption of Chiang's government and its policies favoring large land owners. Republican leaders disputed the State Department report, insisting that Chiang was sold out by communists in the American government. The Truman administration responded to this criticism by failing to recognize the People's Republic of China, continuing to extend formal diplomatic recognition to Taiwan as the legitimate Chinese government—a policy that was maintained into the 1970s with the United States forging a close economic and political alliance with Taiwan while ignoring the most populous nation in the world.

Korean War

Fears regarding communist expansion in the Far East were further exacerbated in June 1950 when North Korean forces invaded South Korea following a series of border incidents. Korea was colonized by Japan beginning in the late nineteenth century, and the end of World War II offered an opportunity for Korea to assert its independence, but the Cold War turned a civil war over the post war direction of the Korean nation into an international conflict. The division at the 38th parallel was supposed to be a temporary division of historical Korea. North Korea was liberated by Soviet and Chinese communist forces who backed the regime of Kim Il Sung, a leader of the resistance against Japanese rule. South Korea, on the other hand, was liberated from Japanese occupation by the United States and its allies who installed Syngman Rhee in power, although he was an authoritarian leader intolerant of dissent. As South Korean forces were pushed back, President Truman and Secretary of State Dean Acheson made a unilateral decision that American troops under the command of General MacArthur would come to the aid of South Korea, effectively ending the United States occupation of Japan. The North Korean advance was finally halted along the Pusan Perimeter on the southern tip of Korea. Meanwhile, the United States brought the Korean issue before the United Nations Security Council, who branded North Korea an aggressor and authorized a United Nations military command under the direction of the United States to come to the aid of South Korea. The Soviets were at the time boycotting meetings of the Security Council, and, thus, they were unable to veto the resolution authorizing military intervention—and the Chinese seat on the Security Council was still held by the Nationalist government in Taiwan. The tide of the Korean War changed in September 1950 when MacArthur orchestrated a brilliant amphibious assault at Incheon in northwestern South Korea near Seoul, placing MacArthur's forces behind the invading North Korean armies and threatening their supply lines. Fearful of being surrounded, the North Koreans retreated and were pursued across the 38th parallel into North Korea by American and South Korean forces. Concern about the heavy toll American bombing was taking on North Korean civilians and how the Chinese and Soviets might react to Americans invading North Korea led Truman to meet with MacArthur at Wake

Island in October 1950. The General assured the President that he understood the "Oriental" mind, and the Chinese would not intervene. In fact, MacArthur believed that the war would be over by Christmas. MacArthur's estimation of the military situation could not have been more inaccurate. As the American forces approached the Yalu River boundary between China and Korea in late November 1950, thousands of Chinese "volunteers" crossed the border and attacked American forces who after their breakout from the Chosen Reservoir retreated to the 38th parallel where the war bogged down in a bloody stalemate.

The United States considered employing nuclear weapons to break the stalemate, but the President and General MacArthur quarreled over who should have tactical control over these weapons. When MacArthur insisted upon making his case publicly to the press, Truman accused the General of insubordination and relieved MacArthur of his command, setting off a political firestorm in the United States. While Truman's defenders pointed out the President was simply exercising the Constitutional principle of civilian control over the military, anticommunists accused the President of treason. MacArthur's return to the United States was welcomed with a ticker tape parade in New York City and an address to a joint session of Congress. Many Americans assumed that MacArthur would mount a political challenge to the President, but MacArthur's imperial style was more attuned with the military occupation of Japan than the hustle and bustle of American politics and campaigning. MacArthur was replaced by General Matthew Ridgway, and the nuclear option was dropped over concerns that it might widen the war.

The Korean War continued to be fought along the 38th parallel, and on July 27, 1953, after the Eisenhower administration assumed office, an armistice ending the fighting was signed at Panmunjom, providing for the exchange of prisoners and establishment of a demilitarized zone along the 38th parallel. Since the signing of that 1953 agreement, American troops have remained stationed in South Korea, while talks for formally ending the conflict between North and South Korea and allowing for the reunification of families continue and remain complicated as North Korea pursues the development of its own nuclear arsenal. After the victory culture of World War II, the stalemate in Korea was extremely frustrating for many Americans, but the Truman administration could proclaim that containment had worked as communist expansion into South Korea was thwarted. But at what cost? Nearly 37,000 Americans lost their lives in Korea, while the three-year conflict included four million Korean casualties, of which approximately two million were civilians.

Election of 1948

The communist issue cast a cloud over American politics, and when the

Democratic Party splintered in 1948, most observers believed that President Truman would not be re-elected. White Southerners were upset with the President for his executive order ending racial segregation in the armed forces and accepting an invitation to speak before the NAACP. When the Democratic national convention endorsed a civil rights platform championed in a fiery speech by liberal Minneapolis Mayor Hubert H. Humphrey, many white Southerners walked out of the convention, forming the Dixiecrat Party with South Carolina Governor Strom Thurmond as their standard bearer. The Dixiecrats with a platform based upon segregation and state rights enjoyed a strong following in the South where most blacks were still barred from voting. Thurmond hoped that the election would be settled in the House of Representatives where segregationists could barter against further civil rights legislation. Truman also faced defections from more leftist Democrats who found his Cold War and anticommunist policies threatening to both world peace and American traditions of free speech. These liberal Democrats flocked to the Progressive Party candidacy of former Vice President Henry Wallace, who vowed to seek better relations with the Soviets while protecting civil liberties and extending regulation of corporate America. Wallace was initially perceived as a strong third-party candidate, whose progressive platform might allow him to win states such as New York. Wallace's campaign, however, disintegrated under red-baiting accusations that his candidacy was controlled by the Communist Party, and in the final analysis, Wallace only garnered three percent of the popular vote and earned no electoral votes.

The Republicans, meanwhile, again selected New York Governor Dewey, who was viewed as the overwhelming favorite in the election. An overconfident Dewey took his victory for granted, and his campaign took few risks. Believing that he had little to lose, Truman mounted a whistle stop train tour of the country, denouncing Dewey and the Republican Congress in caustic language that encouraged the refrain "Give 'em hell, Harry." Truman was not a gifted orator, but his tendency to pepper his speeches with some salty language appealed to many common Democratic voters. The President promised that he would expand the reforms of the New Deal in what he termed "the Fair Deal." Although many newspapers went to press early on election night with headlines proclaiming Dewey's victory, Truman rallied to an electoral triumph with 303 electoral votes to 189 for Dewey. However, the Dixiecrat candidate Thurmond carried four Southern states with 38 electoral votes, offering a preview of the political resistance that the Civil Rights Movement would encounter in the American South.

Fair Deal

After the election, Truman attempted to implement the reform agenda of his Fair Deal, but Republicans as well as Southern Democrats blocked many of these initiatives. Truman was able to achieve a modest extension of public housing for the poor with the Housing Act of 1949, and he convinced Congress to approve some expansion of Social Security benefits as well as an increase of the minimum wage from 40 to 75 cents an hour. Congress, however, thwarted efforts by Truman to expand his civil rights agenda, defeating a bill to make the Fair Employment Commission a permanent government body and bills to outlaw the poll tax for voting and make lynching a federal crime that would place this racial violence against black Americans under the control of federal judges and juries that would be more willing to render convictions for white defendants than all-white Southern court proceedings. Truman also could not convince Congress to approve a comprehensive national health care plan, with opponents labeling government health care programs as socialized medicine—an argument that continues to be echoed by conservatives and insurance companies into the present day. The President was also unable to bring about repeal of the Taft-Hartley Act passed by a Republican Congress in 1947. Under Taft-Hartley, the power of organized labor which had grown during the 1930s under the New Deal's Wagner Act was limited by forbidding the closed union shop as well as secondary strikes and boycotts in which unions were not directly involved. In addition, unions would have to provide eighty days' notice before a work stoppage, and union leaders were required to sign affidavits affirming that they were not associated with the Communist Party. The political and social goals of the CIO were undermined as activist leaders were removed amid allegations regarding their affiliation with leftist groups. With this purge of CIO leadership, the union lost its crusading zeal and merged with the AFL in 1955, forming the AFL-CIO. During the 1950s, organized labor abandoned larger social goals of reforming America and gaining greater influence over corporate management decisions in favor of returning to more bread and butter unionism focused upon wages, pensions, and benefits. Republicans were also able to secure passage and ratification of the Twenty-second Amendment limiting the President to two elected terms—a measure enacted in reaction to Roosevelt's election to four terms.

Rise of Joseph McCarthy and Hiss case

Truman's efforts to enact the Fair Deal legislative agenda and establish himself within the reform tradition of Franklin Roosevelt was also undermined by the anticommunist movement that made any reform endeavors politically suspect. On February 9, 1950 Republican Senator Joseph McCarthy of Wisconsin gave a Lincoln Day speech in Wheeling, West Virginia during which he charged that he had a list of at least 205 members of the State Department with communist affiliations. Although McCarthy never produced his list and seemed to constantly change the number of State Department communists, his unproven accusations struck a nerve among the American people. Up to this point, McCarthy's career was rather undistinguished. He exaggerated his war record as "tail gunner Joe" to win election to the Senate in 1946, and McCarthy was considered to be a rather ineffective member of the Senate chamber, leading the Washington press corps to dub him the "worst U.S. Senator." Concerned about his prospects for re-election in 1952, McCarthy seized upon the communist issue and reveled in the attention given to his anticommunist accusations. From his position as Chairman of the Committee on Government Operations and its Permanent Subcommittee on Investigations, McCarthy launched hearings into allegations of communist subversion in which the Senator employed the bullying tactics of hearsay and innuendo while offering little hard evidence that become known as McCarthyism.

McCarthy's unfounded accusations gained traction because he played upon the insecurities and fears of the American people stoked by the Cold War, atomic bomb, Rosenberg spy ring, and the Alger Hiss case. While the Rosenberg convictions suggested that virtually anyone, and especially Jews, might be subversives, the Hiss case provided conformation that educated elites and New Dealers were not to be trusted, appealing to what historian Richard Hofstadter called anti-intellectualism in American life and thought. Hiss came from a wealthy Baltimore family and graduated from Harvard Law School before moving on to a distinguished political career within the Roosevelt administration. Hiss played an advisory role in the founding of the United Nations and accepted a post war position as President of the Carnegie Endowment for International Peace. His life changed forever on August 3, 1948, when Whittaker Chambers, who confessed to being a former espionage agent for the Soviet Union, testified before the House Un-American Activities Committee (HUAC), naming Hiss as a former roommate who passed government secrets to Chambers. The testimony of Chambers was questionable to some on the committee due to his past homosexuality, although Chambers at the time of the hearings was an editor at *Time* magazine with a wife and family who found peace in his Quaker faith. Hiss appeared before HUAC to clear his name and denied having ever known Chambers. One member of HUAC, however, was not satisfied with the testimony provided by Hiss. Richard Nixon, a Republican Congressman from California, came from a poor background and resented the privileged background of Hiss. Nixon asked Chambers whether he might provide any evidence to support his allegations against Hiss. Chambers recalled that he had stored microfilm procured by Hiss in a hollowed-out pumpkin, and Nixon delighted in posing for photographers while studying the microfilm contained in the pumpkin. Hiss was recalled by the committee and changed his testimony, now asserting that Chambers was, indeed, a former roommate whom he did not initially recognize because Chambers had fixed his teeth. Hiss vehemently denied the accusations of espionage. As a result of his HUAC testimony, Hiss lost his position with the Carnegie Foundation and was convicted of perjury after a hung jury on his first trial. There were no espionage charges brought against Hiss due to a statute of limitations. Hiss spent the rest of his life proclaiming his innocence, although with the opening of Soviet archives, some scholars assert there is evidence that Hiss may have been a Soviet agent, but the case remains controversial. Some defenders of Hiss believe that he failed to initially acknowledge Chambers not because he was covering up for espionage, but rather because he and Chambers may have engaged in a same sex relationship, and Hiss wanted to spare his family from allegations of homosexuality which was recognized by the American Psychiatric Association at this time as a mental disorder. There was no room in the American consensus for gays and lesbians who were denounced as perverts and forced to keep their sexual identity hidden.

The politics of anticommunism

Truman responded to the growing clamor of conspiracy theories regarding communist subversion in the government by issuing Executive Order 9835, establishing loyalty review boards to examine the patriotism of over three million government employees. The review boards found little evidence of communist subversion, but approximately 300 government employees were dismissed, with many of the cases relating to accusations of homosexuality which the government asserted made them susceptible to blackmail by Soviet agents. In the so-called "lavender scare," same sex attraction and espionage were linked as un-American, and sexual imagery was apparent in the demagoguery of politicians such as McCarthy who asserted that liberals were "soft" on communism. The files of the review boards also contained unsubstantiated charges that anticommunist politicians used to smear government employees throughout the 1950s.

Many states followed suit with required loyalty oaths for schoolteachers, professors, and public employees. The ridiculous oaths failed to uncover spies who would have signed them to cover their activities, while many conscientious Americans lost their jobs, refusing to sign documents which they denounced as attacking traditional American values of free speech and violating civil liberties. In fact, free speech and association were denied for American communists perceived as agents of a foreign ideology seeking to overthrow the American government. The history of an indigenous American radicalism was dismissed as all American communists or radicals were considered to be agents of the Soviet Union. There were, indeed, Soviet spies in the United States, but it was simplistic and paranoid to treat all communists as spies and subversives. The Smith Act provided for the registration of American communists, and in 1952 Congress passed legislation that denied communists entry into the United States and prevented the naturalization of communists. The McCarran Internal Security Act of 1950 established the Subversive Activities Board to monitor the activities of radicals. The act also provided for the incarceration of radicals identified by the FBI during a national emergency, allowing the FBI to secretly spy upon and prepare government files upon tens of thousands of Americans whose loyalty was deemed suspect. Legislation and surveillance limited freedom of expression, while Hollywood responded to a HUAC investigation by establishing a blacklist of performers, writers, and directors whose politics were questioned. The Hollywood Ten refused to answer questions from the committee regarding their political views and affiliations, and they were imprisoned for

Contempt of Congress. After serving their sentences, the Hollywood Ten were blacklisted by the film industry, although some writers such as Dalton Trumbo continued to produce scripts under pseudonyms. Free speech and expression were also stifled as film studios attempted to avoid controversy, and social problem films exploring issues such as racism and anti-Semitism were curtailed in favor of Biblical epics and romantic comedies with Doris Day.

Emergence of Eisenhower and moderate Republicanism

As the Truman administration bogged down under the pressures of the Korean War and anticommunism, the conformity of the era continued under the leadership of President Dwight Eisenhower. After a distinguished military career in World War II as the Supreme Commander of the Allied Expeditionary Force in Europe, Eisenhower was a national hero who expanded his civilian credentials by serving as President of Columbia University in the post war era. Although Eisenhower had avoided politics during his military career, both Republicans and Democrats courted him as a Presidential candidate. After flirtations with both parties, Eisenhower declared himself a Republican and wrested the party's nomination from Ohio Senator Richard A. Taft, son of President William Tâft and a favorite of the party's conservative wing. Beset by the issues of Korea, communism, and corruption, Truman did not seek the Democratic nomination in 1952 which was awarded to Illinois Governor Adlai Stevenson. A favorite of liberal Democrats, Stevenson, however, was derided by many Americans for being "an egghead" and taking a too cerebral approach to the nation's problems. The public seemed to reject Stevenson's intellectualism in favor of the more affable Eisenhower whose common touch was apparent in the slogan "I like Ike." In the midst of the campaign, however, Eisenhower almost decided to dump his running mate, Senator Richard Nixon who was accused of accepting political gifts from supporters. Eisenhower had been forced to accept Nixon on the ticket by the extreme anticommunist wing of the party who admired his exposure of Alger Hiss and successful 1950 California Senate campaign against Helen Gahagan Douglas, whom Nixon called "the pink lady" and a communist sympathizer. Nixon responded to the demands that he resign from the ticket with a nationally televised speech. Citing his humble origins and attacking his political opponents, Nixon asserted that he would return all political gifts except for a puppy named Checkers with whom his two young daughters were in love. The ploy worked, and the popular support for the Checkers speech convinced Eisenhower to keep Nixon on the ticket.

As an affable national hero, Eisenhower rolled to a lop-sided win, becoming the first Republican since Herbert Hoover to assume the Presidency. Many Republicans viewed the Eisenhower Presidency and control of Congress as an opportunity to roll back New Deal programs. But after twenty years of New Deal legislation,

Eisenhower took a more moderate approach. While Eisenhower believed there was little need for additional social and welfare measures, New Deal programs such as Social Security would be maintained, but they could be more efficiently managed under Republican control. Accordingly, Eisenhower proposed a modest increase for Social Security benefits and an expansion of the federal bureaucracy with creation of the cabinet level Department of Health, Education, and Welfare (HEW). On the other hand, Eisenhower presided over the largest public works project in American history with passage of the National Interstate and Defense Highway Act in 1956 which expanded the nation's interstate highway system. The legislation pleased liberals by providing jobs, while conservatives were moved to support this massive spending as providing for the national defense. The Interstate Highway system was sold as a measure that would assure the rapid evacuation of American cities in the case of a national emergency such as a nuclear attack.

Sputnik

Fears of the Soviet Union also propelled other major expansions of the federal government during the Eisenhower Presidency. On October 4, 1957, the Soviet Union launched Sputnik, the first manmade satellite to orbit the earth. Although Sputnik only orbited the planet for a few months before crashing back to earth, it set off a panic among Americans who feared they might soon be the target of lasers and weapons launched from space. The Eisenhower administration responded to the national panic by gaining passage of the 1958 National Defense Act which sought to address the perception that Soviet education was surpassing the United States. The legislation provided for low-interest loans to college students majoring in math and science, establishing a precedent for government loans to cover college tuition and expenses that was eventually expanded to other fields of study. Although the United States was not as far behind the Soviets in the space race as many Americans feared, Sputnik also led to the creation of the National Aeronautics and Space Administration (NASA) that would centralize space travel and research under one government agency that succeeded in placing a man on the moon by the end of the 1960s.

Eisenhower's conservative nature

The more conservative side of the Eisenhower administration was apparent in the President's appointments, management of the economy, and response to McCarthyism and the Civil Rights Movement. The Eisenhower cabinet included such conservative figures as Secretary of State John Foster Dulles, a staunch anticommunist, and Secretary of Defense Charles Wilson, the head of General Motors who declared "what's good for General Motors is good for the country" and assured that corporate interests would continue to maintain a significant influence over American politics. Eisenhower, however, was most disappointed with the liberal direction taken by the Supreme Court under his appointee, former California Governor Earl Warren. Eisenhower was also reluctant to intervene economically during the Recession of 1958, preferring that the private sector and market rather than the government guide the country toward economic recovery.

Eisenhower had little use for Senator McCarthy who even questioned the President's loyalty. But rather than directly confront McCarthy, Eisenhower believed that the best way to deal with the Senator was to ignore him and trust that his political overreach would eventually lead to his demise. Eisenhower lacked the courage of Republican Senator Margaret Chase Smith of Maine, the only female member of the Senate chamber, who was willing to publicly challenge McCarthy, This silence among most Republicans allowed the Senator from Wisconsin to smear and destroy the reputations of many distinguished Americans. The Army-McCarthy hearings finally led to McCarthy's downfall. The Army asserted that McCarthy's accusations of communist influence within the military institution were the result of the Army's failure to provide preferential treatment for McCarthy's aide David Schine who was drafted. McCarthy's associate and attorney Roy Cohn, whom President Donald Trump has cited as a mentor, was accused by the Army of intervening on behalf of Schine, and although not publicly addressed at the time except through innuendo, Cohn and Schine likely shared a same sex relationship—with sexual politics again casting a shadow over Cold War security issues. The Army was represented by Boston attorney Joseph Welch, who was attacked by McCarthy for having a young attorney in his firm who was a former member of the National Lawyers Guild, which anticommunists considered to be a communist front organization. This was a classic example of McCarthy's guilt by association tactics, and Welch responded angrily that the Senator had ruined a young man's career. Welch left the hearing room to applause after asserting that the Senator had no sense of decency. After the confrontation, public opinion shifted away from McCarthy, and the Senate voted to censure him in December 1954. McCarthy continued to serve in the Senate, but his influence was considerably diminished. The Senator was rumored to be drinking heavily, and Vice President Nixon reported that he discovered McCarthy wandering aimlessly late one night in a grocery store parking lot clad in his pajamas. The abuse of alcohol contributed to his declining health, and McCarthy died of hepatitis on May 2, 1957. While McCarthy was discredited by the time of the Senator's death, some anticommunists still perceive him as a martyr to their cause.

Eisenhower was also uncomfortable with black people and opposed to the political activism of the Civil Rights Movement. While not a champion of the *Brown v. Board* (1954) Supreme Court decision on school desegregation, Eisenhower believed that it was his duty to enforce the law. Accordingly, when Arkansas Governor Orval Faubus refused to follow a court order calling for the integration of Central High in Little Rock, Eisenhower reluctantly sent federal troops to safeguard black students attempting to enter the school. We will return to this issue in the chapter focusing upon the Civil Rights Movement. Despite his reluctance to confront McCarthy and segregationists, Eisenhower remained popular with most Americans. In 1956, he won re-election, once again defeating Adlai Stevenson, but he was unable to translate his personal popularity to the Republican Party as the Democrats regained control of Congress in 1954, a position they maintained through the Eisenhower administration.

Containment rather than rollback

Rather than the representing a complete rollback of the New Deal, the moderate Republicanism of Eisenhower may be perceived as somewhat of a consolidation of the New Deal and Fair Deal. In the realm of foreign policy, Eisenhower's Secretary of State John Foster Dulles asserted that the United States would abandon cowardly containment and pursue a policy of rolling back communism around the world. However, the administration's New Look Policy of reducing spending on the troops and conventional weapons in favor of a cheaper reliance upon nuclear weaponry considerably reduced the administration's flexibility; unless one were willing to risk a nuclear war in what Dulles called "brinksmanship." When confronted with this reality, the Eisenhower Presidency ended up adhering to the containment strategy introduced by the Truman administration. In Asia, the Eisenhower administration continued the support of Taiwan and nonrecognition of the People's Republic of China, while negotiating an armistice to end the fighting in Korea with the status quo preserved along the demilitarized zone of the 38th parallel. Concerns about communist aggression in Vietnam led the United States to support French colonialism, and the Eisenhower administration even considered employing nuclear weapons to aid the French during the siege of Dien Bien Phu. Continuing support for Israel was tested in the 1956 Suez Crisis. Following the nationalization of the Suez Canal by Egyptian leader Gamal Abdel Nasser, Egypt was invaded by Israel with support from Britain and France. The Soviets vowed to oppose the invasion and back the Egyptians, and the Eisenhower administration feared a larger war, prevailing upon the Israelis, French, and British to withdraw their forces from Egypt. Following the Suez Crisis, the Egyptians retained control of the canal, and Soviet prestige was increased among Arab states in the Middle East. To counter Soviet influence in the region, the United States proclaimed the Eisenhower Doctrine, promising American aid to any government in the Middle East that was the target of foreign aggression by international communism, expanding the reach of the Truman Doctrine into the troubled Middle East.

The chief concern of the Eisenhower administration remained Soviet expansion in Europe. West Germany, accordingly, was allowed to remilitarize and join NATO as a bulwark against Soviet aggression. The Soviets, meanwhile, were undergoing a power struggle following the death of Stalin in 1953, out of which Nikita Khrushchev emerged as the First Secretary of the Communist Party of the Soviet Union. Although he had served as one of Stalin's loyal lieutenants, Khrushchev, in a secret speech before the 20th Party Congress in February 1956, denounced Stalin for his purges, executions, and mass arrests of Soviet citizens. The speech appeared to signify a liberalization of the Soviet regime, and the Hungarians sought to take advantage of the situation with an uprising that overthrew the Soviet-backed government. Fearing that this sense of rebellion might spread throughout Eastern Europe and even into the Soviet Union, Khrushchev in November 1956 authorized an invasion that suppressed the Hungarian Revolution with the death of over 2,000 Hungarians. Many Hungarians appealed to the United States and NATO to rescue their revolution with a military intervention, but the Eisenhower administration was distracted by the Suez Crisis and no intervention was forthcoming. After all, the Hungarian invasion by the Soviet Union was not a new territorial grab, but rather an effort to retain control in an area already aligned with the Soviets; thus, there was no violation of the containment policy opposing further Soviet expansion.

As the end of his Presidency approached, Eisenhower hoped to leave a legacy of better relations with the Soviets. A May 1960 summit meeting between Eisenhower and Khrushchev was sabotaged when shortly before the Paris meeting, an American U-2 spy plane was shot down over the Soviet Union. The United States initially dismissed the allegations, but Eisenhower was put on the defensive when the Soviets produced the American pilot, Francis Gary Powers, who had parachuted to safety after his plane was hit by a Soviet missile. Clearly, it was foolhardy for the United States to be conducting such espionage activities on the eve of an important summit meeting. The incident increased tensions between the Americans and Soviets that carried over into the Presidency of John F. Kennedy.

Covert CIA operations

The foreign policy of the Eisenhower administration also left a troubling legacy with covert CIA operations in the Middle East and Latin America. In 1953, Iranian Prime Minister Mohammad Mosaddegh moved to nationalize the country's oilfields, antagonizing Western oil companies profiting off Iranian oil. In conjunction with their British counterparts, American agents maneuvered to remove Mosaddegh from power in favor of monarchial rule under Mohammad Reza Pahlavi. The pro-American Shah of Iran ruled his country with dictatorial force and a despised secret police force until he was overthrown in the Iranian Revolution of 1978. The American coup in 1953 against a legitimate democratic government has poisoned the relationship between the United States and Iran down to the present day.

Another short-run successful covert operation toppled a democratic government in Guatemala. The United States was opposed to the land reforms of democratically elected President Jacobo Arbenz which were denounced as socialistic and threatening to the economic power of the United Fruit Company in Central America. Also, Secretary of State John Foster Dulles and his brother, CIA Director Allen Dulles, were major stockholders in the American corporation. The CIA schemed to topple Arbenz in a coup that placed General Carlos Castillo Armas in power, fostering political and economic destabilization which continues to plague Guatemala. Latin American resentment toward United States intervention and support for military dictatorships in the region was evident in the demonstrations that greeted Vice President Richard Nixon's 1958 goodwill tour of South America. In Venezuela, Nixon's motorcade was attacked, although the Vice President emerged unarmed. Security for Nixon was increased following a threat of military intervention to rescue him. The incident demonstrated the discontent in the region toward American support for dictators such as Fulgencio Batista in Cuba.

In 1959, Batista was overthrown in a popular revolution led by the charismatic Fidel Castro. After Castro nationalized the property of American companies in Cuba, the Eisenhower administration severed diplomatic relations with the Castro regime and imposed an economic embargo on Cuba. Fearing the collapse of his revolutionary government that did institute educational and health care reforms, Castro turned toward the Soviet Union as a market for Cuban sugar and military protection from the United States. The Eisenhower administration also began to explore military options to depose Castro which culminated in the disastrous Bay of Pigs invasion implemented in the early days of the Kennedy Presidency.

Legacy of the liberal consensus

Eisenhower's policies exacerbated the Cold War tensions formulated during the Truman administration, but in an eloquent farewell address the former General issued a warning about the growing power of the military-industrial complex that fostered a permanent war footing and posed a threat to American democracy. Eisenhower seemed to foresee the future as the Cuban Missile Crisis nearly produced a nuclear war, while the Vietnam War killed millions of Vietnamese and brought about a political and moral crisis within the United States.

The post-World War II liberal consensus extolled the utopia of suburbia in which all Americans could achieve their dreams through hard work and an expanding capitalist economy, with the only threat to this Eden being the serpent of communism. But the reality of life in post-World War II America was far more complex. Beneath the conformity of the white picket fences of suburbia were issues of race, class, gender, and war that continued to threaten the promise of

American life. The next chapter will concentrate upon the efforts of the Kennedy and Johnson Presidencies to maintain the consensus façade when confronted by the challenges of the Civil Rights Movement and Vietnam War. The Civil Rights Movement confronted the giant shadow that race and the original sin of slavery cast over the American experiment. The black Civil Rights Movement also provided an important model for women, Natives, Hispanics, the LGBTQ community, and other minorities who have fought and struggled for America to implement the ideas of Jefferson's Declaration of Independence. The Civil Rights Movement and the responses of the John Kennedy and Lyndon Johnson Presidencies to a changing America will be supplemented by a separate chapter analyzing the Vietnam War, generational conflict, and counterculture that sought to redefine American life during the upheaval of the 1960s when the chickens ignored by the consensus came home to roost.

Further Reading:

Ambrose, Stephen. *Eisenhower: The President*. New York: Simon and Schuster, 1983.

Cohn, Lizabeth. *A Consumers' Republic: The Politics of Mass Consumption in Postwar America*. New York: Vintage Books, 2003.

Coontz, Stephanie. *The Way We Never Were: American Families and the Nostalgia Trap*. New York: Basic Books, 1992.

Cumings, Bruce. *The Korean War: A History*. New York: Modern Library, 2010.

Halberstam, David. *The Fifties*. New York: Villard Books, 1993.

Hamby, Alonzo. *Beyond the New Deal: Harry S. Truman and American Liberalism*. New York: Columbia University Press, 1973.

Immerman, Richard. *The CIA in Guatemala: The Foreign Policy of Intervention*. Austin, TX: University of Texas Press, 1982.

Jackson, Kenneth. *The Crabgrass Frontier: The Suburbanization of the United States*. New York: Oxford University Press, 1988.

Kaledin, Eugenia. *Mothers and More: American Women in the 1950s*. Boston: Twayne Publishers, 1984.

Leffler, Melvyn P. *A Preponderance of Power: National Security, the Truman Administration, and the Cold War*. Stanford, CA: Stanford University Press, 1992.

May, Elaine. *Homeward Bound: American Families in the Cold War Era*. New York: Basic Books, 1988.

Schrecker, Ellen. *Many are the Crimes: McCarthyism in America*. Boston: Little Brown, 1998.

25

JFK and the New Frontier

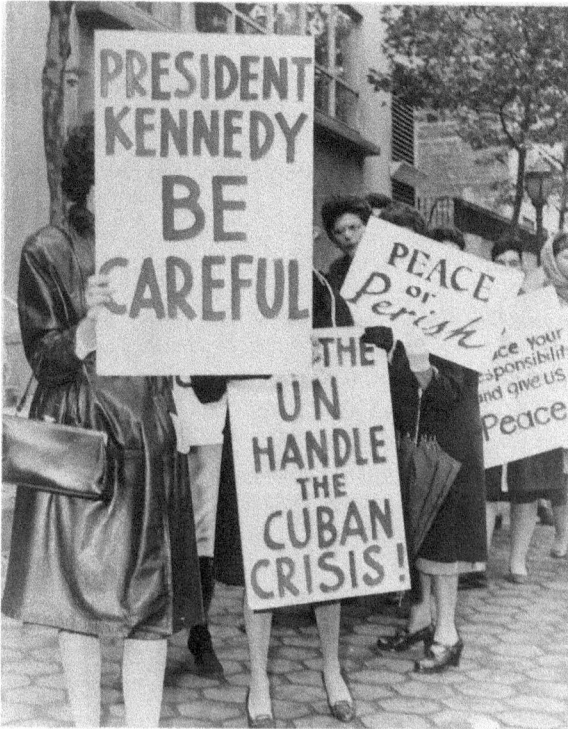

"800 Women Strikers for Peace on 47th St. Near U.N. Building." Phil Stanzida, photographer, *New York World Telegram & Sun* photo, 1962. Prints and Photographs Division, Library of Congress. Promising a New Frontier, President John F. Kennedy was, nevertheless, essentially a Cold Warrior who increased the American commitment to Vietnam and brought the world to the brink of nuclear annihilation in the Cuban Missile Crisis. In this photograph, women protesters urge the President to exercise restraint in his approach to the situation in Cuba.

John Fitzgerald Kennedy claimed that his election in 1960 marked the passing of the torch to a new generation of Americans, and, borrowing from historian Frederick Jackson Turner, the President called his administration The New Frontier. But behind the glamour of a handsome young President and his beautiful wife, Jacqueline "Jackie" Bouvier Kennedy, which some infatuated reporters insisted upon referring to as King Arthur's Camelot, the Kennedy Presidency marked a continuation of the consensus politics followed by the Eisenhower administration. In his farewell address, Eisenhower raised important reservations about the impact of the Cold War and anticommunist crusade upon the American economy and democratic institutions. Despite Eisenhower's warnings, Kennedy embraced the Cold War, with his policies dragging the United States deeper into the Vietnam quagmire and bringing the world to the brink of nuclear war with the Cuban Missile Crisis. Also, his narrow electoral victory over Nixon provided Kennedy with no popular mandate for change, and his legislative agenda languished in Congress. Kennedy also feared that continued agitation on behalf of civil rights would cost him Southern white political support and deny him re-election in 1964. Kennedy was, therefore, a man of the consensus who believed that the promotion of capitalist expansion would solve the nation's ills, while the only real threat to American greatness was international communism promoted by Soviet expansionism. The President devoted considerable time and vigor to the containment of communism, while reluctantly being pushed into engagement with civil rights through the actions of Martin Luther King Jr. and other crusaders for racial justice. This chapter will provide an overview of the Kennedy Presidency and his successor Lyndon Johnson who employed his legislative skills to enact much of Kennedy's stalled agenda after the President's assassination. More detailed analysis of the Civil Rights Movement and Vietnam War will be offered in subsequent chapters.

Today, Kennedy is one of America's most admired Presidents, but in his lifetime public opinion was more divided. Much of the adoration expressed for JFK came after his martyrdom by an assassin's bullet on November 22, 1963. The tragic assassination of his brother Robert, who was murdered while seeking the 1968 Presidential nomination, also contributes to the legend of JFK as a martyr for American freedom. The reality of the Kennedy saga is far more complex than the legend, and, thus, it is necessary to explore the history of the Kennedy family in a little more detail.

Background of JFK

John Kennedy was born into an Irish Catholic family on May 29, 1917 in Brookline, Massachusetts. His grandparents on both sides of the family migrated from Ireland, and JFK's father, Joseph P. Kennedy, seemed obsessed with gaining respect from the Anglo-Saxon establishment and making one of his sons the first Irish Catholic President. Initially, these ambitions fell upon Joseph Jr., but when the eldest son perished on a bombing mission during the Second World War, these patriarchal pressures were transferred to his second son, JFK. The father acquired a fortune in the stock market, and a friendship with Franklin Roosevelt led to significant political appointments as the first head of the Securities and Exchange Commission and as Ambassador to the United Kingdom. In addition to putting considerable pressure upon his sons to excel, the father displayed habits of womanizing and sexual exploitation that were incorporated into the behavior of his sons, including the youngest brother Ted whose Presidential ambitions were forever haunted by the death of a young woman in a car which he drove off a bridge in Chappaquiddick, Massachusetts. While their mother Rose was away from home, the father often openly dated starlets from Hollywood studios in which he invested and exerted some management control. The idea of beautiful women as objects for the sexual gratification of powerful and wealthy men seemed deeply ingrained into JFK and his brothers.

His father helped to secure JFK's admission to Choate, a prestigious New England boarding school, and after graduation he joined his family in England. Joseph Kennedy was eventually removed from his Ambassadorship for his criticism of the British government, and JFK returned to his studies at Harvard University. His senior thesis *While England Slept*, criticizing British appeasement of Nazi Germany, was published at the insistence of his father, although Arthur Krock of *The New York Times* is believed to have rewritten much of the thesis before publication. During the Second World War, JFK joined the Navy and became a war hero, earning decorations after getting his crew to safety following the sinking by the Japanese of *PT Boat 109* commanded by Kennedy. After the war, Kennedy was elected to the House of Representatives, and in 1952 the voters of Massachusetts elevated him to the Senate where he served until assuming the Presidency. Although Democrats, the Kennedy family often socialized with Republican Senator Joseph McCarthy, and JFK was reluctant to criticize McCarthy's extreme anticommunism, and his brother Robert worked for the Wisconsin Senator's committee. Majority Leader Lyndon Johnson was not impressed with the Massachusetts Senator, whom Johnson considered overly ambitious and somewhat of a playboy. While Johnson was not pleased with JFK's work ethic and intellect, the American public purchased his book *Profiles in Courage* (1956) about courageous Senators who placed adherence to principle above their political careers. The book won the Pulitzer Prize, although today it is generally acknowledged that his speechwriter Ted Sorenson had ghost written the book for Kennedy.

After being associated with many women, including actress Gene Tierney, Kennedy married Jacqueline Bouvier in 1953, but there is considerable evidence that he continued to have extramarital affairs throughout his Senate career and into his Presidency. It seems almost impossible that his wife did not have knowledge of his affairs, but the press, Secret Service, and the President's friends were committed to keeping these relationships out of the public eye. The attitude of the press toward covering the private lives of prominent politicians would change following the Watergate crisis. Perhaps the Presidential relationship that has gained the most attention is that between JFK and actress Marilyn Monroe. There seems to be evidence to support the affair, and brother Robert may have also been involved with the actress, but there is no real factual basis for the conspiracy theory that the Kennedys were responsible for Monroe's death. In addition to his extramarital affairs, Kennedy's private life was governed by serious health issues; he suffered from intense back problems and Addison's disease, a painful endocrine disorder. To relieve his pain, the President was given numerous injections which sometimes impacted his decision making—although it seems a bit far-fetched to assume, as some of his defenders argue, that the injections contributed to his strong sexual appetite. The strong family image manufactured by the Kennedy White House did not reflect the reality of the President's life, and much of the Kennedy mystique was built upon style rather than substance.

Election of 1960

In 1960, Kennedy announced his Presidential candidacy and did well in the primaries against Minnesota Senator Hubert Humphrey, and by the time of the party convention in Los Angeles, his main opponent was Senator Johnson who had not entered the primaries. At the convention, JFK, much to the chagrin of his brother Robert, offered the Vice Presidency to Johnson, believing that the more experienced politician could help secure legislative approval for the Kennedy agenda and aid Kennedy in carrying crucial Southern states such as Texas. Robert attempted to block the agreement, producing a personal animosity that carried over into the Johnson Presidency. Johnson helped JFK to carry Texas, but the President and Johnson were never close with Kennedy perceiving the Texan to be rather crude and unsophisticated.

Vice President Richard Nixon easily won the Republican Presidential nomination, citing his experience and expecting to inherit the mantle of a popular Eisenhower. Kennedy also had the problem that many Protestants expressed reservations about a Catholic President, believing that Kennedy's election would result in the Pope dictating American domestic and foreign policies. The Catholic issue had also hindered Al Smith's 1928 campaign, so Kennedy decided to directly confront the question of his religion. On September 12, 1960, Kennedy addressed the Greater Houston Ministerial Alliance, asserting that while he was proud of his Catholicism, the candidate was also dedicated to the Constitutional separation of church and state, and the Catholic Church would not order the policies of his administration. Kennedy also benefitted from the nation's first televised debates. Nixon believed that the first debate offered an opportunity to demonstrate his mastery of the issues, but proving Marshall McLuhan's observation that "the medium is the message," the handsome Kennedy came across to television audiences as cool, calm, and relaxed, while Nixon, who was recently released from the hospital due to an injured knee which he bumped against a car door stuck on a curb, appeared pale with sweat glistening above his upper lip and "five o'clock shadow" visible on his face. The television audience overwhelmingly favored Kennedy, although Nixon supporters claim the smaller radio audience believed Nixon to be the winner of the debate due to his factual grasp of the issues. Both candidates embraced the Cold War consensus and promised to oppose the Soviets, with Kennedy even complaining that under Eisenhower's watch there was a "missile gap" and the United States had fallen behind the Soviets—the same "soft" on communism label that Senator McCarthy had attempted to hang on Eisenhower.

As the final weeks of the 1960 campaign approached, the race remained close, but Kennedy's appeal to black voters may have made the difference. Martin Luther King Jr. was arrested in Georgia shortly before the election for protesting state segregationist facilities and laws. Respecting the concept of states' rights, Nixon refused to issue a statement, while Kennedy was afraid that voicing support for King would cost him with white Southern voters. On the weekend before the election, Kennedy did telephone Reverend King's wife and father, expressing his concern for the incarcerated minister. The network of black churches and ministers got the word out to their parishioners on the Sunday before the election, while the mainstream press generally missed this story, and many white Southerners did not learn of Kennedy's call to the King family until after the election. With the final margin in the popular vote being less than 1 percent, the black vote may have pushed Kennedy over the top.

The promise and limitations of the New Frontier

The youngest American President since Theodore Roosevelt excited many Americans with his energy and promise of a New Frontier. In his inaugural address, the articulate President called for a new sense of national sacrifice, asserting "ask not what your country can do for you—ask what you can do for your country." This sense of sacrifice and Kennedy's call for a new generation to seize the reins of government, however, were still dedicated to the pursuit of the anticommunist crusade in which Americans would "pay any price, bear any burden, meet any hardship, support any friend, oppose any foe to assure the survival and the success of liberty." This idealist rhetoric resulted in a younger generation fighting and dying in the jungles of Southeast Asia for a South Vietnamese government whose commitment to liberty was questionable at best. Kennedy also pledged that his administration would bring the best and the brightest into government service. He recruited Robert McNamara, whose management had revolutionized the Ford Motor Company, to serve as Secretary of Defense, while Walt Rostow, an academic from the University of Texas, served as a Special Assistant for National Security under the guidance of McGeorge Bundy, who left his position at Harvard to assume the position of Kennedy's National Security Adviser. Harvard historian Arthur Schlesinger Jr. also served as a special assistant to the President and provided the administration with somewhat of "a court historian." But perhaps Kennedy's most trusted adviser was his brother Robert, whom he appointed as Attorney General. Nevertheless, the impressive group of Ivy League-educated professors, business leaders, and politicians helped to guide both Kennedy and Johnson deeper into a military commitment in Southeast Asia.

On the domestic front, Kennedy's legislative agenda stalled as the narrow electoral victory in 1960 failed to provide the President with a mandate to wield over recalcitrant legislators. Kennedy was committed to a tax cut for both individuals and corporations that he believed would stimulate the economy. The President wanted to reduce the Eisenhower tax rates on upper incomes which he considered almost confiscatory, but this taxation had provided an economic foundation for the G.I. Bill and Interstate Highway Act. Kennedy also hoped to address the problems of medical expenses for Americans over age sixty-five, many of whom did not have health insurance and were dependent upon Social Security. And bowing to the pressure of the Civil Rights Movement, the President finally came to support a civil rights bill. Kennedy also sought immigration reform that would move the nation away from the discriminatory national origins policy of the 1920s. He did, however, gain Congressional approval for the Trade Expansion Act of 1962 that provided the President with the authority to increase trade by negotiating tariff reductions. Kennedy also captured the public's imagination with his proposal to place a man on the moon before the end of the decade. Responding to the April 1961 flight of Soviet cosmonaut Yuri Gagarin as the first person into space, Kennedy prevailed upon Congress to provide the funds that would allow the United States to surpass the Soviet space program. And at great expense and personal sacrifice, exemplified by the deaths of American astronauts Virgil "Gus" Grissom, Ed White, and Roger B. Chaffee in a January 1967 training accident, the United States achieved the moon landing on July 20, 1969—with Kennedy's old adversary Nixon serving as President and basking in the glory of this achievement as Neil Armstrong took "one giant leap for mankind."

Peace Corps and Alliance for Progress

In foreign policy, Kennedy's idealism and appeal to young Americans was apparent in the creation of the Peace Corps. Under the initial program, young American volunteers after graduation from college would serve two years abroad as goodwill ambassadors for the United States, fostering the growth of developing nations. Kennedy envisioned the program as benefitting American interests in the Cold War by promoting positive personal relationships between young Americans and people from around the world, negating communist propaganda depicting Americans as imperialists and selfish capitalists. While American military interventions in the developing world would continue, the idealistic young Peace Corps volunteers offered an alternative vision of America. And young Americans flocked to the program, although Congressional opponents complained about the cost of the program administered by Kennedy's brother-in-law Sargent Shriver, while others observed that older and more experienced participants would provide greater skills and assistance for the development of needed infrastructure abroad. Although some young people on the political left in the 1960s became suspicious of the Peace Corps as a tool for American imperialism, the program continues to exist with over 200,000 Americans having participated, including older citizens with skills to share.

The Kennedy administration also proposed the Alliance for Progress as an idealistic program for economic development within Latin America, although the unstated purpose was to promote capitalism within the region and limit the appeal of revolutionary Cuba, whom the United States helped expel from the Organization of American States in 1962. While the Alliance spent billions of dollars in Latin America, large amounts of these funds went back to American corporations from whom the Latin nations were supposed to purchase goods and services. The funds allocated for development were supposed to promote democratic changes such as land reform, but much of the money went to authoritarian regimes that did not want to offend local elites. Seeking to prevent Castro from spreading communism, the United States became increasingly close to anticommunist military and dictatorial governments in Latin America, providing training in torture, assassination, and interrogation for Latin American military and police personnel at the School of the Americas located at Fort Benning in Georgia.

Bay of Pigs

While the Peace Corps and Alliance for Progress appeared to promote a sense of idealism, President Kennedy also sought to project a sense of toughness in his personal approach to foreign policy. With an elite family background and Ivy League education, JFK seemed to go out of his way to convince the media and Americans that he exemplified the rugged individualism of the nation. The family delighted in playing competitive games of touch football that often produced bumps and bruises. JFK was also attracted to the Green Berets and arranged demonstrations of their skills for the press and family friends. He was enamored with counter-insurgency tactics which he believed would allow the Americans and their allies in the developing world to defeat insurgent leftist forces. This admiration for counter insurgency also extended to the covert operations of the CIA that toppled perceived leftist governments in Iran and Guatemala during the 1950s. Thus, Kennedy signed on to a CIA proposal for invading Cuba, whose planning was launched under the Eisenhower administration.

The CIA plan called for the training of Cuban exiles who would launch an invasion of Cuba at the isolated Bay of Pigs. Once the Cuban people learned of the invasion, they would join with the invading "liberators" to overthrow the Castro dictatorship. While the United States would provide covert training and support for the invasion, unmarked aircraft and ships would allow the United States to plausibly deny any involvement with the invasion. The U.S. military would be on alert, if anything went wrong, but the CIA assured the President that the operation would be a success and not require U.S. military intervention. The invasion was launched on April 17, 1961, but the exiles along with their CIA operatives were soon pinned down on the beach by Cuban defense forces under the command of Castro. The uprising of the Cuban people forecast by the CIA failed to materialize. Many of the Cubans most opposed to the Castro regime had either fled the country or were imprisoned. The CIA also failed to recognize that the overthrow of the repressive Batista regime plus Castro's reforms in areas such as education and health care enjoyed popular support. In fact, Castro's victory over the United States in the Bay of Pigs increased enthusiasm for the regime. As the military situation became perilous for the invaders and their CIA supporters, the spy agency admitted their failure, but Kennedy could still save the day by openly committing U.S. forces to the invasion and overthrow of the Castro government. Believing that a full-scale American invasion of Cuba would discredit the United States in Latin America and around the world, Kennedy refused to commit forces to the Cuban operation. The President also assumed that the damage suffered to American prestige would be limited, and the American Ambassador to the United Nations, former Democratic Presidential nominee Adlai Stevenson, asserted that there was simply no proof that the United States had any connection with the ill-fated invasion. However, overconfident CIA agents had entered the Bay of Pigs carrying their government credentials. Castro was able to produce evidence that some of the captured invaders were connected to the CIA and United States, catching the Americans in a public lie.

Kennedy personally accepted blame for the Bay of Pigs fiasco, but he moved to replace the leadership of the CIA, such as Allen Dulles, left over from the Eisenhower administration with his own people. However, the Kennedy infatuation with counter insurgency would produce no better results in Southeast Asia. While

Castro's prestige was enhanced by his handling of the Bay of Pigs invasion, the Cuban leader recognized that if Kennedy had ordered American planes and troops into the invasion, the Cuban Revolution would have been crushed. Accordingly, an important legacy of the Bay of Pigs was Castro's growing reliance upon the Soviets for military assistance, culminating in the Cuban Missile Crisis. While Kennedy's foreign policy actions often focused upon Cuba and Southeast Asia, he never waived in his belief in a monolithic international communist movement directed by the Kremlin.

Berlin Wall

Following the Bay of Pigs disaster, an embarrassed and weakened Kennedy, accordingly, went through with his planned summit meeting in Vienna, Austria with Soviet Premier Khrushchev on June 4, 1961. Much of their discussion centered upon the situation in Berlin. The Soviet leader asserted that his country would proceed to negotiate a unilateral treaty with East Germany, and Kennedy pledged that the United States would not abandon Berlin. Kennedy appeared unprepared for the belligerence displayed by the Soviet leader, and some observers believe that the President was bullied by Khrushchev who found Kennedy intelligent but weak. Some Kennedy partisans argue that the President's discomfort at the Vienna summit was exacerbated by injections for a painful backache. Nevertheless, Khrushchev followed up the summit in August 1961 by beginning construction of what would become the Berlin Wall, cutting off movement into West Berlin by refugees fleeing East Germany and the Soviet bloc. The Kennedy administration replied to the wall's construction by reconfirming America's obligations to West Berlin, but no military action to halt construction and possibly start a world war was approved. Instead, the United States projected the Berlin Wall as a symbol of Soviet tyranny, and in June 1962, Kennedy traveled to Berlin and announced his solidarity with the citizens of the city by declaring, "Ich bin ein Berliner."

Cuban Missile Crisis

Berlin was a flashpoint in the Cold War that could have provoked a military confrontation between the United States and Soviet Union; however, the crisis that nearly fostered a nuclear war occurred in Cuba from October 22 to November 2, 1962. The origins of the Cuban Missile Crisis may be traced to the failed Bay of Pigs invasion. Castro feared that the next time troops from the United States would be employed to overthrow his regime. Therefore, Castro negotiated an agreement with

Khrushchev for the Soviets to construct missile bases in Cuba that would thwart any future U.S. invasion of the island. The Soviets were also responding to deployment of U.S. ballistic missiles in Turkey on the border with the Soviet Union. On the eve of the 1962 American midterm elections, surveillance flights confirmed rumors that the Soviets were constructing missile sites; only ninety miles from the United States as alarmed Americans perceived the situation. The President immediately formed an executive committee of national security advisers to address the crisis. The consensus of the group was that a military response by the United States was warranted. After considering a full-scale military invasion of Cuba, Kennedy initially opted for air attacks that would take out the Soviet missile installations. While somewhat less aggressive than an invasion, the air strikes would certainly kill Soviet military and technical personnel, raising a strong possibility of a Soviet counter strike and the likelihood of an escalation toward nuclear war. As planning for the air strike continued, Robert Kennedy expressed some reservations to his brother, remarking how the air attack made him feel like the Japanese planning the 1941 attack on Pearl Harbor. His brother's doubts gave JFK pause, and he prevailed upon military planners to instead provide for a Naval blockade of Cuba; an action which the President announced in a televised address to the nation on October 22. A blockade could certainly be perceived by the Soviets and Cubans as an act of war, but it provided some time for the Soviets and their Cuban allies to assess the situation. The President, asserting a right to self-defense, maintained that the United States would stop any Soviet ships hauling cargo to complete the missile installations.

As Soviet vessels approached the quarantine zone established by the U.S. Navy, the world seemed on the brink of war. The Soviet ships, however, halted and did not challenge the blockade, leading to the assertion that the Americans "had gone eyeball to eyeball with the Russians, and the other guy blinked." It was later revealed that war was closer than many observers thought as a Russian submarine commander, believing that war was already underway, responded to the dropping of depth charges near his vessel by ordering the launch of the submarine's nuclear weapons. Soviet protocol, however, required that the launch command be approved by three officers on board, and one disagreed, averting a nuclear scenario that would certainly have accelerated.

Kennedy and Khrushchev, meanwhile, were pursuing negotiations to end the crisis and prevent war, although Castro still feared an American attack and urged the Soviet leader to take a harder stance. In the final analysis, the Soviets agreed to dismantle their missiles in Cuba under inspection by the United Nations. In return, Kennedy pledged that the United States would not invade Cuba. This gave Khrushchev some cover as he could now argue that the missiles were no longer required as they had served their purpose in protecting Cuba from American aggression. In a secret provision to the negotiations, the United States also agreed to remove its missiles from Turkey. In the wake of the missile crisis, there seemed to be somewhat of a thaw in relations between the Soviet Union and United States. In 1963, the Kennedy administration pleased American farmers by negotiating a massive wheat deal with the Soviets, and in August of that year the Soviets and

Americans agreed to the Nuclear Test Ban Treaty, prohibiting atmospheric testing of nuclear weapons along with similar bans on nuclear testing in space and under water. The treaty did reduce the amount of radioactive material in the atmosphere threatening world health, but it allowed underground testing to continue, and in the final analysis, the Nuclear Test Ban Treaty did not prove to be the first step toward nuclear disarmament that some of its proponents had envisioned. In fact, some Soviet hardliners were disappointed with what they perceived as Khrushchev's weakness during the Cuban Missile Crisis. Khrushchev was removed from power in 1964, and the Soviets pursued a policy of expanding their nuclear muscle to adequately confront the United States. The American response, of course, was to insist that the United States must have nuclear superiority, and the arms race continued. The close call of the Cuban Missile Crisis and the threat of nuclear annihilation did little to halt the growing power of the military-industrial complex.

Many JFK supporter, however, insist that after the missile crisis, the President was committed to reducing world tensions. They point to Kennedy's June 10, 1963 commencement address at American University. In the speech titled "A Strategy of Peace," Kennedy abandoned his harsh anticommunist rhetoric, praising the Nuclear Test Ban Treaty as the first step toward better relations with the Soviets and a more peaceful world. Some point to the speech as evidence that Kennedy would never have made the massive military commitment to South Vietnam implemented by Lyndon Johnson. Yet, the September 1963 military coup against South Vietnam's autocratic President Diem, which the Kennedy administration had approved, only brought the United States deeper into the Vietnam quagmire. Of course, we will never know for sure how Kennedy might have handled Vietnam as his life was cut short by an assassin's bullet.

JFK assassination

In November 1963, Kennedy was traveling to Texas in order to mend fences within the state's Democratic Party between conservative Governor John Connally and liberal Senator Ralph Yarborough. As the President's motorcade wound through Dealy Plaza in Dallas on November 22, 1963, shots were fired, seriously wounding Connally and killing the President who was accompanied by his wife. Kennedy was rushed to Parkland Hospital, where he was pronounced dead. The body was dispatched back to Washington on Air Force One, where Vice President Johnson took the oath of office alongside a blood-splattered Jackie Kennedy. Meanwhile, the Dallas police moved quickly to arrest Lee Harvey Oswald, who had fled the Texas Schoolbook Depository Building where the shots that killed Kennedy were supposedly fired. Oswald allegedly killed a Dallas police officer before he was apprehended in a downtown movie theater. Although Oswald maintained his innocence, Dallas authorities believed they had the assassin. On Sunday November

24, television networks were broadcasting the transfer of Oswald from the police station to the Dallas County Jail, when a man emerged from the crowd and shot the handcuffed Oswald, who was also pronounced dead at Parkland Hospital. Oswald was killed by Dallas nightclub owner Jack Ruby, who maintained that he was trying to spare Jackie Kennedy the pain of a trial for Oswald. Ruby was convicted of Oswald's murder and died of cancer in 1967 while serving a life sentence.

Concerned with conspiracy theories regarding the involvement of foreign governments such as the Soviets or Cubans, Johnson appointed a Presidential Commission headed by Supreme Court Chief Justice Earl Warren to investigate the assassination. The seven-man commission was composed of prominent political leaders, including former CIA head Allen Dulles and Michigan Congressman Gerald Ford, who later ascended to the Presidency during the Watergate crisis. After examining scores of witnesses and documents, the Warren Commission issued a nearly 900-page report whose conclusions were rather straight forward and rejected any notions of a conspiracy. Lee Harvey Oswald, working alone, fired the shots that killed Kennedy from a window in the Texas Schoolbook Depository Building with a mail order rifle he had purchased. Furthermore, Ruby had worked alone in murdering Oswald. Many Americans have never accepted the conclusions of the Warren Commission, and the shady backgrounds of both Oswald and Ruby have provided ample evidence for conspiracy theorists.

Oswald was a loner and struggled in high school, dropping out of school at age seventeen to join the Marines, where he gained training as a marksman. After his discharge from the Marines, Oswald, who considered himself a Marxist, defected to the Soviet Union, where he lived for several years and married a Russian woman with whom he fathered a child. In 1962, Oswald and his family returned to the United States, where he struggled to find steady employment, while still proclaiming himself a Marxist opposed to American treatment of Cuba. Thus, Oswald's background certainly placed him on the radar screen of the FBI, and many speculate that it was strange that Oswald was not taken into custody during Kennedy's visit to Dallas. On the other hand, this may offer evidence of incompetence rather than conspiracy. Ruby's background was also rather suspect as he was alleged to have organized crime links in his native Chicago. After moving to Dallas, Ruby operated several night clubs, including a strip club often frequented by Dallas police officers. Ruby was well known to the police, and he had little problem gaining access to the police station where he killed Oswald. Conspiracy theorists maintain that Ruby was part of some organized crime plan to murder Kennedy because the mob was angry with government prosecutions and the failure to invade Cuba, where the mob was headquartered in Havana before they were ousted by Castro.

Perhaps the best-known conspiracy theory on the Kennedy assassination was perpetuated in the popular film *JFK* (1991) by director Oliver Stone and based upon the investigations conducted by New Orleans District Attorney Jim Garrison. According to Stone and Garrison, as well as other conspiracy theorists, JFK was murdered by the CIA in conjunction with the military-industrial complex because the President was threatening to make peace with the Soviets and end the Cold War while withdrawing from Vietnam. This theory assumes that Kennedy was a threat to the defense establishment and places too much faith in the American University speech. The evidence is ambiguous at best, and at the end of his life, Kennedy was still a man of the consensus. Despite the cottage industry of conspiracy theories, the conclusions of the Warren Commission remain the official explanation of the Kennedy assassination.

LBJ and the Great Society

Upon assuming the Presidency, Lyndon Baines Johnson moved to consolidate his power, often antagonizing Robert Kennedy who emerged as a major political rival. Johnson's background was considerably different from that of the privileged Kennedy family. Born into a Texas Hill Country family of relatively modest means, Johnson graduated from Southwest Texas State Teacher's College in San Marcos, Texas, teaching Mexican American students in segregated schools. An admirer of Franklin Roosevelt and the New Deal, Johnson served as a state administrator for the National Youth Administration and was elected to Congress. In 1948, Johnson was elected to the Senate by a margin of eighty-seven votes, earning him the pejorative nickname of "landslide Lyndon." After winning re-election in 1954 by a more substantial margin, the ambitious Johnson was selected for the post of Senate Majority Leader and established a reputation for his mastery of the legislative process. During his Senate career, Johnson was generally a reliable Southern conservative, who made sure that a civil rights bill passed in 1957 contained few enforcement provisions to antagonize white Southerners. It surprised many when Kennedy tapped the Texan as his running mate in 1960, but Johnson was perceived as appealing to white Democrats in the South. As Vice President, Johnson was given few major responsibilities, and he feared that Kennedy might drop him from the ticket in 1964.

After assuming the Presidency, Johnson insisted that Congress honor Kennedy's memory by passing the slain President's legislative agenda of the Civil Rights Act and a tax cut to stimulate the economy. Former Southern colleagues such as Senator Richard Russell from Georgia were shocked by Johnson's support for civil rights legislation, and the President recognized that the bill would hurt the Democratic Party with Southern white voters, but he thought it was the right thing to do, and nationally it would improve his 1964 electoral position—and in the long run it did increase support for the Democratic Party. In the 1964 campaign, Johnson promised a reform agenda that would achieve what he called the Great Society. In that campaign, Johnson revealed that he could be a ruthless politician. Fearing further erosion of white Southern votes, he refused to support seating of the Mississippi Freedom Democratic Party in place of segregationist Mississippi

Democrats at the party's Atlantic City convention. Johnson also deserted his top aide and friend Walter Jenkins, who was arrested in a public bathroom with another man on charges of public indecency. Considering the public attitude toward homosexuality—to use the language at the time—Johnson distanced himself from Jenkins while his wife sent a message of support to Jenkins and his family. While nervous and insecure about his election, Johnson easily defeated conservative Republican Senator Barry Goldwater of Arizona, who had voted against the Civil Rights Act and whose extreme anticommunism scared many voters.

With the backing of a sympathetic Democratic Congress, Johnson succeeded in passing much of his Great Society agenda, creating many popular programs which are embedded into American life despite Republican efforts to roll back the legislation. Among the Congressional triumphs of Johnson's Great Society were federal aid to education, the Immigration and Nationality Act of 1965 that ended the quota system and encouraged a more diverse immigration policy, expanded public housing, Medicare providing government-subsidized health care for the elderly and Medicaid to address the health needs of America's poor, federal aid to transportation, and the creation of public broadcasting corporations for radio and television. Responding to violence against peaceful marchers in Selma, Alabama, Johnson pushed for passage of the 1965 Voting Rights Act, and recognizing the need to address the national legacy of racial and class inequality so well-articulated in Michael Harrington's *The Other America* (1962), Johnson declared a War on Poverty. With programs such as food stamps, the Job Corps, work-study for students, and Head Start for early childhood education, the Johnson administration emphasized education and job training as the means through which individuals might escape poverty, rather than what was perceived as a more radical approach of addressing the historical legacy of inequality through the redistribution of wealth. While the War on Poverty did succeed in reducing levels of poverty within the United States, Johnson's programs were never fully funded as money was siphoned off to the anticommunist crusade in Southeast Asia.

Fate of the liberal consensus under Kennedy and Johnson

Johnson sacrificed the Great Society on the altar of the Vietnam War as he devoted precious resources and blood to the Vietnam quagmire. The Texan was an anticommunist who feared the legacy of McCarthyism and that his liberal reform agenda would be dismissed as promoting communist principles, so Johnson believed an aggressive anticommunist foreign policy would protect the Great Society. In addition to expanding the Vietnam War, Johnson authorized an American military invasion of the Dominican Republic in April 1965 to depose the reform administration of Juan Bosch, who was perceived as an ally of Cuba's Castro, in favor of Joaquin Balaguer who established a military dictatorship similar to that of

Dominican dictator Rafael Leonidas Trujillo whom the United States had supported from the 1930s until his assassination in 1962.

The liberal anticommunist consensus which Kennedy and Johnson sought to perpetuate into the 1960s was shattered by the winds of change as exemplified by the Civil Rights Movement and Vietnam War, which are the focus of the next two chapters. War and racism revealed the hypocrisy of the consensus, convincing many young Americans to fundamentally question capitalism and pursue more communitarian solutions with the counterculture to the ills of American society. They would rediscover the historical legacy of American radicalism, but when the turbulence of the 1960s and 1970s abated, the conservative forces of corporate capitalism, preaching the mythology of American individualism, maintained control as personified in the Presidency of Ronald Reagan. During the 1960s, the liberal consensus was attacked from both the political left and right, and while much media attention in the era was devoted to hippies, radicals, and minority activists, the real story was the triumph of the right.

Further Reading:

Beschloss, Michael. *The Crisis Years: Kennedy and Khrushchev, 1960–1963*. New York: Edward Burlingame Books, 1991.

Bugliosi, Vincent. *Reclaiming History: The Assassination of President John F. Kennedy*. New York: W. W. Norton and Company, 2007.

Caro, Robert. *The Years of Lyndon Johnson: The Path to Power*. New York: Knopf, 1982.

Dallek, Robert. *Flawed Giant: Lyndon Johnson and His Times, 1961–1973*. New York: Oxford University Press, 1998.

Goodwin, Doris Kearns. *Lyndon Johnson and the American Dream*. New York: Harper & Row, 1976.

Kennedy, Robert F. *Thirteen Days: A Memoir of the Cuban Missile Crisis*. New York: W. W. Norton and Company, 1969.

McDougall, Walter. *Heavens and the Earth: A Political History of the Space Age*. New York: Basic Books, 1985.

Patterson, James T. *America's Struggle Against Poverty, 1900–1980*. Cambridge, MA: Harvard University Press, 1981.

Reeves, Thomas. *A Question of Character: A Life of John F. Kennedy*. New York: Free Press, 1991.

Schlesinger, Arthur M. Jr. *The Thousand Days: John Fitzgerald Kennedy as President*. Boston: Houghton Mifflin, 1965.

Wyden, Peter. *Bay of Pigs: The Untold Story*. New York: Simon and Schuster, 1979.

Zeitz, Joshua. *Building the Great Society: Inside Lyndon Johnson's White House*. New York: Viking, 2018.

26

The Civil Rights Movement and the Struggle for Equality

"Fannie Lou Hamer, Mississippi Freedom Democratic Party Delegate at the Democratic National Convention, Atlantic City, New Jersey." Photographer Warren K. Leffler, August 22, 1964. Prints and Photographs Division, Library of Congress. The grassroots nature of the Civil Rights Movement was evident in the activism of Mississippi sharecropper Fannie Lou Hamer. She testified at the 1964 Democratic National Convention detailing how she was beaten by Mississippi authorities for registering to vote, and Hamer also opposed the compromise that would deny the Mississippi Freedom Democratic Party representation as the official state delegation to the convention.

The premature conclusion of Reconstruction and development of the Lost Cause mythology regarding white Southern victimhood made it virtually impossible to confront and deal with the legacy of American racial slavery. Instead of assuring equal treatment of all Americans before the law and taking measures to address economic inequality wrought by the institution of slavery, the legacy of the Civil War and Reconstruction in the American South was the development of a racial apartheid society called Jim Crow, a terminology based upon a minstrel show stereotype. Although not as rigidly codified in law as Southern Jim Crow, segregation and inequality were also a daily reality for black Americans living in the more urban North. While racial inequality remained a fact of life during the Second World War, the conflict, nevertheless, helped to provide an economic foundation for the black community and organizations such as the NAACP to mount expensive legal challenges by lawyers such as Thurgood Marshall to the economic, social, political, and legal structure of racism and segregation. Black veterans returned from the war determined to assert their equal rights and do battle with a legal system and organizations such as the KKK that perpetuated hate and discrimination. They had fought against an ideology of racism embodied in Hitler's Nazi Party, and those black veterans were going to bring this conflict to the home front.

This chapter will chronicle the courage of black Americans and their white allies who in many cases sacrificed their lives in the Civil Rights Movement struggle to overthrow Jim Crow in the South. We will also examine the challenges of taking the movement for racial equality into the North where frustrations over economic inequality exploded in urban uprisings in the late 1960s. The African American Civil Rights Movement provided a model and encouraged other groups such as women, Hispanics, Natives, and the LGBTQ community to fight for their rights and inclusion within the promise of American life. This chapter will concentrate upon the black struggle for equality in the interests of time and space, but the stories of these other crusaders for justice deserve to be included in the rich fabric of American life.

De jure and *de facto* segregation

Before examining the chronology of the Civil Rights Movement, it is worth pointing out some of the successes as well as failures of this struggle. In many ways this will be a triumphant story in which Americans heroically rose up and abolished Jim Crow in the South and fought for equal rights throughout the nation. The Civil Rights Movement may take credit for abolishing *de jure* segregation based upon law, and this achievement brought significant change to American life. Middle-class blacks—and this pattern was similar for middle-class Hispanics and other minorities—were able to move out of the inner city and integrate into the suburbs with many professional and legal obstacles to their rise removed. This transformation, however, made the economic infrastructure of America's racially segregated inner cities even poorer as affluent blacks fled to the suburbs. It is ironic that in some ways the Civil Rights Movement unintentionally furthered the racial and economic divide.

We remain a racially segregated society in our schools and daily lives due to *de facto* segregation, a racial apartheid based upon economics and housing patterns. Some conservatives like to say this situation is simply a matter of choice, but the reality of the racial economic divide in America provides little proof for this assertion. The Kerner Commission in 1968 suggested that the United States would continue to suffer racial conflict if this economic discrepancy was not addressed. Policies of affirmative action in the workplace along with school admissions and busing to pursue integration of the public schools in the 1960s and early 1970s led to charges of reverse discrimination against whites, and some whites abandoned their black allies. In the 1980s, the Reagan administration retreated from policies to address the racial economic divide, refusing to confront the reality that dealing with this issue and addressing the legacies of slavery and segregation will require a redistribution of resources and incomes that many white Americans will resist. Some observers believed that the election of Barack Obama heralded a post racial America, but the refusal of some Americans to accept the legitimacy of Obama's Presidency by claiming that he was born outside of the United States demonstrates the false optimism of this belief. The inflammatory racial rhetoric of President Donald Trump has fanned the flames of racial discord as hate crimes against blacks, Jews, Hispanics, Natives, Asians, Muslims, Sikhs, Hindus, and members of the LGBTQ community have increased. The economic racial gap continues to grow, and as James Baldwin suggested "the fire next time" may challenge the very fabric of our society. While there is much to celebrate when examining the history of the Civil Rights Movement, there is much that needs to be done to bring about Jefferson's vision of a society in which all Americans are born and created equal.

Jackie Robinson

In attempting to assign a date for the beginning of the Civil Rights Movement, many historians point to the landmark 1954 Supreme Court decision *Brown v. Board of Education*. But perhaps we might look back a few years to 1947 when Jackie Robinson joined the Brooklyn Dodgers and integrated Major League Baseball

(MLB). The black community had enjoyed entertainment and sport heroes such as heavyweight boxing champion Joe Louis, who thrilled black and white audiences with his exploits during the 1930s and 1940s. The affable Louis, however, refused to challenge American racism. Robinson was more outspoken. After playing college athletics at UCLA, Robinson joined the Army during the Second World War and survived a court martial for challenging military segregationist policies. Recruited by Brooklyn executive Branch Rickey to integrate the lily-white institution of MLB—which was the national pastime until the rise of professional football in the 1960s—Robinson was told that he could not fight back against racial insults. The athlete swallowed his pride and took out his frustrations on the playing field where he was acknowledged as one of the sport's fiercest competitors. Ricky finally allowed Robinson to fight back, and he became an outspoken critic of racism in baseball and American society, earning induction into the Baseball Hall of Fame in Cooperstown, New York. MLB has long proclaimed Robinson as evidence of the sport's egalitarianism, but as is often the case, reality was a little more complicated. While other black players were added to MLB rosters following Robinson, racial progress in the sport was slow. When Robinson retired after the 1956 season, the Detroit Tigers and Boston Red Sox maintained they could not find a black athlete of MLB caliber. Also, Robinson was used to denounce black activist and entertainer Paul Robeson for his assertion that due to their second-class citizenship black Americans would not support the United States in a conflict with the Soviet Union. Appearing before HUAC, Robinson proclaimed the loyalty of black Americans and dismissed the charges made by Robeson, although the ballplayer later complained that he felt used by MLB.

Brown v. Board

While Robinson was an important symbol for black Americans, the Brown decision directly impacted far more Americans. In the Brown decision, involving public schools in Topeka, Kansas and not the South, Chief Justice Earl Warren helped to craft a unanimous opinion that overturned the court's 1896 *Plessy v. Ferguson* decision upholding the doctrine of "separate but equal." The Plessy decision dealt with railroad cars in Louisiana, with the court ruling that racial segregation and Jim Crow were perfectly Constitutional as long as the racially separate facilities were equal. Of course, neither segregated Southern transportation nor educational facilities were equal, but the separate but equal doctrine was the law of the land from 1896 to 1954. In the Brown case, expert witnesses such as psychologists Kenneth and Mamie Phipps Clark provided evidence regarding the negative impact of segregation upon black school children, leading the court to conclude that "segregation is inherently unequal." Thurgood Marshall, the chief attorney for the NAACP who was later appointed to the court in 1967, believed that the ruling in Brown should be interpreted as toppling the entire structure of Jim Crow.

Murder of Emmett Till

The murder of young Emmett Till in Mississippi provided the nation with a horrid example of the racial hate and violence underlying Jim Crow and the opposition to school integration. Till was a fourteen-year old black youth from Chicago visiting relatives on the Mississippi Delta in August 1955. He was accused of violating Southern sexual norms by flirting with or whistling at an attractive young white woman, Carolyn Bryant. Several days later Bryant's husband and his half-brother abducted Till, and his badly beaten and mutilated body was found thrown into the Tallahatchie River. Roy Bryant and J. W. Milam were arrested for murder, but they were quickly acquitted by an all-white Mississippi jury. Protected by the Constitution's denial of double jeopardy, the killers bragged of their deed in a national periodical. Meanwhile, Till's mother insisted her son's funeral include an open casket so that everyone could see Emmett's battered face and understand the brutality and hatred of American racism. She sought to encourage the fight for racial justice, and Emmett Till was one of the most publicized martyrs of a bloody civil rights struggle.

Resistance to the Brown decision and Central High in Little Rock

Against the background of Till's murder, enforcing the Brown decision became a major issue as many Southern politicians vowed to resist the court. The Brown decision provided little guidance on how to implement school integration and how the Brown precedent might be applied to other segregated facilities and institutions. In 1955, the court attempted to clarify its position by asserting that the Brown decision be implemented in the schools "with all deliberate speed." There was little speed in the process, and the forces of resistance seemed far more deliberate than the federal government supporting integration of Southern public education. The state of Virginia temporarily closed the public schools rather than integrate, while throughout the South private white academies were created, often leaving the public schools with a primarily black student population. Angry white demonstrators blocked school entrances and proclaimed that integration would lead to miscegenation in states that already outlawed interracial marriage—which was not overturned until the Supreme Court's 1967 *Loving v. Virginia* decision. Those supporting integration were the targets of Klan violence as the KKK enjoyed a resurgence in the South. The Brown decision also led to the formation of White Citizens Councils in which local business elites urged resistance to integration. While supposedly representing upper-and-middle-class Southern whites and publicly urging economic weapons such as boycotts rather than violence, the White Citizens Councils often cooperated with the Klan with whom they shared similar racist sentiments. Resistance to integration also encouraged Southern local and state governments to build public monuments to the Confederacy, suggesting that those fighting against racial integration were continuing the struggle for the Lost Cause. These were monuments to racism rather than simply a celebration of Southern culture and history.

The best-known confrontation over enforcing the Brown decision occurred in Little Rock, Arkansas. After a court order for Central High to accept nine black students, white mobs blocked entrance to the school, and Governor Orville Faubus employed the Arkansas National Guard to turn the students away. The nation was shocked by the images of hatred directed toward the young black students. Locals also recognized that television coverage of the Little Rock crisis was discrediting the segregationist cause and making them look bad before a national audience. Considerable violence, accordingly, was directed against reporters and news organizations, but a free press played an essential role in documenting events in Little Rock and throughout the civil rights struggle. When President Eisenhower was unable to convince Faubus that he should abandon his opposition to the Brown decision, the President reluctantly ordered the Army's 101st Airborne Division, absent black troopers who might antagonize local whites, to Little Rock and nationalized the Arkansas National Guard, removing these units from the Governor's control. The troops escorted the students to school and employed bayonets to make a path for the Little Rock Nine through angry white crowds. The black students were also escorted to classes where soldiers stood guard. The female members of the Little Rock Nine, however, suffered harassment and physical attack in the bathrooms as the male soldiers were forbidden to enter the school's restroom facilities for women. The deployment was maintained for the school year, and not all of the Little Rock Nine were able to cope with the harassment, but in 1955 Ernest Green became the first black graduate of Little Rock's Central High.

Montgomery Bus Boycott

While the battles for school integration raged in the South, civil rights leaders also attempted to integrate other facilities such as public transportation. In Montgomery, Alabama, black customers made up 75 percent of business for the city's bus company. But the city hired no black drivers and enforced rigid segregationist ordinances that blacks must sit at the back of the bus and surrender their seats if a white patron was standing. On December 1, 1955, seamstress Rosa Parks refused to surrender her seat to a white man. She was arrested and fined for her actions, but Parks was determined to appeal her arrest and challenge the city's segregationist ordinances. Parks was more than simply a seamstress who refused to surrender her seat after working all day. An official in the local NAACP, Parks had received training in civil rights resistance, and the cause of the well-respected young woman was embraced by local NAACP President E. D. Nixon and a young minister new to Montgomery, Martin Luther King Jr. King was elected President of the Montgomery Improvement Association (MIA) and used his oratorical and organizational skills to implement a black boycott of the bus system until the bus company treated its black customers with respect and hired black drivers.

The Montgomery Bus Boycott marked the emergence of King as a civil rights leader. He was born January 15, 1929 in Atlanta, Georgia, where his father was an influential minister and the family enjoyed a relatively affluent lifestyle. Growing up in Atlanta's black community, King described a boyhood relatively free from incidents of racial discrimination. He graduated from Morehouse College in Atlanta, then moved north to pursue a career in the ministry, graduating from Crozer Theological Seminary in Chester, Pennsylvania and earning a doctorate from Boston University. He married Coretta Scott in 1953 and planned on conducting his ministry in the North, where he and his family could avoid the rigid segregation of the South. After considerable prayer, King concluded that God's plan was for him to return to his native region, and in 1954 he accepted a position at the Dexter Avenue Baptist Church in Montgomery. Assuming leadership of the Montgomery Bus Boycott, King began his civil rights career that would alter the state of race relations in America, seemingly embodying the background and characteristics that W. E. B. Du Bois envisioned for the "talented tenth" leadership of the black community.

And the bus boycott would certainly test King's leadership skills. The city of Montgomery did not believe that the black community could maintain the boycott which lasted a little over one year. Besides urging his constituents to stay the course, King and the MIA organized private rides so that workers could reach their jobs as most black residents of Montgomery did not own automobiles. Many black domestics walked miles across town to their work in the more affluent white sections of Montgomery. Concerned that the "help" was sometimes arriving late for their domestic duties, some white women began to drive their maids and housekeepers to and from work, often much to the chagrin of their husbands. Seeking to destroy the boycott, King was arrested, and his home firebombed, but he was undeterred, and the boycott persisted. Losing money and suffering defeat in the U.S. District Court ruling of *Browder v. Gayle* (1956) which was upheld by the Supreme Court, the city of Montgomery caved and agreed to abandon its segregationist bus policies. A great victory was won, and King emerged as a national civil rights leader, but angry whites in Montgomery perpetuated a legacy of violence against local blacks in the wake of the victory.

Expansion of civil rights protest and organization

Spurred by the example of Montgomery, civil rights organizations began to stage sit-ins and boycotts to challenge segregationist policies. In Greensboro, North Carolina, four black students from North Carolina Agricultural and Technological State University entered the local Woolworth department store, purchased some items, and then sat down at the store's segregated lunch counter. They were refused service, but they returned the next day with several other students, occupying the seats at the lunch counter and halting service. As the number of protesters increased in the ensuing days and impacted the chain's business, Woolworth opened lunch counter service to black customers. The successful 1960 Greensboro sit-in action encouraged similar activities throughout the South, including Nashville and Richmond. While demonstrating the power of passive resistance, civil rights activists sitting-in at lunch counters were often met with violence and arrests. When taken into custody, the activists would usually put up no resistance and go limp, forcing the police to carry them out of department stores, offering a degree of chaos that was certainly not good for business. While many department stores in the urban South opened their lunch counters to black patrons, others closed their dining facilities rather than accept integration.

The growth of civil disobedience and boycotts against Jim Crow were organized by black-dominated civil rights groups such as the NAACP, Urban League, Congress of Racial Equality (CORE), Southern Christian Leadership Conference (SCLC), and the Student Non-violent Coordinating Committee (SNCC). The nation's oldest and best-funded civil rights organization was the NAACP, which mounted legal challenges to segregation that culminated in the landmark Brown decision. Under the leadership of Whitney Young, the Urban League with a primarily middle-class constituency emphasized economic improvement for the black community. Formed in 1942, CORE took an activist role in the 1960s Civil Rights Movement under the leadership of James Farmer. CORE championed direct action to confront segregation of interstate bus facilities. Farmer antagonized some more pacifistic elements in the movement by embracing the Deacons for Defense and Justice from Louisiana, who provided armed defense for black nationalists as well as CORE organizers. The SCLC was led by King and his lieutenant Reverend Ralph Abernathy, reflecting the importance of Christianity and black churches within the black community going back to the days of slavery. Black churches in the South were used as organization centers and meeting places for the Civil Rights Movement, but this made them the targets for bombings and arson from the KKK. The SCLC modeled the philosophy outlined in King's 1963 *Letter from Birmingham Jail*, borrowing from Jesus's message of love and the civil disobedience of Gandhi and Thoreau, while asserting that it was the duty of Americans who believed in justice and the higher law to confront and disobey unjust laws such as segregation based upon racism and prejudice. It was one's Christian obligation and moral responsibility to peacefully resist unjust laws. An injustice to one is an injustice to all, and King was proud to be in jail while fighting for justice. While King displayed considerable courage in confronting racial hatred and discrimination, many young blacks grew increasingly restive with what they often perceived as his passive turn the other cheek philosophy of nonviolence. Initially organized by Ella Baker at Shaw University in Raleigh, North Carolina following the Greensboro sit-ins in 1960, SNCC included both white and black students who directly challenged Jim Crow by registering black voters and providing freedom schools, teaching the role of abolitionists and indigenous American radicals in combatting slavery and racism. Sometimes referred to as the new abolitionists, SNCC organizers were often the targets of violence by the Klan, and the organization was increasingly radicalized during the late 1960s under the leadership of Stokely Carmichael and H. Rap Brown, opposing the Vietnam War, expelling whites from the organization, and embracing the concept of black power. While these civil rights organizations were often denounced as un-American and outside agitators under the influence of the Communist Party, the courageous men and women of the Civil Rights Movement were much in the tradition of indigenous American radicalism and protest that sought to achieve the promises of equality proclaimed in the nation's founding principles and documents.

Freedom Riders

The growing civil rights agitation put pressure on traditional politicians such as John Kennedy, whose narrow election in 1960 was based upon black votes as well as white Southerners who for the time being continued to vote Democratic. Kennedy was generally supportive of racial justice, but he was not willing to associate his administration with civil rights demonstrators that might antagonize his re-election. Therefore, King and other civil rights leaders believed that it was their responsibility to seize the initiative and force the President to put the federal government behind the struggle for equal rights. The Freedom Riders were efforts, organized primarily by CORE and SNCC, to influence the Kennedy administration to implement court orders desegregating interstate transportation, including bus station facilities such as water fountains and restrooms. In the late spring and early summer of 1961, both black and white civil rights activists boarded interstate buses headed into the South, where they were met by angry white mobs in many cities such as Montgomery and Birmingham, Alabama. When the buses arrived, the police withdrew and allowed whites armed with baseball bats to attack the Freedom Riders when they attempted to disembark from the busses and challenge the segregated facilities. After the Freedom Riders were severely beaten, local police would often return to the scene and arrest the activists for disturbing the peace. In Anniston, Alabama, a mob led by the local KKK firebombed a Greyhound bus, and the occupants were fortunate to escape with their lives. The mob violence was filmed by reporters, and the disturbing images again shocked the nation, leading to the beatings of reporters and photographers. Among the beaten was Justice Department representative and observer John Seigenthaler, a friend of Attorney General Robert Kennedy. The Kennedy administration had initially sought to dissuade the Freedom Riders, fearing they would provoke white Southerners. Confronted by the extreme brutality of white mobs, and especially the beating of his friend and departmental representative, Attorney General Kennedy ordered federal marshals to provide security for the Freedom Riders, and the Interstate Commerce Commission implemented the court orders desegregating the interstate commerce facilities at bus stations.

James Meredith and the University of Mississippi

The brave men and women who risked their lives as Freedom Riders pushed the Kennedy administration to act, as did black military veteran James Meredith, when he entered the University of Mississippi in the fall of 1962. Mississippi Governor Ross Barnett resisted the integration of the university, but the Kennedy administration believed that it had worked out an agreement with the Governor that would avoid violence. Following a football game on September 30, a mob attacked Meredith and the federal marshals guarding the student. Under assault at a university dormitory, the marshals feared for their safety and believed Meredith's life was in danger. They appealed to the President to rescue them, and on October 1, 1962, Kennedy dispatched federal troops onto the campus in Oxford, Mississippi, restoring order after two people were killed and providing security for Meredith, who two years later became the first black to graduate from the University of Mississippi. Seeking to avoid further violence, in June 1963, the Kennedy administration allowed Alabama Governor George C. Wallace to symbolically stand at the "schoolhouse door" at the University of Alabama and make a speech before withdrawing before the threat of federal troops and allowing blacks students to enter the state university. In his speech, Wallace proclaimed his belief in "segregation now, segregation tomorrow, and segregation forever," and the Alabama Governor was provided with a national forum which he employed to become a thorn in the side of the Kennedy and Johnson administrations.

March on Washington

Both John and Robert Kennedy lobbied Martin Luther King Jr. to cancel his proposed August 28, 1963 March on Washington for Jobs and Freedom, believing that the anticipated large crowd and gathering would lead to violence and rioting that would discredit the Civil Rights Movement as well as cost the Kennedy administration support among white Southerners. The Kennedys also insisted that SNCC leader John L. Lewis, now a respected member of Congress, would have to tone down his comments before he would be allowed to speak to the crowd. The march brought approximately 200,000 Americans to the Washington Mall, where they gathered peacefully listening to music and speeches that encouraged the nation to achieve its mission of political equality and economic opportunity for all its citizens. The activities were well organized by veteran civil rights leaders A. Philip Randolph and King's associate Bayard Rustin—whose role in the movement was reduced after he was outed as a gay man. The large crowd was also inspired by the oratory of King in which the minister evoked his dream of an America in which all children would be judged by the content of their character rather than the color of their skin—it is a dream which we are still struggling to attain.

Murder of Medgar Evers and a church bombing in Birmingham

While the March on Washington again reiterated the Civil Rights Movement's commitment to nonviolence and even encouraged President Kennedy to endorse a comprehensive civil rights bill, the movement continued to meet with the violence that had characterized the opposition to the Freedom Riders. On June 12, 1963, Medgar Evers, Mississippi Field Secretary of the NAACP and a World War II veteran dedicated to taking the fight against racism to the home front, was murdered in the driveway of his home. His assassin was a white supremacist who was finally convicted of the murder in 1994. Meanwhile, King and the SCLC challenged Jim Crow in Birmingham, Alabama, often described as the most segregated city in the United States. As Commissioner of Public Safety for the city, Bull Connor employed police dogs, beatings, and fire hoses to attack civil rights demonstrators, many of them children. The violence culminated in the bombing of the 16th Street Baptist Church from which much of King's campaign was organized. The bombing killed four young black girls, Addie Mae Collins, Cynthia Wesley, Carole Robertson, and Carol Denise McNair, who were attending a Sunday school class. The FBI attributed the bombing to four local Klansman, but prejudice and intimidation of witnesses limited convictions until 1977 and later.

Freedom Summer and passage of the 1964 Civil Rights Act

The murder of the four young girls did increase support for Kennedy's civil rights bill, but the President was unable to guide the legislation through Congress before his own murder in November 1963. After assuming the Presidency in wake of Kennedy's assassination, Lyndon Johnson sought to honor the slain President's memory by enacting civil rights legislation. Impetus for passage was also provided by the violent reaction in Mississippi to the voter registration efforts of SNCC organizers. In the Freedom Summer of 1964, white and black college students volunteered to spend the summer living with black families in the Mississippi Delta, where they would teach freedom schools for black children and help register black voters. SNCC field secretary Bob Moses warned participants they would face a violent response, a fact that was borne out. On June 21, civil rights activists James Chaney, a black from Mississippi, and Andrew Goodman and Michael Schwerner, whites of Jewish ancestry from New York, disappeared after they were released from jail for a traffic infraction near Philadelphia, Mississippi. Local authorities conspired with the Klan to murder the young men. The situation was initially treated as a missing persons case, but the bodies of the civil rights activists were eventually discovered buried within an earthen dam. Despite the attention given to the case, heightened by the murder of two young white men, the state of Mississippi refused to move forward with murder indictments, but the federal government was able to avoid state courts and secure seven convictions for violation of the victims' civil rights in federal courts. In 2005, one conspirator was finally convicted of manslaughter in the case.

The disappearance and murders of Chaney, Goodman, and Schwerner did provide further momentum for passage of the Civil Rights Act of 1964, which expanded civil rights protections by employing the commerce power to ban discrimination in education, employment, and accommodations based upon race, color, religion, sex, or national origin. Although many Republicans, including Arizona Senator Barry Goldwater, who was the Republican Presidential nominee in 1964, voted against the bill, arguing that it was un-Constitutional, Republican Senate Minority Leader Everett Dirksen helped secure passage of the bill. Johnson recognized that the bill would antagonize many Southern whites, remarking that the Democrats had lost the South for a generation. The President was prophetic, but overly optimistic with his time frame. Fifty years after the Civil Rights Act, Republican domination of the region has only intensified. In fact, many civil rights leaders were suspicious of Johnson's support for the bill as during his tenure as the Democratic Senate Majority Leader, he was not particularly friendly to civil rights legislation. The President did appear to have sincerely changed his mind on issues of race and believed that in the long term embracing civil rights would benefit the Democratic Party. However, Johnson's handling of the Mississippi Freedom Democratic Party (MFDP) at the 1964 Democratic National Convention in Atlantic City raised questions about the President's commitment. Excluded from participating in the Mississippi Democratic Party, black residents, who constituted 40 percent of the state's population, worked with SNCC organizers to form the MFDP and seek recognition by the national party as the state's legitimate delegation at the Democratic National Convention. Fearing that the seating of the MFDP would further antagonize white Southern Democrats and endanger his electoral prospects, Johnson dispatched Senator Hubert Humphrey to organize a compromise that helped secure the Minnesota Senator a spot on the Democratic ticket as Johnson's running mate. The President then pre-empted the powerful testimony of MDFP delegate and sharecropper Fannie Lou Hamer, testifying how she was beaten by Mississippi authorities for simply registering to vote, to announce a compromise in which the MFDP would be awarded two seats with the regular Democratic and all-white delegation. The MFDP refused to accept the compromise, increasing the distrust of many younger SNCC members with Johnson and the civil rights establishment.

"Bloody Sunday" and the 1965 Voting Rights Act

Johnson easily secured his 1964 victory over Goldwater, but activists were determined to place pressure on the President to secure passage of a voting rights bill. In 1965, King and the SCLC joined a SNCC effort to register black voters in Selma, Alabama, where they encountered fierce opposition from Sheriff Jim Clark. To draw attention to the struggle, King led a fifty-mile march from Selma to the state capital in Montgomery. On what became known as "Bloody Sunday," nonviolent marchers were brutally attacked on March 7, 1965 as they attempted to cross the Edward Pettis Bridge. State troopers on foot and horseback, looking like Russian Cossacks, savagely beat the marching men and women, including SNCC activist John Lewis. Joined by supporters from around the nation—which included Unitarian minister James Reed from Boston who was murdered by a mob—and protected by federal troops, the march was completed on March 24 and 25, providing significant impetus to passage of the 1965 Voting Rights Act.

A landmark piece of legislation, the Voting Rights Act provided federal protection for registration and voting, outlawing discriminatory practices such as literacy tests. The law also asserted that areas, primarily in the South, which had an established historical record of promoting disenfranchisement would be required to seek approval from the Attorney General before implementing changes in voting laws and procedures. In *Shelby County v. Holder* (2013), the Supreme Court struck down these provisions to cover areas of historical discrimination as the court determined they were no longer needed. Since that decision, numerous Southern state legislatures have passed bill suppressing the black vote, offering evidence that the court's decision was premature. For some Americans, passage of the 1964 Civil Rights Act and 1965 Voting Rights Act abolished *de jure* segregation and provided the equality before the law called for in the Fourteenth Amendment. Therefore, the Civil Rights Movement had achieved its goals.

War on Poverty

To his credit, Johnson recognized that the legacy of economic inequality and *de facto* segregation wrought by slavery and Jim Crow needed to be addressed. The President called for the implementation of a Great Society, providing economic security and freedom of opportunity. Johnson gained Congressional approval of federal aid to education, expanded health care in Medicare for the elderly and Medicaid for the poor, and improvements in public housing and transportation. Johnson also enlisted the country in a war on poverty aimed at rural areas such as Appalachia as well as the inner city. Rather than providing for a redistribution of income, the antipoverty programs of the Johnson administration embraced traditional American perceptions of the self-made man and woman by emphasizing education and job training programs such as the Job Corps. The War on Poverty attempted to provide a degree of community control over projects which often led to conflicts between government bureaucrats and community activists. While conservatives objected to the spending of poverty programs, the efforts of the Johnson administration did reduce poverty rates. One of the major problems for the War on Poverty was that most programs were not fully funded for enough time to achieve their goals as Johnson increasingly focused resources on the growing quagmire in Vietnam.

Meanwhile, the Johnson administration was the victim of rising expectations as many black Americans, especially those living in the urban North, perceived little change in their daily lives despite the passage of landmark civil rights legislation. Schools and housing remained inadequate, while jobs in the inner city were scarce, and many black Americans lacked the transportation facilities to reach jobs located outside of city centers. This growing frustration, especially among young blacks, resonated with urban unrest and calls for black power.

Black power, Malcolm X, and the Black Panther Party

The term black power was supposedly coined by charismatic SNCC leader Stokely Carmichael (later known as Kwame Ture) in Greenwood, Mississippi after James Meredith was shot and wounded during his 1966 March Against Fear across the state of Mississippi. Carmichael and other civil rights activists finished the march for Meredith, but more established leaders such as King were uncomfortable with the phrase, believing that it might antagonize white allies. Indeed, many whites were afraid of the black power slogan and the accompanying symbol of a clinched and uplifted black fist. While many whites perceived militancy and violence, Carmichael saw black power as providing a sense of unity and pride. "Say it loud, black and proud" may have scared some whites, but for a community in which some historically consumed products to make one's appearance more white, black pride and power were an essential foundation for empowerment. Black power was also a call for black Americans to assume both political and economic direction over their lives.

Nevertheless, many white Americans viewed black power as furthering racial separation rather than integration and fostering reverse racism. Malcolm X was a voice for black pride and separatism whose uncompromising manner frightened many whites, suggesting development of the black community so that eventually there could be an integration of equals rather than blacks having to be accepted into a white America. Born Malcolm Little, the black leader grew up in a broken home following the murder of his father who was a follower of Marcus Garvey. He fell into a life of crime, but while serving time in prison, Malcolm converted to the Nation of Islam. Following his release from prison, Malcolm became a powerful minister for the faith and disciple of Elijah Muhammad, indicting white America for its racism and recruiting new members to the cause such as heavyweight champion Cassius Clay who became Muhammad Ali. Malcolm eventually broke with his mentor, whom he accused of moral and financial corruption. After a pilgrimage to Mecca, Malcolm denounced racism and formed the Organization of African Unity, continuing to advocate for black pride and self-defense. On February 21, 1965, Malcolm was assassinated in front of his family by Nation of Islam members who were assumed to be carrying out the orders of Elijah Muhammad. One wonders in what directions Malcolm might have moved if his life and voice were not cut short and silenced. The many transformations in Malcolm's brief life are well chronicled in his captivating autobiography.

Whites were also terrified by the Black Panthers with their guns, revolutionary rhetoric, and black berets and jackets. The Black Panther Party (BPP) was founded in October 1966 by Huey Newton and Bobby Seale to protest police brutality in Oakland, California. Standing up to the police and carrying their guns into the California state house earned the Panthers respect within the black community. The BPP was in the tradition of American radicalism, denouncing the capitalist exploitation of black Americans and criticizing American imperialism. While their rhetoric was often revolutionary, the BPP established a strong foothold in the black community, sponsoring breakfast programs for school children and health clinics to address such concerns as sickle cell anemia. As the national membership of the BPP grew during the late 1960s, J. Edgar Hoover described the organization as the greatest internal threat to the security of the United States. Under the direction of Hoover, the government of the United States launched a systematic campaign of intimidation, disinformation, surveillance, and murder against the Panthers. In Chicago, Panther leader Fred Hampton was murdered in his bed during a police raid, while Panther leaders Newton, Seale, and Eldridge Cleaver argued amongst themselves in a factionalism encouraged by FBI spies and informants. The BPP membership deteriorated throughout the 1970s and was essentially defunct by 1980.

Watts and urban uprisings

While the BPP represented an organized challenge to the white establishment, other black uprisings, or riots as they were termed in the mainstream media, were more spontaneous and demonstrated the frustration of black communities with unemployment and police surveillance. The black neighborhood of Watts in Los Angeles exploded from August 11-16, 1965, sparked by the arrest of a black motorist. In addition to concerns with police harassment, the Watts community suffered from overcrowding, a problem exacerbated by voter approval of Proposition 14 which overturned California's fair housing law and was sponsored by the state real estate industry. In six day of unrest, thirty-four people were killed, and an estimated $40 million worth of property destroyed, while the California National Guard was deployed to bring an end to the uprising. Many whites could simply not comprehend why black rioters were burning down their own neighborhoods, failing to understand the frustrations over absentee landlords and business owners from outside the neighborhood taking money away from the community and protected by the police force. Johnson feared that Watts would produce a white backlash against his Great Society legislation, making blacks appear ungrateful for the reform programs and legislation.

Black urban impatience increased in the 1960s as the promises of the Civil Rights Movement and Great Society produced little immediate change in their lives, and young black men were increasingly drafted into the Vietnam War. The "long hot summer" of 1967 witnessed almost 160 racial uprisings in urban America, with Newark and Detroit being two of the deadliest. By 1967, Newark, New Jersey was predominantly a black city, while much of the city's white population and industrial base had retreated to the suburbs, leaving the core city with few jobs and resources. Meanwhile, the city's police force and political structure remained predominantly white, with urban renewal projects increasing residential overcrowding. During the summer evenings of 1967, residents were often in the streets, driven outside by the heat as most residences lacked air conditioning. On the evening of July 12, the city began to explode after police arrested and beat a black taxi driver. Newark erupted in violence that continued until July 17. As police and firefighters were reported being fired upon by snipers, troops were dispatched to the city, and some residents were killed in their apartments, suspected of being snipers. After days of fighting, order was restored with twenty-six dead and millions lost in property damage. Conditions in Detroit were similar, and racial discrimination that led to violence in 1943 had only grown worse. Black unemployment was double that of whites as jobs and the white population fled the city for the suburbs, where discriminatory lending practices and restricted covenants barred black home ownership. The Detroit rebellion began on July 23 when the predominantly white police force raided a blind pig, the local term for unlicensed after-hours bars, where about fifty residents were celebrating the return of two soldiers from Vietnam. The community rebelled against these mass arrests, and Detroit was consumed by looting and rioting. Like Newark, reports of snipers brought in both National Guard and Army units, who again fixated upon apartments which they suspected to be the source of hostile snipers, leading to the death of a four-year old girl. In five days of fighting, forty-three people died, thirty-three of whom were black and shot by police and soldiers dispatched to quell the uprising. The death total also included three young black men killed by the police at the Algiers Motel under suspicious circumstances.

Assassination of Martin Luther King Jr.

Martin Luther King recognized that the growing urban violence reflected anger and frustration over the nation's racial economic inequality, and the minister concentrated his efforts to denounce the economic divide. The civil rights leader also believed that the Vietnam War was morally wrong and sapping resources that could be employed to address poverty in the United States. The decision to speak out against the war took courage as it induced a break with President Johnson, while the FBI continued to harass the minister. J. Edgar Hoover believed that the Civil Rights Movement was a conspiracy financed by the Soviet Union to discredit the United States in the ideological Cold War, and he intimidated the Kennedy brothers—threatening to expose the President's sexual infidelities—into authorizing wire taps and surveillance of King. The FBI investigation failed to uncover any evidence of communist activities by King and his associates; however, Hoover discovered that King had a weakness. The civil rights leader was found to sometimes patronize prostitutes, and Hoover threatened to provide evidence of these infidelities to his wife, Coretta Scott King, if the minister did not abandon his political efforts on behalf of the Civil Rights Movement.

The courageous King, despite personal pain and exposure, refused to retreat from the struggle, expanding his efforts to deal with difficult economic issues by demonstrating for fair housing in Chicago. As he was preparing his Poor People's Campaign to march on Washington and demand a redistribution of resources to address poverty, in the spring of 1968 King was in Memphis, Tennessee supporting a strike by sanitation workers, most of whom were black. On April 4, 1968, King was on the balcony of his Lorraine Motel room speaking to his lieutenants, such as Jesse Jackson, when he was shot by a sniper. King was brought to a Memphis hospital where he was pronounced dead. A manhunt was launched for the white gunman, a loner by the name of James Earl Ray, who evidently fired at King from a boarding house across the street from the Lorraine Motel—which has today been converted to a civil rights museum. Ray was on the run for almost two months before being apprehended in London's Heathrow Airport and extradited to the United States, where he pleaded guilty to the assassination and was sentenced to life in prison and died in 1998. The assassin supposedly worked alone, but the fact that Ray, who had no visible means of financial support, was able to lead law enforcement on a two-month international search has provided considerable fodder for conspiracy theories, including FBI involvement in the murder. Ray's later efforts to recant his confession and seek a jury trial were dismissed, but the King family has expressed reservations about the conclusion regarding Ray working alone.

Despite cries for calm from the King family, President Johnson, New York Senator Robert Kennedy, and civil rights leaders such as Roy Wilkins of the NAACP, in the immediate aftermath of the assassination over 100 American cities erupted in frustration and anger that the nonviolent spokesman for racial equality was gunned down at age thirty-nine. The insurrections led to over forty deaths and millions of dollars in damage as again the Army and National Guard were dispatched to bring order to the streets of America at the same time that the United States was fighting a bloody war in Vietnam and recovering from the Tet Offensive. Violence and looting were especially severe in Washington DC, where some blamed Stokely Carmichael for encouraging looting as fires raged within blocks of the White House, where troops established machinegun positions to guard against looters. On April 20, the Washington Senators opened the baseball season with free tickets provided to National Guardsmen bivouacked in the DC Stadium. The guardsmen watched the game in uniform and were told that if they were needed to quell further disturbances, they would be notified over the public address system. In this surreal atmosphere, the United States buried its greatest advocate of nonviolence.

Kerner Commission

Seeking to understand the cause of urban unrest throughout the country, Johnson appointed a Presidential Commission headed by Illinois Governor Otto Kerner. The Kerner Commission rejected Hoover's assertion that the insurrections were the product of communist agitation; instead, the Commission concluded that the urban unrest of the 1960s was due to the racial economic divide, and if issues of housing and jobs were not addressed, Americans could expect continued periodic racial conflict in the nation's cities. Despite the dire warnings of the Commission's report, the Johnson administration eschewed redistribution of income and resources, pursuing programs of affirmative action, later rejected by the Nixon administration, and busing plans for school integration that caused considerable racial backlash in Northern cities such as Boston. The Civil Rights Movement assault upon Jim Crow and *de jure* segregation enjoyed considerable success, but the struggle against *de facto* segregation and economic inequality has proven more elusive in a capitalist America. Black consciousness and pride were essential products of the movement which continues today. In the 2018 elections, voter suppression resulted in narrow defeats for black gubernatorial candidates in Florida and Georgia, but sixty years earlier such candidates would never have been nominated and might have been killed. The struggle to fully implement the ideas of the Declaration and Fourteenth

Amendment for black Americans continues. In addition, the black Civil Rights Movement served as an inspiration for other oppressed groups.

Chicano Civil Rights Movement

The term Chicano had long been considered a derogatory term among Hispanics, but in the 1960s many young Latino/as embraced the word for displaying a new sense of pride and change beyond the reforms of traditional Hispanic organizations such as the G.I. Forum and The League of United Latin American Citizens (LULAC). In New Mexico, Reis Lopez Tijerina, a former evangelical minister, founded *La Alianza* to fight for the restoration of Spanish land grant claims to their original owners as called for by the Treaty of Guadalupe Hidalgo (1848). The land grant movement brought Tijerina into conflict with the federal government, who owned vast amounts of New Mexico forest land. After several of his followers were arrested for trespassing on national forest land, Tijerina on June 5, 1967 led an armed raid on the Rio Arriba Courthouse in Tierra Amarilla, New Mexico to free the prisoners and arrest the local district attorney, who was not present at the courthouse as it turned out. The raid resulted in a shootout, with Tijerina and his followers retreating into the nearby mountains where they were pursued by the military and state police. Tijerina eventually surrendered to authorities and served a lengthy prison term. His insurrection captured the imagination of many Chicanos who perceived Tijerina as a heroic freedom fighter in the mode of a Che Guevara during the revolutionary 1960s. The religiously conservative Tijerina proved to be less of a revolutionary than some of his followers envisioned, but the land grant movement persists today as litigants seek to have their land claims recognized.

A former boxer, Rodolfo "Corky" Gonzales was an admirer of Tijerina who established the Crusade for Social Justice in Denver, Colorado, advocating self-determination for the Chicano community and expressing distrust of federal anti-poverty programs. His philosophy was best exemplified with his epic poem *I Am Joaquin* (1967), in which Gonzales developed the concept of the Chicano, a unique race of people who were neither European nor Indian, neither Mexican nor American, who laid claim to the southwestern ancestral land of Aztlan. Convening the first Chicano Youth Liberation Conference in March 1969, Gonzales empowered Mexican American youth and activists to create a cultural and educational foundation for Chicano communities. Gonzales encouraged Chicano students to oppose discriminatory education practices and demand that the history of their people be included in the curriculum, while also calling for a Chicano political party; *La Raza Unida*. The influence of Gonzales, however, was limited after a Denver police raid on the headquarters of the Crusade for Justice resulted in violence and a bomb explosion.

Gonzales, nevertheless, successfully encouraged Chicano or Mexican American students to fight for their rights and self-determination. In Crystal City, Texas, the majority of students were Mexican American, but the white school board maintained a rule that a majority of the high school's cheerleaders must be Anglo. In the fall of 1969, Mexican American students walked out of classes over the cheerleading issue, but the student demands soon encompassed other issues such as the right to speak Spanish on the school grounds, education on Mexican American history and culture, and the hiring of Mexican American teachers. The students eventually won acceptance for most of their demands, in addition to encouraging their elders to assert their political power, and the school board and city offices in Crystal City were soon in the hands of the Mexican American community. Leaders of the Mexican-American Youth Organization (MAYO), such as José Angel Gutiérrez, hoped to use the Crystal City walkouts to form a Chicano political movement with the *La Raza Unida* Party in the Southwest, but charges of corruption against the inexperienced Crystal City Chicano politicians as well as internal divisions limited the effectiveness of this challenge to the established political parties.

School rebellions were also prominent in East Los Angeles as Mexican American students walked out of classes in 1968, protesting overcrowded classrooms, understaffing, high dropout rates, poor quality of instruction which included few Mexican American teachers, and the lack of attention paid to Chicano history and culture. The students also demanded that bi-lingual instruction be provided for Mexican Americans in the schools. Teacher Sal Castro was arrested and fired for his support of the walkouts, and student leaders insisted that he be reinstated by the school board. While Castro was eventually allowed to resume his teaching career and students returned to class, many of the issues regarding overcrowding and understaffing continued to plague the Los Angeles schools serving the Chicano community.

Chicano youth were also vocal in their protest of the Vietnam War, where it is estimated that over 3,000 soldiers of Hispanic descent died. On August 29, 1970, a national Chicano Moratorium demonstration and march against the war was held in Los Angeles. The approximately 25,000 marchers were met by sheriff deputies who claimed they were responding to the reported robbery of a local liquor store. As tempers rose between the authorities and demonstrators, the deputies employed force to halt the march. In the midst of the chaos, Ruben Salazar, covering the march for the *Los Angeles Times*, was killed by a teargas pellet fired by a deputy, but no one was charged with the murder. As with groups such as the Black Panthers, Chicano activists were attacked and infiltrated in violation of their civil rights.

Cesar Chavez and the United Farm Workers

Perhaps the best-known of the Chicano leaders was Cesar Chavez, who recognized the priority of economic concerns for many Mexican Americans mired in poverty. Chavez grew up in a family of field workers in Arizona and California, abandoning his formal education at grade seven in order to work in the fields and help support his family. After serving in the Navy, Chavez was an organizer for the Community Service Organization. In 1962, he joined with Dolores Huerta to organize Filipino and Mexican workers in the California fields to form what would become known as the United Farm Workers (UFW). His efforts to organize grape pickers and other farm workers in the state was supported by Walter Reuther of the United Auto Workers. Envisioning himself as a civil rights activist in the mode of Martin Luther King Jr., Chavez advocated nonviolence as he employed marches, strikes, national grape boycotts, and even personal fasts to gain respect for the farmworkers and their cause. In 1970, the UFW signed contracts with a number of growers, but their influence in the fields was challenged by the Teamsters Union who often employed violent tactics. In 1975, Chavez lobbied Governor Jerry Brown to sign the California Agricultural Labor Relations Act recognizing collective bargaining and bringing peace to the fields. Conditions, however, deteriorated under Governor Ronald Reagan who failed to provide sufficient funding and support for regulating collective bargaining. In 1993, Chavez died after he was weakened from overwork and the strain of his fasts. His labors certainly improved conditions in the fields, although the wages for farmworkers who harvest the food for our tables remain low.

The militancy of the Chicano movement has to a great extent disappeared, but the Latino/a population is the fastest growing demographic group in the United States, and it is increasing throughout the country. It is a diverse group extending beyond Mexican Americans to include migrants from Central America to South America to Cuba and Caribbean nations such as Haiti and the Dominican Republic. The growing Latino/a population has led to fears by an aging white population regarding the changing face of America, and demagogic politicians such as President Donald Trump have sought to exploit these insecurities by demonizing the Latino/a citizens and migrants. The anti-immigration campaign directed at those of Latino/a descent entering the United States reminds us that the struggle for respect and equal rights for all residents of the United States remains an essential part of the American experience.

American Indian Movement

During the 1960s and 1970s, the American Indian Movement (AIM) also fought to restore Native sovereignty after the termination policy of the Eisenhower administration forced many Native people off their land and into urban areas where they were separated from their people and culture. To gain national attention for the plight of Native Americans, AIM organized an occupation of the abandoned prison island of Alcatraz which lasted from 1969 to 1971, pointing out the rights of Alcatraz's original inhabitants. In 1972, AIM promoted the Trail of Broken Treaties, a march upon the Bureau of Indian Affairs to highlight the long history of the United States government failing to honor treaties with sovereign Native nations. Perhaps the best-known action taken by AIM was the occupation of the village of Wounded Knee on the Lakota Sioux reservation of Pine Ridge. The site was known for the so-called last battle of the Indian Wars in which Natives were massacred for observing the forbidden Ghost Dance. AIM leaders sought to emphasize the extreme poverty and mismanagement of the Pine Tree Reservation under the Bureau of Indian Affairs and tribal governorship of Richard Wilson. The occupation of Wounded Knee in 1973 by AIM supporters resulted in a seventy-one-day siege in which the Native forces were surrounded by National Guardsmen and federal agents exchanging fire and resulting in several casualties. The siege of Wounded Knee certainly reminded Americans of the nation's violent history of taking Native land by force. After the siege was lifted, AIM leaders Dennis Banks and Russell Means were indicted on conspiracy charges, but the case against them was dismissed due to prosecutorial misconduct—a problem in many political trials of the era. Meanwhile, conditions in Pine Ridge worsened as the Wilson administration was accused of employing tactics of intimidation and murder against its opponents. In 1975, two FBI agents were murdered on the reservation, and AIM activist Leonard Peltier was sentenced to life imprisonment for the murders. Peltier still proclaims his innocence and is the subject of numerous petitions for pardon, insisting that he is a political prisoner of the United States. While the militancy of AIM is missing today, and the federal government has abandoned the policy of termination, poverty and inequality remain a problem for America's Native population. Benefits from industries such as gaming are not equally distributed, and extractive industries continue to exploit Native resources. The treatment of the Native population in contemporary America reminds us of how far we still need to go in addressing the troubled national history of territorial acquisition and subjugation of America's original inhabitants.

Women's liberation

While women were quite active in the civil rights struggle of blacks, Chicanos, and Natives, these liberation movements, including supposedly more radical student and countercultural groups, were often guilty of assigning women to more subsidiary tasks such as making the coffee. Thus, the patriarchy had to be assaulted on both the political right and left, and women would need their own liberation movement. Feminists recognized that the personal was political, as issues such as family leave and daycare facilities necessitated government intervention and regulation. Issues of class, however, limited the effectiveness of the women's movement with the unintended consequence of fostering the feminization of poverty.

The 1963 publication of Betty Friedan's *The Feminine Mystique* is often viewed as the linchpin for the women's movement. In this landmark study, Friedan exposed the discontent of women in the suburbs who found that simply living to serve their husbands and children did not necessarily produce happiness and personal fulfillment. What Friedan described as the problem with no name led some middle-class women to seek escape in pills and alcohol. Friedan argued that women needed to find personal growth and development within their own interests, education, and careers. She joined with other feminists to form the National Organization of Women (NOW) to lobby for equal opportunity in the workplace, education, and politics. NOW succeeded in making some inroads on the pay gap between men and women, abolishing some educational and business barriers to women's advancement, electing more women to political office, and getting some states to address issues such as family leave. Even the 1964 Civil Rights Act barred discrimination based upon gender, although conservatives had initially introduced this amendment hoping it would deter passage of the bill. Feminists such as Gloria Steinem exposed the hypocrisy of the patriarchy, while the birth control pill and sexual revolution provided women with greater control over reproduction and their bodies. In *Roe v. Wade* (1973), the Supreme Court struck down a Texas law banning abortions, allowing women access to safe and legal abortions. The women's liberation movement also supported the Equal Rights Amendment (ERA) to the Constitution, a proposal initially put forth by Alice Paul and the Woman's Party in the 1920s. The amendment was ratified by thirty-five states but fell short by three states as a backlash developed among conservative women who saw the ERA as a threat to the traditional family. Phyllis Schlafly and her Eagle Forum argued that the ERA would endanger women's exemption from the draft and separate gender public restrooms—an argument today employed against transgender rights.

Although organizations such as NOW were successful in attaining more opportunities for their white, educated middle-class constituency, the women's movement of the 1960s and 1970s, similar to their reforming ancestors from the Seneca Falls Conference, provided less relief to their working-class sisters and women of color. Lacking education, poor women were not in position to take advantage of career opportunities available to middle-class women. In addition, poor women were increasingly the head of families living below the poverty line, as the welfare laws of the era denied benefits to families with unemployed fathers in the home, encouraging high divorce rates and children born to single mothers. The class gap among women was similar to what was happening in the black community as middle-class residents fled the inner city for the suburbs. Poor women also lacked the resources to provide affordable and adequate childcare for their families as the United States refused to provide subsidies for working mothers, often leaving the children to virtually raise themselves and perpetuate the cycle of poverty.

While the feminization of poverty persists, the women's movement of the 1960s and 1970s raised consciousness and improved conditions, especially for the middle class. Some dents have been made in the patriarchy, and some husbands are willing to assume a greater role in caring for their children, relieving working women somewhat from the duties of being the primary caregiver in addition to pursuing a career. Yet, American corporations make this difficult by opposing family leave and not promoting talented women for fears of pregnancy and missing work. The contemporary Me Too Movement challenges the sexual exploitation wielded over women in the workplace for all social classes, and the economic gap in equivalent jobs between men and women has been narrowed. And more women have been elected to public office, but the power of the patriarchy persists, and many Americans in 2020 remain uncomfortable accepting a woman as the nation's chief executive.

Stonewall and gay liberation

The sense of personal liberation that governed the women's movement and civil rights struggle also encouraged members of the LGBTQ community to come out of the closet and assert their rights for inclusion in the body politic, even though the American Psychiatric Association continued to view homosexuality as a mental disorder until 1973. Same sex attraction was viewed as a subversive threat to the American family and liberal consensus, and the police in major cities such as San Francisco and New York would routinely raid bars or venues frequented by members of the LGBTQ community. On June 28, 1968, the police in New York City conducted a raid on the Stonewall Inn in Greenwich Village, except that this time the local community clashed with police in a series of disturbances that lasted for several days. The Stonewall riots or uprising encouraged gays, lesbians, and transgender individuals to adopt a more assertive stance, leading to the Gay Liberation Front and Gay Activists Alliance in New York City, out of which grew the national movement for gay rights. In 1977, the openly gay Harvey Milk was elected a city supervisor in San Francisco, where he helped enact a city ordinance banning discrimination on the basis of sexual orientation. The following year, however, Milk was assassinated by a former supervisor colleague. Milk remains an icon within the LGBTQ community, and in 2019 the gay Mayor of South Bend, Indiana, Pete Buttigieg emerged as a serious candidate for the Democratic Presidential nomination. Even some radicals, nevertheless, were uncomfortable with gay rights, and the movement grew slowly, suffering through the AIDS epidemic of the 1980s which President Reagan attempted to ignore, but developing a sense of pride and even embracing the pejorative word "queer." The LGBTQ movement culminated in the *Obergefell v. Hodges* (2015) Supreme Court decision that the right to marry for same sex couples was guaranteed under the due process and equal protection clauses of the Fourteenth Amendment. The five to four decision continues to be attacked by various Christian groups who also oppose the rights of transgender Americans. The civil rights revolution of the 1960s provided a foundation for the LGBTQ community to assert their right to be included within the promise of American life.

Legacy of the civil rights struggle

The 1960s have been denounced by some conservatives and reactionaries as a period in which American history got off track and descended into an era of anarchy, riots, and violence. Many of these people would like to make America great again by returning to the early days of the 1950s when the United States was ruled by white men, and when women, gays, lesbians, blacks, Natives, Hispanics, and other minorities knew to stay in their subservient positions. Instead of viewing the Civil Rights Movement and the other liberation struggles it inspired as aberrations, perhaps the turbulent 1960s should be perceived as a time during which courageous Americans got their country back on the path proclaimed by Jefferson's Declaration of Independence. In addition, to the challenges provided by the Civil Rights Movement and liberation struggles, the Vietnam War raised profound questions regarding the role of the United States in the world, leading many young Americans to interrogate national values and capitalism, suggesting that more communal values and a counterculture might create an egalitarian America and world based upon principles of self-determination, but many of those seeking change underestimated the power of the establishment.

Further Reading:

Acuna, Rodolfo. *Occupied America: A History of Chicanos*. New York: Harper & Row, 1981.

Branch, Taylor. *Parting the Waters: America in the King Years, 1954–1963*. New York: Simon and Schuster, 1988.

Carson, Clayborne. *In Struggle: SNCC and the Black Awakening of the 1960s*. Cambridge, MA: Harvard University Press, 1981.

Dittmer, John. *Local People: The Struggle for Civil Rights in Mississippi*. Urbana, IL: University of Illinois Press, 1994.

Duberman, Martin. *Stonewall*. New York: Dutton, 1993.

Haley, Alex, ed. *The Autobiography of Malcolm X*. New York: Grove Press, 1965.

Rosen, Ruth. *The World Split Open: How the Modern Women's Movement Changed America*. New York: Viking, 2000.

Sitkoff, Harvard. *The Struggle for Black Equality, 1954–1992*. New York: Hill and Wang, 1981.

Smith, Paul Chaat and Robert Allen Warrior. *Like a Hurricane: The Indian Movement from Alcatraz to Wounded Knee*. New York: New Press, 1996.

Sugrue, Thomas. *Origins of the Urban Crisis: Race and Inequality in Postwar Detroit*. Princeton, NJ: Princeton University Press, 1996.

Tygiel, Jules. *Baseball's Great Experiment: Jackie Robinson and His Legacy*. New York: Oxford University Press, 1983.

Tyson, Timothy B. *The Blood of Emmett Till*. New York: Simon and Schuster, 2017.

27

Vietnam War and Social Protest in the 1960s

"A Man and Woman Watching Film Footage of the Vietnam War on a Television in their Living Room." Warren K. Leffler, photographer, February 13, 1968. Prints and Photographs Division, Library of Congress. The violence of the Vietnam War was brought home to Americans every day on the evening news, making it impossible to escape the conflict which became known as the living room war.

The convulsions that tore apart the fabric of American society in the 1960s were due to many factors that exposed the fissures within the liberal consensus. The Civil Rights Movement and other liberation struggles revealed the gap between myth and reality in realizing the American dream of equal opportunity, shedding light on the economic barriers, racism, and discrimination that have placed the promise of American life beyond the reach of many citizens. In addition, for the families of baby boomers, mostly white, who did attain middle-class status in the suburbs, the post-World War II era did not exactly provide security. While there were more material possessions available than their depression era parents would have envisioned in their youth, the baby boomers were raised under the shadow of the atomic bomb and duck and cover drills with the knowledge that their middle-class existence might be destroyed at any moment. Although nuclear annihilation was avoided in the Cold War, with a close call in the Cuban Missile Crisis, the anticommunist crusade limited reform and freedom of expression by labeling dissent and departures from orthodox thought as promoting communism and undermining American traditions. The dangers of this conformity were brought home to the baby boomer generation during the Vietnam War, a conflict waged in Southeast Asia to ostensibly prevent communist expansion.

With the military draft supplying many of the estimated 2.5 million Americans who served in Vietnam, it was difficult to escape the repercussions of the war. Many fathers expected their sons to step up and serve just as they had during World War II, but many young men questioned whether the North Vietnamese really constituted a threat to the United States. And as American bombs and napalm rained down upon Vietnamese villagers, some Americans wondered whether it was moral for the United States to be waging such a war of terror against people of color in the jungles of Vietnam. These moral questions divided American families as the body bags returned home from Vietnam, while demonstrations against the conflict increased on campuses and the streets of major American cities. The war divided Americans, and many young Americans began to wonder if their parents were wrong on such vital issues as civil rights and Vietnam, then perhaps they were also wrong regarding capitalist values along with traditional morality and institutions such as marriage. Thus, the Vietnam conflict laid bare consensus values, encouraging young Americans to experiment with sexuality, drugs, and communal living in a counterculture challenging traditional values. The establishment, however, proved more resistant than many countercultural radicals expected, and, while making some concessions, corporate control of American democracy was able to survive the challenges of the Vietnam War and counterculture.

Historical background of the Vietnam War

The commitment of the United States government to the defense of South Vietnam was based upon many false assumptions and repeated mistakes from the Korean War. In Korea, the United States Congress abandoned its Constitutional obligations to declare war and allowed the President to unilaterally commit American forces to the defense of South Korea. In addition, neither the South Korean nor South Vietnamese governments were the bastions of democracy claimed by American authorities. Both wars also committed American forces to conflicts in which soldiers encountered difficulty in distinguishing friend from foe, contributing to the atrocities that marred both conflicts. Also, most Americans as well as policymakers know little about indigenous Asian conditions that contributed to the hostilities.

In the case of Southeast Asia, the United States perceived the regional war as part of the expansionist efforts of international communism under the direction of the Soviet Union and Red China. Pursing the strategy of containment, the United States would block communist expansion, fighting the communist aggressors in the jungles of Indochina rather than on the streets of American cities. The communists were accused of fomenting violence in Indochina, but this perception ignored the history of the region. The Vietnamese and their Chinese neighbors to the north historically clashed over control of Indochina, while the Vietnamese and their Cambodian rivals to the west have a tradition of hostilities in the region. Thus, after the Untied States withdrew from Southeast Asia in 1975, it is not surprising that the Vietnamese fought a war with the communist government in China, while Vietnam invaded Cambodia to overthrow the extremist communist Khmer Rouge government. Historical rivalries that had little to do with communism quickly reasserted themselves following America's departure from the region. The United States failed to acknowledge the role played by nationalism in Indochina, refusing to make accommodations for communist nationalists such as Ho Chi Minh in Vietnam and insisting upon a monolithic approach to dealing with international communism.

And nationalist ambitions in the region were certainly furthered by experience with European imperialism. In the 1850s the French occupied Indochina, establishing colonial regimes in Laos, Cambodia, and Vietnam, while exploiting resources such as the rubber tree plantations of Vietnam. The French control over Vietnam was characterized by brutality and exploitation, provoking numerous rebellions. During World War II, the Vichy regime in France was in no position to defend its colony from Japanese occupation, seeking to obtain control of Vietnam's vital rubber sources. While opposed to French colonization, the Vietnamese people certainly did not welcome the Japanese as liberators. The resistance to the Japanese was led by the Viet Minh, Vietnamese communists and their leader, the charismatic Ho Chi Minh. Like many communist partisans fighting the Nazis in Europe, the

Viet Minh received military supplies from the United States and cooperated with the Office of Strategic Services, the predecessor of the CIA. Allied with the United States in the struggle against fascism, Ho Chi Minh seemed to assume that the Americans would support independence for Vietnam under his control after the Japanese were expelled. In appreciation of American support, Ho even prepared a Vietnamese declaration of independence modeled upon Jefferson's document, but the Vietnamese leader felt betrayed when the Truman administration supported the return of the French imperialists to Indochina. This decision was based upon the emergence of the Cold War, and Truman perceived an independent Vietnam under the control of Ho as perpetuating the spread of international communism. While the Americans at this time did not sent troops to Vietnam, the French, still reeling from German occupation and internal divisions, could not have afforded a return to Indochina without the financial backing of the United States.

Dien Bien Phu and 1954 Geneva Conference

Ho opposed the French colonial regime, and the Viet Minh were soon involved in a bitter war with the French. The Eisenhower administration followed the Vietnamese policy of containment pursued by Truman, citing the domino theory that the expansion of communism into one nation in Southeast Asia would begin a process of falling dominos (nations) that would extend to Thailand and India, eventually threatening the United States. Despite American support, the war in Indochina did not go well for the French, who found themselves surrounded at Dien Bien Phu in March 1954. The French strategy was to create a base in northwestern Vietnam that would draw the Viet Minh into a major battle where the French could employ their superior fire power. Instead, the Viet Minh under the command of General Nguyen Giap methodically moved artillery and anti-aircraft guns into the mountains surrounding the French position, rendering the airfield at Dien Bien Phu useless. As the French withered under the Viet Minh siege, Vice President Nixon floated the idea of the United States employing nuclear weapons to bail out their French allies, but the suggestion was eventually rejected. With the Viet Minh breaking through their lines, the French surrendered after a three-month siege.

Following this defeat the French had enough of Vietnam, and at the 1954 Geneva Conference, they agreed to withdraw from Indochina. Vietnam was to be temporarily divided at the 17th parallel, with Ho Chi Minh and the Viet Minh controlling the Democratic Republic of Vietnam or North Vietnam, while the South was to be governed by Emperor Bao Dai, who was deposed by his Prime Minister Ngo Dinh Diem. Although the United States failed to sign the Geneva agreement because it would also constitute *de facto* recognition of the People's Republic of China as a signatory power, the Americans still feared the expansion of communism in the region and were willing to replace the French as the major supporters of

Diem's anticommunist government in the South. Under the Geneva agreement, North and South Vietnam were to be unified under free elections scheduled for 1956. However, Diem, who assumed the Presidency of the Republic of Vietnam or South Vietnam, canceled the elections with the backing of the United States. Eisenhower later explained this anti-democratic action by observing that the communists would likely cheat at the ballot box, and even if the elections were fair, the popular Ho Chi Minh might well have prevailed and communist expansion, even via free elections, was unacceptable.

Unable to achieve his dream of a unified and independent Vietnam through the electoral process, Ho shifted his strategy to supporting the National Liberation Front (NLF) as a revolutionary force that would overthrow the Diem regime and seek unification with the North. The NLF was initially a coalition of anti-Diem groups that included the Viet Cong (South Vietnamese communists), Buddhists, and liberal reformers who received supplies and support from the North through the Ho Chi Minh Trail located in Laos. As the conflict in the South expanded, the NLF was dominated by the Viet Cong, and the Ho Chi Minh Trail was employed as an avenue through which to move North Vietnamese troops into the South.

The Kennedy Administration and the Diem regime

Despite the promises of change and a New Frontier, the Kennedy administration continued American support for the Diem regime, believing that the best and the brightest such as Defense Secretary Robert McNamara would be able to master the situation. With his faith in counter-insurgency tactics, Kennedy expanded the deployment of Green Berets to Vietnam who would help train their South Vietnamese allies in combating guerrilla forces. The Green Berets were also to help the South Vietnamese government institute the Strategic Hamlet policy to neutralize Viet Cong influence among the peasantry. Under this ill-advised policy, villages threatened by the Viet Cong were to be relocated to sites where they could be protected by the Green Berets and South Vietnamese forces. What policymakers failed to understand was the Vietnamese culture in which ancestors were venerated and buried in the traditional villages, but in the process of relocation the peasants were deserting their ancestors. In addition, the Strategic Hamlets were often nothing more than stockades surrounded by barbed wire and armed guards. Cut off from their ancestral homes and living often in squalid conditions, the villagers placed in Strategic Hamlets became excellent recruiting targets for the Viet Cong. The Phoenix Program under the direction of the CIA was also of little help in protecting the Vietnamese people. Responding to Viet Cong assassinations of local anticommunist leaders in the South, the CIA developed its own program to kill South Vietnamese politicians suspected of having ties to the Viet Cong, further destabilizing South Vietnamese politics.

The Diem regime also refused to implement reforms suggested by the Kennedy administration. Diem came from a wealthy Catholic family and was educated under the French system, isolating him culturally from the majority Buddhist population. In addition to the failure to institute land reform, the large land-holding Diem family was perceived as corrupt, and Diem's brother Ngo Dinh Nhu, who headed the nation's special forces that essentially served as a private army for the Diem family, was especially feared by the people. As popular support for the government deteriorated, the Diem regime reacted by suppressing Buddhist religious leaders and raiding monasteries. These actions only increased popular discontent, and on July 11, 1963 Buddhist monk Thich Quang Doc burned himself to death at a busy Saigon intersection protesting the religious persecution of the Diem administration. Quang Doc's self-immolation certainly gained the attention of the world as it was captured by photographers and film crews who brought the disturbing image of the burning monk into American homes. As other monks followed the example of Quang Doc, pressure mounted on the Kennedy administration to do something about Diem.

As Diem dragged his heels on reforms, South Vietnamese generals approached U.S. South Vietnamese Ambassador Henry Cabot Lodge Jr. as to whether the United States would oppose a coup to overthrow Diem. Reluctantly, Kennedy agreed to the coup, assuming that Diem would be exiled. The military coup on November 7, 1963 quickly toppled the government, and Diem along with his brother surrendered with the promise they would be allowed to leave the country. Instead, Diem and his brother were murdered, antagonizing President Kennedy who felt betrayed by the plotters. But the generals were now America's South Vietnamese clients, and the charade that the American intervention was about supporting democracy was further discredited. The coup to which the Americans had agreed simply brought the United States deeper into the Vietnam quagmire, but Vietnam became Lyndon Johnson's problem as three weeks after the Diem coup, Kennedy was killed in Dallas.

LBJ and the Gulf of Tonkin Resolution

While Presidents Truman, Eisenhower, and Kennedy provided the foundation for the Vietnam War, it was under the leadership of Johnson that millions of Americans, most of them draftees, were sent to Southeast Asia. Johnson was also a member of the anticommunist consensus, even fearing that his Great Society reforms might be subject to the criticism of McCarthyism if he did not demonstrate his Cold War credentials in Indochina. To Johnson, Vietnam was also personal. He had shaken Diem's hand and promised to support the man he called "the Winston Churchill of Southeast Asia," expressing discomfort with the coup that removed Diem. Also, some historians suggest that it was unfortunate that Johnson was a Texan, raised on the mythology of the heroic last stand at the Alamo. Thus, as the situation in Vietnam deteriorated, Johnson could not abandon the conflict, repeating the poker cliché, "in for a dime, in for a dollar." But as he campaigned for election in 1964, Johnson hoped to remove Vietnam as an issue.

The opportunity to create a consensus on Vietnam was offered by the Gulf of Tonkin Resolution. On August 2, 1964, an American destroyer the *USS Maddox* was involved in a military operation to activate North Vietnamese radar installations that could then be attacked by South Vietnamese demolition teams. The *Maddox* was sailing in the Gulf of Tonkin, territorial waters claimed by the North Vietnamese, when North Vietnamese patrol boats approached the *Maddox* and firing broke out. After suffering damage and casualties, the North Vietnamese ships withdrew. The *Maddox* emerged without damage and continued with its mission, initially reporting a second incident which proved, however, to simply be a blip on the radar screen, perhaps a flock of birds. Although the Johnson administration knew that the second attack on the *Maddox* was a false report, Congress was informed that an American Navy vessel was attacked, not once but twice, by North Vietnamese forces while sailing peacefully in international waters. The President used these reports to convince Congress to pass the Gulf of Tonkin Resolution, providing the President with full military authority to respond to communist aggression in Vietnam and Southeast Asia. This document which was approved unanimously in the House with only two dissenting votes in the Senate, Wayne Morse of Oregon and Ernest Gruening of Alaska, provided the foundation for the expansion of the Vietnam War.

However, overwhelming passage of the Gulf of Tonkin Resolution removed Vietnam as an issue in the 1964 Presidential campaign in which Johnson ran as a peace candidate, portraying his Republican opponent Senator Barry Goldwater as a dangerous extremist who might lead the nation into nuclear war. Johnson as the peace candidate was perhaps best depicted in the controversial Daisy Girl television advertisement. A young innocent-looking girl is picking daisies and counting down from ten, but her world is destroyed by the blast of a nuclear weapon. A black screen replaces the girl with the message, "Vote for President Johnson on November 3rd. The stakes are too high for you to stay home." After his landslide victory, Johnson returned his attention to Vietnam, instituting a bombing campaign against North Vietnam that rained terror from the sky against innocent Vietnamese children like the Daisy Girl.

Operation Rolling Thunder in the air—search and destroy on the ground

Cashing in on the blank check accorded him by the Gulf of Tonkin Resolution, Johnson initiated a sustained bombing campaign called Operation Rolling Thunder against the North Vietnamese. The goals of the bombing campaign were to destroy North Vietnamese morale and its industrial base while interdicting support of insurrection in South Vietnam. From 1965 to 1968, Operation Rolling Thunder dropped more tons of bombs than were employed in the entire Pacific theater during World War II, killing over 50,000 civilians. Yet, Operation Rolling Thunder failed to deter the North Vietnamese. Conservative critics of the bombing campaign assert that it was ineffective because the North Vietnamese port of Haiphong was declared off limits as a target, reflecting fears of sinking Soviet and Chinese ships, not to mention NATO allies who continued to trade with North Vietnam. The North Vietnamese were also supplied with sophisticated anti-aircraft weapons from the Soviets and Chinese, inflicting considerable damage on American aircraft and capturing over 200 pilots, including later Republican Presidential candidate John McCain.

Such a massive air campaign required heavy bombers and could not simply be launched from aircraft carriers. Operation Rolling Thunder necessitated the construction of large air bases such as Da Nang in South Vietnam. To protect the bases from attacks, President Johnson began the deployment of hundreds of thousands of American troops to Vietnam. In order to find the enemy who blended into the jungles and civilian villages of South Vietnam, the United States military began to send out search and destroy missions to engage the Viet Cong and North Vietnamese. Since the purpose of these missions was not the traditional military goal of seizing territory from the enemy, another objective had to be established in order to rate their effectiveness. Thus, the measuring tool of the kill ratio was employed to demonstrate that the United States and its South Vietnamese allies were winning the war. These kill figures were reported on the evening news in the United States as if they were the scores of some bizarre ballgame. In addition, this strategy encouraged the killing of Vietnamese civilians who could be added to the body count. And the kill ratio begged the question of what if the other side were willing to pay a high price in pursuit of their national independence. Nevertheless, William Westmoreland, the commanding general in Vietnam, offered the kill ratio as proof that the war was being won.

Tet Offensive

This illusion was shattered on January 30, 1968 when the Viet Cong and North Vietnamese launched the Tet Offensive during the Vietnamese New Year. The communist forces had infiltrated South Vietnam, and more than 80,000 troops attacked over 100 cities, catching the Americans and their Vietnamese allies by surprise. General Westmoreland considered the cities to be securely in American hands and believed the attacks were a feint to draw attention from the siege of Khe Sanh near the Laotian border in the western highlands of Vietnam. After communist forces infiltrated the American Embassy in Saigon and gained control over the imperial capital of Hue, Westmoreland recognized the seriousness of the situation and launched counterattacks that eventually drove the occupying communist fighters out of the cities. The heaviest fighting was in Hue where American and

South Vietnamese troops did not regain control of the city until early March. Casualties on both sides totaled over 10,000, while approximately 5,000 civilians were killed by American shelling and executions carried out by the Viet Cong. The Tet Offensive proved to be a military failure for the North Vietnamese. They hoped that the offensive would spur a massive uprising in the South that would greet them as liberators, but this popular insurrection failed to materialize. In addition, North Vietnamese losses were so great that the ability to wage offensive warfare was severely limited.

While American soldiers, initially caught by surprise, fought well and helped win the Tet Offensive, the battle was, nevertheless, a turning point in the war for the North Vietnamese. As one North Vietnamese official observed, "we may have lost the battle on the streets of Hue and Saigon, but we won the war on the streets of Chicago and New York City," as protests against the war intensified. The Tet Offensive shattered the illusion that the United States was winning the war, and the demonstrations against the Vietnam War—which will be discussed in greater detail below in the section on social protest—expanded from students into the middle class. The Tet Offensive also had major ramifications for American politics.

Election of 1968

As American commanders in Vietnam asked Washington for more troops, Democratic Senator Eugene McCarthy of Minnesota challenged Johnson for the party's Presidential nomination. Campaigning against the war and supported by idealistic young people who insisted they were "getting clean for Gene," McCarthy shocked Johnson by nearly defeating the President in the New Hampshire Democratic Primary. Observing Johnson's vulnerability, Senator Robert Kennedy of New York announced his candidacy and denounced the war. Many of McCarthy's supporters accused Kennedy of being an opportunist and dividing the antiwar vote, but Johnson surprised Americans by proclaiming that he was suspending the bombing of North Vietnam and would not be a candidate for re-election. To represent the administration, Vice President Hubert Humphrey then announced his candidacy, although he did not enter the primaries. Meanwhile, McCarthy and Kennedy waged a vigorous primary campaign that culminated with Kennedy's triumph in the pivotal California contest. After claiming victory, Kennedy, however, was assassinated by Sirhan Sirhan, a Palestinian ostensibly angry with Kennedy's pro-Israeli views. The charismatic Kennedy, whose early political career was characterized by a reputation for ruthlessness, had captured the imagination of many young people and minorities who saw him as the voice of change. McCarthy continued his campaign to the Democratic National Convention in Chicago, where despite massive protest and police violence in the streets, party regulars awarded the nomination to Humphrey.

Meanwhile, Richard Nixon re-emerged as a force in Republican politics and received the party's Presidential nomination. Nixon recognized the importance of the Vietnam issue, but the man who made his political reputation as an anti-communist attacking Alger Hiss and Helen Gahagan Douglas was not going to become an antiwar candidate. While third party American Independent Party candidate Governor George Wallace of Alabama and his running mate General Curtis LeMay advocated winning the war, Nixon advanced what he called "peace with honor." Nixon was vague in defining this term, insisting that he had a secret plan to end the war in Vietnam, but he could not yet share these details with the American people. With a huge lead in the polls, this vague strategy seemed to benefit the front runner, but as the race tightened, Nixon was afraid of an "October surprise." Thus, the Republican candidate worked behind the scenes to prevent any last-minute peace deal with North Vietnam that might benefit Humphrey. Although not widely known at the time, in private conversations Johnson believed Nixon was guilty of treason. In the final analysis, there was no peace treaty, support for the Wallace candidacy declined amid concerns regarding the violent rhetoric of the Alabama Governor, and Nixon defeated Humphrey in an extremely close election.

Nixon and his National Security Adviser, Harvard Professor Henry Kissinger who would later serve the President as Secretary of State, were now in charge of implementing "peace with honor." Framing his policy as Vietnamization, Nixon announced that he would begin withdrawing American troops from Vietnam who would be replaced by South Vietnamese forces. Meanwhile, the United States would continue to prosecute the war in Vietnam. Nixon also made it clear to his supporters, whom he called the "silent majority," that his administration would have no use for draft dodgers and antiwar protestors. Vietnamization, however, proved to be a sham as the South Vietnamese forces often lacked the vigor and discipline of their North Vietnamese and Viet Cong adversaries, perhaps reflecting the corruption that often characterized the South Vietnamese regime.

My Lai

American protest of the war increased when in November 1969, investigative journalist Seymour Hersh reported that on March 16, 1968 American soldiers from Charlie Company entered the South Vietnamese village of My Lai in search of Viet Cong fighters. After finding no enemy combatants in My Lai, frustrated soldiers marched the villagers, primarily old men, women, and children into a ditch where they proceeded to massacre between 350 and 500 civilians. Some of the women were raped before they were killed, and some bodies were mutilated. Helicopter pilot Hugh Thompson and his crew intervened, rescuing some villagers while helping to bring the killing to a halt. Thompson reported the massacre, but military officials sought to cover up the atrocity until it was reported by Hersh. After the cover up was exposed, twenty-six soldiers were charged in the My Lai Massacre, but only Lieutenant William Calley, who evoked the Nuremburg defense that he was only following orders, was found guilty and sentenced to life imprisonment. While many Americans were shocked by the massacre, there was also popular sentiment that Calley was a scapegoat for the military and politicians who had gotten the United States into the Vietnam War. Nixon, seeking to take political advantage of discontent over the verdict, reduced the sentence to house arrest at Fort Benning while the case was appealed. After three and one-half years of house arrest, a federal judge found irregularities in the trial, and Calley was released. For many Americans, the My Lai Massacre provided graphic evidence of the immoral war the United States was conducting against the Vietnamese people. Other critics focused upon the American soldiers. The average age for combat soldiers in Vietnam was nineteen, and these young conscripts with little training or maturity were placed in an impossible dilemma where atrocities were seemingly bound to occur.

Nixon's invasion of Cambodia

Despite the atrocities and obvious failure of Vietnamization, Nixon continued the war effort while simultaneously announcing troop withdrawals. On April 30, 1970 the president informed the American people during a televised address that U.S. and South Vietnamese forces had invaded neutral Cambodia from which the North Vietnamese were launching attacks into the South. The President believed the invasion would reduce military pressure on the implementation of Vietnamization. Instead, the situation in Southeast Asia deteriorated due to the ill-conceived invasion. Many Americans were outraged that Nixon had just widened the conflict which he was supposedly winding down. Protests erupted at universities throughout the nation, with four students killed at Kent State in Ohio. Congressional opposition to the invasion culminated in the Cooper-Church Amendment which forced Nixon to withdraw from Cambodia after cutting off funding for military operations in Cambodia.

The American intervention also destabilized the political situation in Cambodia as neutralist Prince Norodom Sihanouk was replaced by pro-American General Lon Nol. Following the withdrawal of American combat support, the Lon Nol government struggled against the Cambodian communist insurgency known as the Khmer Rouge. In 1975, the Khmer Rouge seized power in Cambodia, and under the leadership of Pol Pot instituted a policy of re-education in which all Cambodians would denounce Western influence and embrace the peasantry in what was called the new nation of Kampuchea. Attempting to erase the past resulted in a policy of genocide in which through starvation and murder in the killing fields perhaps two million Cambodians perished out of an estimated population of eight to nine million. The genocide in Cambodia was finally stopped when the government of Vietnam, unified under communist rule, intervened in 1979 and overthrew the Khmer Rouge regime. The United States, distracted by the Watergate crisis and having no desire to become further involved in the region after the end of the Vietnam War in 1975, refused to intervene even though Nixon's invasion of Cambodia destabilized a nation that eventually descended into genocide.

Détente

After the failure in Cambodia, Nixon and Henry Kissinger, desperate to end the war and maintain the fiction of peace with honor, pursued a policy of détente with the Soviet Union and People's Republic of China, hoping to convince the two powerful communist nations into pressuring their North Vietnamese allies to negotiate a deal with the United States to end the conflict in Vietnam. With his reputation as an anticommunist in the 1950s, Nixon believed that he could make these overtures to the communist powers without being subject to McCarthyism and charges that he was "soft" on communism. Accordingly, Nixon met with Soviet leader Leonid Brezhnev in 1972 and signed the Strategic Arms Limitations Treaty, limiting nuclear arsenals, and the Anti-Ballistic Missile Treaty, placing limitations upon the deployment of anti-ballistic missile systems. Even more surprising was Nixon's decision that he would travel to communist China, a regime which the United States had ostracized since Mao's revolution in 1949. Kissinger secretly traveled to China and paved the way for Nixon's February 1972 visit. The President met with Mao, and the two nations opened trade while agreeing that the future of Taiwan was to be peacefully resolved. Although the United States still officially recognized Taiwan as the legitimate Chinese government, Nixon's visit to China paved the way for a change in policy which culminated in 1979 with full diplomatic relations between the United States and People's Republic of China.

Believing that détente provided a carrot for bringing the Vietnam War to a conclusion, Nixon also thought that the North Vietnamese would only respond to the stick or military pressure. Accordingly, the President resumed the bombing of North Vietnam in what he called Operation Linebacker, demonstrating Nixon's perception of himself as the nation's leading sports fan. In late December 1972 as negotiations seemed on the verge of collapse, Nixon announced what was called the Christmas Day bombings with 20,000 tons of bombs dropped on Hanoi and Haiphong. Nixon supposedly wanted the North Vietnamese to believe that he was a madman who might do anything to end the war, including the deployment of nuclear weapons.

Paris Peace Accords

While there is considerable dispute as to whether the North Vietnamese really subscribed to the madman theory, they did return to the negotiating table, and the Paris Peace Accords ending American participation in the war were signed in January 1973. In the agreement, the United States promised to withdraw from Vietnam, and there was to be an exchange of prisoners—although some critics of the agreement maintain that not all the American captives were returned, but these allegations have not been documented. The United States also pressured the South Vietnamese government of Nguyen Van Thieu to accept a cease fire in place which allowed North Vietnamese and Viet Cong forces to maintain the positions they had occupied in the South. The future of Vietnam was to be resolved peacefully; however, as soon as the United States forces withdrew, fighting resumed. Although technically the United States could have used these hostilities as offering grounds for resuming its military role in the region, Nixon, increasingly focused upon Watergate, had no intention of returning to Vietnam. From 1973 to 1975, the North Vietnamese forces continued their advance until the fall of Saigon on April 30, 1975. The final images of the Vietnam War were disturbing with American helicopters departing from the embassy, while desperate Vietnamese who had cast their lot with the Americans attempted to cling to the aircraft.

Hanoi won the war and unified Vietnam under communist rule. While there were certainly major repercussions for Vietnamese who had cooperated with the Americans, sparking a flood of refugees, the dire predictions of the domino theory were not forthcoming. The collapse of Saigon did not lead to falling dominos of nations in Southeast Asia and around the world. Losing in the streets of Saigon did not mean fighting communists in the streets of major American cities. While nearly 60,000 Americans died in Vietnam and perhaps several million Vietnamese, today the United States and Vietnam are important trading partners and Vietnam is a major destination for American tourists. The question remains as to why so many Vietnamese and Americans had to endure so much in this bloody episode of the Cold War. The war continues to haunt many Vietnam veterans, drafted right out of high school and sent off to the horrors of war, who continue to suffer from inadequate health care and post-traumatic stress syndrome. And there was a racial and class dynamic to who served in Vietnam. With student deferments available to the middle class who could work the system and afford higher education, poor whites, blacks, and Hispanics provided much of the manpower for the war. The conscript army generally fought well, but as the war wound down, discipline declined as soldiers did not want to the last one to die in Vietnam. Military authorities reported insubordination, war resistance, and in extreme cases "fragging" attacks against officers. When disillusioned soldiers returned to the United States, there were no victory parades, and some Vietnam veterans reported being harassed by protestors—

although some historians argue that the image of protestors spitting upon returning soldiers is an exaggeration. Other veterans joined the demonstrations, denouncing the war and returning their decorations of valor from the military.

Thus, the Vietnam War led many Americans to ponder the role war had played in American history and question the anticommunist crusade that fostered a military-industrial complex with global reach. This interrogation of American militarism and empire, however, proved to be short lived. The War on Terror replaced the Cold War as a source of perpetual military preparedness, and more widespread resistance to conscription was thwarted by relying upon a volunteer fighting force with an expanded role for female recruits. Presidents Nixon and Reagan embraced the returning prisoners of war as heroes and branded critics of the war as unpatriotic. Anyone criticizing U.S. military policy was branded as failing to support the troops. Americans were told that the nation must not repeat the mistake of Vietnam and fail to back the sacrifice of soldiers. This unquestioning embrace of militarism seeks to silence debate, and the country finds itself mired in Afghanistan with the longest war in American history.

Alienated youth

During the 1960s and 1970s, however, the Vietnam War along with the Civil Rights Movement led many young Americans to interrogate the values of their parents' generation. There is always somewhat of a clash of values between generations, but the generation gap in the 1960s was often a chasm. After living through the depression and World War II, many Americans in the 1950s sought security in the materialism and conformity of the suburbs. When the consensus was threatened by the serpent of communism in Vietnam, it was time for their sons to assume the responsibility of defending the American way of life. But many of their children questioned a way of life that required the exclusion of blacks from the suburbs while justifying the dropping of napalm on people of color in Southeast Asia. Just as the nation split apart during the 1960s, so did many families. Young people were alienated from a middle-class existence that provided for their material needs but propagated a life of conformity. The outer-directed lives of their parents seemed to afford little opportunity for individual happiness and fulfillment. Instead, the children were expected to behave and do well in school so that they could enter college and attain the credentials for a professional career as an accountant, doctor, or lawyer so that they could assume their position in the consumer wasteland of suburbia. Rather than a quest for the meaning of life, formal education was to mold the individual to fit into the consensus. Corporate America required complacent workers and consumers, not individuals who might question Vietnam or the racial apartheid of the suburbs.

This sense of alienation induced many young people in America, and around the world as well, to reject mainstream society and seek meaning by dropping out of the traditional rat race, forming an alternative society or counterculture in which the individual could find personal fulfillment in a community that tolerated differences and did not evaluate people based upon their possessions. The counterculture attempted to balance the somewhat conflicting American values of individual freedom and egalitarianism, suggesting that individual happiness might be best realized in a more communal rather than capitalist environment. However, the counterculture, much like the communal experiments of the Jacksonian era, failed to fundamentally alter the marketplace orientation of American society due to internal contradictions and excesses as well as the commercialism and repressive power of the dominant culture.

Beats, hippies, and the counterculture

The counterculture of the 1960s, or the hippie movement as it was usually identified in the mainstream media, had its origins in the 1950s with the beatniks or beats who rejected the post war liberal consensus, seeking an alternative and more natural community with sexuality, reefers, jazz, poetry, black Americans, and the freedom of the open road. The beats were exemplified by an eclectic literary movement that included such works as William Burroughs's *Naked Lunch* (1950), Allen Ginsberg's epic poem *Howl* (1956), and Jack Kerouac's *On the Road* (1957). The beat movement found a home in San Francisco and New York City's Greenwich Village, where their hipster approach to life evolved into the larger hippie generation of the 1960s who found the beats more inspirational than their parents. Ginsberg and Neal Cassady, the basis for the character of Dean Moriarty in *On the Road*, transitioned from the beats into the hippie movement, but Kerouac, a former football player at Columbia University, became a critic of the hippies and a supporter of the Vietnam War.

As part of the baby boom generation, the hippies were a much larger group of young men and women who challenged their parents' generation by dropping out of school, the job market, and traditional society in favor of more communal living arrangements. Hippies also interrogated traditional gender roles with young men wearing their hair long, and both men and women adhering to open sexual relationships that undermined the concept of monogamy. To foster the search for authenticity in comparison to the artificial life of the suburbs, hippies turned to drugs. Marijuana, for example, was a natural herb with healing powers, unlike the artificial distilled liquor of their parents. The hippies also embraced hallucinogens such as mushrooms to develop a new sense of consciousness. Timothy Leary was a Harvard psychologist who conducted experiments on the therapeutic possibilities of psychedelic drugs such as LSD for the military. His experimental use of LSD convinced Harvard to fire Leary and his associate Richard Alpert (later Ram Dass), but Leary continued to advocate for the use of LSD as a means through which individuals might reach a higher degree of consciousness and realize their full potential. A less scientific approach to the use of psychedelic drugs was pursued by novelist Ken Kesey, author of the influential *One Flew Over the Cuckoo's Nest* (1962), and his band of Merry Pranksters, including Neal Cassady from the beat generation, who traveled around the country in a psychedelic school bus touting the liberating impact of hallucinogenic drugs. Kesey also sponsored multimedia Acid Tests in San Francisco that featured rock bands such as the Grateful Dead.

And rock music was a key element within the counterculture, promoting freedom of expression and a separation from the music of an older generation. In the early 1960s, folk musicians such as Bob Dylan promoted the Civil Rights Movement and criticized the military-industrial complex in protest songs such as "Blowin' in the Wind" (1963), "The Times They Are a-Changin'" (1964), and "Masters of War" (1963). By the late 1960s, Dylan moved in more personal directions with his music and lyrics which eventually earned him the Nobel Prize in Literature (2017). In the late 1960s, rock transformed in a more psychedelic direction influenced by hallucinogenic drugs with prominent San Francisco bands such as The Grateful Dead, Big Brother and the Holding Company featuring Janis Joplin, and the Jefferson Airplane. While the counterculture had initially championed drugs as a way to free your mind and creativity, by the late 1960s the use of drugs was primarily about the pleasure principle and simply getting high, dropping the intellectual justifications of Timothy Leary. The expanding drug culture moved into heroin and later cocaine, with many young people suffering "bad trips" and mental health breakdowns, in addition to deaths from drug overdoses. Prominent among the overdoses were musicians such as guitarist Jimi Hendrix, blues singer Janis Joplin, and poet-vocalist Jim Morrison of the Doors. The excesses of the drug culture were a significant factor in the eventual collapse of the counterculture.

Communal living and the Woodstock festival

Seeking alternative living experiences, many hippies formed communes, where they hoped to grow their own food and live in harmony with nature. Many of these communes, however, experienced the same type of problems that plagued the communal farms of the 1830s and 1840s. Many of the young people drawn to the hippie lifestyle lacked the practical skills and experience to build structures and grow crops. The communes were also plagued by internal discord with rivalries over free love, excessive drug use, and members who failed to do their fair share of work—especially some males who perpetuated the patriarchal attitudes of the dominant culture by assigning domestic duties and childcare to the women of the community. Thus, most communes did not prove to be self-sustaining with many collapsing when the members were unable to feed themselves. This proved to be a problem for urban hippies who flocked to cities such as San Francisco where they celebrated the Summer of Love in 1967. Hippies moved into the Haight-Ashbury section of the city that had provided a home for many of the beats. The Diggers, a group who rejected a society based upon the marketplace, attempted to provide food for the growing hippie population, but their efforts were overwhelmed by the sheer number of young people migrating to the area. The dream of Haight-Ashbury as a hippie Mecca degenerated into overcrowding with high crime, sanitation problems, and drug overdoses.

Despite these problems, the hippie movement appeared to achieve its promise at the Woodstock, New York music festival scheduled for August 15-18, 1969. Promising three days of peace and love, Woodstock attracted far larger crowds than the promoters anticipated, leading them to abandon efforts at collecting tickets. With massive traffic jams blocking access to the concert, many of the musical acts had to be flown in via helicopter. The crowd swelled to over 400,000 people who slept on the ground and tents while being pelted by rain. Despite these difficult conditions, the crowd sat back and listened to the music while smoking marijuana and partaking of other drugs. Three days of peace ensued with two births, while there were two deaths from overdoses. Listening to the sounds of such major artists as Jimi Hendrix, Janis Joplin, Credence Clearwater Revival, Country Joe and the Fish, and Jefferson Airplane, the counterculture at Woodstock demonstrated that it offered a peaceful alternative to the violence of mainstream America. At Woodstock, it did, indeed, seem that it was the "dawning of the Age of Aquarius."

Dark side of the 1960s

But beyond the peace and love of Woodstock there was a dark side to the counterculture. Many hippies were white and middle class, seeking to flee the artificial and materialistic lifestyle of their parents for the authenticity of black, Native, and Hispanic culture. Thus, many hippies moved into the inner city or places such as Taos, New Mexico, where in the early twentieth century writer D. H. Lawrence retreated to escape the ills of industrial society while celebrating the Native and Hispanic populations and their living in harmony with nature. While the hippies' intentions may have been sincere, to many blacks, Natives, and Hispanics, they were condescending and slumming, celebrating poverty when they enjoyed the option of returning to their middle-class roots when the going was too rough. The hippies, accordingly, were not always welcomed with open arms, provoking resistance from communities where they were considered cultural appropriators or economic freeloaders. Perhaps the best-known case of how "slumming" could be dangerous was the 1967 murder of eighteen-year old Linda Rae Fitzpatrick, who was killed in the East Village of New York City by a black nationalist and former convict. Fitzpatrick had deserted her wealthy parents to pursue a life of authenticity on the streets of New York City. Her death was a warning of the danger lurking in the hippie lifestyle, confirming white middle-class fears and suspicions of the black community.

The peace and love image of Woodstock was also shattered by the Rolling Stones December 1969 concert at the Altamont Speedway near San Francisco. The free festival sparked numerous problems regarding overcrowding and security. In an incredibly bad idea, the Hells Angels Motorcycle Club was lured with free beer to provide security. The festival deteriorated with confrontations between the Hells Angels and musical performers, culminating in the murder of a black concert attendee who attempted to reach the stage. The murder was captured in the documentary film *Gimme Shelter* (1970) by Albert and David Maysles. The image of a peaceful Woodstock West was shattered by the violence, and a series of California murders attributed to hippie guru Charles Manson further discredited the reputation of the counterculture in the eyes of mainstream Americans.

In the late 1960s, Manson, who spent much of his life incarcerated, fancied himself a songwriter and had even ingratiated himself with some music celebrities such as Dennis Wilson of the Beach Boys. The charismatic Manson also was surrounded by a cult of followers, many of them vulnerable young women, who lived on a desert California commune. The Manson Family was heavily involved with drugs, and the young women were expected to demonstrate their devotion by engaging in sexual acts with the cult leader. Manson was convinced that the Beatles had recorded a secret message to him in their song "Helter Skelter" from the *White Album* (1968), telling Manson to provoke a war between whites and blacks, and after the racial bloodshed, Manson would emerge from the desert as a messiah to restore the peace. Accordingly, on August 8, 1969, Manson's followers murdered pregnant actress Sharon Tate, wife of the well-known director Roman Polanski, and four others at the estate of Tate and Polanski, who was away at a film shoot. The bodies were butchered with a fork stuck in the stomach of Tate, also killing her child, and the word "pigs" was smeared in blood on the walls. The next evening, the Manson Family murdered supermarket executive Leno La Bianca and his wife Rosemary in a similar fashion. The idea seemed to be that the murders would be blamed on blacks, provoking "Helter Skelter." Residents of Los Angeles were alarmed, but the murder trail soon led to the Manson Family. After a widely publicized trial in which Manson and his followers were convicted of murder—his death sentence was later commuted to life imprisonment after California abolished the death penalty—the dark underside of the counterculture was confirmed for many Americans.

Commercialization of the counterculture

In addition to suffering from its own excesses, the counterculture was undermined by repression and commercialization from the dominant culture. The student and political radicals of the 1960s, including groups such as the Black Panthers, were subject to illegal wiretaps, searches, and intimidation from the FBI—and will be discussed below. Also, anyone in the 1960s who adopted the hippie lifestyle and appearance can remember the constant harassment and threats from authorities and the dominant culture, which sometimes descended into violence. On the other hand, the mainstream capitalist culture recognized that aspects of the hippie lifestyle were appealing to members of the consensus. Accordingly, rock songs, such as "Light My Fire" by the Doors, initially intended to promote a sense of rebellion against the corporate community, found their way into commercials selling products like automobiles, promoting the capitalist consumption to which the counterculture was supposedly offering an alternative. Also, long hair for men, bell bottom jeans, and peace medallions became fashionable throughout the culture in the 1970s. Perhaps this commercialization of the counterculture has reached its crescendo in the early twenty-first century with the legalization of recreational marijuana. Capitalist entrepreneurs are seeking to cash in on this lucrative market, while governments perceive the once "demon weed" as a significant new source of revenue. While the dominant corporate culture was able to commercialize symbols of the counterculture such as music, fashion, and marijuana into harmless recreational activities, the radical politics of the 1960s with their connection to the indigenous radicalism of America's past were a far more serious threat and elicited a much more repressive response.

Port Huron Statement, Berkeley Free Speech Movement, and student rebellion

Students have historically often played an important role in political protest, seeking to put the ideas they are studying into practice and having not yet established families and careers which political activities might endanger. The college generation of the 1950s, however, was in no mood to challenge the status quo, perceiving education as providing a security blanket to protect them from the vicissitudes of depression and war. Their baby boomer children, including many first-generation college students, were encouraged by the Civil Rights Movement and Vietnam War to ask more questions of their materialistic society. The interrogation of the liberal consensus by a new generation was perhaps best exemplified by *The Port Huron Statement* (1962) written by Michigan student Tom Hayden during a retreat for Students for a Democratic Society (SDS) sponsored by the United Auto Workers.

Hayden's manifesto criticized American racism, materialism, and imperialism. Rejecting the old left of the Communist Party, *The Port Huron Statement* called for nuclear disarmament and a participatory democracy in which all Americans would work together to create a more egalitarian society. Calling for a new student left, Hayden insisted that it was the mission of the university to help forge a new democratic order rather than employ its resources to maintain the status quo. *The Port Huron Statement*, the Civil Rights Movement, the growing war in Vietnam, and the Free Speech Movement at the University of California, Berkeley, helped foster the growth of SDS on college campuses.

The free speech struggle at the University of California grew out of the student concerns expressed in *The Port Huron Statement* as well as the doctrine of *loco parentis* in which the university acted as a parental supervisor to monitor the behavior of students. After returning from summer activities in the civil rights struggle, students in the fall of 1964 were informed that university regulations forbid the distribution of political literature on topics such as civil rights. The arrest of students for distributing leaflets from civil rights organizations set off campus demonstrations, including the blocking of a police car containing the arrested defendants. Speaking from atop the police car, graduate student Mario Savio emerged as one of the student leaders. Savio placed the student rebellion in the broadest of perspectives, asserting that individuals must take risks to disrupt the gears of bureaucracy and authority that seek to control them and deny personal expression. Expanding protests and an occupation of the administration building led to the arrest of over 800 students. Responding to the arrests, the faculty senate censured the administration, which backed down and opened the campus to political debate, returning university life to what many students and professors considered to be the real purpose of higher education: a free exchange of ideas.

The free speech movement expanded to other campuses, encouraging discussion and "teach-ins" on the expanding war in Southeast Asia. With conscription quotas increasing, campus protests of the war grew, often organized by university SDS chapters, including the burning of draft cards. The Reserve Officers Training Corps (ROTC), a required course at some universities for many males during the early 1960s, also drew criticism from antiwar protestors, who also resented the presence of military recruiters and war industries on campus. No only were students concerned about their draft status and that of friends and family members, but they sought a way to express their moral concerns and responsibility for the actions their government was taking in Vietnam.

Despite the growing protest, the war persisted and increased student frustration. The Presidential election year of 1968 witnessed increased violence in Vietnam and on the streets of America. The Tet Offensive demonstrated that the war was not winding down, and the assassination of Martin Luther King Jr. led to insurrection in many American cities. Just weeks after King's death, Robert Kennedy was murdered as he sought the Presidency on an antiwar platform. Meanwhile, violence erupted on the Ivy League campus of Columbia University in New York

City. The campus SDS led by Mark Rudd called for student demonstrations against the university's connections with the military-industrial complex as well as the university's construction of a gym in the nearby predominantly black neighborhood of Morningside Heights that would be accessible to privileged students but not members of the community. The protest culminated in the violent removal of student demonstrators from the library and administration building by police. These violent arrests increased student support for the demonstrators as many non-protestors and bystanders were beaten by the police, inducing Columbia University into surrendering to many of the protestors' demands. As for Mark Rudd, he was expelled from Columbia, emerging as one of the radical leaders of the Weather Underground.

A police riot and the Chicago Seven

The violence of 1968 seemed to reach a crescendo in the protests at the Chicago Democratic National Convention which resulted in a police riot and ensuing trial of the Chicago Seven. As the Democrats prepared to nominate Vice President Hubert Humphrey and ignore the antiwar candidacy of Eugene McCarthy, approximately 10,000 protestors sponsored by SDS, the National Mobilization Committee to End the War in Vietnam, and the Youth International Party (Yippies) prepared to descend upon the city of Chicago. Mayor Richard Daley pledged that his city's streets would not be controlled by protestors, arranging for the deployment of over 20,000 police and National Guard troops to control the protests. Refusing to grant permits for demonstrators or allow them to sleep in the city parks, Daley's tactics guaranteed there would be confrontations in the streets of Chicago. The protests began in a more frivolous atmosphere with rock concerts, and the Yippies led by Jerry Rubin and Abbie Hoffman nominated a pig named Pigasus for President. However, when the authorities attempted to force demonstrators out of Grant Park and into the streets of Chicago, fighting broke out between the police and protestors chanting, "the whole world is watching." As tear gas engulfed downtown Chicago, the police turned their clubs on television crews, reporters, and Democratic Convention delegates who expressed support or sympathy for the mostly young demonstrators. Meanwhile, in the convention hall where Humphrey was nominated, Democratic delegates denounced Daley for employing Gestapo tactics in the streets of Chicago. When the smoke cleared, hundreds of police, demonstrators, and bystanders were injured in what the Walker Commission, appointed to study the violence, later called a police riot.

Daley refused to apologize, and the Justice Department indicted eight protest leaders for conspiracy and incitement to riot. The defendants and their attorney William Kunstler were confrontational and succeeded in frustrating Judge Julius Hoffman. Abbie Hoffman (no relation to the judge) would show up for trial dressed in judicial robes and turn cartwheels in the courtroom, and the judge ordered Black Panther leader Bobby Seale to be bound and gagged due to his courtroom outbursts—with Seale's trial eventually being severed from the other seven defendants. Judge Hoffman issued long contempt penalties for attorney Kunstler and his clients, who were convicted of crossing state lines to incite a riot, but the convictions and contempt citations were overturned on appeal.

The trial of the Chicago Seven was an example of guerrilla theater designed to highlight the hypocrisy of the system, but Richard Nixon was not impressed as both the harassment of suspected radicals and the war in Vietnam continued. While Nixon was beginning troop withdrawals, more American soldiers died during his Presidency than that of Johnson. In October 1969, students across the nation left their classrooms to participate in campus demonstrations and teach-ins on ending the war in Vietnam, followed the next month by a Moratorium March on Washington, which attracted hundreds of thousands of participants, demonstrating that the antiwar movement extended beyond America's colleges campuses. Yet the war continued despite these massive protests, and many of the New Left grew impatient and frustrated, leading to the breakdown of SDS during its June 1969 national convention.

Weather Underground and COINTELPRO

The organization splintered between the Progressive Labor Party, advocating for students to abandon college and infiltrate the American working class, and the Revolutionary Youth Movement, which favored revolutionary action in conjunction with the Black Panthers and global insurgent movements to bring about world communism. The Revolutionary Youth Movement evolved into the Weather Underground based on Bob Dylan's "Subterranean Homesick Blues" (1965) line that "you don't need a weatherman to know which way the wind blows." Led by radicals Mark Rudd, Bernardine Dohrn, and Bill Ayers, the Weather Underground launched a bombing campaign that they believed would bring the war home to the United States and American people. Following a March 6, 1970 bomb explosion in a Greenwich Village safe house that killed three of their colleagues, membership in the Weather Underground declined, and the organization abandoned plans for bombings whose main purpose was to inflict casualties in favor of more symbolic military and police targets with warning phone calls before the detonation of a bomb. Living as fugitives exhausted the Weather Underground, and most surrendered to authorities in the mid-1970s following the end of the Vietnam War. They had failed to achieve their revolutionary dreams, underestimating the power of the establishment as well as overestimating the appeal of their violent rhetoric and actions.

Most of the Weather Underground, however, served little time incarcerated when the illegal search and surveillance activities of the FBI were revealed. The Counter-Intelligence Program (COINTELPRO) began in the 1950s as a FBI program for the surveillance and infiltration of the Communist Party as well as right-wing groups such as the KKK. In the 1960s, J. Edgar Hoover expanded these activities to target the Civil Rights Movement, Black Panther Party, student organizations such as SDS, and the antiwar movement. Hoover ordered the FBI to expose, disrupt, discredit, and neutralize organizations and their leaders whom the FBI chief deemed radical and a threat to national security. The FBI tactics included illegal wiretaps and searches without warrants, as well as encouraging factional violence and in the case of the Black Panthers participating in the "neutralization" of leadership. The existence of COINTELPRO was exposed in 1971 when the Citizens Commission to Investigate the FBI broke into the FBI office in Media, Pennsylvania, sharing their findings with the press.

Following this public exposure, Hoover announced the termination of COINTELPRO, but Nixon's war on free speech and dissent was hardly curtailed. Vice President Spiro Agnew drew headlines with his employment of alliteration in denouncing the press, dissenters, and the liberal elite. Agnew referred to the free press as the "nattering nabobs of negativism" and called leftists an "effete corps of impudent snobs." Nixon encouraged Agnew's divisive rhetoric, while praising "hard hat" construction workers who violently attacked citizens who were peacefully protesting Nixon's invasion of Cambodia. The "hard hat" riot in New York City was promoted by the leadership of the AFL-CIO who supported Nixon and the war as opposed to the rank and file membership of the union whose sons were fighting and dying in Vietnam.

Attica, Kent State, and Jackson State

The coercive powers of the establishment in the early 1970s were on display in the violent crushing of the Attica prison uprising and the shooting of protesting students at Kent State and Jackson State Universities. On September 9, 1971 a group of inmates, predominantly black, seized control of Attica Correctional Facility in Attica, New York, taking correctional officers as hostages and demanding improved living conditions in the overcrowded prison. After four days of negotiations, Governor Nelson Rockefeller refused to recognize amnesty demands for actions taken during the rebellion and ordered the retaking of the prison by force. In a bloody attack, thirty-three inmates and ten hostages were killed. Authorities insisted that the civilian and correctional officer hostages were murdered by the inmates, but autopsies later revealed that they were killed by troopers and guards who fired indiscriminately. Inmates who surrendered were subject to beatings and intimidation, although eventually the Attica uprising contributed to some prison reform measures, and the state settled financial claims from families whose relatives were slain in the retaking of the prison.

Attica again demonstrated that the state would ruthlessly crush black rebellion, and students learned this lesson as well in the aftermath of campus protests erupting against the May 1970 invasion of Cambodia. At Kent State, the Governor of Ohio dispatched the National Guard to quell further violence after the ROTC building on campus was burned. On May 4, after the Guard had dispersed an angry crowd on the university campus, the situation seemed somewhat under control when suddenly Guardsmen turned and fired into the crowd, killing four students and wounding nine others, some of whom were bystanders and had nothing to do with the protests. The Guardsmen would later maintain they heard shots fired and believed that their lives were in danger. Many student and faculty witnesses insisted that the Guardsmen were in no danger, and the Kent State shootings were premeditated murder. No Guardsmen were ever convicted in the Kent State shootings, although the state would later approve payments to the victims and their families. The Kent State shooting set off massive student protests and strikes on campuses throughout the country. Police and Guardsmen were ordered to many campuses, with the bayonetting of students at the University of New Mexico and two black students killed at Jackson State University in Mississippi, although the Jackson State shootings of black students never captured the public imagination in the same way as the killing of white students at Kent State. Many universities shut down in wake of the protests and violence, with many cancelling final examinations in the spring of 1970. However, when universities reopened in the fall, passions had cooled and the atmosphere on campus was more tranquil. Students had won greater freedoms, especially regarding issues of *loco parentis* governing curfews and sexuality, but a fundamental rebellion against the university as an institution of the corporate capitalist order was crushed. The triumph of the establishment and military-industrial complex was seemingly ratified in the 1972 Presidential election with the overwhelming re-election of Nixon over antiwar Democratic candidate George McGovern of South Dakota who only carried the state of Massachusetts.

Patty Hearst and the legacy of rebellion in the 1960s

Yet, the cultural and political dissent of the era had one last bizarre episode in the kidnapping of Patty Hearst that sheds some light on what happened to the counterculture. In 1974, Patty Hearst, the granddaughter of millionaire publishing magnate William Randolph Hearst, was kidnapped by radicals who called themselves the Symbionese Liberation Army. She was held for a ransom that included the Hearst family contributing several million dollars to feed the poor in the San Francisco area. Several months later, Hearst emerged as the revolutionary Tonia and joined her captors in a bank robbery. Tonia escaped a gun battle in which many of her Symbionese Liberation Army colleagues were killed, and she remained on the run until she was captured in September 1975. She was placed on trial for her crimes as an "urban guerrilla" in 1976, dropping her radical posturing and claiming to be a victim of the "Stockholm syndrome" and had been brainwashed by her captors. Hearst was found guilty by a jury; however, President Jimmy Carter commuted her sentence, and Bill Clinton issued a full pardon for the heiress. The Patty Hearst saga seems to epitomize the story of many white hippies who dropped out of their middle and upper social class life to experiment with the communal alternatives of the counterculture, only to escape back into the security of their parents and consensus capitalist values.

The Vietnam War tore apart American society and fostered an environment in which many young Americans experimented with the new consciousness of a counterculture, but the violence, excesses, and repression of the 1960s culminated in the triumph of conservativism in the guise of Richard Nixon and Ronald Reagan. The Vietnam experience encouraged a questioning of authority figures and the establishment in American society whether in government, education, religion, the workplace, or the family. Americans emerged from the era with a healthy disrespect for authority and greater sense of personal freedom, but the changes were often more style than substance. American imperialism and corporate capitalism were challenged in the 1960s, but they retained their core influence over a nation where the Civil Rights Movement and personal liberation struggles had expanded opportunities for minorities and women beyond the patriarchy and white middle class. The conservative forces that employed fear and prejudice to crush the rebellion of the 1960s, however, had another scare in the 1970s when the abuses of power in the Watergate scandal threatened the American political establishment.

Further Reading:

Bowden, Mark. *Hue 1968: A Turning Point of the American War in Vietnam*. New York: Atlantic Monthly Press, 2017.

Farber, David. *The Age of Great Dreams: America in the 1960s*. New York: Hill and Wang, 1994.

Gaillard, Frye. *A Hard Rain: America in the 1960s: Our Decade of Hope, Possibility and Innocence Lost*. Montgomery, AL: NewSouth Books, 2018.

Gitlin, Todd. *The Sixties: Years of Hope, Days of Rage*. New York: Bantam Books, 1987.

Herring, George. *America's Longest War: The United States and Vietnam, 1950–1975*. New York: Wiley, 1979.

Isserman, Maurice and Michael Kazin. *America Divided: The Civil War of the 1960s*. New York: Oxford University Press, 2000.

Karnow, Stanley. *Vietnam: A History*. New York: Viking, 1983.

Logevall, Fredrik. *Embers of War: The Fall of an Empire and the Making of America's Vietnam*. New York: Random House, 2012.

Matusow, Allen J. *The Unraveling of America: A History of Liberalism in the 1960s*. New York: Harper & Row, 1984.

Oglesby, Carl. *Ravens in the Storm: A Personal History of the 1960s Anti-War Movement*. New York: Scribner, 2008.

Thompson, Heather Ann. *Blood in the Water: The Attica Prison Uprising of 1971 and Its Legacy*. New York: Pantheon Books, 2016.

Young, Marilyn. *Vietnam Wars, 1945–1990*. New York: HarperCollins, 1991.

28

The Triumph of the Right: America in the 1970s and 1980s

Ronald Reagan, 1981. Prints and Photographs Division, Library of Congress. Reagan asserted that he would reinvigorate the Cold War and reduce the size of government. Yet, his administration recorded record deficits, and the "Great Communicator" was fortunate to find a Soviet leader in Mikhail Gorbachev who partnered with him to end the Cold War and avoid a nuclear nightmare.

The liberal consensus, as exemplified by President Johnson's allegiance to reform in the Great Society and the Cold War with the conflict in Southeast Asia, was challenged from both the political right and left during the 1960s. The leftist attack from the counterculture, Black Panthers, SDS, and other radicals received the most attention from the media as well as consensus politicians who perceived the left as threatening corporate capitalism. Following the overwhelming defeat of Barry Goldwater in the 1964 Presidential election, the liberal consensus seemed to give little thought to what they assumed was a discredited extremist movement that had been rejected by the American people. The political right, however, took a differing approach to the lessons one might draw from the 1964 election. Political defeat did not lead them to question their essential values such as adherence to the marketplace and rejection of government interference in the economy as undermining American individualism and fostering dependency.

Rise of the New Right

This rather libertarian philosophy was akin to the rugged individualism of Herbert Hoover, and the goal of the New Right was to dismantle the New Deal and welfare state. The problem with this strategy was that many working-class Americans were quite pleased with and even dependent upon New Deal programs such as Social Security. Thus, the New Right focused much of their attention upon criticizing government programs such as affirmative action and busing to achieve school integration as favoring minorities at the expense of the white working class. The New Right also aligned with conservative fundamentalist Christian ministers such as Jerry Falwell to form the Moral Majority—which critics argued was neither—to mobilize evangelicals as a conservative voting bloc to oppose abortion, gay rights, and feminism which were perceived as threats to the traditional family. Social issues, thus, dominated the political ideology of many New Right voters who seemed to acquiesce in the dismantling of the New Deal and Great Society programs if they were protected from the rise of welfare cheats, gays, minorities, feminists, and radicals whom the liberal consensus was accused of fostering and pandering.

The rise of the New Right was also encouraged by the formation of conservative think tanks such as the American Enterprise Institute and Heritage

Foundation that provided intellectual justification for the movement along with Nobel Prize-winner in Economics, Milton Friedman from the University of Chicago. The influential Friedman rejected the government intervention of Keynesian economics and advocated personal choice and responsibility as the solution to most of America's problems, and his views were widely circulated in a weekly column for *Newsweek* magazine. Meanwhile, the conservative think tanks, financed by wealthy industrialists such as Charles and David Koch opposed to government regulation, emerged as spokespersons for limited government and private enterprise, whose lack of intellectual and financial independence from corporate America is rarely challenged in the mainstream media. In addition to the intellectual support provided by the think tanks, the New Right proved to be quite successful in raising funds through the direct mailing strategy of Richard Viguerie who targeted politically conservative voters and contributors.

The conservative reaction to the New Deal, Great Society, and upheavals of the 1960s led to the elections of Republican Presidents Nixon and Reagan. In the midst of the cultural and political wars of the 1960s, Nixon's Presidency in many ways reflected the resentment of many in the middle class to the rise of the counterculture, but the blooming of the New Right in American politics came a decade later. The influence of the New Right was to reach its zenith with the affable Reagan who was able to somewhat disguise his ideological proclivities as a spokesman for corporate America under the guise of a self-effacing personality with which many Americans felt comfortable. The triumph of conservatism seemed almost institutionalized with the elections of Republican George H. W. Bush and a fairly conservative Democrat in Bill Clinton, but in the twenty-first century the growing gap between rich and poor in America increased, exacerbating social tensions and exposing Americans to the specter of terrorism which replaced communism as an international threat. While the narrow election of Donald Trump in 2016 demonstrated that the politics of conservatism, fear, and resentment still enjoyed some appeal, a younger generation and the demographics of a more diverse nation seemed to provide an alternative to the conservative victory of the 1980s, offering a new opportunity for the country to achieve a more inclusive incarnation of its founding principles.

Economic challenges of the 1970s

It is also important to recognize that the triumph of the New Right conservativism, with its agenda of marketplace economics, dismantling the New Deal, and emphasizing the divisiveness of social issues, took place during a period of economic decline that terrified many Americans who were encouraged by the right to blame scapegoats such as hippies, minorities, liberals, and welfare queens—a favorite phrase of President Reagan—for their plight. Plowing the ground of resentment, the right discouraged Americans from a more honest appraisal of how the policies of corporate America were impacting their daily lives. The period after World War II from 1945 to the late 1960s was the most sustained period of economic growth in American history with many working Americans able to attain their own homes and even send their children to college. This growth and such massive infrastructure projects as the Interstate Highway Act along with the G.I. Bill were financed by large corporate tax rates as well as high rates on individuals with significant incomes, demonstrating that government expenditures and taxation were not an obstacle to growth. The post war prosperity was also a product of the competitive advantage enjoyed by American businesses who dominated world markets. American industries shifted from producing war materials to consumer goods, and there was little competition from other nations whose factories were damaged or destroyed by the global conflict. However, nations such as Germany and Japan, whose industrial base was devastated had to rebuild from scratch, which meant that over time they could incorporate the latest technology into their plants. Thus, foreign competition moved ahead of American industries who did not plan for this contingency and changing consumption patterns. A good example of this is the American automobile industry which had once dominated the world but failed to recognize in the words of Bob Dylan that the times were "a' changin.'" World oil prices were rising, and the United States was increasingly dependent upon foreign oil from the Middle East. In 1973, the Organization of Exporting Petroleum Countries (OPEC), dominated by Arab states, announced an oil embargo of Western nations such as the United States for supporting Israel during the Yom Kippur War. While having little impact on policies toward Israel, the embargo sent a shock wave through the American economy as rising oil prices contributed to inflation and long lines at gasoline stations with limited supplies for Americans who valued the freedom of the open road that was limited by Congressional action establishing a national speed limit set at fifty-five miles per hour. As the world and American consumers began to value smaller and more gasoline efficient automobiles, the major American car companies such as General Motors, Ford, and Chrysler continued to produce gas-guzzling large automobiles, while emerging companies such as Honda, Toyota, and Hyundai in Japan and Korea responded to the changing market by producing cheaper and more fuel-efficient automobiles. The result was declining sales and the loss of American jobs in an industry that had helped to propel the post war prosperity. A similar fate befell American industries such as steel and rubber production.

As the American manufacturing jobs moved abroad to cheaper sources of production, the foundation of the American economy shifted from manufacturing to the service industry with retail, restaurant, and hotel jobs paying less than industrial occupations. In addition, the loss of the manufacturing base contributed to the decline of American unions. With their reduction in membership, the unions were unable to serve as a countervailing power to corporate influence. Losing jobs, benefits, and pensions, American workers blamed minorities and immigrants along with policies such as affirmative action for their plight rather than automation and the failure of corporate America to plan ahead and look to the retraining of the job force in a more competitive and technological marketplace. The white ethnic working class identified with Rocky Balboa in the film *Rocky* (1976); a boxer whose gym locker is taken by a more promising black fighter, but Rocky realizes his dream of going the distance with the black champion.

In addition to recession and rising unemployment, America in the 1970s had to deal with inflation, creating the seemingly impossible economic dilemma of "stagflation." While rising oil prices were a significant cause of inflation, perhaps the most important factor was the reluctance of the Johnson administration to raise taxes. The President was afraid that if he let the American people know how much the Vietnam War was really costing, Congress might reduce funding for his Great Society programs. The result of the failure to raise taxes was growing deficits and inflation, while in the final analysis much of Johnson's Great Society and War on Poverty was sacrificed to the Vietnam War. Thus, after his narrow election over Humphrey in 1968, Nixon inherited a nation mired in an unpopular war with a declining economy. This state of affairs seemed to fit well with Nixon's self-perception as the perpetual outsider who had to always battle against the entrenched wealthy elites of the American establishment. This sense of resentment and anger helped foster the isolation and abuses of power that eventually led to Nixon's political demise during the Watergate scandal.

The return of Richard Nixon

Richard Nixon was born into a California Quaker family of modest means and attended public school rather than elite private schools. Although he was accepted at Harvard, Nixon was needed to work in the family store and attended nearby Whittier College, where he excelled at debate and rarely played on the school football squad. He was awarded a full scholarship to the newly established Duke Law School. After graduation from Duke, Nixon returned to California in order to practice law, and during World War II he served in the Naval reserves. Following the war, Nixon was elected to Congress, where he established a reputation as a staunch anticommunist, serving as a member of HUAC and denouncing Alger Hiss as a Soviet agent, whom he also detested for Hiss's privileged background. In 1950, Nixon ran for the Senate, defeating liberal Democrat and former actress Helen Gahagan Douglas whom Nixon derided as a member of the Hollywood elite and "the pink lady" sympathetic to communist causes. Two years later, anticommunist Republicans insisted that Eisenhower accept Nixon as his running mate, although the Senator was almost dumped from the Republican ticket for accepting illegal campaign contributions, but he saved himself in the Checkers speech in which he depicted the Nixon family as poor and asserted that he would not return the gift of a family dog whom his daughters adored. After serving eight years as Vice President, Nixon was narrowly defeated for the Presidency in 1960 by Kennedy, only increasing his disdain for wealthy liberal elites who enjoyed unfair advantages over a common man like Dick

Nixon. Two years later, Nixon was defeated in a contest for the Governorship of California by Democratic incumbent Pat Brown, and Nixon angrily announced his retirement from politics.

After a few years in the political wilderness, Nixon determined that the Democrats were vulnerable in 1968, and he was able to receive the Republican nomination. While much of the campaign was focused upon the issue of Vietnam, Nixon sought to take advantage of middle-class white fears of black lawlessness and rioting by asserting that he was the candidate who could restore law and order to the streets of America. In this regard, Nixon was stealing the thunder of independent candidate Governor George Wallace of Alabama, whose appeal was limited by the violence of his rhetoric and the skirmishes that sometimes marred his campaign rallies. Borrowing upon his own sense of resentment and ostracism, Nixon identified with middle-class white voters who believed that liberal judges were fostering an environment of permissiveness that tolerated dissent, reverse discrimination, and the destruction of traditional American moral standards. In office, Nixon developed the Southern strategy, hoping to take advantage of regional discontent over Democratic passage of civil rights legislation such as the Civil Rights Act of 1964 and Voting Rights Act of 1965. The Nixon administration announced its opposition to court-mandated busing to achieve racial integration, and Nixon endeavored to appoint judges that opposed expansion of civil rights and the imposition of racial busing plans to integrate the schools. Nixon's Southern strategy worked as the Republican Party continues to dominate Southern politics, winning dominant percentages of the white vote, while minority blacks formed an allegiance to the Democratic Party.

Nixon and the Warren Court

Nixon also railed against the liberal decisions of the Supreme Court presided over by Chief Justice Earl Warren, a Republican appointee of President Eisenhower, whom the extremist John Birch Society insisted should be impeached. Although two of his initial appointments were rejected by the Senate, Nixon eventually had the opportunity to appoint four justices, but the court disappointed conservatives and Nixon by rejecting the President's claims of executive privilege during the Watergate crisis and approving the right of women to privacy and access to abortion in the *Roe v. Wade* (1973) decision.

The *Brown v. Board* (1954) case was only one of many Warren Court decisions that confounded conservatives. In *Gideon v. Wainwright* (1963), the Supreme Court ruled that the state must provide an attorney for a defendant who could not afford legal counsel, while in *Miranda v. Arizona* (1966) the court decreed that defendants facing police interrogation must be appraised of their Constitutional rights, including the right to an attorney. In *Baker v. Carr* (1962), the court called for the concept of "one man, one vote," outlawing electoral districts that discriminated against urban areas in favor of rural voters; although gerrymandering by state legislatures has been able to thwart the purpose of the court's ruling. *Griswold v. Connecticut* (1965) overturned a state law that banned the use of any device or drug for the purpose of contraception, establishing an expectation of privacy that provided a foundation for the court's 1973 abortion ruling. One of the court's most controversial decisions was *Engel v. Vitale* (1962) which declared state-mandated prayer in the public schools to be an un-Constitutional violation of the separation between church and state; although as one politician observed "as long as there are math tests, there will be prayer in the public schools." In *Roth v. United States* (1957), the court was accused of expanding the limits of pornography by ruling that material could only be banned if the dominant theme was an effort to appeal to the prurient interest of an average citizen, applying "contemporary community standards." Dissent was protected in *Tinker v. Des Moines Independent School District* (1969) which upheld that students could protest the Vietnam War by wearing arm bands as long as their actions did not constitute "substantial disruption" of school activities.

Eager to demonstrate his opposition to the permissive Warren Court and currying support in the white South, Nixon welcomed the opportunity in 1969 to replace the retiring Warren with conservative jurist Warren Burger. Later that year, Nixon was able to make another appointment when embattled Justice Abe Fortas resigned from the court. Nixon selected Clement Haynsworth, an appellate judge from South Carolina, who was opposed by liberal groups who challenged his rulings on labor and civil rights issues. Haynsworth became the first Supreme Court nominee to be rejected by the Senate since the Hoover Presidency in 1930, and Nixon had no better luck with his next nominee to fill the Fortes vacancy. Again seeking to implement his Southern strategy, Nixon selected G. Harrold Carswell, a federal judge in Florida. Carswell's decisions regarding civil rights for blacks and women also drew criticism amid allegations that the judge belonged to a private segregated club. Nixon once again suffered defeat at the hands of the Senate. As for Carswell, he returned to Florida, resigned his judicial position, and ran for the Senate, but his candidacy was rejected by Florida voters. To fill the vacant court seat, a frustrated Nixon appointed Burger's Minnesota associate, Harry Blackmun, who was confirmed unanimously by the Senate. Blackmun, however, antagonized many conservatives and Nixon by authoring the court's majority opinion in the *Roe v. Wade* abortion case. Nixon's conservative appointees also failed to provide legal cover for the President during the Watergate crisis. Conservatives, however, were pleased with the Burger Court in the *Milliken v. Bradley* (1974) case that prohibited school busing desegregation plans from crossing school district lines, in effect recognizing *de facto* segregation in America's suburbs. Also. the *Bakke* decision (1978) ruled against the employment of racial quotas in college admissions; although the court concluded that race or ethnicity might be employed along with other factors to create a more diverse student body.

Progressive legislation and environmental protections

While Nixon battled with Congress over the Vietnam War and the Supreme Court, significant progressive legislation was enacted during the Nixon Presidency. Nixon signed into law the Education Amendment of 1972 to the 1964 Civil Rights Act, which included Title IX prohibiting sexual discrimination in educational programs or activities receiving federal funds. Although the original intent of the legislation was not focused on athletics, much of the subsequent controversy surrounding the implementation of Title IX has involved gender equity in school and collegiate athletic programs. While critics of Title IX lamented that the legislation would destroy traditional male sports, men's football and basketball programs have maintained their dominant position in the lucrative world of intercollegiate athletics. On the other hand, Title IX may be credited with promoting the opportunity for a new generation of young women to participate in athletic competition like their male counterparts while attending school and college. Nixon, however, refused to aid working women when he vetoed legislation that would have provided for nationwide public daycare.

Nixon's greatest legislative achievements were an enlargement of the federal government's responsibility for safeguarding the nation's environment. The origins of the modern environmental movement are often traced to the publication of marine biologist Rachel Carson's *Silent Spring* (1962), exposing the danger posed by pesticides to America's food supplies and suburbs. In this interpretation, environmentalism is perceived as a middle-class movement rooted in the suburbs. In reality, the history of environmentalist activism traces its origins to people of color and the working class confronting dangerous industrial pollution in the workplace and their daily living conditions. This overlooked history runs from the efforts of nineteenth-century New England mill workers to deal with the pollution and damming of streams to the twentieth-century efforts of Cesar Chavez and the United Fruit Workers to address the dangers of pesticides to workers as well as consumers. Hippies and the counterculture built upon this rich working-class history of protest to promote the first Earth Day on April 22, 1970. Also championed by politicians such as Senator Gaylord Nelson of Wisconsin, a staunch conservationist, Earth Day was to foster national attention upon the damage done to the environment by industrial pollution as well as question the assumption that resources are infinite, and prosperity is based upon continuous economic expansion. This production ethic embraced by European colonists replaced the conservation ethos of America's Native population, but Earth Day was an effort to redress this balance, culminating in some significant pieces of legislation such as the Clean Air Act of 1970, Clean Water Act of 1970, and Endangered Species Act of 1973, in addition to the creation of the Environmental Protection Agency (EPA) and Occupational Safety and Health Administration (OSHA) in 1970. While these environmental reforms have certainly contributed to the reduction of industrial pollution, they have not adequately addressed carbon emissions which continue to plague the world with climate change. In addition, administrations unfriendly to regulation such as the Trump Presidency may appoint regulators from industry to rollback safeguards and protections.

Pinochet coup in Chile

While it is possible to point to some progressive accomplishments from the Nixon administration, the Nixon Presidency was eventually destroyed by a sense of paranoia and secrecy that sought to place the President above the law. The autocratic nature of Nixon's imperial Presidency was evident in his handling of Vietnam, the Pentagon Papers and Watergate, and the 1973 military coup in Chile. In 1970, Marxist Salvador Allende was elected President of a democratic Chile. American business interests in Chile such as Anaconda Copper and International Telephone & Telegraph, which controlled about three-quarters of the Chilean phone system, were opposed to nationalization policies pursued by the Allende government, demanding that the Nixon administration protect American corporations. Nixon and Secretary of State Kissinger denounced Allende's Marxist agenda with Cold War rhetoric, claiming that Castro was attempting to garner influence in Latin America after the CIA had foiled the efforts of his chief lieutenant Che Guevara to foment insurrection in Bolivia. Relying upon the covert operations which had proven so successful for the Eisenhower administration in Iran and Guatemala, Nixon and Kissinger employed the CIA to foster opposition toward Allende among business groups, unions, and the military. On September 11, 1973, the Chilean military, with the approval of the CIA, launched a military coup that overthrew democratically elected Allende. As troops stormed the Presidential palace, Allende took his own life. The Chilean military rounded up thousands of dissidents whom they placed in Santiago's national stadium for interrogation, torture, and murder, including poet Victor Jara who was often called the Chilean Bob Dylan. The coup culminated in the repressive regime of General Augusto Pinochet, who reopened Chilean resources for American investment and whose regime apparently carried out the murder of Chilean political dissident Orlando Letelier on the streets of Washington DC in 1976. Nixon's opposition to democratic institutions was quite evident in the U.S. backing for the Pinochet coup.

Pentagon Papers and Election of 1972

Nor was Nixon necessarily an advocate for democratic institutions within the United States as is evidenced by his handling of the Pentagon Papers and ensuing

Watergate scandal. The Pentagon Papers were a report on the origins of the Vietnam War prepared for the Defense Department by the RAND Corporation. The detailed study concluded that American entrance into the Vietnam War was a mistake and especially criticized President Johnson for misleading the American people about the nature of the conflict. Although the report was quite critical of the Democrats, Nixon decided to keep the Pentagon Papers classified as he feared their release might further undermine support for the war. Believing that the American people had a right to see the information that Nixon refused to release, Daniel Ellsberg, a former Marine and Defense Department consultant for the RAND Corporation, secretly made copies of the study and gave them to the *New York Times*. When the *Times* began publication of the Pentagon Papers, the Nixon administration sought a prior restraint injunction to halt publication. While the *Times* appealed the injunction, other newspapers such as the *Washington Post* also received copies of the report which they printed. On June 30, 1971, the Supreme Court ruled that the administration had failed to meet the burden of proof for prior restraint of publication, and the newspapers were allowed to continue with publication. As for Ellsberg, the Nixon administration planned to make an example of him by charging the former Marine with espionage. The case against Ellsberg, however, was compromised and eventually dismissed due to an illegal burglary of Ellsberg's psychiatrist's office authorized by John Erlichman, Assistant to the President for Domestic Affairs.

Nixon was furious over publication of the Pentagon Papers and obsessed with security and leaks to the press. This paranoia led to the formation of a secret group known as the plumbers under the direction of E. Howard Hunt, a former CIA operative, and Gordon Liddy, who previously worked for the FBI, and placed under the overall control of former Attorney General John Mitchell who was heading the Committee to Re-elect the President (CREEP). Although there is little evidence to suggest that the President authorized the illegal entry, on June 17, 1970, the plumbers broke into the Democratic headquarters at the Watergate Hotel in Washington. Five burglars were arrested and appeared before U.S. District Judge John Sirica, who decided to pursue the case after Watergate burglary defendant James McCord insisted that the action was part of a larger conspiracy. While most of the mainstream media initially paid little attention to the burglary, metro reporters Bob Woodward and Carl Bernstein of the *Washington Post* pursued the story with the aid of a secret source, Deep Throat—who later proved to be Associate FBI Director Mark Felt who resented Nixon administration efforts to curtail the investigation, but Felt would have his own legal problems for authorizing illegal wiretaps in pursuit of 1960s radicals such as the Weather Underground.

On the eve of the 1972 election, the *Washington Post* published an article describing a "dirty tricks" campaign to disrupt the Democratic primaries, spreading rumors and discrediting such candidates as Maine Senator Ed Muskie. These tactics helped to assure the nomination of South Dakota Senator George McGovern, whose liberal views and vehement opposition to the Vietnam War made him the opponent Nixon believed he could most easily defeat. But some of the damage to the McGovern campaign was self-inflicted. For a running mate, McGovern selected

Missouri Senator Tom Eagleton. Shortly after the Miami Beach Democratic Convention, however, it was revealed that Eagleton in the past had suffered from mental health issues. The ensuing controversy convinced McGovern that he had to dump Eagleton, whom he replaced with Kennedy family in-law Sargent Shriver. The Eagleton affair also demonstrates the stigma attached to issues of mental health in the United States.

Watergate crisis

Nixon trounced McGovern in both the popular vote and Electoral College, but the Watergate issue that voters ignored refused to die. Investigations by Archibald Cox, who was appointed as the Justice Department's Special Prosecutor for Watergate, and a Senate panel, headed by Senator Sam Ervin of North Carolina, uncovered evidence that the President was involved in efforts to cover up connections between the Watergate burglary and White House. Former White House Counsel John Dean testified that the President had discussed making cash payments to guarantee the silence of the burglars. Nixon denied these accusations, but when it was revealed that the President secretly taped all of his White House conversations, the Senate Watergate Committee demanded that the President surrender the tapes to them or the Special Prosecutor as the tapes would apparently determine whether Dean or Nixon were lying to the American people. Nixon refused to surrender the tape recordings, and on October 20, 1973, in an episode that would become known as the Saturday Night Massacre, Attorney General Elliot Richardson and his deputy William Ruckelshaus resigned rather than follow the President's order to fire Special Prosecutor Cox. Solicitor General Robert Bork finally agreed to implement the Presidential demands, but the dismissal of Cox turned popular opinion against Nixon with demands for his impeachment growing. In the midst of the Watergate crisis, on October 10, 1973 Vice President Spiro Agnew, who had served as the President's most vocal critic of liberals, resigned after being accused of accepting bribes and income tax evasion when he served as Governor of Maryland. Under the provisions of the Twenty-fifth Amendment, Nixon appointed House Minority Leader Gerald Ford of Michigan to fill the Vice-Presidential vacancy, and Congress ratified the choice of a popular colleague despite increasing discontent with the President.

Meanwhile, Nixon attempted to convince Congress to accept White House-edited transcripts of the Presidential recordings. Instead, on July 24, 1974, the Supreme Court unanimously rejected Nixon's claims of executive privilege, ordering the President to surrender the tapes which appeared to substantiate Dean's accusations and offer proof of the President's intentions to obstruct justice, despite Nixon's assurance that he was "not a crook." The House Judiciary Committee then approved articles of impeachment, and Republican Senators led by 1964 standard bearer Goldwater journeyed to the White House, informing Nixon that the House would support impeachment, and the President lacked the votes to survive a Senate trial. A distraught Nixon then announced his resignation on August 8, 1974. Choking back tears, the President still refused to acknowledge wrongdoing in the Watergate affair as Gerald Ford assumed the Presidency. Many scholars insist that the Watergate Crisis validates the wisdom of the nation's founders in establishing three separate branches of government. When an executive like Nixon attempted to extend his power beyond Constitutional limits, the Congressional and judicial branches of the government moved to check the President who was forced to resign. The system worked, but numerous Nixon aides remained fearful during the final days of his Presidency that Nixon, who was reportedly drinking heavily, might provoke a confrontation with the other branches of the government by relying upon his control of the military to stay in office. In the wake of the revelations of Presidential abuses of authority uncovered by the Watergate-related investigations such as the Church Committee, headed by Idaho Democratic Senator Frank Church, into the activities of the U.S. intelligence community, Congress sought to reassert their authority over American foreign relations. This reassertion of Congressional oversight was short lived, as during the 1980s President Reagan reinvigorated the Cold War and the power of the imperial Presidency. Also, Nixon denounced the free press; one of the cornerstones of democratic government for exposing his scandals, while today the press is under attack from the Trump administration as fake news. Watergate represents the essential truth that power in America must be interrogated by an informed and educated citizenry.

Ford Presidency

President Ford sought to end America's long Watergate nightmare by pardoning Nixon for any crimes he may have committed while serving as President. While Nixon's former Attorney General John Mitchell and other members of the Nixon administration, including John Dean, were convicted and served prison sentences, Ford believed that he was sparing the nation the pain of a Nixon trial. Critics, however, asserted that the pardon was a *quid pro quo* for Ford's appointment as Vice President, and the Nixon pardon cast a cloud over the short Ford Presidency. Ford assumed office amid the stagflation that plagued the economy and presided over the collapse of Saigon as the Vietnam War finally concluded. The President also antagonized conservatives in his party by appointing liberal Republican Nelson Rockefeller to the vacated Vice Presidency and signing of the Helsinki Accords, an agreement on human rights which critics claimed the Soviets violated in their treatment of their Jewish population. In addition, some traditional Republicans resented the President's wife, Betty Ford, who was outspoken in her support of the Equal Rights Amendment and women's rights. The courageous First Lady also admitted her own problems with alcohol and encouraged expanded government support for substance abuse treatment; a rare public political commitment to America's need for improved mental health care.

Conservatives convinced former California Governor Reagan to challenge Ford for the Republican nomination in 1976. Ford narrowly prevailed over Reagan at the party's convention, where Kansas Senator Bob Dole was selected to replace the controversial Rockefeller as Ford's running mate. The Democrats nominated a relatively unknown national figure, former Georgia Governor Jimmy Carter, who seemed to represent the New South and counted black leaders such as Andrew Young and Julian Bond as important advisers. Casting himself as a common Georgian peanut farmer, Carter enjoyed a reputation for honesty and openly talked about his Baptist faith, offering a refreshing counter to the murky politics of Watergate. However, his openness sometimes got Carter in trouble as when he admitted in a *Playboy* magazine interview that he had committed "lust in his heart." Carter's large lead evaporated, but Ford hurt his cause when in a televised debate he seemed ignorant about Soviet domination of Eastern Europe.

The promise of Jimmy Carter

Carter won a narrow victory over Ford, and it seemed that the nation had finally put Watergate behind it. But even the celebration of America's Bicentennial in 1976 seemed somewhat forced, and Carter inherited an economy still mired by large budget deficits and rising inflation along with an energy crisis arising from the dependency on foreign oil. A technocrat and Naval Academy graduate who was seemingly obsessed with detail, Carter struggled in his dealings with Congress, limiting his legislative achievements. Although he had little experience in foreign affairs, the Carter Presidency was beset by international events that undermined the promise of his election. Seeking to move beyond the militarism of the Vietnam War, Carter offered pardons to draft resisters and presided over the negotiations that completed the return of the Panama Canal to the Panamanian nation, although the United States reserved the right to intervene if the canal was in danger of falling into the hands of forces unfriendly to the interests of the United States. The Carter administration also completed the process of assuming full diplomatic relations with the People's Republic of China who would now hold the Chinese veto power on the UN Security Council; although Taiwan remained an important trading partner with the United States. The emphasis of the Carter administration upon human rights was evident in opposition to the white minority governments of Rhodesia and South Africa, while withdrawing support for the corrupt Somoza family that had ruled Nicaragua with the aid of the United States since the 1930s.

Perhaps Carter's greatest diplomatic achievement was the Camp David Accords between Egypt and Israel. Carter invited Israeli Prime Minister Menachem

Begin and Egyptian President Anwar Sadat to the Camp David Presidential retreat in Maryland for negotiations that the President hoped would introduce a model for peace in the volatile Middle East. In the 1978 agreement, for which Sadat and Begin received the Nobel Peace Prize, Egypt agreed to diplomatically recognize Israel in exchange for restoring Egyptian control over the Sinai Peninsula which Israel seized during the 1967 Six-Day War. The hope was that the Israeli-Egyptian formula could be extended throughout the region, and Arab states would recognize Israel's right to exist in exchange for the territory such as the West Bank which Israel captured in 1967. In 1979, Israel and Egypt signed a peace treaty, but the assassination of Sadat by fundamentalist Egyptian military officers prevented the spread of the Camp David solution.

Iranian Hostage and energy crises

In 1979, the Iranian Revolution overthrew the despotic rule of Mohammad Reza Pahlavi as the Shah of Iran who had gained power in a 1953 coup sponsored by the CIA. The Iranian Revolution culminated in the rise of religious fundamentalists led by Ayatollah Khomeni who opposed Western influence upon Iranian politics and culture. The political upheaval in Iran disrupted oil supplies to the United States, sparking another energy crisis. With gasoline supplies scarce, long lines formed at gas stations, and consumers were forced to deal with rationing that limited when they could purchase gasoline—if your license plate ended in an even number, then you could fill your tank only on an even-numbered calendar day. Carter responded to the energy crisis by retreating to Camp David for ten days where he consulted with political and business leaders. On July 15, 1979, Carter shared his conclusions with the American people in a televised address that would become known as the "malaise" speech, although the President never employed that particular word. Carter asserted that Americans must end their dependency upon foreign oil and proclaimed that his administration would foster development of synthetic fuels. But rather than a policy speech, the President talked about the need for a spiritual revival among the American people, criticizing materialism and shallow consumerism while asserting the need for sacrifice and conservation. In pursuit of this conservation theme, Carter urged Americans to turn down their thermostats, and he placed solar panels on the White House; although Reagan would later have them removed. While Carter's critics and big business panned the speech, public opinion polls indicated that the President's message resonated with average Americans. Carter, however, failed to take advantage of this popular momentum, when following the speech he fired four of his cabinet members, including Secretary of Energy James Schlesinger, sowing political uncertainty.

The Iranian situation worsened when on November 4, 1979, radical Iranian students stormed the American Embassy in Teheran, taking fifty-two American diplomats as hostages. It remains unclear as to whether the revolutionary government authorized the attack, but they decided to back the students, insisting that the hostages would be released if Carter returned the despised Shah, who had entered the United States for cancer treatment, to Iran to stand trial for his crimes. Carter refused to surrender the Shah, asserting that the Iranians had violated international law and the principle of diplomatic immunity be seizing the hostages. To pressure Iran, the Carter administration initiated a series of economic sanctions, including the freezing of Iranian assets held by American banks, to destabilize the revolutionary regime, but the crisis persisted into the 1980 electoral season. Voters seemed to be losing their patience with Carter as the hostage situation was perceived as an insult to American prestige and honor, projecting a sense of impotence toward the nation's adversaries. Finally, Carter approved a challenging military operation to rescue the hostages on April 24, 1980. However, the helicopter rescue by American special forces was aborted when technical problems and the difficult desert terrain of Iran rendered several of the aircraft inoperable. The rescue debacle resulted in a crash between American aircraft that left eight soldiers dead. The failed mission further damaged American morale, while encouraging Iranian intransigence and anger with Carter. As a final insult to Carter, the hostages were finally released on January 20, 1981, after 444 days of captivity, just as Reagan was taking the oath of office to replace Carter.

Soviet invasion of Afghanistan and election of 1980

Carter's final year in office was also marred by a deteriorating relationship with the Soviet Union. On December 27, 1979, Soviet troops invaded Afghanistan to bolster a teetering pro-Soviet regime in a strategically important nation on the borders of Iran and India. The Soviets seemed to perceive the invasion as not violating the principle of containment, for it was only in support of a regime already allied with the Soviet Union. Carter saw the situation in quite different terms, believing that Soviet aggression was targeting the Persian Gulf. In his 1980 State of the Union Address, the President proclaimed the Carter Doctrine, asserting that the United States was prepared to employ military force in defense of the Persian Gulf, an essential trade route for Middle Eastern oil into the United States and other Western nations. Carter also initiated economic sanctions against the Soviets such as an embargo on American grain and high technology exports to the Soviet Union. In addition, Carter called for the U.S. Olympic Committee to boycott the 1980 Moscow Summer Olympic Games, a move which probably did more damage to American athletes than the Soviet economy. In retaliation, the Soviets boycotted the 1984 Los Angeles Summer Olympic Games. The invasion of Afghanistan also tanked Senate ratification of the SALT II Treaty limiting the Soviet and American nuclear arsenals. The aid to Afghan rebels fighting the Soviets initiated by Carter was expanded during the Reagan administration, and the Soviets became bogged down in what many termed "the Soviet Union's Vietnam War."

Confronted with the energy crisis, the holding of American hostages by the Iranians, and the Soviet invasion of Afghanistan, Carter entered the 1980 Presidential election at a considerable disadvantage, and he was challenged within his own party by Massachusetts Senator Ted Kennedy, the surviving Kennedy brother, who won several Democratic primaries. Kennedy's candidacy was tarred by a reputation for womanizing that lingered from the 1969 Chappaquiddick incident in which a young woman drowned in Kennedy's car. Nevertheless, the Kennedy challenge further damaged Carter politically. The Republicans nominated former California Governor Reagan who selected primary rival George H. W. Bush of Texas as his running mate. Carter attempted to portray his opponent as a dangerous right-wing extremist in the Goldwater mold; however, the grandfatherly Reagan, with his optimistic rhetoric that it "was morning again in America," failed to scare most Americans, and Reagan won an overwhelming electoral victory. Carter may have lost the election in 1980, but his career as an ex-President was noteworthy and perhaps more significant than his Presidency. In addition to bringing his carpentry skills to Habitats for Humanity and building homes for poor Americans, Carter established the Carter Center in Atlanta to promote international human rights and democratic elections, earning the 2002 Nobel Peace Prize for his efforts.

Emergence of Ronald Reagan

The victory of Reagan and his two terms as President are often heralded as the triumph of conservatism with the defeat of the Soviet Union and end of the Cold War, coupled with a scaled down government and attack on the welfare state. The legacy of Reagan, however, is far more complex, and the growing economic gap between rich and poor in America, along with the instability of areas such as Central America and Afghanistan, indicate that the victory of conservatism and Reagan was perhaps not a "triumph" at all. Reagan, who was sixty-nine when he took the oath of office, was born on February 6, 1911 to a family of modest means in Tampico, Illinois. His father was a salesman with a drinking problem, and the young boy was very close to his religious mother. Reagan was athletic and enjoyed drama in school, often working as a lifeguard in the summer, leading some biographers to conclude that the lifeguard analogy was important to the Reagan psyche, as he wanted to save his mother, distressed swimmers, and as President the American people. After graduating from little Eureka College in Iowa, Reagan was employed as a radio announcer, whose specialty was recreating baseball games based on minimal wire service accounts of the contests, fostering a sense of exaggeration and hyperbole which many critics argue characterized his Presidency. In 1937, the handsome announcer who recreated the games of the Chicago Cubs took a screen test and was awarded with a contract from Warner Brothers. Although not exactly a Hollywood "star," Reagan enjoyed a solid career, marrying actress Jane Wyman and appearing in numerous films as the sidekick to action hero and leading man Errol Flynn, with his most famous role probably as George Gipp in *Knute Rockne, All-American* (1940). After stateside military service during the Second World War, Reagan struggled to regain momentum in his film career. He ended up divorcing Wyman whose star was rising following an Oscar winning-performance in *Johnny Belinda* (1948). Reagan would later marry actress Nancy Davis who played opposite him in *Hell-cats of the Navy* (1957). As his acting career wound down, Reagan turned his attention to hosting television shows such as *General Electric Theater* as well as politics.

In the 1930s, Reagan was an enthusiastic supporter of Franklin Roosevelt and the New Deal, but during the post-World War II atmosphere of the liberal consensus and anticommunism, Reagan's politics moved to the right. A turning point was apparently Reagan's period as President of the Screen Actors Guild from 1947 to 1952. During this time, Hollywood was plagued by fierce labor disputes regarding union recognition, and Reagan sided with management in favoring the anticommunist International Alliance of Theatrical Stage Employees. In addition, Reagan testified before HUAC when the committee was invited to Hollywood by the reactionary Motion Picture Alliance for the Preservation of American Ideals, and the union president secretly supplied HUAC with information on members of his union whose politics were suspect. After serving as a host for *General Electric Theater*, Reagan began appearing as a political spokesman for the conservative General Electric (GE) corporation opposed to extending the regulatory powers of the state. Reagan's performances as a corporate spokesman for GE proved quite popular, and on the eve of the 1964 election, he delivered a televised speech praising Senator Goldwater and denouncing the socialist trappings of Johnson's Great Society. The speech was not enough to save the Goldwater campaign, but it impressed California conservatives and business interests who prevailed upon the actor to challenge incumbent Democratic Governor Pat Brown. Campaigning against what he termed the coddling of protesting hippies and bums at the University of California, Reagan was elected Governor in 1966. Seeking to fulfill his campaign promises, Reagan dispatched the California National Guard to Berkeley during the 1969 People's Park protests that culminated in violence when residents attempted to construct a public park on university property. Reagan won re-election in 1970, but he declined to seek a third term, opting to carry his campaign against government to the national stage. When Reagan was unsuccessful in wresting the 1976 Republican nomination from Ford, he spent the next four years delivering speeches and serving as a radio commentator that kept his name and political philosophy before the American people.

Reagan political philosophy and personal popularity

Reagan's 1980 electoral victory certainly benefitted from the problems plaguing America and the Carter administration, but his popularity with some

Americans certainly grew out of his communication skills honed as a radio, Hollywood, and television personality. No intellectual, Reagan liked to place his key points on three by five notecards, and part of his appeal was to consistently adhere to a few core principles. Unlike Carter, Reagan did not believe that America was experiencing an existential crisis of confidence. Instead, Reagan served as a cheerleader for the American economy, urging expansion and growth rather than conservation. According to Reagan, the only obstacles to American greatness were government and the Soviet Union. Rather than government programs such as the New Deal and Great Society providing relief for the problems of inequality and insecurity confronting Americans, Reagan insisted that government was the problem and not the solution. Continuing to sound the refrain of Herbert Hoover, Reagan argued that government programs were a threat to individual freedom of choice and attacked the welfare state, advocating for reductions in government assistance programs such as food stamps. The President believed that the full potential of the American economy would be unleashed by lowering taxes and abolishing government regulation of business and industry. Going back to the notion of trickle-down economics, the Reagan administration advocated reduced taxation on the wealthy who would invest their tax savings into corporate expansion, creating more employment opportunities for the working class. Relying upon the theory of supply side economics, the Reagan administration insisted that a reduced tax rate would encourage so much increased economic activity that the government would generate more revenue by reducing high tax rates. The numbers for Reagan's economic program, however, did not quite add up as the tax reductions and decreased spending on government programs failed to compensate for vast increases in the military budget for both tactical and nuclear weapons, contributing to growing budget deficits. Reagan referred to the Soviet Union as the "evil empire," embarking upon a defense spending binge that would bankrupt the Soviets who could not keep up with the Americans. The eventual dissolution of the Soviet Union and end of the Cold War are considered to be Reagan's greatest achievements, but the strategy was dangerous as rather than negotiating when the Soviet system could not produce both guns and butter, Soviet hardliners might have chosen to go down in a blaze of nuclear glory rather than a whimper.

Reagan's popularity was enhanced when he survived an assassination attempt on March 30, 1981, in which he was shot at point blank range in the chest outside the Washington Hilton Hotel. The motives for the attempted assassination proved to be rather bizarre. John Hinckley Jr. was a mentally disturbed young man who wanted to impress the actress Jodie Foster, who portrayed a child prostitute who had to be violently rescued from a pimp in Martin Scorsese's film *Taxi Driver* (1976). Hinckley was found not guilty by reason of insanity and committed to a mental institution. Reagan's Press Secretary James Brady suffered a head wound in the attack and was permanently disabled, working alongside his wife for gun control legislation that eventually culminated in the 1993 Brady Bill providing for federal background checks for the purchase of handguns. As for Reagan, he walked out of the hospital after two weeks, an amazing recovery for a man of his age.

Dark side of the Reagan domestic agenda

While the attempted assassination and Reagan's rapid recovery tended to increase the President's popularity, there was a darker side to the Reagan Presidency that is important to note. He continued to pursue the Southern strategy forged by Nixon, opening his 1980 Presidential campaign in Philadelphia, Mississippi, near the site where the three civil rights workers were murdered in 1964. Reagan's constant rhetorical references to "welfare queens" were an effort to employ images of unemployed black women collecting welfare checks that played upon the racial prejudices of the disgruntled white ethnic working-class voters whom Reagan was attempting to entice from their traditional home within the Democratic Party. Concerned about the growing crack cocaine epidemic in America's inner cities, Reagan expanded Nixon's war on drugs, targeting the black population and exacerbating the racial discrepancy within the nation's growing prison population. The Reagan administration also opposed sanctions against the racial apartheid regimes of Rhodesia and South Africa.

The legislative agenda of the New Right and evangelicals was honored with the appointment of conservative judges who opposed affirmative action and abortion rights; although *Roe v. Wade* was not overturned, the courts allowed limitations to be imposed upon a woman's right to choose and maintain control over her body. One of Reagan's appointments to the Supreme Court was Sandra Day O'Connor, the first woman selected for the nation's highest court, but conservative ideologue Robert Bork, who executed Nixon's order to fire Special Prosecutor Cox, was rejected by the Senate.

In addition to focusing upon opposition to abortion, Reagan's evangelical supporters were concerned about what they perceived to be growing acceptance of the gay and lesbian community. Thus, many evangelical ministers such as Jerry Falwell asserted that the emergence of AIDS in the early 1980s was God's punishment for homosexual behavior. As thousands died, Reagan placated his evangelical constituency by remaining silent on the need for compassion and additional funding to combat the scourge of AIDS. Reagan only spoke out on the epidemic late in his second term following the death of his Hollywood friend Rock Hudson, a leading man whose sexual orientation was obscured by the studios until shortly before he died from AIDS. It is interesting how evangelicals clung to Reagan's rhetoric, as in his daily life the President did not always adhere to their conservative religious values. Reagan was the first divorced President, and while devoted to his second wife, Nancy, his relationship with his children and stepchildren was often stormy. Often evoking religion in his oratory, the President was an infrequent participant in Sunday services. The affable Reagan had many acquaintances, but few close friends beyond Nancy.

While cutting taxes for the wealthy and slashing programs for the poor, including job training centers, Reagan, the only American President to ever lead a union when he headed the Screen Actors Guild, made his opposition to the labor movement clear when he fired over 11,000 striking members of the Professional Air Traffic Controllers Organization (PATCO) in August 1981. The President's actions endangered public safety, but Reagan considered the strike by the union of public employees to be an illegal work stoppage. Union membership had declined during the 1970s, but the one major area of growth was in the public sector. The crushing of PATCO would send a message to public employees and the labor movement in general that Reagan and his corporate allies would not tolerate labor as a countervailing power to their control of the economy.

Reagan and foreign policy

Reagan devoted much of his first term to reinvigorating the Cold War and fighting for freedom around the globe, although many of the regimes and freedom fighters supported by the United States hardly promoted the concept of liberty. Many Americans were alarmed by Reagan's Cold War rhetoric and expansion of the nuclear arsenal, fearing Reagan's aggressive policies might lead to thermonuclear war. As thousands marched in the streets of the United States and Western Europe in opposition to Reagan and his British ally Prime Minister Margaret Thatcher, the President was undeterred. Reagan also called for an end to the Anti-Ballistic Missile Treaty which would be replaced by the Strategic Defense Initiative (SDI), or Star Wars program as it was popularly known, that would employ laser weapons to destroy incoming missiles, making the United States invulnerable to nuclear attack. If deployed, the system threatened to destabilize the Cold War as the United States could launch a first strike at the Soviets and then be able to resist nuclear retaliation. While many scientists questioned whether SDI technology could ever realistically be employed, its potential was disconcerting to the Soviets who lacked the technology to keep up with the Americans. Reagan's distrust of the Soviets was seemingly confirmed for many Americans in September 1983 when a Soviet aircraft accidentally shot down a South Korean passenger plane. However, when the United States Navy mistakenly downed an Iranian passenger jet in July 1988, there was far less coverage and outrage over the incident.

Reagan, nevertheless, recognized that the United States was still recovering from the Vietnam War and reluctant to approve placing American troops in harm's way. Thus, Reagan generally relied upon surrogates to do the fighting for the United States, while continuing to bestow honors upon the Vietnam era prisoners of war in pursuit of convincing Americans that in future was it would be essential to support the troops and not coddle war protestors. One of the groups that the Reagan administration funded was the Islamic Mujahideen fighters recruited throughout the Middle East to oppose the Soviet occupation of Afghanistan. The CIA trained young men such as the scion of a wealthy Saudi family, Osama bin Laden, who wanted to drive foreigners from the region. Reagan referred to the Mujahideen as freedom fighters in the mold of men like Patrick Henry and George Washington. They fought well against the Soviets, forcing them to withdraw from Afghanistan in 1989, after losing considerable soldiers, money, and prestige in the ill-conceived military occupation that turned out to be their Vietnam. Following the Soviet retreat, American policymakers paid little attention to the rebuilding of Afghanistan after years of fighting and bloodshed, losing interest after the Mujahideen had served their purpose. The legacy of the war in Afghanistan was the rise of the Taliban to power in a destabilized nation, while Osama bin Laden formed the al-Qaeda network to drive the Americans from Saudi Arabia and the Middle East. Meanwhile, the United States supported the Iraqi dictator Saddam Hussein in the bloody war between Iran and Iraq that relied upon the outdated mass wave attacks of the Western front in World War I.

Lebanon, Grenada, and Central America

When Reagan did send American troops into the Middle East, things did not go well. In June 1982, Israeli forces invaded neighboring Lebanon from which Palestinian fighters were launching attacks against Israel. The result of the invasion was the destabilization of Lebanon and the massacre of Palestinian civilians by local militias allied with the Israelis. To restore order, American troops joined an international peacekeeping force, but on October 23, 1983 a suicide bomber driving an explosives-laden truck crashed into an American barracks, killing over 200 Marines. Reagan's response to the attack was to withdraw American troops from the Lebanon mission, seemingly undermining the militaristic rhetoric of the administration. However, only days after the fiasco in Lebanon, U.S. forces launched an invasion of the tiny Caribbean island nation of Grenada, claiming that Castro's Cuba was gaining a foothold on the island and that American medical students were in danger. An overwhelming invading force quickly gained control over the island and rescued the medical students who did not seem to realize they were in danger. While the invasion was denounced by the United Nations, the military action in Grenada seemed to restore some of the American pride lost in Lebanon.

American intervention in Central America under the Reagan administration proved to be far bloodier for the people of the region. The Reagan administration was concerned with the triumph of the Sandinista Liberation Front, named after Augusto Sandino who led the Nicaraguan opposition to American occupation in the 1930s, and the overthrow of the Somoza family dictatorship controlling the Central American nation. Reagan viewed the Sandinistas as a Marxist group that would seek to export the Cuban Revolution to El Salvador, Guatemala, and Honduras. The

Reagan administration began to supply arms to the Contras, an opposition force in Nicaragua dominated by former members of the Somoza national guard. In addition, right-wing governments in El Salvador and Guatemala received American supplies and training in counter-insurgency tactics and torture from the CIA and American military missions. Government death squads murdered tens of thousands of peasants, who favored land reform and sympathized with the guerillas. The death squads were especially abhorrent in El Salvador, where the Catholic Church was targeted for supporting liberation theology and the peasantry. Salvadorian Archbishop Oscar Romero was assassinated while conducting mass, and three American nuns were raped and murdered with their bodies left in a ditch. Reagan credited his intervention with preventing domino theory communist expansion in Central America that would have eventually threatened the security of the United States and Mexico. However, his support for the Contras in violation of Congressional restrictions threatened him with impeachment, and the civil wars of the 1980s in Central America contributed to an economic and political instability that continues to plague the region and fosters desperate people hoping to find asylum within the United States.

Reagan's foreign adventures, nevertheless, did not seem to hurt him politically, leading to the depiction of Reagan as the "Teflon" President whose mistakes did not seem to stick with the electorate. Politically, the President was fortunate that the implementation of his economic agenda, which had initially led to rising unemployment, seemed to stabilize in the mid-1980s, and Reagan was able to easily win re-election over Minnesota's Walter Mondale, who had served as Carter's Vice President, and Congresswoman Geraldine Ferraro of New York, the first woman to be nominated on the ticket of a major American political party—although black New York Congresswoman Shirley Chisholm had campaigned for the Democratic Presidential nomination in 1972.. During his second term, many of the economic contradictions of Reaganomics became more apparent, but the President could point to ending the Cold War—however technically the global conflict was concluded during the watch of his successor George H. W. Bush.

Ending the Cold War

Reagan's Cold War strategy of expanding American defense spending to levels beyond which the Soviets could not compete, as they were also bogged down in Afghanistan, worked, and the Soviet Empire eventually collapsed. The Soviet economy was not strong enough to provide both military hardware and a minimum of consumer goods, while the United States was able to produce both—although the economic gap between rich and poor continued to increase. Reagan and the world, however, were lucky that during the 1980s a reformer, Mikhail Gorbachev, rose to power in the Soviet Union. Gorbachev believed that he might be able to save the Communist Party in the U.S.S.R. by introducing reforms. The Soviet leader advocated *glasnost*, which would introduce a degree of free speech and liberty to politics in the Soviet Empire, and *perestroika*, a concept that included the introduction of market capitalism into the Soviet Union. In the final analysis, Gorbachev's reforms were unable to prevent the dissolution of the Soviet Empire in Eastern Europe as well as the disintegration of the Soviet Union. However, Gorbachev and Reagan, after a series of summit meetings, did reach agreement in December 1987 on the Intermediate-Range Nuclear Forces Treaty that eliminated the short and intermediate range nuclear missiles and weapons from the arsenals of the U.S. and U.S.S.R. It was a considerable achievement for Reagan to wind down the Cold War, but in 1991 these accomplishments almost unraveled in an attempted coup by Communist Party hardliners against Gorbachev. The coup was defeated by Russian Federation President Boris Yeltsin and a campaign of civil disobedience. Reagan got Gorbachev and reform rather than hardliners bringing down the world with nuclear annihilation, but it was a close call.

Iran-Contra

Reagan's reputation for the handling of foreign affairs was also called into question by the Iran-Contra Affair which led some critics to call for the President's impeachment. Although the administration had a policy of not negotiating with terrorists, arms sales were made to the Iranian regime for their assistance in freeing American hostages held in Lebanon. Lieutenant Colonel Oliver North of the National Security Agency authorized employing the funds from the Iranian arms deal to aid the Contras in overthrowing the Sandinista regime in Nicaragua even though Congress had passed legislation outlawing U.S. assistance to the Contras. Investigations into the Iran-Contra Affair determined that the President did not have full knowledge of the scheme, but several of the President's subordinates were convicted before being pardoned by President George H. W. Bush. Reagan's critics pointed out that if he had not violated the law, then the Iran-Contra Affair certainly demonstrated that he was at best a disengaged and sloppy administrator.

Limitations of the Reagan Revolution

Reagan's second term also highlighted problems with the President's economic policies. The tax cuts for the wealthy and massive defense expenditures produced record deficits. During his eight years in office, Reagan added more than two trillion dollars to the national deficit—more than all his predecessors combined.

Interest rates remained high as the government borrowed large sums of money to pay down on the debt, contributing to an international trade deficit for the United States. However, inadvertently the deficits allowed Reagan to achieve one of his goals—a reduction of the role of government. With massive deficits there were simply no funds available for new government social programs such as health care for all the American people. The trickle-down impact of the tax cuts failed to materialize for most Americans. Rather than using their tax savings to invest in job creation, wealthy individuals and corporations purchased art collections whose values soared in the era. Corporate raiders also engaged in hostile takeovers of corporations, raising the stock value and then selling for immense profits when the company was liquidated, and workers laid off. Jobs were created during the 1980s, but many of these positions were in the low paying service sector rather than high wage manufacturing jobs. In addition, the gap between the compensation for a corporate chief executive officer and a median worker skyrocketed during the 1980s and continues to grow with corporate officials earning a 1,000 percent more than their workers, while labor has little power to resist this trend. While the post-World War II economic boom helped ease income inequality, the gap between rich and poor increased during the 1980s and continues to grow. Corporate and banking deregulation also contributed to the Savings and Loan Crisis of the late 1980s as over a thousand financial institutions closed their doors. The greed of America in the 1980s was symbolized in the character of Gordon Gekko, loosely based upon the career and imprisonment of Wall Street financier Ivan Boesky, in Oliver Stone's film *Wall Street* (1987). Gekko, as portrayed by Oscar-winning actor Michael Douglas, epitomized the young urban professionals or yuppies of the 1980s who rejected the countercultural values of the 1960s and 1970s and focused upon the accumulation of wealth and consumer goods in opposition to the historical struggles for a more egalitarian America.

As Reagan rode off into the sunset in 1988—and soon disappeared from the public stage suffering from Alzheimer's disease—conservatism had seemingly triumphed on both the domestic and international stages. Reagan's successor, George H. W. Bush presided over the end of the Cold War, but he soon led the nation into a new military crusade in the Middle East, complicated by the policies of his son President George Bush, and today the War on Terror has replaced the Cold War as a perpetual source for the military-industrial complex to keep the nation on a war footing. And deteriorating relations between the United States and Russia indicate that the ghosts of the Cold War have yet to be exorcised. The Reagan Revolution did not usher in prosperity for all Americans, instead exacerbating the class and racial divisions within the United States. The Presidencies of Bill Clinton and Barack Obama offered some opportunities for liberal reform, but Obama retreated from making any fundamental changes to the corporate capitalist order following the Great Recession of 2008. In 2016, frustrated white working-class Americans, afraid of changing demographics and their economic futures, narrowly elected demagogic businessman Donald Trump to the Presidency, while millions of young voters flirted with the Presidential candidacy of Democratic Socialist Senator Bernie

Sanders from Vermont. The future is uncertain, but the unequivocal triumph of the right seems short lived as the nation transitions to the twenty-first century, and the achievement of a more inclusive and egalitarian America still seems within our grasp.

Further Reading:

Bill, James A. *The Eagle and the Lion: The Tragedy of American-Iranian Relations*. New Haven: CT: Yale University Press, 1988.

Bernstein, Carl and Robert Woodward. *All the President's Men*. New York: Simon & Schuster, 1974.

Gaddis, John Lewis. *The United States and the End of the Cold War: Implications, Reconsiderations, Provocations*. New York: Oxford University Press, 1992.

Johnson, Haynes. *Sleepwalking Through History: America in the Reagan Years*. New York: W. W. Norton and Company, 1991.

Kaufman, Burton. *The Presidency of James Earl Carter*. Lawrence, KS: University Press of Kansas, 1993.

Kutler, Stanley. *The Wars of Watergate: The Last Crisis of Richard Nixon*. New York: Knopf, 1990.

LaFeber, Walter. *Inevitable Revolutions: The United States in Central America*. New York: W. W. Norton and Company, 1984.

Martin, William. *With God on Our Side: The Rise of the Religious Right in America*. New York: Broadway Books, 1996.

McGirr, Lisa. *Suburban Warriors: The Origins of the New American Right*. Princeton, NJ: Princeton University Press, 2001.

Morris, Edmund. *Dutch: A Memoir of Ronald Reagan*. New York: Random House, 1990.

Phillips, Kevin. *The Politics of Rich and Poor: Wealth and the American Electorate in the Reagan Aftermath*. New York: Random House, 1990.

Wills, Garry. *Reagan's America: Innocents at Home*. Garden City, NY: Doubleday, 1987.

29

Post-Cold War America: The Age of Terror, The Great Recession, the Politics of Hope, and Living in Trump's America

"Skyline of Manhattan with Smoke Billowing from the Twin Towers following September 11th Terrorist Attacks on World Trade Center, New York, September 11, 2001." *New York World Telegram & Sun* Newspaper Photograph Collection (Library of Congress). The end of the Cold War and collapse of the Soviet Union did not constitute the end of history as some predicted. The American people were challenged by the Terrorist attacks of 9/11, wars in Iraq and Afghanistan, and the Great Recession of 2008. Hope for a more progressive America was encouraged by the election of Barack Obama, the nation's first black President, but the elevation of Donald Trump to the Presidency in 2016 raised new challenges for American democracy.

The last thirty years of American history have been somewhat of a roller coaster ride, registering both hope and despair as political divisions have seemingly exacerbated. The collapse of the Soviet Union and the victory of the United States in the Cold War encouraged some pundits to declare the end of history with the triumph of capitalism over Soviet communism. As usual, the train of history has proven resistant to such oversimplifications. The communist government in China has abandoned much of its Marxist ideology, but the powerful nation presents a strong challenge to American hegemony. The fears and insecurities of the Cold War have been replaced by the War on Terror which was brought home to the American people by the terrorist attacks of 9/11, and this insecurity was employed to justify increased government surveillance under legislation such as the Patriot Act, trading civil rights and liberty for assurances of safety and security. Meanwhile, the invasions of Afghanistan and Iraq by the United States have only increased Middle Eastern and global instability, seemingly constituting a never-ending military commitment. While the 1990s witnessed a brief economic boom under the Clinton administration, the Great Recession raised serious questions about the unfettered triumph of capitalism. Nevertheless, the liberal Obama Presidency authorized a series of economic bailouts that rescued American banks and corporation from their own excess and greed that had fostered the financial crisis. A slow economic recovery was achieved under President Obama, but an opportunity to fundamentally restructure American capitalism was missed. Continuing economic and security fears were employed by Donald Trump to win the Presidency in 2016, representing a populist authoritarian movement gaining a foothold in Western democracies by blaming scapegoats such as immigrants, racial minorities, and the LGBTQ community for national decline. The Trump regime, however, has provoked a large resistance movement that offers an opportunity to forge a more inclusive United States embracing the visions of Thomas Jefferson and Martin Luther King Jr. that all Americans are created equal and should be judged on their character rather than their race, class, gender, or sexual identity.

George H. W. Bush and the election of 1988

Despite the problems plaguing the Reagan administration after eight years in office, the continuing popularity of Reagan was evident in the 1988 election during which Reagan's support helped propel his Vice President George H. W. Bush to the White House. Bush lacked the common touch and oratorical skills of his predecessor, but he had compiled an impressive resumé. Born into a wealthy New England family, Bush's father, Prescott served as a U.S. Senator from Connecticut. Following service in World War II as a combat Naval aviator and graduation from

Yale, the young Bush moved his family to Texas, where he established a foothold in the booming oil business. Although he failed to win a Senate seat in his adopted state, Bush was elected to Congress. Under Nixon, Bush served as Ambassador to the United Nations and Chairman of the Republican National Committee, while President Ford tapped Bush to head the CIA and serve as Chief of the Liaison Office in China. In 1980, Bush sought the Republican Presidential nomination, but after several primary defeats, he accepted Reagan's offer to serve as his running mate.

After eight years as Vice President, Bush sought to inherit the Reagan mantle. Although in the 1980 Republican primaries Bush had criticized Reagan's agenda as "voodoo economics," in 1988 he promised Republicans that he was a loyal follower of Reagan who would never raise taxes even with the increasing deficits of Reaganomics. The Democrats in 1988 nominated Massachusetts Governor Michael Dukakis, a candidate who shared Bush's lack of charisma. Although Bush's civility was touted during his 2018 funeral, he attacked the character of Dukakis who initially enjoyed a lead in the polls. Playing upon racial stereotypes, Bush accused Dukakis of being soft on crime, running ads that featured the case of Willie Horton, a black convicted Massachusetts felon who was released from prison under a weekend furlough program. While on furlough, Horton committed a robbery and rape which were exploited in racially charged messages from the Bush campaign. The aggressive Bush candidacy succeeded in discrediting Dukakis, and the Texan won the 1988 election by a healthy margin.

The New World Order

As President, Bush presided over the end of the Cold War in which Eastern European nations broke from the Soviet Empire, the Berlin Wall was destroyed, and the Soviet Union dissolved. While Reagan dramatically demanded of Gorbachev that he tear down the Berlin Wall, Bush's style was pedestrian and steady, for he did not want to slow the pace of change and reform by gloating over American and Western victories. Bush was reassuring when many European allies expressed qualms over the reunification of Germany, insisting that the new Germany did not represent a threat to peace. The President spoke about a New World Order that would assure global peace and prosperity in the post-Cold War era, but the concept proved to be rather ambiguous, and there was little protest when the major powers employed force to assert their hegemony and limit dissent. The United States made little effort to restrain the Russian Federation when they brutally suppressed the breakaway Republic of Chechnya in the Caucasus region. While the fighting in Chechnya was off the radar screen for most Americans, considerable international attention was focused upon the 1989 Chinese democracy movement that led students to convene on Tiananmen Square in Beijing, demanding democratic reforms such as free speech, press, and elections. While the Chinese communist government was open to some marketplace and capitalist reforms of the economic system, the democratic changes sought by the students could lead to the overthrow of the Chinese Communist Party. Accordingly, the government declared martial law, pulled the plug on Western media coverage, and dispatched tanks and troops to Tiananmen Square to crush the democratic protests. The Chinese government has prohibited discussion of the ensuing massacre, but some critics of the regime maintain that perhaps as many as 10,000 dissidents were murdered. The Chinese Communist Party seemed to conclude that upper and middle-class Chinese could enjoy capitalist consumer goods, but in exchange there was to be no questioning of the party's political supremacy. Many Chinese appear to have accepted this brutal compromise, as did President Bush and the United States. While the massacre was denounced, the Bush administration failed to impose sanctions on the regime. The lucrative China market was just too enticing for American corporations to resist. Again, capitalism seemed to trump democratic values.

And President Bush did not hesitate to unilaterally order American forces to invade Panama, indicating that the legacy of the Roosevelt Corollary was still alive and well. The United States had soured upon Panamanian leader Manuel Noriega, a former ally of Washington, accusing him of corruption, drug trafficking, and that favorite American bugaboo of supporting Cuba's Fidel Castro. After Noriega annulled the election of Guillermo Endara to the Presidency, Bush launched a military invasion of Panama in which Noriega was captured and sent to the United States, where he was tried and imprisoned for illegal money laundering and drug trafficking. The United States then installed Endara in power, justifying the invasion as both an effort to restore democracy in Panama and assure that the Panama Canal did not fall into the hands of a dictator unfriendly to the interests of the United States. The fighting was relatively short-lived, but approximately 500 Panamanians were killed in the invasion, while another 20,000 were left homeless. The invasion of Panama was denounced by the Organization of American States and UN General Assembly, and it was an event consistently omitted in the funeral eulogies praising the Bush Presidency.

First Gulf War

Bush, however, abandoned the unilateral Latin American approach when he formed an international coalition to drive Iraqi dictator Saddam Hussein from the oil fields of neighboring Kuwait which he seized in August 1990. Although Saddam Hussein was presented as an arch enemy of the United States, provoking two Middle Eastern wars, it is often forgotten that the Iraqi dictator was once considered a valuable anticommunist American ally who blocked Iranian expansion in the Iran-Iraq War of the 1980s. And some historians speculate that Saddam's ill-conceived invasion of Kuwait grew out of a misunderstanding with the U.S. Ambassador to

Iraq, April Glaspie. Nevertheless, American opposition to the occupation of Kuwait was soon apparent as the Bush administration imposed economic sanctions on Iraq and assembled a thirty-six-nation coalition headquartered in Saudi Arabia to drive Saddam out of Kuwait. To convince the American people that the military build up was not simply about oil, the Bush administration resorted to false propaganda, arguing that Iraqi invaders were entering Kuwait hospitals and pulling babies out of incubators, leaving them on the floor to die. As it turned out, the nurse who provided this testimony before a Congressional committee was a member of the Kuwait royal family who lived in the United States and was not present in Kuwait during the Iraqi invasion.

The propaganda, however, worked, and Congress authorized what became known as the First Persian Gulf War. In January 1991, American-led coalition forces launched air attacks against Iraqi positions, and the Iraqis retaliated with Scud missiles directed against Israel and Saudi Arabia, although the Iraqi missiles proved to be rather unreliable. On February 24, Operation Desert Storm was launched to drive the Iraqis out of Kuwait. While Saddam was viewed as having a powerful army at his disposal, the Iraqi troops proved to be no match for the U.S.-led coalition forces. After 100 hours, the American assault was halted as the Iraqis retreated toward Baghdad. Bush was criticized for limiting the offensive, but the President asserted that overthrowing Saddam would force the United States to occupy Baghdad and become militarily engaged in Iraq with no conceivable exit strategy—a piece of advice his son would later refuse to follow. Saddam was allowed to stay in power and turned his attention to suppressing groups such as the Kurds who had hoped to use the Gulf War to overthrow the Iraqi dictator who now employed biological and chemical weapons against his own people. As for President Bush, he emerged as a national hero whose Persian Gulf War had seemingly erased the ghosts of Vietnam. The United States had won a great military victory with little loss of American lives, and the returning soldiers were greeted with ticker tape parades—a popular recognition denied veterans of the Vietnam War.

Domestic problems for the Bush administration

With huge public opinion poll approval ratings after the war, Bush was considered politically invulnerable. However, the economic problems of the Reagan administration continued to plague the nation, and the President was forced to violate his pledge that he would not raise taxes. Bush acknowledged that the deficit left him little choice, but he also recognized that going back on his promise, "read my lips, no new taxes," would hurt him politically. The continuing racial divide in America was also apparent in the violence that exploded in Los Angeles in April 1992 after police officers were acquitted in the beating of black motorist Rodney King that had been captured on videotape. After days of rage, sixty-three people were dead with over a billion dollars in property damage—confirming the Kerner Commission's dire warning about the consequences of the economic racial divide in America.

The Bush administration was also marred by the controversial Senate Judiciary Committee hearings on the confirmation of Supreme Court appointee Clarence Thomas, who was only the second black to be nominated to the nation's highest court. Anita Hill, a young black attorney, accused Thomas of sexual harassment while he was her supervisor at the Department of Education and the Equal Employment Opportunity Commission. In nationally-televised hearings, Thomas denied the charges and accused his opponents of engaging in a symbolic lynching—referencing a long history in which innocent black men were accused of rape and hanged by white mobs. The all-white male Judiciary Committee did not know how to handle Hill's testimony, with several Senators suggesting that she was simply a scorned woman seeking revenge. A woman accusing a powerful man of harassment was ignored, and Thomas was narrowly confirmed to the court, where he remains a reliable conservative vote. Hill has gone on to an outstanding career as a law professor, but the hesitancy of powerful men to believe women was again apparent during the 2018 confirmation hearings of Judge Brett Kavanaugh. On a more positive note, perhaps the greatest domestic legislative achievement of the Bush administration was passage of the Americans with Disabilities Act (ADA) that expanded civil rights protections to a class of citizens all too often ignored— although some business interests complained that the legislation was too expensive and would place undue burdens upon business and commerce.

Election of 1992

Despite the accomplishments of the ADA and Persian Gulf War, Bush was saddled with concerns about the economy. And while Bush later believed that his tax increase helped pave the way for the prosperity of the 1990s, in 1992 it endangered his prospects for re-election. His Democratic challenger, Arkansas Governor Bill Clinton, was a member of the baby boomer generation, making Bush appear rather out of touch with contemporary America. Nevertheless, the campaign raised questions regarding Clinton's character that seemingly related to generational conflict in America. Clinton was accused of being a draft dodger during the Vietnam War when he sought a student deferment to study abroad at Oxford University. In addition, he responded to allegations that he smoked marijuana during his college years by insisting that he had tried pot but had never inhaled. More serious allegations were made regarding Clinton's extramarital affairs, especially with an aspiring Arkansas model and singer, Geniffer Flowers. With his wife at his side, Clinton denied the allegations but confessed that the Clintons had worked through some difficult times in their relationship—Clinton would later acknowledge a brief sexual encounter with Flowers. Despite the character issues, Clinton was an attractive candidate who seemed to embody the Horatio Alger qualities so admired by the American people. Initially raised by his single mother and maternal grandparents in Hope, Arkansas, the young Clinton exhibited intelligence, charm, and ambition as he matriculated to Georgetown, Oxford, and Yale Law School, before returning to Arkansas in pursuit of a political career. In addition, the white Southerner demonstrated a strong affinity for black Americans and culture, earning him the accolade of being "America's first black President."

The 1992 Presidential contest contained the wildcard factor of independent candidate, Ross Perot, a Texas billionaire, whose no-nonsense campaign concentrated on the deficit and featured the employment of charts and graphs much to the delight of many voters. In a hotly contested election, Clinton captured only 43 percent of the popular vote, but he was able to gain a majority in the Electoral College. Bush finished second, but Perot received almost 20 percent of the popular vote, the strongest showing for a third party since Theodore Roosevelt and the Progressive Party in 1912. Perot would fade from view, but America had not heard the last from the Bush family.

Early problems for the Clinton administration

The Clinton administration got off to a somewhat awkward start when the President seemed to overestimate the political support for transforming American culture. Efforts to openly recruit gays and lesbians into the American military were rebuffed in Congress, and the Clinton administration was left with the rather hypocritical policy of "don't ask, don't tell," which allowed gays and lesbians to serve if they did not publicly acknowledge their sexual preference. Clinton also proposed an ambitious overhaul of the health care system under the guidance of his wife, Hillary Rodham Clinton. Born in Chicago, Hillary was an outstanding student who graduated from Wellesley College and earned a law degree from Yale. She served as a consultant to the House Judiciary Committee during the Watergate hearings, and Bill Clinton believed she was well qualified to guide the administration's efforts at health care reform. A government-run national health care system was opposed by the powerful health insurance industry which insisted that government bureaucrats would now make family health decisions—as if this was worse than having for profit insurance companies dictating such decisions. Opponents of Clinton's plan also aimed much of their criticism at Hillary, an intelligent and ambitious woman who has always raised the ire of conservatives who seem threatened by her talent and willingness to challenge traditional gender barriers.

Health care reform was defeated, and in the 1994 Congressional elections, the Republicans gained control of both houses of Congress for the first time in forty years. A brash young Congressman from Georgia, Newt Gingrich was selected as Speaker of the House, and he promised to implement a Contract with America agenda reducing government spending and slashing welfare programs. Clinton responded to the election returns by moving his administration to the right, signing into law modified versions of conservative legislation. In addition, Gingrich tended to overplay his hand, provoking government shutdowns in 1995 and 1996 and proclaiming such harsh ideas as that the solution to the cycle of poverty might require that the children of welfare recipients be separated from their parents. And efforts to impeach Clinton on a party line vote backfired in the 1998 Congressional elections, and Gingrich resigned from the House in 1999 after revelations of an extramarital affair with a younger Congressional employee.

The depth and dangers of anti-government sentiments in America were revealed with the Oklahoma City bombing on April 19, 1995 that destroyed the Alfred P. Murrah Federal Building and killed at least 168 people, many of them children at a daycare center in the building. This act of domestic terrorism was perpetrated by Terry Nichols and Timothy McVeigh, a veteran of the Persian Gulf War and a member of a right-wing militia who was supposedly seeking revenge for the government's handling of the Branch Davidian siege in Waco, Texas two years earlier. The Branch Davidian cult led by David Koresh was accused of illegally storing guns and ammunition at their compound, in addition to holding members against their will. During a government assault, the compound caught fire and seventy-one people perished. For the Oklahoma City bombing, Nichols was sentenced to life imprisonment and McVeigh executed by lethal injection, but they perceived themselves as patriots fighting against a tyrannical central government opposing the interests of white working-class Americans. The dangers of right-wing extremism were certainly exposed by the Oklahoma City bombing, while the militia movement and acts of violence by the radical right have increased following the election of President Trump in 2016.

Clinton moves in a more conservative direction

The success of congressional Republicans, however, did force the Clinton administration into a more conservative direction. President Clinton signed into law the Omnibus Crime Bill of 1994 that increased funding for law enforcement and federal penalties for drug-related crimes, expanding the number of black Americans incarcerated in the nation's prisons. The legislation also included a ten-year ban on assault weapons which has since lapsed. The President also greatly reduced the federal role in welfare, imposing work requirements for any able-bodied adult receiving welfare benefits. Although only a small segment of the federal budget, the bill stigmatized individuals receiving government assistance and suggested that poverty was a result of personal responsibility and choice. Blaming the poor for poverty deflected any role for corporate America in fostering the economic divide.

Clinton also angered the LGBTQ community when he agreed to sign the Defense of Marriage Act (DOMA), which defined marriage on the federal level as a union between a man and a woman. The President defended his action as necessary to prevent passage of a Constitutional amendment that would have prohibited any state from recognizing gay marriage. The Supreme Court eventually struck down DOMA in the case of *United States v. Windsor* (2013).

This more conservative course change for Clinton was buoyed by a growing economy. The tax increases of the Bush administration, coupled with modest revenue enhancements from the Clinton White House, helped to erase the deficit, and the federal budget briefly registered a surplus. In addition, the Clinton administration implemented the North American Free Trade Agreement (NAFTA), negotiated under the Bush administration, to foster trade among Canada, Mexico, and the United States. Critics of NAFTA, however, argue that the agreement has harmed American labor and failed to provide adequate environmental safeguards. With a strong economy and his conservative flank covered, Clinton rolled to an easy re-election victory over his Republican opponent, Senator Robert Dole of Kansas. His second term, however, was to be marred by scandal.

Clinton's Foreign Policy

Although Clinton focused most of his attention upon domestic affairs, he was unable to avoid global conflicts that were not silenced by the end of the Cold War. President Bush had committed American forces to nation building and peacekeeping in the war-torn African nation of Somalia. On October 3-4, 1993, an ill-fated mission to arrest a Somali warlord in the capital of Mogadishu led to the downing of two American helicopters and the killing of eighteen servicemen, some of whose bodies were dragged through the streets after a gun battle in which hundreds of civilians were killed. Clinton responded to the debacle by withdrawing American troops from Somalia. Wishing to avoid further misadventures on the African continent, Clinton refused to become involved in the Rwandan genocide of 1994 during which perhaps as many as one million ethnic Tutsi were slaughtered by the majority Hutu who controlled the government. The charge that Clinton did nothing to prevent ethnic cleansing and genocide in Rwanda induced the President to become involved in the Balkans; however, the Balkan intervention still made it appear that white lives mattered more than their black counterparts in Africa. The state of Yugoslavia disintegrated into ethnic conflict in 1990 following the death of communist leader Josip Broz Tito who had ruled the country since the end of World War II. Tito had kept the lid on ethnic tensions in the region, but local leaders seeking to increase their power and influence encouraged ethnic violence. The Serbs under the direction of President Slobodan Milosevic and local militias pursed a policy of genocide directed against the Muslim population of Bosnia, while they also targeted the majority Albanian ethnic population of Kosovo which was coveted by the Serbs. The U.S. and NATO intervened with a bombing campaign that eventually led to the overthrow of Milosevic and introduction of American peacekeeping forces into the region. While no American pilots were killed in this action, the intervention was not without cost as technical mistakes resulted in the bombing of the Chinese Embassy in Belgrade and the destruction of a busy Belgrade bridge at noon rather than midnight.

Scandal and impeachment

Congressional accusations of corruption against Bill and Hillary Clinton in an Arkansas real estate deal called Whitewater led to the appointment of a special prosecutor to investigate the Clintons. While Special Prosecutor Kenneth Starr brought no charges against the Clintons in the Clearwater matter, he broadened his mandate to consider accusations of sexual misconduct against the President. While questioning the President regarding the allegation that while Governor of Arkansas he had propositioned and exposed himself to a woman named Paula Jones, the Starr team questioned Clinton about rumors that he was sexually involved with a twenty-two-year old White House intern, Monica Lewinsky. In his testimony, and later public statements, Clinton denied having sexual relations with Lewinsky. Hillary Clinton stood by her husband, suggesting that the allegations were politically inspired by a right-wing conspiracy to discredit the Clinton Presidency. However, a semen stain on a dress worn by Lewinsky was found to contain the President's DNA. Clinton backtracked and apologized to the nation for his actions. Although Lewinsky testified that the affair was consensual, the differences in age and positions of power between the President and the young intern certainly constituted a degree of abuse by Clinton. Meanwhile, Republicans in Congress moved to impeach the President for lying under oath about the Lewinsky affair. On a party-line vote, Republicans in the House approved Articles of Impeachment against Clinton, and he became the first President to face a Senate impeachment trial since Andrew Johnson during Reconstruction. Clinton's defenders insisted that while the President had behaved badly, his sexual activities and efforts to conceal them did not constitute the "high crimes and misdemeanors" outlined by the Founders in the Constitution for impeachment. Also, with a two-thirds majority in the Senate required for conviction, the Republicans simply did not have the votes to remove Clinton from office. However, they pursued impeachment to politically discredit and embarrass the President but overplayed their hand. As expected, Clinton was acquitted by the Senate, and in the 1998 Congressional elections, the Republicans lost seats in the House. The Lewinsky scandal and impeachment proceedings, nevertheless, cast a shadow over the 2000 Presidential election as well as the Clinton legacy.

Disputed election of 2000

With the economy strong, the Democrats nominated Clinton's Vice President, Al Gore of Tennessee, who made little use of Clinton in the campaign as he sought to avoid any connection with the Clinton sex scandal. This may have been a mistake in a close electoral contest as Clinton remained popular with many Americans. The Republicans surprised many observers by nominating George H. W. Bush's son, George, who as a young man had earned a reputation for drinking and partying before undergoing a religious conversion and family obligations that changed his life. After two terms as a conservative Governor in Texas, Bush sought the Presidency. In debate with Gore, Bush proved to be less informed on the issues than his opponent, but many Americans found the personable Bush to be more likeable than the cerebral and more aloof Gore. On election night, Gore moved out to any early lead and won the popular vote, but a majority in the Electoral College came down to the state of Florida, where Bush's brother, Jeb served as Governor. With the results in limbo for weeks, the Florida Supreme Court ordered a hand recount, which Bush's lawyers challenged as lacking uniform standards that would protect their client's Fourteenth Amendment rights of equal protection under the law. Breaking along partisan lines, the Supreme Court voted five to four to halt the Florida recount, awarding the Presidency to Bush. For many Americans, the court decision exposed the fiction that the Supreme Court was a nonpartisan body dedicated to the rule of law and above political influence. Out of over six million votes cast in Florida, Bush prevailed by 537 votes and earned all twenty-five of Florida's Electoral College votes. The final Electoral College count was 271 to 266 in favor of Bush, and Democrats lamented the 22,198 votes in Florida garnered by Green Party candidate Ralph Nader, the majority of which they assumed would have gone to Gore if consumer advocate Nader had not been on the ballot. A full Constitutional crisis was averted when Gore reluctantly conceded to Bush, and the President-elect called for national unity in the language Thomas Jefferson employed following the disputed election of 1800. After coming so close, Gore did not make another run for the Presidency, devoting his time and energy to environmental concerns such as climate change questioned by Republican Presidents George Bush and Donald Trump. While some called for a Constitutional amendment to abolish the Electoral College in wake of the 2000 election, the institution of the Electoral College remains enshrined in the Constitution, protecting minority state interests against majority rule.

The disputed election initially cast a large shadow over the Bush Presidency, whose inauguration was jeered by protestors, who shouted "hail to the thief." And Bush seemed to further the partisan divide during his early days in office. Seeking to place himself within the Reagan tradition rather than that of his father, Bush pushed through Congress a tax cut that soon erased the budget surpluses of the Clinton administration and returned the nation's finances into a deficit. In addition, Bush challenged the findings of the scientific community by repudiating the Kyoto Treaty, negotiated by the Clinton administration, that limited greenhouse gas emissions, earning the support of large energy corporations such as the Koch brothers. Bush's popularity, however, turned after the terrorist attacks of 9/11.

9/11 terrorist attacks and their aftermath

On that fateful day of September 11, 2001, nineteen terrorists, most of whom held Saudi passports, hijacked four domestic airliners. Two of the jets were crashed into New York City's World Trade Center, a symbol of American global economic power. As the twin towers collapsed, approximately 3,000 people, including hundreds of police and fire department personnel attempting to carry out rescue operations, were killed. Another plane struck the Pentagon with the loss of 189 people. A final hijacked plane was headed toward the White House, when courageous passengers launched an assault to regain control over the aircraft. In the ensuing struggle, the plane crashed into a field in Pennsylvania, killing everyone on board. Americans were stunned and angry in wake of the tragedy, demanding revenge against the perpetrators of the atrocity, but there was little self-examination of why so many in the world perceived the United States guilty of economic exploitation and supporting military dictatorships. Viewing themselves as perpetual innocents, Americans are woefully ignorant of the nation's imperialistic history with people of color. In some ways the tragedy of 9/11 was the chickens of American imperialism coming home to roost, but the victims of that day were innocent men, women, and children simply going about the routine of their daily lives.

In response to the attacks, Congress passed the Patriot Act that surrendered civil liberties to a government promising to provide security; a recipe for fascism too often associated with national emergencies. The legislation provided for government surveillance of telephone calls, emails, and business records of Americans overseen by secret courts. In addition, these secret courts could authorize searches whose targets would not be notified of these investigations. Immigrants suspected of abetting terrorists were subject to detention and deportation. In the weeks following the attacks, hundreds of immigrants, mostly of Middle Eastern origins, were rounded up by the Justice Department and denied habeas corpus rights. While Bush called for toleration and respect for Muslim Americans, asserting that the United States did not want to repeat the World War II mistake of Japanese American internment, the period after the terrorist attacks witnessed widespread acts of violence against American Muslims and mosques. Some of the more stringent provisions of the Patriot Act have expired, but the legacy of the legislation, like the Alien and Sedition Acts of the 1790s, is troubling and suggests that liberty must be defended in times of crisis.

The nation rallied around President Bush who sent out somewhat mixed signals to the American people. While asserting that those who perpetrated the attacks would be punished, Bush urged Americans to go about their daily lives as usual, shopping and taking those family trips to Disneyland. Instead of the sacrifices called for during the Second World War, the President insisted that resistance to terrorism would be realized in the resilience of capitalism and corporate activity as the reasons for the attacks were jealousy toward the American way of life. Meanwhile, Bush announced that Osama bin Laden and his al-Qaeda terrorist network, now headquartered in Afghanistan under the protection of the Taliban, were responsible for the 9/11 attacks. Bin Laden was already on the radar screen of American intelligence for attacks launched during the Clinton administration, but Bush elected to treat 9/11 as an act of war rather than a criminal conspiracy, declaring a war against terrorism that placed the United States in an open-ended conflict with radical Islam in the Middle East. The President authorized a military invasion of Afghanistan in conjunction with America's NATO allies, who fulfilled their commitments to aid a member nation under assault. Fighting alongside local warlords, the Americans and their allies drove the Taliban from power, but bin Laden eluded them and escaped. The United States then commenced a policy of nation building that has not brought stability to Afghanistan amid continuing government corruption and a growing Taliban insurgency in the countryside. An exit strategy for Afghanistan continues to elude the United States almost twenty years after the invasion.

Invasion of Iraq

Influenced by the neo-conservatives, or neocons, cloistered around Vice President Dick Cheney and Secretary of Defense Donald Rumsfeld, Bush began to speak about the War on Terror in broader terms, employing World War II imagery to label North Korea, Iran, and Iraq as the "axis of evil" in the world. The neocons concentrated upon the oil rich nation of Iraq, whose dictator Saddam Hussein was said to possess weapons of mass destruction that threatened the security of Israel and the entire Middle East. The Vice President, a former president of the Halliburton Energy Corporation who earned massive profits from government contracts following the Iraq War, had a somewhat Svengali influence over the younger President, who increasingly embraced an invasion of Iraq as a way to complete the overthrow of Saddam that his father began in the First Gulf War. Sounding like Woodrow Wilson, Bush championed regime change in Iraq as a means through which to promote the spread of democracy in the Middle East. Meanwhile, Cheney and the neocons were growing impatient with the intelligence community who could find no connections between Iraq and the 9/11 terrorists. Cheney and his neocon cohorts, however, attempted to push the case against Iraq, even bullying Secretary of State General Colin Powell to deliver a speech before the United Nations employing doctored evidence to make the case against Iraq. While the UN failed to authorize the use of force against the Iraqi regime, the Bush administration was able to secure Congressional approval, with even New York Senator Hillary Clinton voting in favor of the measure. Fearful of being called "soft" on terrorism, American politicians seemingly had learned nothing from the Cold War, Vietnam, and the Gulf of Tonkin Resolution.

Despite massive protests in the United States and around the world, the Bush administration launched the long-anticipated invasion of Iraq on March 19, 2003, with many Americans believing the fiction that the action was warranted because of Iraq's involvement in 9/11. The invasion of Iraq did not enjoy the support of America's NATO allies who failed to perceive the United States as the target of Iraqi aggression. An exception was Great Britain and Prime Minister Tony Blair, whose promising political career was eventually ended because of his decision to support the Americans in Iraq. Despite the large size of Saddam's armed forces, the superior American firepower captured Baghdad in less than a month, while Saddam was found hiding in a ditch, and the dictator was eventually executed by the American-dominated Iraqi government. On May 1, 2003, President Bush triumphantly declared mission accomplished in Iraq, but the American misadventure in Iraq was only beginning.

The invasion was seemingly conducted with little understanding of Iraqi politics or the division between the Sunni and Shia branches of Islam. While the Sunnis constitute a majority of Muslims worldwide, the Shia are a majority in Iraq and Iran. Under Saddam, the Sunni minority exercised power in Iraq, but in elections sponsored by the United States the majority Shia gained control of the government, increasing Iranian influence—not exactly what the Bush administration had in mind. Civil war soon threatened the stability of the new Iraq, with Shia militias carrying out savage attacks against the Sunni population. The increasing violence led to a Sunni insurgency against the American military occupation. By 2006, a surge of American troops seemed to bring the insurgency under control, but by that time the U.S. had lost nearly 2,500 soldiers, and somewhere between 500,000 and 1,000,000 Iraqis had perished in the violence. Corruption and exploitation were also evident as American corporations secured lucrative contracts to reconstruct Iraq. American civilians were protected behind the so-called green zone in Baghdad, while the National Museum was looted with valuable antiquities lost, and private security firms such as Blackwater demonstrated little respect for Iraqi lives. The Bush administration was further embarrassed when the invaders were unable to locate the weapons of mass destruction supposedly possessed by the Saddam regime.

America's prestige in the world also suffered as evidence mounted of torture tactics employed against many combatants captured in Afghanistan and Iraq. Prisoners from Afghanistan were taken to the American Naval base in Guantanamo, Cuba, which the United States had forced the Cubans to cede following the Spanish-American War. Since the prisoners were technically not on American soil and under the protection of American courts, the Bush Justice Department ruled that they could be subjected to "enhanced interrogation" or torture such as waterboarding, sleep and sensory deprivation, sexual intimidation, extreme temperatures and noise, nudity, and barking attack dogs. Some of the prisoners suffered mental breakdowns and committed suicide, but many have been released today, while others remain incarcerated without ever having their day in court. When the CIA sought to avoid direct involvement with torture, they resorted to extreme rendition in which suspected terrorist targets were captured and turned over to authorities in nations such as Syria, where no restrictions were placed on the use of torture. To his credit, Republican Senator John McCain of Arizona, who faced torture after being shot down over Vietnam, took a leading role in denouncing this shameful episode in American history.

The Bush administration also faced criticism for its handling of the intelligence leading to the 9/11 attacks. Some conspiracy theorists argue that the Bush administration benefitted politically from 9/11, insisting that the attacks were an inside job that provided the government with an opportunity to increase its powers both domestically and globally. Others countered that the administration was simply negligent in their failure to thwart the terrorists. The bipartisan 9/11 Commission, however, rejected the conspiracy charges, while urging better communication and coordination among the agencies entrusted with national security and intelligence gathering. Much like the assault upon Pearl Harbor, it was easy to connect the dots leading up to the attack after the target was clear.

Bush re-election, Hurricane Katrina, and the Great Recession

Bogged down in Iraq and Afghanistan, Bush seemed politically vulnerable as he sought re-election in 2004. Critical of Bush's handling of the Iraq War, the Democrats were, nevertheless, concerned about being perceived as an antiwar party and did not want to suffer the type of devastating defeat visited upon George McGovern in 1972. Accordingly, they nominated Massachusetts Senator John Kerry, who was a decorated hero from the Vietnam conflict, while Bush's service record was questionable. Bush avoided Vietnam by landing a coveted spot with the Texas Air National Guard, but critics maintained that Bush often failed to fulfill his required service commitments. Nevertheless, Bush supporters attacked Kerry about his antiwar activities after he returned from Vietnam, and a group called "Swift Boat Veterans" questioned Kerry's combat record, placing the candidate on the defensive. The election was close with Bush holding a narrow lead in the popular vote, while the electoral vote came down to the state of Ohio, where Democrats claimed irregularities with the state's voting machines. But the election lacked the drama of 2000, and this time Bush did not have to depend upon the nation's highest court.

His narrow re-election, however, tended to make the President overly confident, and Bush overestimated his mandate by calling for the privatization of Social Security. This proposal frightened many older Americans, and there was considerable pushback from Congress, leading the President to abandon the privatization scheme. Americans may have re-elected a Republican President, but they were hardly ready to abandon the New Deal safety net. The President also stumbled in his handling of Hurricane Katrina which struck the city of New Orleans and Gulf Coast on August 29, 2005. The levee system designed by the Army Corps of Engineers failed New Orleans, and over 80 percent of the city was flooded. Especially hard hit were the poorest wards of the city populated primarily by black Americans, many of whom lacked the money and transportation facilities to evacuate. Poor residents became trapped in their homes as well as overcrowded shelters such as the New Orleans Super Dome and Convention Center. Desperate and starving citizens raided grocery stores in search of food, but they were shot as looters by the police. Failing to recognize the humanitarian disaster engulfing New Orleans, President Bush announced that the Federal Emergency Management Agency (FEMA) was doing a great job. This callous approach made Bush and the federal government appear unresponsive to the needs of black Americans. Eventually the government arranged for the evacuation of New Orleans residents who had lost their homes to cities such as Houston. Many of those evacuated from New Orleans have never been able to return home, while the rebuilding of the city has prioritized commercial and tourist sites, and the poorest wards of the city have not been reclaimed. Bush's leadership was repudiated in the 2006 Congressional elections as the Democrats gained control of both the House and Senate, while also picking up Governorships. Following the Democratic victories, Congresswoman Nancy Pelosi of California was selected as the first female Speaker of the House, placing a woman third in line to the Presidency.

The final disaster of the Bush Presidency occurred with the Great Recession of 2007-2008 that coincided with the Presidential race of 2008. The Great Recession demonstrates the economic dangers of income inequality and unregulated capitalism. The financial meltdown was the most severe setback for international capitalism since the Great Depression of the 1930s. Financial institutions such as investment banks were marketing assets globally backed by subprime mortgages, which had targeted Americans whose low incomes made mortgage payments challenging, and the failure of these high-risk borrowers to make their payments led to a financial crisis. Many financial institutions were in danger of collapse after encouraging the housing bubble of the early twenty-first century. Both bankers and low-income Americans might be criticized for attempting to live beyond their means, but bankers and lending institutions were bailed out by the federal government, while no such relief was forthcoming for the poor Americans who lost their homes. Bankers were rewarded for their greed, while citizens seeking to attain the American dream of owning their own homes were given no relief—with some ending up homeless and on the streets. It was determined that banks and financial institutions were too big to fail, demonstrating the power of corporate America over the political system.

Election of Barack Obama

Following Iraq, Katrina, and the financial meltdown, 2008 was going to be a difficult time for the Republicans, who nominated John McCain, a political maverick who antagonized many in his party with calls for limitations to be placed upon corporate and individual campaign contributions. Although McCain was a national hero to many Americans for his service during the Vietnam War, 2008 was a challenging year for any Republican. McCain hoped to shake up the campaign by bestowing the Vice-Presidential nomination upon the first-term Republican Governor of Alaska, Sarah Palin. Initially a fresh and attractive new voice on the national political scene, Palin proved to be a political liability as she struggled with questions during interviews, and McCain regretted his choice. After the losing 2008 campaign, Palin resigned as Alaska's Governor, seeking to forge a career as a conservative media personality, but she has largely fallen off the national stage. On the Democratic side, Hillary Clinton, who had effectively served New York as a Senator after her White House years, was expected to garner the nomination. However, she got a surprise challenge from an Illinois Senator serving his first term. Barack Hussein Obama was a new national voice with an American family story that seemed to epitomize the American dream. A biracial man who identifies as black, Obama was the product of the union between a Kenyan father and white mother. He was raised in Hawaii by his maternal grandparents from the Midwest. He attended Occidental College in Los Angeles, before earning degrees from Columbia and Harvard. Building upon his experience as a community organizer, Obama followed graduation from Harvard Law School by serving as a civil rights attorney and teaching Constitutional Law at the University of Chicago. His life story was well captured in the best-selling memoir *The Audacity of Hope: Thoughts on Reclaiming the American Dream* (2006). And in his 2008 campaign, the skilled orator preached the politics of hope, as he and Clinton waged a fierce competitive primary battle across the nation before Clinton conceded defeat. Needing her support, Obama would later appoint Clinton as his Secretary of State.

Obama's triumph over McCain was heralded by some commentators as the end of racial politics with the United States finally achieving the dream of Martin Luther King Jr. And, indeed, the election of a black President was a remarkable achievement considering the national history of racial slavery, segregation, and discrimination. The election of Obama, however, hardly marked the end of race as a factor in American politics and society. Some Americans struggled with the concept of a black President, sparking the racist "birther" movement asserting that Obama was born in Kenya rather than Hawaii, and, thus, he was ineligible to serve as President. It was simply inconceivable to some that there could be a black man in the White House. Among those who perpetuated this conspiracy theory was Donald Trump. Accordingly, throughout his Presidency, Obama was forced to address issues of race, often reluctantly it seemed, explaining why black parents cautioned their children to be particularly careful with the police and exposing why Black Lives Matter resonated with so many black families who experienced unpleasant confrontations with police authority figures. Obama, nevertheless, articulated a politics of hope that resonated beyond the United States, earning him a global following and seemingly a 2009 Nobel Peace Prize based more upon his potential rather than accomplishments in office. The reality of the Obama Presidency, however, was more complicated as the politics of hope were often stymied by Republican intransigence and Obama's own willingness to accept compromise.

The Great Recession

As President, Obama inherited the Great Recession, and he deserves credit for guiding the nation to a gradual economic recovery. The financial crisis, however, offered an opportunity for Obama to fundamentally alter corporate control of American politics and the economy. Instead, Obama followed the lead of the Bush administration and supported the bailout of the financial industry. Rather than indicting bankers for their negligence, they were rewarded with funds from the national treasury. The Dodd-Frank Wall Street Reform and Consumer Protection Act provided for greater regulation of the financial community, but the corporate managers maintained their incomes and influence. Obama would later rail against the Supreme Court for their ruling in the *Citizens United* case (2010) that corporate campaign contributions were free speech that could not be limited by Congress. The President was correct to point out how this decision encouraged corporate domination of the nation's politics, but he also hedged when corporate America was on the political defensive in 2008-2009 and more fundamental changes in the corporate economy were feasible.

To address the significant unemployment brought about by the financial crisis, Obama proposed generous loans to the country's major auto companies as well as a stimulus package of $787 billion to be spent on improving infrastructure, education, health care, internet service, and other projects. Somewhat borrowing upon the New Deal's PWA and WPA, the Obama stimulus was to generate new jobs and replace decreased consumer spending in order to jump start the American economy. Over time, the Obama stimulus did seem to work, and the nation slowly pulled itself out of recession, although some economists criticized Obama for not proposing an even larger financial stimulus, considering the severity of the recession.

Affordable Care Act

Obama displayed a similar timidity with his approach to what has become the most significant legislation of his Presidency, the Affordable Care Act of 2010 or Obamacare as it is commonly known. Since the New Deal, Democrats and reformers have sought to bring the universal health care system that characterizes Western Europe and other industrialized nations to the United States, asserting that health care is a universal human right. Conservatives have opposed government health care as socialized medicine that will undermine individual responsibility and destroy the relationship between doctor and patient. Although Medicare and Medicaid did expand government subsidized health care for the elderly and poor, the powerful health insurance lobby successfully blocked further changes until by the early twenty-first century, millions of Americans could not afford health care coverage. While Democratic majorities in both the House and Senate provided an opportunity to enact universal or single payer health care, Obama balked at this political confrontation, instead opting for reforms that would work through the health insurance industry. The Affordable Care Act sought to reduce health care costs by forcing all Americans to obtain health insurance through a tax upon those who did not purchase insurance. Health insurance companies would not be able to use pre-existing conditions to deny coverage, and parents could keep their children on their plan until the child reached age twenty-six. The forced inclusion of younger and healthier Americans in the insurance pool would supposedly allow the insurance industry to profitably serve all Americans. Although the Affordable Care Act borrowed ideas previously endorsed by the Republican Party, the legislation passed on a partisan basis with no Republican votes. The complex bill expanded health care coverage, but the rising cost of health care remained a problem.

Republicans terrified Americans with visions of government death panels deciding the fate of loved ones—although this was a role insurance companies had been playing. Campaigning against what they pejoratively called Obamacare, the Republicans regained control of the House in 2010, while gaining seats in the Senate and state legislatures. Republicans claimed that they would repeal and replace Obamacare, but they could not seem to agree upon any replacement legislation other than returning to the status quo where many Americans were left uninsured. While Republicans continued to attack Obamacare, it was soon apparent that many Americans appreciated provisions such as the ban on denying coverage to those with pre-existing conditions. Despite repeated attacks in Congress and the courts, Obamacare continues to exist, while support for health care solutions such as Medicare for all is gaining traction regardless of opposition from the health insurance lobby.

Setbacks for the politics of hope

Recovery from the Great Recession was slow, but Obama won re-election in 2012 over Republican and former Governor of Massachusetts Mitt Romney. The Obama coalition of young people, blacks, and Hispanics, many of whom seemed to sit out the 2010 Congressional elections, returned to the ballot box. The Romney campaign never appeared to recover from a secretly recorded speech at a Republican fund raiser in which Romney claimed that 49 percent of the electorate was dependent upon government programs and would never vote for him, injecting an element of class conflict into the election. While House Democratic candidates received more votes, the House of Representatives remained in Republican hands as gerrymandering and demographics concentrated Democratic support in large urban areas.

With Obama not on the ballot in 2014, the Republicans, who pushed voter identification laws and reduced ballot access that negatively impacted the poor and people of color, captured control of the Senate as well as increasing their majority in the House. As Congress increasingly blocked his agenda, Obama relied upon executive orders and regulatory agencies to promote change; although this approach could easily be overturned by the election of a more conservative President. While many in the Republican Party continued to deny the scientific community consensus on climate change, Obama spoke eloquently of the necessity for conservation and reducing carbon emissions, ordering regulatory agencies such as the EPA to push for more fuel- efficient automobiles and reduced industrial pollution, while fostering alternatives to fossil fuels with solar and wind power. On the other hand, oil and coal production increased during his watch as America still remained dependent upon the profitable and influential fossil fuel industry and corporations such as Exxon. Failing to get Congressional approval for comprehensive immigration reform, Obama issued an executive order creating the Deferred Action for Childhood Arrivals (DACA) policy that allows individuals brought to the United States illegally when they were children to register for a renewable two-year period of immunity from deportation and become eligible for a work permit as long as they do not have a criminal record. Many progressives hope that DACA will eventually provide a path to citizenship for these young immigrants classified as "dreamers," while the Trump administration has attempted to discontinue the policy. While DACA and Obama's rhetoric offered hope to many crossing America's southern border, the Obama administration also forged a complex legacy by deporting more than 2.5 million people who entered the United States illegally, leading some of his critics to label Obama as "the deporter in chief." Obama's record in regard to the LGBTQ community is less ambiguous. While initially favoring civil unions rather than gay marriage, the Obama administration repealed the "don't ask, don't tell" provisions of the Clinton Presidency, allowing gays and lesbians to openly serve in the military. The Obama administration also added gender identity to the categories protected against discrimination by the federal government, an important extension for the transgender community; however, the Trump administration has attempted to abandon these protections. The embracing of the LGBTQ community by Obama, nevertheless, helped to pave the way for many Americans to accept the Supreme Court decision upholding gay marriage and the right of all citizens, regardless of their sexual orientation and identity, to be subject to the equal protection of the laws.

The Obama Presidency was far less successful in enacting meaningful gun control legislation through a Congress whose members were often beholding to the gun lobby. The National Rifle Association (NRA) claims to be a citizen group fighting for fundamental American freedoms such as the Second Amendment right to bear arms, when the organization is actually a well-financed and organized lobby group for American arms manufacturers. And repeated school shootings across the country—from Columbine High School in 1999 to the murder of elementary school students and teachers in Newton, Connecticut in 2012 to the 2018 killing of seventeen at Marjory Stoneman High School in Florida—have not moved the NRA to abandon their position that only more guns and arming teachers will solve the problem. Hopes and prayers, along with the rhetoric of Obama, failed to move Congress, but perhaps a new generation forced to submit to the tyranny of active shooter drills will break the stranglehold of the gun lobby upon American politics. Obama was stymied by the Republican Senate when he nominated distinguished Court of Appeals Judge Merrick Garland to replace conservative Associate Justice Antonin Scalia who died suddenly in early 2016. Although the Senate had earlier confirmed Obama appointees Sonia Sotomayor and Elizabeth Kagan to the court, Republican Senate Majority Leader Mitch McConnell of Kentucky asserted that he would refuse to even grant Garland a hearing during an election year. Ignoring the Constitution, McConnell increased the partisanship surrounding the court by holding out for a Republican electoral victory in 2016 that would allow for the appointment of another conservative judge to replace Scalia. McConnell also fanned the flames of partisanship which divided the country over Trump's appointment of Brett Kavanaugh to the nation's highest court.

Obama on the global stage

The global legacy of the liberal Obama is also a contested one. Obama entered the Presidency as a man of peace dedicated to challenging the global reach of American militarism and empire. Obama pledged to close the Guantanamo detention center in Cuba while removing American troops from Iraq and Afghanistan, but things did not go as planned. Efforts to shut the Guantanamo facility and transfer inmates to the United States were thwarted by the Congress, who insisted that the public would be threatened by the presence of the dangerous criminals upon American soil, although their greatest fear might be exposure of the torture tactics pursued by the Bush administration. While enhanced interrogation was discontinued by the Obama administration, prisoners who have been denied a day in court remain indefinitely incarcerated in Guantanamo. Obama scaled back American troop levels in Afghanistan, but the United States remains bogged down in an Afghan civil war with no clear exit strategy. Obama did implement a military withdrawal from Iraq, but the Bush invasion and ensuing civil war left the country devastated. With the Iraqi government mired in partisanship, ethnic and sectarian violence, and corruption, the instability provided a power vacuum filled by radicals such as the Islamic State of Iraq and Syria (ISIS), a jihadist fundamentalist group who gained power in western Iraq and Syria, undergoing a civil war aimed at overthrowing the dictator and President of Syria, Bashar al-Assad. The rise of ISIS in Iraq and Syria, along with the terrorist group's sponsorship of violence in the United States and the world, forced the Obama administration to commit forces to Iraq and Syria to defeat ISIS, although much of the fighting on the ground was delegated to groups such as the Kurds who have essentially carved out an autonomous government in northern Iraq. Yet, the role of the Kurds raises problems with America's NATO ally Turkey who fears the impact of an independent Kurdistan upon its ethnic Kurdish population.

Continuing to pursue the War on Terror, Obama took credit for ordering the special forces raid on Osama bin Laden's secret enclave in Pakistan which resulted in the death of al-Qaeda's founder. The Obama administration also made extensive use of clones to eliminate terrorist leaders. The employment of clones had the advantage of reducing American casualties, but the civilian collateral damage from these weapons was often quite high, perhaps creating more enemies for the United States. The Arab Spring of 2011 failed to bring the democratization of the Middle East anticipated by the Obama White House, and, like Bush's invasion of Iraq, an American military intervention in Libya only made matters worse. When rebellion broke out against Libyan dictator Muammar Gaddafi, the United States aided the rebels with a bombing campaign. The overthrow of Gaddafi, however, led to a civil war in Libya, and the ensuing instability made Libya an attractive home for many terrorist groups. Amid the chaos, the American Ambassador to Libya, Christopher Stevens, and three other Americans were murdered in the Libyan city of Benghazi, with Republican Congressional leaders placing blame upon Secretary of State Hillary Clinton for a lack of security. While an American military presence in Syria contributed to the territorial losses suffered by ISIS, the Obama administration was unable to prevent President Assad from using chemical weapons against his own people, and with the backing of Russia, Assad crushed the democratic rebellion against his rule. A man who was awarded the Nobel Peace Prize, Obama left the Presidency with American forces still bogged down in the Middle East, again demonstrating that it is easier to initiate than end an international conflict.

On some other international fronts, the Obama administration concluded on a more positive note. Obama visited Cuba and initiated a process of normalizing relations between the United States and Cuba and lifting the trade embargo that has existed since the 1959 Cuban Revolution. The United States and other Western European nations negotiated an agreement with Iran that limited the Iranian nation from attaining nuclear weapons—although the Trump administration has abrogated the Iranian deal. In pursuing a normalization of relations with Cuba and Iran, Obama was moving away from the foreign policy legacy of the Cold War. On the other hand, relations with Russia, led by former KGB intelligence officer Vladimir Putin, deteriorated as the Obama administration placed sanctions upon the Russian government following the annexation of Crimea from the Ukraine. The incoming Trump administration sought to reverse these policies by taking a tougher stand with Iran and Cuba, while reaching out to Russia and Putin.

Election of 2016

The Presidential election of 2016 resulted in major party nominations for two candidates with high negative polling. After serving as Obama's Secretary of State, Hillary Clinton appeared as the heir apparent to the Obama mantle, but she faced a serious primary challenge from Vermont Senator Bernie Sanders, who identified himself as a democratic socialist. The fact that Sanders was almost able to wrest the nomination from Clinton indicates that the red scare mentality of McCarthyism may be losing its appeal among the electorate, and especially with young voters who embraced the Sanders candidacy. With control of the party apparatus and a strong showing among black primary voters, Clinton became the first woman nominated for President by a major political party. With her experience as an attorney, First Lady, U.S. Senator from New York, and Secretary of State, Clinton was a well-qualified candidate, yet her campaign was subjected to relentless questioning of her character. In addition to accusations of dereliction of duty during the attack on the American mission in Benghazi, Republicans complained that her use of a private server for her emails while Secretary of State was a criminal conspiracy. Clinton confessed to making a misjudgment on the emails, but the FBI cleared her of any criminal charges. The candidate was also criticized for accepting extravagant speaking fees from corporate America, and the Clinton Foundation raised questions about favorable treatment for contributions to the charitable organization. She also continued to be hounded about the sexual indiscretions of her husband, and Hillary was accused of unfairly treating Bill's victims such as Monica Lewinsky. On the other hand, one would think traditionalists might have embraced Hillary for standing by her man during difficult days. Hillary was also depicted as a Lady McBeth character and denounced for her ambition, a quality admired in male politicians, which leads to the conclusion that much of the venom generated against her candidacy was the sexual discrimination and misogyny that continues to exist within the culture despite the many advances women have achieved in American history.

Meanwhile, a crowded field of seventeen Republican candidates culminated in the surprising nomination of businessman Donald Trump, a New York City real estate developer, who owed his notoriety to self-promotion, manipulation of his brand name, and celebrity status as host of the popular television reality show, *The Apprentice*. No hard-working product of the American dream, Trump got his start with an inheritance from his wealthy father, who was criticized for his racially discriminatory policies as a New York City real estate developer, and it seems that the fruit did not fall far from the tree as Trump pursued a divisive campaign strategy. In debates, he bullied and belittled his Republican opponents, focusing his campaign upon fears of immigration from Mexico. Trump denounced Mexicans entering the country as murderers and rapists who threatened the jobs and lives of white Americans. His solution to what Trump described as a crisis at the nation's southern border was to construct a concrete wall along the border for which Mexico would pay. Trump conducted rallies throughout the nation in which enthusiastic supporters chanted "build that wall" and urged that Hillary be arrested and "locked up." The rallies were also marred by violence against protestors encouraged by candidate Trump, who insisted that his rabid followers would continue to support him even if he openly shot someone on Fifth Avenue in New York City.

This theory was seemingly tested when a 2004 tape from the *Access Hollywood* show was discovered with Trump, who had a reputation for sexual infidelities, declaring that since he was a celebrity, he could do whatever he wanted with women, including grabbing them by their private parts. Despite vulgar language essentially embracing sexual assault, many evangelical women stood by Trump as he promised to appoint judges that would outlaw abortion. Despite his loyal following, public opinion polls on the eve of the election indicated that Hillary would win. And she polled over 3,000,000 more votes than Trump, but a shift of approximately 100,000 votes in the usually reliable Democratic industrial states of Wisconsin, Michigan, and Pennsylvania provided Trump with a victory in the Electoral College. Electoral divisions in American society were also exacerbated by Russian interference and propaganda which tended to favor the Trump candidacy. Many predominantly white voters in the Midwest and South felt left out of the country's recovery from the Great Recession. While unemployment was declining, wages remained stagnant, and many Trump voters in more rural areas had witnessed the departure of their industrial economic base. In addition, many of these voters who responded positively to Trump's promise that he "would make America great again" felt threatened by cultural and demographic change. The white birth rate in America was declining, and the nation was becoming more diverse with immigration growing, especially from Mexico and Central America. The Civil Rights Movement, which had launched a frontal assault on *de jure* segregation and prejudice in the 1950s and 1960s, continued to fight against *de facto* segregation, economic inequality, and discrimination by law enforcement against the black community. The LGBTQ community was also asserting their rights to be included within the promise of American life, with the Supreme Court recognizing gay marriage and schools working to accommodate the needs of transgender students. Those who took comfort in the dream of a homogenous white heterosexual America safely encased behind the white picket fences of suburbia in the 1950s were attracted to Trump's illusive vision.

Living in Trump's America

To many progressives, Trump's electoral victory seemed a repudiation of their struggles to achieve a country embodying the principles of equality and opportunity championed by Jefferson's Declaration, Lincoln's Gettysburg Address, and Martin Luther King Jr.'s "I have a dream." The global populism and nationalism of racial prejudice had seemingly found a home in America with Trump and his corporate backers. Trump may have raised some legitimate issues with his critique of globalization and open-ended military commitments, but his first acts as President demonstrated his allegiance to corporate backers rather than his threatened and frightened rural base. Surrounding himself with a cabinet of wealthy white corporate representatives, Trump abandoned his pledge to pursue an extended program of infrastructure improvement that would have provided jobs and increased the quality of life for all Americans. Instead, the Trump administration pushed through Congress a massive tax cut for the wealthy that promoted Wall Street and corporate America. Energy conglomerates sponsored by the Koch brothers were rewarded with Presidential denials of global warming, the deregulation of business and industry, and withdrawal from the Paris Accords on climate change, endangering the lives of every American as well as the world's population. Although he had developed no health plan of his own, Trump launched an assault upon Obamacare and the natural right of all to adequate health care.

The Trump administration has also appealed to America's dark history of racial, ethnic, and gender discrimination, while refusing to denounce white supremacists marching in America's streets. He has demonized immigrants in the tradition of the Know Nothings, encouraging an environment in which the number of hate crimes committed by right-wing white nationalists have increased. One of Trump's first acts as President was to decree a travel ban on nations with predominantly Muslim populations. While on the Southern border, Trump has separated families in deplorable detention centers and cut aid to the Central American nations of Guatemala, Honduras, and El Salvador whose population is fleeing poverty, violence, and the economic impact of climate change. The rights of transgender Americans are violated by executive orders against transgender enlistment in the military and dismissing civil rights protection for sexual identity. Trump's court appointees are dictated by evangelical supporters, seeking to implement protections of religious freedom that will blur the separation between church and state while denying a woman's right to choose and allowing religious discrimination against the LGBTQ community. As President, Trump has consistently attacked the free press, an essential cornerstone of democracy, as fake news.

On the international scene, Trump describes himself as a nationalist who wants to renegotiate trade deals while imposing tariffs, disengage with alliances such as NATO, and end the American military presence in Iraq, Syria, and Afghanistan. On the other hand, the President has withdrawn the United States from the nuclear deal with Iran and threatened that Middle Eastern nation with war. And while he speaks of disengagement on the global stage, Trump also surrounds himself with generals and calls for increased government expenditures on both conventional and nuclear weapons. He also encourages the militarization of American life and culture, stating that the country needs large demonstrations of military might such as those that characterize dictatorial and authoritarian regimes. Indeed, Trump's admiration for authoritarianism is quite disturbing as is evident in his friendship with Russia's Putin and North Korea's Kim Jong-un in which discussions over de-nuclearization of the Korean peninsula are clouded by Trump's praising of his dictatorship. Responding to concerns regarding Trump's proclivity toward dictators, the Department of Justice appointed former FBI Director Robert Mueller to investigate allegations that the Trump campaign conspired with the Russian government to defeat Clinton and place Trump in the White House. After an extensive investigation, Mueller concluded that the Russians had, indeed, interfered in the American election on behalf of Trump. Mueller's report documented numerous contacts between the Russians and the Trump campaign; however, the Special Counsel was unable to establish proof of a conspiracy. Mueller also examined whether the President committed obstruction of justice by seeking to limit any inquiry into the Russian allegations. The final report described numerous incidents of the Trump administration engaging in questionable activities; however, Mueller adhered to a Justice Department directive that a sitting President may not be indicted. Accordingly, Mueller did not exonerate the President as Trump claimed, and many Democrats in Congress called for the President's impeachment—although a conviction in the Republican-controlled Senate seems unlikely. However, evidence that Trump pressured the Ukranian government to investigate former vice-president Joe Biden has reignited the impeachment debate. The best chance, nevertheless, to rid the nation of Trump appears to be the 2020 election, and over twenty candidates sought the Democratic nomination—including progressives Bernie Sanders and Elizabeth Warren.

For many progressives, the Trump Presidency represents the dark side of American history and the threat of fascism in the modern world. But the history of democratic struggle in America should provide hope and inspiration for those laboring to create a modern America worthy of its founding principles. This fundamental conflict goes back to the country's origins as those seeking liberty and economic opportunity fled from Europe to forge a new life free from oppression, yet this vision was grounded upon seizing land from the Native population and destroying their way of life, while introducing a forced labor system based upon racial slavery. In more modern times, the exploitive nature of American history has been perpetuated by faceless corporations exercising political and economic power over democratic institutions, fostering American imperialism, and threatening the world with global warming.

The arc of justice

While President Trump attempts to brand his opposition as un-American, there is a rich tradition of progressive reform and resistance upon which those living in Trump's America may draw. Among the many Americans who have labored to erase the gap between the myth and reality of the American dream and experience are freedom fighters such as Nat Turner, John Brown, and Harriet Tubman; Patriot Chiefs and Native leaders such as Tecumseh, Sitting Bull, and the American Indian Movement; abolitionists such as Frederick Douglass, William Lloyd Garrison, and Angelina Grimké; labor leaders and organizations such as the Knights of Labor, IWW, Elizabeth Gurley Flynn, CIO, and Walter Reuther; suffragists and women's rights champions such as Susan B. Anthony, Elizabeth Cady Stanton, Alice Paul, Ida B. Wells, Margaret Sanger, Betty Friedan, and Gloria Steinhem; anti-imperialists such as Robert LaFollette, Jane Addams, and Mark Twain; conservationists and naturalists such as Henry David Thoreau, John Muir, and Rachel Carson; artists and writers such as Woody Guthrie, Walt Whitman, James Baldwin, Joan Baez, Langston Hughes, John Steinbeck, Toni Morrison, Kate Chopin, and Allen Ginsberg; radicals such as Emma Goldman, Lucy Parsons, Big Bill Haywood, Eugene V. Debs, and the Socialist Party of the United States; antiwar activists and organizations such as Tom Hayden, William Sloan Coffin, and SDS; Civil Rights icons such as W. E. B. DuBois, Rosa Parks, Medgar Evers, Martin Luther King Jr., Malcolm X, the Black Panthers, and Fannie Lou Hamer; reform politicians such as Abraham Lincoln, Franklin Roosevelt, and Robert Kennedy; Chicano leaders such as Cesar Chavez, Corky Gonzales, and Dolores Huerta; LGBTQ activists such as Harvey Milk and the patrons of the Stonewall Inn; and American working people who have labored every day to assure the dignity and respect for all Americans regardless of race, class, or gender. This progressive tradition continues into the present day with the Me-Too Movement, Black Lives Matter, and women's marches and growing political participation symbolized by female members of the Congress and Senate along with governorships and local offices—not to mention the record number of women seeking the 2020 Democratic Presidential nomination. And hope also rests in the hands of a younger generation who, although perhaps a little too smitten by screens and social media, are less addicted to consumerism, and more open to new ideas and acceptance of differences. Embracing the LGBTQ community, they seem shorn of earlier prejudices, and, free from the legacy of the Cold War, are even willing to examine the possibilities of socialism. Economic inequality exacerbated by issues of race and immigration presents a continuing challenge, as does America's flirtation with fascism and authoritarianism under the leadership of Donald Trump. Nevertheless, the United States has experienced considerable progressive change since the 1960s, and some of the current reactionary politics are a response to that change. Building upon this progressive legacy with courage and compassion, the promise of American life as outlined in Jefferson's Declaration, Lincoln's Gettysburg Address, and King's "I have a dream" are within our grasp. As Martin Luther King Jr. observed in 1964, "The arc of the moral universe is long, but it bends toward justice."

Further Reading:

Boyer, Paul. *Promises to Keep: The United States Since World War II*. Lexington, MA: D. C. Heath, 1995.

Bacevich, Andrew J. *America's War for the Greater Middle East: A Military History*. New York: Random House, 2016.

Chafe, William H. *Bill and Hillary: The Clintons and the Politics of the Personal*. Durham, NC: Duke University Press, 2014.

Ehrenreich, Barbara. *Nickel and Dimed: On (Not) Getting by in America*. New York: Metropolitan Books, 2001.

Garrow, David. *Rising Star: The Making of Barack Obama*. New York: HarperCollins, 2017.

Krugman, Paul. *The Great Unraveling: Losing Our Way in the New Century*. New York: W. W. Norton and Company, 2003.

Kruse, Kevin H. and Julian E. Zelizer. *Fault Lines: A History of the United States Since 1974*. New York: W. W. Norton and Company, 2019.

Meacham, Jon. *Destiny and Power: The American Odyssey of George Herbert Walker Bush*. New York: Random House, 2015.

Obama, Barack. *The Audacity of Hope: Thoughts on Reclaiming the American Dream*. New York: Crown Publishers, 2006.

O'Neil, William. *A Bubble in Time: America During the Interwar Years, 1989–2001*. Chicago: Ivan R. Dee, 2009.

Posner, Richard. *An Affair of State: The Investigation, Impeachment, and Trial of President Clinton*. Cambridge, MA: Harvard University Press, 1999.

Zelizer, Julian E. *The Presidency of Barack Obama: A First Historical Assessment*. Princeton, NJ: Princeton University Press, 2016.

INDEX

Chinese Exclusion Act 209-210, 216-217

Choctaw 120

Church of England 18, 27, 29

Churchill, Winston 337-340, 344, 356

Citizens United v. Federal Election Commission 202, 487

City Manager 260

City on a Hill 29-30

Civil Rights Act of 1964 405

Civil Rights Movement 392-416

Civil Service Reform Act 216

Civil War 161-171, 173-185

Civilian Conservation Corps 316

Clark, George Rogers 72

Clayton Anti-trust Act

Clay, Cassius Marcellus 138

Clay, Henry 105, 108, 117, 119, 123, 151, 162

Cleveland, Grover 217-218, 222-223, 247

Climate Change 204

Clinton, Bill 475-479

Clinton, Hillary Rodham 476, 479, 486, 492-493

Cohens v. Virginia 110

Cohn, Roy 370

COINTELPRO 439-440

Cold War 354-363, 371-373, 463-468

Colombia 282-283

Colonial American Society 47-51

Columbia University 438

Committees of Correspondence 63-67

Committee on Public Information 286

Compromise of 1850 161-163

Compromise of 1877 198

Confederacy 170, 176-177

Congress of Industrial Organization (CIO) 321-322

Congress of Racial Equality 399-400

Congressional Reconstruction 193-195

Constitution of the United States 81-87

Continental Congress 65-66

Convention of 1800 97

Coolidge, Calvin 303-304

Lavender Scare 366-367

Lebanon 464

Leary, Timothy 424-425

Lee, Robert E. 182, 175

Leisler, Jacob 39

Lend-Lease 331

Lewinsky, Monica 479

Lewis and Clark Expedition 101

Lewis, John L. 404

Lewis, Sinclair 301

Lexington and Concord 65-66

Liberal Consensus 352-353, 373-374, 389-390

Liberty League 319

Lincoln, Abraham 167-170, 179, 184, 191-192

Lincoln-Douglas Debates 167-168

Little Rock (Central High) 370-371, 397

Locke, John 40, 68

Lodge, Henry Cabot 288

London, Jack 259

Long, Huey P. 320

Louisiana Purchase 100

Lost Cause 142, 174, 188

Lovejoy, Elijah 140

Loyalists 73

Ludlow Amendment 352

Ludlow Massacre 251-252

Lusitania 285

MacArthur, Douglas 334-335, 342-343, 362-363

Madison, Dolly 107

Madison, James 86, 97, 100, 105, 109

Mahan Alfred T. 275

Maine 277

Malcolm X 144, 406

Manhattan Project 344-345

Manifest Destiny 150-151, 156-158

Mann Act 262

Mann, Horace 132

Mao Zedong 361-362, 429

Marbury v. Madison 100

March on Washington 401-402

Marion, Francis 72

Marshall, John 97, 100, 109-110, 120

Marshall Plan 358-359

Marshall, Thurgood 395

Massachusetts Bay Company 30

Matewan Massacre 295

Manson, Charles 435

Mayflower Compact 27-28

McCain, John 486-487

McCarthy, Eugene 426

McCarthy, Joseph 365-366, 370

McClellan, George 180-181, 184

McCulloch v. Maryland 109

McGovern, George 453-454

McKinley Tariff 218

McKinley, William 223-224, 278-281

Mercantilism 53

Meredith, James 401

Mexican-American Youth Organization 411

Mexican Revolution 284

Metacom 31

Methodism 137

Mexican War 153-158

Miller, William 134

Military-Industrial Complex 373

Military Reconstruction Act 194

Milk, Harvey 415-416

Mining Frontier 228-229

Mississippi Freedom Democratic Party 403-404

Missouri Compromise 112-113

Moderate Republicanism 368-369

Mongrel Tariff of 1883 216

Monopoly 210-211

Monroe Doctrine 111, 157, 282

Monroe, James 110-112

Morgan, J. P. 208

Mormonism 135

www.ingramcontent.com/pod-product-compliance
Lightning Source LLC
Chambersburg PA
CBHW020447270326
41926CB00008B/519